# The Oxford Guide to International Humanitarian Law

# Preface

The prevalence, and ever-present threat, of armed conflict ensures the continuing importance of international humanitarian law (IHL), which seeks to balance the military necessity of fighting war with the humanitarian protection of those affected by it. IHL governs 'old' and 'new' wars alike, from conventional inter-state wars to complex, contemporary transnational insurgencies involving non-state 'terrorist' organizations. While the implementation and enforcement of IHL rules and principles is always challenging, not least because of new actors and technologies, these challenges have often also led to flexible new interpretations, adaptations, or applications of IHL, enabling IHL to maintain and reassert its relevance.

This *Oxford Guide to International Humanitarian Law* is intended as a practical yet sophisticated overview of the subject for professionals who are not necessarily IHL experts, but who work in fields where IHL may be relevant. These may include government officials (lawyers and decision- or policy-makers in defence, foreign affairs, foreign aid and development, policing, human rights, or other areas); military officers (such as military lawyers, judges, planners, or commanders); civilian judges, prosecutors, and defence lawyers in national or international courts; United Nations entities; peacekeepers; humanitarians; development actors; the human rights community; investors or corporations; and civil society (including media, non-governmental organizations (NGOs), and think tanks), as well as university students and researchers.

The *Oxford Guide to IHL* aims to serve as a first port of call, and an essential reference work, for such non-experts dealing with IHL matters. It provides an accurate, objective, and accessible overview of IHL by leading and emerging experts. It is intended to be more detailed and nuanced, and less descriptive, than some of the many introductory surveys or student textbooks on IHL which have proliferated in recent years,[1] precisely as a result of the burgeoning interest in the practice of IHL in many conflicts and countries. It is not, however, as technical as the various practical manuals[2] or expert commentaries on IHL;[3]

---

[1] Leslie Green, *The Contemporary Law of Armed Conflict* (3rd edn, Manchester University Press 2008); Frits Kalshoven and Liesbeth Zegveld, *Constraints on the Waging of War: An Introduction to International Humanitarian Law* (4th edn, CUP 2011); Marco Sassòli, Antoine Bouvier, and Anne Quintin, *How Does Law Protect in War?* (3rd edn, ICRC 2011); Laurie Blank and Gregory Noone, *The International Law of Armed Conflict: Fundamental Principles and Contemporary Challenges in the Law of War* (Wolters Kluwer 2013); Jonathan Crowe and Kylie Weston-Scheuber, *Principles of International Humanitarian Law* (Edward Elgar 2013); Robert Kolb, *An Advanced Introduction to International Humanitarian Law* (Edward Elgar 2014); Emily Crawford and Alison Pert, *International Humanitarian Law* (CUP 2015); Yoram Dinstein, *The Conduct of Hostilities under the Law of International Armed Conflict* (3rd edn, CUP 2015); Françoise Bouchet-Saulnier, *The Practical Guide to International Humanitarian Law* (Rowman & Littlefield 2016); Nils Melzer, *International Humanitarian Law: A Comprehensive Introduction* (ICRC 2016); Geoffrey Solis, *The Law of Armed Conflict: International Humanitarian Law in War* (2nd edn, CUP 2016); Gary Corn, Christopher Jenks, Richard Jackson, and Victor Hansen, *The Law of Armed Conflict: An Operational Approach* (2nd edn, Wolters Kluwer 2018); Nicholas Tsagourias and Alasdair Morrison, *International Humanitarian Law* (CUP 2018).

[2] UK Ministry of Defence, *The Manual of the Law of Armed Conflict* (OUP 2004); Dieter Fleck (ed), *The Handbook of International Humanitarian Law* (3rd edn, OUP 2013). For an extensive list of national military manuals, see ICRC, 'Military Manuals' https://ihl-databases.icrc.org/customary-ihl/eng/docs/src_iimima.

[3] ICRC Commentaries on the four Geneva Conventions (GCs) of 1949: GCI (1952 and 2016); GCII (1960 and 2017); GCIII (1960); GCIV (1960). See also Andrew Clapham, Paola Gaeta, and Marco Sassòli, *The 1949*

nor is it as conceptual, theoretical, or argumentative as academic works covering IHL as a whole[4] or specialized areas of it.[5] Rather, this *Handbook* fills a gap in the middle of this spectrum, in between student texts, practitioner manuals, and academic treatises.

The *Handbook* covers all of the classical IHL topics: history and sources; classification of conflicts (international—including occupation—and non-international), and their temporal and geographical scope; the different domains of warfare (air, land, and sea, and potentially outer space and the cyber domain); how IHL categorizes actors (fighters, civilians, and others) and what general and special protections apply to them (from humanitarian aid to detention and trial); the conduct of hostilities (including basic principles such as humanity, necessity and proportionality, and the means and methods of warfare, including weapons); humanitarian relief operations; and implementation and enforcement (including war crimes liabilities).

Along the way, the chapters discuss contemporary challenges and controversies in IHL, including, among others, the interaction of IHL with human rights, with terrorism and counter-terrorism, and with United Nations Security Council measures; new technologies (such as cyber operations and autonomous weapons); how to classify conflicts involving non-state armed groups on the territory of more than one state; the targeting of civilians taking a direct part in hostilities; and the lawfulness of detention in non-international armed conflict. Many of these issues remain unsettled, and the *Handbook* deftly charts their contours, so that interested professionals can readily grasp and seek to navigate through them.

This *Handbook* was originally conceived by Jelena Pejic (Senior Legal Adviser at the International Committee of the Red Cross) and Michael Schmitt (Professor of Public International Law at Exeter Law School and Emeritus Professor at the United States Naval War College's Stockton Centre for International Law). They graciously invited the present editors to assume carriage of the project at an early stage and we are grateful to them for entrusting us with the responsibility. Any errors or omissions are, of course, our own. We also thank our publisher, Oxford University Press, particularly Merel Alstein and Jack

---

*Geneva Conventions: A Commentary* (OUP 2015). Commentaries on the Additional Protocols of 1977: Michael Bothe, Karl Josef Partsch, and Waldemar A Solf, *New Rules for Victims of Armed Conflicts: Commentary on the Two 1977 Protocols Additional to the Geneva Conventions of 1949* (Martinus Nijhoff 1982); Yves Sandoz, Christophe Swinarski, and Bruno Zimmermann (eds), *Commentary on the Additional Protocols to the Geneva Conventions* (Martinus Nijhoff/ICRC 1987). On customary IHL, see Jean-Marie Henckaerts and Louise Doswald-Beck, *Customary International Humanitarian Law, Volume 1: Rules* (ICRC 2005).

[4] Daniel Thürer, *International Humanitarian Law: Theory, Practice, Context* (Hague Academy of International Law 2011); Andrew Clapham and Paolo Gaeta (eds), *The Oxford Handbook of International Law in Armed Conflict* (OUP 2014); Rain Liivoja and Tim McCormack (eds), *Routledge Handbook of the Law of Armed Conflict* (Routledge 2016); Marco Sassòli, *Problems Arising in Warfare* (Edward Elgar 2019).

[5] Nils Melzer, *Targeted Killing in International Law* (OUP 2008); Emily Crawford, *The Treatment of Combatants and Insurgents under the Law of Armed Conflict* (OUP 2010); Anthony Cullen, *The Concept of Non-international Armed Conflict in International Humanitarian Law* (OUP 2010); Andrea Bianchi and Yasmin Naqvi, *International Humanitarian Law and Terrorism* (Hart 2011); Mélanie Jacques, *Armed Conflict and Displacement: The Protection of Refugees and Displaced Persons under International Humanitarian Law* (CUP 2012); Sandesh Sivakumaran, *The Law of Non-International Armed Conflict* (OUP 2012); Elizabeth Wilmshurst (ed), *International Law and the Classification of Conflicts* (OUP 2012); Robert Kolb and Gloria Gaggioli (eds), *Research Handbook on Human Rights and Humanitarian Law* (Edward Elgar 2013); Mariëlle Matthee, Brigit Toebes, and Marcel Brus (eds), *Armed Conflict and International Law: In Search of the Human Face* (Asser Press 2013); Derek Jinks, Jackson Maogoto, and Solon Solomon (eds), *Applying International Humanitarian Law in Judicial and Quasi-Judicial Bodies International and Domestic Aspects* (Springer 2014); Sharon Weill, *The Role of National Courts in Applying International Humanitarian Law* (OUP 2014); Emily Crawford, *Identifying the Enemy: Civilian Participation in Armed Conflict* (OUP 2015).

McNichol. At Sydney Law School, for editorial assistance we thank research assistants Ellen Moore and Katya Pesce, and student volunteers Sulithi Dewendra, Umar Ikram, Kirsty Jones, Jonathan Malka, August Reinisch, and Arsh Shah.

Ben Saul and Dapo Akande
Sydney and Oxford, June 2019

# Contents

# Table of Cases

## International Criminal Tribunal for Rwanda (ICTR)

## International Criminal Tribunal for the Former Yugoslavia (ICTY)

## Permanent Court of International Justice

## The Special Court for Sierra Leone

## UN Human Rights Committee

## UN Special Tribunal for Lebanon

DOMESTIC CASES

# Table of Legislation

Great Clarendon Street, Oxford, OX2 6DP,
United Kingdom

Oxford University Press is a department of the University of Oxford.
It furthers the University's objective of excellence in research, scholarship,
and education by publishing worldwide. Oxford is a registered trade mark of
Oxford University Press in the UK and in certain other countries

Published in the United States of America by Oxford University Press
198 Madison Avenue, New York, NY 10016, United States of America

British Library Cataloguing in Publication Data
Data available

Library of Congress Control Number: 2019954554

ISBN 978–0–19–885530–9 (hbk.)
ISBN 978–0–19–885531–6 (pbk.)

Printed and bound by
CPI Group (UK) Ltd, Croydon, CR0 4YY

# The Oxford Guide to International Humanitarian Law

*Edited by*

BEN SAUL AND DAPO AKANDE

OXFORD

UNIVERSITY PRESS

# List of Contributors

**Dapo Akande** is Professor of Public International Law and Co-Director of the Oxford Institute for Ethics, Law and Armed Conflict at the University of Oxford, and a Fellow of Exeter College, Oxford.

**Stuart Casey-Maslen** is Honorary Professor at the Centre for Human Rights of the University of Pretoria.

**Emily Crawford** is Associate Professor of International Law at the University of Sydney.

**Robert Cryer** is Professor of International and Criminal Law at Birmingham Law School and Extraordinary Professor of Law at the University of the Free State in South Africa.

**Gloria Gaggioli** is Swiss National Science Foundation Professor at the University of Geneva, Lecturer at the University of Neuchâtel, and a former Legal Adviser at the ICRC.

**Robin Geiß** is Professor of International Law and Security at the University of Glasgow, Director of the Glasgow Centre for International Law and Security and Swiss Chair of International Humanitarian Law at the Geneva Academy of International Humanitarian Law and Human Rights.

**Jean-Marie Henckaerts** is head of the ICRC project to update the Commentaries on the Geneva Conventions of 1949 and the Additional Protocols of 1977, and co-editor of the ICRC's Customary International Humanitarian Law Study.

**Lawrence Hill-Cawthorne** is an Associate Professor in Law at the University of Reading.

**Eve Massingham** is a Senior Research Fellow in the Law and the Future of War research group at the University of Queensland, and a former Legal Adviser at the ICRC.

**Sarah McCosker** is Partner at Lexbridge Public International Lawyers, Canberra, and a former Legal Adviser at the ICRC, Geneva.

**Robert McLaughlin** is Professor of Military and Security Law at UNSW Canberra, Professor of International Law at the Australian National Centre for Oceans Research and Security, and former Director of the Australian Naval Legal Service.

**Nils Melzer** is Human Rights Chair of the Geneva Academy of International Humanitarian Law and Human Rights, Professor of International Law at the University of Glasgow, and UN Special Rapporteur on Torture and Other Cruel, Inhuman or Degrading Treatment or Punishment.

**Christophe Paulussen** is a Senior Researcher at the Asser Institute and Research Fellow at the International Centre for Counter-Terrorism, The Hague.

**Cymie R Payne** is Associate Professor in the Department of Human Ecology and the School of Law at Rutgers University.

**Jelena Pejic** is Senior Legal Adviser at the ICRC, Geneva.

**Marco Sassòli** is Professor of International Law at the University of Geneva and Director of the Geneva Academy of International Humanitarian Law and Human Rights.

**Ben Saul** is Challis Chair of International Law at Sydney Law School, Visiting Professor at Harvard Law School, and Visiting Chair of Australian Studies at Harvard University.

**Michael N Schmitt** is Professor of International Law, University of Reading; Francis Lieber Distinguished Scholar, West Point; Strass Center Distinguished Scholar and Visiting Professor of Law, University of Texas; and Professor Emeritus, United States Naval War College.

**Kelisiana Thynne** is a Legal Adviser with the Advisory Services in the Legal Division of the ICRC, Geneva.

**David Turns** is Senior Lecturer in International Law at the Defence Academy of the United Kingdom (Cranfield University).

**Sylvain Vité** is a Legal Adviser at the ICRC, Geneva.

# 1

# History and Sources

*Jean-Marie Henckaerts**

## 1. Introduction

As its name indicates, international humanitarian law (IHL) is a branch of international law. It is also known as the international law of armed conflict, or simply the law of armed conflict (LOAC) or law of war. It must be distinguished from the law on the use of force which is regulated, for inter-state relations, by the UN Charter.[1] This distinction is often referred to by the Latin designations of both bodies of law: IHL is thus known as the *jus in bello* (law applicable in armed conflict) while the law on the use of force is known as the *jus ad bellum* (the law applicable to recourse to armed conflict).[2]

The rules and principles of IHL seek to limit the effects of armed conflict and at its core, IHL aims to preserve a sense of humanity in time of war.[3] At the same time, IHL has been developed to regulate the social reality that is armed conflict. In order to provide a realistic, and hence useful, legal framework IHL must also take into account the military needs of parties to an armed conflict in their pursuit of defeating the adversary. The development of particular treaties and specific rules of IHL over time reflects what is at times the difficult exercise of finding the correct balance between these humanitarian and military considerations.[4]

As a branch of international law, IHL is subject to the general rules of international law, such as those related to sources, treaty interpretation, and state responsibility. The sources of international law are set out in article 38 of the Statute of the International Court of Justice. This provision lists international conventions, international custom, and general principles of law as the main sources of international law, in accordance with which the Court is to decide disputes submitted to it. It further stipulates that judicial decisions and the teachings of the most highly qualified publicists of the various nations are subsidiary means for the

---

* The author wishes to acknowledge the valuable assistance of Ellen Nohle in finalizing this chapter. The views expressed in this chapter are personal and do not necessarily reflect those of the ICRC.

[1] See UN Charter 1945 articles 2(4) (prohibition of threat or use of force against another state) and 51 (right of individual or collective self-defence). For further analysis, see Yoram Dinstein, *War, Aggression and Self-Defence* (5th edn, CUP 2011). It should be noted that there is no equivalent body of international law regulating recourse to force by or against non-state armed groups.

[2] For a detailed analysis, see Keiichiro Okimoto, *The Distinction and Relationship between Jus ad Bellum and Jus in Bello* (Hart 2011).

[3] See Amanda Alexander, 'A Short History of International Humanitarian Law' (2015) 26 *EJIL* 111–12 and Jeroen C van den Boogaard, 'Fighting by the Principles: Principles as a Source of International Humanitarian Law', in Mariëlle Matthee et al (eds), *Armed Conflict and International Law: In Search of the Human Face* (Asser Press 2013) 4.

[4] For a discussion of the principles of humanity and military necessity, see chapter 7, 'International Humanitarian Law and the Conduct of Hostilities'.

determination of rules of law. These are also the main sources of IHL, although in recent years a number of soft-law instruments have emerged with a view to providing guidance on the application and interpretation of IHL.

This chapter examines each of these sources of IHL, which in a particular way represent techniques of law-making or law clarification. Each source also interacts with the others in what is a constant dialogue leading to new treaties, customary rules, and principles, under the influence of case law, expert opinion, scholarship, and of course, world events.

## 2. Treaties

While international conventions—or treaties—establish rules 'expressly recognized by the contesting states', international custom is defined in article 38 of the ICJ Statute as 'evidence of a general practice accepted as law'. Even though article 38 lists 'international conventions' (treaties) as the first source, this does not reflect a hierarchy among the main sources of international law. Historically, customary international law has often preceded treaty law and provided a reservoir of principles and concepts on which much of the codification of IHL is based.[5]

The history of the codification of IHL, resulting in a long series of treaties with a global scope, started in 1864 with the adoption of the first Geneva Convention for the Amelioration of the Condition of the Wounded in Armies in the Field.[6] During the centuries leading up to this first codification, rules regulating warfare existed but were based mainly on tradition and custom. It is fair to say, therefore, that humanitarian law started as a body of customary rules and remained so for centuries, and that its codification is a much more recent phenomenon.[7]

The codification and conventional development of IHL have often occurred against the background of particular battles that exposed weaknesses in the existing legal framework, and in response to developments in the means and methods of warfare.[8]

---

[5] See eg Christopher G Weeramantry, 'The Revival of Customary International Humanitarian Law', in Larry Maybee and Benarji Chakka (eds), *Custom as a Source of International Humanitarian Law* (ICRC 2006) 25.

[6] Geneva Convention for the Amelioration of the Condition of the Wounded in Armies in the Field of 22 August 1864.

[7] For a discussion, see Frits Kalshoven, 'The History of International Humanitarian Law Treaty-Making', in Rain Liivoja and Tim McCormack (eds), *Routledge Handbook of the Law of Armed Conflict* (Routledge 2016) 33.

[8] In the codification of IHL, the ICRC has played an important role, in particular with respect to the Geneva Conventions. According to the Statutes of the Movement, the role of the ICRC includes in particular 'to work for the understanding and dissemination of knowledge of international humanitarian law applicable in armed conflicts and *to prepare any developments thereof*'. The ICRC has prepared the draft Conventions and Protocols and these have been considered at the International Conference of the Red Cross and Red Crescent, which 'contributes to the respect for and development of international humanitarian law'. See Statutes of the International Red Cross and Red Crescent Movement, adopted by the 25th International Conference of the Red Cross (Geneva, 23–31 October 1986, as amended in 1995 and 2006) article 5(2)(g) and article 10(2), respectively. For example, the 1949 Geneva Conventions are based on drafts prepared by the ICRC and discussed at the 1948 Stockholm Conference. In addition, the ICRC has published commentaries on each of the Conventions and Protocols and a project is currently underway to update these Commentaries. See Lindsey Cameron, Bruno Demeyere, Jean-Marie Henckaerts, Eve La Haye, and Heike Niebergall-Lackner, 'The Updated Commentary on the First Geneva Convention—A New Tool for Generating Respect for International Humanitarian Law' (2015) 97 *IRRC* 1209.

## A. The General Framework: The Geneva Conventions and Their Additional Protocols

### 1. The Geneva Conventions

The battle of Solferino in northern Italy in 1859 acted as a catalyst for the adoption of the very first Geneva Convention in 1864.[9] Henry Dunant, a businessman from Geneva, witnessed the horrific effects of the fighting during this battle and played a key role in the collection and caring for the wounded soldiers. In his book, *A Memory of Solferino*, Dunant proposed the peacetime creation of permanent aid societies in all countries to ensure that qualified volunteers would be available in the event of war to help the wounded of all parties. Dunant also suggested that states meet 'to formulate some international principle, sanctioned by a Convention inviolate in character' to regulate the functioning of such societies and to give legal protection to the wounded soldiers in the field. These proposals inspired the foundation of the Red Cross Movement and the convening by the Swiss Federal Council of a Diplomatic Conference in Geneva that, on 22 August 1864, adopted the 1864 Geneva Convention.[10]

The 1864 Convention, a mere ten articles, laid down several principles that have been maintained as core principles of IHL to this date: the protection of the wounded and sick without any distinction, whether friend or foe; the inviolability of medical personnel, establishments, and transports; and the use of a distinctive emblem of the red cross on a white ground (later supplemented by other emblems).

This Convention has been the subject of continuous update and adaptation. Thus, new versions were adopted in 1906, 1929, and 1949, and protocols were added in 1977 and 2005. Consideration of a possible revision of the 1864 Convention was, however, excluded from the agenda of the International Peace Conferences held at The Hague in 1899 and 1907.[11] This led to a split of the law of armed conflict into two branches, each with their own path of development.[12] Named after the respective cities in which their treaty rules were adopted, Geneva law was concerned mainly with the protection of the victims of armed conflict, while Hague law focused largely on limiting or prohibiting certain means and methods of warfare. With the adoption in 1977 of Additional Protocol I (AP I) to the Geneva Conventions of 1949, the two strands of law could be seen to merge.[13] As is discussed below, that protocol reaffirms and develops the rules on methods and means of warfare embodied in the Hague Conventions and Regulations, as well as setting out rules on the wounded, sick, and shipwrecked, combatant, and prisoner-of-war status, and it contains a long section on the civilian population.

The first update of the 1864 Geneva Convention in 1906 more than tripled the size of the convention, from ten to thirty-three articles, adding more details and precisions, in addition to new provisions. For example, the 1906 Convention introduced provisions concerning the burial of the dead and the transmission of information concerning the wounded and

---

[9] The *Instructions for the Government of Armies of the United States in the Field*, General Orders No 100 (24 April 1863) (*Lieber Code*) also had an important influence on subsequent efforts at codifying IHL. The *Lieber Code* was written to regulate the conduct of Union Forces during the American Civil War (1861–1865) and largely reflected existing laws and customs of war. For a discussion, see Kalshoven (above n 7) 35.

[10] Kalshoven (above n 7) 34.

[11] ibid 39.

[12] See Alexander (above n 3) 111.

[13] See Kalshoven (above n 7) 44.

sick and the dead.[14] The protection of personnel of voluntary aid societies was also recognized for the first time.[15]

The third version of the Geneva Convention concerning the protection of the wounded and sick was adopted in 1929 in the wake of the First World War, taking into account the experience of that conflict.[16] It contained new provisions on the protection of medical aircraft[17] and the use of the distinctive emblem in time of peace.[18] The emblems of the red crescent and of the red lion and sun were moreover recognized for countries that already used them instead of the red cross.[19]

In addition, the Diplomatic Conference of 1929 adopted an entirely new Convention relative to the treatment of the prisoners of war.[20] This regime had previously been subject to the Hague Regulations of 1899 and 1907, which proved insufficient during World War I. Informed by the experiences of that war, the International Red Cross Conference held in Geneva in 1921 expressed the wish that a special Convention on the treatment of prisoners of war be developed. This new Convention did not replace the Hague Regulations, but complemented them. It is much more detailed, containing ninety-seven articles, compared to the previous seventeen articles found in the Hague Regulations (articles 4–20). Influenced by the practices during the First World War, the 1929 Convention on Prisoners of War moreover introduced new rules prohibiting reprisals against prisoners of war (POWs),[21] regulating the work by POWs and their pay,[22] and regulating the relations of POWs with the exterior[23] and with the authorities,[24] including the appointment of representatives.[25]

The 1949 Geneva Conventions represent the third update of the 1864 Geneva Convention. While the initial diplomatic conference had been planned for the early 1940s, it could not take place due to the outbreak of the Second World War. As a result, the whole process was delayed for nine years, but with the consequence that the new Conventions could take into account the experience from the Second World War. The new Conventions include an update of the 1929 Geneva Conventions on Wounded and Sick (GCI of 1949),[26] as well as an update of the Hague Convention (X) of 1907 for the Adaptation to Maritime Warfare of the Principles of the Geneva Convention.[27] The latter update expanded the Hague Convention from a mere twenty-eight articles to a more complete and self-standing convention of sixty-three articles (Second Geneva Convention of 1949). The 1929 Convention on Prisoners of War was updated and became the Third Geneva Convention of 1949, making the regime of the protection of prisoners of war more detailed, increasing from ninety-seven articles in

---

[14] Convention for the Amelioration of the Condition of the Wounded and Sick in Armies in the Field (6 July 1906) articles 3–4.

[15] ibid articles 10–11.

[16] Geneva Convention for the Amelioration of the Condition of the Wounded and Sick in Armies in the Field (27 July 1929) 118 LNTS 303.

[17] ibid article 18.

[18] ibid article 24.

[19] ibid article 19.

[20] Geneva Convention relative to the Treatment of Prisoners of War (27 July 1929) 118 LNTS 343.

[21] ibid article 2.

[22] ibid articles 27–34.

[23] ibid articles 35–41.

[24] ibid articles 42–67.

[25] ibid articles 43–44.

[26] Geneva Convention (I) for the Amelioration of the Condition of the Wounded and Sick in Armed Forces in the Field (adopted 12 August 1949, entered into force 21 October 1950) 75 UNTS 31 (GCI).

[27] Geneva Convention (II) for the Amelioration of the Condition of Wounded, Sick and Shipwrecked Members of Armed Forces at Sea (adopted 12 August 1949, entered into force 12 August 1949) 75 UNTS 85 (GCII).

1929 to 143 articles in 1949.[28] This level of detail was meant to avoid certain misinterpret-ations and abuses that had occurred during the Second World War.

An important gap in the protection of victims of armed conflict had remained after 1929 and was sorely felt during the two World Wars, namely the protection of civilians. This protection has two aspects: the protection of civilians in the hands of a party to the conflict, and the protection of civilians against the dangers arising from warfare. The need to regulate the first aspect had become overwhelmingly clear during the Second World War and in response, states adopted the Fourth Geneva Convention in 1949.[29] The need to update the second aspect, already addressed in the Hague Regulations, was also clear during the Second World War, but would only be addressed in 1977 with the adoption of the Additional Protocols to the Geneva Conventions. With the increasing use of aerial warfare affecting populated areas, the rules on the conduct of hostilities were in dire need of up-dating. This was a long and difficult process for a variety of reasons, not least because of the thorny issue of nuclear weapons.

The Fourth Convention contains a short part concerning the general protection of populations against certain consequences of war, covering the whole of the populations of the countries to the conflict.[30] This includes an important provision on enquiries by members of families dispersed owing to the conflict, with a view to renewing contact and meeting.[31] The bulk of the Convention deals with civilians in enemy territory and in oc-cupied territory. The Hague Regulations already contained some provisions on occupied territory (articles 42–56) but these had proven inadequate already during the First World War. That is why the ICRC developed a new draft convention on the subject, approved by the International Red Cross Conference of 1934 in Tokyo. However, due to the out-break of the Second World War the diplomatic conference planned for 1940 had to be can-celled. The consequences for populations in occupied territories would be dire. The 1949 Convention expands and makes the protection of the civilian populations more detailed and complete. With a total of 159 articles, the Fourth Convention is the longest of the four Conventions.

One of the major innovations of the 1949 Conventions was the regulation of non-international armed conflicts (NIACs) in Common Article 3. This article was the outcome of protracted negotiations. Two options had become available: either to make the en-tire Geneva Conventions applicable to a limited number of NIACs, or to make a limited number of rules applicable to a wide range of NIACs broadly defined. The latter option was ultimately chosen. Common Article 3 has become one of the most important provisions of IHL, since most conflicts today are non-international in nature, and since all states are party to the Geneva Conventions, and thus bound by Common Article 3. In addition, the International Court of Justice (ICJ) has recognized the fundamental character of this provi-sion as a reflection of 'elementary considerations of humanity' and as a 'minimum yardstick' binding in all armed conflicts.[32] Common Article 3 has been supplemented by Additional

---

[28] Geneva Convention (III) Relative to the Treatment of Prisoners of War (adopted 12 August 1949, entered into force 21 October 1950) 75 UNTS 135 (GCIII).
[29] Geneva Convention (IV) Relative to the Protection of Civilian Persons in Time of War (adopted 12 August 1949, entered into force 21 October 1950) 75 UNTS 287 (GCIV).
[30] ibid Part II articles 13–26.
[31] ibid article 26.
[32] See *Case concerning Military and Paramilitary Activities in and against Nicaragua* (*Nicaragua v USA*) (Advisory Opinion) [1986] ICJ Reports paras 218–219.

Protocol II (APII, by other treaty rules applicable in NIACs) and by the continuous development of customary international law in this area (see below).

## A. *The additional protocols*
As explained above, the Geneva Conventions were continuously updated through successive treaties replacing the previous ones. Updates since 1949, on the other hand, have taken place via a system of additional protocols. The advantage of this system is to preserve the acquis of the main Conventions, while states may adhere to the additional rules in the Protocols.[33]

After 1949, the importance of the protection of the civilian population against the effects of hostilities or the conduct of hostilities, became clear. In 1956 the ICRC prepared Draft Rules for the Limitation of the Dangers Incurred by the Civilian Population in Time of War. These were approved a year later by the International Red Cross Conference in New Delhi and submitted to governments for examination. However, there was virtually no response from governments and no further action was taken to convert the Draft Rules into a treaty. It would not be until 1969 that the International Conference asked the ICRC to work out proposals to address these issues. As a result, the ICRC convened two expert meetings in 1971 and 1972 to prepare two draft protocols additional to the Geneva Conventions, one on international armed conflict (IAC) and the other on NIAC. The ICRC published the draft protocols in 1973 and Switzerland convened a diplomatic conference to adopt them which would meet during four sessions between 1974 and 1977. The outcome was the adoption of two Protocols Additional to the 1949 Geneva Conventions, updating the rules on the conduct of hostilities and on the protection of war victims and providing the first international convention specifically applicable in NIACs (APII).[34] The four years of negotiation show how the development of IHL had become more difficult, compared to the adoption in 1949 of four Geneva Conventions during a diplomatic conference that lasted less than four months.

The two Additional Protocols of 1977 were negotiated against the background of the decolonization process and the Vietnam/Second Indochina War (1955–1975), which had brought to the fore the issues of liberation wars and the status of guerrilla fighters.[35] One of the main objectives of countries of the South was to have fights against colonial domination, alien occupation, and racist regimes recognized as IACs. When this was achieved with the adoption of what is now article 1(4) of API, these countries lost interest in the regulation of NIACs. The result was a simplification of APII and its reduction to a mere twenty-eight articles, compared to 102 in API.

The most important developments in API relate to the rules on the conduct of hostilities (articles 35–60), which contain a much-needed update of the Hague Regulations of 1899 and 1907. The experience of the Vietnam War had demonstrated the importance of reaffirming and developing the rules on the conduct of hostilities in order to enhance the

[33] Other IHL treaties have also used this system of development, including treaties on the protection of cultural property and the regulation or prohibition of the use of certain weapons.
[34] Protocol Additional to the Geneva Conventions of 12 August 1949 and Relating to the Protection of Victims of International Armed Conflicts (adopted 8 June 1977, entered into force 7 December 1978) 1125 UNTS 3 (API); Protocol Additional to the Geneva Conventions of 12 August 1949 and Relating to the Protection of Victims of Non-International Armed Conflicts (adopted 8 June 1977, entered into force 7 December 1978) 1125 UNTS 609 (APII).
[35] See Kalshoven (above n 7) 48.

protection of the civilian population.[36] API thus elaborates on the principle of distinction between civilians and combatants and between civilian objects and military objectives and prohibits indiscriminate attacks. It contains a definition of military objectives,[37] and it spells out the obligations to take precautions in attack[38] and against the effects of attack.[39] The practices during the Vietnam War moreover focused the drafters' attention on topics such as starvation as a method of warfare, area bombardment, and the destruction of the natural environment.[40] For example, the prohibition in article 35(3) 'to employ methods of means of warfare which are intended, or may be expected, to cause widespread, long-term and severe damage to the natural environment' was inspired by the considerable environmental destruction brought about by that conflict.[41] Another important aspect of API is the extension of the protection of the Conventions to civilian medical personnel, equipment, and supplies and to civilian medical units and transports.[42]

As mentioned above, the draft APII was simplified in the last days of the Conference. The original drafts of both protocols submitted by the ICRC to the 1974–1977 diplomatic conference were very similar.[43] Even during the diplomatic conference, Committee III, which worked on the draft of APII, accepted a substantial number of the draft provisions submitted by the ICRC, often with consensus, although sometimes with minor changes. Yet in the last weeks of a four-year long negotiation, many parts of draft APII were simply deleted. The main reason was that a consensus could only be reached on a much-simplified text, not on the version elaborated by Committee III on the basis of the ICRC draft. This simplification process consisted, in particular, of removing or revising all articles that referred to the 'parties to the conflict'. A good example of this diplomatic manoeuvre is the provision on dissemination in the Additional Protocols. Whereas API imposes an obligation on all 'High Contracting Parties' to disseminate the Conventions and the Protocol as widely as possible,[44] APII summarily requires that '[t]his Protocol shall be disseminated as widely as possible'—without specifying to whom this obligation is addressed.[45] At the time, a number of states could not accept that armed groups as 'parties to the conflict' would have specific rights and obligations under international law, for example the obligation to disseminate humanitarian law.[46]

This reticence was based on the reasoning of the then newly independent states that recognizing such rights and obligations and, in general, a detailed regulation of NIACs would encourage rebellion and secession, threatening their frail sovereignty.[47] However,

[36] Michael Bothe, Karl Josef Partsch, and Waldemar A Solf, *New Rules for Victims of Armed Conflicts. Commentary on the Two 1977 Protocols Additional to the Geneva Conventions of 1949* (Martinus Nijhoff 1982) xix.

[37] API article 52(2).

[38] ibid article 57.

[39] ibid article 58.

[40] See Hans Blix, 'Arms Control Treaties Aimed at Reducing the Military Impact on the Environment', in Jerzy Makarczyk (ed), *Essays in International Law in Honour of Judge Manfred Lachs* (Martinus Nijhoff 1984)710.

[41] ibid 712 and Kalshoven (above n 7) 47.

[42] API articles 8–31.

[43] Draft Additional Protocols of June 1973 to the Geneva Conventions of 12 August 1949, Official Records of the Diplomatic Conference on the Reaffirmation and Development of International Humanitarian Law Applicable in Armed Conflicts (Geneva, 1974–1977), Federal Political Department, Bern, 1978, Vol I, Part III.

[44] API article 83(1).

[45] See APII article 19.

[46] For more details, including references to the preparatory work, see Bothe et al (above n 36) 604–08 (general) and 701 (dissemination in particular) and Sylvie S Junod, 'General Introduction to the Commentary on Protocol II', in Yves Sandoz, Christophe Swinarski, and Bruno Zimmermann (eds), *Commentary on the Additional Protocols to the Geneva Conventions* (Martinus Nijhoff/ICRC 1987) paras 4405–4418.

[47] See ibid.

this reasoning was misleading as recognition of rights and obligations of non-state armed groups (NSAGs) under international law predated the Protocol by at least thirty years. Indeed, Common Article 3 of the Geneva Conventions already imposed obligations on 'each Party to the conflict' not of an international character and even encouraged the parties to 'further endeavour to bring into force, by means of special agreements, all or part of the other provisions of the present Convention' and so went further than APII. Common Article 3 specifies, on the other hand, that its application 'shall not affect the legal status of the Parties to the conflict', a provision that is repeated in a number of later treaties applicable to NIACs.[48]

The simplification process of APII has, unfortunately, left the Protocol with an awkward structure. The basic rules on the distinction between military objectives, civilian objects, and their subsequent definitions are missing, though the Protocol retained mention of detailed rules on specific objects, namely objects indispensable to the survival of the civilian population, works, and installations containing dangerous forces, and cultural objects and places of worship.[49]

As a result, an important impediment in applying humanitarian treaty law is that it offers only a rudimentary framework for the regulation of NIACs, in particular with respect to the conduct of hostilities. Common Article 3 of the Geneva Conventions, the only provision of the Geneva Conventions that is formally applicable to NIACs, does not as such deal with the conduct of hostilities. APII failed to remedy this and does not deal with the conduct of hostilities and a number of other issues in sufficient detail. For example, unlike API, APII does not provide for the obligation to distinguish between military objectives and civilian objects. As a result, it does not contain any protection for civilian objects in general, nor does it define civilian objects and military objectives. This is problematic in practice because NIACs require armed forces (both state armed forces and NSAGs) to actually limit their military operations to military objectives. APII moreover lacks other key provisions on the conduct of hostilities, such as the prohibition and definition of indiscriminate attacks and the obligation to take precautions in attack and against the effects of attack.

These shortcomings in APII have somewhat been rectified in subsequent treaties applicable to NIACs.[50] But more importantly, these gaps have been filled by the development of customary rules of IHL (see below).

Finally, it should be mentioned that in 2005 a Third Additional Protocol to the Geneva Conventions was adopted. It recognizes an additional distinctive emblem: the 'Red Crystal', providing a further option to the Red Cross and Red Crescent.[51]

---

[48]  See eg the Hague Convention for the Protection of Cultural Property in the Event of Armed Conflict of 14 May 1954 (Hague Convention 1954) and the Convention on Conventional Weapons (CCW). Article 19 of the 1954 Convention is modelled on Common Article 3: (i) it provides a minimum set of rules applicable to a broad range of armed conflicts not of an international character; (ii) it requires parties to the conflict to endeavour to bring into force, by means of special agreements, all or part of the other provisions of the Convention; (iii) it provides that UNESCO may offer its services to the parties to the conflict; and (iv) it provides that the application of this provision shall not affect the legal status of the parties to the conflict.

[49]  See APII article 14 (objects indispensable to the survival of the civilian population); APII article 15 (works and installations containing dangerous forces); AP II article 16 (cultural objects and places of worship).

[50]  For an overview of some of these treaties, see the section on customary humanitarian law.

[51]  Protocol additional to the Geneva Conventions of 12 August 1949, and Relating to the Adoption of an Additional Distinctive Emblem (8 December 2005).

## B. Specialized Conventions

In addition to the Geneva Conventions and their Protocols IHL is also characterized by different strands of substantive developments and specialization. Different areas of IHL are governed by different specialized treaties.[52] Prominent examples are the protection of cultural property and the regulation of specific weapons.

With respect to the protection of cultural property, such property is, in principle, a civilian object and therefore protected under the general IHL rules on the conduct of hostilities. Nevertheless, cultural property has been protected by specific treaty rules since 1899.[53] The wanton destruction and forced exportation of cultural property during World War II reinforced the need for new treaty law on the subject. To that end, an intergovernmental conference convened by UNESCO in 1954 adopted the Convention for the Protection of Cultural Property in the Event of Armed Conflict.[54] Weapons law is another area where special treaty regulation has emerged, even though the use of any weapon in armed conflict must comply with the general rules of IHL on the conduct of hostilities. Among the numerous treaties that have been adopted to specifically regulate the use of certain weapons, the 1980 Convention on Conventional Weapons (CCW) deals with the use of certain conventional weapons that may be considered excessively injurious or to have indiscriminate effects.

In both these fields, the technique of adding protocols to the basic treaties have been used, similar to the Geneva Conventions which are supplemented by three additional protocols. The advantage of using additional protocols is to preserve the acquis of the original convention while allowing states flexibility in choosing which protocols to join. Thus, the 1954 Convention for the Protection of Cultural Property is supplemented by two Protocols, one of 1954, which aims to prevent the exportation of cultural property from occupied territory and to provide for restitution of illegally exported objects, and the second one of 1999 which updates the 1954 Convention in relation to the conduct of hostilities and individual criminal responsibility and established a new system of enhanced protection.[55] The CCW is different in that it is an 'umbrella' convention, providing the general framework but containing no regulation of specific weapons, which is the subject of its protocols. Three original Protocols were adopted the same year as the CCW, prohibiting the use of any weapon which primary effect is to injure by fragments that in the human body escape detection by X-ray;[56] restricting the use of mines, booby-traps and similar devices;[57] and restricting

---

[52] For a discussion, see Jann Kleffner, 'Sources of the Law of Armed Conflict', in Livoja and McCormack (eds) (above n 7) 71, 72–3.

[53] Thus the 1899 and 1907 Hague Regulations first protected 'buildings dedicated to religion, art, science, or charitable purposes, historic monuments, ... provided they are not being used at the time for military purposes'. The Regulations further specify that 'the besieged must indicate the presence of such buildings or places by distinctive and visible signs, which shall be notified to the enemy beforehand'.

[54] Hague Convention 1954. See Kalshoven (above n 7) 45.

[55] First Protocol for the Protection of Cultural Property in the Event of Armed Conflict of 14 May 1954; Second Protocol to the Hague Convention of 1954 for the Protection of Cultural Property in the Event of Armed Conflict of 26 March 1999 (Hague Protocol II).

[56] Protocol on Non-Detectable Fragments (Protocol I) (10 October 1980).

[57] Protocol (II) on Prohibitions or Restrictions on the Use of Mines, Booby-Traps and Other Devices (10 October 1980). Protocol II to the CCW was replaced in 1996 by Amended Protocol II, which sets stricter limitations on the use of mines, booby-traps, and similar devices. A total ban on the use of anti-personnel land mines (as opposed to anti-vehicle land mines) was adopted just a year later by the Mine Ban Convention, which was adopted outside the framework of the CCW.

the use of incendiary weapons, ie weapons that use fire as their means of injury or destruc-tion.[58] In 1995 and 2003 respectively, two further protocols were adopted, prohibiting laser weapons specifically designed to cause permanent blindness to unenhanced vision (so-called 'blinding laser weapons'),[59] and seeking to minimize the risks and effects of explosive remnants of war (ERW) in post-conflict situations.[60] In addition, there are several 'stand alone' treaties prohibiting the development, production, stockpiling, transfer and/or use of certain types of weapons, in particular chemical and biological weapons, anti-personnel landmines, cluster munitions, and nuclear weapons.

For a discussion of the substantive protection of cultural property and regulation of spe-cific weapons, see chapters 8 'Specifically Protected Persons and Objects' and 11 'Weapons', respectively.

## C. IHL Mainstreaming in Human Rights Treaties

In addition to the adoption of specialized treaties on specific issues, another codification technique is to mainstream IHL by including it in human rights treaties. It is generally accepted that human rights law constitutes a relevant source of law in armed conflict, in addition to IHL.[61] The ICJ has confirmed that international human rights law re-mains applicable during armed conflict, subject only to derogation.[62] The relationship between IHL and human rights law is, however, complex and requires devoted separate consideration in chapter 17 'International Humanitarian Law and International Human Rights Law'.

The incorporation of IHL in human rights treaties has, for example, taken place in rela-tion to the protection of children, women, and persons with disabilities. The first example is article 38(1) of the Convention on the Rights of the Child, which provides that 'States Parties undertake to respect and to ensure respect for rules of international humanitarian law applicable to them in armed conflicts which are relevant to the child'. Through this re-ferral, the Convention on the Rights of the Child incorporates all relevant IHL rules.[63] This is important because it means that the relevant IHL rules come within the mandate of the supervision system of the Convention, a system which does not (yet) exist under IHL. The Convention also contains a substantive rule aimed to prevent children under the age of fifteen being recruited and taking a direct part in hostilities. This age limit was increased to eighteen years in a 2000 Protocol to the Convention on the Involvement of Children in Armed Conflict.[64]

[58] Protocol on Prohibitions or Restrictions on the Use of Incendiary Weapons (Protocol III) (10 October 1980).

[59] Protocol on Blinding Laser Weapons (Protocol IV to the 1980 CCW Convention) (13 October 1995).

[60] Protocol on Explosive Remnants of War (Protocol V to the 1980 CCW Convention) (28 November 2003).

[61] See eg Hans-Joachim Heintze, 'On the Relationship between Human Rights Law Protection and International Humanitarian Law' (2004) 86 IRRC 789.

[62] See Legality of the Threat or Use of Nuclear Weapons (Advisory Opinion) [1996] ICJ Rep 266 (Nuclear Weapons) para 26 and Legal Consequences of the Construction of a Wall in the Occupied Palestinian Territory (Advisory Opinion) [2004] ICJ Rep 136 paras 102–106.

[63] See eg GCIV articles 16 and 49 and GCIII, articles 14, 16–18, 21–27, 38, 49–51, 68, 76, 81, 82, 85, 89, 91, 94, 119, 127, 132, 136–140; API articles 8, 52, 70, 74, 75–78; APII articles 4–6; as well as relevant rules of customary international humanitarian law, as expressed for example in Rules 120 and 135–137 of Jean-Marie Henckaerts and Louise Doswald-Beck, Customary International Humanitarian Law, Vol 1: Rules (ICRC 2005) (CIHL).

[64] Optional Protocol to the Convention on the Rights of the Child on the involvement of children in armed con-flict of 25 May 2000.

The second example is a regional instrument, the Protocol to the African Charter on Human and Peoples' Rights on the Rights of Women in Africa.[65] Article 11(1) on protection of women in armed conflict stipulates: 'States Parties undertake to respect and ensure respect for the rules of international humanitarian law applicable in armed conflict situations, which affect the population, particularly women.' By the method of *renvoi*, this provision incorporates relevant provisions of IHL into the Protocol.[66]

The third example is the International Convention on the Protection and Promotion of the Rights and Dignity of Persons with Disabilities (CRPD).[67] Article 11 of this Convention provides:

> States Parties shall take, in accordance with their obligations under international law, including international humanitarian law and international human rights law, all necessary measures to ensure the protection and safety of persons with disabilities in situations of risk, including situations of armed conflict, humanitarian emergencies and the occurrence of natural disasters.

This reference to IHL in this treaty is less direct than in the two previous examples.

## D.  Criminalization

The fact that serious violations of IHL are recognized as war crimes attracting individual criminal responsibility goes back at least to the First World War.[68] It was first recognized in the 1929 Convention. It was more firmly established in the grave breaches of regime of the 1949 Geneva Conventions, as complemented by API. This regime only applied to IACs; neither Common Article 3 nor APII contain such provisions.

However, over the past few decades, a level of convergence has been achieved in terms of the criminalization of conduct in IACs and NIACs.[69] The atrocities committed in the former Yugoslavia and in Rwanda in the 1990s led to the establishment of the ad hoc International Criminal Tribunal for the Former Yugoslavia (ICTY) and the International Criminal Tribunal for Rwanda (ICTR), both of which list war crimes committed in the context of NIACs.[70] This development paved the way for the adoption in 1998 of the Statute

---

[65]  Adopted at Maputo, 11 July 2003.

[66]  Relevant provisions include GCI article 12(4), GCII article 12(4), GCIII article 14(2), GCIV article 27(2), API article 76(1), and APII articles 4–5, as well as relevant rules of customary international humanitarian law, including CIHL Rules 119 and 134.

[67]  Adopted by UN General Assembly Resolution 61/106 (13 December 2006) Annex I.

[68]  See Treaty of Versailles 1919 articles 227–229.

[69]  See eg Statute of the International Tribunal for the Prosecution of Persons Responsible for Serious Violations of International Humanitarian Law Committed in the Territory of the Former Yugoslavia since 1991 (adopted by UN Security Council Resolution 827 (25 May 1993), as amended by Resolutions 1166 (13 May 1998) and 1329 (30 November 2000) (ICTY Statute) article 3 (as interpreted by the Tribunal in *Prosecutor v Tadić* (Decision) [1995] IT-94-1-AR72, Appeals Chamber paras 71–93); Statute of the International Criminal Tribunal for the Prosecution of Persons Responsible for Genocide and Other Serious Violations of International Humanitarian Law in the Territory of Rwanda and Rwandan citizens responsible for genocide and other such violations committed in the territory of neighbouring States between 1 January 1994 and 31 December 1994 (adopted by UN Security Council Resolution 955 (8 November 1994), as amended by Resolutions 1165 (30 April 1998), 1329 (30 November 2000), 1411 (17 May 2002), and 1431 (14 August 2002)) (ICTR Statute) article 8(2)(c) and 8(2)(e). See also Eve La Haye, *War Crimes in Internal Armed Conflicts* (CUP 2008); Theodor Meron, 'International Criminalization of Internal Atrocities' (1995) 89 *AJIL* 554; and Lindsay Moir, 'Grave Breaches and Internal Armed Conflicts' (2009) 7 *JICJ* 763.

[70]  ICTY Statute, article 3; ICTR Statute, article 8(2)(c) and 8(2)(e).

of the International Criminal Court (ICC) defining war crimes in IACs and NIACs,[71] as amended in 2010.[72]

While there is thus a growing tendency to consider serious violations of IHL applicable in NIACs under the broader concept of 'war crimes', liabilities are still less extensive in NIACs compared to IACs. This is demonstrated by the fact that the list of war crimes in relation to which the International Criminal Court has jurisdiction is more extensive for IACs compared to NIACs.[73]

From a sources point of view, this field of law is moreover complicated by the existence of different liabilities, depending on the international instrument in question.[74] Notably, API extends the concept of 'grave breaches' laid down in the Geneva Conventions to cover various violations of the rules governing the conduct of hostilities.[75] While both the ICTY and the ICC have jurisdiction to take cognizance of grave breaches of the Geneva Conventions, neither Statute mentions grave breaches of API. On the other hand, the ICTY is competent to take cognizance of 'violations of the laws or customs of war'—a concept which the tribunal has interpreted broadly to include violations committed on the battlefield.[76] Moreover, the Statute of the ICC lists, in addition to grave breaches of the Geneva Conventions, 'other serious violations' of the law of IAC. These other 'serious violations' cover some, but not all, of the grave breaches set out in API.[77] For example, there is no reference in the ICC Statute to unjustified delays in repatriating prisoners of war and civilians.

## E.  General Observations on Codification

Based on this overview of the codification of IHL, a number of general observations can be made:

### 1. Universalization
The history of codification of IHL is marked by two strands of universalization. The first one is the increased participation of states in the development and codification of IHL. Whereas only sixteen states were present at the 1864 diplomatic conference that led to the adoption of the first Geneva Convention, by 1949 their number had increased to sixty-three states participating, and between 1974 and 1977 between 106 and 126 states took part in the four sessions of the diplomatic conference that adopted the Additional Protocols. This development reflects the general expansion of the community of states, mainly through

---

[71] Rome Statute of the International Criminal Court (adopted 17 July 1998, entered into force 1 July 2002) 2187 UNTS 3 (Rome Statute).

[72] An amendment to article 8 of the Rome Statute in Kampala on 10 June 2010 extended the criminalization of the use of three categories of weapons to situations of non-international armed conflict (employing poison or poisoned weapons; employing asphyxiating, poisonous or other gases, and all analogous liquids, materials, and devices, and employing bullets that expand or flatten easily in the human body). See 2868 UNTS 195.

[73] See Rome Statute article 8(2)(b) on international armed conflict and article 8(2)(c) and (e) on non-international armed conflict.

[74] See eg Philippe Xavier, 'Sanctions for Violations of International Humanitarian Law: The Problem of the Division of Competences between National Authorities and between National and International Authorities' (2008) 90 *IRRC* 359.

[75] API articles 11 and 85.

[76] See *Tadić* (Decision) (above n 69) paras 86–136.

[77] See Rome Statute, article 8(2)(e).

decolonization and the breaking up of a number of states. The result is that today's IHL treaties have been developed with the cooperation of the global community of states and no longer by a limited number of (mostly Western) states. This increases the legitimacy of the treaties and their acceptance as reflective of global traditions.

Related thereto, the second strand is the universalization in the participation of the main treaties of IHL. The most notable example is the Geneva Conventions themselves, which enjoy universal adherence.[78] After their adoption, the Geneva Conventions immediately had huge success. They entered into force as soon as 21 October 1950, after the first two ratifications. They were ratified by seventy-four states in the 1950s and obtained a further forty-eight ratifications in the 1960s. The ratification steadily increased in the 1970s (twenty ratifications) and 1980s (twenty ratifications). A wave of twenty-six new ratifications occurred in the early 1990s, resulting in particular from the break-up of the Soviet Union, Czechoslovakia, and the former Yugoslavia. With the last nine ratifications since the year 2000, the applicability of the Geneva Convention has today become universal, with 196 states party.

Other IHL treaties also enjoy increasing participation.[79] For example, API has 174 states parties and APII 168. While this is an impressive (and increasing) ratification record, an important number of states still remain outside the framework of this treaty regime.[80] This situation implies that in different conflicts, different treaty regimes apply, which is unsatisfactory from the perspective of the legal protection of war victims. The fact that different treaties have different levels of ratification also has an impact on coalition warfare when different coalition partners have not subscribed to the same treaties.[81] In such cases, customary humanitarian law provides a common set of rules that is applicable to all coalition partners. Therefore, even if a state is a party to a particular treaty, it may still be relevant to know to what extent that treaty reflects customary law and is, as such, binding on coalition partners which have not ratified it.

Moreover, while IHL is marked by increased universalization in terms of state participation, it remains the case that NSAGs cannot be parties to IHL treaties.[82] This fact poses a challenge to universalization understood in a broad sense. As mentioned in section 1.A.1 ('The Geneva Conventions') above, most contemporary armed conflicts are of a non-international nature. Armed groups thus constitute important actors in the social reality which IHL seeks to regulate.[83] Indeed, recent decades have witnessed an expansion of the

[78] South Sudan and Palestine were the most recent states to adhere to the Geneva Conventions, on 13 January 2013 and on 2 April 2014, respectively. As a result, the Conventions are binding on all states as a matter of treaty law, regardless of whether they are also part of customary international law.

[79] To the knowledge of this author, as of December 2017, no state has denounced a current IHL treaty to which it adhered.

[80] UN member states that are not yet party to Additional Protocol I as of December 2017 are Andorra, Azerbaijan, Bhutan, Eritrea, India, Indonesia, Iran, Israel, Kiribati, Malaysia, Marshall Islands, Myanmar, Nepal, Pakistan, Papua New Guinea, Singapore, Somalia, Sri Lanka, Thailand, Turkey, Tuvalu, and the United States of America. UN member states that are not yet party to Additional Protocol II are Andorra, Angola, Azerbaijan, Bhutan, Democratic People's Republic of Korea, Eritrea, India, Indonesia, Iran, Iraq, Israel, Kiribati, Malaysia, Marshall Islands, Mexico, Myanmar, Nepal, Pakistan, Papua New Guinea, Singapore, Somalia, Sri Lanka, Syrian Arab Republic, Thailand, Turkey, Tuvalu, United States of America, and Vietnam.

[81] For discussion on the applicability and application of IHL to multinational operations, see 'Multinational Operations and the Law' (2013) 95 *IRRC* 472–742 (special issue).

[82] Vienna Convention on the Law of Treaties 1969 article 2(a) defines a treaty as 'an international agreement concluded between States in written form and governed by international law'.

[83] See Jean-Marie Henckaerts, 'Binding Armed Opposition Groups through Humanitarian Treaty Law and Customary Law' Spring 2003 27 *Proc Bruges Coll: Relevance of International Humanitarian Law to Non-State Actors* 128.

IHL rules regulating the conduct of states and organized armed groups in NIACs. Yet, the traditional doctrine of sources remains largely intact: states are the primary law-makers of international law, with near-exclusive capacity to enter into treaties and create customary rules of international law.[84] Although NSAGs are bound by IHL applicable in NIACs to which they are party, their exclusion from the process of creation and formal ratification of the rules that bind them may have an adverse effect on their ability and/or willingness to comply with the applicable IHL rules.

There are, however, a limited number of ways in which organized armed groups can express their commitment to uphold IHL rules applicable in NIACs. One way is by means of unilateral declaration, through which the armed group expresses its intent to be bound by (certain) IHL treaties or rules.[85] API contains a specific provision that envisages unilateral declarations by national liberation movements. In view of article 1(4), which brings national liberation wars within the ambit of the Protocol and the category of IACs, article 96(3) opens up the possibility for the 'authority representing a people' fighting a liberation war to unilaterally 'undertake to apply the Conventions and this Protocol'. This construct remained a dead letter for many years, but was applied for the first time in 2015.[86]

Another method in which armed groups party to a NIAC can formally make commitments under IHL is by means of special agreements. Article 3(3) of the Geneva Conventions encourages the parties to the conflict 'to bring into force, by means of special agreements, all or parts of the other provisions of the present Convention'. Such agreements could implement IHL obligations already incumbent on the parties, or contain provisions 'drawn from humanitarian law'.[87]

## 2. *Regionalization*
Unlike human rights law, IHL has not (yet) been subject to regionalization in the sense of the development of regional IHL instruments. Limited examples of regional IHL treaties or treaties that are related to IHL include the 1935 Treaty on the Protection of Artistic and Scientific Institutions and Historic Monuments (the Roerich Pact);[88] the 1974 European Convention on the Non-Applicability of Statutory Limitations to Crimes against Humanity and War Crimes;[89] the 1977 Organization of African Union (OAU) Convention for the Elimination of Mercenarism in Africa,[90] and the 1994 Inter-American Convention on the Forced Disappearance of Persons.[91]

---

[84]   See eg Anthea Roberts and Sandesh Sivakumaran, 'Lawmaking by Nonstate Actors: Engaging Armed Groups in the Creation of International Humanitarian Law' (2012) 37 *Yale J Int'l L* 107 and Marco Sassòli, 'Taking Armed Groups Seriously: Ways to Improve their Compliance with International Humanitarian Law' (2010) 1 *Int'l Hum Legal Stud* 7.

[85]   Such declarations can either be of a general nature, encompassing whole IHL treaties, or focus on particular rules or issues, such as in the form of 'Deeds of Commitment' made under the auspices of Geneva Call to ban anti-personnel mines. See Kleffner (above n 52) 83 and Liesbeth Zegveld, *Accountability of Armed Opposition Groups in International Law* (CUP 2002) 25.

[86]   See the unilateral declaration by the POLISARIO Front of 23 June 2015 www.eda.admin.ch/content/dam/eda/fr/documents/aussenpolitik/voelkerrecht/geneve/150626-GENEVE_en.pdf.

[87]   For a discussion, see ICRC, *Commentary on the First Geneva Convention* (CUP 2016) paras 846–855.

[88]   The Treaty has ten American states parties, all of which have since joined the Hague Convention 1954 on the subject.

[89]   The Convention only has three European states parties (the UN Convention on the Non-Applicability of Statutory Limitations to War Crimes and Crimes against Humanity 1968 has fifty-five states parties).

[90]   The Convention has thirty African states parties (the International Convention against the Recruitment, Use, Financing and Training of Mercenaries (adopted by UN General Assembly Resolution 44/34) (4 December 1989) has thirty-four states parties).

[91]   Adopted by the 24th Regular Session of the OAS General Assembly Resolution 1256 (XXIV-O/94) at Belém do Pará, 9 June 1994. It has fifteen American states parties. (The International Convention for the Protection of

The most recent, and perhaps most prominent, example is the 2009 African Union Convention for the Protection and Assistance of Internally Displaced Persons in Africa ('the Kampala Convention'). This is the first binding instrument on the protection of and assistance of internally displaced persons.[92] At the universal level, there is no specific treaty on this topic, only a soft-law instrument, the Guiding Principles on Internal Displacement.[93]

### 3. Institutionalization

It also noteworthy that most IHL treaties foresee meetings of states parties to discuss the state of implementation of the treaty and any issue with respect to their application. Meetings of state parties are, for example, envisaged in the treaties on the ICC,[94] conventional weapons,[95] chemical weapons,[96] anti-personnel mines,[97] cluster munitions,[98] arms trade,[99] and cultural property.[100]

The main and important exceptions are the Geneva Conventions and their Additional Protocols.[101] An ICRC-Swiss government proposal to create a voluntary meeting of states, based on discussions among states that were held between 2011 and 2015, was not accepted at the 32nd International Conference of the Red Cross and Red Crescent in 2015.[102] It was agreed instead that there should be a continuation of:

> an inclusive, State-driven intergovernmental process based on the principle of consensus after the 32nd International Conference ... to find agreement on features and functions of a potential forum of States and to find ways to enhance the implementation of IHL using the potential of the International Conference and IHL regional forums in order to submit the outcome of this intergovernmental process to the 33rd International Conference.

The further years of work were unfortunately unsuccessful due to deep political divisions among States. The Swiss-ICRC facilitated process came to an end in 2019 with the submission of a purely procedural report to the 33rd International Conference on the

---

all Persons from Enforced Disappearance (adopted by UN General Assembly Resolution 61/177 (20 December 2006), has fifty-two states parties, including all states parties to the Inter-American Convention on the Forced Disappearance of Persons 1994, with the exception of Guatemala and Venezuela).

[92] The Kampala Convention has twenty-five states parties.
[93] Presented to the UN Commission on Human Rights by the Special Representative of the UN Secretary General on Internally Displaced Persons (11 February 1998).
[94] Rome Statute of the International Criminal Court 1998 (Assembly of States Parties).
[95] Convention on Prohibitions or Restrictions on the Use of Certain Conventional Weapons Which May Be Deemed to Be Excessively Injurious or to Have Indiscriminate Effects as amended on 21 December 2001 (Review Conference).
[96] Convention on the Prohibition of the Development, Production, Stockpiling and Use of Chemical Weapons and on their Destruction 1993 (Conference of States Parties).
[97] Anti-Personnel Mine Ban Convention 1997 (Meeting of States Parties).
[98] Convention on Cluster Munitions 2008 (Meeting of States Parties).
[99] Arms Trade Treaty 2013 (Conference of States Parties).
[100] Hague Convention 1954 (Meeting of the High Contracting Parties).
[101] Additional Protocol I, Article 7, foresees a possibility for the depositary to convene a meeting of states parties at the request of one or more and the approval of the majority of them. However, such a meeting has, to date, not taken place.
[102] See Jelena Pejic, 'Strengthening Compliance with IHL: The ICRC-Swiss Initiative' (2017) 901 IRRC 315–330.

exchanges that were held among States and on the documents that had been produced by the co-facilitators.[103]

One of the aims of API was to add more teeth to the system of execution of the Conventions and the Protocol, ie measures aimed at ensuring respect for IHL.[104] One of the novelties of the Protocol was the provision for the establishment of an International Humanitarian Fact-Finding Commission.[105] Constituted in 1991, the Commission is a permanent body the primary purpose of which is to investigate allegations of grave breaches and other serious violations of IHL. While potentially a powerful mechanism to promote compliance with IHL, it has remained ineffective for a long time, but was activated for the first time in 2017.[106]

Another way in which IHL is increasingly being institutionalized is through its application by human rights bodies and courts.[107] According to O'Donnell, this 'is perhaps the inevitable consequence of years promoting the idea that human rights and IHL are complementary and dedicated to the same objective'.[108] In addition, human rights mechanisms are increasingly called upon to deal with situations of armed conflict as their geographical and thematic coverage expand.[109]

## 3. Customary International Law

International custom is defined in article 38 of the ICJ Statute as 'evidence of a general practice accepted as law'. It is thus generally agreed that the formation of custom requires two elements: general practice and an indication that this practice is followed as a matter of law (so-called *opinio juris*). The methodology to establish customary law has been clarified

[103] For further details, see https://www.icrc.org/en/document/strengthening-compliance-international-humanitarian-law-ihl-work-icrc-and-swiss-government.

[104] See API articles 80–91.

[105] ibid article 90.

[106] An Independent Forensic Investigation (IFI) team was assembled and deployed by the International Humanitarian Fact-Finding Commission at the request of the OSCE to look into an incident whereby an OSCE armoured vehicle was struck by an explosion, resulting in the death of an OSCE paramedic and the injury of two other patrol members. This occurred on 23 April 2017 during a routine patrol of the OSCE Special Monitoring Mission to Ukraine in the non-government-controlled area of Ukraine near Pryshyb. The aim of the IFI was to establish the facts of the incident by conducting a post-blast scene forensic investigation and technical assessment against the background of international humanitarian law. It was not within the mandate of the IFI to establish criminal responsibility or accountability for the incident. For an executive summary of the report, see OSCE 'Executive Summary of the Report of the Independent Forensic Investigation in relation to the Incident affecting an OSCE Special Monitoring Mission to Ukraine (SMM) Patrol on 23 April 2017' (OSCE, 7 September 2017) www.osce.org/home/338361. For information about the Commission, see www.ihffc.org/index.asp?page=home.
The Commission's effective utilization has been impeded by a number of features. First, a state is not bound by the authority of the Commission simply by acceding to the Protocol; it must additionally make a declaration specifically accepting the Commission's competence (currently seventy-six states parties to Additional Protocol I have made such a declaration). Second, the Commission does not have the power to act on its own initiative, but is dependent on a state (that has recognized its competence) to make a request for an investigation. Third, the Commission is only competent to inquire into situations arising in an international armed conflict. It should be noted, however, that the Commission has expressed its willingness to inquire into alleged violations of IHL arising from non-international armed conflicts, provided that the parties involved consent. See eg Charles Garraway, 'The International Humanitarian Fact-Finding Commission' (2008) 34 *Commonwealth Law Bull* 813.

[107] One example is the Human Rights Division of the UN Observer Mission in El Salvador (ONUSAL), which had an express mandate to monitor violations of IHL as well as violations of human rights law. Another example is the work of the Committee on the Rights of the Child, which has evaluated compliance with IHL in its examination of the reports submitted by states parties involved in armed conflict.

[108] See Daniel O'Donnell, 'Trends in the Application of International Humanitarian Law by United Nations Human Rights Mechanisms' (1998) 324 *IRRC* 481.

[109] ibid.

in several cases by the ICJ and is the subject of a recent study by the International Law Commission (ILC).[110]

Without being comprehensive, important material sources of customary rules of IHL include actual battlefield behaviour, the treatment of different categories of persons in armed conflict, and the use of certain weapons, in addition to certain verbal acts by states.[111] Military manuals, in particular, can constitute an important source for ascertaining both state practice and *opinio juris* with respect to customary rules of IHL.[112] An increasing number of states have sophisticated manuals that are publicly available for consultation. Domestic case law is another relevant source, as domestic courts are organs of the state and their decisions constitute practice of the state.[113] This is independent of the fact that the decisions of national courts can also serve as a supplementary means for the determination of rules of law (see section 5 'Judicial Decisions' below). Other examples of relevant verbal acts include national legislation, diplomatic protests, comments by governments on draft treaties, executive decisions and regulations, pleadings before international tribunals, statements in international organizations and at international conferences, and government positions taken with respect to resolutions of international organizations.[114]

By nature, customary international law is unwritten. The 'discovery' or 'identification' of customary law happens usually through judicial decisions or legal writings. States may also declare which parts of IHL they consider customary, but such statements are not binding on other states.

Notwithstanding the high degree of codification of IHL, customary humanitarian law continues to be relevant, due to the impediments that affect the application of treaty law in practice today. These have been highlighted: the fact that not all IHL treaties are universally ratified and that treaty law governing NIACs is still rudimentary, in particular concerning the conduct of hostilities.

These impediments came to the forefront during the conflicts in the former Yugoslavia and Rwanda in the first half of the 1990s and explain why a study on customary IHL was commissioned at that time. The Intergovernmental Group of Experts for the Protection of War Victims met in Geneva in January 1995 and adopted a series of recommendations aimed at enhancing respect for humanitarian law, in particular by means of preventive measures that would ensure better knowledge and more effective implementation of the law. Recommendation II of the Intergovernmental Group of Experts proposed that:

[t]he ICRC be invited to prepare, with the assistance of experts in IHL [international humanitarian law] representing various geographical regions and different legal systems, and in consultation with experts from governments and international organizations, a report on customary rules of IHL applicable in international and non-international armed conflicts, and to circulate the report to States and competent international bodies.[115]

---

[110] Draft Conclusions on Identification of Customary international Law, *Yearbook of the International Law Commission*, 2018, vol. II, Part Two, (A/73/10, para. 65).

[111] See CIHL xxxvii and International Law Association Committee on Formation of Customary (General) International Law, Final Report of the Committee (London Conference 2000) 12–14.

[112] See eg François Bugnion, 'Customary International Humanitarian Law' (2007) 7 *ISIL YB Int'l Hum Ref L* 10.

[113] See Conclusion 6 (2), Draft Conclusions on the Identification of Customary International Law (above n 107).

[114] CIHL (above n 63) xxxvii and Conclusion 6(1) and 6 (3) (above n 110) .

[115] Meeting of the Intergovernmental Group of Experts for the Protection of War Victims (23–27 January 1995), Recommendation II, published in , 62(1996) 78 *IRRC* 198.

In December 1995, the 26th International Conference of the Red Cross and Red Crescent endorsed this recommendation and officially mandated the ICRC to prepare a report on customary rules of IHL applicable in IACs and NIACs.[116] Nearly ten years later, in 2005, after extensive research and widespread consultation of experts, this report was published.[117]

The Conference gave this mandate to the ICRC particularly in light of the rudimentary nature of treaty law governing NIACs. Indeed, both Yugoslavia and Rwanda had ratified APII when their armed conflicts broke out but, as explained above, the Protocol contains many gaps. Therefore, states wanted to know to what extent these gaps had been filled by customary international law.[118]

One of the main outcomes of the ICRC's customary law study was a confirmation of the gradual rapprochement of the law on IACs and the law of NIACs. This outcome should not come as a surprise, since it is part of a general evolution in IHL and practice.

The same evolution has taken place in the development of humanitarian treaty law. The dichotomy between the regulation of IACs and NIACs that had been the hallmark of humanitarian treaty law since its inception gradually came undone. After the adoption of two separate Additional Protocols in 1977, API on IACs and APII on NIACs, the CCW and its three protocols adopted in 1980 were limited to IACs.[119] Protocol IV to the CCW, adopted on 13 October 1995, just two weeks after the decision of the ICTY Appeals Chamber in *Tadić*, was the last humanitarian law treaty so far to cover only IACs (and it was amended in the meantime to also cover NIACs). The shift in treaty law came with the adoption the next year of the Amended Mines Protocol on 3 May 1996.[120] The scope of application of the Amended Mines Protocol includes situations referred to in Common Article 3 of the Geneva Conventions.[121] The Mine Ban Convention adopted a year later in 1997 does not explicitly define its scope of application in terms of international or NIAC, but prohibits the use, development, production, acquisition, stockpiling, retention, or transfer to anyone, directly or indirectly, of anti-personnel mines 'under any circumstances'.[122] This means effectively that it applies equally in NIACs.

Next, in 1998, the adoption of the ICC Statute formally approved the extension of the concept of war crimes to NIACs in treaty law.[123] A year later, in 1999, the Second Protocol to the Hague Convention for the protection of cultural property was made applicable to NIACs.[124] In 2001, the CCW was amended to extend the scope of application of all then

---

[116] 26th International Conference of the Red Cross and Red Crescent (3–7 December 1995) Resolution 1, published in 60 (1996) 78 *IRRC*.

[117] CIHL vols I (Rules) and II (Practice).

[118] However, the development of customary law is an ongoing process and no doubt future practice will continue to influence and shape customary law. Therefore, the ICRC decided to keep the collection of practice up to date in the form of a database. See ICRC, 'Customary IHL Database' https://ihl-databases.icrc.org/customary-ihl/eng/docs/home.

[119] CCW; CCW Protocol I; CCW Protocol II; CCW Protocol III.

[120] CCW Protocol II (as amended, 3 May 1996).

[121] ibid article 1(2). See also article 1(3) and 1(6).

[122] Convention on the Prohibition of the Use, Stockpiling, Production and Transfer of Anti-Personnel Mines and on their Destruction (18 September 1997) article 1(1).

[123] Rome Statute article 8(2)(c) and (e).

[124] Second Protocol to the Hague Convention of 1954 for the Protection of Cultural Property in the Event of Armed Conflict (adopted 26 March 1999, entered into force 9 March 2004) 2253 UNTS 212 article 7 (containing a list of detailed precautionary measures very similar to those listed in API article 57(2)). For an analysis, see Jean-Marie Henckaerts, 'The Protection of Cultural Property in Non-International Armed Conflicts', in Nout van Woudenberg and Liesbeth Lijnzaad (eds), *Protecting Cultural Property in Armed Conflict. An Insight into the 1999 Second Protocol to the Hague Convention of 1954 for the Protection of Cultural Property in the Event of Armed Conflict* (Martinus Nijhoff 2010) 81.

existing Protocols (I–IV) to NIACs, as defined in Common Article 3 of the Geneva Conventions.[125] Until then, only Amended Protocol II had applied in NIACs. The subsequent CCW Protocol V on explosive remnants of war adopted in 2003 applies to both IACs and NIACs.[126] The 2008 Convention on Cluster Munitions uses the same approach as the Mine Ban Convention. Under the Convention on Cluster Munitions, states undertake 'never under any circumstances' to engage in prohibited acts.[127] The Kampala Convention on Internally Displaced Persons adopted in 2009 equally extends to NIACs.[128] Finally, the amendments to the ICC Statute adopted at the in 2017, 2019 and 2010 go in the same direction, as they extend the list of war crimes in NIACs, bringing it more in line with the list of war crimes in IACs.[129]

Similar developments took place in international fora, most notably the UN Security Council and General Assembly, as well as regional organizations and international conferences of states, which adopted numerous resolutions calling for respect for humanitarian law in general or for specific aspects of it. These resolutions dealt mostly with NIACs, being the most widespread form of armed conflicts in the recent decades.[130] Similarly, in national practice, military manuals, and legislation, case law and official statements increasingly focus on the application of humanitarian law in NIACs.[131]

This is not to say that the law on IACs and NIACs is now exactly the same. In *Tadić*, the ICTY Appeals Chamber famously noted that:

only a number of rules and principles governing international armed conflicts have gradually been extended to apply to internal conflicts; and this extension has not taken place in the form of a full and mechanical transplant of those rules to internal conflicts; rather, the general essence of those rules, and not the detailed regulation they may contain, has become applicable to internal conflicts.[132]

Later in the *Hadzihasanović* appeal on command responsibility, the ICTY Appeals Chamber stated that 'the rules applicable to international armed conflicts do not automatically apply to an internal armed conflict and what may constitute a war crime in the context

---

[125] CCW (21 December 2001) Amendment of article 1.

[126] Protocol on Explosive Remnants of War (Protocol V) (28 November 2003) article 1(3).

[127] Convention on Cluster Munitions (30 May 2008) article 1(1).

[128] African Union Convention for the Protection and Assistance of Internally Displaced Persons in Africa (23 October 2009) articles 1(k), 3(1)(e), 4(1) and (4)(b), and 7.

[129] For instance, the list of war crimes in the Rome Statute article 8, as adopted in 2002, was considerable shorter for non-international armed conflicts than for international armed conflict and did not include such customary prohibitions as intentionally causing starvation, launching an indiscriminate attack, making civilian objects the object of attack, using human shields, and using prohibited weapons. At the 2010 ICC Review Conference in Kampala, the use of poison and poisoned weapons, asphyxiating, poisonous, or other gases, and all analogous liquids, materials, and devices, and expanding bullets were added to the list of war crimes in article 8(2)(e). see https://asp.icc-cpi.int/iccdocs/asp_docs/Resolutions/RC-Res.5-ENG.pdf. Other war crimes in non-international armed conflicts were added to that list by the ICC Assembly of States Parties in 2017 and 2019, see https://asp.icc-cpi.int/iccdocs/asp_docs/Resolutions/ASP16/ICC-ASP-16-Res4-ENG.pdf.

[130] See the numerous resolutions concerning the conflicts in, among others, Afghanistan, Angola, Bosnia-Herzegovina, Burundi, DRC, Liberia, Rwanda, Sierra Leone, Russia (Chechnya), Somalia, Sudan (Darfur), Tajikistan and Yemen, comprehensively catalogued in the ICRC's 'Customary International Humanitarian Law Database' www.icrc.org/customary-ihl.

[131] For a comprehensive overview of national practice, see ibid.

[132] *Prosecutor v Tadić* (Decision) (above n 69) para 126.

of an international armed conflict does not necessarily constitute a war crime if committed in an internal conflict'.[133]

Similarly, the ICRC study shows that a difference continues to exist in customary IHL between the regulation of IACs and NIACs. Of the 161 rules the study has identified, twelve apply to IACs only. These relate to what continues to be considered the 'reserved domain' of IACs, which are the definition of combatants and armed forces, conditions for POW-status, the regulation of occupied territory, and the regulation of belligerent reprisals.[134] On the other hand, two rules were found to apply to NIACs. These relate to the prohibition of belligerent reprisals and the granting of amnesty at the end of active hostilities.[135] With respect to the remaining 146 rules applicable in both IACs and NIACs, three important nuances exist. First, several rules were found to be only 'arguably' customary in NIACs, recognizing that practice was not as dense in certain areas.[136] Second, the wording of some rules of customary humanitarian law is different for IACs and NIACs.[137] Finally, some rules of customary international humanitarian applicable in NIACs could only be identified as applicable to states.[138] Hence, important differences in substance and scope continue to exist.

However, the main rules on the conduct of hostilities, the use of means and methods of warfare, and the treatment of persons in the hands of a party to the conflict are now the same. The divide between the law on IACs and NIACs that existed in the past has been significantly narrowed down, but is not totally closed.

## 4. General Principles

Article 38(1) lists as one of the sources of international law '[g]eneral principles of law recognized by civilized nations'. This source is the least 'developed' or studied. It is also subject to controversy as to its exact place and content.

---

[133] *Prosecutor v Hadžihasanović and Kubura* (Decision on Command Responsibility) para 12.

[134] These are CIHL Rules 3 (definition of combatants), 4 (definition of armed forces), 41 (export and return of cultural property in occupied territory), 49 (war booty), 51 (public and private property in occupied territory), 106–108 (conditions for POW-status, spies, mercenaries), 130 (transfer of own civilian population in occupied territory), and 145–147 (reprisals). For an analysis of whether even these areas could be merged, see Emily Crawford, 'Blurring the Lines between International and Non-International Armed Conflicts: The Evolution of Customary International Law Applicable in Internal Armed Conflicts' (2008) 15 *AILJ* 29 and E Crawford, *The Treatment of Combatants and Insurgents under the Law of Armed Conflict* (OUP 2010).

[135] These are CIHL Rules 148 (reprisals in non-international armed conflicts) and 159 (amnesty).

[136] The following rules were only 'arguably' customary in non-international armed conflicts: CIHL Rules 21 (target selection), 23–24 (specific precautions against the effects of attack), 44–45 (specific rules on the natural environment), 62–63 (improper use of flags, military or military emblems, insignia or uniforms), and 82 (recording of the placement of landmines). For Rule 114 (return of the remains and personal effects of the dead), the study argues that the rule should apply equally in both international and non-international armed conflicts. See Jean-Marie Henckaerts and Louise Doswald-Beck (eds), *Customary International Humanitarian Law, Vol II: Practice* (ICRC and CUP 2005) 412.

[137] The following rules have different formulations for international and non-international armed conflicts: CIHL (above n 63) Rules 124 (ICRC access to persons deprived of their liberty), 126 (visits to persons deprived of their liberty), 128 (release and return of persons deprived of their liberty), and 129 (displacement).

[138] The following rules were found to be customary applicable to states only: CIHL Rules 141 (legal advisers for armed forces), 143 (dissemination among the civilian population), 144 (ensuring respect *erga omnes*), 149–150 (responsibility and reparation), 157–158 (jurisdiction over and prosecution of war crimes), and 161 (international cooperation in criminal proceedings).

International courts and tribunals rarely discuss how general principles of law are generated or their existence ascertained. However, it is generally accepted that general principles of law can be based on a number of material sources.[139] Doctrine typically refers to general principles of law derived from those principles of domestic law that are common to all legal orders, as well as principles of legal logic.[140]

Although listed as a source on a par with convention and custom in article 38, general principles of law primarily play a supplementary function, filling gaps left by treaty and customary law.[141] General principles also assist in the interpretation of conventional and customary rules.[142]

IHL contains its own general principles, specific to this body of law.[143] The principles most often referred to are the principles of humanity,[144] distinction, necessity, and the prohibition of causing unnecessary suffering. These principles have a triple legal basis: in addition to constituting general principles of law, they are also based on international conventional and customary law.[145] Albeit derived from existing rules, these principles also constitute an inspiration for the rules and a means of interpreting them.

The Martens Clause confirms the importance of general principles in IHL.[146] This clause, which first appeared in the preamble of the 1899 Hague Convention II, and which is contained in a number of IHL treaties, is phrased as follows in article 1(2) of API:

In cases not covered by this Protocol or by other international agreements, civilians and combatants remain under the protection and authority of the principles of international law derived from established custom, from the principles of humanity and from the dictates of public conscience.

In the *Krupp et al.* case, the Nuremberg Tribunal explained that:

The Preamble is much more than a pious declaration. It is a general clause, making the usages established among civilized nations, the laws of humanity and the dictates of public conscience into the legal yardstick to be applied if and when the specific provisions of the

---

[139] See eg van den Boogaard (above n 3) 7.

[140] For instance, if it is prohibited to attack civilians, logic dictates that an attack directed at a military objective has to be cancelled if it becomes apparent that the target is civilian. In addition, Kleffner mentions general principles that emanate from international relations (such as the principle of good faith) and general principles that develop from a fundamental rule in one particular treaty into a principle of a more general scope through express invocation in case law and doctrine, and through reaffirmation in resolutions of international organizations or statements of international conferences. See Kleffner (above n 52) 80–1.

[141] Indeed, this was the main reason for including general principles as a source of law in the Statute of the Permanent Court of International Justice and later in the statute of the ICJ, ie to prevent the court from having to conclude a *non-liquet*. See van den Boogaard (above n 3) 8.

[142] For instance, van den Boogaard writes that the principles of international law may be invoked to provide guidance in one direction or another in the event that there is already a rule of treaty or customary international law in place, but its interpretation in a given situation is not clear. See van den Boogaard (above n 3) 6–10.

[143] For a more detailed discussion, see chapter 7 'International Humanitarian Law and the Conduct of Hostilities'.

[144] See Kjetil Mujezinović Larsen, Camilla Guldahl Cooper, and Gro Nystuen (eds), *Searching for a Principle of Humanity in International Humanitarian Law* (CUP 2013).

[145] Kleffner (above n 52) 82.

[146] See van den Boogaard (above n 3) 19–21.

Convention and the Regulations annexed to it do not cover specific cases occurring in warfare, or concomitant to warfare.[147]

Although it has been pointed out that the 'regulatory density' of IHL means that exclusive reliance on general principles of law in any given case will be rare,[148] and while the exact meaning of 'the laws of humanity and the dictates of public conscience' is debated,[149] the ICJ has confirmed the continued relevance of the Martens Clause.[150] Its importance arguably lies in affirming that not everything that is not prohibited by a specific rule is necessarily lawful in war, recognizing 'the existence of wider principles behind specific rules of IHL and point[ing] to the principles of IHL that fill the gaps left by customary and treaty rules'.[151]

# 5. Judicial Decisions

The subsidiary sources listed in the ICJ Statute are judicial decisions and publications by legal scholars. As subsidiary sources, they do not create legal rules but assist in their identification (eg their identification as customary law) or in their clarification (eg their interpretation). Although these sources are 'subsidiary', in practice they are extremely important because issues of rule identification and clarification almost always come up when rules have to be applied to concrete cases or in new situations.

The ICJ Statute mentions 'judicial decisions' as the first supplementary source of international law. In the realm of IHL, judicial decisions help to clarify and flesh out the content of the law. This is useful as many notions of IHL remain quite general or vague or their practical application to specific facts raises issues which judicial decisions can usefully clarify—and have done so on many occasions.

The ICJ has on several occasions clarified the content of the Geneva Conventions, for example in the *Nicaragua* case, where it clarified the scope of Common Article 1 by recognizing the negative obligation 'not to encourage persons or groups engaged in the conflict in Nicaragua to act in violation of the provisions of Article 3 common to the four 1949 Geneva Conventions'.[152] IHL issues were also assessed by the ICJ in its Advisory Opinions on the *Legality of the Threat or Use of Nuclear Weapons*,[153] and on the *Legal Consequences of the Construction of a Wall in the Occupied Palestinian Territory*.[154] The Court moreover examined IHL issues at depth in the *Armed Activities* case *(Congo v Uganda)*,[155] and in the *Arrest*

---

[147] *Krupp et al* [1948] Case No 214, Judgment of 31 July 1948, United States Military Tribunals (reprinted *Annual Digests and Reports of Public International Cases*, 1948 (Lauterpacht, ed.) 620, 622.

[148] Kleffner (above n 52) 81.

[149] ibid 85–6.

[150] *Nuclear Weapons* paras 78 and 87.

[151] van den Boogaard (above n 3) 20.

[152] *Military and Paramilitary Activities in and against Nicaragua (Nicaragua v USA) (Merits)* [1986] ICJ Rep 3 para 220. See also *Legal Consequences of the Construction of a Wall in the Occupied Palestinian Territory* (Advisory Opinion) [2004] ICJ Rep 136 paras 158–159 and *Armed Activities on the Territory of the Congo (Judgment)* [2005] ICJ Rep 168 paras 211 and 345.

[153] *Nuclear Weapons*.

[154] *Legal Consequences of the Construction of a Wall in the Occupied Palestinian Territory* (Advisory Opinion) [2004] ICJ Rep 136.

[155] *Armed Activities on the Territory of the Congo (Democratic Republic of the Congo v. Uganda) (Judgment)* [2005] ICJ Rep 168.

*Warrant* case *(Democratic Republic of Congo v Belgium)* the Court considered the scope of universal jurisdiction in the prosecution of war criminals.[156]

There has been a significant growth in IHL litigation in both domestic and international courts and tribunals over the past decades. This is partly owing to the growth of international criminal law and the creation of tribunals tasked with the prosecution of war crimes. The role played by judicial decisions as a subsidiary source of IHL has come to the forefront since the establishment of the ICTY, followed by other ad hoc tribunals[157] and the establishment of the ICC.

These tribunals have clarified a number of notions and aspects of IHL. To give an example, the ICTY famously defined IAC and NIAC. In its decision on jurisdiction in *Tadić* in 1995, the ICTY Appeals Chamber stated that 'an [international] armed conflict exists whenever there is a resort to armed force between States'.[158] This definition has since been adopted by other international bodies and is generally considered as the contemporary reference for any interpretation of the notion of armed conflict under humanitarian law. In the same decision, the Chamber found that the threshold of a NIAC is crossed 'whenever there is ... protracted armed violence between governmental authorities and organized armed groups or between such groups within a State'.[159] In its trial judgment in the same case in 1997, the ICTY further developed this approach by holding that the 'test applied by the Appeals Chamber ... focuses on two aspects of a conflict ... the intensity of the conflict and the organization of the parties to the conflict'.[160] These conclusions were subsequently reaffirmed in the case law of the ICTY, the ICTR, and the ICC.[161] Another example is the clarification by the ICTY of the concept of torture under IHL.[162]

Arbitral proceedings have also played an important role in the clarification of IHL. One notable example is the work of the Ethiopia–Eritrea Claims Commission (EECC). This

---

[156] *Arrest Warrant (Democratic Republic of Congo v Belgium) (Judgment)* [2000] ICJ Rep 168, 3.
[157] For a discussion, see Guénaël Mettraux, *International Crimes and the Ad Hoc Tribunals* (OUP 2005).
[158] *Tadić* (Decision) (above n 69) para 70.
[159] ibid.
[160] See *Tadić* (Trial Judgment) [1997] ICTY para 562:

> (a) *Protracted armed violence between governmental forces and organized armed groups*
>
> 562. The test applied by the Appeals Chamber to the existence of an armed conflict for the purposes of the rules contained in Common Article 3 focuses on two aspects of a conflict; *the intensity of the conflict* and *the organization of the parties to the conflict*. In an armed conflict of an internal or mixed character, these closely related criteria are used solely for the purpose, as a minimum, of distinguishing an armed conflict from banditry, unorganized and short-lived insurrections, or terrorist activities, which are not subject to international humanitarian law. Factors relevant to this determination are addressed in the Commentary to Geneva Convention for the Amelioration of the Condition of the Wounded and Sick in Armed Forces in the Field, Convention I, ('*Commentary*, Geneva Convention I') [emphasis added].

[161] See eg *Limaj* (Trial Judgment) [2005] ICTY para 84, and *Boškoski and Tarčulovski* (Trial Judgment) [2008] para 175. See also eg *Akayesu* (Trial Judgment) [1998] ICTR paras 619–620 and *Rutaganda* (Trial Judgment) [1999] paras 91–92.
[162] Departing from its earlier case law (see *The Prosecutor v Zejnal Delalić et al*, ICTY Trial Chamber Judgment, 16 November 1998, IT-96-21-T, para 549, and, *Prosecutor v Furundzija* ICTY AC Judgement, 21 July 2000,IT-95-17/1-A, para 111), the ICTY in the *Kunarac* case [*Prosecutor v Kunarac* ICTY Appeals Chamber Judgement, 12 June 2002, IT-96-23/1-A at para 147] concluded that 'the definition of torture under international humanitarian law does not comprise the same elements as the definition of torture generally applied under human rights law' and that 'the presence of a state official or of any other authority-wielding person in the torture process is not necessary for the offence to be regarded as torture under international humanitarian law'. The tribunal defined torture as the intentional infliction, by act or omission, of severe pain or suffering, whether physical or mental, in order to obtain information or a confession, or to punish, intimidate or coerce the victim or a third person, or to discriminate on any ground, against the victim or a third person.

Commission was set up after the end of the armed conflict between Ethiopia and Eritrea in 2000 to:

> decide through binding arbitration all claims for loss, damage or injury by one Government against the other, and by nationals (including both natural and juridical persons) of one party against the Government of the other party or entities owned or controlled by the other party that are (a) related to the conflict that was the subject of the Framework Agreement, the Modalities for its Implementation and the Cessation of Hostilities Agreement and (b) result from violations of international humanitarian law, including the 1949 Geneva Conventions, or other violations of international law.[163]

The Claims Commission has clarified several aspects related to the treatment of prisoners of war. For example, with regard to the humane treatment of prisoners of war, the Claims Commission has held that the evacuation of prisoners of war from the battlefield after their footwear had been seized, forcing them to walk barefoot through harsh terrain, which 'unnecessarily compounded their misery', was in violation of article 20 of the Third Convention requiring evacuations to be 'effected humanely'.[164] And with respect to the level of medical care to be provided to the wounded and sick, the Commission found that:

> Eritrea and Ethiopia cannot, at least at present, be required to have the same standards for medical treatment as developed countries. However, scarcity of finances and infrastructure cannot excuse a failure to grant *the minimum standard of medical care* required by international humanitarian law. The cost of such care is not, in any event, substantial in comparison with the other costs imposed by the armed conflict [emphasis added].[165]

The Claims Commission thereby confirmed that a basic minimum of medical care can reasonably be expected whatever the circumstances, even when a state lacks significant resources.

The Commission also ruled on other issues, such as the definition of occupied territory, holding that the term 'occupation' covers cases in which a state occupies territories with a controversial international status.[166]

Domestic courts can also play an important role in clarifying rules of IHL, independent of the potential value of national case law for the process of customary law formation. In other words, the decisions of domestic courts can constitute both a 'formal' source (a process that creates rules of law) and an 'evidential source' (evidence of an existing rule) of IHL.[167]

The negotiation of the Geneva Conventions made it apparent that states considered national courts to be the most appropriate fora for judicial consideration of matters relating to conduct during armed conflict, and it remains the case that judicial enforcement of IHL

---

[163] Agreement between the Governments of the State of Eritrea and the Federal Democratic Republic of Ethiopia, Algiers of 12 December 2000, article 5(1).

[164] Eritrea–Ethiopia Claims Commission (*Prisoners of War, Eritrea's Claim*) (Partial Award) [2003] para 68.

[165] ibid paras 138 and 115–119; Eritrea–Ethiopia Claims Commission (*Prisoners of War, Ethiopia's Claim*) (Partial Award) [2003] paras 104–107.

[166] Eritrea–Ethiopia Claims Commission (*Central Front, Ethiopia's Claim*) (Partial Award) [2004] para 29.

[167] See eg Kleffner (above n 52) 84.

'relies primarily on domestic courts'.[168] A recent example of a domestic court ruling seeking to clarify a controversial issue of IHL is the decision by the Swedish District Court that a non-state party to a NIAC can establish courts in order to (i) maintain discipline in the actor's own armed units; and (ii) maintain law and order in a given territory which the actor is controlling.[169]

## 6. Teachings of the Most Qualified Publicists

Today we would call this source 'legal writings'. In the area of IHL, writings abound and anyone deciding on IHL may find it difficult to select from among the large amount of recent writings. There are a number of handbooks and guides that stand out and have been referred to on many occasions.[170] As a subsidiary source, the writings of publicists may assist courts and lawyers to determine or clarify the law, but they are in no way binding as such.

One particular type of legal writings is commentaries. These are article-by-article commentaries on the provisions of a treaty that provide interpretations of the provisions, examples of their application, references to case law, state practice, and academic commentary. Such commentaries exist on the Geneva Conventions[171] and their Additional Protocols,[172] as well as a range of other IHL treaties.[173]

Another type of legal writing is expert restatements. These are particularly popular today to update areas of law, address new areas of law, or to provide expert clarifications.[174] As a restatement, they may reflect existing treaty or customary law, but they may also contain suggested new rules as a kind of 'progressive development'. The first, recent restatement is the *San Remo Manual on International Law Applicable to Armed Conflicts at Sea*.[175] This manual was adopted to update the law applicable to naval warfare, and also includes some 'progressive development'. Another example is the 2009 *HPCR [Humanitarian Policy and Conflict*

---

[168] Sharon Weill, *The Role of National Courts in Applying International Humanitarian Law* (OUP 2014) 7.

[169] Stockholm District Court, Case No B 3787-16 (Judgment of 16 February 2017) para 31.

[170] See eg D. Fleck (ed.) *The Handbook of International Humanitarian Law* (OUP, 3rd edn, 2013) and E. David, *Principes de droit des conflits armés* (Bruylant, 5th edn, 2012); on occupation see eg Dinstein (above n 1); on non-international armed conflicts, see eg S Sivakumaran, *The Law of Non-International Armed Conflict* (OUP 2012); and on classification of conflicts, see E Wilmshurst (ed), *International Law and the Classification of Conflicts* (OUP, 2012).

[171] See ICRC Commentaries available at Andrew Clapham, Paola Gaeta, and Marco Sassòli (eds), *The 1949 Geneva Conventions: A Commentary* (OUP 2015).

[172] Sandoz et al (above n 46); Bothe et al (above n 36).

[173] See eg Jiří Toman, *The Protection of Cultural Property in the Event of Armed Conflict: Commentary on the Convention for the Protection of Cultural Property in the Event of Armed Conflict and its Protocol*, (Dartmouth 1996) and Jiří Toman, *Commentary on the Second Protocol to the Hague Convention of 1954 for the Protection of Cultural Property in the Event of Armed Conflict* (UNESCO 2009); Stuart Maslen (ed), *Commentaries on Arms Control Treaties, Volume I: The Convention on the Prohibition of the Use, Stockpiling, Production, and Transfer of Anti-Personnel Mines and on their Destruction* (OUP 2004); William Schabas, *The International Criminal Court: A Commentary on the Rome Statute* (OUP 2010); Gro Nystuen and Stuart Casey-Maslen (eds), *The Convention on Cluster Munitions: A Commentary* (OUP 2010); Andrew Clapham, Stuart Casey-Maslen, Gilles Giacca, and Sarah Parker (eds), *The Arms Trade Treaty: A Commentary* (OUP 2016); and Otto Triffterer and Kai Ambos (eds), *The Rome Statute of the International Criminal Court: A Commentary* (3rd edn, Hart 2016).

[174] These are not new, as even in 1880 the Institute of International Law had adopted a manual *The Laws of War on Land*, which was a restatement of the law as it then existed.

[175] Louise Doswald-Beck and international lawyers and naval experts convened by the International Institute of Humanitarian Law: Louise Doswald-Beck (ed), *San Remo Manual on International Law Applicable to Armed Conflicts at Sea* (CUP 1995).

*Research] Manual on International Law Applicable to Air and Missile Warfare.*[176] Under the auspices of the International Society for Military Law and the Law of War, a similar manual has been developed for peace operations.[177] Expert restatements can also be used to address new areas of law where no specific treaties or custom may exist. The first example is the *Tallinn Manual on the International Law Applicable to Cyber Warfare.*[178] A similar manual is being developed for outer space (the *Manual on International Law Applicable to Military Uses of Outer Space*, MILAMOS for short).[179]

An example of an expert clarification is the ICRC report on the notion of 'direct participation in hostilities'. The report reflects the ICRC's interpretation of this notion but was the outcome of a multi-year project where experts met and discussed the notion of direct participation.[180] Another example is the 2016 Oxford Guidance on the Law Relating to Humanitarian Relief Operations in Situations of Armed Conflict commissioned by the UN Office for the Coordination of Humanitarian Affairs.[181]

## 7. Soft Law

With a few exceptions, for example in the area of weapons law, there seems today to be a reticence of states to adopt further IHL treaty law. The last comprehensive update of the Geneva Conventions dates from 1977 and no new treaties appear to be on the horizon. Instead, states have preferred to use the technique of soft-law developments. Soft law can be described as 'principles, rules, and standards governing international relations which are not considered to stem from one of the sources of international law enumerated in article 38 of the ICJ Statute'.[182]

Like treaties and custom, they can 'create' rules and standards, but unlike them they are not formally binding. That being said, soft-law instruments have a certain—undefined— normative value because they can be used as arguments in various fora (eg in negotiations in international organizations or in pleadings before courts) and violating them would have certain (political) consequences. Sometimes soft-law instruments can also resemble expert restatements and reflect existing treaty or customary rules but applied to new phenomena, although they may also contain 'new' rules.

Examples of soft-law instruments are the Montreux Document on Private Military and Security Companies,[183] and the *Copenhagen Process on the Handling of Detainees in*

---

[176] *HPCR Manual on International Law Applicable to Air and Missile Warfare*, Program on Humanitarian Policy and Conflict Research (HPCR) at Harvard University, Bern, 15 May 2009 and HPCR, *HPCR Manual on International Law Applicable to Air and Missile Warfare: Commentary* (CUP 2013).

[177] Terry Gill, Dieter Fleck, William H Boothby, and Alfons Vanheusden (eds), *Leuven Manual on the International Law Applicable to Peace Operations* (CUP 2017).

[178] Michael N Schmitt (ed), *Tallinn Manual on International Law Applicable to Cyber Warfare* (CUP 2013).

[179] *Manual on International Law Applicable to Military Uses of Outer Space* www.mcgill.ca/milamos/about.

[180] Nils Melzer, *Interpretive Guidance on the Notion of Direct Participation in Hostilities under International Humanitarian Law* (ICRC 2009).

[181] See www.unocha.org/sites/dms/Documents/Oxford%20Guidance%20pdf.pdf.

[182] Daniel Thürer, 'Soft Law', in Rüdiger Wolfrum (ed), *Max Planck Encyclopedia of Public International Law* (OUP 2009) www.mpepil.com.

[183] The Montreux Document on pertinent international legal obligations and good practices for states related to operations of private military and security companies during armed conflict (adopted at Montreux 17 September 2008, ICRC/Swiss Federal Department of Foreign Affairs August 2009).

*International Military Operations.*[184] These soft-law instruments were adopted by groups of states at the initiative of one of them, in this case Switzerland and Denmark, respectively.

Soft-law instruments can also result from multilateral organizations, in particular the UN, such as the UN Guiding Principles on Internal Displacement,[185] and the Basic Principles and Guidelines on the Right to a Remedy and Reparation for Victims of Gross Violations of International Human Rights Law and Serious Violations of International Humanitarian Law.[186] Both of these are not only limited to IHL, but also draw upon international human rights law (and refugee law).

## 8. Conclusion

The ever-increasing codification of humanitarian law, starting in 1864 and continuing well on to this day, means that this part of international law is highly codified. Nevertheless, in the big picture of human history and of warfare, this codification is still a recent phenomenon. Customary rules have regulated warfare for centuries prior to the start of this wave of codification and continue to do so today. Impediments to the application of the wealth of existing humanitarian treaty law, as well as the predominance of NIACs today, have contributed to a 'revival' of customary humanitarian law.[187] Hence, any description or analysis of humanitarian law that does not include an important section on customary humanitarian law will be considered deficient and, in the end, of limited practical value in today's world. Furthermore, today, general principles continue to act to fill gaps and as guidance for the interpretation of treaty or customary law. The subsidiary sources of judicial decisions have taken on an increasingly important role and international courts in particular have contributed greatly to the definition of IHL notions. Scholarly writings have flourished and key publications have a wide impact and some expert restatement are of significant importance. Finally, several soft law instruments have emerged as a preferred manner for States to fill gaps and develop the law without committing to new formally binding rules.

---

[184] The Copenhagen Process, *Principles and Guidelines, The Copenhagen Process on the Handling of Detainees in International Military Operations* (Copenhagen Process 2012).

[185] Guiding Principles on Internal Displacement, presented to the UN Commission on Human Rights by the Special Representative of the UN Secretary General on Internally Displaced Persons UN Doc E/CN.4/1998/53/Add.2 (11 February 1998).

[186] Adopted by UN General Assembly Resolution 60/147 (16 December 2005).

[187] The term is borrowed from Meron (above n 69).

# 2

# Classification of Armed Conflicts

*Dapo Akande**

## 1. Introduction

International humanitarian law (IHL) governs the conduct of participants in an armed conflict. Thus, to determine whether this body of law applies to situations of violence, it is necessary to assess first of all whether the situation amounts to an 'armed conflict'. However, IHL does not recognize a unitary concept of armed conflict but two types of it: international (IACs) and non-international (NIACs).

This chapter examines the history of the distinction between these two categories, the consequences of it, and whether it still has validity. It then discusses legal concepts relevant to the two categories, including the differences between a NIAC and other violence, extraterritorial hostilities by one state against a non-state armed group (NSAG), and conflicts in which multinational forces are engaged.

## 2. History of the Distinction between IAC and NIAC

The distinction between IACs and NIACs arises out of the history of the regulation of wars and armed conflicts by international law. In the period following the peace of Westphalia in 1648 until the end of the Second World War (WWII), the international laws of war applied only to inter-state wars.[1] This was a consequence of the fact that international law was concerned only with relations between states[2] and eschewed regulation of matters considered to be within 'domestic jurisdiction'. Internal armed conflicts, or civil wars, were not considered to be 'real war[s] in the strict sense of the term in International Law'.[3] The laws of war could only apply to civil wars where there was recognition, either by the state involved or a third state, of the belligerency of the insurgent party.[4] Thus, the application of international law to what was prima facie an internal situation was not automatic but the result of recognition of the insurgent party's state-like qualities. At that time, the international laws of war did not distinguish between international and other wars. There was only one body of law which applied either *in toto* to international conflicts between states (or conflicts treated as such) or not at all.[5]

---

* [1] See Lorand Bartels, 'Timelines, Borderlines and Conflicts: The Historical Evolution of the Legal Divide between International and Non-International Armed Conflicts' (2009) 91 *IRRC* 35, 44–8.
[2] See Lassa Oppenheim, *International Law, Vol I: The Law of Peace* (Longmans 1912) 12 para 13.
[3] Lassa Oppenheim, *International Law, Vol II: War and Neutrality* (Longmans 1906) 67.
[4] ibid 65; Lindsay Moir, *The Law of Internal Armed Conflict* (CUP 2002) 5ff.
[5] See Bartels (above n 1) 51; Moir (above n 4) 10.

The extension of international regulation to internal armed conflicts changed decisively after WWII. This period was marked by the gradual expansion of international rights and obligations to individuals, as exemplified by the post-war prosecutions for international crimes and the development of international human rights law. It is therefore not surprising that around the same time consideration was given to extending the laws of war to internal armed conflicts. These developments were foreshadowed by the practice of some states and the League of Nations during the Spanish Civil War (1936–39). Although there was no recognition of belligerency during that conflict, there was an emerging view that international law applied to the conduct of hostilities during a civil war.[6]

The four Geneva Conventions 1949 not only decisively established that IHL would apply to certain conflicts involving non-state entities, but they also bifurcated IHL into the law of IAC and that of NIAC. Article 2 common to all four Conventions specifies that the Conventions apply 'to all cases of declared war or of any other armed conflict which may arise between two or more High Contracting Parties'. The International Committee of the Red Cross (ICRC) had proposed to extend the Conventions in their entirety to internal conflicts.[7] However, this was rejected by most states. Instead, only a single provision (article 3 common to the four Geneva Conventions, or 'Common Article 3') was made applicable to 'armed conflict not of an international character occurring in the territory of one of the High Contracting Parties'. Thus, a division was established between the law applicable to IACs and NIACs.

This division was reinforced with the adoption of the Protocols Additional to the Geneva Conventions (API and II) in 1977.[8] While API deals with 'the Protection of Victims of International Armed Conflicts,' APII 'relat[es] to the Protection of Victims of Non-International Armed Conflicts'. Likewise, the Rome Statute of the International Criminal Court of 1998 distinguishes between war crimes (that is, serious violations of the laws and customs of war) committed in IACs[9] and NIACs.[10]

## 3. Consequences of the Distinction between IAC and NIAC

It is essential to distinguish between IACs and NIACs as differences exist in the content of the law applicable to each type of conflict. Under treaty law, the differences are vast. The entirety of the Geneva Conventions 1949, the Hague Conventions which preceded them, and API 1977 apply to IACs. These contain hundreds of articles which establish a detailed body of rules relating to the conduct of hostilities ('Hague Law'), as well as those concerning the protection of persons who do not, or who no longer, take part in hostilities ('Geneva Law').

By contrast, the treaty rules applicable to NIACs are rather limited. They are largely to be found in Common Article 3 of the Geneva Conventions 1949, the provisions of APII 1977, and article 8(2)(c) and (e) of the ICC Statute. Common Article 3 provides basic protection

---

[6] Antonio Cassese, 'Civil War and International Law', in Antonio Cassese (ed), *The Human Dimension of International Law: Selected Papers* (OUP 2008) 114–16. See also Bartels (above n 1) 56; *Prosecutor v Tadić* (Decision on Defence Motion for Interlocutory Appeal on Jurisdiction) IT-94-1-AR72 (2 October 1995) para 63.

[7] See Cassese 'Civil War' (above n 6) 116–17; Bartels (above n 1) 57.

[8] See also Hague Convention for the Protection of Cultural Property in the Event of Armed Conflict (1954) articles 18 and 19; Roger O'Keefe, *The Protection of Cultural Property in Armed Conflict* (CUP 2006) 96–8.

[9] ICC Statute ('ICCSt') article 8(2)(a) and (b).

[10] ibid article 8(2)(c) and (e).

to those who do not or no longer take part in hostilities and does not regulate the conduct of hostilities. APII, which has fewer than twenty substantive provisions, and those parts of the ICC Statute dealing with NIACs, extend the rules protecting victims of conflict and introduce modest rules on the conduct of hostilities,[11] but fall far short of approximating the IHL rules applicable in IACs.[12]

Notwithstanding this difference in the applicable treaty rules, the distinction between IACs and NIACs is being eroded such that there is now greater, though incomplete, unity in the law applicable to these two forms of conflict.[13] First, some treaties governing the conduct of hostilities apply to all conflicts without distinction. Examples include the Biological Weapons Convention 1972, Chemical Weapons Convention 1993, Convention Prohibiting Anti-Personnel Land Mines 1997, Second Protocol to the Hague Convention for the Protection of Cultural Property 1954, and the Amendment of 2001 extending the Convention on Conventional Weapons 1980 and its Protocols to NIACs.

Second, and more importantly, customary international law now provides for a broader set of rules governing NIACs and fills many of the gaps in treaty law. This was the position taken by the International Criminal Tribunal for the former Yugoslavia (ICTY) Appeals Chamber in the *Tadić* case, which held that the rules of IHL applicable in IAC concerning the protection of civilians, of persons *hors de combat* and of civilian objects, as well as the prohibitions relating to means and certain methods of warfare also apply in NIACs.[14] The ICTY justified its position on the basis of state practice and that 'elementary considerations of humanity and common sense' would 'make it preposterous' that weapons prohibited in IACs could be used by states 'to put down rebellion by their own nationals on their own territory'.[15]

Further, the ICRC, in its 2005 comprehensive study of customary IHL ('the ICRC Study'),[16] found evidence that nearly all customary IHL rules applied to both IACs and NIACs. It noted, in particular, that the gaps in APII 'have largely been filled through State practice', leading to 'the creation of rules parallel to those in [API], but applicable as customary law to [NIACs]'.[17] Although this suggestion contradicted earlier assumptions,[18] and questions have been raised as to the ICRC Study's methodology for identifying custom,[19] it is now generally accepted (including by states) that customary IHL has expanded in NIACs beyond the rules in Common Article 3 and APII. That expansion is reflected in the war crimes provisions of the ICC Statute.[20]

---

[11] See Jelena Pejić, 'Conflict Classification and the Law Applicable to Detention and the Use of Force', in Elizabeth Wilmshurst (ed), *International Law and Classification of Conflicts* (OUP 2012), ch 4.

[12] See section 6 'The Scope of Application of IHL: NIACs' below.

[13] See Lindsay Moir, 'Towards the Unification of International Humanitarian Law?', in Richard Burchill, Nigel White, and Justin Morris (eds), *International Conflict and Security Law* (CUP 2005) 108.

[14] *Tadić* Jurisdiction (above n 6) para 127.

[15] ibid para 119.

[16] Jean-Marie Henckaerts and Louise Doswald-Beck, *Customary International Humanitarian Law Study: Vol I: Rules and Vol II: Practice* (ICRC and CUP 2005).

[17] ibid Vol I xxxv.

[18] See eg 'Final Report of the Commission of Experts Established Pursuant to Security Council Resolution 780(1992)', S/1994/674 (27 May 1994) 13 para 42.

[19] See Daniel Bethlehem, 'The Methodological Framework of the Study' and Iain Scobbie, 'The Approach to Customary International Law in the Study', in Elizabeth Wilmshurst and Susan Breau (eds), *Perspectives on the ICRC Study on Customary International Humanitarian Law* (CUP 2007) 3, 15; and also John Bellinger and William Haynes, 'A US Government Response to the International Committee of the Red Cross Study on Customary International Humanitarian Law' (2007) 89(866) *IRRC* 443.

[20] It should, however, be noted that the ICCSt's list of war crimes in IACs is longer than that of war crimes in NIACs, even though the difference has been narrowed through amendments. Compare ICCSt articles 8(2)(a)–(b)

Although the distinction between the law in IACs and NIAC is blurring, it remains important. This is particularly so in two key areas where the law still differs: the status of fighters and the detention of combatants and civilians.[21]

## 4. Why Does the Distinction Exist and Should it be Abolished?

The main reason for the persistence of the distinction is the view by some states that equating NIAC and IAC would undermine state sovereignty, particularly national unity and security.[22] There are concerns that uniform rules would not only encourage secessionist movements, by giving them a status under international law, but also restrain the hand of the state when seeking to put down rebellions.[23] For example, if the IAC principle of combatant immunity—which prevents prosecutions of combatants merely for taking part in the conflict—were applied in NIACs, states would be unable to criminalize acts which are traditionally regarded as treasonous.[24] This is why article 3 of APII states that nothing in APII restricts the responsibility of the state 'by all legitimate means, to maintain or re-establish law and order'.[25] States have also feared that abolishing the distinction would give international status to non-state groups and encourage international intervention in internal conflicts.[26] Hence, paragraph 4 of Common Article 3 states that '[t]he application of the preceding provisions shall not affect the legal status of the Parties to the conflict'.

In light of the saving clauses in Common Article 3 and article 3 of APII, the above concerns are hardly justifiable. Also, the idea that foreign intervention follows from the classification of a conflict is to some extent erroneous. First, the UN Security Council (UNSC) now regularly intervenes in non-international conflicts.[27] Second, international law does not permit unilateral 'humanitarian intervention'[28] or any kind of forceful intervention by a state in another state based on the nature of a conflict. It is, however, true that the more rules of IHL apply to NIACs, the greater the opportunity for other states to use countermeasures in response to alleged breaches.[29]

---

and 8(2)(c) and (e). The ICC Pre-Trial Chamber I has regarded this difference as reflecting IHL. See *Abu Garda*, ICC-02/05-02/09, Confirmation of Charges Decision, 8 February 2010.

[21] For these differences, see chapters 5 'Persons Covered by International Law: Main Categories' and 12 'Detention in Armed Conflict' in this book. See also Pejić 'Conflict Classification' (above n 11).

[22] Cassese 'Civil War' (above n 6) 116; Bartels (above n 1) 61–4. See also Howard Levie (ed), *The Law of Non-International Armed Conflict: Protocol II to the 1949 Geneva Conventions* (Martinus Nijhoff 1987) for government statements made, during the drafting of AP II.

[23] François Bugnion, '*Jus Ad Bellum, Jus in Bello* and Non-International Armed Conflicts' (2003) 6 *YIHL* 167, 168.

[24] See Dieter Fleck, 'The Law of Non-International Armed Conflicts', in Dieter Fleck (ed), *The Handbook of International Humanitarian Law* (3rd edn, OUP 2013) 590–1; Waldemar Solf, 'Non-International Armed Conflicts: Commentator' (1982) 31 *AULR* 927.

[25] See also ICCSt article 8(3).

[26] See Levie (above n 22) for statements made, during the drafting of AP II by Yugoslavia (47 para 6) and Mexico (49 para 14).

[27] See eg UNSC Resolution 1973 (2011) with respect to Libya. See also the World Summit Outcome Document, UNGA Resolution 60/1 (2005) para 139.

[28] See generally Simon Chesterman, *Just War or Just Peace: Humanitarian Intervention and International Law* (OUP 2001).

[29] See International Law Commission, Articles on the Responsibility of States for Internationally Wrongful Acts and accompanying commentary (2001) II-2 ILCYB ('ARSIWA') article 54 (referring to sanctions imposed on the former Yugoslavia for actions that occurred during armed conflict).

While states may have legitimate concerns about extending the IAC rules relating to the status of fighters to NIACs, this should not prevent the extension of other norms to NIACs.[30] However, since IHL applies equally to all sides in a conflict, transposing some IAC rules to NIACs might be problematic where those rules assume or require state authority.

## 5. The Scope of Application of IHL: IACs

### A. Inter-State Conflict

Article 2 common to the Geneva Conventions 1949 states that the Conventions 'shall apply to all cases of declared war or of any other armed conflict which may arise between two or more High Contracting Parties, even if the state of war is not recognised by one of them'. It follows that an IAC is essentially an inter-state conflict.[31] However, the key question for the application of IHL is 'When does an armed conflict exist between two States such that this body of law applies?'

The question may be difficult to answer where one party claims to be a state and the other rejects this, as during the dissolution of the former Socialist Federal Republic of Yugoslavia. A NIAC may turn into an IAC when an internal rebel group successfully becomes a state. Nevertheless, except in the case of entities possessing the right of external self-determination, such as colonial or other non-self-governing peoples,[32] secession without the consent of the parent state is rarely recognized as successful in international law.[33] Conversely, in cases of state dissolution or where the parent state consents to secession but continues to fight (perhaps indirectly by providing support for groups within the new state), the conflict may be 'internationalized'.[34]

### 1. War

Prior to the Geneva Conventions, the international laws of war applied to 'war'. The concept had a technical meaning and referred to the opposite of peace in the relations between states.[35] According to the Hague Convention (III) relative to the Opening of Hostilities 1907, a formal declaration of war was a pre-condition for the laws of war to apply.[36] Today, IHL will apply once an armed conflict factually exists between states, even if neither party formally considers itself at war.[37] However, the Geneva Conventions will still apply to cases of declared war, even if no hostilities take place. Although there are no modern cases of

---

[30]  See Fleck (above n 24) 590–1.

[31]  Except in situations covered by AP I article 1(4), on which see section 5.B 'Self-determination Conflicts of National Liberation under Article 1(4) of API' below.

[32]  See UNGA Resolutions 1514 (1960) and 2625 (1970).

[33]  James Crawford, *The Creation of States in International Law* (OUP 2006) ch 9. The main exception is Bangladesh, which was admitted to the UN before consent by Pakistan.

[34]  See eg *Prosecutor v Milošević* (Decision on Motion for Judgment of Acquittal under Rule 98 bis) IT-02-54-T (16 June 2004) (holding that Croatia had become a state following the dissolution of the former Socialist Federal Republic of Yugoslavia). See generally Kubo Mačák, *Internationalized Armed Conflicts in International Law* (OUP 2018) ch 2.3.

[35]  Christopher Greenwood, 'Scope of Application of Humanitarian Law', in Dieter Fleck (ed), *The Handbook of International Humanitarian Law* (OUP 2008) 45.

[36]  See René Provost, *International Human Rights and Humanitarian Law* (CUP 2002) 249.

[37]  See Greenwood 'Scope of Application' (above n 35) 47; J Pictet (ed), *Commentary on the Geneva Conventions of 12 August 1949, Vol IV* (ICRC 1952) 2.

formal declarations of war,[38] there are statements by states to the effect that they are at war with another state.[39] Whether these are to be regarded as bringing into effect IHL is essentially a question of intention. For there to be a war in the technical sense, there needs to be an *animus belligerendi*. Yet '[t]here is probably a presumption that nations do not intend to create a state of war'[40] and '[s]o serious a matter as the existence of a state of war is not lightly to be implied'.[41]

## 2. Armed conflict

Both IHL and the rules prohibiting recourse to force in international relations have moved away from the formal concept of war and towards much more factual criteria. In the UN Charter, it is the 'use of force' that is prohibited. Likewise, the application of IHL depends on the existence of an 'armed conflict'. Although the Geneva Conventions lack a definition of 'armed conflict', the ICTY Appeals Chamber in *Tadić* found that:

> an armed conflict exists whenever there is a resort to armed force between States or protracted armed violence between governmental authorities and organised armed groups or between such groups within a State. International humanitarian law applies from the initiation of such armed conflicts and extends beyond the cessation of hostilities until a general conclusion of peace is reached; or in the case of internal conflicts, a peace settlement is achieved. Until that moment, international humanitarian law continues to apply to the whole territory of the warring States or, in the case of internal conflicts, the whole territory under the control of a party, whether or not actual combat takes place there.[42]

### A. Threshold for IACs

By asserting that an IAC exists *whenever* there is resort to armed force by states, the *Tadić* decision suggests a very low threshold for an IAC.[43] As Vité notes, 'it is ... not necessary for the conflict to extend over time or for it to create a certain number of victims'.[44] Almost any use of armed force by one state against another is sufficient,[45] except perhaps where it is unintended (eg arising out of error).[46] This view has been endorsed in the ICRC's Commentaries to the Geneva Conventions.[47]

The alternative view requires a minimum intensity for an IAC to exist[48] and thereby seeks consistency with the definition of NIAC, which has an intensity requirement.[49] However,

[38] Greenwood 'Scope of Application' (above n 35) 49.
[39] See examples cited in Christopher Greenwood, 'The Concept of War in Modern International Law' (1987) 36 *ICLQ* 283.
[40] Greenwood 'Scope of Application' (n 35) 49.
[41] Lord McNair and Arthur D Watts, *The Legal Effects of War* (4th edn, CUP 1966) 8.
[42] *Tadić* Jurisdiction (above n 6) para 70.
[43] Sylvain Vité, 'Typology of Armed Conflicts in International Humanitarian Law: Legal Concepts and Actual Situations' (2009) 91 *IRRC* 69, 72; William Fenrick, 'Article 8, War Crimes', in Otto Triffterer (ed), *Commentary on the Rome Statute of the International Criminal Court* (Hart 1999).
[44] Vité (above n 43) 72.
[45] See Greenwood 'Scope of Application' (n 35) 46 para 202.
[46] UK Ministry of Defence, *The Manual of the Law of Armed Conflict* (OUP 2004) 29.
[47] Jean Pictet (ed), *Commentary on the Geneva Conventions of 12 August 1949, Vol III* (ICRC 1960) 23; ICRC, *Commentary on the First Geneva Convention*, (2nd edn, ICRC 2016) paras 236–244.
[48] See International Law Association, 'Final Report of the Meaning of Armed Conflict in International Law' (ILA 2010).
[49] See section 6 'The Scope of Application if IHL: NIACs' below.

this analogy is misplaced, as it would result in a regulatory gap for inter-state military operations below that level, including the opening phase of hostilities. Unlike in NIACs, domestic law is not fully applicable to such inter-state military operations.

## B. Geographical and temporal scope of IACs

The geographical and temporal scope of application of IHL in both IACs and NIACs are explored more fully in chapter 3 'The Temporal and Geographic Reach of International and Humanitarian Law' in this book and is addressed more briefly here. Where an armed conflict exists between two states, military operations may only be carried out by the parties on their territories and the high seas, including the airspace above them, the seafloor below, and the exclusive economic zones (that is, outside the territorial waters) of neutral states.[50] IHL will apply to the hostilities in these areas and any other area where military operations are actually carried out.

As *Tadić* indicates,[51] IHL applies to IACs until a general peace is concluded. Peace treaties may end an IAC, but they have not been common since WWII (the 1979 peace treaty between Israel and Egypt being a notable exception[52]). Beyond that, the issue has arisen as to whether a ceasefire or an armistice agreement can end an armed conflict. Under the Hague Regulations 1907, these merely suspended military operations rather than ended a war.[53] This question remains significant, as there is not yet a peace treaty terminating the Korean conflict of the early 1950s or the conflict between Israel and some of her Arab neighbours since 1949. The better view, espoused by Greenwood, is that 'since armed conflict is not a technical, legal concept but a recognition of the fact of hostilities, the cessation of active hostilities should be enough to terminate the armed conflict'.[54] A fortiori, a ceasefire or armistice agreement will end a conflict where it is intended to do so[55] and is effective in practice.

The cessation of hostilities triggers certain duties, including to release prisoners of war[56] and detainees.[57] However, the termination of a conflict does not terminate the application of all IHL rules. Just as IHL imposes some obligations on states prior to the commencement of a conflict (eg the obligation to disseminate IHL and to train armed forces in it[58]), certain rules apply beyond the cessation of hostilities or even the conclusion of an occupation. For example, those detained in the conflict continue to be protected.[59]

---

[50] See Greenwood 'Scope of Application' (n 35) 59 para 216. Note that military operations are prohibited in certain areas, such as hospital and safety, demilitarized and neutralized zones. ibid paras 219–20. See also chapter 3 'The Temporal and Geographic Reach of International Humanitarian Law' in this book.
[51] *Tadić* Jurisdiction (above n 6) para 70.
[52] Peace Treaty between Egypt and Israel (1979) 18 ILM 362.
[53] Regulations Respecting the Laws and Customs of War on Land, annexed to Hague Convention IV Respecting the Laws and Customs of War on Land (1907) article 36.
[54] See Greenwood 'Scope of Application' (n 35) 72 para 250.
[55] Yoram Dinstein, *War, Aggression and Self-Defence* (CUP 2017) 47.
[56] Geneva Convention (III) Relative to the Treatment of Prisoners of War (adopted 12 August 1949, entered into force 21 October 1950) 75 UNTS 135 (GCIII) article 118.
[57] Geneva Convention (IV) Relative to the Protection of Civilian Persons in Time of War (adopted 12 August 1949, entered into force 21 October 1950) 75 UNTS 287 (GCIV) articles 133 and 134.
[58] See Protocol Additional to the Geneva Conventions of 12 August 1949, and Relating to the Protection of Victims of International Armed Conflicts (adopted 8 June 1977, entered into force 7 December 1978) 1125 UNTS 609 (API) article 83.
[59] See GCIII article 5 and GCIV article 6.

*C. Occupation*

**(i) The definition of occupation**   Chapter 13 'Occupation' in this book addresses the law of occupation, including its commencement and termination. In brief, Common Article 2 to the Geneva Conventions 1949 states that the Conventions shall also apply to all cases of partial or total occupation of the territory of a party, even if there is no armed resistance (as in the case of the German annexation of Czechoslovakia before WWII). Although the Geneva Conventions do not define occupation, article 42 of the Hague Regulations 1907 does. That provision, which is regarded as customary international law,[60] states that 'territory is considered occupied when it is actually placed under the authority of the hostile army'. This means that the occupier must exercise effective territorial control, substituting its own authority for the authority of the territorial state without the consent of the latter's government.[61] This usually requires the deployment of troops, as opposed to a brief incursion. A state may also occupy the territory of another state (or parts thereof) through a subordinate (or puppet) administration, where there is complete dependence or effective control.[62]

The Fourth Geneva Convention imposes obligations with regard to occupation and occupied territory, including with regard to the status and treatment of protected persons (Part III, Section III) and internees (Part III, Section IV). According to article 6 of the Fourth Convention, its provisions apply 'from the outset of any conflict or occupation'. The ICRC had previously suggested ('the Pictet theory') that the definition of occupation for the purposes of the Fourth Geneva Convention was broader than the definition of occupation in the Hague Regulations of 1907.[63] On this theory, the Fourth Geneva Convention applies from the invasion phase of a conflict without requiring stable control of the territory.[64] However, although the Pictet theory was applied by the ICTY,[65] the ICRC, in its later Commentary to article 6, concluded that the concept of occupation used in the Geneva Conventions 'is not distinct from that used in the Hague Regulations'.[66]

**(ii) Conflicts with non-state armed groups in the context of occupation**   During an occupation, the occupying power may be engaged in hostilities with, or otherwise take military action against, a local non-state group, as in Iraq after the 2003 US–UK invasion and the fall of Saddam Hussein's regime. To determine the applicable law, one must first determine that the situation involves hostilities governed by IHL, as opposed to internal disturbances or riots (in which case, domestic law and international human rights law apply). But questions

---

[60] See *Case concerning Armed Activities on the Territory of the Congo (Democratic Republic of the Congo v Uganda)* (2005) ICJ Rep 168 ('*Armed Activities* case') paras 172ff.

[61] See generally Adam Roberts, 'What is Military Occupation?' (1984) 55 *BYBIL* 249.

[62] See *Armed Activities* case (above n 60) para 177 (finding that rebel groups operating in the Democratic Republic of Congo outside of the Ituri region were not under complete dependence or effective control of Uganda); Vité (above n 43) 74–5 (arguing that Armenia indirectly occupies Nagorno-Karabakh in Azerbaijan); *Loizidou v Turkey*, ECtHR App No 15318/89, 18 December 1996 (on Turkey's effective control over Northern Cyprus, which could qualify as indirect occupation).

[63] See Pictet *Vol III* (above n 47) article 6, quoted with approval by the ICTY Trial Chamber in *Prosecutor v Rajić* (Review of the Indictment) IT-95-12 (13 September 1996).

[64] See Knut Dörmann, 'The Legal Situation of "Unlawful/Unprivileged Combatants"' (2003) 85 *IRRC* 45, 61–3 and chapter 13 'Occupation' in this book.

[65] See *Prosecutor v Naletilić & Martinović* (Trial Chamber Judgment) IT-98-34 (31 March 2003) paras 218–222. However, this theory was rejected by the English High Court in *Alseran v MoD* [2017] EWHC 3289 (QB) paras 266–272.

[66] ICRC, *Commentary on the First Geneva Convention* (2nd edn, ICRC 2016) para 299; and paras 294–298.

arise as to whether the law of IACs or NIACs applies in those situations, as the context is one of occupation but the fighting is between a state and a non-state group.[67]

There are two possibilities. First, the non-state group may be fighting on behalf of the occupied state or under a command responsible to the occupied state (within the meaning of article 4(A)(2) of the Third Geneva Convention or article 43 of API).[68] Second, the non-state group may be independent of the occupied state. In the first case, it is clear that the conflict is governed by the law applicable to IAC, since the group, though irregular, qualifies as part of the state's armed forces.

The second scenario is less straightforward. In the *Targeted Killings* case, the Israeli Supreme Court found that confrontations between the occupying party and non-state groups in occupied territory are governed by the law applicable to IAC, even where the non-state group is not fighting on behalf of a state.[69] To some degree this conclusion is arguably correct.[70] It follows from the fact that the Geneva Conventions and other rules concerning IAC, including API, apply to the *acts of the occupying power* and regulate its relationship both to the occupied state and the people in the occupied territory. However, it is also possible that *alongside the occupation* there exists a NIAC between the occupying power and an organized armed group (provided the criteria for NIAC, discussed below, are met).[71]

The critical question is not, however, what type of conflict exists between the state and the non-state group but what law applies to the acts of an occupying power in occupied territory. The law of occupation is not just about the relationship between two contending states or simply a means of indicating the temporary nature of the occupier's authority vis-à-vis the territorial state. It also regulates what may well be the tense relationship between the occupying power and persons within the occupied territory, particularly by restraining how the former treats the latter, including where there are confrontations. The fact that the local population has chosen to rise up in arms does not free the occupier from its obligations, but ought to reinforce them. Moreover, the law of occupation foresees that those who are not members of the occupied state's armed forces may engage in hostilities against the occupier, or commit acts of sabotage or other acts which imperil the occupier's security.[72] Various IHL provisions accordingly address such activities.[73]

---

[67] See Andreas Paulus and Mindia Vashakmadze, 'Asymmetrical War and the Notion of Armed Conflict—A Tentative Conceptualization' (2009) 91 *IRRC* 95, 113–15.

[68] See section 7.A 'Foreign Intervention on the Side of a Non-State Armed Group against the State' below.

[69] *Public Committee against Torture in Israel v Government of Israel*, High Court of Justice, HCJ 769/02 (11 December 2005) ('*Targeted Killings* case') paras 16–23.

[70] Similarly Antonio Cassese, *International Law* (OUP 2005) 420–3; Antonio Cassese, 'On Some Merits of the Israeli Judgment on Targeted Killings' (2007) 5 *JICJ* 339; Yoram Dinstein, *The International Law of Belligerent Occupation* (CUP 2009) 100. *Contra* Marko Milanovic, 'Lessons for Human Rights and Humanitarian Law in the War on Terror: Comparing *Hamdan* and the Israeli *Targeted Killings* Case' (2007) 89 *IRRC* 373, 383–6; Yutuka Arai-Takahashi, *The Law of Occupation: Continuation and Change of International Humanitarian Law, and its Interaction with International Human Rights Law* (Brill 2009) 300–3. See also section 6.A.1 below, 'Criteria for the Existence of NIACs'.

[71] See Milanovic 'Lessons for Human Rights' (above n 70); Kubo Mačák, 'The Ituri Conundrum: Qualifying Conflicts between an Occupying Power and an Autonomous Non-State Actor' (*EJIL: Talk!*, 15 July 2019) https://www.ejiltalk.org/the-ituri-conundrum-qualifying-conflicts-between-an-occupying-power-and-an-autonomous-non-state-actor.

[72] Nils Melzer, *International Humanitarian Law: A Comprehensive Introduction* (ICRC 2016) 62.

[73] For instance, articles 5 and 68 of GCIV contemplate persons who engage in sabotage, and the provisions of GCIV on internment deal with persons who may imperil the security of the State. Likewise, article 45(3) of API recognizes that persons engaging in hostilities during occupation, and who are not entitled to POW status, are entitled to the protections of GCIV or of the fundamental guarantees in article 75 of API (which mirrors customary law). See generally Dörmann (above n 64).

Thus, the law of occupation and other IAC rules (including on targeting) continue to regulate how the occupier may respond to an uprising in the foreign territory. This conclusion finds supports in the International Court of Justice (ICJ)'s judgment in the *Armed Activities* case, where it applied the law of occupation and the law of IAC to Uganda's acts in the Ituri region of the Democratic Republic of Congo (DRC). This was despite the fact that Uganda was acting primarily against non-state groups.[74] However, this is not to suggest that the law of NIAC will never apply in occupied territory. Such a conflict might arise between two non-state groups who engage in hostilities, with the result that those parties are bound by the rules applicable to NIACs.[75] Also, where there is a NIAC between the occupier and an armed group, the conduct of the armed group will be subject to the law of NIACs, even if the occupier continues to have obligations under the law of IACs.[76]

**(iii) End of occupation** Occupation 'ends when [the occupying] State no longer *de facto* exercises its control over the territory'.[77] Usually, this will coincide with the forced or voluntary removal of the occupying power's troops. Nevertheless, control may extend beyond such removal, for example, where the direct control of the occupier is replaced by indirect occupation. More difficult is the situation, as in Gaza, where the armed forces of the occupier leave the territory and no longer exercise control over its governance, but continue to exercise control over other aspects of it (namely, control over Gaza's airspace, certain borders, and adjacent sea areas). Opinion is divided over whether such a situation constitutes a continuation of occupation.[78] Yet, it may be argued that, like the criteria for statehood (where creation and continuation are assessed by different standards[79]), the criteria for the establishment of occupation may differ from the ones required for its maintenance. This suggests that even where a former occupying power no longer exercises the level of control used to establish the occupation, if such control is exercised to prevent another power from gaining full control, the occupation continues.

## B. Self-Determination Conflicts of National Liberation under Article 1(4) of API

Although an IAC usually involves two (or more) states fighting each other, API 1977 also applies the laws of IAC to a special category of internal armed conflict. Under article 1(4), API extends to armed conflicts where 'peoples are fighting against colonial domination and alien occupation and against racist regimes in the exercise of their right of self-determination [ ... ]'.

[74] *Armed Activities* case (above n 60). For a similar view, see *Lubanga* (Decision on Confirmation of Charges) ICC-01/04-01/06 (29 January 2007) para 220.
[75] See *Lubanga* (Trial Judgment) ICC-01/04-01/06 (14 March 2012) paras 563–565; *Katanga* (Trial Judgment) ICC-01/04-01/07-3436-tENG (7 March 2014) para 1182; Paulus and Vashakmadze (above n 67) 115.
[76] *Ntaganda* (Trial Judgment) ICC-01/04-02/06-2359 (8 July 2019) paras 725 and 728.
[77] Hans-Peter Gasser and Knt Dörmann, 'Protection of the Civilian Population', in Fleck (ed) 2013 (above n 24) 280 para 537.
[78] See the discussion in chapter 13 'Occupation' in this book; and Vité (above n 43) 83–5 (with extensive references to the opposing views); Iain Scobbie, 'Gaza', in Wilmshurst (ed) (above n 11) ch 9.
[79] Crawford (above n 33) 667ff.

The provision reflects concerns prevailing at the time of API's negotiation and responds to the desire, mainly of developing countries, for legitimation of liberation struggles. The provision was primarily aimed at Israel's occupation of Palestine, the struggle in South Africa and Rhodesia (as it was then called), and the colonial struggles of the time.[80] However, API has never been applied in any of those situations. This is because the situations to which it applies are difficult to define. One key question is whether a movement is indeed fighting in the exercise of the right of self-determination. That matter is determined by general international law. However, in addition, a national liberation movement that seeks the application of article 1(4) to a conflict it is engaged in, may, under article 96(3), make a unilateral declaration undertaking to apply the provisions of the Geneva Conventions and API in that conflict. Such a declaration was first made in 2015 by the Polisario Front, which seeks independence for Western Sahara from Moroccan administration and control (of a non-self-governing territory previously administered by Spain until 1975). Most authors consider that article 1(4) is not part of customary international law.[81]

## C. Recognition of Belligerency

As noted earlier in section 2 'History of the Distinction between IAC and NIAC', even before WWII, the laws of war applied to civil wars between a state and a rebel group where the latter was recognized as a belligerent.[82] Such recognition could be done either by the opposing government or third states, usually through a declaration of neutrality by the foreign state. According to Oppenheim, recognition is warranted if the insurgents '(1) [ ... ] are in possession of a certain part of the territory of the legitimate Government; (2) [ ... ] have set up a Government of their own; and (3) [ ... ] conduct their armed contention with the legitimate Government according to the laws and usages of war'.[83]

The effect of a recognition of belligerency, by the state fighting against the rebel group, is the application of all laws of war between the parties. But these effects only operate between the recognizing state and the belligerent group, without prejudice to the relations between other states and the belligerent group.[84]

The practice of recognizing belligerencies has declined since the regulation of NIAC and the doctrine is said to be obsolete or to have fallen into desuetude. However, while the Boer War (1899–1902) was the last instance of recognition of belligerency by a belligerent government, there have been cases of third states recognizing belligerency of insurgents operating in other countries.[85] Moreover, recognition of belligerency was mostly implied in

---

[80] See George Aldrich, 'Prospects for United States Ratification of Additional Protocol I to the 1949 Geneva Conventions' (1991) 85 *AJIL* 1, 6.

[81] See eg Mačák *Internationalized Armed Conflicts* (above n 34) 73–4 and Yoram Dinstein, *The Conduct of Hostilities under the Law of International Armed Conflict* (CUP 2010) 28; cf Antonio Cassese, 'Wars of National Liberation and Humanitarian Law' reprinted in Antonio Cassese (ed), *The Human Dimension of International Law: Selected Papers* (OUP 2008) 99, 106.

[82] See Eibe Riedel, 'Recognition of Belligerency', in Rudolf Bernhardt (ed), *Encyclopedia of Public International Law, Vol 4* (North-Holland 2000) 47 and Mačák *Internationalized Armed Conflicts* (above n 34) 74–82.

[83] Lassa Oppenheim, *International Law, Vol II: Disputes, War and Neutrality* (2nd edn, Longmans 1912) 92.

[84] Lassa Oppenheim, *International Law, Vol II: Disputes, War and Neutrality* (7th edn, Longmans 1952) 251.

[85] For instance, the recognition of the belligerency of the Nicaraguan Sandinistas by the Andean Group in 1979, cited in Nieto Navia, 'Hay o no hay conflicto armado en Colombia' (2008) 1 *Anuario Colombiano de Derecho Int'l* 139, 147; the recognition, in 1981, by France and Mexico of El Salvadoran rebels; recognition by Venezuela of the FARC group in Colombia in 2008.

the nineteenth century, such as through declarations of neutrality and acquiescence in the confiscation of contraband or a blockade.[86] Since 1949, blockades have been instituted in NIACs and these may be regarded as implicit recognition, thus internationalizing the conflict. It is worth noting that desuetude of a customary principle does not extinguish it.[87]

## 6. The Scope of Application of IHL: NIACs

It is not always easy to determine when violence within a state is to be classified as a NIAC. Where it is regarded as merely internal strife or civil disturbance, the threshold of 'armed conflict' is not reached and IHL does not apply. Conversely, where the threshold is reached, IHL applies. The question, therefore, is what is the threshold for a NIAC to exist?

## A. NIACs under Common Article 3

### 1. Criteria for the existence of NIACs

Unfortunately, Common Article 3 does not specify when it will apply, referring only to an 'armed conflict not of an international character occurring in the territory of one of the High Contracting Parties'. Whether or not such a conflict is taking place is determined by criteria which have been fleshed out by customary international law. In the *Tadić* case, the ICTY Appeals Chamber referred to a NIAC as a situation of 'protracted armed violence between governmental authorities and organised armed groups or between such groups within a State'.[88] This test is also adopted in article 8(2)(d) and (f) of the ICC Statute, which excludes from the definition of NIACs 'situations of internal disturbances and tensions, such as riots, isolated and sporadic acts of violence or other acts of a similar nature'.[89]

The first criterion for determining whether a NIAC exists is the involvement of an '*organised armed group*'.[90] Under customary law, a NIAC governed by Common Article 3 may be a conflict between a state and a non-state group, or between non-state groups. Thus, at least one side must be a non-state group. To be a party to an armed conflict a non-state group must have a certain level of organization with a command structure.[91] Relevant factors that *may* be taken into account include the existence of a command structure and disciplinary rules and mechanisms; the existence of headquarters; control over territory; access to weapons, other military equipment, recruits, and military training; the ability to plan, coordinate, and carry out military operations, including troop movements and logistics; a unified military strategy and use of military tactics; and an ability to speak with one voice, to negotiate and conclude agreements such as ceasefire or peace accords.[92]

Although groups involved in NIACs usually have a political purpose or aim, this is not a requirement under IHL. Thus, violence involving criminal groups acting for private,

---

[86] Riedel (above n 82) 48.
[87] Scobbie 'Gaza' (above n 78) 303.
[88] *Tadić* Jurisdiction (above n 6) para 70.
[89] See also APII article 1.
[90] *Tadić* Jurisdiction (above n 6) para 70.
[91] Jelena Pejić, 'Status of Armed Conflicts', in Wilmshurst and Breau (eds) (above n 19) 85–6.
[92] *Haradinaj et al* (Trial Judgment) IT-04-84-T (3 April 2008) para 60.

non-political motives may NIACs. What is important is that the group is sufficiently organ-ized and is involved in an armed campaign reaching the required degree of intensity (the second criterion for a NIAC, discussed below). Factually, it is unlikely that these conditions will be met by criminal gangs, but the possibility cannot be ruled out and the UNSC has ac-knowledged the applicability of IHL to the fight against piracy.[93]

The second criterion required for a NIAC is that the violence must reach a certain degree of *intensity*.[94] In *Tadić* the ICTY spoke of 'protracted armed violence'.[95] While the word 'protracted' implies a certain duration, it is generally accepted that the key requirement is the intensity of the force rather than its timing. This indicates that the threshold of violence for NIACs is higher than in IACs. While an IAC exists from the initiation of inter-state vio-lence, the situation with respect to NIACs is more fluid as often the violence pre-dates the armed conflict and the application of IHL. Thus, it will often be necessary to assess *when* the violence crosses the threshold of applicability of IHL.

In *Haradinaj et al*, a case relating to the conflict in Kosovo between the Federal Republic of Yugoslavia and the Kosovo Liberation Army, the ICTY relied on several indicative factors to assess the two criteria of 'intensity' and 'organisation of armed groups'.[96] These include the number, duration, and intensity of individual confrontations; the type of weapons and other military equipment used; the number and calibre of munitions fired; the number of persons and type of forces partaking in the fighting; the number of casualties; the extent of material destruction; and the number of civilians fleeing combat zones. The involvement of the UNSC may also be a reflection of the intensity of a conflict.[97] This is a case-by-case evaluation of the overall situation and no particular formula exists for weighting the dif-ferent factors.

Thus, it may be that violence of relatively short duration amounts to a NIAC where its scale and the destruction is particularly high. In the *Abella* case, the Inter-American Commission of Human Rights held that a thirty-hour confrontation between the Argentinian military and a dissident group of soldiers was covered by Common Article 3.[98] Alternatively, pro-longed violence may suffice even though the individual confrontations are not destructive. However, where fighting involves state authorities, violence should be equivalent to that used by its armed forces, even if it is the activity rather than the state arm that is decisive.[99] Thus even operations conducted by law enforcement could be classified as NIACs.

---

[93] See UNSC Resolution 1851 (2008) and Robin Geiss, 'Armed Violence in Fragile States: Low Intensity Conflicts, Spill Over Conflicts, and Sporadic Law Enforcement Operations by External Actors' (2009) 91(873) *IRRC* 127, 139ff; Michael Passman, 'Protections Afforded to Captured Pirates under the Law of War and International Law' (2008) 33 *Tulane Maritime L J* 1; cf Douglas Guilfoyle, 'The Law of War and the Fight against Somali Piracy: Combatants or Criminals?' (2010) 11 *MJIL* 141.

[94] For a summary of the two criteria, see Dietrich Schindler, 'The Different Types of Armed Conflicts According to the Geneva Conventions and Protocols' (1979) 163 *Recueil des cours* 147.

[95] *Tadić* Jurisdiction (above n 6) para 70.

[96] *Haradinaj* (above n 92). See also *Milošević* (above n 34) para 14ff; *Katanga* (above n 75) paras 1186–1187; *Ntaganda* (above n 76) paras 704, 716–717. See generally Anthony Cullen, *The Concept of Non-International Armed Conflicts in International Humanitarian Law* (CUP 2010) and Sandesh Sivakumaran, *The Law of Non-International Armed Conflict* (OUP 2012) ch 5.

[97] *Haradinaj* (above n 92) para 49.

[98] *Abella v Argentina*, IACmHR, Case No 11.137, Report No 55/97, 8 November 1997. However, this case is criticized by Michael Schmitt and Noam Lubell in Wilmshurst (ed) (above n 11) chs 9 and 11.

[99] Note that the threshold of derogation from human rights treaties in case of a 'public emergency threat-ening the life of the nation' is separate from the threshold of a Common Article 3 conflict. See UN Human Rights Committee, 'General Comment 29: States of Emergency (article 4)', CCPR/C/21/Rev.1/Add.11 (2001).

## 2. Geographical scope of NIACs

Two questions arise with regard to the geographical scope of the application of IHL in a NIAC. The first relates to the territorial extent of application of IHL *within* a state in which the NIAC takes place. In the *Tadić* case, the ICTY Appeals Chamber stated that in a NIAC, IHL 'continues to apply ... in the whole territory under the control of a party, whether or not actual combat take place there'.[100] However, since fighting in some NIACs is confined to only a part of the state with large parts of the state being unaffected, the view that IHL applies throughout the state has been questioned as being overbroad.[101]

The second question relates to whether NIACs, and thus the application of IHL, can extend beyond the boundaries of one state. Although many NIACs are internal conflicts confined to the territory of one state, particularly between the government of that state and a non-state group within that state, it is possible for the fighting in a NIAC to span more than the state. This will happen where the NSAG operates in more than one state. Where this is the case, the question may arise whether the hostilities that take place in different states between the same parties are: (i) part of the same armed conflict, for instance by aggregating the violence in the different states to cross the threshold of intensity for a NIAC; or (ii) to be regarded as separate conflicts, with the effect that the focus must be on whether the hostilities in each state separately meet the threshold for a NIAC.

Although Common Article 3 speaks of NIACs occurring in the territory of 'one of the High Contracting Parties', it is accepted that this provision was not intended to, and does not, limit NIACs to the territory of one state. It simply means that Common Article 3 will only apply where the conflict occurs on the territory of at least one High Contracting Party. It has been generally accepted that where a non-state armed group is based (or retreats) across the border, hostilities which spill across that border will be regarded as part of the same NIAC.[102]

However, the US claimed that it is involved in a 'global war' with a number of terrorist groups and that its actions in many states are part of that same NIAC. It is more likely that hostilities will spill over across a land border than to a more distant country. However, where the same non-state group in a NIAC operates in another country, there seems to be no reason as a matter of law or logic why the same NIAC would not also extend there too.[103] If this approach is followed, the intensity requirement for NIACS could be met by aggregation of violence in the different countries, rather than by examining the level of violence in each country.[104] Even if a NIAC may exist in more than one country under IHL, it is the law

---

[100] *Tadić* Jurisdiction (above n 6) para 70.

[101] See Sivakumaran (above n 96) 250–1 and ch 3 'The Temporal and Geographic Reach of International Humanitarian Law' in this book.

[102] See the position of the ICRC on spillover conflicts at ICRC, *International Humanitarian Law and the Challenges of Contemporary Armed Conflicts* (Report of the 31st Conference of the International Red Cross and Red Crescent), pp. 9–10 https://www.icrc.org/en/doc/resources/documents/report/31-international-conference-ihl-challenges-report-2011-10-31.htm: 'it is submitted that the relations between parties whose conflict has spilled over remain at a minimum governed by Common Article 3 and customary IHL. This position is based on the understanding that the spill over of a NIAC into adjacent territory cannot have the effect of absolving the parties of their IHL obligations simply because an international border has been crossed.'

[103] See eg Noam Lubell and Nathan Derejko, 'A Global Battlefield? Drones and the Geographical Scope of Armed Conflict' (2013) 11 *JICJ* 65. See also Chapter 3 'The Temporal and Geographic Reach of International Humanitarian Law' in this book for a more general discussion.

[104] See Lubell and Derejko (above n 102) 78; Christoph Heyns, Dapo Akande, Lawrence Hill-Cawthorne, and Thompson Chengeta, 'The International Law Framework Regulating the Use of Armed Drones' (2016) 65 *ICLQ* 791, 806–9.

governing resort to force under the UN Charter and customary international law that determines whether a state may lawfully use force on the territory of another state. That such force will be part of a NIAC regulated by IHL does not authorize or determine the legality of such resort to force.

## B.  NIACs under APII

Both Common Article 3 and APII do not apply to situations of internal disturbance and tensions such as riots, or isolated and sporadic acts of violence (the threshold for 'armed conflict'). However, under article 1(1) of APII, the rules therein only apply to armed conflicts taking place on the territory of a party 'between its armed forces and dissident armed forces or other organised armed groups which, under responsible command, exercise such control over a part of its territory as to enable them to carry out sustained and concerted military operations and to implement this Protocol'. This threshold of application of APII is higher than that of Common Article 3 in a number of ways. The effect of the different thresholds is that there are at least two types of NIAC: those covered by both sources, and those covered only by Common Article 3.

The APII test, which is similar to the one for the recognition of belligerency,[105] is more stringent in various ways than the threshold in Common Article 3. First, it applies only if government forces are involved and APII does not apply to conflicts solely between organized armed groups. Second, the organized armed group must exercise control over territory, typically where a rebel group is fighting against the government for authority over the state or part thereof. While the actual carrying out of sustained and concerted military operations and compliance with APII are not strictly required (and only the ability to do so is required), in practice it is difficult to conceive of territorial control without such operations.

A third difference between APII and Common Article 3 is that the former applies to NIACs on the territory of a party between '*its* armed forces' and organized armed groups. This means that in NIACs where a third state intervenes in an internal conflict with the consent of the territorial state, APII will not apply to the acts of the intervening state, even if both states are parties to it. After all, the conflict does not take place on its territory and is not between its armed forces and armed groups. Applying this interpretation to the NIAC in Afghanistan since 2002 (after the formation of a new Afghan government) is illustrative. It would mean that although Afghanistan became party to APII in 2009, and some of the countries fighting there with its consent are also parties to it, the Protocol does not apply to the conflict between those intervening countries and armed groups.[106] It is not clear whether this was intended by the Protocol's drafters.

An alternative interpretation would be to consider the forces of the intervening state to be part of the armed forces of the territorial state.[107] Although this would be a desirable extension of the Protocol's humanitarian protections, this test for armed forces does not find

---

[105] See eg the criteria set out by Oppenheim *International Law, Vol II: Disputes, War and Neutrality* 2nd edn (above n 83) 92.

[106] Dapo Akande, 'Afghanistan Accedes to Additional Protocols to Geneva Conventions: Will APII Govern the Conflict in Afghanistan?' (*EJIL Talk!*, 30 June 2009) https://www.ejiltalk.org/afghanistan-accedes-to-additional-protocols.

[107] See Vité (above n 43) 80.

support in the rest of IHL. The forces of a co-belligerent are not usually regarded as part of the armed forces of a party. Also, it would be a stretch to say that a state is responsible not only for the acts of own forces but also for those of the co-belligerent.[108] Nevertheless, APII could apply to acts of invited foreign forces if their acts are attributable to the territorial state under the law of state responsibility, as where the foreign forces are 'placed at the disposal of' the territorial state.[109] This means that they must act under the exclusive direction and control of the territorial state rather than the sending state.[110] This test will rarely be satisfied in practice.

## 7. Foreign Intervention in NIACs

Despite the significance of the distinction between IACs and NIACs, drawing this distinction in practice is often difficult. This is particularly so where there is foreign intervention in a NIAC. Since the end of WWII, NIACs have become more common than IACs. During the Cold War, this trend was coupled with the phenomenon of 'proxy wars' where foreign states intervened in many NIACs. Similarly, in the twenty-first century, there continues to be increased foreign intervention in what would otherwise be internal conflicts, as in Yemen, Syria, Iraq, Afghanistan, the DRC, and South Ossetia.

Since IACs are essentially inter-state conflicts, whether or not intervention in a NIAC transforms it into an IAC (or at least grafts an IAC onto an existing, and perhaps continuing, NIAC) will depend on which side of the conflict the foreign state intervenes. A proposal by the ICRC for all such conflicts to be deemed international was rejected during the negotiation of the Additional Protocols.[111]

### A. Foreign Intervention on the Side of a Non-State Armed Group against a State

Where the armed forces of a foreign state intervene on the side of the non-state group fighting against a state, there will be two opposing states involved in a conflict and, therefore, an IAC. This situation is hardly any different from a quintessential IAC. However, the fact that there is an IAC between two states does not necessarily affect the classification of the NIAC between the territorial state and non-state group, in so far as the latter does not act on behalf of the intervening state. Accordingly, there will be a mixed conflict with an IAC alongside a continuing NIAC, as in the *Nicaragua* case, where the actions of the US in and against Nicaragua were governed by the rules of IAC but the conflict between Nicaraguan forces and the Contra rebels remained a NIAC.[112]

It is more difficult where a foreign state does not send its own armed forces to fight alongside rebel forces but provides other means of support to them. It is accepted that where a

---

[108] For IAC see API article 91.
[109] See ARSIWA article 6. See also discussion in Akande (above n 106).
[110] See ARSIWA commentary to article 6.
[111] ICRC, 'Protection of Victims of Non-International Armed Conflicts' (1971) cited by Vité (above n 43) n 31.
[112] *Military and Paramilitary Activities in and against Nicaragua (Nicaragua v United States of America)* (Merits) [1986] ICJ Rep 14 para 219. See section 7.C below for a discussion of 'Mixed Conflicts'.

non-state group fighting a state acts on behalf of a different state, there is an IAC. However, there has been much controversy as to what level of involvement by the intervening state internationalizes the conflict.[113] In *Tadić*, the ICTY Appeals Chamber held that this question depends on whether the non-state group 'belongs to' a party to the conflict, within the meaning of article 4 of the Third Geneva Convention.[114] This in turn relates to whether the non-state group is a de facto state organ; that is, whether its acts are attributable to the state under the law of state responsibility,[115] in which case an IAC exists. The Appeals Chamber also found that the test of attribution is 'overall control', as opposed to the 'effective control' test developed by the ICJ in the *Nicaragua* case.[116] It considered the ICJ's test to be too strict in cases of organized groups. The 'overall control' test would be satisfied:

> when the State [ … ] *has a role in organising, coordinating or planning the military actions* of a military group, in addition to financing, training and equipping or providing operational support to the group. Acts performed by the group or members thereof may be regarded as acts of *de facto* State organs regardless of any specific instruction by the controlling State concerning the commission of each of those acts.[117]

On that basis, the Appeals Chamber held that the Bosnian Serbs were under the overall control of the Federal Republic of Yugoslavia, so that the conflict between such group and the Muslim-led Bosnian government was an IAC.[118] The overall control test has been endorsed by the ICC in several cases.[119]

Although the decision on the facts in *Tadić* was probably correct, the reasoning for it has rightly been criticized.[120] The ICTY misinterpreted the *Nicaragua* test of attribution. As the ICJ confirmed in the *Bosnia Genocide* case,[121] the *Nicaragua* case, customary international law, and the International Law Commission's (ILC) articles on State Responsibility do not contain one single test for the attribution of acts of non-state groups to a state, but at least two. The first is the test to determine whether a non-state group can be considered a de facto state organ under article 4 of the ILC's articles. If that test is satisfied, then *all* the acts of a non-state group are attributable to a state. In some ways, this is precisely what the Appeals Chamber was seeking to achieve in *Tadić*. But according to the ICJ, this is not a question of 'overall control' but requires a much stricter test of 'complete dependence and control', under which the group is seen as the mere instrument of the state.[122] Thus, under the law of state responsibility the fact that a non-state group is under the 'overall control' of a state would not make it a state organ.

---

[113] See generally Christine Byron 'Armed Conflicts: International or Non-International' (2001) 6 *JCSL* 63.

[114] *Prosecutor v Tadić* (Appeal Judgment) IT-94-1-A (15 July 1999) paras 92–95.

[115] ibid paras 96–97.

[116] ibid paras 120–138.

[117] ibid para 139.

[118] ibid paras 146–162.

[119] *Lubanga* Decision on Confirmation of Charges (above n 74) para 541; *Katanga* (above n 75) para 1178; *Bemba* (Trial Judgment) ICC-01/05-01/08-3343 (21 March 2016) para 130; *Ntaganda* (above n 76) paras 726–727.

[120] See Stefan Talmon, 'The Responsibility of Outside Powers for Acts of Secessionist Entities' (2009) 58 *ILCQ* 493; Marko Milanovic, 'State Responsibility for Genocide' (2006) 17 *EJIL* 553; Marko Milanovic, 'State Responsibility for Genocide: A Follow-Up' (2007) 18 *EJIL* 669.

[121] *Case concerning Application of the Convention on the Prevention and Punishment of the Crime of Genocide (Bosnia and Herzegovina v Serbia and Montenegro)* (Merits) (*Bosnian Genocide* case) [2007] ICJ Rep 43 paras 385–395.

[122] ibid paras 392–93.

The second test applies where a group is not a de facto state organ under article 4, but *specific acts* of that group can be attributed to a state, under article 8 of the ILC's articles, where such acts are carried out on that state's instructions or under its direction or 'effective control'.[123] Thus, the tests for state responsibility are stricter than the one put forward by the ICTY and there are good reasons for this.[124] A state should only be held legally responsible for its own acts. Otherwise, depending on the primary rules in question, it may be held responsible for its failure to control others or for creating a situation which permitted particular acts to occur.[125]

Nevertheless, the internationalization of armed conflict is not necessarily dependent on rules of attribution in the general international law of state responsibility, so that the test required for the former may not be equivalent to the latter. To be sure, as the ICTY noted, where a non-state group is a de facto state organ or is under its effective control when fighting against another state, the conflict will be international, as the group acts on behalf of the state. But the question remains whether IHL provides for a lower threshold of attribution for the purpose of conflict classification. This point was raised by the ICJ itself in the *Bosnian Genocide* case, where it stated:

> Insofar as the 'overall control' test is employed to determine whether or not an armed conflict is international, which was the sole question which the Appeals Chamber was called upon to decide, it may well be that the test is applicable and suitable; the Court does not however think it appropriate to take a position on the point in the present case, as there is no need to resolve it for purposes of the present Judgment. [ ... ]
>
> [L]ogic does not require the same test to be adopted in resolving the two issues, which are very different in nature: the degree and nature of a State's involvement in an armed conflict on another State's territory which is required for the conflict to be characterized as international, can very well, and without logical inconsistency, differ from the degree and nature of involvement required to give rise to that State's responsibility for a specific act committed in the course of the conflict.[126]

If *Tadić* is wrong on the specific point that the 'overall control' test is the test of state responsibility under general international law, there are three further views on the test for internationalization of a NIAC as a result of state support for non-state groups. One view would agree with *Tadić* that the key question is whether the non-state group 'belongs to' a foreign state but would argue that this question depends on specific IHL rules, as opposed to the general law of state responsibility. Under those rules, an armed group would be regarded as belonging to a state, in particular under article 4 of the Third Geneva Convention, regardless of effective control by a state, provided that there is a de facto agreement or relationship

---

[123] ibid paras 396–402. See in particular para 400, where the Court stated that: 'It must [ ... ] be shown that this "effective control" was exercised, or that the State's instructions were given, in respect of each operation in which the alleged violations occurred, not generally in respect of the overall actions taken by the persons or groups of persons having committed the violations.'

[124] See Talmon (above n 120) 517.

[125] See eg *Bosnian Genocide* case (above n 121) (holding that while Serbia was not responsible for the genocide in Bosnia, it breached its duty to prevent and to punish the genocide).

[126] ibid paras 404–405. See Marina Spinedi, 'On the Non-Attribution of the Bosnian Serbs' Conduct to Serbia' (2007) 5 *JICJ* 829.

between the state and the group.[127] This test draws from the ICRC commentary to article 4[128] and it is probably even looser than the 'overall control' test. This approach postulates a *lex specialis* rule in the regime of state responsibility[129] for breaches of IHL. Thus, a state would be responsible for the acts of non-state groups that belong to it under a lower threshold of attribution.[130]

A second approach is to argue that the 'overall control' test is simply a rule of IHL which exists for the classification of armed conflict, as opposed to being a more general rule of state responsibility. This view has been adopted by the ICC[131] and it has the advantage of reconciling the conflicting views of the ICJ and the ICTY. However, it contrasts with the approach in *Tadić* in that it does not claim (as *Tadić* does) that the 'overall control' test is derived from general international law.

A third approach was adopted by Judge Shahabuddeen in his Separate Opinion in the *Tadić* Appeal Judgment. In his view, the question is whether a foreign state can be said to have used force against another state. With regard to the Bosnian conflict, he framed it as follows:

> *Ex hypothesi*, an armed conflict involves a use of force. Thus, the question whether there was an armed conflict between the FRY [Federal Republic of Yugoslavia] and BH [Bosnia Herzegovina] depended on whether the FRY was using force against BH through the Bosnian Serbian Army of the Republika Srpska ('VRS').[132]

If a foreign state has used force against another state, albeit indirectly by supporting a non-state group, there is an IAC between the two states. To determine whether one state uses forces against another we must turn to the international law rules prohibiting the use of force. Ironically, the leading case here is *Nicaragua*,[133] but not the parts referred to by the majority in *Tadić*. According to the ICJ's case law and customary international law, a state is taken to have indirectly used force against another state where it arms and trains non-state forces, without having sent its own troops or having used forces that are de facto its own.

While it is the second view, that the 'overall control' approach is simply a rule for classification of conflicts that appears to have greater judicial support, it is problematic to separate the rules of state responsibility from those for classification of conflicts. This is because that approach leads to the possibility that one side of an IAC, there is no state that is responsible for violations of the rules of IHL, because a state has sufficient 'overall' control over a non-state armed group for the conflict to be international but insufficient control to be held responsible for the acts of the group. For that reason, it would be better to align the test for classification and that of state responsibility using one of the other approaches (or a modified version of the second approach whereby the 'overall control test' is considered a *lex specialis* rule of responsibility for breaches of IHL.

---

[127] See Katherine del Mar, 'The Requirement of Belonging under International Humanitarian Law' (2010) 21 *EJIL* 105.

[128] Pictet *Vol III* (above n 47) 23.

[129] A possibility contemplated by ARSIWA article 55.

[130] See API article 91.

[131] See (n 119).

[132] See *Tadić* Appeal Judgment (above n 114), Separate Opinion of Judge Shahabuddeen para 7.

[133] *Nicaragua* (above n 112) para 227. See also *Armed Activities* case (above n 60) paras 160–165.

## B. Foreign Intervention at the Invitation (or with Consent) of a State against a Non-State Group

Where there is intervention by a foreign state in a NIAC on the side of the government (or at its invitation) against a non-state group, such intervention will not transform the NIAC into an IAC.[134] As noted above in section 2 'History of the Distinction between IRC and NIAC', the ICRC's proposal in the 1970s, that all conflicts involving foreign intervention are to be regarded as international, was rejected by states.[135]

It may be that a foreign state intervenes initially on the side of rebels, who subsequently become the government and continue to fight against the former government. In those instances, when the foreign state was supporting a non-state group the conflict would have been international. Once a new government is formed and the foreign forces intervene at its the invitation, the conflict is in principle transformed into a NIACs.[136] However, taking this position without safeguards would undermine the law of occupation, since establishing a puppet regime and consent from that regime would suffice to de-internationalize the conflict. Thus, some assurance that the new government is indeed independent from the foreign forces is necessary. For this purpose, one should look at the degree of effectiveness of its control over the territory of the state and its international recognition,[137] factors which also determine whether the rebels can be considered the new government representing the state.

## C. Mixed Conflicts

IACs and NIACs may go on simultaneously in the same area, as the aforementioned example of the *Nicaragua case* in section 7.A 'A Foreign Intervention on the Side of a Non-State Armed Group against a State' demonstrated. Likewise, the ICTY Appeals Chamber held in *Tadić*[138] that the conflict in the former Yugoslavia had both international and non-international characteristics, thus requiring a determination in each particular case. This approach, allowing for mixed (international and non-international) conflicts in the same factual situation, has been criticized for creating 'a crazy quilt of norms applicable in the same conflict'.[139] However, this possibility is neither new nor

---

[134] See Fleck (above n 24) 582; *Bemba* Trial Judgment (n 119) 649–66; *Bemba* (Confirmation of Charges Decision) ICC-01/05-01/08 (15 June 2009) para 246 (finding that the conflict in the Central African Republic (CAR) was non-international, despite the presence of foreign troops in the country, as those troops were there to support CAR's government).

[135] But see George Aldrich, 'The Laws of War on Land' (2000) 94 *AJIL* 42, 62–3 (arguing that such conflict should be regarded as international as it would be practically impossible to apply both the rules on IACs and NIACs, using the example of the Vietnam War).

[136] See the letter to the UK House of Commons by Philip Spoerri, Legal Adviser to the ICRC www.publications. parliament.uk/pa/cm200203/cmselect/cmintdev/84/84ap09.htm (asserting that conflict in Afghanistan could no longer be viewed as an IACs following the establishment of an Afghan transitional government on 19 June 2002). Others have suggested this happened earlier: see Yutuka Arai-Takahashi, 'Disentangling Legal Quagmires: The Legal Characterisation of the Armed Conflicts in Afghanistan since 6/7 October 2001 and the Question of Prisoner of War Status' (2002) 5 *YIHL* 61, 97 (citing the signature of the Bonn Agreement of 5 December 2001 as the date when the conflict became a NIAC).

[137] For a similar situation in Libya, see Marko Milanovic, 'How to Qualify the Armed Conflict in Libya' (*EJIL: Talk!*, 1 September 2011) https://www.ejiltalk.org/how-to-qualify-the-armed-conflict-in-libya.

[138] *Tadić* Jurisdiction (above n 6) paras 72–77.

[139] See Theodor Meron, 'Classification of Armed Conflict in the Former Yugoslavia: *Nicaragua's* Fallout' (1998) 92 *AJIL* 236, 238.

illogical.[140]

Granted, it has made the application of IHL much more complicated in many recent conflicts. Standards for detention will sometimes depend solely on who happened to capture or to detain a particular person, since the Third and Fourth Geneva Conventions only apply to internment by state forces in an IAC.

In cases where there is intervention by foreign state forces alongside a non-state group fighting against the territorial state, whether the conflict is mixed or fully internationalized will depend on whether the non-state group is seen as 'belonging to' the intervening state. Where the foreign intervening state exercises the requisite degree of control over the group,[141] the entire conflict will be an IAC, including confrontations between the group and the territorial state.

## 8. Intervention by Multinational Forces under UN Command or Authorized by the UN

Particular problems of classification arise when forces authorized by the UN or another international organization are involved in a conflict. The UN does not have any forces of its own and UN authorized forces are always composed of contingents from national armed forces. The key question is whether UN authorization of force affects the classification of a conflict. This requires, first, a determination of whether a particular UN force is simply a national armed force or one for whose acts the UN bears responsibility under international law.

Under article 7 of the ILC's Draft Articles on Responsibilities of International Organizations, an international organization is only responsible for the acts of a state organ, including armed forces, placed at its disposal.[142] For instance, this would be the case if the forces of a peace-keeping or peace-enforcement operation are placed at the disposal, or are under the effective control, of the organization. Contrary to the view of the European Court of Human Rights,[143] the UN or another international organization will only have effective control of a national contingent if the organization has operational control of it.[144] Ultimate control over the force and the ability to terminate its mandate are immaterial. Without effective control, the force simply belongs to the state and the armed conflict is classified according to the principles discussed earlier.

Three types of armed forces may be authorized to use force by the UNSC. First, the UNSC may authorize states, acting individually, in coalition, or through regional arrangements, to

---

[140] Christopher Greenwood, 'Development of International Humanitarian Law by the ICTY' (1998) 2 *Max Planck YB UN Law* 98, 117.

[141] See section 7.A 'Foreign Intervention on the Side of a Non-State Armed Group against a State' above.

[142] See ILC, 'Draft Articles on the Responsibility of International Organizations' (2011) A/CN.4/L.778 ('DARIO') article 7.

[143] See *Behrami and Saramati v France and others*, ECtHR Apps No 71412/01 and 78166/01, 2 May 2007 (holding that the UN was responsible for forces in Kosovo). But see *Al Jedda v UK*, ECtHR App No 27021/08, 7 July 2011 para 84 (where the Court mentioned effective control together with ultimate control).

[144] In its commentary to article 6 (now art 7) of DARIO, the ILC has pointed out that the ECtHR's decision in *Behrami and Saramati* (above n 143) misunderstood the scope of article 6. See ILC, 'Report on the Work of its 61st Session', A/64/10 (2009) ch IV: 'Responsibility of International Organizations', 67. The ECtHR decision has been criticized by many scholars. See eg Marko Milanovic and Tatjana Papic, 'As Bad as it Gets: The European Court of Human Rights' *Behrami and Saramati* Decision and General International Law' (2009) 58 *ICLQ* 267.

take enforcement action under Chapter VII of the UN Charter. Examples include the authorization to remove Iraq from Kuwait in 1990 and to protect civilians in Libya in 2011.[145] In these cases, the forces are not under UN command but remain under national command or some other unified command. Second, the UN may create and authorize a traditional peacekeeping mission, where the force is under UN command, operates with the consent of the host state and in a neutral manner, and uses force only in self-defence.[146] Third, the UN may authorize a 'robust' peacekeeping force, where the national contingents operate under UN command but the force is authorized to use 'all necessary means', including military force, to achieve certain objectives, such as protecting civilians, usually in an armed conflict. The second and third categories of forces are in principle subsidiary UN organs, as they are under UN command.[147] However, where a force is in fact under the effective control of a state, the UN will not be responsible for its acts.

While in the past there was much debate on the applicability of IHL to UN forces,[148] it is now generally accepted that these forces are bound by customary IHL when engaged in armed conflict.[149] The provisions of Status of Forces Agreements, concluded between the UN and host States, refer, in particular, to principles and rules mirrored in the Geneva Conventions and the APs.[150]

Where multinational forces are involved in an armed conflict, it will be necessary to consider whether the conflict is an IAC or a NIAC. If they fight against the armed forces of a state, such as occurred with the United Nations Operation in the Congo (ONUC) in the 1960s, the conflict seems to be international.[151] Although the conflict per se is between an international organization and a state, the actual fighting is carried out by national forces. However, as discussed earlier, in the unlikely scenario when those forces are under the effective control of the UN only, they are a UN organ only so no armed conflict exists between contributing states and the state against whose forces they engage.[152] Still, there is either a customary rule broadening IACs to include conflicts involving international organizations and states, or the conflict could be regarded as international because contributing states remain bound by their treaty obligations to 'ensure respect' for IHL.[153]

Where the UN fights against a non-state group within a state and its presence is with the consent of the host state, the conflict should be classified as NIAC, in line with the analysis above regarding foreign intervention. However, the situation is more difficult if the UN's presence lacks consent and is solely grounded in a Security Council resolution. Some argue

[145] See UNSC Resolutions 678 (1990) and 1973 (2011), respectively.
[146] Examples include the UN Emergency Forces I and II deployed in the Middle East after the conflicts in 1956 and 1973 and the UN Missions in Ethiopia and Eritrea. See https://peacekeeping.un.org/en.
[147] See Letter of 3 February 2004 by the UN Legal Counsel to the Director of the Codification Division, A/CN.4/545 (2004) section II.G.
[148] See Hialaire McCoubrey and Nigel White, *The Blue Helmets: Legal Regulation of United Nations Military Operations* (Ashgate 1996).
[149] See Christopher Greenwood, 'International Humanitarian Law and United Nations Military Operations' (1998) 1 YIHL 3; Zagreb Resolution on the Conditions of Application of Humanitarian Rules of Armed Conflict to Hostilities in which United Nations Forces may be Engaged (1971) 54 (II) Annuaire de L'Institut de Droit International 465.
[150] Greenwood 'International Humanitarian Law' (above n 149) 21. See also 'Secretary-General's Bulletin: Observance by United Nations Forces of International Humanitarian Law', ST/SGB/1999/13 (6 August 1999).
[151] Vité (above n 43) 88. See also Greenwood 'International Humanitarian Law' (above n 149) 27; McCoubrey and White (above n 148) ch 8; Zagreb Resolution (above n 149) art 2.
[152] Unless one accepts that attribution of the acts to the UN does not also preclude attribution to the State.
[153] UK Ministry of Defence (above n 46) 376.

that such conflicts are NIACs.[154] Yet the sovereignty concerns behind the less expansive regulation of NIACs by IHL are clearly absent in this case. Others take the view that any armed conflict involving the UN is an IAC, since the operations concerned are decided and carried out by international organizations.[155]

It is difficult to determine when peacekeepers become direct participants in hostilities such that they are engaged in an armed conflict. Their mere presence or their use of force in self-defence does not necessarily imply involvement therein.[156] However, the mere fact that peacekeepers are using force in defence of their mandate also does not itself mean that they are *not* taking a direct part in hostilities, nor does it mean they have *not* become a party to an armed conflict.[157]

Holding that UN peacekeepers are involved in an armed conflict with another entity when carrying out their mandate, but are not involved when exercising their individual right of self-defence, leads to an imbalance in the application of IHL to UN forces. It appears that UN forces are engaged in an armed conflict when the UN force uses force against another entity, but are not when the other entity has targeted the UN force. In that latter scenario, the UN force is acting in self-defence, is not involved in an armed conflict, and its members are protected as civilians. Thus, UN forces gain an advantage as they may carry out initial acts of targeting which would be lawful if they comply with IHL. By contrast other forces may not initiate attacks on UN forces as there would be no armed conflict with the UN at that point and those other forces would even be committing a war crime if they act in the context of another armed conflict (eg, the one that the peacekeeping force is trying to bring an end to).[158]

This result appears on one level, to be contrary to the principle of equal application of IHL. However, from a formal perspective it is not, given the fact that once an armed conflict is initiated between the UN forces and others, both sides are equal. All that the result being discussed here leads to is an imbalance as to who may start an armed conflict when UN forces are involved. In this way, the UN's special role has an impact on the application of IHL.

An alternative approach is to say that acts of individual self-defence by peacekeepers do not make them direct participants in an armed conflict, but where there is a sustained attack on such peacekeeping forces, which would normally pass the intensity threshold for an armed conflict, there should be recognized an armed conflict between the UN forces and the attackers (albeit one initiated by other forces). The difficulty with this approach is that it would mean that those attacks on UN peacekeepers would be made lawful (in terms of IHL) if they are sustained and draw the UN into a conflict, while lower-level attacks would not be lawful, since there would be no armed conflict with the UN and the peacekeepers would remain protected as civilians.

The temporal and geographical scope of armed conflicts involving UN peacekeepers is unclear. As in the case of inter-state conflicts, the involvement of one contingent in an armed

---

[154] Vité (above n 43) 88 (asserting that this is also the ICRC's position).

[155] See Vité (above n 43) and the extensive literature referred to in n 70.

[156] *Abu Garda* (above n 20) para 83 and *Sesay, Kallon and Gbao* (Trial Judgment) SCSL-04-15-T (2 March 2009) para 233.

[157] Sivakumaran (above n 96) 326. The opposite assumption appears to have been made *Sesay, Kallon and Gbao* (above n 156) para 233, final sentence.

[158] ICCSt article 8(2)(b)(iii) and (2)(e)(iii).

conflict in principle means that all UN peacekeeping forces in the country are engaged in it. However, this would deprive all UN peacekeepers of the protected status they ordinarily enjoy. In addition, there is no definite answer as to when such armed conflicts end. It is unclear whether it is the end of hostilities or a general conclusion of peace. However, to require a general conclusion of peace seems artificial, as UN peacekeepers have been authorized to use force precisely to achieve that aim.

## 9. Extraterritorial Conflicts with Non-State Armed Groups

There are many situations where a state uses force on the territory of another state but does not directly target the territorial state, but only an NSAG based therein. Examples include the use of force by Israel in Lebanon against Hezbollah; acts by Uganda and Rwanda in the DRC; Colombian attacks on the FARC in Ecuador; US targeting of persons connected with Al-Qaeda in countries such as Yemen, Somalia, and Pakistan; Turkey's attacks on PKK targets in Northern Iraq and other Kurdish groups in Syria; and the strikes by the US, UK, and France, and others in Syria against Islamic State of Iraq and the Levant (ISIL) strongholds. In most of these cases, the extraterritorial attacks on non-state groups abroad are an extension of a pre-existing conflict in the foreign state, between the latter and the non-state group.

Whether such situations are IACs or NIACs has been controversial. On the one hand, although the foreign state uses force without the consent of the territorial state, the hostilities do not engage the armed forces of two states. Thus, they are factually different from the quintessential IAC. On the other hand, though the confrontations are between a state and a non-state group, they are not purely internal given their location on foreign territory. Furthermore, as discussed earlier in section 6 'The Scope of Application of ILH: NIACs', both Common Article 3 and APII, dealing with NIACs, appear on their face to confine such conflicts to the territory of one Contracting Party.

In light of this mismatch between the facts and the law, some have suggested that a new category of armed conflict should be recognized to account for the transnational aspects of these conflicts, as well as the fact they occur between states and non-state groups.[159] These new approaches have not been generally accepted. Rather, most commentators propose to apply existing rules of IHL to such conflicts and to determine whether the situation involves an IAC or NIAC.[160]

Following this approach, some have concluded that a NIAC exists to the extent that the force is directed solely at the non-state group.[161] They rightly argue that the wording of Common Article 3 does not prevent a NIAC from straddling more than one state. The reference to *one* of the High Contracting Parties simply means that fighting must occur in the

---

[159] See Geoffrey Corn, 'Hamdan, Lebanon, and the Regulation of Armed Hostilities: The Need to Recognize a Hybrid Category of Armed Conflict' (2006) 40 *Vanderbilt J Transn'l L* 295; Roy Schöndorf, 'Extra-State Armed Conflicts: Is There a Need for a New Legal Regime?' (2004) 37 NYUJILP 26.

[160] Marco Sassòli, 'Transnational Armed Groups and International Humanitarian Law' (2006) Harvard University Program on Humanitarian Policy and Conflict Research, Occasional Paper No 6, 5; Paulus and Vashakmadze (above n 67) 111; Noam Lubell, *Extraterritorial Use of Force against Non-State Actors* (OUP 2010) Part II (particularly ch 4); Claus Kreß, 'Some Reflections on the International Legal Framework Governing Transnational Armed Conflicts' (2010) 15 *JCSL* 245.

[161] See (above n 160) (with the exception of Sassòli).

territory of *at least one* party to the Conventions.[162] It is also argued that the conflict should be classified as a NIAC because the opposing parties are not two states but a state and a non-state group. Furthermore, it is said that non-state actors cannot comply with many rules applicable to IACs and states are unwilling to grant them combatant immunity.[163]

## A.  A State Consent-Based Approach

The law that governs transnational conflicts between a state and a non-state group will depend, in the first place, on whether the territorial state in which the non-state group is based has given its consent to the foreign state using force against that group. Where such consent exists, then the conflict will be governed exclusively by the law of NIACs.[164] The situation is no different from one in which the territorial state is itself fighting the non-state group and invites the foreign state to intervene. The consent of the territorial state has the effect that there are not two opposing states involved in the conflict.[165]

However, as indicated in section 7.C 'Mixed Conflicts' above, a state may be involved in a NIAC with an NSAG at the same time as it is involved in an IAC with another state. In the situation being considered, the conflict between the state and a non-state group would be a NIAC, but there would also be an IAC between the state using force and the state on whose territory the force is being used, *if such force is being used without the latter's consent.* This is because such use of force without consent is *against* the territorial state, even if it is not directed at its governmental structures or designed to coerce it. State practice and the jurisprudence of international tribunals supports this approach.[166]

An IAC is no more than the use of armed force by one state against another.[167] It matters not whether the territorial state responds to the attack nor does it matter, as Common Article 2 of the Geneva Conventions makes clear, whether either state acknowledges the state of armed conflict. It is also irrelevant whether the targeted entities are part of the governmental structure of the state or whether the purpose of the use of force is to affect the government. In the first place, there is a distinction between a state and a government. IACs are conflicts between states. A government is but one part of a state. A state is also made of people and territory in addition to a government in control of the territory.[168] Attacks against people in a state or against the territory of a state are also attacks against the state.

Second, if it were attempted to limit IACs to cases where attacks were initiated against the governmental infrastructure of a state, it would be difficult to discern what is meant by the governmental infrastructure of a State and no uniform answer can be given to that question. Whether airports, sea ports, electricity-generating plants, roads, bridges and so forth are owned by the government of a state or by private parties (as is the case in some countries)

[162] See Vité (above n 43); Lubell *Extraterritorial Use* (above n 160) ch 4; Sassòli (above n 160); ICRC *Commentary* 2016 (above n 66) paras 465–472. See also *Hamdan v Rumsfeld,* 548 US 557 (2006); cf *Situation in Afghanistan* (Decision Pursuant to Article 15 of the Rome Statute on the Authorisation of an Investigation into the Situation in the Islamic Republic of Afghanistan) ICC-02/17-33 (12 April 2019) para 53.
[163] See Noam Lubell, 'The War (?) against Al-Qaeda', in Wilmshurst (ed) (above n 11) ch 13.
[164] *Katanga* (above n 75) para 1184; ICRC *Commentary* 2016 (above n 66) paras 259, 263.
[165] See section 7.B 'Foreign Intervention at the Invitation (or with Consent) of a State against a Non-State Group' above. Similarly Fleck (above n 24) 582.
[166] *Armed Activities* case (above n 60) para 163.
[167] *Tadić* Jurisdiction (above n 6) para 70; Greenwood 'Scope of Application' (above n 35) 46 para 202.
[168] Montevideo Convention on the Rights and Duties of States 1933 article 1.

will depend on the economic approach adopted by that country. None of these things are intrinsically governmental.

Third, and most importantly, to attempt to distinguish between force directed at a non-state group and force intended to influence the government is to condition the application of IHL on the mental state or motive of the attacker. It is to suggest that the very same acts of force directed by one state against the territory of another state would yield different legal results, depending on the intention of the intervening state regarding whom it seeks to affect. The protections afforded to the civilian population and to the infrastructure of the territorial state ought not to depend on such motives, which additionally may not be easily discernible. What is important are the objective facts, which are: that force is being used by one state *against* another state (ie on its territory and without its consent).

The view that any use of force by a state on the territory of another without the consent of the latter brings into effect an IAC between the two states has been endorsed by several international tribunals. The ICJ only applied the law of IAC to Uganda's activities in the DRC, including its acts outside the Ituri province under Ugandan occupation, despite the fact that Uganda was in the DRC's territory primarily to fight non-state groups.[169] The view taken here also finds support in the decision of Judge Shahabuddeen in *Tadić*[170] and the Israeli Supreme Court in the *Targeted Killings* case.[171] The UN Commission of Inquiry into the 2006 conflict in Lebanon found that there was an IAC between Israel, Hezbollah, and Lebanon, though the Lebanese forces were not involved in the fighting between Israel and Hezbollah.[172] Both Israel and Lebanon accepted this view.[173] The same view has been clearly taken by the ICC in *Ntaganda* with respect to Uganda's intervention in the DRC.[174] It also has the support of the ICRC in its updated Commentary to Common Article 2,[175] and of some scholars.[176]

The US Supreme Court decision in *Hamdan* might, at first glance, be read as taking a contrary view. This is because it held that Common Article 3 applied to the conflict between the US and Al-Qaeda in Afghanistan.[177] Yet, a more plausible interpretation is that the Court was simply referring to Common Article 3 as a minimum yardstick of protection in all armed conflicts. This is precisely what the ICJ held in *Nicaragua*, which was cited in that part of *Hamdan*.[178] Moreover, the Supreme Court explicitly abstained from determining the nature of the armed conflict, as the application of Common Article 3 made it unnecessary.[179] For those reasons, *Hamdan* cannot be decisive as to the classification of said conflict.[180]

---

[169] *Armed Activities* case (n 60) paras 163 and 165.

[170] See *Tadić* (Appeal Judgment) (above n 114), Separate Opinion of Judge Shahabuddeen.

[171] See *Targeted Killings* case (above n 69) para 18.

[172] UN HRC, 'Report of the Commission of Inquiry on Lebanon pursuant to Human Rights Council Resolution S-2/1*', A/HRC/3/2, 23 November 2006 paras 50–62.

[173] ibid paras 59 and 62.

[174] *Ntaganda* (above n 76) paras 726, 728. See also *Lubanga* Decision on Confirmation of Charges (above n 74) para 541, implicitly reaching the same result.

[175] ICRC *Commentary* 2016 (above n 66) paras 257–262.

[176] See Fleck (above n 24) 584; Sassoli (above n 160) 5; James Stewart, 'The UN Commission of Inquiry on Lebanon: A Legal Appraisal' (2007) 5 *JICJ* 1043.

[177] *Hamdan* (above n 162) part C.ii.

[178] ibid n 63.

[179] ibid sentence with n 61 attached.

[180] See also Harold Koh, 'The Obama Administration and International Law' (25 March 2010) Remarks at the Annual Meeting of the American Society of International Law, 25 March 2010 (noting that the same ambiguity exists in the position of the Obama administration as to the conflict between the US and Al Qaeda).

Where a state uses force against a non-state armed group on the territory of another state, without the consent of the territorial state, there will (depending on the intensity of the violence) be two simultaneous conflicts: a NIAC between the state and the non-state group, and an IAC between the state using force and the territorial state (irrespective of the involvement of the latter's armed forces). The question that then arises with respect to the state using force is whether its conduct will be governed by the law applicable in IACs or NIACs. Since the conflict with the non-state group will be so bound up with the IAC between the two states, it will be impossible, from the perspective of the state using force, to separate the two conflicts. With respect to the conduct of hostilities and targeting in general, every act of targeting by the foreign state will not only be an attempt to target the non-state group (or members thereof), but will also be at the same time a use of armed force against the territorial state (being a use of force on its territory without its consent). This means that every act of targeting or opening fire must comply with the law of IACs in addition to that of NIACs. At the same time, the non-state group continues to be bound by the laws applying to NIACs, as it does not have obligations under the rules applicable to IACs.

With regard to detention and the status of combatants, one anxiety expressed by some authors is that saying that there is an IAC between a state and non-state group would imply that the latter's fighters are entitled to combatant immunity or to prisoner-of-war (POW) status. However, this conclusion does not follow. It is one thing to assert that the law of IAC applies; it is another matter *how* that law applies. Applying the law of IACs would not grant combatant immunity or POW status to non-state fighters as they would not, in practically all cases, fulfil the criteria for these statuses: they do not fight on behalf of the state or belong to it; and they would be unlikely to fulfil the other legal conditions of combatancy.

Questions remain as to whether members of that non-state group should be entitled to the benefits that the rest of the population are entitled to. In particular, if they are detained should they be accorded the protections to which civilians are entitled under the Fourth Geneva Convention? In principle, and leaving aside important threshold questions regarding the personal and territorial scope of the application of the Fourth Geneva Convention, there is no reason why persons in the territory of the conflict, or removed to the territory controlled by the state using force, should be deprived of protections that they ordinarily enjoy under the Geneva Conventions. If a person were to be picked up by the foreign state and detained, it is impossible to see how the person's status as a protected person under the Geneva Conventions should be superseded by a claim that the person is a fighter in a NIAC. Such protected persons under the Geneva Conventions do not lose that status because they may have engaged in hostile acts, though where they are so engaged some derogations may be made, under article 5 of the Fourth Convention, in relation to protections to which they may otherwise be entitled.

Irrespective of the consent of the territorial state, there are at least two situations where a transnational conflict between a state and a non-state group will be governed by the law of IAC. First, where the non-state group belongs to a state other than the intervening foreign state: here there will be two opposing states. This would be the case of the conflict between Israel and Hezbollah if the latter was regarded as belonging to Lebanon or a third state. Second, where a state occupies another state to act against a non-state group or as a result of a conflict with the latter, the actions of the occupying state during the occupation will be governed by the law of occupation and other rules of IACs.[181] This is the position of the ICJ and the ICC in relation to Uganda's occupation of the DRC's Ituri province.[182]

## 10. Conclusion

This chapter has shown that the definition of armed conflict has been fleshed out over the years through state practice, international case law, and the writings of scholars. NIACs need to cross a threshold of intensity and take place between a state and a non-state group or between non-state groups themselves. Nevertheless, they are not restricted to purely internal contexts but may have a cross-border dimension. The clearest and most objective definition of IACs, in turn, is that which holds that two states are in conflict when one uses force against the other; that is, on its territory of another and without its consent. However, IACs are not limited to traditional confrontations between state forces. Rather, they extend to cases where one or more states use force indirectly through non-state actors. We have also seen that conflict classification, though often cumbersome, remains important for reasons of law and policy. Yet the lines between the two types of armed conflict have been gradually blurred under conventional and customary international law. While there have been calls to abandon the distinction, this is not likely to happen until certain sovereignty concerns and related issues relating to targeting and detention in NIACs are resolved.

---

[181] See section 5 'The Scope of Application of IHC: IACs' above.
[182] See (n 75).

# 3

# The Temporal and Geographic Reach of International Humanitarian Law

*Emily Crawford*

## 1. Introduction

Understanding the geographical and temporal scope of international humanitarian law (IHL) is a fundamental component in the process of applying IHL norms to armed conflicts. Knowing where and when the provisions of IHL start—and cease—to apply is vital to ensuring that the rules are respected, and to identifying where other rules of international and domestic law are pertinent or more relevant. This chapter canvasses both the temporal and geographical scope of application of IHL, charting when and where the law applies and when and where it is deemed to cease applying. In doing so, it examines some of the more complex issues raised by the temporal and geographical aspects of IHL, such as the changing level of intensity of hostilities and the geographical location of participants in armed conflict.

## 2. The Temporal Scope of IHL

As a general rule, IHL applies from the commencement of hostilities, whether such hostilities are international or non-international in character. In international armed conflicts (IACs), situations of belligerent occupation also trigger the applicability of IHL, even if there are no active hostilities. However, there are different thresholds applicable in international and non-international armed conflicts (NIACs).

## A. Start of Application of IHL

### *1. International armed conflicts*
In IACs, IHL applies as soon as an armed conflict exists between states. Common Article 2 of the four Geneva Conventions of 1949 states that the Conventions apply to 'all cases of declared war or of any other armed conflict which may arise between two or more of the High Contracting Parties, even if the state of war is not recognized by one of them'. A formal declaration of war is no longer required. The Geneva Conventions dispensed with this requirement, previously outlined in article 1 of Hague Convention (III) of 1907 Relative to the Commencement of Hostilities, that 'the contracting Powers recognize that hostilities between themselves must not commence without previous and explicit warning, in the form

either of a declaration of war, giving reasons, or of an ultimatum with a conditional declaration of war'.[1]

Given that IHL applies as soon as an armed conflict exists between states, it is necessary to define 'armed conflict'. Chapter 2 'Classification of Armed Conflicts' in this book explores this concept in more detail, but for the purposes of this chapter it is useful to note that the test for determining the existence of an IAC was outlined by the International Criminal Tribunal for the Former Yugoslavia (ICTY) in the *Tadić* Jurisdiction decision: 'an armed conflict exists whenever there is a resort to armed force between States'.[2] Any time there is 'any difference arising between two states and leading to the intervention of members of the armed forces',[3] an IAC will be deemed to exist. Additional Protocol I to the Geneva Conventions (API)[4] adds so-called 'wars of national liberation' to the categories of IAC, as being those armed conflicts 'in which peoples are fighting against colonial domination and alien occupation and against racist regimes in the exercise of their right to self-determination'.[5]

In situations of belligerent occupation, IHL is applicable to all situations of total or partial belligerent occupation, even if the occupation meets with no armed resistance.[6] Territory will be considered occupied when it is placed under the authority of a hostile army.[7] This determination involves a bipartite objective test: the establishment of authority by the occupying force over the territory, and the ability of the occupier to actually exercise authority over the territory.[8] Once territory is considered occupied, IHL relating to belligerent occupation is applicable.[9]

## 2. Non-international armed conflicts

Determining when IHL starts to apply in situations of NIAC is slightly more difficult than for IACs. The first treaty provision regulating NIAC was Common Article 3, which did not explicitly state any temporal grounds for application—rather, it was only to apply in 'armed conflict not of an international character occurring in the territory of one of the High Contracting Parties'. Therefore, it is necessary to determine when exactly an armed conflict

[1] Hague Convention (III) Relative to the Opening of Hostilities (adopted 18 October 1907; entered into force 26 January 1910) 205 CTS 263 (Hague Convention III) article 1.
[2] *Prosecutor v Tadić* (Decision on Defence Motion for Interlocutory Appeal on Jurisdiction) IT-94-1-AR72 (2 October 1995) para 70.
[3] Jean Pictet (ed), *Commentary to the First Geneva Convention for the Amelioration of the Condition of the Wounded and the Sick in Armed Forces in the Field* (ICRC 1952) 32.
[4] Protocol Additional to the Geneva Conventions of 12 August 1949, and Relating to the Protection of Victims of International Armed Conflicts (adopted 8 June 1977; entered into force 7 December 1978) 1125 UNTS 3 (API). Also adopted at the time was the Protocol Additional to the Geneva Conventions of 12 August 1949, and Relating to the Protection of Victims of Non-International Armed Conflicts (adopted 8 June 1977; entered into force 7 December 1978) 1125 UNTS 609 (APII). The Protocol Additional to the Geneva Conventions of 12 August 1949, and Relating to the Adoption of an Additional Distinctive Emblem (adopted 8 December 2005, entered into force 14 January 2007) 2404 UNTS 261 (APIII) adds an additional protected emblem—that of the Red Crystal—to the existing Red Cross and Red Crescent emblems.
[5] API article 1(4).
[6] Geneva Convention (I) for the Amelioration of the Condition of the Wounded and Sick in Armed Forces in the Field of 12 August 1949 (GCI) article 2.
[7] Hague Convention (IV) Respecting the Laws and Customs of War on Land and its Annex: Regulation concerning the Laws and Customs of War on Land (adopted 18 October 1907; entered into force 26 January 1910) 205 CTS 227 (Hague Convention IV) article 42.
[8] See the *Armed Activities on the Territory of the Congo (Democratic Republic of the Congo v Uganda)* [2005] ICJ Rep 168 (*Armed Activities* case) 172-3.
[9] See chapter 2 'Classification of Armed Conflicts' for more detailed examination of how to determine the existence in fact of occupation.

of a non-international character is deemed to exist. The current accepted definition is outlined in the *Tadić* Jurisdiction decision, which states that a NIAC exists whenever there is 'protracted armed violence between governmental authorities and organized armed groups or between such groups within a State'.[10] There are thus two elements to this test: the intensity of the hostilities, and the level of organization of the groups involved.[11]

Additional Protocol II (APII) sets the threshold higher for its applicability. For an APII NIAC to exist, the conflict must:

> … take place in the territory of a High Contracting Party between its armed forces and dissident armed forces or other organized armed groups which, under responsible command, exercise such control over a part of its territory as to enable them to carry out sustained and concerted military operations and to implement this Protocol.[12]

Therefore, in addition to the intensity and organization criteria outlined in *Tadić* and required for application of Common Article 3, APII will only apply where the organized armed group maintains some territorial control to the exclusion of the High Contracting Party (ie the state). Furthermore, APII only applies to armed conflicts taking place between the armed forces of a state and organized armed groups; it does not apply to armed conflicts taking place between organized armed groups that do not also involve a state.

Once a NIAC is deemed to have started, and depending on what kind of NIAC it is, IHL will be applicable. However, when exactly IHL will begin to apply in NIACs is often difficult to ascertain, as internal tensions and disturbances will likely precede the conflict. For instance, the Arab Spring of 2011 started as a series of widespread public protests in states such as Libya, Syria, Egypt, and Tunisia.[13] In Syria, protests were met with military force in an attempt to suppress the demonstrations.[14] In response, the Syrian protestors gradually became more organized, changing from protestors and rioters to more organized armed opposition groups; by July 2011, the Free Syrian Army (FSA) had proclaimed its formation.[15] By May 2012, the FSA claimed at least 40,000 members and was able to launch systematic attacks against the military assault launched against them by the Syrian government.[16]

Determining when the violence in Syria became an armed conflict for the purposes of the application of IHL was difficult. An examination of the facts on the ground in November 2011 by a United Nations Independent International Commission of Inquiry found that, despite the deaths of nearly 4000 Syrian civilians and the widespread military operations taking place throughout Syria, they were unable to verify whether the FSA maintained a

---

[10] *Tadić* Jurisdiction decision (above n 2) para 70.

[11] See chapter 2 'Classification of Armed Conflicts' for more detailed examination of how to determine the existence in fact of a non-international armed conflict.

[12] APII article 1(1).

[13] See Fouad Ajami, 'The Arab Spring at One: A Year of Living Dangerously' (*Foreign Affairs*, April 2012) www.foreignaffairs.com/articles/libya/2012-01-24/arab-spring-one.

[14] 'Middle East Unrest: Three Killed at Protest in Syria' *BBC News* (London, 18 March 2011) www.bbc.com/news/world-middle-east-12791738.

[15] The formation of the Free Syrian Army, one of the first organized opposition groups to emerge in the Syrian conflict, was announced via video release on YouTube on 29 July 2011: thesyrianinterpreter, 'Defected Officers Declare the Formation of "Syrian Free Army", 29-7-2011' (29 July 2011) www.youtube.com/watch?v=Rk7Ze5jVCj4.

[16] Suheil Damouny and Emily Benammar, 'Syria Opposition Parties: Explained' *ABC News* (Sydney, 10 June 2014) www.abc.net.au/news/2013-08-29/syria-opposition-parties/4913162#FSA.

sufficient degree of organization, or whether the hostilities were of such an intensity, as to warrant the designation of NIAC and the application of IHL.[17] The Commission's second[18] and third[19] reports, in February and August 2012 respectively, noted the increasing intensity and violence of the situation in Syria, and the increasingly organized opposition groups, but only in its third report was any mention made of the possible applicability of IHL, even though there was no express designation of the conflict as being non-international in character.[20] This came after the July 2012 report from the International Committee of the Red Cross (ICRC) where it stated that it believed that an armed conflict existed in Syria and that IHL was applicable throughout the state.[21] When IHL begins to apply in NIACs can often be difficult to ascertain, and requires careful examination of the facts on the ground.

## B.  End of Application of IHL

### 1. General rule: cessation of active hostilities

As a general rule, in both IACs and NIACs, IHL will cease to apply when there is a 'general close of military operations'.[22] This concept of a close of military operations is understood to mean when there has been the adoption of a 'general or definitive armistice, of a general capitulation by a belligerent, or at the point in time that witnesses any form of *debellatio* [total defeat]'.[23]

While a seemingly straightforward statement, in practice determining when an armed conflict has ceased can be difficult. There have, of course, been situations where military operations have been terminated at a precise date and time, pursuant to a peace treaty or armistice treaty. For example, Germany signed documents indicating its unconditional surrender at the end of the Second World War; the instrument included a sentence stating that:

> ... the German High Command will at once issue orders to all German military, naval and air authorities and to all forces under German control to cease active operations at 2301 hours Central European time on 8 May and to remain in the positions occupied at that time. No ship, vessel, or aircraft is to be scuttled, or any damage done to their hull, machinery or equipment.[24]

---

[17]  UNHRC, 'Report of the Independent International Commission of Inquiry on the Syrian Arab Republic' UN Doc A/HRC/S-17/2/Add.1 (23 November 2011) paras 97–99.

[18]  UNHRC, 'Report of the Independent International Commission of Inquiry on the Syrian Arab Republic' UN Doc A/HRC/19/69 (22 February 2012).

[19]  UNHRC, 'Report of the Independent International Commission of Inquiry on the Syrian Arab Republic' A/HRC/21/50 (15 August 2012).

[20]  UNHRC A/HRC/19/69 (above n 18) paras 105–109; ibid paras 26–29.

[21]  Martin Chulov Julian Borger, 'Bashar al-Assad could face prosecution as Red Cross rules Syria is in civil war' *The Guardian* (16 July 2012) https://www.theguardian.com/world/2012/jul/15/syria-civil-war-red-cross?newsfeed=true. By contrast see UNHRC A/HRC/S-17/2/Add.1 (above n 17) para 62, where the Commission of Inquiry states that while the acts of violence discussed in the report 'may be linked to non-international armed conflict and thus assessed under international humanitarian law', the Commission was not able to definitively 'make such an assessment'.

[22]  See Geneva Convention (IV) Relative to the Protection of Civilian Persons in Time of War (adopted 12 August 1949, entered into force 21 October 1950) 75 UNTS 287 (GCIV) article 6(2) and API article 3(b). See also APII article 2(2), which refers to the 'end of the conflict'.

[23]  Robert Kolb and Richard Hyde, *An Introduction to the International Law of Armed Conflicts* (Hart 2008) 102. See also Yoram Dinstein, *War, Aggression and Self-Defence* (5th edn, CUP 2011) 34–51.

[24]  Act of Military Surrender, signed by of the Chief of Operations Staff of the Armed Forces High Command General Alfred Jodl on behalf of the German High Command (Rheims 7 May 1945) www.ourdocuments.gov/doc.

However, such clear-cut situations, where military operations are terminated at precise times, are infrequent. For example, despite definitive statements as to the 'end' of the conflict in places such as Iraq[25] and Afghanistan,[26] active hostilities in those locations continued for some time afterward.[27] In NIACs, the situation is even more complex. Should the *Tadić* criteria regarding the commencement of hostilities be applied to the cessation of hostilities? That is to say, if the NIAC, once started, falls below its initial triggering criteria of group organization and intensity of hostilities, is IHL also suspended? Such an approach could potentially see IHL applicable one day and non-applicable the next, depending on whether hostilities of a sufficient degree of intensity were taking place at the time.[28] This approach seems operationally unworkable and would require parties to the conflict to undertake daily—perhaps even hourly—assessments of active hostilities and group organizational structure, to examine whether IHL was applicable at the time. Indeed, the *Tadić* jurisprudence seems to reject this approach, stating that only when a 'peaceful settlement is achieved'[29] will IHL cease to apply. Therefore, lulls in the intensity of hostilities in certain regions will not suspend the operation of IHL. Once the conflict reaches the necessary levels of group organization and intensity of violence, IHL remains applicable, even if the intensity of hostilities falls below the initial threshold required to trigger its application.

However, if one takes the view that IHL, once triggered, applies until a peace settlement is negotiated, different problems arise. NIACs can often become protracted, low-intensity affairs. For instance, the four-decade-long NIAC in Colombia against FARC[30] and the ELN[31] has been, at times, considered an APII conflict[32] as well as a Common Article 3[33] conflict. Ongoing, low-level hostilities continued for much of that period, despite efforts to negotiate

---

php?flash=false&doc=78. There is, as of this writing, no extant formal peace treaty between Japan and Russia regarding the Second World War (Carol Williams, 'Russia, Japan Renew Quest for Elusive WWII Peace Treaty' *Los Angeles Times* (Los Angeles, 1 May 2013) http://articles.latimes.com/2013/may/01/world/la-fg-wn-russia-japan-peace-treaty-20130430; 'Tokyo Wants 'New Level' in Relations with Moscow—PM Abe' *RT Question More* (21 May 2015) http://rt.com/business/260701-japan-russia-relations-development). This, however, does not mean that IHL continues to apply between Japan and Russia.

[25] Following the 2003 invasion and occupation of Iraq, ongoing hostilities against insurgents continued until the Iraq War was declared 'over' on 31 August 2010, when President Barack Obama declared an 'end of the combat mission' in Iraq. White House, 'Remarks by the President on Ending the War in Iraq' https://obamawhitehouse.archives.gov/the-press-office/2011/10/21/remarks-president-ending-war-iraq.

[26] Mark Thompson, 'US Ends its War in Afghanistan' *Time* (28 December 2014) http://time.com/3648055/united-states-afghanistan-war-end.

[27] In Iraq, US strikes in Iraq against Islamic State continued until the purported 'defeat' of ISIS in 2018; (see further 'Syria conflict: US officials withdraw troops after IS "defeat"' *BBC News* (London, 19 December 2018) https://www.bbc.com/news/world-middle-east-46623617; US troops remain in Afghanistan, with hostilities continuing, despite the supposed end of the war (see further The U.S. War in Afghanistan 1999–2019, Council on Foreign Relations https://www.cfr.org/timeline/us-war-afghanistan).

[28] Indeed, in the *Tadić* Jurisdiction decision (above n 2), this phenomena of regional lulls in fighting was noted (at para 70), when the Chamber, in assessing the existence of an armed conflict, stated that IHL had been triggered within the former Yugoslavia due to the intensity of hostilities and the organization of the groups involved, and continued to apply 'even if substantial clashes were not occurring in the Prijedor region at the time' that the alleged crimes for which Tadić was on trial occurred.

[29] *Tadić* Jurisdiction decision (above n 2) para 69.

[30] Fuerzas Armadas Revolucionarias de Colombia (Revolutionary Armed Forces of Colombia).

[31] Ejército de Liberación Nacional (the National Liberation Army).

[32] See the Organization of American States (OAS), 'Third Report on the Situation of Human Rights in Colombia' (OEA/Ser.L/V/II.102, Doc 9 rev 1) (26 February 1999) 4; see also the Colombian Constitutional Court, Sentencia No C-574/92, and Ruling on the Constitutional Conformity of Protocol II, Sentencia No C-225/95, and the Supreme Court of Colombia case *Gian Carlo Gutierrez Suarez*, Radicado No 32.022, 59.

[33] OAS (above n 32), where it is stated that:

peace. (A lasting peace was only concluded in 2016.[34]) To continue to apply APII, or even Common Article 3, to situations that had for some time fallen well below the threshold for the application of those norms is fraught with problems, such as the potential displacement of international human rights law norms that apply in peacetime.[35]

Armed conflicts can also be cyclical in intensity. For example, Afghanistan, due to its climate, has seasonal periods of hostilities, colloquially known as 'fighting seasons'.[36] Winter snows make the mountainous regions of the country impassable, but as the snows melt in spring, Taliban fighters are able to move more freely and engage in hostilities against the Afghan National Security Forces.[37] The winter season, followed by the poppy harvest, generally sees little in the way of active hostilities.[38] However, there is a clear intent, certainly on the part of the Taliban, that such a cessation of hostilities is merely temporary and that 'the Islamic Emirate of Afghanistan [the Taliban] has ambitions of continuing the sacred obligation of Jihad with the backing of its Muslim nation until the expulsion of every last infidel invader and establishment of an Islamic government'.[39] Indeed, terrorist activities more generally are by their nature sporadic and unpredictable. As such, reaching the requisite threshold of intensity, and determining when the campaign or attacks have permanently stopped, is particularly problematic. This is also because instances of terrorist organizations publicly declaring their intent to cease hostilities are infrequent.[40]

As with determining the beginning of an armed conflict, determining its cessation requires an objective assessment of the facts. It is the actual conduct of the parties on the ground that will indicate whether a conflict has terminated, rather than subjective statements of intent to terminate hostilities.[41]

> Colombia, unlike other States that all too frequently choose to deny the existence of such hostilities within their territory for political or other reasons, has openly acknowledged the factual reality of its involvement in such a conflict and the applicability of Article 3 common to the four 1949 Geneva Conventions (Common Article 3), the 1977 Protocol Additional to the Geneva Conventions of August 12, 1949, Relating to the Protection of Victims of Non-International Armed Conflicts (Protocol II), and other customary law rules and principles governing internal armed conflicts.

[34] Government of Colombia and FARC-EP, Final Agreement for Ending Conflict and Building a Stable and Long-Lasting Peace (24 November 2016).

[35] Indeed, the applicability of international human rights law in times of armed conflict generally remains contentious—especially in non-international armed conflicts, where recent case law in the UK has queried the legal basis under which persons may be detained in relation to non-international armed conflicts; see further Gabor Rona, 'Guest Post: Rona on *Mohammed v Ministry of Defence* and Detention in NIAC', *Opinio Juris* (22 May 2014) http://opiniojuris.org/2014/05/22/guest-post-rona-mohammed-v-ministry-defence-detention-niac.

[36] See Neil Shea, 'The Talking Season' *Virginia Q Rev* (2010) www.vqronline.org/vqr-portfolio/talking-season; Joseph Goldstein, 'Afghan Army is Tested by the Taliban as Fighting Season Begins' *New York Times* (New York, 13 April 2015) www.nytimes.com/2015/04/14/world/asia/afghan-army-is-tested-by-the-taliban-as-fighting-season-begins.html?_r=0. See also Bill Roggio, 'Taliban Announce this Year's Spring Offensive' *The Long War Journal* (9 May 2014) www.longwarjournal.org/archives/2014/05/taliban_announce_thi.php?utm_source=rss&utm_medium=rss&utm_campaign=taliban-announce-this-years-spring-offensive.

[37] See Jonah Blank, 'Is There a Hidden Message in the Taliban's 2014 Fighting Season Plan?' *Foreign Policy* (29 May 2014) http://foreignpolicy.com/2014/05/29/is-there-a-hidden-message-in-the-talibans-2014-fighting-season-plan.

[38] See Jay Price, 'Cyclical Nature of Afghan Fighting May Mask Deeper Trends, Experts Warn' *McClatchy DC* (Washington, 18 March 2013) https://www.mcclatchydc.com/news/nation-world/world/article24746842.html.

[39] See Islamic Emirate of Afghanistan, 'Statement of Leadership Council of Islamic Emirate Regarding the Commencement of the Annual Spring Operation Named "Khaibar"' (8 May 2014), reprinted in Bill Roggio, 'Taliban announce this year's spring offensive' (above n 36).

[40] See eg the declaration of the complete cessation of hostilities by the IRA on 31 August 1994. P O'Neill, 'IRA Announce Cessation of Military Operations—31 August 1994' *Sinn Fein* (29 August 2014) www.sinnfein.ie/contents/31310.

[41] Jann Kleffner, 'Scope of Application of International Humanitarian Law', in Dieter Fleck (ed), *The Handbook of International Humanitarian Law* (3rd edn, OUP 2013) 61.

Finally, note should be made regarding temporary termination or suspension of hostilities. Temporary cease-fires are often negotiated by parties to the conflict to allow for further discussions preparatory to permanent cease-fire and for peace treaties to be concluded,[42] or for reasons such as the removal of the wounded or sick (or shipwrecked) left on the battlefield or in other areas.[43] However, these agreements are temporary; as Dinstein notes, 'the pause in the fighting, brought about by a cease-fire, is no more than a convenient juncture for direct negotiations … a cease-fire in and of itself is, consequently, no harbinger of peace'.[44] Indeed, the repeated cease-fires and breaches of cease-fires in the Israeli–Palestinian conflict are demonstrative of how cease-fires do not always lead to a complete termination of hostilities and lasting peace.[45]

## 2. Sui generis rules: occupied territories and persons detained in relation to the conflict
In addition to the general rules on the cessation of hostilities, the law of armed conflict contains specific rules regarding its termination in situations of occupied territory and relating to the detention of persons, such as civilian internees and prisoners of war.

### A. Occupied territories
Occupation, as a matter of fact, continues until the territory in question is no longer occupied; that is, when the occupying power no longer exercises effective control in the territory.[46] The cessation of the law of occupation is different according to different treaties. Article 6 of Geneva Convention IV (GCIV) provides that the Convention ceases to operate on the general close of military operations, except in occupied territory. In occupied territory, GCIV will continue to operate for one year following the general close of military operations,[47] with a number of its other provisions continuing to bind the occupying power for as long as it exercises the functions of government in the territory.[48] Furthermore, protected persons 'whose release, repatriation or reestablishment may take place after such dates shall meanwhile continue to benefit'[49] from the protections of GCIV.

However, the one-year limitation rule outlined in article 6 is not repeated in API, which instead states in article 3(b) that in occupied territory the provisions of the Geneva Conventions and API will only cease to operate on the termination of the occupation. Thus, under API, the operation of the entirety of GCIV is extended to the end of occupation.[50] The API approach operates on a factual control framework, similar to that of

---

[42]  See further Dinstein *War, Aggression and Self-Defence* (above n 23) 57.

[43]  See eg GCI article 15. See also the armistice provisions in Regulations Annexed to the Hague Convention (IV) Respecting the Laws and Customs of War on Land and Its Annex: Regulation concerning the Laws and Customs of War on Land (adopted 18 October 1907, entered into force 26 January 1910) 187 CTS 227 (Hague Regulations) articles 36–41.

[44]  Dinstein *War, Aggression and Self-Defence* (above n 23) 57.

[45]  For instance, there have been a number of cease-fires agreed between Israel and Palestinian groups, including in 2008, 2012, and 2014. None of these have led to lasting peace and a permanent cessation of hostilities.

[46]  The Hague Regulations of 1907 do not specify when they cease to operate; however, a teleological approach to the Regulations, and to article 42 in particular, would suggest that if the Regulations apply once territory is actually placed under the control of a hostile power, then the rules would cease to apply once the territory is no longer actually controlled by that hostile power. See further Kolb and Hyde (above n 23) 104.

[47]  GCIV article 6(3).

[48]  These provisions are ibid articles 1–12, 27, 29–34, 47, 49, 51, 52, 53, 59, 61–77, and 143.

[49]  ibid article 6(3).

[50]  Yoram Dinstein, *The International Law of Belligerent Occupation* (CUP 2009) 281; see also Yutaka Arai-Takahashi, *The Law of Occupation: Continuity and Change of International Humanitarian Law, and its Interaction with International Human Rights Law* (Koninklijke Brill 2009) 16–24.

article 42 of the Hague Regulations. That is to say, if the law on occupation comes into effect when the territory is actually placed under the authority of the hostile power, then, logically, the law ceases to operate when the territory is no longer under the authority of the hostile power.[51]

The customary status of article 3 of API is 'unclear'.[52] However, as Kolb and Hyde suggest, in effect the substance of article 3 prevails in the form of article 42 of the Hague Regulations and article 6(3) of the Geneva Conventions—namely that:

> ... the Hague Regulations apply as long as the occupation lasts, and the rules of the Geneva Convention IV continue to apply to the extent that they are expressive of customary international law. Virtually all substantive rules of occupation law are now considered to be reflected in customary international law. The limitation of Article 6(3) therefore seems now largely obsolete.[53]

## B. End of captivity and detention

For those persons who have been detained in relation to the conflict, IHL continues to apply up until the time of their release or repatriation. For prisoners of war (POWs), article 5(1) of Geneva Convention III (GCIII) provides that POWs are protected under the Convention from the time of their capture until their final release and repatriation.[54] Similar provisions in Geneva Convention I (GCI) and API cover any other protected persons 'who have fallen into the hands of the enemy'.[55] For protected persons who have been detained in relation to the hostilities in occupied territory, article 6(4) of GCIV provides that such persons continue to enjoy the benefits of the Convention until their 'release, repatriation or re-establishment'.[56] This continuing protection is necessary to ensure that no one in a position of vulnerability finds themselves bereft of international legal protections, even if there has been a permanent cessation in hostilities. There have been a number of examples of POWs or protected persons being detained by parties to the conflict long after the termination of hostilities. For example, following the Iran–Iraq War in the 1980s, thousands of detainees from both sides of the conflict experienced significant delays in their repatriation—indeed, the last group of detainees held by Iran was only released in 2003.[57] The provisions in IHL are a vital measure to ensure that such protected persons remain protected until they are no longer under the control of the adverse party.

---

[51]   Arai-Takahashi (above n 50) 17.

[52]   ibid 18.

[53]   Kolb and Hyde (above n 23) 104; see also Robert Kolb, 'Étude sur l'Occupation et sur l'article 47 de la IVème Convention de Genève du 12 Août 1949 Relative à la Protection des Personnes Civiles en Temps de Guerre: Le Degree d'Intangibilité des Droits en Territoire Occupé' (2002) 10 *AYIL* 267, 291, 295.

[54]   GCIII article 5(1).

[55]   GCI article 5; API article 3(b). GCI article 5 is worded in the same way at GCIII article 5; API article 3(b) states that the Protocol and Conventions apply 'for those persons whose final release, repatriation or re-establishment takes place thereafter. These persons shall continue to benefit from the relevant provisions of the Conventions and of this Protocol until their final release, repatriation or re-establishment.'

[56]   GCIV article 6(4).

[57]   'Iran Frees "Last Iraqi Prisoners"' *BBC News* (London, 5 May 2003) http://news.bbc.co.uk/2/hi/middle_east/3001751.stm. See also John Quigley, 'Iran and Iraq and the Obligations to Release and Repatriate Prisoners of War after the Close of Hostilities' (1989) 5 *Am U Int'l L Rev* 73.

### 3. End of application of IHL due to denunciation

For the sake of completeness, it is worth noting that IHL's application may be terminated due to a state denouncing the Conventions. All four Geneva Conventions, and the Hague Regulations, contain provisions allowing for denunciation.[58] Denunciation has the effect of making the treaty no longer in force for the denouncing party. However, the Hague Regulations and the Geneva Conventions outline strict rules regarding denunciation, stating that denunciation will only take effect one year after the receipt of such denunciation by the depository of the treaty.[59] Further, if a state currently engaged in an armed conflict denounces the Conventions, such denunciation will not take effect until 'peace has been concluded, and until after operations connected with the release and repatriation of the persons protected by the present Convention have been terminated'.[60] Therefore, states may not denounce the Conventions as a means by which to avoid their treaty obligations. Furthermore, all applicable customary international law obligations will endure;[61] indeed, given that the vast bulk of the substantive provisions of the Conventions has attained customary status,[62] there seems little to be achieved by denunciation.

## 3. Geographical Scope of IHL

The geographical or spatial scope of IHL depends on what kind of armed conflict is taking place—international or non-international.

### A.  International Armed Conflicts

#### 1. The principle of unity of territory

In IACs, the principle of unity of territory prevails—IHL is applicable throughout the entire territory of the parties to the conflict, including their territorial waters[63] as well as the airspace above their territories.[64] Thus, IHL applies beyond the immediate areas of active hostilities to encompass all the territory under the control of belligerent parties. This ensures

---

[58] Hague Convention IV article 8; GCI article 63; Geneva Convention (II) for the Amelioration of the condition of the Wounded, Sick, and Shipwrecked Members of the Armed Forces at Sea (adopted 12 August 1949, entered into force 12 October 1949) 75 UNTS 85 (GCII) article 62; GCIII article 142; GCIV article 158.

[59] Hague Convention IV article 8; GCI article 63; GCII article 62; GCIII article 142; GCIV article 158.

[60] GCI article 63; GCII article 62; GCIII article 142; GCIV article 158.

[61] This is explicitly stated in GCI article 63(4); GCII article 62(4); GCIII article 142(4); and GCIV article 158(4), which provide that any denunciation of the treaty:

> shall in no way impair the obligations which the Parties to the conflict shall remain bound to fulfil by virtue of the principles of the law of nations, as they result from the usages established among civilised peoples, from the laws of humanity, and from the dictates of public conscience.

[62] See eg the findings of the Eritrea–Ethiopia Claims Commission, 'Prisoners of War—Ethiopia's Claim 4' (1 July 2003) paras 30–31, where the Commission stated that 'given the nearly universal acceptance of the four Geneva Conventions of 1949 … the Geneva Conventions of 1949 have largely become expressions of customary international law'. See also the *Advisory Opinion on the Legality of the Threat or Use of Nuclear Weapons* [1996] ICJ Rep 226 para 79.

[63] Defined in customary international law and treaty law as twelve nautical miles from the low-water mark baseline of a coastal state (United Nations Convention on the Law of the Sea (adopted 10 December 1982, entered into force 14 November 1994) 1833 UNTS 3 (UNCLOS) article 3).

[64] See section 3.A.2 'Air and outer space and the high seas' below for a more detailed explanation of the geographical scope of IHL in relation to airspace, the exclusive economic zones (EEZ) and high seas, and outer space.

that certain situations—like occupied territory, internment camps, or POW detention facilities—remain covered by IHL, even if no active hostilities take place in the immediate vicinity. This was noted by the ICTY in *Tadić*:

> Although the Geneva Conventions are silent as to the geographical scope of international 'armed conflict', the provisions suggest that at least some of the provisions of the Conventions apply to the entire territory of the Parties to conflict, not just to the actual vicinity of the hostilities. Certainly, some of the provisions are clearly bound up with the hostilities and the geographical scope of those provisions should be so limited. Others, particularly those relating to the prisoners of war and civilians, are not so limited.[65]

Thus, areas where prisoners of war or other protected persons are detained are covered by IHL. In addition to territory under the jurisdictional control of the belligerent parties, IHL also applies in areas where there are 'actual hostilities or relationships between belligerents outside the territory of the belligerents'.[66] IHL will therefore apply on the high seas and in the exclusive economic zones (EEZ, defined as 200 nautical miles from the low-water-mark baseline of a coastal state[67]), including the EEZs of neutral states.[68]

### 2. Air and outer space and the high seas

As noted above, IHL applies to the airspace over the territorial lands and waters of the belligerent parties. There is no international treaty that delimits national airspace, but in practice national airspace is considered to be all airspace above the territorial lands and waters of a state that is capable of generating aerodynamic lift and thus sustaining powered flight. Airspace is perhaps best understood as what it is not—that is, national airspace (and thus sovereignty over such space) ends where outer space begins. The Fédération Aéronautique Internationale proposes the delimitation between airspace and outer space at the so-called Kármán Line—sixty-two miles (or 100 km) from sea level.[69] All territorial airspace would be considered as coming within the purview of IHL, as would any hostile acts that take place in international airspace (that is, airspace superadjacent to the high seas).[70]

Existing international law treaties place limitations on certain kinds of hostile activities in outer space. Article IV of the 1967 Treaty on Outer Space[71] obliges parties to the treaty

---

[65] *Tadić Jurisdiction decision* (above n 2), para 68.

[66] Kolb and Hyde (above n 23).

[67] See UNCLOS article 57.

[68] Note, however, UNCLOS article 58(3), which provides that any activities carried out by States in the EEZ must 'have due regard to the rights and duties of the coastal State and shall comply with the laws and regulations adopted by the coastal State in accordance with the provisions of this Convention and other rules of international law'. As such, any military operations in the EEZ of a neutral state must be carried out in accordance with any existing rights and duties retained by the coastal state.

[69] The *HPCR Manual on the International Law Applicable to Air and Missile Warfare* defines airspace as 'the air up to the highest altitude at which an aircraft can fly and below the lowest possible perigee of an earth satellite in orbit' (article 1(a)) (*HPCR Manual on International Law Applicable to Air and Missile Warfare* CUP 2013). The Fédération Aéronautique Internationale defines such a space at the so-called Kármán Line—see FAI, '100km Altitude Boundary for Astronautics' https://www.fai.org/page/icare-boundary, accessed 14 January 2020.

[70] See generally the Hague Declaration (XIV) Prohibiting the Discharge of Projectiles and Explosives from Balloons (adopted 18 October 1907; 27 November 1909), the non-binding Rules concerning the Control of Wireless Telegraphy in Time of War and Air Warfare (adopted 19 February 1923) (also known as the Hague Rules on Air Warfare), and *HPCR Manual on the International Law Applicable to Air and Missile Warfare* (ibid n 69).

[71] Treaty on Principles Governing the Activities of States in the Exploration and Use of Outer Space, Including the Moon and Other Celestial Bodies (adopted 27 January 1967; entered into force 10 October 1967) 610 UNTS 205.

not to place in orbit any objects carrying nuclear weapons or any other weapons of mass destruction, or to install such weapons on celestial bodies, or otherwise station them in outer space. Furthermore, parties to the treaty are under an obligation to use the moon and other celestial bodies 'exclusively for peaceful purposes'.[72] Additional regulation, in the form of the 1979 Agreement Governing the Activities of States on the Moon and Other Celestial Bodies,[73] reaffirms the principles of the 1967 treaty and prohibits the threat or use of force either on the moon (or other celestial bodies in the solar system other than Earth) or from the moon (in relation to Earth or other human-made spacecraft).[74] However, none of the extant treaties prohibit the use of conventional weapons in outer space—only weapons of mass destruction, such as nuclear weapons, are prohibited. Outer space must therefore be considered as coming within the geography of armed conflict and within the purview of existing IHL rules.[75]

Armed conflict may also occur on the high seas—that is, all waters that are not part of a coastal state's territorial sea, archipelagic waters, or internal waters. With regards to armed conflict on the high seas, note must first be made of article 88 of the 1982 United Nations Convention on the Law of the Sea, which states that 'the high seas shall be reserved for peaceful purposes'.[76] Thus, any acts of hostilities on the high seas would seem to violate article 88 of the Law of the Sea Convention. However, state practice[77] and the writings of experts[78] would suggest that an overly literal application of article 88 is unwarranted. Indeed, the most recent definitive statement of the existing law of naval warfare, the *San Remo Manual on the International Law Applicable to Armed Conflicts at Sea*, expressly rejects an interpretation of article 88 prohibiting naval warfare on the high seas.[79] The high seas and the seabed under the high seas are therefore legitimate theatres of war and governed by IHL.[80]

### 3. Special areas—hospital zones and neutralized zones

IHL provides that certain areas within the territory of a party to the conflict (or in any other territory) may be rendered off-limits to military activity, through designation of the area as a demilitarized zone, a neutralized zone, a non-defended locality (or safe zone), or a hospital or safety zone. Thus IHL provisions and protections still apply, but these zones are not to be made the location of active hostilities.

Non-defended localities can be any town, village, dwelling, or building which is declared to be an undefended place.[81] Non-defended localities are open to occupation by the adverse

---

[72]  ibid article IV.
[73]  (adopted 5 December 1979; entered into force 11 July 1984) 1363 UNTS 3.
[74]  ibid article 3(2).
[75]  See further Jackson Maogoto and Steven Freeland, 'The Final Frontier: The Laws of Armed Conflict and Space Warfare' (2007-2008) 23 *Conn J Int'l L* 169; and Michael Schmitt, 'International Law and Military Operations in Space' (2006) 10 *MPYUNL* 89.
[76]  UNCLOS article 88. Note also UNCLOS article 58(2), which applies the same principle to the EEZ.
[77]  See eg UK Ministry of Defence, *Manual on the Law of Armed Conflict* (OUP 2004) 350-1.
[78]  See Robin R Churchill and Vaughan Lowe, *The Law of the Sea* (3rd edn, Manchester UP 1999) 208; Rudiger Wolfrum, 'Military Activities on the High Seas: What are the Impacts of the UN Convention on the Law of the Sea?', in Michael Schmitt and Leslie Green (eds), *The Law of Armed Conflict: Into the Next Millennium* (1998) 71 ILS 505; Dinstein *War, Aggression and Self-Defence* (above n 23) 23.
[79]  Louise Doswald-Beck (ed), *The San Remo Manual on International Law Applicable to Armed Conflicts at Sea* (CUP 1995) 82.
[80]  Dinstein *War, Aggression and Self-Defence* (above n 23) 23.
[81]  Hague Regulations article 25; API article 59.

party,[82] but are immune from attack provided that all combatants and mobile military equipment are evacuated from the locality;[83] that no hostile use is made of fixed military installations or establishments within the locality;[84] that no acts of hostility are committed by the authorities or population within the locality;[85] and that no activities in support of the hostilities take place within the locality.[86] The presence of the police force or of medical units of the adverse party, or of enemy sick and wounded, does not result in the loss of a locality's non-defended status.[87] Undefended localities may be established by unilateral act by any of the parties to the conflict; it is not necessary for all parties to the conflict to agree to them being established. While attacking undefended localities is contrary to IHL, respect for the rule has not always been absolute. A recent example was seen in the conflict in the former Yugoslavia, where the UN established a number of safe zones,[88] all of which were, by the end of the conflict, attacked and occupied. One of these safe areas—Srebrenica—was the site of the murder of over 8000 Bosnian Muslims.[89]

Hospital and safety zones may also be established by parties to the conflict—though these zones require agreement by all parties. Article 23 of GCI and article 14 of GCIV provide that parties to the conflict may establish, both in their own territory and in occupied territory, hospital zones and localities to ensure protection for the wounded and sick, and for medical personnel and others who tend to the wounded and sick. While article 23 of GCI covers the wounded and sick in armies in the field, article 14 of GCIV goes further and provides protection for aged persons, children under fifteen, expectant mothers, and mothers of children under seven years of age. Such safety zones may also be established on the high seas; one such zone was established during the Falklands/Malvinas conflict in 1982. This so-called 'Red Cross Box' was approximately twenty nautical miles in diameter and enabled hospital ships to maintain their position and assist in the transfer of British and Argentinian wounded.[90]

Finally, neutralized or demilitarized zones may also be established by parties to a conflict. Unlike undefended localities, demilitarized or neutralized zones are not open to occupation by adverse parties. The scope of the provisions is slightly different in each case. In GCIV, article 15 refers to neutralized zones, which can be established, by agreement of the parties, with the intention to 'shelter from the effects of war … wounded and sick combatants and non-combatants [and] … civilian persons who take no part in hostilities, and who, while they reside in these zones, perform no work of a military character'.[91] Demilitarized zones are outlined in article 60 of API and are intended to protect civilians living within such zones from attack by parties to the conflict. The provisions for establishing a demilitarized zone are similar to those for an undefended locality; however, demilitarized zones can

[82]  API article 59(2).
[83]  ibid article 59(2)(a).
[84]  ibid article 59(2)(b).
[85]  ibid article 59(2)(c).
[86]  ibid article 59(2)(d).
[87]  ibid article 59(3).
[88]  See UNSC Resolutions 819 (16 April 1993), 824 (6 May 1993), and 836 (4 June 1993).
[89]  See *Prosecutor vs Krstić* (Appeals Judgment) IT-98-33 (19 April 2004); and *Application of the Convention on the Prevention and Punishment of the Crime of Genocide (Bosnia and Herzegovina v Serbia and Montenegro)* (Judgment) [2007] ICJ Rep 43.
[90]  Sylvie Junod, 'Protection of the Victims of Armed Conflict: Falkland-Malvinas Islands (1982)', in ICRC, *International Humanitarian Law and Humanitarian Action* (2nd edn, ICRC 1985) 23–4, 26.
[91]  GCIV article 15(a)–(b).

only be created by agreement of the parties to the conflict. As the ICRC Commentary to the Protocols notes, the 'essential character of the zones created in Article 60 ... [is] that they have a humanitarian and not a political aim; they are specially intended to protect the population living there against attack'.[92] Demilitarized zones in API are thus to be distinguished from demilitarized zones that have been established pursuant to an armistice treaty[93] (or indeed, any treaty[94]), from zones or areas which have been designated as *permanently* neutral,[95] or from zones established as 'buffer' zones between belligerent parties.[96]

### 4. *The law of neutrality and IHL*

On the outbreak of hostilities, the law of armed conflict applies to those states that are the belligerent parties in the conflict. All other states must determine whether to become involved in the hostilities, and thus become a co-belligerent state, or else refrain from becoming involved in the hostilities.[97] For those states that refrain from involvement in hostilities, the law on neutrality will apply. Specific rights and duties attach regarding neutrality, both for the state that chooses neutrality and for belligerent parties to the conflict. The law of neutrality provides that the neutral state has a right to remain separate from the hostilities, and not be adversely impacted by such hostilities. This is given practical effect in the extant laws on neutrality—the 1907 Hague Convention (V) Respecting the Rights and Duties of Neutral Powers and Persons in Case of War on Land[98] and the 1907 Hague Convention (XIII) concerning the Rights and Duties of Neutral Powers in Naval War.[99] Article 1 of Hague Convention V provides that the territory of a neutral state is inviolable; it is prohibited to conduct any hostilities on the territory of a neutral state, including the transport of troops or munitions through neutral territory.[100] The rules on neutrality apply to neutral land, as well as territorial waters and airspace.[101] However, to enjoy these benefits, neutral states must fulfil certain duties. A neutral state must abstain from participating in

---

[92] Yves Sandoz, Christophe Swinarski, and Bruno Zimmerman (eds), *Commentary on the Additional Protocols of 8 June 1977 to the Geneva Conventions of 12 August 1949* (ICRC/Martinus Nijhoff 1987) 709 (AP Commentary).

[93] For instance, following the First World War, the Treaty of Versailles (signed 28 June 1919) (1919) 225 CTS 189 article 42 provided that 'Germany is forbidden to maintain or construct any fortifications either on the left bank of the Rhine or on the right bank to the west of a line drawn 50 kilometres to the East of the Rhine'.

[94] For instance, The Antarctic Treaty (adopted 1 December 1959; entered into force 23 June 1961) 402 UNTS 71 article 1 provides that 'there shall be prohibited, inter alia, any measure of a military nature, such as the establishment of military bases and fortifications, the carrying out of military manoeuvres, as well as the testing of any type of weapon' in Antarctica.

[95] The Panama Canal is permanently neutral, pursuant to the Treaty concerning the Permanent Neutrality and Operation of the Panama Canal (adopted 7 September 1977; entered into force 1 October 1979) 1161 UNTS 177 article 1.

[96] The demilitarized zone (DMZ) between the Democratic People's Republic of Korea and the Republic of Korea was the result of the Panmunjom Armistice Agreement (North Korea–People's Republic of China–UNC) (27 July 1953) 4 UST 234; it acts as a buffer between the two states, and while there are no military installations within the DMZ, both sides of the zone, within North and South Korea respectively, are heavily militarized. See further Don Oberdorfer and Robert Carlin, *The Two Koreas: A Contemporary History* (Basic Books 2014), specifically chs 1 and 3 on the post-war division of Korea and the ongoing tensions which have often played out in the DMZ.

[97] Note that some states have declared their permanent neutrality, such as Switzerland, Austria, Sweden, Ireland, and Finland (as reported by NATO, 'Neutral European Countries: Austria, Switzerland, Sweden, Finland, Ireland' http://nato.gov.si/eng/topic/national-security/neutral-status/neutral-countries; see also Paul Seger, 'The Law of Neutrality', in Andrew Clapham and Paolo Gaeta (ed), *The Oxford Handbook of International Law in Armed Conflict* (OUP 2014) 259–60.

[98] (adopted 18 October 1907; entered into force 26 January 1910) 205 CTS 299 ( (Hague Convention V).

[99] (adopted 18 October 1907; entered into force 26 January 1910) 205 CTS 395 (Hague Convention XIII).

[100] Hague Convention V article 2.

[101] See Hague Convention XIII articles 1–2; see also Hague Rules of Aerial Warfare (above n 70) article 40, and the *HPCR Manual on the International Law Applicable to Air and Missile Warfare* 170–1.

the conflict, either directly or indirectly, on behalf of any of the parties to the conflict. If it wishes to remain neutral, it may not provide any military assistance to parties to the conflict, whether through supply of personnel, material, or financial aid.[102] The prohibition on aid applies only to acts of the neutral state which are 'of military relevance to the belligerents'.[103] Furthermore, states may make political statements criticizing one party or the other without violating the law of neutrality.

Neutral states are also under an obligation to ensure that their territory remains neutral. As well as abstaining from participating in the hostilities, the neutral state must ensure that its territory is not used in any way in violation of the principle of neutrality. This includes a duty to ensure that its territory is not used by parties to the conflict as a base from which military operations may be conducted. Furthermore, a neutral state may not allow passage by a belligerent through its land territory.[104]

Finally, neutral states are obliged to 'defend' their neutrality, by repelling any violation of their neutrality by a belligerent party.[105] How such defence is carried out varies in state practice. Some states, such as Switzerland and Austria, take a position of 'armed neutrality'—operating on the idea that 'neutral states are indeed obliged to undertake military efforts in order to repel a violation of neutrality by the use of armed force'.[106] Other states, such as Costa Rica, take the approach of 'unarmed neutrality', having disbanded their armed forces.[107] There is no 'formal obligation'[108] on states to use armed force to defend their neutrality, but states are obliged to repel or suppress attempts to violate their neutrality. States are thus entitled to use proportionate measures, including armed force, to prevent or repress violations of their neutrality. Such 'defence' of neutrality remains governed by the law of neutrality; that is to say, states engaged in such actions must act *only* to restore their territorial integrity and neutrality. They must not take any additional steps which would render their defensive action an act of belligerency and result in their participation in the hostilities, at which point their acts would be governed by the law of armed

---

[102] This relates solely to the provision of financial aid for the purposes of the conflict. Neutrality and the duty of non-participation do not mean that states may not maintain commercial relationships with belligerent parties. Hague Convention V article 5 and Hague Convention XIII article 7 outlines this principle. As a general rule, neutral states are under an obligation to treat the belligerent parties equally, and not favour one or the other—ie by granting new commercial rights to one belligerent, or placing new economic restrictions on one belligerent state. As Kolb and Hyde (above n 23) note:

> usual State practice is to continue commerce with the belligerents on the same basis as existed prior to the commencement of hostilities … changes to the pre-existing trade relationships to the detriment of one belligerent, or, in some cases, extreme imbalances in the pre-existing trading relationship being maintained without giving the other belligerent the chance to take part in trade on an equal basis, are prohibited.

See also Seger (above n 97) 256–7.

[103] Seger (above n 97) 257.

[104] Hague Convention V article 2. It is noteworthy that while the Hague Convention V on neutrality on land clearly prohibits the movement of troops or supplies through neutral territory, the Hague Convention XIII article 10 on maritime neutrality only states that neutrality will not be lost by a state if a warship or other belligerent vessel transits its territorial waters or else is forced to remain within its territorial waters (for instance, due to inclement weather or for urgent repairs to the vessel) for up to a period of twenty-four hours. This right of innocent passage is found in articles 10, 12, 14, and 17 of Hague Convention XIII.

[105] See Hague Convention V article 5 and Hague Convention XIII articles 2, 9, and 24.

[106] Michael Bothe, 'The Law of Neutrality', in Fleck (ed) (above n 41) 560.

[107] Seger (above n 97) 256.

[108] Peter Hostettler and Olivia Danai, 'Neutrality in Land Warfare', *Max Planck Encyclop Public Int'l L* (September 2013) http://opil.ouplaw.com/view/10.1093/law:epil/9780199231690/law-9780199231690-e347?rskey=qQk2nI&result=1&prd=EPIL.

conflict. If belligerent forces enter the territory of a neutral state, such forces must be disarmed and interned.[109]

## B. Non-International Armed Conflicts

*1. Intrastate issues—does IHL apply only where there are active hostilities in NIAC?*
In NIACs, the geographical scope of IHL depends on the type of NIAC taking place. For NIACs that are purely internal—that is, are conducted solely within the territorial boundaries of the affected state—one approach posits that IHL will apply to the entire territory of the affected state. This approach was outlined by the International Criminal Tribunal for Rwanda in the *Akayesu* decision:

> There is no clear provision on applicability *ratione loci* either in Common Article 3 or Additional Protocol II. However, in this respect Additional Protocol II seems slightly clearer, in so far as it provides that the Protocol shall be applied 'to all persons affected by an armed conflict as defined in Article 1'. The commentary thereon specifies that this applicability is irrespective of the exact location of the affected person in the territory of the State engaged in the conflict. The question of applicability *ratione loci* in non-international armed conflicts, when only Common Article 3 is of relevance should be approached the same way, i.e. the article must be applied in the whole territory of the State engaged in the conflict. This approach was followed by the Appeals Chamber in its decision on jurisdiction in *Tadić*, wherein it was held that 'the rules contained in [common] Article 3 also apply outside the narrow geographical context of the actual theatre of combat operations'.[110]

According to this interpretation of the law, IHL will apply in all areas of the state, including those areas that are not sites of active hostilities.[111]

However, there is a case to be made for a more restricted approach, limiting the application of IHL. Indeed, that the law relating to NIACs should have strict territorial and geographical limitations was envisaged by those involved in the drafting of APII. At the 1972 Conference of Government Experts, it was considered 'inconceivable that, in the case of a disturbance in one specific part of the territory (in a town, for instance) the whole territory of the State should be subjected to the application of the Protocol'.[112] This is borne out in practice, where some conflicts have been highly geographically restricted; the conflict between the Aceh separatist movement and the Indonesian government on the island

---

[109] Hague Convention V articles 11–15.

[110] *Prosecutor v Akayesu* (Judgment) ICTR 96-4-T (2 September 1998) para 635.

[111] See *Tadić* Appeal Judgment (above n 65) para 69. See also *Kunarac*, where the ICTY stated that 'there is no necessary correlation between the area where the actual fighting takes place and the geographic reach of the laws of war'. (*Prosecutor v Kunarac et al* (Judgment) IT-96-23 and IT-96-23/1-A (12 June 2002) para 57). It was sufficient, from the Tribunal's perspective, that the acts are 'closely related' to the hostilities (*Kunarac* Judgment, ibid). The *Tadić* approach seems to have been followed by institutions such as the UN and the Inter-American Commission on Human Rights (in, respectively, UN Economic and Social Council, 'Report on the Situation of Human Rights in Somalia' UN Doc E/CN.4/1997/88 (3 March 1997) para 55; and the Inter-American Commission on Human Rights, 'Report on Terrorism and Human Rights' Doc No OEA/Ser.L/V/II.116 Doc 5 rev 1 corr (22 October 2002) para 60. See further Sandesh Sivakumaran, *The Law of Non-International Armed Conflict* (OUP 2012) 250–2.

[112] Conference of Governments Experts on the Reaffirmation and Development of International Humanitarian Law Applicable in Armed Conflicts, *Report on the Work of the Conference*, Vol I, at 68 para 2.59.

of Sumatra is one such example.[113] For all of the rules of IHL to apply to the totality of Indonesian territory for the duration of such a conflict would seem to create problems for, at the very least, the application of international human rights law norms. Certain international human rights law provisions may be derogated from in a time of public emergency which threatens the life of the nation; thus, too broad an application of IHL norms could potentially see human rights norms suspended for protracted periods of time, even in locations far removed from active hostilities, resulting in, for example, broad application of the law on permissible lethal targeting of persons.[114]

That being said, it is equally possible to apply IHL too narrowly. The *Akayesu* formula for the geography of NIAC, a formula drawn from the *Tadić* and *Kunarac* cases, applies 'the laws of war ... in the case of internal armed conflicts, [to] the whole territory *under the control* of a party to the conflict, whether or not actual combat takes place there'.[115] The use of the phrase 'under the control' would seem to exclude from the operation of IHL parts of the territory that are *not* under the control of parties to the conflict. This would create the 'curious consequence'[116] of having IHL cease to apply in areas where no one party held exclusive control of the territory.

The *Akayesu/Tadić/Kunarac* approach seems to suggest that IHL attaches to certain participants and acts only where territorial control is effected. It would thus seem to exclude from the operation of IHL those conflicts that take place in territory not under the territorial control of the participants to the conflict. This raises the question: does IHL have extra-territorial effect?

## 2. *Extraterritorial applicability for trans-national actors in NIAC: does IHL 'follow' the participants everywhere they are found in the world?*

The *Tadić* formula—that 'the rules contained in [common] Article 3 also apply outside the narrow geographical context of the actual theatre of combat operations'[117] and that IHL applies in the whole territory of the state engaged in the conflict—raises an obvious question: what happens when the conflict crosses the territorial boundary? What happens when a NIAC, either between non-state armed groups (NSAGs), or between a state and an NSAG—'spills over' into the territory of other states? Indeed, what happens when participants in a NIAC engage in hostilities at a distinct geographical remove from their adversaries? Does IHL follow the participants in these so-called 'transnational'[118] NIACs wherever they are found in the world?

---

[113] See generally Kirsten Schulze, *The Free Aceh Movement (GAM): Anatomy of a Separatist Organization* (East-West Center Washington, 2004); and Human Rights Watch, *Indonesia: The War in Aceh* (August 2001) www.hrw.org/reports/2001/aceh. See also Sivakumaran (above n 111) 250.

[114] See eg International Covenant on Civil and Political Rights (adopted 16 December 1966; entered into force 23 March 1976) 999 UNTS 171 (ICCPR) article 4, which allows for derogations from the Covenant in situations of states of emergency, such as armed conflict. However, the Human Rights Committee has made it clear that derogations from fundamental human rights principles must be 'limited to the extent strictly required by the exigencies of the situation. This requirement relates to the duration, geographical coverage and material scope of the state of emergency and any measures of derogation resorted to because of the emergency' (Human Rights Committee, *General Comment 29: States of Emergency (Article 4)* UN Doc CCPR/C/21/rev.1/Add.11 (31 August 2001) para 4.

[115] *Kunarac* (above n 111) 57 (emphasis added).

[116] Michael Schmitt, 'Charting the Legal Geography of Non-International Armed Conflict' (2013) 51 *Rev Dr Milit* 93, 102.

[117] *Tadić* (Appeal Judgment) (above n 65) para 69.

[118] For further discussion of the concept of 'transnational armed conflict', see Geoffrey Corn and Eric Jensen, 'Transnational Armed Conflict: A "Principled" Approach to the Regulation of Counter-Terror Combat Operations'

One line of thinking about the geography of NIAC suggests that IHL—specifically the rules on targeting and military necessity[119]—applies wherever the participants in the conflict are found.[120] Thus, the moment a direct participant crosses an international boundary, he or she 'brings the law with them' into that territory, and the state into which that participant crosses comes under the ambit of IHL. In certain situations, this approach is entirely logical. An armed non-state group may utilize a poorly guarded border region of a neighbouring state as a base from which to conduct hostilities. In such a situation, the NIAC does not suddenly stop because a border is crossed: 'the applicable law does not suddenly cease when it reaches a territorial frontier.'[121] Indeed, as the ICRC has stated:

> [The] spillover of a NIAC into adjacent territory cannot have the effect of absolving the parties of their IHL obligations simply because an international border has been crossed. The ensuing legal vacuum would deprive of protection both civilians possibly affected by the fighting, as well as persons who fall into enemy hands.[122]

A broad application of IHL would thus be warranted, to ensure that anyone possibly impacted by the conflict finds due protection under the law.

However, a broad approach might be problematic, depending on how far away from the hostilities such participants are located. High-level leaders of organized armed groups often locate themselves far from active hostilities, sometimes even well beyond the state where the armed conflict is taking place.[123] The general consensus regarding such leaders is that they are lawful targets due to their involvement in the hostilities.[124] But how far is too far, for the purposes of the application of IHL? In 'geographically unfocused conflicts',[125] the central command of an organized armed group may be located far away from active hostilities, perhaps even operating in a putatively neutral state. The quintessential example of this was Osama bin Laden. Bin Laden was head of the Al Qaeda armed group from 1988 to 2011.[126] During that time, Al Qaeda conducted hostilities in Afghanistan, Yemen, Iraq, Somalia, the Maghreb,[127] and Syria.[128] Following the attacks on the US in September 2001,

---

(2009) 42(1) *Israel L Rev* 33–4; Geoffrey Corn, 'Geography of Armed Conflict: Why it is a Mistake to Fish for the Red Herring' (2013) 89 *Int'l L Stud* 77, 80–83.

[119] See further chapter 7 'International Humanitarian Law and the Conduct of Hostilities' in this book, in which Michael Schmitt details the substance of these principles.

[120] The idea of participants raises the issue of direct participation in hostilities (DPH)—see further chapter 7.

[121] Sivakumaran (above n 111) 251.

[122] ICRC, *International Humanitarian Law and the Challenges of Contemporary Armed Conflicts* (Report of the 31st Conference of the International Red Cross and Red Crescent) www.icrc.org/eng/assets/files/red-cross-crescent-movement/31st-international-conference/31-int-conference-ihl-challenges-report-11-5-1-2-en.pdf. See also Dapo Akande, 'Classification of Armed Conflicts: Relevant Legal Concepts', in Elizabeth Wilmshurst (ed), *International Law and the Classification of Armed Conflicts* (OUP 2012) 70–2 and Nils Melzer, *Targeted Killing in International Law* (OUP 2008) 259–60. This broad approach is evidenced in article 7 of the Statute of the International Tribunal for Rwanda (UNSC Resolution 955 UN Doc S/RES/955 (8 November 1994)), which states that its temporal jurisdiction shall extend to the territory of Rwanda including its land surface and airspace, as well as to the territory of neighbouring states in respect of serious violations of international humanitarian law committed by Rwandan citizens.

[123] See below nn 127, 130 regarding Osama bin Laden.

[124] Sivakumaran (above n 111) 251.

[125] Schmitt 'International Law' (above n 75) 104.

[126] See further Michael Scheuer, *Osama bin Laden* (OUP 2011), specifically ch 5.

[127] The Maghreb encompasses Algeria, Chad, Mali, Mauritania, Morocco, Niger, and Tunisia.

[128] Scheuer (above n 126) ch 6.

Bin Laden was allegedly smuggled out of Afghanistan into Pakistan, from where he oversaw the group's activities.[129] Thus, Bin Laden was geographically removed from the site of active hostilities. Was his targeting by the US in May 2011 governed by IHL? Did Bin Laden 'carry' the conflict, and thus the law, with him wherever he was located?

Critics of this perspective, including the ICRC, have rejected taking an overly broad approach to the geographical application of IHL in NIACs, stating that to do so 'would have the effect of potentially expanding the application of rules on the conduct of hostilities to multiple states according to a person's movement around the world as long as he is directly participating in hostilities in relation to a specific NIAC'.[130] Such an approach would create a 'global battlefield',[131] with the flow-on effect of having IHL apply to all states where conflict-related activities occur, even if such states host no active hostilities, and are not parties to the conflict.[132]

A third approach, and one that seems to have some support in both treaty and case law, avoids the drawing of 'arbitrary boundaries'[133] and proposes a case-by-case approach to the geography of armed conflict and the applicable law—namely, is there a sufficient nexus between the relevant law and the conduct in question? The language of APII suggests such an approach, by providing for its applicability to 'all persons affected by an armed conflict',[134] an interpretation confirmed by the Commentary to the Protocols, which states that APII is triggered by criteria related to 'persons, and not to places'.[135] This approach is congruent with that espoused by the 1972 Conference of Government Experts, which affirmed that, for the purposes of APII, 'what is important is that persons affected by the armed conflict should be entitled to the protection of the Protocol, wherever they might be'.[136] This case-by-case approach was evidenced by the International Criminal Tribunal for Rwanda (ICTR) in the *Kayishema* trial judgment, where the Tribunal stated that 'violations of [Common Article 3 and APII] could be committed outside the theatre of combat ... every crime should be considered on a case-by-case basis taking into account the material evidence'.[137]

This 'third approach' provides a different possibility of examining the geographical scope of armed conflict. Rather than hewing to a strict geographical limit on the applicability of the law, or espousing a broad, potentially vast, scope of applicability, this approach suggests that it is the 'persons, objects, and the like that are affected by the armed conflict and the conduct at issue rather than any geographic location [that] would provide a more appropriate solution to the question of the geographic scope of application of the law'.[138] This approach suggests implementation of IHL in a more nuanced manner: rather than the entirety of IHL applying to the entirety of a state as soon as a participant or combatant is physically

---

[129] Tim Ross, 'WikiLeaks: Osama bin Laden "Protected" by Pakistani Security' *The Telegraph* (London, 2 May 2011) www.telegraph.co.uk/news/worldnews/asia/pakistan/8488236/WikiLeaks-Osama-bin-Laden-protected-by-Pakistani-security.html. See also Abdel Bari Atwan, *After Bin Laden: Al Qaeda, The Next Generation* (New York: New Press 2012) 24–6 regarding Bin Laden's residency in Pakistan following the 9/11 attacks.

[130] ICRC Report of the 31st Conference of the International Red Cross and Red Crescent (above n 122) 22.

[131] ibid.

[132] Schmitt 'International Law' (above n 75) 107.

[133] Sivakumaran (above n 111) 251.

[134] APII article 2(1).

[135] AP Commentary 1360.

[136] ICRC, *Commentary on the Draft Additional Protocols to the Geneva Conventions of August 12, 1949* (ICRC 1973) 134.

[137] *Prosecutor v Kayishema and Ruzindana* (Judgment) ICTR-95-1-T (21 May 1999) para 176.

[138] Sivakumaran (above n 111) 252; see also Louise Arimatsu, 'Territory, Boundaries and the Law of Armed Conflict' (2009) 12 *YBIHL* 157, 189.

present in that territory, the IHL relevant to NIACs instead applies to specific territory only in so far as either active hostilities are taking place or to the geographically limited areas where participants are found. Thus, in the case of the Bin Laden targeting, IHL rules would not have applied to the entirety of Pakistani territory, but rather only to that locale where Bin Laden himself was found.

## 4. Conclusion

Knowing when and where to apply the law of armed conflict is a vital first step for states and non-state actors engaged in armed conflict. Developments in the conduct of armed conflicts over recent years have made this process notably more complicated. However, case law and commentary from experts has contributed greatly to better understanding the geographical and temporal scope of the law and will, no doubt, continue to fill in the gaps that exist in the law, especially in the area of NIAC.

# 4

# Domains of Warfare

*Sarah McCosker\**

## 1. Introduction

'Domains' of warfare are generally understood as the operational environments in which armed conflict occurs, and to which international humanitarian law (IHL) therefore applies. Until recent decades, domains of armed conflict have been largely predicated on geospatial conceptions, denoting the physical places where armed conflict has customarily occurred: land, sea, and air. General IHL applies across all these areas—including the fundamental principles of humanity, military necessity, and proportionality; restrictions or prohibitions of certain means and methods of warfare; and basic rules requiring humane treatment of persons and respect for civilians and civilian property. Over time however, the particular exigencies of land, sea, and air warfare have led to the development of some specific IHL rules and principles tailored to each of those environments. Discussing domains of armed conflict therefore offers a window into the historical development of IHL. It shows how the emergence of new operational environments and new means and methods of armed conflict catalyses efforts at legal regulation, which can lead to the development of new domains or sub-sets of IHL. In this way, IHL has become more specialized over time, organized into sub-fields of interpretation and application.

This chapter first examines the land, air, and sea domains, and then considers how the idea of a domain might apply to armed conflict in outer space, and armed conflict involving cyber operations and other emerging capabilities. The aim is to give a general overview of the development of IHL in relation to these different operational contexts, and to analyse the concept itself of a 'domain of armed conflict' and show how it shapes the way we think about and apply IHL. The chapter argues that the concept remains useful when analysing how IHL applies to armed conflict occurring in specific physical environments. However, it is perhaps less useful in the contexts of armed conflict occurring in multiple domains simultaneously, and armed conflict carried out through some new technologies and capabilities. Such contexts show the limitations of the concept and suggest that the increasingly complex nature of armed conflict may require the future development of more sophisticated ways of thinking about armed conflict and IHL.

* The views expressed in this chapter are those of the author in her personal capacity and do not reflect the views of any organization or other entity. The author is grateful to Matthew Teh for his excellent research assistance, to Chris Hanna for his very helpful feedback on an earlier draft of the chapter, and to Bruce Oswald for his valuable comments in early discussions.

## 2. The Evolving Concept of 'Domain': From Physical Battlefield to Figurative Field of IHL Application

The traditional concept of a battlefield is the physical location of armed conflict. Accordingly, IHL is underpinned by several fundamental geospatial concepts, essentially prescribing what parties to armed conflict can and cannot do in certain places. Two such concepts are the 'area of war' and the 'area of operations'. The 'area of war' is the area within which the military operations of the parties to an armed conflict may be carried out.[1] This is an extensive area, comprising all the territories of the parties, the high seas (including the airspace above and the sea floor), and exclusive economic zones.[2] Certain areas may be excluded from the area of war, for example neutralized zones (such as Antarctica), demilitarized zones, or the territory of neutral states. Within the area of war are the places where military operations actually take place at any given time, known as the 'theatre of war' or the 'area of operations'.[3] Domains of armed conflict are traditionally understood as the specific environments in which military operations may be conducted. The three main physical domains are land, sea, and air, where particular means and methods of armed conflict are conducted by states' armies, navies, and air forces respectively.

As indicated earlier, much of IHL is not domain-specific and applies generally, including most weapons-related treaties and treaties regarding cultural property. However, general IHL is supplemented by some domain-specific IHL rules and principles. This regulatory development began with armed conflict on land, was followed by sea and air, and now debates are occurring about possible extension into other operational environments such as outer space and cyberspace. The diversification of domains of IHL therefore reflects technological developments, as humans have evolved different environments in which to fight and new capabilities. This is not, of course, a clear linear progression; there are ongoing efforts to refine various aspects of IHL regarding land, sea, and air warfare.

In general, however, the history of IHL is one of increasing detail and specificity in legal regulation, as warfighting capabilities have become more sophisticated and specialized. Over time, domains of *armed conflict* have given rise to domains of *IHL*: the particular bodies of law, practice, and interpretation that have developed to guide behaviour in certain operational environments. Land, sea, and air warfare now represent bodies of specialized IHL and professional communities of expertise and practice. The latter comprise both those who engage directly in armed conflict, and those who advise on and/or interpret the relevant rules and principles—principally state defence forces, government ministries, relevant international organizations, the International Committee of the Red Cross, and legal academics.

While some might use the terms 'domains of armed conflict' and 'domains of IHL' interchangeably, it is important to recognize that these are different concepts. As will be discussed further in sections 6–8 of this chapter, not all domains of armed conflict necessarily correlate to specific fields of IHL. That is, while all domains of armed conflict may be understood as domains of IHL in the broad sense that general IHL applies to all activities

---

[1] Hersch Lauterpacht (ed), *Oppenheim's International Law, Vol II: Disputes, War and Neutrality* (7th edn, David McKay 1952) (*Oppenheim*) 236–44.

[2] Christopher Greenwood, 'Scope of Application of Humanitarian Law', in Dieter Fleck, *The Handbook of International Humanitarian Law* (2nd edn, OUP 2008) 45, 59 para 216.

[3] ibid 53 para 220; *Oppenheim* (above n 1) 237.

undertaken in the course of armed conflict, they are not all domains of IHL in the more narrow sense of being the subject of sub-sets of specialized IHL rules and principles.

Within military forces, the domain is a fundamental concept for organizing particular expertise, resources, and operations. For international lawyers, the 'domain' similarly serves as an organizational concept, which helps to structure our thinking about the application of IHL to a given context. That is, a basic first step in analysing the application of IHL is to ask where the armed conflict is occurring, which helps us to identify the applicable specialized sources of law and commentary. The way many lawyers structure their legal analysis therefore reflects traditional spatial conceptualizations of the battlefield.

In recent decades, the idea of discrete geographic domains has been challenged by two interrelated features of contemporary warfare. The first feature is that armed conflict increasingly involves integrated operations carried out simultaneously across multiple domains. The second feature is the increasing technological sophistication of armed conflict, with new capabilities changing the ways and spaces in which armed conflict is being fought. In turn, this is opening up new spaces for consideration by lawyers about how to apply and interpret IHL. This is demonstrated by the recognition by some states of outer space, cyberspace, and the electromagnetic spectrum as domains of armed conflict, and debates about whether other emerging capabilities may lead to the future recognition of additional domains. With some of these technologies, it is not possible to pinpoint a specific place where armed conflict occurs. In these contexts, understanding 'domains' is less about the physical theatre or locus *where* parties fight, than about *how* they fight and using what means and methods. In this way the concept of a domain as an environment is evolving into a broader concept, encompassing methods and means of warfare. For example, the Australian Army has recently defined domains as 'the physical or conceptual areas in which human activity and interaction occurs, including the four environmental domains of maritime (including subsurface), land, air and space, and the three non-environmental domains of cyberspace, the electromagnetic spectrum, and information'.[4]

The next sections will examine briefly the three main physical domains of armed conflict: land, sea, and air. Each section will flag key IHL treaties and other relevant instruments. It should be noted that both international and non-international armed conflict may occur in all of the domains discussed in the chapter. The classification of conflicts will not be discussed here, other than to note that most domain-specific IHL has developed initially in the context of international armed conflict.

## 3. Land

Land is the oldest domain of warfare, where humans first began fighting each other. As most contemporary armed conflicts are conducted at least partially on land, questions about land warfare remain as topical as ever.[5] Treaty law regarding the means and methods of land warfare stretches back well over a century. Early instruments include the *Lieber Code*

---

[4] Australian Army, *Land Warfare Doctrine 3-0, Operations* (2018) 13 www.army.gov.au/sites/default/files/lwd_3-0_operations_full.pdf.
[5] Yves Sandoz, 'Land Warfare' in Andrew Clapham and Paolo Gaeta (eds), *The Oxford Handbook of International Law in Armed Conflict* (OUP 2014) 91, 91.

1863[6] and the Hague Convention (II) with Respect to the Law and Customs of War on Land 1899, and its annexed Regulations,[7] which are considered declaratory of customary rules regarding armed conflict in general.[8] This Convention was replaced and amended as Hague Convention IV at the 1907 Hague Conference.[9] Other important treaties regarding armed conflict on land are the Hague Convention III (Opening of Hostilities) 1907;[10] Hague Convention V (Respecting the Rights and Duties of Neutral Powers and Persons in Case of War on Land) 1907;[11] Hague Convention IX (Respecting Bombardment by Naval Forces in Time of War) 1907;[12] and the First, Third, and Fourth Geneva Conventions 1949,[13] as well as Additional Protocols I and II of 1977.[14] IHL regarding land warfare has largely been applied and adapted to other domains, including maritime and air warfare.[15]

## 4. Sea

The maritime domain is a three-dimensional space, as military operations may be conducted on, under, or over the sea.[16] More specifically, hostile actions by naval forces may be conducted in, on, or over the land territory of the parties to armed conflict; their internal and archipelagic waters; territorial seas; neutral contiguous zones; fishery zones; continental shelf areas and exclusive economic zones; the high seas; and the airspace above those areas. The general principles of IHL are applicable in naval warfare as they are in land and air warfare. However, a significant body of treaty law and other instruments has developed to cater for the specificities of armed conflict in the maritime context, in particular the fact that the emphasis is on ships taking part in hostilities rather than individuals,[17] and also the involvement of neutral interests to a much greater extent than with land operations.[18]

---

[6] *Instructions for Government of Armies in the United States in the Field*, General Orders No 100 (24 April 1863). Another early instruments was the Institute of International Law's *Oxford Manual on the Laws of War on Land* (1880), and both were influential in the negotiations at the 1899 and 1907 Hague peace conferences.

[7] (signed 29 July 1899, entered into force 4 September 1900).

[8] Leslie Green, 'Conduct of Hostilities: Maritime' in Leslie Green, *The Contemporary Law of Armed Conflict* (3rd edn, Manchester UP 2008) 188, 188.

[9] Dietrich Schindler and Jiří Toman, *The Laws of Armed Conflicts* (4th edn, Martinus Nijhoff 2004) 55.

[10] (signed 18 October 1907, entered into force 26 January 1910), USTS 538.

[11] (signed 18 October 1907, entered into force 26 January 1910), USTS 540.

[12] (signed 18 October 1907, entered into force 26 January 1910), USTS 542.

[13] Geneva Convention (I) for the Amelioration of the Condition of Wounded and Sick in Armed Forces in the Field (adopted 12 August 1949, entered into force 21 October 1950) 75 UNTS 31 (GCI); Geneva Convention (III) Relative to the Treatment of Prisoners of War (adopted 12 August 1949, entered into force 21 October 1950) 75 UNTS 135 (GCIII); Geneva Convention (IV) Relative to the Protection of Civilian Persons in Time of War (adopted 12 August 1949, entered into force 21 October 1950) 75 UNTS 287 (GCIV).

[14] Protocol Additional to the Geneva Conventions of 12 August 1949, and Relating to the Protection of Victims of International Armed Conflicts (adopted 8 June 1977, entered into force 7 December 1978) 1125 UNTS 3 (API); Protocol Additional to the Geneva Conventions of 12 August 1949, and Relating to the Protection of Victims of Non-International Armed Conflicts (adopted 8 June 1977, entered into force 7 December 1978), 1125 UNTS 609 (APII).

[15] Leslie Green, 'Conduct of Hostilities: Land', in Green, *The Contemporary Law of Armed Conflict* (above n 8) 147, 147 (internal footnotes omitted).

[16] *The San Remo Manual on International Law Applicable to Armed Conflicts at Sea* (adopted 1994, reproduced 1995) No 309 IRRC 583 (*San Remo Manual*); Louise Doswald-Beck (ed), *San Remo Manual on International Law Applicable to Armed Conflicts at Sea* (CUP 1995) para 10ff.

[17] Natalino Ronzitti, 'Naval Warfare', in Frauke Lachenmann and Rudiger Wolfrum, *The Law of Armed Conflict and the Use of Force: The Max Planck Encyclopedia of Public International Law, Thematic Series, Vol II* (OUP 2017) 757, 758.

[18] *San Remo Manual* (above n 16).

Certain means and methods of armed conflict are unique to the maritime domain, such as blockade, visit and search, and naval mine warfare.[19] In maritime warfare only warships may take part in hostilities and exercise belligerent measures, not merchant vessels.[20]

How IHL applies often depends on the particular maritime area in which the relevant activity occurs. For example, armed conflict in a belligerent's sovereign waters (internal waters and territorial sea) is largely analogous to fighting on a belligerent's land territory, and includes fighting in the adversary's national airspace.[21] This contrasts to armed conflict occurring in the maritime zones beyond states' territorial seas, and the airspace above them—commonly referred to respectively as 'international waters' and 'international airspace'.

Although naval battles have been fought for several thousand years, legal regulation occurred later than for armed conflict on land. Following some early instruments adopted in the late nineteenth century,[22] most of the international instruments governing naval armed conflict were developed in 1907 through eight Hague Conventions (Hague Conventions VI–XII).[23] They concern the conduct of hostilities (the laying of underwater mines, bombardment by naval forces, and protection of the sick, wounded, and shipwrecked);[24] and the protection of certain ships (the status of merchant ships and their conversion into warships,[25] the right of capture,[26] and the rights and duties of neutral powers).[27] Technological progress led to further codification efforts, including the Declaration of London concerning the Laws of Naval War 1909;[28] the 1913 Oxford Manual of the Laws of Naval War;[29] agreements in 1922 regarding the use of submarines and noxious gases;[30] and further instruments

[19] Ronzitti 'Naval Warfare' (above n 17) 761–2.

[20] 'Warship' is defined in the Convention on the High Seas (done 29 April 1958, entered into force 30 September 1962), 450 UNTS 11 article 8(2) and the United Nations Convention on the Law of the Sea (adopted 10 December 1982, entered into force 16 November 1994), 1833 UNTS 3 (UNCLOS) article 29; see also W Heintschel von Heinegg, 'Warships', in Lachenmann and Wolfrum (above n 17) 1358.

[21] David Letts and Rob McLaughlin, 'Law of Naval Warfare', in Rain Liivoja and Tim McCormack (eds), *Routledge Handbook of the Law of Armed Conflict* (Routledge 2016) 264, 266.

[22] Paris Declaration Respecting Maritime Law (signed and entered into force 16 April 1856, 115 CTS 1); Hague Convention (III) for the Adaptation to Maritime Warfare of the Principles of the Geneva Convention of 22 August 1864 (adopted 29 July 1899, entered into force 4 September 1900).

[23] See further Schindler and Toman (above n 9) 1059–93; W Heintschel von Heinegg, 'Maritime Warfare', in Clapham and Gaeta (above n 5) 145; Marco Sassòli, Antoine Bouvier, and Anne Quintin, *How Does Law Protect in War? Vol 1* (ICRC 2011), ch 10 Letts and McLaughlin (above n 21) 269–73.

[24] Hague Convention (VIII) Relative to the Laying of Automatic Submarine Contact Mines (adopted 18 October 1907, entered into force 26 January 1910) 205 CTS 331; Convention (IX) concerning Bombardment by Naval Forces in Time of War (adopted 18 October 1907, entered into force 26 January 1910) 205 CTS 345; Convention (X) concerning the Adaptation to Maritime Warfare of the Principles of the Geneva Convention (adopted 18 October 1907, entered into force 26 January 1910) 15 LNTS 340.

[25] Convention (VI) Relating to the Status of Enemy Merchant Ships at the Outbreak of Hostilities (adopted 18 October 1907, entered into force 26 January 1910) 205 CTS 305; Convention (VII) Relating to the Conversion of Merchant Ships into War-Ships (adopted 18 October 1907, entered into force 26 January 1910) 205 CTS 319.

[26] Convention (XI) Relative to Certain Restrictions with Regard to the Exercise of the Right of Capture in Naval War (adopted 18 October 1907, entered into force 26 January 1910) 205 CTS 367; and Convention (XII) Relative to the Creation of an International Prize Court (adopted 18 October 1907, entered into force 26 January 1910) 205 CTS 381.

[27] Convention (XIII) concerning the Rights and Duties of Neutral Powers in Naval War (adopted 18 October 1907, entered into force 26 January 1910) 205 CTS 395.

[28] Signed 26 February 1909 [1908–09] 208 CTS 341; Schindler and Toman (above n 9) 1111.

[29] 'The Oxford Manual of Naval Warfare' (9 August 1913) [1913] 26 AnnIDI 610; in D. Schindler and J. Toman, *The Laws of Armed Conflicts* (Martinus Nijhoff 1988), 858–75.

[30] Treaty for the Limitation of Naval Armament (6 February 1922), 25 LNTS 202; Treaty Relating to the Use of Submarines and Noxious Gases in Warfare (6 February 1922, not in force), 16 AJIL Supp 57.

in the 1930s on the limitation and reduction of naval armaments, and on submarines.[31] The Second World War saw numerous torpedo attacks on neutral vessels, merchant ships, and hospital ships, as well as indiscriminate laying of underwater mines. This led to the development in 1945 of the Geneva Convention II, providing a regime for the protection of the wounded, sick, and shipwrecked in armed conflict at sea.[32] However, since 1945 there have been no new treaties specifically concerning naval warfare, with attempts to promote further codification being generally unsuccessful.[33] This means that interpreting and updating the law has been entrusted to state practice, which is reflected largely in states' naval manuals.[34]

The main contemporary reference document for the law of naval warfare is the *San Remo Manual on International Applicable Armed Conflicts at Sea*.[35] Developed between 1987 and 1994 by a Committee of Experts under the auspices of the International Institute of Humanitarian Law and the International Committee of the Red Cross (ICRC), it restated and significantly clarified the rules applicable to naval warfare, taking into account developments over the previous century. Although non-binding, it is often used as the basis of national military manuals.[36] While some consider it expressive of customary law,[37] others argue that not all its details necessarily reflect custom.[38]

In comparison with armed conflicts on land, armed conflicts at sea (or in other waters) have been uncommon over the past decades.[39] While the basic principles of the Hague Conventions and other early treaties are still generally recognized as customary in character,[40] the age of the instruments understandably means that aspects are significantly outdated, and need to be adapted to contemporary naval warfare,[41] as well as to take into account the major changes in the law of the sea.[42] An ongoing challenge is therefore how to interpret existing law to apply to the modern realities of the maritime domain. Particular topical issues include how to apply existing law to non-international maritime conflict; the blurring of paradigms from constabulary operations into armed conflict; and how to characterize unmanned and autonomous surface and sub-surface combat vehicles.[43]

---

[31] Treaty for the Limitation and Reduction of Naval Armaments (Part IV) (22 April 1930), 112 LNTS 88; Procès-Verbal Relating to the Rules of Submarine Warfare set forth in Part IV of the Treaty of London of 22 April 1930 (signed and entered into force 6 November 1936), 173 LNTS 353; Green, *The Contemporary Law of Armed Conflict* (above n 8) 45, citing Schindler and Toman (above n 9) 1139–49.

[32] Geneva Convention (II) for the Amelioration of the Condition of Wounded, Sick and Shipwrecked Members of Armed Forces at Sea (adopted 12 August 1949, entered into force 21 October 1950), 75 UNTS 85 (GCII).

[33] Letts and McLaughlin (above n 21) 274. API contains provisions concerning naval attacks on land targets (arts 50–60), but otherwise just states that the provisions concerning protection against the effects of hostilities similarly apply to naval operations which may affect civilians: API article 49(3).

[34] Ronzitti 'Naval Warfare' (above n 17) 767; eg UK Ministry of Defence, *Joint Service Manual of the Law of Armed Conflict* JSM 383 (Ministry of Defence 2004) (as updated to 21 May 2014) (*UK Manual*) 347–61 www.ihlresearch.org/amw.

[35] *San Remo Manual* (above n 16); Sassòli et al (above n 23) 302.

[36] eg the UK, German, and US military manuals: Sassòli et al (above n 23) 302, n 289.

[37] Green, *The Contemporary Law of Armed Conflict* (above n 8) 45.

[38] Vaughan Lowe and Antonios Tzanakopoulos, 'Ships, Visit and Search', in Lachenmann and Wolfrum (above n 17) 1153, 1158.

[39] Bruno Demeyere, Jean-Marie Henckaerts, Heleen Hiemstra, and Ellen Nohle, 'The Updated ICRC Commentary on the Second Geneva Convention: Demystifying the Law of Armed Conflict at Sea' (2016) 98 *IRRC* 401, 417.

[40] Heintschel von Heinegg 'Maritime Warfare' (above n 23) 146.

[41] ibid 146, 180–1.

[42] eg through the Convention on the High Seas 1958 (above n 20) and UNCLOS; see Ronzitti 'Naval Warfare' (above n 17) 758.

[43] Letts and McLaughlin (above n 21) 265.

# 5.  Air

Airpower plays a critical role in twenty-first-century armed conflict, and yet it remains the operational domain least regulated by IHL treaty law.[44] To date, unlike for land and maritime warfare, states have not adopted any treaty exclusively devoted to air warfare—understood as hostilities conducted during armed conflict by or against aircraft.[45] The limited existing treaty law concerning air and missile warfare mainly deals with medical aircraft.[46] However, much of the vacuum has been filled by customary international law, combined with some provisions in general IHL treaties that constrain air operations and non-binding instruments.[47] IHL applicable to air and missile warfare draws on both the land and naval domains, either directly or indirectly, for relevant legal rules and principles.[48] Air attacks against targets on land are governed by the rules of war on land. When aircraft fly over open sea or engage in combat with naval forces, the law of naval warfare applies.[49] Though the *San Remo Manual* does not deal with aviation, it looks at aerial activity in conjunction with naval operations— for example, it contains special rules on the interception, visit, and search of civil aircraft.[50]

Airspace is divided into national airspace and international airspace (airspace over the exclusive economic zones of other states, and the high seas). Under customary international law each state has exclusive sovereignty over the airspace above its land and territorial sea.[51] The vertical extent of airspace, and the beginning of outer space, is unsettled in international law.[52] It has been argued that anything in orbit or beyond is in outer space,[53] which reflects the view that airspace means 'the air up to the highest altitude at which an aircraft can fly and below the lowest possible perigee of an earth satellite in orbit'.[54] In international armed conflict air operations may be conducted over the territory of belligerent states, and also in international air space.[55] There is no settled definition of the term 'aircraft' in international law,[56] though one suggested definition is craft 'deriving their support in the atmosphere from the reactions of the air', with military aircraft understood as all aircraft (whether manned or unmanned, armed or unarmed) that are operated by the armed forces or a state and bear its military markings.[57] Only military aircraft are entitled to engage in hostilities, unlike other state aircraft or civilian aircraft.[58]

---

[44]  Michael Schmitt, 'Air Warfare', in Clapham and Gaeta (above n 5) 118, 119, 144. See also Javier Guisández Gómez, 'The Law of Air Warfare' (1998) 323 IRRC 347; *UK Manual* (above n 34) ch 12 ('Air Operations').

[45]  Yoram Dinstein, 'Air Warfare', in Lachenmann and Wolfrum (above n 17) 13, 14.

[46]  Ian Henderson and Patrick Keane, 'Air and Missile Warfare', in Liivoja and McCormack (above n 21) 282; GCI ch VI; API articles 24–31.

[47]  Schmitt 'Air Warfare' (above n 44) 119, 144.

[48]  Henderson and Keane (above n 46) 282–98.

[49]  Sassòli et al (above n 23) 314.

[50]  *San Remo Manual* (above n 16) rules 125–158; Harvard University Program on Humanitarian Policy and Conflict Research, *Manual on International Law applicable to Air and Missile Warfare* (2009) www.ihlresearch. org/amw; Yoram Dinstein, Bruno Demeyere, and Claude Bruderlein (eds), *Harvard Manual on International Law Applicable to Air and Missile Warfare* (CUP 2010) (*Harvard Manual*) rules 37, 38, 40, 41, 55, 57, 70, and 134–46.

[51]  Convention on International Civil Aviation (7 December 1944), 15 UNTS 295 articles 1–2; *Military and Paramilitary Activities in and against Nicaragua (Nicaragua v US)* [1986] ICJ Rep 14 para 251.

[52]  Henderson and Keane (above n 46) 288; Gbenga Oduntan, 'The Never Ending Dispute: Legal Theories on the Spatial Demarcation Boundary Plane between Airspace and Outer Space' (2003) 1 *Hertfordshire LJ* 64.

[53]  eg *UK Manual* (above n 34) para 12.13.

[54]  *Harvard Manual* (above n 50) rule 1(a).

[55]  Schmitt 'Air Warfare' (above n 44) 125; *UK Manual* (above n 34) para 12.14.

[56]  *UK Manual* (above n 34) para 12.4.

[57]  Dinstein (above n 45) 14.

[58]  ibid 15.

Following the beginnings of air warfare through use of balloons in the late eighteenth century,[59] the first attempt to develop principles concerning air warfare was at the 1899 Hague Peace Conference, where declarations were adopted banning the launching of projectiles and explosives by balloons or by similar methods, and the use of certain kinds of projectiles.[60] The Balloons Declaration was replaced in 1907 by a further Declaration to the same effect,[61] although few states ratified either Declaration. At the time of the 1899 and 1907 Hague Conferences air technology was insufficiently advanced to allow precise targeting of military objectives, but by the First World War air operations played a critical role, with aircraft widely used for observation, bombing, and dog fighting.[62] It became apparent that some rules were necessary to regulate conflict in this theatre of activity, which led to the 1923 development of the 'Hague Rules of Air Warfare'.[63] Although not in treaty form, much of the Hague Rules are understood as reflecting customary law.[64] Two particularly important provisions—early versions of the principle of distinction (between military aircraft and other aircraft) and IHL's first definition of 'military objectives'—became custom and were later codified in API in 1977.[65]

The Second World War involved extensive bombing offensives which resulted in the destruction of many civilian areas, and during this period there was no written law binding specifically governing air warfare.[66] While much of the law of air warfare has developed through analogies drawn from the laws of armed conflict on land and at sea, since the Second World War 'it has become quite clear ... that such analogies are often inadequate, inasmuch as conditions of air warfare differ radically from those prevailing on land and at sea', such as '[t]he high speed, the vast space, and the state-of-the-art sophistication of air warfare'.[67]

However, overall there seems to have been a reluctance to address the broad issues of air warfare through treaty law, with only a few specific aspects selected for regulation through binding rules.[68] The four Geneva Conventions of 1949 mention aircraft primarily regarding their medical functions rather than their use in the conduct of hostilities,[69] and certain other instruments not specific to armed conflict also contain rules restricting air operations.[70] API contains several provisions regarding medical aircraft,[71] and rules concerning

---

[59]   Schmitt 'Air Warfare' (above n 44) 120.

[60]   Declaration (IV, 1) to Prohibit for the Term of Five Years the Launching of Projectiles and Explosives from Balloons, and Other New Methods of a Similar Nature (20 July 1899); Green, *The Contemporary Law of Armed Conflict* (above n 8) 40, citing Schindler and Toman (above n 9) 95.

[61]   Declaration (XIV) Prohibiting the Discharge of Projectiles and Explosives from Balloons (18 October 1907).

[62]   Schmitt 'Air Warfare' (above n 44) 121.

[63]   Commission of Jurists, The Hague, Rules concerning the Control of Wireless Telegraphy in Time of War and Air Warfare (drafted December 1922–February 1923), Parliamentary Papers, Cmd 2201, (Hague Rules of Air Warfare) Miscellaneous No 14 (1924); Schmitt 'Air Warfare' (above n 44) 121–2.

[64]   Sassòli et al (above n 23) 314; Schmitt 'Air Warfare' (above n 44) 122–3; *Prosecutor v Galić*, IT-98-29-A, ICTY Appeals Chamber (30 November 2006) n 275; *UK Manual* (above n 34) para 1.26.3. Their customary status is debated by some: see Green, *The Contemporary Law of Armed Conflict* (above n 8) 46–7.

[65]   Hague Rules of Air Warfare (above n 63) articles 22 and 24; API articles 51 and 52; Schmitt 'Air Warfare' (above n 44) 122.

[66]   *UK Manual* (above n 34) para 1.28.1.

[67]   Dinstein (above n 45) 13.

[68]   ibid 14.

[69]   GCI articles 13, 36, 37; GCII articles 12, 13, 15, 39, 40; GCIII articles 4, 75; GCIV articles 22, 111.

[70]   eg the Convention on Prohibitions or Restrictions on the Use of Certain Conventional Weapons which may be Deemed to be Excessively Injurious or to Have Indiscriminate Effects (adopted 10 April 1981, entered into force 2 December 1983), 1342 UNTS 137; Convention on Cluster Munitions (adopted 3 December 2008, entered into force 1 August 2010), 2688 UNTS 39; Schmitt 'Air Warfare' (above n 44) 123.

[71]   API articles 8(f)–(g) and (i) 24–31.

air-to-ground attacks, but does not address air-to-sea, sea-to-air, ground-to-air, or air-to-air combat except as they have incidental effects on civilians or civilian objects on the ground.[72] Despite this incompleteness, API's general norms regarding issues like proportionality and precautions in attack are regarded by most states as reflective of custom applicable in all air operations.[73] API is therefore understood as prohibiting attacks on the civilian population and civilian property, regardless of whether the attack is on land, from the air or from the sea.[74]

In an effort to restate and update the law applicable to air warfare, between 2002 and 2010 a group of military and humanitarian experts developed the *Harvard Manual on International Law Applicable to Air and Missile Warfare*,[75] which now represents 'the most authoritative and comprehensive treatment of air warfare to date'. Although non-binding, it is regarded by many as reflecting customary rules, and as a subsidiary means to determine international law applicable to air and missile warfare.[76] Its 175 Rules and detailed accompanying commentary focus on where air operations may be conducted; who and what may be attacked; how air operations must be conducted; and what weapons may be used.[77] It has been noted, however, that in many cases the *Manual* only includes 'the least common denominator, in particular in the crucial area of protection of the civilian population on land against air attacks'.[78]

Topical issues in recent years include how to apply IHL in relation to unmanned aerial vehicles (UAVs) or 'remotely piloted aerial systems' (RPAS).[79] While UAV/RPAS are governed by the fundamental rules of IHL just as non-remotely piloted aircraft or any other weapon system,[80] some interpretative challenges remain, such as how UAVs should be marked; how to apply the concept of 'command' to the operation of a UAV, and how the concept of 'crew' applies to those who are remotely operating or programming a UAV.[81] Several aspects of the existing law of air warfare need further updating. Given that air capabilities are continuing to evolve rapidly and to be relied on heavily by states, it has been argued that '[t]here is a constant and obvious need to adapt the law of armed conflict to the changing and challenging contingencies of air warfare'.[82]

---

[72] Schmitt 'Air Warfare' (above n 44) 124, citing API article 49(3); Michael Bothe, Karl Josef Partsch, and Waldemar A Solf, *New Rules for Victims of Armed Conflicts: Commentary on the Two 1977 Protocols Additional to the Geneva Conventions of 1949* (Martinus Nijhoff 1982) 290.

[73] Schmitt 'Air Warfare' (above n 44) 125.

[74] Sassòli et al (above n 23) 315.

[75] (above n 50).

[76] Schmitt 'Air Warfare' (above n 44) 125; Henderson and Keane (above n 46) 283.

[77] Harvard University Program on Humanitarian Policy and Conflict Research, *Commentary on the Manual on International Law Applicable to Air and Missile Warfare* (2010) www.ihlresearch.org/amw/manual; Schmitt 'Air Warfare' (above n 44) 125.

[78] Sassòli et al (above n 23) 314.

[79] The *Harvard Manual* divides the definition of RPAS into 'Unmanned Aerial Vehicles' (unmanned aircraft of any size which does not carry a weapon and which cannot control a weapon' (rule 1(dd)) (commonly referred to as a 'drone') and 'Unmanned Combat Aerial Vehicle' which 'carries and launches a weapon, or which can use on-board technology to direct such a weapon to a target' (rule 1(ee)).

[80] See eg New Zealand Defence Force, *Manual of Armed Forces Law: Vol 4, Law of Armed Conflict*, DM 69 (2nd edn, New Zealand Defence Force 1982) (*NZDF Manual*) para 10.7.2–10.7.3.

[81] Henderson and Keane (above n 46) 285–6; *Harvard Manual* (above n 50) rule 1(x) para 6; see Markus Wagner, 'Unmanned Aerial Vehicles', in Lachenmann and Wolfrum (above n 17) 1280–6.

[82] Dinstein (above n 45) 24.

# 6. Outer Space

Outer space[83] is another physical environment in which armed conflict may potentially occur, and is considered by some as a 'fourth domain' of armed conflict.[84] There is significant interest in developing more detailed guidance on the application of IHL to it.[85] Although long recognized that IHL applies to military operations in outer space, there is little state practice, both because of the legal requirement to use space only for peaceful purposes, and because not all states are capable of conducting military operations in space.[86] It was not until the 1960s that armed conflict in space began to be possible, following space research and missions in the 1950s, and the US and Soviet launch of satellites and manned space missions during the Cold War.[87] In 1959 the UN Committee on the Peaceful Uses of Outer Space was established[88] and was instrumental in the creation of five space-related treaties[89] and five non-binding instruments and sets of principles.[90] However, these treaties have few states parties and provide little detailed guidance for modern military uses of space. Inter alia, they provide that the moon and other bodies in outer space must only be used for peaceful purposes,[91] and prohibit the establishment of military bases, installations and fortifications, testing of weapons, and conduct of military manoeuvres.[92] Thus far, much of the military use of outer space has been considered in the context of disarmament and arms control issues rather than IHL.[93]

Over the ensuing decades, space capabilities have increased significantly, such that now many states rely heavily on space and satellites for communications; transportation; global positioning systems; reconnaissance; surveillance; and early warning and navigation

---

[83] As noted earlier in section 5 'Air', there is no treaty law definition of 'outer space', but it is understood to mean the space beyond the upper atmosphere: eg *NZDF Manual* (above n 80) para 8.11.8.

[84] eg the US refers to space as a 'warfighting domain' in its 2018 National Defense Strategy: US, 'Summary of the 2018 National Defense Strategy of the USA' (2018) 6 https://dod.defense.gov/Portals/1/Documents/pubs/2018-National-Defense-Strategy-Summary.pdf. See also Sean Hall, 'Cyberspace at the Operational Level: Warfighting in all Five Domains' (2016) 5 https://apps.dtic.mil/dtic/tr/fulltext/u2/1045557.pdf.

[85] See eg Dale Stephens and Cassandra Steer, 'Conflicts in Space: International Humanitarian Law and its Application to Space Warfare' (2015) XL *Annals of Air and Space Law* 1.

[86] Adelaide Law School, 'The Woomera Manual: Legal Framework and Context' https://law.adelaide.edu.au/woomera/legal-framework.

[87] Hall (above n 84) 5; Manfred Lachs, 'The International Law of Outer Space' (1964) 113(3) *Recueil des Cours* 1.

[88] UN Office for Outer Space Affairs, 'Committee on the Peaceful Uses of Outer Space' www.unoosa.org/oosa/en/ourwork/copuos/index.html.

[89] Treaty on Principles Governing the Activities of States in the Exploration and Use of Outer Space, including the Moon and Other Celestial Bodies (opened for signature 27 January 1967, entered into force 10 October 1967), 610 UNTS 205 (Outer Space Treaty) article V; Agreement on the Rescue of Astronauts, the Return of Astronauts and the Return of Objects Launched into Outer Space (opened for signature 22 April 1968, entered into force 3 December 1968); Convention on International Liability for Damage Caused by Space Objects (opened for signature 29 March 1972, entered into force on 1 September 1972); Convention on Registration of Objects Launched into Outer Space (opened for signature on 14 January 1975, entered into force on 15 September 1976); Agreement Governing the Activities of States on the Moon and Other Celestial Bodies (opened for signature 18 December 1979, entered into force 11 July 1984), 1363 UNTS 21 (Moon Treaty) articles 3–4.

[90] eg Declaration of Legal Principles Governing the Activities of States in the Exploration and Use of Outer Space, UNGA Resolution 1962 (XVIII) (13 December 1963); Declaration on International Cooperation in the Exploration and Use of Outer Space for the Benefit and in the Interest of All States, Taking into Particular Account the Needs of Developing Countries, UNGA Resolution 51/122 (13 December 1996). The other three sets of principles concern broadcasting, remote sensing, and nuclear power sources.

[91] Outer Space Treaty articles 3 and 4; Moon Treaty articles 3(1)–(2).

[92] Outer Space Treaty article 4; Moon Treaty article 3(4).

[93] See Colleen Sullivan, 'The Prevention of an Arms Race in Outer Space: An Emerging Principle of International Law' (1990) 2 *Temple Int'l Comp LJ* 211.

systems[94]—all capabilities with potential dual uses for civilian and military purposes. As a consequence, the possibility of armed conflict extending to outer space is considered by some to be growing,[95] with space now being described as 'a critical security and conflict domain'.[96] It can be understood both as a 'supporting domain' of armed conflict, in that space capabilities play an important role in supporting military operations in land, sea, and air warfare,[97] and also as a potential domain itself.

With these growing space capabilities is an increasing interest in legal regulation.[98] There is currently no intergovernmental instrument specifically examining the application of IHL to armed conflict in outer space. However, two independent expert-led projects are underway to develop manuals to clarify existing international laws applicable to military space operations, including IHL. One initiative, which began in 2016, is being led by the McGill University Centre for Research in Air and Space Law and aims to develop a 'Manual on International Law Applicable to Military Activities in Outer Space'.[99] Another, launched in 2018, aims to develop the 'Woomera Manual on the International Law of Military Space Operations'.[100] Both projects comprise experts from academia, the private sector, government, and military service, contributing in their personal capacities. These processes seek to avoid some of the challenges associated with space-related discussions in intergovernmental fora. For example, a lack of consensus has prevented progress on international law issues through the UN Committee on the Peaceful Uses of Outer Space and the UN Conference on Disarmament.[101] Current UN-facilitated intergovernmental initiatives therefore focus more on broader issues, for example the UN General Assembly Group of Government Experts on the Prevention of an Arms Race in Outer Space, and the UN Group of Governmental Experts on Transparency and Confidence-Building Measures in Outer Space Activities.[102]

## 7. New and Emerging Technologies

As discussed earlier, the development of new technologies has been a force driving the recognition of new domains of armed conflict. Technological innovation led to expansion of armed conflict from land into the naval and air environments, spurring efforts at legal

---

[94] See Christopher Dixon, Jessica Clarence, Amelia Meurant-Tompkinson, and Melissa Liberatore, 'The Five-Domains Update' Australian Strategic Policy Institute (29 May 2018) www.aspistrategist.org.au/the-five-domains-update-16/#.

[95] University of Adelaide, 'The Woomera Manual' https://law.adelaide.edu.au/woomera/home; eg in 2019 the US directed the creation of a US Space Force: US Presidential Memoranda, 'Space Policy Directive-4: Establishment of the United States Space Force' (19 February 2019) www.whitehouse.gov/presidential-actions/text-space-policy-directive-4-establishment-united-states-space-force; Joan Johnson-Freese, *Space Warfare in the 21st Century: Among the Heavens* (Routledge 2017).

[96] Rob McLaughlin, cited in 'Conflict in Outer Space will Happen: Legal Experts', Adelaide Law School Blog (20 April 2018) https://blogs.adelaide.edu.au/law/2018/04/20/conflict-in-outer-space-will-happen-legal-experts.

[97] Hall (above n 84) 6.

[98] See Ram Jakhu, Cassandra Steer, and Kuan-Wei Chen, 'Conflicts in Space and the Rule of Law' (2016) *Space Policy* 1.

[99] <www.mcgill.ca/milamos>.

[100] University of Adelaide (above n 95).

[101] John Goehring, 'International Law Manuals for Military Operations in Space', Guest Post (10 October 2018) *Lawfire* https://sites.duke.edu/lawfire/2018/10/10/guest-post-john-goehring-on-international-law-manuals-for-military-operations-in-space.

[102] UN Office of Disarmament Affairs, 'Outer Space' www.un.org/disarmament/topics/outerspace.

regulation that led eventually to the development of new domains of IHL. Throughout history there is 'a clear tendency initially for the law to follow the technology, with new platforms as well as weapons prompting attempts to regulate'.[103] Technological change is therefore not a new challenge for IHL; however, the speed of change is now much faster, which exacerbates the problem of law lagging behind technology.[104] Below is a discussion of three areas of new technologies and capabilities that some states and commentators have identified as constituting new or future domains of armed conflict: activities conducted through cyber space; the electromagnetic spectrum; and computer–human body interfaces.

## A. Information Technology/Cyberspace

For many states, critical areas of defence capability have become increasingly reliant on information technology and cyber operations—such as command-and-control, navigations, communications, intelligence, surveillance and reconnaissance, and weapons employment.[105] Cyberspace has therefore been described by some as the 'fifth domain' or 'dimension' of armed conflict.[106] For example, the US Department of Defence recognized cyberspace as an operational domain in 2011.[107] It has been described as 'a global domain within the information environment' which 'is dependent on the physical domains of air, land, maritime, and space'.[108] The US regards it both as a 'critical enabler for other warfighting domains and a new domain itself'.[109] Other countries are following suit by acquiring cyber capabilities and developing their force structures to leverage these capabilities.[110] In 2016 NATO Allied Ministers formally recognized cyberspace as an 'operational domain' along with land, air, and sea operations, noting that '[m]ost crises and conflicts today have a cyber dimension'.[111] By 2015 more than 100 states had reportedly established dedicated cyber-warfare units within their armed forces or intelligence agencies.[112]

Most states and commentators would appear to recognize cyber capabilities as new means of supporting the conduct of armed conflict through kinetic operations. In this sense cyber capabilities can be understood as representing a 'domain' of armed conflict, although their non-geospatially bounded nature makes use of a term like 'domain' figurative rather

---

[103] Steven Haines, 'The Developing Law of Weapons: Humanity, Distinction, and Precautions in Attack', in Liivoja and McCormack (above n 21) 273, 275.

[104] Rain Liivoja, 'Technological Change and the Evolution of the Law of War' (2015) 97 *IRRC* 1157, 1173.

[105] Michael Schmitt, 'Rewired Warfare: Rethinking the Law of Cyber Attack' (2014) 96 *IRRC* 189 190.

[106] John R Wilson, 'Cyber Warfare Ushers in 5th Dimension of Human Conflict' (2014) 25(12) *Military & Aerospace Electronics* 8–15.

[107] US Department of Defense, 'Strategy for Operating in Cyberspace' (2011) 5–6 https://csrc.nist.gov/CSRC/media/Projects/ISPAB/documents/DOD-Strategy-for-Operating-in-Cyberspace.pdf.

[108] US Office of the Chairman of the Joint Chiefs of Staff, *Cyberspace Operations: Joint Publication 3–12* (CJCS 8 June 2018) Glossary, 4 and main text, vii https://fas.org/irp/doddir/dod/jp3_12.pdf.

[109] Matthew H Swartz, Director, Communications & Networks Division and Task Force Cyber Awakening Lead, Office of the Deputy Chief of Naval Operations for Information Dominance, Media Roundtable (31 October 2014), cited in George I Seffers, 'Task Force Cyber Awakening Recommendations Due', *Signal* (3 November 2014) www.afcea.org/content/task-force-cyber-awakening-recommendations-due.

[110] Schmitt 'Rewired Warfare' (above n 105) 190.

[111] NATO Secretary General J Stoltenberg, Press Conference: following the North Atlantic Council meeting at the level of NATO Defence Ministers (14 June 2006) www.nato.int/cps/en/natohq/opinions_132349.htm?selectedLocale=en.

[112] Liivoja (above n 104) 1158, citing Fergus Hanson, 'Waging War in Peacetime: Cyber Attacks and International Norms', *The Lowy Interpreter* (20 October 2015) www.lowyinterpreter.org/post/2015/10/20/Waging-war-in-peacetime-Cyber-attacks-and-international-norms.aspx.

than actual. Despite the common use of the term cyber-'space', cyber operations cannot easily be conceptualized spatially.[113] Cyber capabilities denote a complex range of technologies, together understood loosely as a medium or dimension through which certain kinds of activities may be conducted, with real-world effects in the domains of land, sea, air, and space.[114] IHL is applied by states to 'cyber operations that occur in the context of armed conflict or which have effect comparable to armed conflict'.[115] The ICRC has described 'cyber warfare' as encompassing 'operations against a computer or a computer system through a data stream, when used as means and methods of warfare in the context of an armed conflict, as defined under IHL'.[116]

As an emergent capability in armed conflict it poses several challenges for our existing constructs—including debate about whether actions such as cyber-attacks fall within the definition of 'armed' conflict, or a military 'attack'; and whether data is an 'object' whose targeting is regulated by IHL.[117] Some commentators have therefore argued that it is an error to think of cyberspace as a warfighting domain analogous to the traditional domains, and have critiqued the narrative that seems to suggest that 'cyberspace has become the new high ground of warfare, the one domain to rule them all and in the ether bind them'.[118]

While it is clear that the fundamental rules and principles of IHL apply to computer network attacks conducted in the course of armed conflict, as with other means and methods of warfare,[119] the issue is specifically *how* they should apply and be interpreted. This has been the topic of considerable debate since the late 1990s[120]—together with the question of whether cyber operations should be considered a new and distinct domain of IHL. This is a context in which commentary and analysis of academics and non-state experts is far ahead of the law, as well as state practice. There is currently no treaty law explicitly addressing the use of military computer network operations in armed conflict. The most in-depth attempt so far to clarify the international legal framework was the 2013 *Tallinn Manual on the International Law Applicable to Cyber Warfare*,[121] a statement of rules by an international group of experts facilitated and led by the NATO Cooperative Cyber Defence Center of Excellence. This was followed in 2017 by *Tallinn Manual 2.0*, an updated and expanded edition.[122]

---

[113] Hall (above n 84) 9–10.

[114] ibid 1, 12.

[115] *NZDF Manual* (above n 80) para 5.2.23; Michael Schmitt (gen ed), *Tallinn Manual on the International Law Applicable to Cyber Warfare* (CUP 2013) (*Tallinn Manual*) rule 20.

[116] ICRC, 'International Humanitarian Law and the Challenges of Contemporary Armed Conflicts', Report No 32IC/15/11 (October 2015) 39.

[117] Respectively: *NZDF Manual* (above n 80) para 5.2.22;, *Tallinn Manual 2.0 on the International Law Applicable to Cyber Operations* (Cambridge: CUP 2017) (*Tallinn Manual 2.0*) Rule 92; *Tallinn Manual 2.0* Rule 100.

[118] Martin C Libicki, 'Cyberspace is Not a Warfighting Domain' (2012) 8(2) *I/S: A Journal of Law and Policy for the Information Society* 321, 322.

[119] ICRC, 'Cyber Warfare' (29 October 2010) www.icrc.org/en/document/cyber-warfare. See eg 'Report of the Group of Governmental Experts on Developments in the Field of Information and Telecommunications in the Context of International Security', UN Doc A/68/98 (24 June 2013) paras 19, 20–23 and report of same name UN Doc A/70/174 (22 July 2015) para 28.

[120] See eg Rain Liivoja, Kobi Leins, and Tim McCormack, 'Emerging Technologies of Warfare', in Liivorja and McCormack (above n 21) 603, 605–11; Schmitt 'Rewired Warfare' (above n 105) 189; Cordula Droege, 'Get Off My Cloud: Cyber Warfare, International Humanitarian Law, and the Protection of Civilians' (2012) 94 *IRRC* 533.

[121] *Tallinn Manual* (above n 115).

[122] NATO Cooperative Cyber Defence Centre of Excellence, 'Tallinn Manual 2.0' https://ccdcoe.org/research/tallinn-manual.

In intergovernmental fora such as the UN Group of Governmental Experts on cyber security, discussion of the applicability of IHL to cyberspace operations has proved very sensitive and difficult. Between 2004 and 2017 it made modest progress in discussing norms, rules, and principles for responsible state behaviour in cyberspace, but it concluded its deliberations in the final session without arriving at a consensus outcome report.[123] It is widely considered to have failed in its objective, due to fundamental disagreements among members, including on the applicability of IHL.[124]

State practice on this issue is either contradictory or classified, and thus undetectable. Although there are some emerging sprouts of *opinio juris* to be found in some states' national cyber-security strategies and other sources, overall states have been reluctant to express *opinio juris* in this rapidly evolving area.[125] The ICRC has acknowledged this is a difficult area, observing that '[c]yber warfare adds a new level of complexity to armed conflict that may pose novel questions for IHL.'[126] While many states appear to consider cyber operations as constituting a potential domain of armed conflict, it remains debatable whether it can be considered a distinct sub-field of IHL.

## B. Electromagnetic Spectrum

The electromagnetic spectrum (EMS) appears to be considered by several states as a separate domain of armed conflict. The EMS encompasses infrared, radar, TV, and radio waves. There is increasing discussion about the possible uses of EMS in armed conflict, such as sensor technology, electronic jammers, and radars.[127] For example, military radar and military communications networks require increasing access to the radio frequency spectrum.[128] The phrase 'electronic warfare' is being used by several states to denote 'manipulation of the electromagnetic spectrum for military advantage.'[129] It is closely related to the concept of 'cyber warfare' (both being forms of electronic communication), but their relationship is the subject of debate.[130] Australia has recognized the EMS as one of 'three

---

[123] Elaine Korzak, 'UN GGE on Cybersecurity: The End of an Era?' *The Diplomat* (31 July 2017) https://thediplomat.com/2017/07/un-gge-on-cybersecurity-have-china-and-russia-just-made-cyberspace-less-safe.

[124] Eg Stefan Soesanto and Fosca Incau, 'The UNGGE is Dead: Time to Fall Forward', European Council on Foreign Relations, Commentary (15 August 2017) www.ecfr.eu/article/commentary_time_to_fall_forward_on_cyber_governance; Michelle Markoff, US Deputy Coordinator for Cyber Issues, 'Explanation of Position at the Conclusion of the 2016–2017 UNGGE on Developments in the Field of Information and Telecommunications in the Context of International Security' (23 June 2017) paras 2, 5 https://www.state.gov/explanation-of-position-at-the-conclusion-of-the-2016-2017-un-group-of-governmental-experts-gge-on-developments-in-the-field-of-information-and-telecommunications-in-the-context-of-international-sec/.

[125] Ann Väljataga, 'Tracing *Opinio Juris* in National Cyber Security Strategy Documents' (NATO CCD COE, Tallinn 2018) 3, 4 https://ccdcoe.org/library/publications/tracing-opinio-juris-in-national-cyber-security-strategy-documents; Michael Schmitt and Sean Watts, 'The Decline of International Humanitarian Law *Opinio Juris* and the Law of Cyber Warfare' (2015) 50 *Texas Int'l LJ* 189, 217.

[126] ICRC 'Cyber Warfare' (above n 119).

[127] US Defense Advanced Research Projects Agency (DARPA), 'Electromagnetic Spectrum and Bandwidth' www.darpa.mil/tag-list?tt=61.

[128] DARPA, 'Congested Frequencies: How to Improve Bandwidth Access for Military and Commercial Use' (2 August 2013) www.darpa.mil/news-events/2013-02-08.

[129] DARPA, 'Electronic Warfare' www.darpa.mil/tag-list?tt-=21.

[130] Patrick Tucker, 'How the Army Plans to Fight a War across the Electromagnetic Spectrum', *Defense One* (26 February 2014) www.defenseone.com/technology/2014/02/inside-armys-first-field-manual-cyber-electromagnetic-war/79498; US Army, 'Field Manual on Cyber Electromagnetic Activities', FM 3-38 (12 February 2014) iv https://fas.org/irp/doddir/army/fm3-38.pdf; Sydney J Freedberg, 'DoD CIO Says

non-environmental domains', alongside 'cyberspace' and 'information'.[131] In 2016, the US Defense Advanced Research Projects Agency (DARPA) has described the EMS as 'the sixth domain of modern warfare',[132] explaining that:

> The effectiveness of combat operations in the land, sea, air, space, and cyber domains depends on our ability to control and exploit the spectrum, because it is critical to our capabilities in navigation. While the spectrum is at the heart of current and future warfare, it remains highly contested and congested, and future info-centric warfare will require more access than ever before.[133]

In 2018 a US Navy policy appeared to recognize the EMS as a warfighting domain 'on par with sea, land, air, space and cyber',[134] while in 2019 a US Defense Primer on Electronic Warfare characterized it somewhat differently, noting that '[a]s electronic warfare affects all military domains—land, air, sea, space, and cyberspace—each of the military services has its own EW capabilities and programs'.[135] Like the use of cyber technologies, the EMS is not a discrete geographic area and it potentially traverses several existing physical domains. A question for future consideration may be whether to regard the EMS solely as a means or method of armed conflict, or as a domain of armed conflict. It remains to be seen whether over time specific IHL rules and principles might be developed in this area.

## C. The Human Mind?

Another emerging area of capability to mention briefly concerns the human mind, and brain–computer interface (BCI) technologies, which connect the brain to certain kinds of devices. This has led some commentators to forecast the human mind as being 'the next domain of warfare'.[136] This body of debate discusses matters such as the potential for brain-controlled drones, metal exoskeletons, and other BCIs aimed at enhancing the power, efficiency, and lethality of soldiers.[137] It has been observed that military research arms like the

---

Spectrum May Become Warfighting Domain', *Breaking Defense* (9 December 2015) www.afcea.org/content/task-force-cyber-awakening-recommendations-due.

[131] Australian Army (above n 4) 13.
[132] DARPA, 'The Sixth Domain of Warfare: DARPA' Excerpt from DARPA-SN-16-59, MTO Office-wide Proposers Day, 20 September 2016 https://alphabetics.info/2016/09/13/the-sixth-domain-of-warfare-darpa (DARPA 2016); Sandra Jontz, 'DoD Tinkering with Making EMS New Warfare Domain', *Signal* (28 January 2016) www.afcea.org/content/Article-dod-tinkering-making-ems-new-warfare-domain.
[133] DARPA 2016 (above n 132).
[134] US Department of the Navy, Chief Information Officer, 'SECNAV Instruction 2400.3 Recognizes the Electromagnetic Spectrum Environment as a Warfighting Battle Space' (12 October 2018) https://www.doncio.navy.mil/ContentView.aspx?id=10869; see also US Under Secretary of the Navy, Thomas B. Modley, 'SECNAV Instruction 2400.3 'Electromagnetic Battle Space' (5 October 2018) https://www.secnav.navy.mil/doni/Directives/02000%20Telecommunications%20and%20Digital%20Systems%20Support/02-400%20Visual%20Information%20Services/2400.3.pdf; Lauren C Williams 'Navy Declares EMS a Full-Fledged Warfighting Domain' (23 October 2018), *Defense Systems* https://defensesystems.com/articles/2018/10/24/navy-electronic-warfare-williams.aspx.
[135] US Congressional Research Service, 'Defense Primer: Electronic Warfare' (30 December 2019) https://fas.org/sgp/crs/natsec/IF11118.pdf.
[136] Chloe Diggins and Clint Arizmendi, 'Hacking the Human Brain: The Next Domain of Warfare': Opinion, *Wired* (12 November 2012) www.wired.com/2012/12/the-next-warfare-domain-is-your-brain; Jonathan D Moreno, *Mind Wars: Brain Science and the Military in the 21st Century* (Bellevue Literary Press 2012).
[137] Diggins and Arizmendi (above n 136) 1.

US DARPA are 'investing in understanding complex neural processes and enhanced threat detection through BCI' and that 'it seems the marriage between neuroscience and military systems will fundamentally alter the future of conflict'.[138] Again, the interrelationships with existing domains has been emphasized:

> Like every other domain of warfare, the mind as the sixth domain is neither isolated nor removed from other domains; coordinated attacks across all domains will continue to be the norm. It's just that military and defense thinkers now need to account for the subtleties of the human mind ... and our increasing reliance upon the brain–computer interface.[139]

Debates about BCIs and IHL are at any early stage, but this brief example illustrates how commentators describe emerging capabilities through the language of 'domains' of warfare.

## D. New Domains or Just New Means/Methods of Armed Conflict?

In addition to the above examples, there are a whole host of other technologies in armed conflict that are the subject of current debate about how IHL should be applied to them, including artificial intelligence and autonomous weapons. Should these kinds of developments be approached as emerging 'domains' of armed conflict or instead thought of as capabilities and/or weapons?

This depends on how broadly one understands the concept of 'domains of armed conflict'. If one interprets it broadly, as new operating environments and capabilities through which armed conflict is conducted, then these new technologies might be regarding as emerging domains of armed conflict. However, whether the extension of armed conflict into new domains has led already to new domains *of IHL*, or will do so in the future, is a separate question. The application of IHL to new technologies in armed conflict is the subject of significant debate[140] and is recognized by the ICRC as one of the key contemporary challenges for IHL.[141] The ICRC is engaged in clarifying the significance of basic IHL concepts, and suggests that although the fundamental rules of IHL apply to new technologies used in armed conflict, '[m]ore tailor-made rules to protect civilians from conflict's future frontlines may be needed'.[142]

Many would argue that land, sea, and air are currently the only three recognized domains of IHL (in the sense of an established sub-set of specialized rules, principles, practice, and analytical commentary) and that, as yet, there are no new sub-sets of IHL applicable to newer technologies. Others would contend that these new capabilities *are* giving rise to

[138] ibid.
[139] ibid.
[140] eg ICRC, 'Special Issue: New Technologies and Warfare' (2002) 94 IRRC 457; Hitoshi Nasu and Rob McLaughlin (eds), *New Technologies and the Law of Armed Conflict* (Asser Press 2014); Dan Saxon (ed), *International Humanitarian Law and the Changing Technology of War* (Martinus Nijhoff 2013).
[141] ICRC 'International Humanitarian Law and the Challenges of Contemporary Armed Conflicts' (above n 116) 38.
[142] ibid.

new domains of IHL. They might support this by arguing either that they are new domains of IHL—in the broad sense of being capabilities subject to general IHL—and/or that they already constitute particular sub-sets of IHL due to the growing body of non-binding guidance instruments that interpret and apply existing IHL by analogy.

The former argument is not contentious; all military activities undertaken by a party in the course of armed conflict are subject to IHL. Although there may be no specific, tailored treaty obligations regarding the conduct of armed conflict through a new technology, the fundamental principles of IHL apply to all military operations, regardless of the specific medium employed. This is reflected in the Martens Clause[143] and the weapons review process of Article 36 of API, requiring states to conduct legal reviews of a new weapon, means, or method of warfare, to determine whether its employment would be prohibited under international law.[144] As the International Court of Justice has affirmed, IHL 'applies to all forms of warfare and to all kinds of weapons, those of the past, those of the present and those of the future'.[145] One just has to apply IHL by analogy to adapt it to new contexts and situations.[146]

The second argument is more contentious, as it raises deeper questions about what constitutes the development of IHL—specifically, whether IHL can be said to be 'developed' through non-legal instruments, and through processes of interpretation and application, rather than only through binding treaty law or customary law. That is, is development through non-binding instruments and commentary sufficient to give rise to a new sub-field of IHL? Some might argue this to be the case, particularly in the current multilateral environment, where state-led development of IHL through binding law is proving so difficult, and where there is an increase in interpretative activity by non-state bodies or groups of experts.[147] Many others, from a more positivist perspective, would argue that such instruments and activities do not give rise to binding legal obligations on states, and are therefore not new IHL—while recognizing of course, that over time some sources may come to be regarded as subsidiary sources for interpreting international law.[148]

This kind of debate shows that the concept of an IHL 'domain' is being used by commentators in different ways. Some use it to denote a physical environment where armed conflict occurs; others use it more broadly to mean a new field of operational activity to which IHL needs to be applied; while yet others use it to refer to a developed sub-set of specialized IHL rules, principles, interpretation, and practice. There is therefore some conflation between the concepts of operational environments and new methods and means of armed conflict, and also between the concepts of 'domains of armed conflict' and 'domains of IHL'.

---

[143] API article 1(2); *NZDF Manual* (above n 80) para 8.10.23; ICRC, *Commentary on the First Geneva Convention* (2nd edn, CUP 2016) para 3296.

[144] API, article 36; see generally ICRC, 'A Guide to the Legal Review of New Weapons, Means and Methods of Warfare' (2006) 88 *IRRC* 931.

[145] *Legality of the Threat or Use of Nuclear Weapons* (Advisory Opinion) [1996] ICJ Rep 266 para 86.

[146] Lachs (above n 87) 19.

[147] For discussion of this increase in activity, see eg Knut Dörmann, 'The Role of Nonstate Entities in Developing and Promoting International Humanitarian Law' (2018) 51 *Vanderbilt J Transn'l L* 713; Michael Schmitt and Sean Watts, 'State *Opinio Juris* and International Humanitarian Law Pluralism', (2015) 91 *Int'l Legal Stud* 171, 175–7.

[148] Statute of the International Court of Justice, as annexed to the Charter of the United Nations (26 June 1945) 1 UNTS xvi, article 38(1)(d).

## 8. Armed Conflict Traversing Multiple Domains

With the trend towards increasing detail and specificity of legal regulation, it is important that each domain (or potential future domain) of IHL is not considered in isolation as a self-contained sub-set, but that they are understood and applied together in a comprehensive, integrated manner.[149] In practice, armed conflict is often conducted across several different operational environments simultaneously. This can occur in different ways. For example, as noted earlier in section 7 'New and Emerging Technologies', military operations on land, at sea, or in the air often use cyber and/or space-based interconnected technologies, which can sometimes make it difficult to isolate precisely where a particular action is occurring. Also, an action may start in one domain and move into, or produce effects in, one or more other domains.

The complexities here are demonstrated by the significant debate about the application of IHL to technologies that produce a remote effect, for example the use of unmanned aerial or underwater vehicles to track and analyse potential targets or to provide platforms for weapons that are activated remotely.[150] Such capabilities challenge the concept of the domain of armed conflict as a discrete physical space, and affect how we understand the area of operations—because the effect may occur in the area of operations while the operator and targeting decisions may be far outside that area.[151] An additional layer of complexity arises due to the fact that military operations are often of a joint nature, undertaken in coalitions with other states[152] who may have different IHL obligations or interpret their obligations differently.

For all these reasons the concept of a battlefield as a discrete, identifiable physical space is now changing,[153] with the importance of integrated approaches to armed conflict evidenced in growing discussions of 'multi-domain battle'[154] (MDB) or 'multi-domain operations'.[155] In essence, the concept concerns the need for a party to armed conflict to synchronize and coordinate its actions across multiple domains, involving both kinetic and non-kinetic operations. It has been explained as having emerged from 'a re-examination of ... previous military concepts and doctrine' caused by 'the rapid growth of capabilities tied to the newly minted space and cyber domains'.[156] It has been argued that the concept 'is being developed

---

[149] This point is underscored throughout the *UK Manual* (above n 34), eg paras 12.1; 13.1; *NZDF Manual* (above n 80) para 1.3.1.

[150] Haines (above n 103) 292. See also Jelena Pejic, 'Extraterritorial Targeting by Means of Armed Drones: Some Legal Implications' (2014) 96 *IRRC* 67.

[151] Vincent Bernard, 'Editorial: Delineating the Boundaries of Violence' (2014) 96 *IRRC* 5.

[152] See Cordula Droege and David Tuck, 'Fighting Together: Obligations and Opportunities in Partnered Warfare', *ICRC Hum Law & Pol* (26 March 2017) https://medium.com/law-and-policy/fighting-together-obligations-and-opportunities-in-partnered-warfare-362c9dfb741a.

[153] Laurie Blank, 'Defining the Battlefield in Contemporary Conflict and Counterterrorism: Understanding the Parameters of the Zone of Combat' (2010) 39 *Georgia J Int'l Comp L* 1.

[154] Kelly McCoy, 'The Road to Multi-Domain Battle: An Origin Story', Modern War Institute at West Point (27 October 2018) https://mwi.usma.edu/road-multi-domain-battle-origin-story.

[155] See eg General SJ Townsend (US Army) 'Accelerating Multi-Domain Operations: Evolution of an Idea': *Military Rev* (September-October 2018) Army University Press www.armyupress.army.mil/Journals/Military-Review/English-Edition-Archives/September-October-2018/Townsend-Multi-Domain-Operations.

[156] Kevin Woods and Thomas Greenwood, 'Multi-Domain Battle: Joint Experiments Needed', *The Australian Naval Institute* (31 March 2018) https://navalinstitute.com.au/multi-domain-battle-joint-experiments-needed. See also David Perkins and James Holmes, 'Multidomain Battle: Converging Concepts Toward a Joint Solution' (2018) 88 *Joint Force Q* 54.

to address the interconnected, *Omni domain* battlespace of the 21st Century',[157] and that it 'promises more fluid, adaptive, and effective operations simultaneously across five domains (land, sea, air, space, and cyber)'.[158]

One illustration is the 2019 US Air Force launch of 'a next-generation airborne surveillance and command and control technology intended to successfully synchronize air, ground, drone and satellite assets onto a single seamless network'.[159] Known as 'Advanced Battle Management and Surveillance', it is planned to reach full maturity in the 2040s and is described by Air Force officials as more of a 'system' than a platform-specific application,[160] intending 'to change the way we execute battlefield management command and control in the multi-domain environment'.[161] More broadly, the US has argued inter alia, that:

> Multi-domain battle is a concept designed to overcome our adversary's integrated defensive capabilities, avoid domain isolation and fracturing, and preserve freedom of action ... The rate and speed of current and future world events will not allow us the time to synchronize federated solutions. In order to present the enemy with multiple dilemmas, we must converge and integrate multi-domain solutions and approaches before the battle starts ... we must maintain a common operating picture.[162]

The MDB concept is the subject of ongoing debate. While it has received some critiques for not being new,[163] others question more fundamentally the heavy military reliance on the concept of domains, arguing for example that the word 'domain' itself 'contains some built-in assumptions regarding how we view warfare that can limit our thinking'.[164] That is, it 'undermines the ability to think holistically', which could 'actually pose an intractable conceptual threat to an integrated joint force'.[165] It appears therefore that the concept needs further testing before its practical utility can be established.[166] For example, how might MDB approaches affect the future drafting of rules of engagement, the delivery of IHL advice, and legal decision-making processes? And more generally, what might be the impact of MDB approaches on the way international lawyers approach IHL?

[157] Amos Fox, 'Multi-Domain Battle: A Perspective on the Salient Features of an Emerging Operational Doctrine', *Small Wars Journal* (21 May 2017) (emphasis added).
[158] Woods and Greenwood (above n 156).
[159] Kris Osborn, 'The Air Force is Creating a System to Manage the Military's Forces in War', *The National Interest* (1 March 2018) https://nationalinterest.org/blog/the-buzz/the-air-force-creating-system-manage-the-militarys-forces-24701M.
[160] ibid.
[161] ibid.
[162] David Perkins, 'Multi-Domain Battle: The Advent of Twenty-First Century War', US Army *Military Rev* (Nov–Dec 2017) www.armyupress.army.mil/Journals/Military-Review/English-Edition-Archives/November-December-2017/Multi-Domain-Battle-The-Advent-of-Twenty-First-Century-War.
[163] Richard Hart Sinnreich, 'Multi-Domain Battle: Old Wine in a New Bottle', *The Lawton Constitution* (30 October 2016); Shmuel Shmuel, 'Multi-Domain Battle: Airland Battle, Once More, With Feeling,' *War on the Rocks* (20 June 2017) https://warontherocks.com/2017/06/multi-domain-battle-airland-battle-once-more-with-feeling.
[164] Erik Heftye, 'Multi-Domain Confusion: All Domains are Not Created Equal', *Real Clear Defense* (26 May 2017).
[165] ibid.
[166] Woods and Greenwood (above n 156) text before n 2.

## A. Moving beyond Specific Domains: Challenges for Legal Analysis

The above points about multi-domain armed conflict and the complex relationships between different domains present challenges for international law interpretation and application, and for the organization and delivery of IHL advice within governments. How may states cultivate deep expertise across all the growing sub-fields of IHL, but also ensure that lawyers 'develop a common operating picture' of how all the sub-fields work together? How is potential 'domain isolation' in IHL to be avoided, and how can we ensure that experts in IHL regarding land, sea, and naval warfare, as well as in space and new technologies, are acting in coordination? If the fast pace of armed conflict requires quick decisions that do not always allow time to 'synchronize federated solutions', it is important to ensure that IHL expertise is made an integral part of the planning, risk assessment, and decision-making involved for MDB approaches. In practice, this underscores the importance of lawyers, with IHL expertise being embedded in joint operations commands; and/or of IHL lawyers advising decision-makers across different parts of a defence force, different military services, and different parts of government to operate in close coordination and ensure their advice is consistent.

MDB appears for now to be more of a planning concept than a concept providing guidance on how to adopt an integrated, holistic approach to IHL application and interpretation. Does existing IHL, together with general international law, already provide an adequate body of rules and principles for evaluating and advising on armed conflict occurring in multiple domains? The reality of contemporary warfare is of operations frequently conducted simultaneously in multiple domains; therefore, applying IHL already requires lawyers to be conversant in multiple sets of rules and principles and to understand how they interact. Applying IHL always relies on the lawyer's interpretive and legal reasoning tools—and these are all that are available in the absence of binding law applicable specifically to new environments or means or methods of armed conflict. An emerging question though may be whether the existing legal reasoning tools continue to be fit for purpose for navigating these challenges in IHL.

The division of IHL into specialized sub-sets reflects the broader trend of fragmentation in international law, with the growing number of fields of particular expertise and practice, and the need for interpretative approaches that help navigate the relationships between them.[167] The issue of norm and regime interaction is therefore not new in international law[168] and certainly not new to IHL—as illustrated by the ongoing, extensive debates about the relationships between IHL and other bodies of international law that also apply in armed conflict (including international human rights law and international criminal law).[169]

---

[167] See M Koskenniemi, *Fragmentation of International Law: Difficulties Arising from the Diversification and Expansion of International Law*, Report of the Study Group of the International Law Commission, UN Doc A/CN.4/L.682 (13 April 2006).

[168] Margaret Young (ed), *Regime Interaction in International Law: Facing Fragmentation* (CUP 2012); Margaret Young, 'Climate Change Law and Regime Interaction' (2011) 5 *Carbon and Climate LR* 147.

[169] See Roberta Arnold and Noelle Quenivet (eds), *International Humanitarian Law and Human Rights Law: Towards a New Merger in International Law* (Martinus Nijoff 2008); Marko Milanovic, 'A Norm Conflict Perspective on the Relationship between International Humanitarian Law and Human Rights Law (2009) 14 *J Conflict & Security L* 459; Sarah McCosker, 'The "Interoperability" of International Humanitarian Law and Human Rights Law: Evaluating the Legal Tools Available to Negotiate their Relationship', in Andrew Byrnes, Mika Hayashi, and Christopher Michaelsen (eds), *International Law in the New Age of Globalization* (Martinus Nijhoff 2013). This is a key reason why some states prefer the terminology 'law of armed conflict' rather than 'IHL', to recognize that there are multiple bodies of law potentially applicable in armed conflict.

General international law already provides several legal tools for managing challenges of coordination and interpretation (including the *lex specialis* principle, among others). Although one might argue that there are no gaps in IHL application because of the lawyers' tools of applying existing law by analogy, it could also be argued that the existing organization of sources of IHL according to specific 'domains' of armed conflict is not sufficiently sophisticated to cater for the increasing complexity of contemporary warfare. Looking to specific domains of armed conflict and domains of IHL may certainly be useful as a first step for an international lawyer to help identify which rules and principles may be most appropriate to apply to a particular situation. However, answering the basic question, 'Is a particular action or set of actions permissible or not permissible within existing IHL?' might not always be answerable simply by recourse to existing domain-specific sources of law or non-binding instruments. Instead, it may potentially require more sophisticated analysis and reasoning. A siloed, source-focused approach may need to be supplemented in the future by more holistic, integrated approaches, perhaps drawing more on systems analysis.

These issues of regime interaction and regulatory fragmentation are faced by multiple areas of law. Several other areas of international law may be further ahead than IHL in developing deeper reflections on these issues, for example in international environmental law, resource management, and climate change, which call for more holistic, integrated approaches to avoid legal silos, and which are sometimes underpinned by systems theory.[170] One illustration is the 'ecosystem' approach, seen as a new paradigm for integrated environmental and biodiversity management.[171] As our conceptualization of the battlefield changes, our legal analytical processes may also need to evolve—perhaps drawing on insights and lessons from these other areas of international law. It may also require recognition that sometimes, legal reasoning will be insufficient to answer particular questions, and that resolution may need to take the form of practical policy decisions.[172]

## 9. Conclusion

Much of the military and academic discourse about contemporary armed conflict demonstrates a continued heavy reliance on the concept of a domain. It serves as a fundamental organizing idea, reflecting the way we conceptualize the battlefield and categorize actions taking place during armed conflict. For much of history, the concept has reflected a fairly simple delineation of different physical battlefield environments, mirrored in the traditional division of states' armed forces into the army, navy, and air force. The domain concept has also exerted a powerful influence in shaping the way we think about, organize, and apply IHL. While much of IHL, including its fundamental principles, applies generally across all armed conflict, it has been supplemented over time by the development of specialized rules

---

[170] Janice Gray, Cameron Holley, and Rosemary Rayfuse, *Trans-Jurisdictional Water Law and Governance* (Routledge 2016) 26, citing Lee Godden, Raymond Ison, and Philip Wallis, 'Water Governance in a Climate Change World: Appraising Systemic and Adaptive Effectiveness' (2011) 25 *Water Resources Management* 3971.
[171] Vito De Lucia, *The 'Ecosystem' Approach in International Environmental Law: Genealogy and Biopolitics* (Routledge 2019).
[172] Milanovic (above n 169); Sarah McCosker, 'The Limitations of Legal Reasoning: Negotiating the Relationships between International Humanitarian Law and Human Rights Law in Detention Situations', in Gregory Rose and Bruce Oswald (eds), *Detention of Non-State Actors Engaged in Hostilities: The Future Law* (Brill/Martinus Nijhoff 2016) 23.

and principles tailored to particular domains. Over the past decades however, major evolutions in warfighting capabilities have caused the emergence of significant challenges to the traditional understanding of the domain and changes in the way the term is used.

The concepts of domains of armed conflict and of specialized sub-sets of IHL still continue to serve us well to the extent that it is possible to isolate certain actions in armed conflict as occurring in a particular physical environment, and to identify what sources of IHL may be applicable to those actions. However, these concepts are less useful in relation to activities occurring in non-physical environments, and to activities occurring across multiple environments, when there are potentially several sub-sets of rules applying simultaneously. Contemporary armed conflict therefore calls for a broader, looser approach to the idea of a domain. When 'domain' is understood less as a physical environment for armed conflict and more broadly as a set of activities that are subject to the application of IHL, then the concept can continue to have some utility in describing new and emerging capabilities.

This chapter has shown that new domains of armed conflict can, over time, sometimes lead to the development of new sub-sets of IHL. However, in the current multilateral environment, many states appear reluctant to develop treaty law to address IHL issues. This means that in the near-to-medium future it is unlikely there will be new treaties with detailed IHL provisions regarding armed conflict in outer space or new warfighting capabilities and technologies—or even amendments to update existing IHL regarding land, sea, and air warfare. Development through customary international law is also likely to be challenging.

It is therefore more likely that many new capabilities would be addressed through non-binding, less-than-treaty status instruments, interpretation, and analysis. This raises fundamental questions about whether such processes can truly be said to constitute 'development' of IHL, or just 'clarification' and 'interpretation', and what the differences are between these concepts (including debates about the relationships between *lex lata* and *de lege ferenda*). In the absence of detailed binding law, one can only apply existing IHL by analogy, informed by the growing number of non-binding sources of interpretation. In this context, the skills of international lawyers in interpreting and applying IHL will have heightened importance—which invites greater attentiveness to the legal reasoning tools, the terminology, and the concepts we deploy as part of those interpretative processes. As this chapter has discussed, the domain concept may no longer be so well adapted or fit for purpose to assess some aspects of contemporary warfare. This suggests there may be value in exploring the potential for more sophisticated analytical approaches for evaluating armed conflict and its compliance with IHL.

# 5

# Persons Covered by International Humanitarian Law: Main Categories

*Lawrence Hill-Cawthorne**

## 1. Introduction

Many of the rules of international humanitarian law (IHL) are structured according to particular categories of persons deemed to be in need of protection in situations of armed conflict. The two principal categories of persons under the law of international armed conflict (IAC) are combatants/prisoners of war (POWs) and civilians. Indeed, this categorization lies at the heart of one of the key principles of IHL, that of the distinction between combatants (being, generally, lawful targets) and civilians (being, generally, not lawful targets). These two principal categories are then further divided, with special (additional) rules applying to certain persons falling within each sub-category, including the wounded, sick, and shipwrecked; women; children; the elderly, disabled, and infirm; refugees and internally displaced persons (IDPs); mercenaries and spies; journalists; and the missing and the dead.

The purpose of this chapter is to offer a taxonomy of these different categories of persons under IHL, elaborating on the distinct features of each. It begins by elaborating on the two principal categories of combatant and civilian. It then moves on to an examination of those sub-categories of persons subject to special rules. For each category examined, we will look in turn at their applicability in the context of IACs and non-international armed conflicts (NIACs).

## 2. Combatants/POWs

### A. International Armed Conflicts

The rules regulating the status and treatment of combatants and POWs in IACs are found principally in the Third Geneva Convention (II) and Additional Protocol I (API).[1] There is considerable overlap between the statuses of combatant and POW. As Knut Ipsen explains, the primary status of combatant gives rise to the secondary status of POW when the

---

* Some of the content of this chapter has been taken from Lawrence Hill-Cawthorne, *Detention in Non-International Armed Conflict*, Oxford Monographs in International Humanitarian and Criminal Law (OUP 2016).

[1] Geneva Convention (III) Relative to the Treatment of Prisoners of War (12 August 1949, entered into force 21 October 1950) 75 UNTS 135 (GCIII); Protocol Additional to the Geneva Conventions of 12 August 1949, and Relating to the Protection of Victims of International Armed Conflicts (adopted 8 June 1977, entered into force 7 December 1978) 1125 UNTS 3 (API).

combatant falls into the power of the enemy.[2] Thus, article 44(1) of API states clearly that '[a]ny combatant . . . who falls into the power of an adverse Party shall be a prisoner of war'.

Article 4 of GCIII specifies upon whom POW status, and thus the protections of GCIII, is conferred. According to this provision, POWs are persons that have fallen into the power of the enemy and belong to one of the following:

    i. The armed forces and the militias and volunteer corps forming part of the forces of a party to the conflict (article 4A(1));

    ii. Other militias or volunteer corps that belong to a party to the conflict and are commanded by a person responsible for subordinates, wear a fixed, distinctive emblem, carry arms openly, and adhere to IHL (article 4A(2));

    iii. Regular forces professing allegiance to an authority not recognised by the detaining power (article 4A(3));

    iv. Non-members authorised to accompany the armed forces (article 4A(4));

    v. Members of crews, including masters, pilots and apprentices of the merchant marine and the crews of civil aircraft of the parties to the conflict where no greater protection is offered under international law (article 4A(5)); and

    vi. Members of a *levée en masse* (that is, a spontaneous civilian uprising) (article 4A(6)).

Article 4B of GCIII specifies two further categories of persons to be *treated as* POWs:

    vii. Demobilised members of the armed forces of occupied territory, if the occupier considers it necessary to intern them, for example, where they have attempted to rejoin the enemy forces, or where they do not comply with a summons for internment, so long as hostilities continue outside the occupied territory (article 4B(1)); and

    viii. Those falling in one of the above categories who are in neutral or non-belligerent states and whom such states are obligated under international law to intern (article 4B(2)).

Persons falling into the above categories are thus entitled to the status of POW should they be captured by enemy armed forces. Though there is considerable overlap between the statuses of combatant and POW, they are not fully coterminous. Thus, whilst all combatants are entitled to POW status upon capture, not all those entitled to POW status are necessarily combatants. This is illustrated by the definition of 'civilian' for the purposes of the rules on the conduct of hostilities in article 50(1) of API:

> A civilian is any person who does not belong to one of the categories of persons referred to in Article 4A(1), (2), (3) and (6) of the Third [Geneva] Convention and in Article 43 of this Protocol [ie combatants].

Persons falling within articles 4A(4) and (5) of GCIII (non-members accompanying the armed forces and members of crews of the merchant marine and civil aircraft) are thus entitled to POW status when captured, yet are civilians rather than combatants. This distinction is an important one, for it is only those entitled to combatant status that have a 'right' to participate in hostilities.[3] By this is meant that such persons are cloaked with

---

[2] Knut Ipsen, 'Combatants and Non-Combatants', in Dieter Fleck (ed), *The Handbook of International Humanitarian Law* (3rd edn, OUP 2013) 79.

[3] Article 43(2) of API.

an immunity from domestic prosecution for their 'ordinary', IHL-compliant acts of war.[4]

For those states that have ratified API, some of the rules on combatant/POW status have controversially been altered.[5] Thus, article 44(1) of API states that, '[a]ny combatant, as defined in Article 43, who falls into the power of an adverse Party shall be a prisoner of war', with article 43(1) of API defining combatants as:

> ... all organized armed forces, groups and units which are under a command responsible to that Party for the conduct of its subordinates, even if that Party is represented by a government or an authority not recognized by an adverse Party. Such armed forces shall be subject to an internal disciplinary system which, *inter alia*, shall enforce compliance with the rules of international law applicable in armed conflict.

API thus brings regular armed forces, as well as organized groups and units, previously dealt with separately under articles 4A(1) and (2) of GCIII, under this single paragraph. The requirements for *all* such forces are now simply that they be organized, operate under a command responsible to a party to the conflict, and have an internal disciplinary system to enforce IHL.[6]

More controversially, article 44(3) of API, after confirming that 'combatants are obliged to distinguish themselves from the civilian population while they are engaged in an attack or in a military operation preparatory to an attack', states that a combatant shall, nevertheless, retain his combatant status if he cannot so distinguish himself, as long as he carries his arms openly during each military engagement and when visible to the enemy whilst deploying for an attack. Article 44(4) then states that failure to honour these requirements shall lead to a forfeiture of POW status, although such persons 'shall, nevertheless, be given protections equivalent in all respects to those accorded to prisoners of war'. The requirement of a fixed, distinctive emblem for combatant/POW status, originally in article 4A(2) (b) of GCIII, has thus been relaxed by article 44(3).[7] Yoram Dinstein argues that this change is to the detriment of the civilian population, for whom the principle of distinction is so essential.[8] That said, article 44(3)'s purpose was to bring the increasingly common phenomenon of guerilla warfare within the POW framework,[9] rather than to change the tradition of the wearing of uniforms by regular state forces.[10]

It was this controversy regarding article 44 of API which was invoked by certain states, including the United States, as a reason for not ratifying API.[11] The ICRC has noted how controversial this provision continues to be, undermining its ability to crystallize as

---

[4] Emily Crawford, *The Treatment of Combatants and Insurgents under the Law of Armed Conflict* (OUP 2010) 52–3.

[5] Yoram Dinstein, *The Conduct of Hostilities under the Law of International Armed Conflict* (2nd edn, CUP 2010) 51.

[6] Ipsen (above n 2) 85.

[7] Leslie Green, *The Contemporary Law of Armed Conflict* (3rd edn, Manchester University Press 2008) 135.

[8] Dinstein, *The Conduct of Hostilities* (above n 5) 53–4. Similarly, see Guy B Roberts, 'The New Rules for Waging War: The Case against Ratification of Additional Protocol I' (1985–86) 26 *VaJ Int'l L* 109, 129; Abraham D Sofaer, 'The Rationale for the United States Decision' (1988) 82 *AJIL* 784, 786.

[9] Yves Sandoz, Christophe Swinarski, and Bruno Zimmerman (eds), *Commentary on the Additional Protocols of 8 June 1977 to the Geneva Conventions of 12 August 1949* (ICRC/Martinus Nijhoff 1987) (AP Commentary) 520–1.

[10] Article 44(7) of API.

[11] Sofaer (above n 8) 786.

customary international law.[12] This controversy is confirmed in doctrine, with a number of commentators considering article 44 of API as binding only on states parties to API.[13] If accurate, this has important consequences for the applicable law in particular conflicts, since, unlike the 1949 Geneva Conventions, the Additional Protocols do not enjoy universal ratification.[14] Indeed, these consequences would be especially pronounced in IACs involving multinational forces, for a captured person may well be entitled to combatant/POW status vis-à-vis one participating state but not vis-à-vis another participating state. It is of course true that API remains widely ratified, even if not by certain states that regularly participate in overseas military operations.[15] Such widespread ratification of treaties has in other contexts been suggested as being capable of contributing to the formation of customary international law.[16] However, some practice of non-state parties in conformity with the conventional rule would ordinarily also be required for that rule to crystallize in custom, unless one were to consider such states to be persistent objectors to the rule.[17]

The treaty law of IAC has thus been developed so as progressively to expand the scope of persons entitled to the status of POW. Indeed, alongside this broadening of the definition of POW has been a desire to ensure persons rightfully entitled to the status are not arbitrarily deprived thereof. Thus, article 5 of GCIII contains the following rule:

> Should any doubt arise as to whether persons, having committed a belligerent act and having fallen into the hands of the enemy, belong to any of the categories enumerated in Article 4, such persons shall enjoy the protection of the present Convention until such time as their status has been determined by a competent tribunal.

There has been some controversy in the practical application of this provision, and it is unclear at what point doubt can be said to have arisen so as to bring into effect the presumption of POW status.[18] Following the 2001 invasion of Afghanistan, for example, the United States did not extend POW status to captured members of the Taliban and al-Qaeda, controversially stating that they had no doubt that such persons were not entitled to that status, thus purporting to exclude the obligation of presumption of POW status under article 5 of GCIII.[19] This position was, however, criticized, for seeking to escape the international

---

[12] Jean-Marie Henckaerts and Louise Doswald-Beck (eds), *Customary International Humanitarian Law, Vol 1: Rules* (CUP 2005) (CIHL) 387–9.

[13] Dinstein, *The Conduct of Hostilities* (above n 5) 54–5; Christopher Greenwood, 'The Law of War (International Humanitarian Law)', in Malcolm D Evans (ed), *International Law* (2nd edn, OUP 2006) 790.

[14] As of 28 January 2020, 196 states are party to the 1949 Geneva Conventions, 174 are party to API, and 169 are party to Protocol Additional to the Geneva Conventions of 12 August 1949, and Relating to the Protection of Victims of Non-International Armed Conflicts (adopted 8 June 1977, entered into force 7 December 1978) 1125 UNTS 609 (APII): http://ihl-databases.icrc.org/applic/ihl/ihl.nsf/xsp/.ibmmodres/domino/OpenAttachment/applic/ihl/ihl.nsf/9EE82DA65960019EC12581E7002F91D2/%24File/IHL_and_other_related_Treaties.pdf?Open.

[15] ibid.

[16] *North Sea Continental Shelf cases (Federal Republic of Germany/Denmark; Federal Republic of Germany/Netherlands)* [1969] ICJ Rep 3 para 73. Though see the caution noted in Peter Tomka, 'Custom and the International Court of Justice' (2013) 12 *Law & Prac Int'l Courts and Tribunals* 195, 207.

[17] *North Sea Continental Shelf* cases (above n 16) para 76.

[18] See eg Yasmin Naqvi, 'Doubtful Prisoner-of-War Status' (2002) 84 *IRRC* 571.

[19] Marie-Louise Tougas, 'Determination of Prisoner of War Status', in Andrew Clapham, Paolo Gaeta, and Marco Sassòli (eds), *The 1949 Geneva Conventions: A Commentary* (OUP 2015) 950.

obligation to presume entitlement to POW status in a situation in which doubt could reasonably be said to have existed.[20]

API sought to prevent the kinds of claims made by the United States in the above case by extending the presumption to a greater number of situations. Thus, article 45(1) of API states:

> A person who takes part in hostilities and falls into the power of an adverse Party shall be presumed to be a prisoner of war, and therefore shall be protected by the Third Convention, if he claims the status of prisoner of war, or if he appears to be entitled to such status, or if the Party on which he depends claims such status on his behalf by notification to the detaining Power or to the Protecting Power. Should any doubt arise as to whether any such person is entitled to the status of prisoner of war, he shall continue to have such status and, therefore, to be protected by the Third Convention and this Protocol until such time as his status has been determined by a competent tribunal.

The consequence of the above provision is that states parties to API must now extend the presumption of POW status to anyone who is captured that has taken part in hostilities, where they claim POW status, they appear to be entitled to such status, or their national state claims it on their behalf.

It is clear from the above provisions that it is assumed that persons will want to be granted POW status. Indeed, the presumptions in articles 5 of GCIII and 45 of API apply, respectively, to persons that have committed a belligerent act and taken part in hostilities. It is especially for such persons that being labelled a POW protected by GCIII (as opposed to a civilian protected by GCIV) would be advantageous, as combatant immunity would apply to ensure that they were not prosecuted for their 'ordinary', IHL-compliant acts of war. In other circumstances, however, this presumption that persons wish to assert POW status may be ill-founded, and certain persons that are detained as POWs solely on the ground of their presumed combatant status may wish to challenge that status; GCIII does not appear to provide any such mechanism. Problems have arisen in this regard in practice, where the detaining authority claims that a person's administrative detention for the duration of hostilities is justified on the basis that they are assumed to be a combatant/POW and thus are detained in accordance with article 21 of GCIII, yet the detainee purports to be a civilian and thus not subject to automatic administrative detention for the duration of the hostilities.[21] Such situations have arisen with respect to United Kingdom and US detentions in the 1990–91 Gulf War and following the 2003 Iraq invasion; in these cases, both states applied the tribunals under article 5 of GCIII to hear challenges by detainees as to their assumed combatant/POW status.[22]

---

[20] See eg Inter-American Commission on Human Rights (IACommHR), *Detainees in Guantanamo Bay, Cuba* (Request for Precautionary Measures) (2002) 41 *ILM* 532.

[21] On the rules governing detention of civilians in IACs, see Geneva Convention (IV) Relative to the Protection of Civilian Persons in Time of War (adopted 12 August 1949, entered into force 21 October 1950) 75 UNTS 287 (GCIV) articles 41–43 and 78.

[22] Nils Mercer, 'The Future of Article 5 Tribunals in the Light of Experiences in the Iraq War, 2003', in Caroline Harvey, James Summers, and Nigel D White (eds), *Contemporary Challenges to the Laws of War* (CUP 2014) (on UK practice in Iraq following the 2003 invasion); Naqvi (above n 18) at 586 (on US policy during the Gulf War) and 588 (on UK practice during the Gulf War); Gordon Risius, 'Prisoners of War and the United Kingdom', in Peter Rowe (ed), *The Gulf War 1990–91 in International and English Law* (Routledge, 1993) 296 (also on UK practice during the Gulf War).

A similar situation was faced by the International Criminal Tribunal for the former Yugoslavia (ICTY), in a case in which the defendants claimed that persons whom they were said to have arbitrarily detained were in fact lawfully held as combatants/POWs. The ICTY held that persons are to be presumed to be civilians, and cannot be arrested as combatants/POWs, *unless clear evidence to the contrary exists.* In *Krnojelac*, the Trial Chamber held that possession of weapons at the time of their arrest did not 'create a reasonable doubt as to the civilian status of most of the Muslim detainees'.[23] Similarly, in *Simić* et al, the Trial Chamber did not accept that:

> ... allegations about weapons possession, in itself, creates a reasonable doubt as to the civilian status of the persons arrested and detained for possession of weapons ... The fact that most of them were arrested from their homes, combined with a lack of evidence that they participated in an armed conflict, clearly shows that they were not combatants, but rather, civilians, and consequently were not taken as prisoners of war.[24]

It seems that, in cases where a person has not clearly taken part in hostilities (in which case a presumption of combatant status and its immunizing of belligerent acts would benefit the individual), the presumption should be of civilian status, such that they can only be detained where the procedures governing detention of civilians are followed.[25]

## B. Non-International Armed Conflicts

The issue of status is especially controversial in the context of NIACs, where persons are not clearly categorized under the applicable rules. Thus, whilst Common Article 3 refers to 'members of the armed forces' and APII refers to 'civilians', suggesting some distinction between categories of persons, no elaborated legal categories of combatant and civilian apply under the treaty law of NIAC. Indeed, there is no combatant or POW status in NIACs, at least in the form in which it exists in IACs, with the consequence that those participating in hostilities on either the state or non-state side are not entitled to combatant immunity under international law; states have consistently rejected the claim that armed opposition groups, even if fighting in compliance with IHL, cannot be prosecuted under domestic criminal law for their actions, which would be the consequence of extending combatant immunity to NIACs.[26] Instead, the current *lex lata*, by laying down no rule of combatant immunity in NIACs, leaves states free to immunize (under their domestic law) their own armed forces from domestic prosecution whilst prosecuting armed opposition groups even for IHL-compliant acts. Indeed, the ICRC in its Customary International Humanitarian Law Study (CIHL Study) makes clear that, under both treaty and customary law, combatant status does not apply in NIACs, though sometimes the term 'combatant' is applied in such situations in a lay manner.[27]

---

[23] *Prosecutor v Krnojelac* (Trial Judgment) ICTY-97-25, Trial Judgment, 15 March 2002 para 117.
[24] *Prosecutor v Simić et al* (Trial Judgment) ICTY-95-9-T (17 October 2003) para 659.
[25] See above n 21.
[26] Sandesh Sivakumaran, *The Law of Non-International Armed Conflict* (OUP 2012) 71; Crawford (above n 4) 104; Yoram Dinstein, *Non-International Armed Conflicts in International Law* (CUP 2014) 219.
[27] CIHL 12–13.

It is thus clear that there is no status of combatant/POW under the law of NIAC in the sense of individuals enjoying combatant immunity and POW status. More controversial, however, is whether IHL draws a distinction between civilians and persons participating in hostilities (whether state or non-state) for the purposes of targeting. Thus:

> While it is generally recognized that members of State armed forces in non-international armed conflict do not qualify as civilians, treaty law, State practice, and international jurisprudence have not unequivocally settled whether the same applies to members of organized armed groups (i.e. the armed forces of non-State parties to an armed conflict).[28]

The question thus remains open as to whether members of non-state armed groups (NSAGs) may be targeted on the basis of their status alone, as is the case for combatants in IACs, or whether they are to be treated as civilians, targetable only if and for so long as they directly participate in hostilities.

There is significant debate on this point.[29] In its CIHL Study, for example, the ICRC notes that 'practice is ambiguous as to whether members of armed opposition groups are considered members of armed forces or civilians'.[30] On the other hand, in its *Guidance on Direct Participation in Hostilities,* the ICRC states that, given the reference to 'civilians' in APII and their general protection from attack, it might reasonably be presumed that there is a category of 'non-civilians' that are not entitled to such immunity from targeting under IHL.[31] Indeed, this has been recognized by the ICTY Appeals Chamber.[32]

However, the question then arises as to what the parameters of such a category are; that is, who constitutes 'non-civilians' for the purposes of conduct of hostilities. There is no guidance in the treaty rules applicable in NIACs on this point. A number of different approaches have been proffered. The ICRC's *Guidance on Direct Participation in Hostilities,* for example, takes the view that, to comply with IHL, only members of the state armed forces and members of armed opposition groups who have a 'continuous combat function' may be targeted *ipso facto,* that is, on the same status-based grounds as combatants in IACs.[33] In pertinent part, 'individuals whose continuous function involves the preparation, execution, or command of acts or operations amounting to direct participation in hostilities are assuming a continuous combat function'.[34] Others, however, have criticized this definition of 'non-civilians' in NIACs on the grounds that it is too narrow, defining those members of armed opposition groups that can be targeted on the basis of their status more restrictively than those members of the state armed forces that are so targetable; this, so the argument goes, undermines IHL's important principle of the equality of obligations between belligerents.[35]

---

[28] Nils Melzer, *Interpretive Guidance on the Notion of Direct Participation in Hostilities under International Humanitarian Law* (ICRC 2009) (*DPH Guidance*) 27.
[29] For an overview of this debate, see Sivakumaran, *Law of Non-International Armed Conflict* (above n 26) 359–63.
[30] CIHL 17.
[31] *DPH Guidance*, 28 ('As the wording and logic of Article 3 GCI–IV and Additional Protocol II (APII) reveals, civilians, armed forces, and organized armed groups of the parties to the conflict are mutually exclusive categories also in non-international armed conflict').
[32] *Prosecutor v Martić* (Appeals Judgment) ICTY-95-11-A (8 October 2008) paras 300–302.
[33] *DPH Guidance*, 27.
[34] ibid 34.
[35] Kenneth Watkin, 'Opportunity Lost: Organized Armed Groups and the ICRC "Direct Participation in Hostilities" Interpretive Guidance' (2010) 42 *NYU J Int'l L & Pol'y* 641, 675–8; Sivakumaran, *Law of Non-International Armed Conflict* (above n 26) 360–2.

Sandesh Sivakumaran, for example, proposes instead a model that contains both a de jure notion of membership, based on the membership rules of the NSAG, and a de facto notion, based on 'ongoing direct participation in hostilities by persons who are not *de jure* members'.[36] By including de jure membership, which itself includes members of armed groups not performing a combat function, a broader definition of membership than the ICRC's *Direct Participation Guidance* is endorsed by Sivakumaran's approach.

Though it might be argued that it is now accepted that the law of NIAC does not prohibit the targeting of members of armed opposition groups on the basis of that status alone, it is clear that there is considerable disagreement over the appropriate definition of membership of such groups. Moreover, it must be emphasized that the above only considers the legality of targeting non-state fighters *under IHL*; other bodies of international law, such as international human rights law, may well place additional legal restrictions on whom state forces may lethally target in a NIAC.[37]

## 3. Civilians

### A.  International Armed Conflicts

When the four Geneva Conventions were adopted in 1949, the first three all 'updated' pre-existing treaties, thus furthering the protections granted to combatants rendered *hors de combat*, either as a result of being wounded, sick, or shipwrecked (in the case of GCI and GCII), or as a result of being taken as a prisoner of war (in the case of GCIII). GCIV, however, in extending protections to *civilians*, represented a novel development, for it was the first treaty that sought to protect this particular category of persons in armed conflict. Prior to 1949, civilians were in a precarious position, regulated (at the international level) principally by custom, which was prone to change in light of state practice. Indeed, such changes in customary law were clearly visible in the first half of the twentieth century. The preceding centuries had seen the gradual development of the notion that war represented a conflict between states and not between entire populations, enabling enemy civilian populations increasingly to be respected during wartime.[38] In contrast, state practice during the First and Second World Wars undermined this considerably:

> There was a tendency in the nineteenth century to draw a dividing line between civilians and the armed forces and to leave the former as much as possible undisturbed. The development, however, since the First World War tends to revert to the original practice of identifying the individual with his home State ... Civilians who are resident in the country of a belligerent and are of enemy nationality may, therefore, be interned like prisoners of war, or be subjected to other restrictions, as may be required in the interest of national security.[39]

---

[36]  Sivakumaran, *Law of Non-International Armed Conflict* (above n 26) 360.

[37]  Marco Sassòli and Laura M Olson, 'The Relationship between International Humanitarian and Human Rights Law Where It Matters: Admissible Killing and Internment of Fighters in Non-International Armed Conflicts' (2008) 90 *IRRC* 599, 613–16.

[38]  John Westlake, *International Law Part II: War* (CUP 1907) 32–8; Norman Bentwich, 'International Law as Applied by England in the War: The Treatment of Alien Enemies' (1915) 9 *AJIL* 642, 646.

[39]  Georg Schwarzenberger, *A Manual of International Law* (Stevens 1947) 80.

The incorporation of civilians as a protected category of persons into the treaty regime governing IACs was thus an important milestone in 1949.

GCIV does not, as such, define the category of 'civilians'. Instead, it defines the category of persons protected by the Convention in article 4, which, with a view to minimizing gaps in the protections accorded to persons in armed conflict, states this in negative terms. Thus, persons protected by GCIV are those that are in the hands of the enemy and are not protected by the first three Geneva Conventions.[40] Further limitations, however, are placed on GCIV's application. First, with some exceptions in the Convention, it generally only applies where the individual is in the hands of a party to the conflict of which they are not a national.[41] Second, it only applies where the individual's national state is bound by the Convention.[42] Third, it does not apply to nationals of neutral states in the territory of a belligerent state, and nationals of co-belligerent states, as long as their states maintain normal diplomatic relations with the state in whose hands they are.[43] The consequence of the way in which article 4 of GCIV is drafted is that the Convention protects only a subset of what might normally be referred to as 'civilians'. GCIV then goes on to specify a range of protections for such persons, including general protections for all civilian populations, as well as specific protections for civilians in enemy territory and occupied territory.

Whereas GCIV focuses on the so-called 'Geneva rules', that is, protection of civilians that are in the hands of an enemy state (such as those interned by that state), API provides further 'Hague' rules on the protection of civilians from attack, such as a prohibition on the direct targeting of peaceful civilians and the obligation not to carry out attacks that may be expected to cause disproportionate harm to civilian persons or objects. In so doing, API specifically defines the category of 'civilians' that are entitled to such immunity from attack as 'any person who does not belong to one of the categories of persons referred to in article 4 A (1), (2), (3) and (6) of the Third Convention and in article 43 of this Protocol. In case of doubt whether a person is a civilian, that person shall be considered to be a civilian.'[44] The category of 'civilians' protected under API from attack is thus framed more broadly than the general category of persons protected under GCIV. In particular, the rules on attacks under API apply with respect to a state's actions on its own territory and towards its own civilian population, whereas the majority of the rules in GCIV, as noted above, apply only with respect to civilians of enemy nationality.[45]

## B.  Non-International Armed Conflicts

As noted above, whilst the combatant/civilian distinction lies at the heart of the law of IAC, such categories are far less elaborated in NIACs. Indeed, Common Article 3 itself does not refer to civilians, but rather lays down basic protections for all persons *hors de combat*, which

---

[40]  GCIV article 4(4).

[41]  ibid article 4(1). The ICTY Appeals Chamber in *Prosecutor v Tadić* (Appeals Judgment) ICTY-94-1-A (15 July 1999) paras 166–169, however, took the view that the drafting history and object and purpose of GCIV, together with the trend in modern warfare that now sees conflicts as being inter-*ethnic* rather than primarily inter-*state*, necessitate a reading of the test for the applicability of GCIV as being based not on nationality but allegiance.

[42]  GCIV article 4(2).

[43]  ibid.

[44]  API article 50(1).

[45]  ibid article 49(2); AP Commentary 604–5.

includes civilians (as ordinarily understood), as well as members of the armed forces that have laid down their arms or been detained. Furthermore, as has already been discussed, though APII does refer to 'civilians' as being entitled to immunity from attack until and for such time as they directly participate in hostilities, this term is not defined, and there is some disagreement over whether members of armed opposition groups are considered civilians for these purposes, targetable only where they directly participate in hostilities.

## 4. A Third Category?

In addition to the basic categories of combatant and civilian, there is a debate regarding a possible third category of persons under the law of IAC—so-called 'unlawful combatants' or 'unprivileged belligerents'—who, it is claimed, directly participate in hostilities without being entitled to POW status under GCIII or protected person status under GCIV. This debate was revived in light of the so-called 'war on terror' and resulting detentions at Guantánamo Bay, Cuba, by the US Department of Defence of those it considered 'unlawful enemy combatants' (including members of the Taliban and al-Qaeda).[46] In examining the status of the Taliban and al-Qaeda, Christopher Greenwood, for example, implied that they fall outside both GCIII and GCIV.[47] Dinstein, similarly, argues that, '[a] person who engages in military raids by night, while purporting to be an innocent civilian by day, is neither a civilian nor a lawful combatant. He is an unlawful combatant.'[48]

Such arguments, however, are difficult to reconcile with the text of the Geneva Conventions. As Knut Dörmann argues, the text makes it clear that no third category of person exists, since the scope of GCIV is defined negatively, as protecting those not protected by the other Conventions.[49] Moreover, given that article 5 of GCIV was designed as a derogation provision for those individuals who may be characterized as unlawful combatants, it is clear that GCIV was intended to cover such persons.[50] Indeed, state practice, much of which has been in response to post-9/11 US detention practices, similarly confirms the non-existence of this alleged third category.[51] Thus, Emily Crawford notes that, '[g]iven the almost uniform resistance to US attempts to proclaim a "Geneva" status of "unlawful enemy combatant", it is doubtful such a legal category exists.'[52] Consequently, where not entitled to POW status, if its article 4 conditions are met, an individual is protected by GCIV, albeit subject to article 5 of GCIV.[53] Moreover, for the purposes of targeting, persons not lawfully

---

[46] Crawford (above n 4) 56–61; Ipsen (above n 2) 83.

[47] Christopher Greenwood, 'International Law and the "War Against Terrorism"' (2002) 78 *Int'l Affairs* 301, 316.

[48] Dinstein, *The Conduct of Hostilities* (above n 5) 36. For a slightly different approach, see Jason Callen, 'Unlawful Combatants and the Geneva Conventions' (2004) 44 *Va J Int'l L* 1025 (arguing that GCIV applies to spies/saboteurs in enemy territory but not to 'unlawful combatants' on the battlefield, invoking the distinction drawn in Richard R Baxter, 'So-Called "Unprivileged Belligerency": Spies, Guerrillas, and Saboteurs' (1951) 28 *BYBIL* 323).

[49] Knut Dörmann, 'The Legal Situation of "Unlawful/Unprivileged Combatants"' (2003) 85 *IRRC* 45, 49.

[50] ibid 50.

[51] See eg Peter Tange, 'Netherlands State Practice for the Parliamentary Year 2007-2008' (2007) 38 *NYIL* 263, 290; HCJ 769/02, *Public Committee against Torture in Israel et al v The Government of Israel et al*, 57(6) PD 285 (Israeli Supreme Court) paras [26]–[28]; *A v State of Israel*, CrimA 3261/08, 11 June 2008 (Israeli Supreme Court) para 12; UK Ministry of Defence, *Joint Doctrine Publication 1-10: Captured Persons (CPERS)* (3rd edn, Ministry of Defence 2015) 1–16 para 141.

[52] Crawford (above n 4) 60.

[53] Similarly, see Jean Pictet (ed), *Commentary: Geneva Convention IV Relative to the Protection of Civilian Persons in Time of War* (ICRC 1958) (GCIV Commentary) 51; Dörmann (above n 49) 49; Derek Jinks, 'The

entitled to combatant status are civilians, targetable only if and for so long as they directly participate in hostilities.

## 5. Persons Entitled to Special Protections

The two fundamental categories of combatant/POW and civilian are further sub-divided into certain categories of persons that are subject to further special protections due to their particularly vulnerable situation. The following sections will explore some of the key sub-categories of special protection, including the wounded, sick, and shipwrecked; women; children; the elderly, disabled, and infirm; refugees and IDPs; journalists; and the missing and the dead.

### A. Wounded, Sick, and Shipwrecked

#### 1. International armed conflicts

The category of wounded, sick, and shipwrecked persons has an important place in the history of IHL. Indeed, it was his witnessing of the terrible suffering and fate of the wounded following the Battle of Solferino in 1859 that led Henry Dunant to call for the establishment of relief societies and the adoption of binding standards at the international level on the protection of the wounded and sick in battle.[54] The consequence was the establishment of what later became the ICRC and the adoption of the first multilateral treaty on the laws of war, the 1864 Geneva Convention for the Amelioration of the Condition of the Wounded in Armies in the Field.[55] This was subsequently updated and extended to wounded, sick, and shipwrecked members of the armed forces at sea[56] and, later, wounded and sick members of the civilian population.[57] These various codifications sought to extend special protections to these categories of persons. For example, GCI prescribes not only the humane treatment of wounded, sick, and shipwrecked members of the armed forces by whatever power in whose hands they fall,[58] but also the more onerous obligation of searching for and collecting wounded and sick combatants.[59]

The categories of persons entitled to protection under this heading have, in line with the other categories of protected persons under IHL, been expanded over time. With respect

---

Declining Significance of POW Status' (2004) 45 *Harvard Int'l LJ* 367, 381–6; Marco Sassòli, 'The Status of Persons Held in Guantánamo under International Humanitarian Law' (2004) 2 *JICJ* 96, 100–2; Crawford (above n 4) 60–1.

[54]  Henry Dunant, *The Battle of Solferino* (ICRC 1986).
[55]  (22 August 1864, entered into force 22 June 1965) 129 CTS 361.
[56]  See eg Hague Convention (III) for the Adaptation to Maritime Warfare of the Principles of the Geneva Convention of 22 August 1864 (adopted 29 July 1899, entered into force 4 September 1900) 187 CTS 443; Geneva Convention for the Amelioration of the Condition of the Wounded and Sick in Armies in the Field (adopted 6 July 1906, entered into force 9 August 1907) 11 LNTS 440; Geneva Convention (I) for the Amelioration of the Wounded and Sick in the Armed Forces in the Field (adopted 12 August 1949, entered into force 21 October 1950) 75 UNTS 31 (GCI), and Geneva Convention (II) for the Amelioration of the Condition of the Wounded, Sick and Shipwrecked Members of Armed Forces at Sea (adopted 12 August 1949, entered into force 12 October 1949) 75 UNTS 85 (GCII).
[57]  GCIV articles 16-22; API Part II.
[58]  GCI article 12; GCII article 12.
[59]  GCI article 15; GCII article 18.

to wounded, sick, and shipwrecked members of the armed forces, whilst the 1864 Geneva Convention applied only to 'combatants',[60] GCI and GCII now extend the relevant protections to all such persons who would otherwise qualify for POW status under article 4 of GCIII (which, as noted in section 2 'Combatants/POWs' above, is a broader category than that of 'combatants').[61] GCI and GCII thus provide additional protections to a specific category of those persons otherwise covered by GCIII; 'the applicability of the latter Convention, will, as a matter of fact rather than law, only materialize in full once wounded and sick military personnel are brought back behind the lines and are on the way to convalescence and cure'.[62]

Though the protective category of wounded and sick civilians is subject to the general scope of application of GCIV (on which see section 3 'Civilians' above), certain general rules on search and protection of wounded and sick civilians, as well as on protection of the infirm and expectant mothers, are laid down that bind all states party to an IAC, even with respect to their own nationals.[63] There are also other specific protections for wounded and sick civilians of enemy nationality when in the territory of a party to the conflict and in occupied territory (including when interned).[64]

These parallel developments in the protection of wounded, sick, and shipwrecked combatants and wounded and sick civilians were brought together under API, which applies the same protective regime to wounded, sick, and shipwrecked persons of combatant and civilian status.[65] This protective regime also does not distinguish between nationals of the relevant state and enemy nationals.[66] These API rules on the protection of wounded, sick, and shipwrecked persons, unlike the API rules noted above on combatant/POW status, are generally accepted as reflecting customary international law; they therefore apply equally to states that are party and states that are not party to API.[67]

Importantly, API, unlike the treaties preceding it, defined what was meant by the term 'wounded', 'sick' and 'shipwrecked'. Thus, article 8(a) of API defines 'wounded' and 'sick' to mean:

> ... persons, whether military or civilian, who, because of trauma, disease or other physical or mental disorder or disability, are in need of medical assistance or care and who refrain from any act of hostilities. These terms also cover maternity cases, new-born babies and other persons who may be in need of immediate medical assistance or care, such as the infirm or expectant mothers, and who refrain from any act of hostility.

Article 8(b) then defines 'shipwrecked' to mean:

> ... persons, whether military or civilian, who are in peril at sea or in other waters as a result of misfortunate affecting them or the vessel or aircraft carrying them and who refrain

---

[60]   Geneva Convention for the Amelioration of the Condition of the Wounded in Armies in the Field (adopted 22 August 1864, entered into force 22 June 1865) article 6.

[61]   GCI article 13, and GCII article 13.

[62]   Jann Kleffner, 'Protection of the Wounded, Sick, and Shipwrecked', in Dieter Fleck (ed), *The Handbook of International Humanitarian Law* (3rd edn, OUP 2013) 323.

[63]   GCIV article 16.

[64]   See eg ibid articles 38(2) and 57.

[65]   API articles 8(a) and (b).

[66]   ibid article 9(1).

[67]   Kleffner (above n 62) 324; CIHL rules 109, 110, and 111.

from any act of hostility. These persons, provided that they continue to refrain from any act of hostility, shall continue to be considered shipwrecked during their rescue until they acquire another status under the Conventions or this Protocol.

API thus helped to clarify and consolidate the existing categories and rules on the protection of wounded, sick, and shipwrecked persons.

### 2. Non-international armed conflicts

From the first codification of the rules applicable in NIACs in 1949, IHL incorporated basic protections on wounded and sick persons. Thus, Common Article 3(1) requires that persons placed *hors de combat* by, inter alia, sickness or wounds, be humanely treated, and Common Article 3(2) requires that '[t]he wounded and sick shall be collected and cared for'. As the ICRC Commentary explains, 'Article 3 here reaffirms, in generalized form, the fundamental principle underlying the original Geneva Convention of 1864'.[68]

More detailed rules on the protection of the wounded, sick, and shipwrecked in NIACs were incorporated in APII.[69] Though these treaty provisions as such only apply in a sub-set of NIACs,[70] the ICRC takes the view that the rules on these particular categories of persons found in the law of IAC also apply as custom in NIACs.[71]

## B. Women

### 1. International armed conflicts

A number of provisions in both GCIV and API extend special protections to female civilians. GCIV, for example, requires that women internees that are protected persons under that Convention have separate sleeping quarters and sanitary facilities to male internees.[72] Moreover, article 27, after setting forth the basic requirement of humane treatment of all persons protected by GCIV, states in paragraph 2 that, '[w]omen shall be especially protected against any attack on their honour, in particular against rape, enforced prostitution, or any form of indecent assault'. Article 76 of API repeats this rule,[73] adding to it a requirement that pregnant women and mothers with dependent children that are arrested or detained as a result of the conflict 'shall have their cases considered with the utmost priority' and, '[t]o the maximum extent feasible', shall not be sentenced to death.[74] Importantly, as noted above, the protections for civilians under API, including these specific protections for women, apply to a broader group of persons than the rules in GCIV, including to the nationals of the state in whose hands they find themselves.[75]

---

[68] GCIV Commentary 40.
[69] APII articles 7–12.
[70] On this, and on the various categories of armed conflict more generally, see Marko Milanovic and Vidan Hadzi-Vidanovic, 'A Taxonomy of Armed Conflict', in Nigel White and Christian Henderson (eds), *Research Handbook on International Conflict and Security Law* (Edward Elgar 2013).
[71] Kleffner (above n 62) 322. Though cf James Benoit, 'Mistreatment of the Wounded, Sick and Shipwrecked by the ICRC Study on Customary International Humanitarian Law' (2008) 11 *YIHL* 175, 199–203, 210–12, 214–15.
[72] GCIV article 85(4).
[73] API article 76(1).
[74] ibid articles 76(2) and (3).
[75] Dinstein, *The Conduct of Hostilities* (above n 5) 156.

These brief provisions on the protection of women in armed conflict appear wholly inadequate when viewed against the background of actual practice. Indeed, practice demonstrates that '[s]exual violence against women in armed conflict is structural, part of the instrumentality of conflict and often inherent to its very aims' (as opposed to being a rare by-product, which these IHL provisions imply).[76] Practice also shows that gender-based discrimination against women in armed conflict goes far beyond sexual violence, such as in the burdensome domestic and bread-winning responsibilities that fall on them.[77]

To a certain extent, international criminal law has helped to address some of these silences in IHL. The ad hoc international criminal tribunals established in the 1990s recognized a number of gender-based violations, including forced labour and forced marriage, as the crimes underlying certain war crimes, certain crimes against humanity, and genocide.[78] Yet many problems remain here, such as the failure to engage with the underlying causes of gender-based crimes and the fact that sexual violence is often a core aspect of the manner in which armed conflict is conducted.[79] There is also the concern that the legal developments in this field have been slow to respond to sexual violence committed against men and boys in armed conflict.[80]

Finally, though the above has focused on protections for civilian women, special treaty provisions also exist for female members of the armed forces. For example, GCIII requires that female prisoners of war are granted treatment as favourable as that of male POWs and are given separate dormitories and bathrooms.[81] Both female civilians and female combatants/POWs are thus the subject of special (albeit limited) rules under IHL.

### 2. Non-international armed conflicts

As with the law of IAC, the basic treaty rules applicable in NIACs on the protection of civilians apply equally to both women and men.[82] With respect to specific rules for the protection of women in armed conflict, Common Article 3 is silent. APII, however, does contain certain rules specific to women, such as a requirement to hold women internees separately from men and under the immediate supervision of women,[83] and a prohibition of carrying out the death sentence on pregnant women or mothers of young children.[84] An absolute prohibition of rape and enforced prostitution also applies under APII and protects both male and female victims.[85] Customary IHL also contains a general rule applicable in all armed conflicts that '[t]he specific protection, health and assistance needs of women affected by armed conflict must be respected'.[86]

---

[76] Christine Chinkin, 'Gender and Armed Conflict', in Andrew Clapham and Paolo Gaeta (eds), *The Oxford Handbook of International Law in Armed Conflict* (OUP 2014) 680.

[77] ibid.

[78] ibid 687.

[79] See also the alternative critique in Karen Engle, 'Feminism and Its (Dis)contents: Criminalizing Wartime Rape' (2005) 99 *AJIL* 778.

[80] Sandesh Sivakumaran, 'Sexual Violence against Men in Armed Conflict' (2007) 18 *EJIL* 253.

[81] See GCIII articles 14, 25 and 29, respectively.

[82] Françoise Krill, 'The Protection of Women in International Humanitarian Law' (1985) 25 *IRRC* 337.

[83] APII article 5(2)(a); CIHL rule 119.

[84] APII article 6(4).

[85] ibid article 4(2)(e); CIHL rule 93.

[86] CIHL rule 134.

As with the law of IAC, these limited rules applicable in NIACs leave a number of gaps. More generally, the different roles of women in armed conflict have traditionally been under-explored. This is true, for example, regarding the position of female members of NSAGs in NIACs, which has received little research.[87] Indeed, it has been reported that certain women join such groups in order to prevent further sexual violence against them.[88] The limited rules in IHL specifically addressing women demonstrate this historical lack of research into their differing roles in armed conflict.

## C. Children

### 1. International armed conflicts

Children are also a specially protected category of person under IHL. GCIV, for example, contains provisions on evacuation of civilian children from besieged areas and care for children under fifteen years of age that are orphaned or separated from their families.[89] Article 77(1) of API contains the basic rule that '[c]hildren shall be the object of special respect and shall be protected against any form of indecent assault. The Parties to the conflict shall provide them with the care and aid they require, whether because of their age or for any other reason.' Other rules include the requirement that children, where detained, shall be held in quarters separate from adults (except where held as a family), and that no person under eighteen years of age shall be executed for committing an offence related to the conflict.[90]

Further rules specific to children focus, inter alia, on recruitment of child soldiers. The upper age limit of this particular category of persons is, however, contentious. Thus, whereas API prohibits recruitment of children under fifteen years of age and requires states to take all feasible measures to ensure that children under fifteen years of age do not take a direct part in hostilities,[91] the Optional Protocol to the 1989 Convention on the Rights of the Child prohibits the *compulsory* recruitment of children under eighteen years of age and requires states to take all feasible measures to ensure that children below that higher age threshold do not take a direct part in hostilities.[92] Under custom, the ICRC has argued that, though there is no 'uniform practice with respect to the minimum age for recruitment, there is agreement that it should not be below 15 years of age'.[93]

Special rules on the protection of children thus exist under both of the two principal categories of persons in IHL, those of combatants/POWs and civilians. This is true also of many of the other categories of special protection explored in this chapter, such as women or wounded and sick persons. However, what is especially interesting here is that these rules on recruitment into the armed forces of children do not focus on the protection of children

---

[87] Geneva Call, 'Women in Armed Opposition Groups in Africa and the Promotion of International Humanitarian Law and Human Rights: Report of a Workshop organized in Addis Ababa by Geneva Call and the Program for the Study of International organization(s) (23–26 November 2005)', cited in Sivakumaran, *Law of Non-International Armed Conflict* (above n 26) 314.

[88] Sivakumaran, *Law of Non-International Armed Conflict* (above n 26) 314.

[89] See GCIV articles 17 and 24, respectively.

[90] API articles 77(4) and (5), respectively.

[91] See eg API article 77(2).

[92] Optional Protocol to the Convention on the Rights of the Child on the Involvement of Children in Armed Conflict (adopted 25 May 2000, entered into force 12 February 2002) A-27531 (2173), articles 1 and 2.

[93] CIHL 485.

vis-à-vis the enemy state (as is the case with many of the other categories of special protection), but rather on their protection vis-à-vis any state (including their state of nationality).

## 2. Non-international armed conflicts

With respect to children in NIACs, Common Article 3 is silent regarding special rules of protection. APII remedied this gap to a certain extent (at least for those NIACs to which APII applies), setting out specific rules on protection of children, requiring that children 'be provided with the care and aid they require'.[94] More specific rules concern, inter alia, education, evacuation, the inapplicability of the death penalty, and a prohibition on the recruitment of children under fifteen years of age into the state or non-state armed forces and their participation in hostilities.[95] These are considered to reflect customary international law.[96]

The same lack of a general definition of 'child' for the purposes of these protective rules exists in NIACs as exists in IACs. This has resulted in a lack of clarity on the point at which a child becomes an adult and thus no longer benefits from this specialized regime of protection, though there is a trend towards eighteen years of age as a general standard.[97] Like API, APII prohibits recruitment and participation in hostilities by states and NSAGs of children under fifteen years of age.[98] As noted, however, the Optional Protocol to the 1989 Convention on the Rights of the Child adopts the higher age limit of eighteen with respect to compulsory recruitment by the state and the obligation of the state to take all feasible measures to ensure that children below that higher age threshold do not take a direct part in hostilities. Interestingly, the Protocol also states that armed groups 'should not, under any circumstances' recruit persons under eighteen years of age, whether it is through compulsory or voluntary recruitment.[99]

## D. Elderly, Disabled, and Infirm

## 1. International armed conflicts

A number of provisions of IHL specifically refer to elderly, disabled, and infirm persons as sub-categories requiring special protection over and above the ordinary rules applicable to all civilian persons.[100] These include, for example, rules on the conclusion of agreements on the evacuation of certain vulnerable persons, including the infirm and elderly, from besieged areas.[101] Other rules provide more generally that a person's age and health must be taken into account in applying the ordinary standards applicable to all protected persons.[102] Importantly, API extended the protections it contains for wounded and sick persons to the infirm and to persons with disabilities.[103]

---

[94] APII article 4(3).
[95] APII articles 4(3) and 6(4).
[96] CIHL rules 135, 136 and 137; Sivakumaran, *Law of Non-International Armed Conflict* (above n 26) 315–24.
[97] Sivakumaran, *Law of Non-International Armed Conflict* (above n 26) 315; CIHL 481–2.
[98] APII article 4(3)(c).
[99] Optional Protocol (above n 92) article 4(1).
[100] See eg GCIV article 16: 'The wounded and sick, as well as the infirm, and expectant mothers, shall be the object of particular protection and respect.'
[101] ibid article 17.
[102] See eg ibid article 85 (on sufficient bedding for internees) and article 119 (on disciplinary punishments).
[103] API article 8(a).

## 2. Non-international armed conflicts

The treaty law of NIAC does not provide specific protections for the elderly, disabled, or infirm. However, importantly, the definition of wounded, sick, and shipwrecked persons under API, which was noted above as extending the protections granted to such persons to the infirm and disabled, is also considered to apply in NIACs.[104] As such, the infirm and disabled are entitled to those same protections for wounded, sick, and shipwrecked persons in NIACs that were outlined above. Moreover, the ICRC Study avers that it is a customary rule applicable in both IACs and NIACs that '[t]he elderly, disabled and infirm affected by armed conflict are entitled to special respect and protection'.[105]

## E. Refugees and Internally Displaced Persons

### 1. International armed conflicts

IHL does not deal in detail with the specific category of refugees and internally displaced persons (IDPs). Instead, it merely refers to them in passing in a few specific provisions and, for the most part, only where they otherwise fall within one of the categories of protected person under IHL (as with the other special categories of protection). It has been noted that:

> On the one hand, its [IHL's] primary function in the field of forced migration is a pre- ventive one. The explicit prohibition of forced displacement aims to prevent civilians from becoming refugees. On the other hand, international humanitarian law is relatively indifferent to the specific needs of refugees who are in the territory of a party to an armed conflict.[106]

Refugees are specifically referred to in only a few provisions of the IHL treaties. First, article 44 of GCIV states that refugees that have the nationality of the enemy state, but do not as a matter of fact enjoy the protection of any state, must not be treated as enemy aliens for the purposes of the various measures of control and security that GCIV permits states to take against enemy aliens. It should be noted that the ICRC Commentary notes that article 44 of GCIV does not require a person to qualify for refugee status as a matter of international or national law; the term rather is used in a factual sense, and is, therefore, broader than it might otherwise be.[107]

Second, article 70(2) of GCIV requires that any nationals of an occupying state that sought refuge in the occupied territory before the outbreak of hostilities:

---

[104] Sivakumaran, *Law of Non-International Armed Conflict* (above n 26) 274.

[105] CIHL rule 138.

[106] Vincent Chetail, 'Armed Conflict and Forced Migration: A Systemic Approach to International Humanitarian Law, Refugee Law, and Human Rights Law', in Clapham and Gaeta (eds (above n 76) 704 (footnotes omitted). The prohibition of forced displacement referred to is that in GCIV article 49 and APII article 17.

[107] GCIV Commentary 264:

> The Convention does not define the term refugee. It merely notes the fact that certain persons do not "enjoy the protection of any government": if a protected person who is in law a national of an enemy State is in actual fact without any diplomatic protection (whether because he has broken with his country's government or because he does not wish to claim its protection), this provision applies to that person. The clause should be interpreted in this broad sense, in accordance with the spirit of the Convention.

Similarly, see Chetail (above n 106) 707.

... shall not be arrested, prosecuted, convicted or deported from the occupied territory, except for offences committed after the outbreak of hostilities, or for offences under common law committed before the outbreak of hostilities which, according to the law of the occupied State, would have justified extradition in time of peace.

It is noteworthy that this provision only prohibits certain measures of control being taken against refugees with the nationality of the occupying state, apparently leaving the occupying power free to introduce measures not explicitly prohibited.[108] The provision also applies only to persons that fled their home state before the outbreak of hostilities, but does not cover persons that fled as a result of the conflict.[109]

Finally, article 73 of API requires that persons that were considered stateless or refugees under international or national law before the outbreak of hostilities are to be considered to be protected persons under GCIV. This was an important clarification, as the nationality requirements in article 4 of GCIV, noted above, mean that many persons entitled to refugee status would not be protected under GCIV at the outbreak of hostilities in the territory in which they sought refuge (other than by the general rules on protection of civilian populations in GCIV).[110] However, entitlement is restricted under article 73 to persons that qualify as stateless or refugees under international or domestic law; determining the application of article 73 thus requires a *renvoi* to the definition of 'refugee' in, for example, the 1951 Geneva Convention Relating to the Status of Refugees. Moreover, only persons considered stateless or refugees before the outbreak of hostilities are to be protected persons under GCIV. If seeking refuge as a result of the conflict, on the other hand, a person is not entitled to protected person status under that Convention. This has been heavily criticized for undermining the protection of refugees in armed conflict.[111]

As noted above, the only way in which IHL deals explicitly with displacement arising from the armed conflict itself is in a preventive sense, with article 49(1) of GCIV prohibiting 'individual or mass forcible transfers, as well as deportations of protected persons from occupied territory', albeit subject, in paragraph 2, to 'the security of the population or imperative military reasons'. This, however, only applies in the case of occupied territory and where the individuals in question are protected persons under GCIV.

## 2. Non-international armed conflicts

Like the law of IAC, the law of NIAC addresses this category of persons principally in a preventative sense.[112] Thus, article 17(1) of APII contains a prohibition on ordering the displacement of the civilian population 'unless the security of the civilians involved or imperative military reasons so demand'; paragraph 2 then contains an absolute prohibition of forced deportation of civilians. The ICRC CIHL Study considers this to reflect customary international law in all NIACs (ie not only those meeting the higher threshold in APII).[113]

---

[108] Yoram Dinstein, 'Refugees and the Law of Armed Conflict' (1982) 12 *Israel YB HR* 94, 104.

[109] Chetail (above n 106) 709.

[110] ibid 708.

[111] See eg ibid 706; Mélanie Jacques, *Armed Conflict and Displacement: The Protection of Refugees and Displaced Persons under International Humanitarian Law* (CUP 2012) 162.

[112] Emanuela-Chiara Gillard, 'The Role of International Humanitarian Law in the Protection of Internally Displaced Persons' (2005) 24 *Refugee Survey Q* 37, 39–41.

[113] CIHL rule 129B.

However, the law of NIAC does not generally set out specific rules on addressing the particular vulnerabilities of refugees and displaced persons in armed conflict. There are only a few exceptions, such as the requirement that, where displacement of civilians does take place, 'all possible measures shall be taken in order that the civilian population may be received under satisfactory conditions of shelter, hygiene, health, safety and nutrition'.[114] Of course, refugees and internally displaced persons will be protected by the general rules in NIAC relating to civilians and, more generally, persons *hors de combat* (assuming they do not join the armed wing of the NSAG or the state's armed forces). This is because there are no nationality requirements attached to these rules, such requirements being, as shown above, problematic for refugees in the context of IACs. Furthermore, other bodies of international law may become relevant in laying down more specific protections for these categories of persons.[115]

## F. Journalists

### 1. International armed conflicts

Journalists, who 'encompass all members of the general media (as distinct from those media that are run by the armed forces of a Belligerent Party)', are civilians at least for the purposes of the Hague rules on the conduct of hostilities (including immunity from direct attack).[116] Journalists reporting from conflict zones are, of course, exposed to significant dangers. The rule that such persons nonetheless must not be considered to have waived their immunity from attack is specifically reiterated in article 79(1) of API.

Slightly more complicated is the position of journalists under the Geneva rules on the protection of war victims. For the purpose of these rules, journalists are divided into two categories: war correspondents, who are entitled to protection as POWs under GCIII in the event that they fall into the hands of the enemy; and all other journalists, who are protected persons under GCIV (assuming they meet the criteria for the application of that Convention). The category of 'war correspondents' under GCIII is defined strictly, referring to journalists that accompany the armed forces without actually being members thereof and who 'have received authorisation from the armed forces which they accompany, who shall provide them for that purpose with an identity card'.[117] Only where these conditions are met can a journalist reporting from a conflict zone fall under GCIII rather than GCIV should they fall into the hands of the enemy state.[118]

Other than these few provisions, the treaty law of IAC does not provide for a special regime of protection for journalists in armed conflict. The ICRC CIHL Study suggests that custom requires not merely that journalists, as civilians, not be attacked, but also that they be respected and protected in carrying out their professional duties. This includes a prohibition on harassment and intimidation of journalists and assaults upon freedom of the

---

[114] APII article 17(1); CIHL rule 131. Other purported exceptions under custom include the right of return for displaced persons and the requirement that the property rights of displaced persons be respected: see, respectively, CIHL rule 133 and rule 132.

[115] Sivakumaran, *Law of Non-International Armed Conflict* (above n 26) 289 (referring to international human rights law and the Guiding Principles on Internal Displacement, the latter of which codifies both hard and soft law).

[116] Dinstein, *The Conduct of Hostilities* (above n 5) 166.

[117] GCIII article 4A(4).

[118] Robin Geiss, 'The Protection of Journalists in Armed Conflicts' (2008) 51 *GYIL* 289, 310.

press.[119] It is unclear, however, whether such protections follow from a special customary status for journalists in armed conflict or simply the ordinary rules applicable to all civilians, including that of humane treatment.[120]

### 2. Non-international armed conflicts

The IHL treaty provisions applicable in NIAC do not provide specific rules on the protection of journalists. Nonetheless, as in IACs, journalists are civilians for the purposes of the Hague rules on the conduct of hostilities and are thus immune from attack.[121] Unfortunately, this rule is not infrequently violated.[122] Moreover, since the law of NIAC does not provide for POW status, all journalists, whether embedded within the armed forces or independent, are treated as persons *hors de combat* and are subject to the protective rules applicable thereto, including the basic requirement of humane treatment. Finally, though the ICRC CIHL Study takes the view that the requirement of respect and protection of journalists applies in all armed conflicts, it is not clear, as noted above, that this adds to the existing treaty and customary framework applicable to civilians generally.

## G. The Missing and the Dead

### 1. International armed conflicts

IHL also provides certain special rules for missing and dead persons (whether civilian or combatant) in armed conflict. With respect to deceased members of the armed forces, GCI, GCII and GCIII require, for example, states party to an IAC to search for, collect, record, and respectfully inter them, as well as respect and maintain their graves and prevent their bodies from being despoiled.[123] Concerning civilians, GCIV requires more basically that parties to the conflict 'facilitate the steps taken to search for the killed' and respectfully bury and maintain the graves of dead civilian internees.[124]

API sets down general rules on the missing and the dead, whether civilian or combatant. Article 33 of API introduces a new obligation on parties to an IAC to 'endeavour to agree on arrangements to search for, identify and recover the dead from battlefield areas'. Article 34 of API then, inter alia, expands the scope of the GCIV rules on respectful interment and maintenance of graves (which only applied to interned protected persons that had died) to include more generally persons that die for reasons related to occupation and non-nationals of the territory in which they die as a result of hostilities.

With respect to missing persons, GCIII and GCIV contain basic rules on the establishment, by agreement between the parties to the conflict, of commissions to search for

---

[119] CIHL rule 34.

[120] On the question of a potential special regime of protection for journalists in armed conflict, see eg Ben Saul, 'The International Protection of Journalists in Armed Conflict and other Violent Situations' (2008) 13 *AJHR* 99; Isabel Düsterhöft, 'The Protection of Journalists in Armed Conflicts: How Can They Be Better Safeguarded?' (2013) 29 *Utrecht J Int'l Eur L* 4. See also Draft United Nations Convention on the Protection of Journalists Engaged in Dangerous Missions in Areas of Armed Conflict UN Doc A/10147 (1 August 1975).

[121] Sivakumaran, *Law of Non-International Armed Conflict* (above n 26) 311.

[122] ibid 312.

[123] GCI articles 15(1), 16, and 17; GCII articles 18(1), 19, and 20; GCIII article 120.

[124] GCIV articles 16(2) and 130.

'dispersed' POWs and civilians. Article 33(1) of API introduced the general rule requiring that, '[a]s soon as circumstances permit, and at the latest from the end of active hostilities, each Party to the conflict shall search for the persons who have been reported missing by an adverse Party'. This new general rule was an important addition to the rules in the Geneva Conventions.[125] Though framed in broad terms, the ICRC Commentary to this article makes clear that:

> The request [for information from the adverse party] must relate to persons who are either nationals of that Party, or in some other way are linked to it—such as, in particular, persons who had been admitted to its territory as refugees or persons who had enlisted in its armed forces—or generally persons in whom it has a genuine interest based on the general principle of Article 32 (General principle), such as members of the family of a person belonging to the two former categories.[126]

Nonetheless, the drafters of this provision rejected the notion of adopting a definition of 'missing persons', lest it be invoked as a basis for refusing a request from an adverse party for information about a person they deem to be missing.[127]

## 2. Non-international armed conflicts

APII introduced the first treaty provisions on the dead in NIACs, setting out the basic obligations to 'search for the dead, prevent their being despoiled, and decently dispose of them'.[128] No treaty provisions applicable in NIACs specifically detail rules relating to missing persons. However, the ICRC considers many of the rules on missing and dead persons in the context of IACs to be of a customary character applicable in both IACs and NIACs.[129] On the one hand, this suggests that these two categories of persons entitled to special protection also exist under IHL applicable in NIACs. On the other hand, the ICRC refers in part to the jurisprudence of human rights treaty bodies in establishing some of these customary rules, such as that on missing persons. As such, one might argue that this obligation in NIACs is not per se one applicable under IHL, but rather one applicable under human rights law.[130] Sandesh Sivakumaran argues that, '[i]n light of the close relationship between this rule [on missing persons] and other customary rules, and the link between norms in various bodies of law, if it is not already a rule of customary international law, it is on its way to becoming one'.[131]

---

[125] Kleffner (above n 62) 334; AP Commentary 350.
[126] AP Commentary 350.
[127] ibid 351.
[128] APII article 8.
[129] Regarding the dead, see CIHL rules 112 (search for the dead), 113 (prohibition of despoliation of the dead), 115 (respectful burial and maintenance of graves), and 116 (record-keeping of the dead). Though cf CIHL rule 114 (return of the remains of the deceased to their next of kin), for which the ICRC states that it is not clear that this has crystallized yet as a rule of custom in non-international armed conflict. Regarding missing persons, see CIHL rule 117 (take all feasible measures to account for persons reported missing as a result of a conflict).
[130] CIHL 425.
[131] Sivakumaran, Law of Non-International Armed Conflict (above n 26) 285. See also Susan Breau and Marie Aronsson, 'Drone Attacks, International Law, and the Recording of Civilian Casualties in Armed Conflict' (2012) 35 Suffolk Transnat'l L Rev 255.

## 6. Mercenaries and Private Military/Security Companies

### A. International Armed Conflicts

The Geneva Conventions make no mention of mercenaries as a specific category of persons in IAC. The assumption, rather, was that they would simply fall within the existing categories of persons established under IHL without the need for further rules. API, however, changed this, with article 47(1) stating that '[a] mercenary shall not have the right to be a combatant or a prisoner of war', with 'mercenary' for these purposes being defined in paragraph 2. It is worth emphasizing that having a provision specifically excluding a particular category of persons from one of the protected statuses is unusual in IHL.[132] Article 47 must be seen in light of the significant use of mercenaries in many of the conflicts in the period between the adoption of the Geneva Conventions and the Additional Protocols.[133] Finally, there is some disagreement over the degree to which article 47 of API represents customary international law. Whereas the ICRC takes the view that this provision reflects custom in IACs,[134] others take the view that article 47 reflects a departure from customary international law.[135]

Where a person is subject to article 47 of API, the consequence is that they are entitled neither to combatant status, thereby preventing them from benefitting from combatant immunity, nor to POW status, thereby preventing them from benefitting from the protections under GCIII. As was made clear in section 4 'A Third Category' above with respect to so-called unlawful combatants, however, persons who, to varying degrees, participate in hostilities but fail to qualify for combatant/POW status are not unprotected by IHL. Thus, mercenaries could, where its conditions are met, be protected by GCIV.[136] The nationality conditions under which article 47 applies, however, do mean that, where persons do fall within that provision, they are unlikely to meet the nationality conditions to be considered protected persons under GCIV—thus also preventing them from benefiting from many of the protections under that Convention. Nonetheless, such persons at a minimum are protected by the fundamental guarantees laid down in article 75 of API, widely considered to reflect customary international law.[137] Furthermore, they would be entitled, as civilians, to protection under the Hague rules on the conduct of hostilities, according to which, inter alia, civilians may not be the object of attack unless and for such time as they directly participate in hostilities.

In reality, '[i]t is virtually impossible to find an individual who falls within the Article 47.2 definition' of mercenary.[138] Moreover, it has been pointed out elsewhere that those

[132] Lindsey Cameron, 'Private Military Companies: Their Status under International Humanitarian Law and Its Impact on their Regulation' (2006) 88 *IRRC* 573, 580.
[133] AP Commentary 572–4.
[134] CIHL rule 108.
[135] Michael Matheson, 'The United States Position on the Relation of Customary International Law to the 1977 Protocols Additional to the 1949 Geneva Conventions' (1987) 4 *Am U J Int'l L & Pol'y* 426; Dinstein, *The Conduct of Hostilities* (n 5) 67; HC Burmester, 'The Recruitment and Use of Mercenaries in Armed Conflicts' (1978) 72 *AJIL* 37.
[136] Emanuela-Chiara Gillard, 'Business Goes to War: Private Military/Security Companies and International Humanitarian Law' (2006) 88 *IRRC* 525, 562–4.
[137] See eg Sandra Krähenmann, 'Protection of Prisoners in Armed Conflict', in Dieter Fleck (ed), *The Handbook of International Humanitarian Law* (3rd edn, OUP 2013) 368.
[138] Katherine Fallah, 'Corporate Actors: The Legal Status of Mercenaries in Armed Conflict' (2006) 88 *IRRC* 599, 605.

falling within the definition of article 47(2) would not be entitled to combatant/POW status in the first place, as the definition excludes members of the armed forces of a party to the conflict, in relation to which API defines combatant status.[139]

With respect to the more modern phenomenon of private military/security companies, while a generalized approach is not possible to determine whether article 47 applies, it seems unlikely that their employees would fall within the strict definition of a mercenary in that provision.[140] Instead, their status as either combatants or civilians would need to be determined on a case-by-case basis. In this respect, it has been noted elsewhere that most employees of private military/security companies would not satisfy the conditions for combatant/POW status under GCIII or API.[141] Instead, so the argument goes, the majority are more likely to be considered civilians, entitled to protection from direct attack unless and for so long as they directly participate in hostilities, and entitled to protection under GCIV should they meet the conditions for that Convention's application.[142] Others have taken the view that, where a private military/security company de facto performs a combat function on behalf of the state, they are no longer civilians and become targetable on the same basis as members of the state armed forces.[143]

## B.  Non-International Armed Conflicts

Given the absence of combatant status in NIAC, there is no equivalent of article 47 of API for such conflicts, though there are mercenary-specific conventions that criminalize mercenaries in all situations, including NIACs (in contrast to IHL, which does not speak to the legality under international law of mercenarism as such, but rather regulates the status of mercenaries).[144] Thus, mercenaries and employees of private military/security companies operating in a NIAC are entitled to the ordinary protections that apply to all persons in such situations where they are *hors de combat*.

The question does arise in such circumstances, however, as to whether employees of private military/security companies operating in a NIAC should be considered as members of the state or non-state armed forces, or whether they should be considered civilians, for the purposes of the rules on targeting. This is related to the controversy, noted above, about the degree to which different statuses of persons exist under the law of NIAC. The ICRC in its Guidance on Direct Participation in Hostilities takes the view that such private contractors can become members of the state armed forces for the purposes of targeting where they are engaged by the state either de jure or de facto in a combat function.[145] Similarly, the ICRC also takes the view that they could be considered members of the armed opposition group where they perform a continuous combat function on behalf of that group.[146] Indeed, it has

---

[139]  ibid 606.
[140]  See eg Cameron (above n 132) 581–2 (on companies operating in Iraq).
[141]  Gillard, 'Business Goes to War' (above n 136) 531–6; Cameron (above n 132) 582–7. Though note Gillard, 'Business Goes to War' (above n 136) at 536–9 (stating that some may be entitled to POW status, though not combatant status, under GCIII article 4A(4) as civilian contractors accompanying the armed forces).
[142]  Gillard, 'Business Goes to War' (above n 136) 539; Cameron (above n 132) 587.
[143]  *DPH Guidance* 39, n 71.
[144]  Cameron (above n 132) 578.
[145]  *DPH Guidance* 39, n 71.
[146]  ibid 39.

also been noted that private contractors could constitute an NSAG party to a NIAC in and of themselves.[147]

# 7. Spies

## A.  International Armed Conflicts

Like mercenaries, spies fall into the unusual category of persons singled out as *not* being entitled to certain protections. Article 29 of the 1907 Hague Regulations provides the customary definition of a spy for these purposes: '[a] person can only be considered a spy when, acting clandestinely or on false pretences, he obtains or endeavours to obtain information in the zone of operations of a belligerent, with the intention of communicating it to the hostile party'. In principle, this could include not only members of the armed forces of a party to the conflict, but also civilians.[148]

The two principal consequences of falling within this definition are set out in article 46 of API: first, that the person is not entitled to POW status even if they otherwise would be (eg because they are members of the opposing armed forces or civilians accompanying the armed forces in accordance with article 4A(4) of GCIII); and second, that they may be prosecuted for their acts of espionage.[149] Again, the position is thus the same as with mercenaries: espionage in itself is not prohibited by IHL; rather, IHL leaves states free to prosecute those engaging in this act.[150] Again, this is not to say that spies are then left unprotected by IHL, for anyone falling within the scope of these provisions could qualify for protected person status under GCIV, should the conditions for that Convention's applicability be met. It should be noted, however, that article 5 of GCIV does permit derogation from certain of the rules in that Convention for persons engaging in, inter alia, espionage.[151]

## B.  Non-International Armed Conflicts

Given that POW status does not exist under the law of NIAC, there is no equivalent rule relating to spies in such situations. Rather, all persons *hors de combat* are entitled to the protections granted by the rules of IHL applicable in NIAC, whilst continuing to be subject to the domestic laws of the state(s) concerned. However, were a member of the state armed forces or a member of the armed group performing a continuous combat function (should one accept the ICRC's approach) to engage in espionage, they would not be entitled to immunity from direct attack under IHL, as discussed in detail above.

---

[147]  ibid 39–40.

[148]  Ipsen (above n 2) 108. Though API article 46 only applies as such to members of the armed forces, Hague Convention (IV) Respecting the Customs of War on Land and Its Annex: Regulations concerning the Customs of War on Land (adopted 18 October 1907, entered into force 26 January 1910) 187 CTS 227 (Hague Regulations) article 29 applies to any person engaging in espionage.

[149]  API article 46(1); Ipsen (above n 2) 109.

[150]  AP Commentary 562.

[151]  ibid 563–4.

## 8. Concluding Remarks

This chapter has explored the key categories of persons in both IACs and NIACs according to which the rules of IHL are structured. It has been shown that the two principal categories are those of combatant/POW and civilian; indeed, this basic framework lies at the heart of the fundamental principle of distinction in the rules on the conduct of hostilities under IHL. Notwithstanding this long-established basic framework, a number of practical and doctrinal debates were shown to continue to exist in determining combatant/POW and civilian status. Indeed, this is especially the case under the more embryonic law of NIAC, to which these categories are not quite so easily transposed.

Furthermore, within each of these categories, a number of sub-categories of specially protected persons were shown to exist, recognizing the vulnerability of particular persons in armed conflict. For some of these categories of persons, such as women and displaced persons, the rules remain very basic and inadequate for the contemporary challenges faced in armed conflicts. What is more, many of these categories are even less clearly defined under the law of NIAC. It is to be remembered, however, that the focus of this chapter has been on the applicable rules under IHL; other bodies of international law, including international human rights law and refugee law, continue to apply in parallel, which may well offer more robust protections for certain persons in armed conflict.

# 6

# Fundamental Guarantees

*Robert McLaughlin*

## 1. Introduction

Cicero's maxim 'Silent enim leges inter arma' is generally interpreted as 'During war, the law falls silent'.[1] Often, however, the context is forgotten—he was advocating for the right to kill in self-defence, albeit in breach of Roman law, in a time of civil riot and conflict. Cicero was no advocate of lawlessness or the absence of law—as a lawyer, advocate, politician, and philosopher, this was against every grain of his being.[2] To use law instrumentally, and to selectively deny the applicability of certain rules—absolutely; this was his stock in trade. But to deny the applicability of law to a sphere of human activity in toto—no, this was not his point. Even the Romans, for whom 'no quarter' across both combatants and civilians was formally permissible in the absence of surrender before engagement, specific law applied in time of war[3]—to designate and assign status,[4] to govern conduct, to provide for fighting in a way that viably left an option for the future incorporation of the defeated entity into the Roman polity.[5] And although not as detailed as modern IHL, Roman law as applicable in times of conflict clearly addressed issues that would today touch upon fundamental guarantees—such as the status of 'deditio' surrender, which entitled the defeated party to favourable treatment and the

---

[1] Marcus Tullius Cicero, *Pro Milone* 2.6, trans NH Watts, ed J Henderson (Harvard University Press 1953): 'I beg and implore you, gentlemen, that, having lost all else, this right at least we may retain—the right of fearlessly defending our life against the unscrupulous weapons of our foes'; Cicero, 4.10–11:

> There does exist therefore, gentlemen, a law which is a law not of the statute-book, but of nature; a law which we possess not by instruction, tradition, or reading, but which we have caught, imbibed, and sucked in at Nature's own breast; a law which comes to us not by education but by constitution, not by training but by intuition—the law, I mean, that, should our life have fallen into any snare, into the violence and the weapons of robbers or foes, every method of winning a way to safety would be morally justifiable. When arms speak, the laws are silent; they bid none to await their word, since he who chooses to await it must pay an undeserved penalty ere he can exact a deserved one.

[2] Anthony Everitt, *Cicero: The Life and Times of Rome's Greatest Politician* (Random House 2003) chapters 6–10, 13, 15.

[3] See eg Alexander Gillespie, *A History of the Laws of War* (Hart 2011) Vol I, 112–15; Vol II, 114–212. For example, Tacitus records that when the town of Uspe (Armenia) offered to surrender and provide 10,000 slaves 'in return for mercy for the freeborn', the Romans felt obliged to refuse it because (as summarized by Gillespie) the Roman force did not have the capacity 'to guard all of the prisoners who would have been taken. Due to the fact that the Romans felt it would have been barbarous to slaughter men who had surrendered, they refused to take the surrender and fought them to their deaths ...': Gillespie, Vol I, 112; Vol II, 115.

[4] See eg the often misunderstood nature of Roman law appertaining to pirates, described succinctly in Tamsin Paige, 'Piracy and Universal Jurisdiction' (2013) 12 *MLJ* 131, 132–4.

[5] See generally, Benedict Kingsbury and Benjamin Straumann, 'Introduction', in Benedict Kingsbury and Benjamin Straumann (eds), *The Roman Foundations of the Law of Nations: Alberico Gentili and the Justice of Empire* (OUP 2010); Clifford Ando, 'Empire and the Laws of War: A Roman Archaeology', in Kingsbury and Straumann (eds); Diego Panizza, 'Alberico Gentili's *De armis Romanis*: The Roman Model of the Just Empire', in Kingsbury and Straumann (eds); David Lupher, 'The *De Armis Romanis* and the *Exemplum* of Roman Imperialism', in Kingsbury and Straumann (eds).

preservation of certain fundamental rights and guarantees.[6] This recognition of the need to ensure that the law of war continued to include explicit regimes for reducing the deleterious effects of armed conflict upon civilians and (to a lesser extent) certain categories of participants, retains its most eloquent canonical expression in the Martens Clause:

> Until a more complete code of the laws of war has been issued, the high contracting Parties deem it expedient to declare that, in cases not included in the Regulations adopted by them, the inhabitants and the belligerents remain under the protection and the rule of the principles of the law of nations, as they result from the usages established among civilised peoples, from the laws of humanity, and the dictates of public conscience.[7]

Yet this admonition to protect those fundamental guarantees of treatment that civilization has progressively endowed should not disguise the unambiguous record of barbarity and atrocity that has generally accompanied warfare, despite Geoffrey Best's poignant description of the law of war as a great but paradoxical achievement.[8] It was still part of the expectation of statesmen in the 1800s that insurgents not entitled to treatment as combatants in accordance with the laws of war, could 'legally' fall into the deep black hole of harsh and unregulated extrajudicial treatment still acquiesced in for rebels.[9] It is not surprising, as Brian Dirck has noted, that in some quarters there remains a persistent assumption that 'humanitarian needs and military necessity are natural enemies of each other and extra scrutiny is necessary to ensure a harmonious balance between the two'.[10] Whilst these two drivers of IHL are not as antithetical to each other as is often asserted—indeed, the concept

---

[6] Arthur Nussbaum, 'The Significance of Roman Law in the History of International Law' (1952) 100 *U Pa L Rev* 678.

[7] The Martens Clause was originally promulgated in the preamble to the Hague Convention (II) with Respect to the Laws and Customs of War on Land (adopted 29 July 1899, entered into force 4 September 1900) 187 CTS 429 (Hague Convention II):

> [u]ntil a more complete code of the laws of war is issued, the High Contracting Parties think it right to declare that in cases not included in the Regulations adopted by them, populations and belligerents remain under the protection and empire of the principles of international law, as they result from the usages established between civilized nations, from the laws of humanity, and the requirements of the public conscience.

The slightly modified version cited above is from the preamble to Hague Convention (IV) Respecting the Laws and Customs of War on Land (adopted 18 October 1907, entered into force 26 January 1910) 205 CTS 227 (Hague Convention IV).

[8] Geoffrey Best, *War and Law since 1945* (Clarendon Press 1997) 3: '[r]esort to the violence of armed conflict, with all its usual chances and accidents, its frequent furies and inhumanities, its lists of casualties, trails of desolation, and legacies of hatred, looks like the antithesis of everything comprised in that ark of civilization's covenant, the rule of law'.

[9] This was well evidenced, eg in Lord Canning's letter to Lord Wellesley, the British Minister in Vienna, concerning Austrian refusals to treat the Greek rebels fighting against the Ottoman Empire as full belligerents:

> The doctrine of Prince Metternich, that the Greeks, as rebels, are not entitled to the same rights of war, as legitimate belligerents, is one, of which, we think His Highness would do well to weigh all the consequences, before he promulgates it to the world. The practical enforcement of that doctrine could have no other effect than to convert the contest which has been brought, in a great measure by our exertions, into one of a regular and civilized character, into one of indiscriminate rapine and massacre (Letter from Lord Canning to Lord Wellesley (31 December 1824) (FO 7/181, no 34), extracted in Herbert Smith, *Great Britain and the Law of Nations* (King & Son 1932) 296.

See similarly the US Supreme Court in *Ford v Suget*, which was also of the view that the application of the international law of war during the American Civil War 'was conceded, in the interest of humanity, and to prevent the cruelties of reprisals and retaliations': *Ford v Suget*, 97 US 594 per Harlan J.

[10] Brian Dirck, *Waging War on Trial: A Handbook with Cases, Laws, and Documents* (ABC-Clio 2003) 35–6.

of counter-insurgency (COIN) warfare is to some extent premised upon achieving each through the other[11]—it is true that scrutiny remains essential to ensuring that humanitarian needs, in particular the IHL fundamental guarantees addressed in this chapter, remain as equally governing of conduct as military necessity. The recent history of US jurisprudence dealing with the iconic and indicative issue of habeas corpus in conflict situations certainly bears witness to this constant tension.[12]

Given the central importance of such fundamental guarantees as a significant counter-weight to military necessity, it is perhaps surprising that there is no central or core instru-ment which coherently and collectively delineates their content: As Emily Crawford notes, analysing the course by which the current state of the law has evolved,

> The question of the scope and content of minimum humanitarian standards or funda-mental standards of humanity as they are now termed—has become clearer with time, especially through the growth of international criminal case law and works such as the International Committee of the Red Cross (ICRC) study into customary international hu-manitarian law. Yet the adoption of a document that outlines these fundamental standards is no more imminent than when the issue first moved to the United Nations.[13]

Thus despite sustained advocacy from, inter alia, Theodor Meron, and regardless of the bur-geoning attention paid to the substantive content of the individual rules within the scheme, a 'short, simple and modest instrument … [detailing the] irreducible and non-derogable core of human rights that must be applied at a minimum in situations of internal strife and violence'[14] still eludes insofar as the fundamental guarantees proscribed under the law of armed conflict (LOAC) are concerned.

In this chapter, I will iteratively address three matters. The first section provides a general overview of the context and background of the IHL fundamental guarantees, with a focus upon describing the concept through reference to three definitional aspects: rationale, sources in law, and scope. Section two provides a brief outline of one indicative example of the category of general, procedural, fundamental guarantees—those that presage, context-ualize, or underpin many of the other, more specific treatment-based fundamental guar-antees. To this end, the analysis will address the requirement of legality. The final section will then deal with a number of specific fundamental guarantees under two broad category headings. The first is humane treatment, which is itself an umbrella fundamental guarantee encompassing: violence to life (such as murder, but not battlefield killing in accordance with LOAC, which is subject to different rules and is dealt with elsewhere in this book); through other violent breaches of fundamental guarantees (such as torture, and rape); to the

---

[11] See US Army-Marine Corps, 'Counterinsurgency', in *Field Manual* 3-24 (Marine Corps Warfighting Publication No 3-33.5 2006); the updated version is US Army-Marine Corps, 'Insurgencies and Countering Insurgencies', in *Field Manual* 3-24 (Marine Corps Warfighting Publication No 3-33.5 2014) paras 1.27–1.33.

[12] See eg Ashley Nikkel, 'Painting Ourselves into a Corner: The Fundamental Paradoxes of Modern Warfare in *Al Maqaleh V. Gates*' (2011–12) 12 *Nevada LJ* 443, 446–51.

[13] Emily Crawford, 'Road to Nowhere? The Future for a Declaration on Fundamental Standards of Humanity' (2012) 3 *Int'l Hum Studs* 43, 45, with background analysis of the course of discussions and attempts outlined at 46–55.

[14] See eg Theodor Meron, 'On the Inadequate Reach of Humanitarian and Human Rights Law and the Need for a New Instrument' (1983) 77 *AJIL* 589; see also Theodor Meron, 'Towards a Humanitarian Declaration on Internal Strife' (1984) 78 *AJIL* 859.

proscriptions relating to degrading treatment. The second broad category is restriction of freedoms, focusing upon forced labour and slavery (but not upon detention, which is dealt with more fully elsewhere in this book). Whilst this provides but a slim and selective assessment across the broad and still evolving concept of fundamental guarantees, it is hoped that it will nevertheless furnish some indication of the scope and content of this externally referencing, inclusive category of IHL rights and obligations.

## 2. 'Fundamental Guarantees' within the Broader IHL/LOAC Scheme

### A. What are 'Fundamental Guarantees'?

Adopting a list-based approach to the concept of the IHL fundamental guarantees certainly accords an appreciation of their scope, but does not adequately describe them as a coherent category of rights and obligations. Additionally, the list-based approach can risk being interpreted as exclusive and fixed, rather than incorporative and still evolving, as is in fact the case. It is, consequently, more meaningful to attempt a generic and holistic approach to concept description. This can be achieved through a brief examination of three components: contextual rationale; the sources from which the rules are drawn; and their scope of application.

### 1. Rationale

The rationale behind the IHL fundamental guarantees is, in short, to ensure that the unique context of armed conflict cannot be cited as strategic or legal authority for dispensing with the de jure applicability of certain key guarantees of treatment, and the availability of certain rights and protections. To this end, there are a number of indicators that may assist in differentiating fundamental guarantees from other rules in IHL. First, the fundamental guarantees apply to both civilians who are not taking a direct part in hostilities ('DPH') and combatants who are *hors de combat*.[15] However, some of the rules do have differing substantive content depending upon the status of the recipient. One example of this, as will be discussed below, is uncompensated or inadequately compensated forced labour, which is prohibited for civilians, but a form of which is permissible in respect of prisoners of war (POWs). Another example is the IHL fundamental guarantee against discrimination,[16] the application of which must nevertheless account for certain sanctioned distinctions that carry significant consequences—such as the specific right to inter former military personnel (which is permissible in LOAC[17]), and the separate and

---

[15] Jean-Marie Henckaerts and Louise Doswald-Beck (eds), *Customary International Humanitarian Law, Vol I: Rules* (CUP 2005) (CIHL) 299.

[16] CIHL rule 88; Common Article 3; Geneva Convention (III) Relative to the Treatment of Prisoners of War (adopted 12 August 1949, entered into force 12 October 1950) 75 UNTS 135 (GCIII) article 16; Geneva Convention (IV) Relative to the Protection of Civilian Persons in Time of War (adopted 12 August 1949, entered into force 21 October 1950) 75 UNTS 287 (GCIV) article 13; Protocol Additional to the Geneva Conventions of 12 August 1949, and Relating to the Protection of Victims of International Armed Conflicts (adopted 8 June 1977, entered into force 7 December 1978) 1125 UNTS 3 (API) articles 9(I), 69(1), 70(1), and 75(I); and Protocol Additional to the Geneva Conventions of 12 August 1949, and Relating to the Protection of Victims of Non-International Armed Conflicts (adopted 8 June 1977, entered into force 7 December 1978) 1125 UNTS 609 (APII) articles 2(1), 4(1), and 18(2).

[17] See eg GCIII article 4(B)(1).

distinct (and prima facie discriminatory) right to inter those whose political views (eg, exhorting acts of sabotage) mean that they constitute an imperative threat to security.[18] Similarly, whilst the fundamental guarantee against discrimination encompasses nationality,[19] LOAC also provides some more specific rules that allow for limited discrimination on exactly these grounds; for example, article 40 of Geneva Convention IV (GCIV), which provides that:

> Protected persons may be compelled to work only to the same extent as nationals of the Party to the conflict in whose territory they are.
>
> If protected persons are of enemy nationality, they may only be compelled to do work which is normally necessary to ensure the feeding, sheltering, clothing, transport and health of human beings and which is not directly related to the conduct of military operations.
>
> In the cases mentioned in the two preceding paragraphs, protected persons compelled to work shall have the benefit of the same working conditions and of the same safeguards as national workers, in particular as regards wages, hours of labour, clothing and equipment, previous training and compensation for occupational accidents and diseases.

The key, it serves repeating, is always to confirm the scope of the specific guarantee in question: whilst the IHL fundamental guarantee of non-discrimination between enemy nationals, own nationals, and other nationals applies to humane treatment, it does not apply to, for example, employment options.

A second indicator—which is to some extent a corollary of the first—is that the IHL fundamental guarantees do not apply during attacks to combatants, members of organized armed groups ('OAGs'), and civilians DPH, and are irrelevant in terms of the infliction of death or injury to civilians in their unwelcome capacity as 'collateral damage'. This is because other rules apply in those situations and the conduct is de jure contextualized and characterized differently. Thus the permissible killing of a civilian in the course of a lawful application of the targeting rules, or the killing of a combatant or civilian DPH/OAG member in compliance with LOAC, cannot equate to murder precisely because it is permissible to kill a combatant/civilian DPH/OAG member in such circumstances; it is also permissible to cause incidental civilian deaths in a proportionate attack. Outside of these circumstances, however, the killing would need to be assessed against the IHL fundamental guarantee in relation to murder or wilful killing, as opposed to the lawfulness of the killings under the targeting law regime. Thus the killing of a civilian, or a POW, outside the accepted bounds of LOAC would constitute prima facie murder.

The third indicator of the need to apply an assessment scheme based in the fundamental guarantees as opposed to another component of LOAC, is where there is a clear disparity in the power relationship within a situation, expressed most clearly in the assertion of control by one of the belligerent parties over a person and their situation.

---

[18]  See eg GCIV articles 5, 41–46.
[19]  See eg API article 75(1):

> … shall be treated humanely in all circumstances and shall enjoy, as a minimum, the protection provided by this Article without any adverse distinction based upon race, colour, sex, language, religion or belief, political or other opinion, national or social origin, wealth, birth or other status, or on any other similar criteria …

That is, the IHL fundamental guarantees come into play in situations where the subject is within the control of an adversary; this is why the fundamental guarantees *do not* apply to combatants/civilians DPH/OAG in the normal course of events during attacks. Conversely, this is exactly why the IHL fundamental guarantees *do* apply to civilians at all times (excepting the issue of targeting law), and to combatants/DPH/OAG when detained or *hors de combat*, and thus within the power/control of the adversary force. Additionally, there are jurisprudential indications that an armed group must also afford—as a minimum—certain of the fundamental guarantees to vulnerable persons within its structure as equally as to those whose allegiance lays with a neutral or an adversary belligerent. In the International Criminal Court (ICC) Appeals Chamber decision on jurisdiction in relation to the prosecution of Bosco Ntanganda for, inter alia, rape and sexual slavery offences against members of his own armed group, the unanimous view of the court was that:

> Having regard to the established framework of international law, members of an armed force or group are not categorically excluded from protection against the war crimes of rape and sexual slavery under article 8 (2) (b) (xxii) and (2) (e) (vi) of the Statute when committed by members of the same armed force or group. Nevertheless, it must be established that the conduct in question 'took place in the context of and was associated with an armed conflict' of either international or non-international character. It is this nexus requirement that sufficiently and appropriately delineates war crimes from ordinary crimes.[20]

## 2. Rule sources

The second component of a holistic description of the concept of IHL fundamental guarantees is that although the notion, as an articulable component of LOAC, dates at least as far back as the Martens Clause, the manner by which this is achieved in modern LOAC is through the integration and iterative construction of a rule set leveraging both LOAC and international human rights law (IHRL). As the UN General Assembly made clear in 1970, 'fundamental human rights, as accepted in international law and laid down in international instruments, continue to apply fully in situations of armed conflict'.[21] This requirement to recall both bodies of law in order to identify the IHL fundamental guarantees is explicitly noted in the preamble to one significant attempt at encapsulating the scope and content of these fundamental guarantees—the *1990 Turku Declaration*:

> Confirming that any derogations from obligations relating to human rights during a state of public emergency must remain strictly within the limits provided for by international law, that certain rights can never be derogated from and that humanitarian law does not admit of any derogations on grounds of public emergency;

---

[20] ICC Appeals Chamber, *Judgment on the appeal of Mr Ntaganda against the 'Second decision on the Defence's challenge to the jurisdiction of the Court in respect of Counts 6 and 9'* No ICC-01/04-02/06 OA5 (15 June 2017) para 2.

[21] UNGA Resolution 2675 (XXV) (9 December 1970) para 1.

Confirming further that measures derogating from such obligations must be taken in strict conformity with the procedural requirements laid down in those instruments, that the imposition of a state of emergency must be proclaimed officially, publicly, and in accordance with the provisions laid down by law, that measures derogating from such obligations will be limited to the extent strictly required by the exigencies of the situations, and that such measures must not discriminate on the grounds of race, colour, sex, language, religion, social, national or ethnic origin.[22]

As to LOAC, for example, the International Court of Justice, in the *Nicaragua* case, determined that:

Article 3 which is common to all four *Geneva Conventions* of 12 August 1949 defines certain rules to be applied in the armed conflicts of a non-international character. There is no doubt that, in the event of international armed conflicts, these rules also constitute a minimum yardstick, in addition to the more elaborate rules which are also to apply to international conflicts, and they are rules which, in the Court's opinion, reflect what the Court in 1949 [*Corfu Channel* case] called 'elementary considerations of humanity'.[23]

As Emily Crawford then goes on to observe of the *Turku Declaration*,

Nearly half of the rules are derived from fundamental rules of international humanitarian law. They include a prohibition on attacks against non-combatants; proportionality in the use of force; prohibition on the use of illegal means and methods of warfare; prohibition on spreading terror throughout the population; special protection for the sick, wounded, and medical and religious personnel; special respect/protection for the dead; and free access to humanitarian organizations.[24]

The 'other half' of the rules, therefore, source their more refined elucidation in IHRL, from both treaty and CIL sources.[25] Thus Natasha Balendra has described the orthodox approach whereby 'IHL and HRL can be applied simultaneously and can complement each other without there being a conflict between the two sets of norms. This is what occurs when some norms of IHL are interpreted by reference to the more developed norms of HRL.'[26] Again, in an oft-cited ICJ passage from the *Nuclear Weapons Advisory Opinion*,

In principle, the right not arbitrarily to be deprived of one's life applies also in hostilities. The test of what is an arbitrary deprivation of life, however, then falls to be

---

[22] 'Declaration of Minimum Humanitarian Standards Adopted by an Expert Meeting Convened by the Institute for Human Rights' (meeting convened by the Institute of Human Rights, Åbo Akademi University, Turku Finland, 2 December 1990) (Turku Declaration) www.ifrc.org/Docs/idrl/I149EN.pdf.
[23] *Military and Paramilitary Activities in and against Nicaragua (Nicaragua v US)* (Merits) [1986] ICJ Rep 14 (*Nicaragua* case) para 218.
[24] Crawford (above n 13) 53.
[25] On the dissolving of hard paradigmatic boarders between IHL and IHRL, see in general: CIHL ch 32; Cyril Laucci, 'Customary International Humanitarian Law Study: Fundamental Guarantees' (2009) 6 *Slovenian L Rev* 191; Natasha Balendra, 'Defining Armed Conflict' (2007–2008) 29 *Cardozo L Rev* 2461; Jeremy Marsh, 'Rule 99 of the Customary International Humanitarian Law Study and the Relationship between the Law of Armed Conflict and International Human Rights Law' (2009) *Army Law* 18.
[26] Balendra (above n 25) 2495.

determined by the applicable *lex specialis*, namely, the law applicable in armed conflict which is designed to regulate the conduct of hostilities. Thus whether a particular loss of life, through the use of a certain weapon in warfare, is to be considered an arbitrary deprivation of life contrary to Article 6 of the Covenant [ICCPR], can only be decided by reference to the law applicable in armed conflict and not deduced from the terms of the Covenant itself.[27]

Thus, as a component of this interaction it is important to also bear in mind that the integration of IHL and IHRL in the construction of the modern IHL fundamental guarantees is not one of unmitigated imperialism by IHRL over IHL—the need to accommodate both rule sets means that they necessarily act upon one another. As Louise Doswald-Beck noted of the ICJ's *Nuclear Weapons Advisory Opinion* formulation:

> This is a very significant statement, for it means that humanitarian law is to be used to actually interpret a human rights rule. Conversely, it also means that, at least in the context of the conduct of hostilities, human rights law cannot be interpreted differently from humanitarian law.[28]

This bivalency and interoperability was further described by the ICJ in the 2004 *Advisory Opinion on the Legal Consequences of the Construction of a Wall in the Occupied Palestinian Territory*:

> As regards the relationship between IHL and HRL, there are thus three possible situations: some rights may be exclusively matters of IHL; others may be exclusively matters of HRL; yet others may be matters of both these branches of international law.[29]

As Laucci notes of the ICRC's Customary International Humanitarian Law Study's (CIHL Study) approach, 'the fundamental guarantees provided for in Rules 87–105' generally 'fall within this third category'.[30]

There is one significant outlier in this clear trend for IHL fundamental guarantees to reflect this IHL–IHRL bivalency—rape. Whilst the prohibition of rape in war has a long and inglorious history as one of the most breached and least enforced 'rules' of combatant conduct, recent treaty and case law—whilst clearly reiterating the place of rape within the highest echelons of IHL fundamental guarantees—has been haphazard. As Shane Darcy notes, rape has been prosecuted and convicted as variously genocide

---

[27] *Legality of the Threat or Use of Nuclear Weapons* (Advisory Opinion) [1996] ICJ Rep 66 para 25.

[28] Louise Doswald-Beck, 'International Humanitarian Law and the Advisory Opinion of the International Court of Justice on the Legality of the Threat or Use of Nuclear Weapons' (1997) *IRRC* 35, 51; see also, Aldo Zammit Borda 'Introduction to International Humanitarian Law' (2008) 34(4) *CLB* 739, 747:

> [b]ut the effective protection of the victims of armed conflict requires not only that they should enjoy certain basic human rights, but also that they should benefit from certain supplementary rights which are necessary precisely because of the armed conflict, such as medical care, the right of prisoners of war to correspond with their families, the right of repatriation in certain circumstances, etc. In these areas, the provisions of IHL go beyond the requirements of basic human rights law.

[29] *Legal Consequences of the Construction of a Wall in the Occupied Palestinian Territory* (Advisory Opinion) [2004] ICJ Rep 136 para 106.

[30] Laucci (above n 25) 194.

(*Akayesu* case), a crime against humanity (*Celebici* case), and torture (*Furunzija* case).[31] It has also been prosecuted as sexual slavery, including as an offence perpetrated within and against members of one's own OAG.[32] But it has rarely been prosecuted as rape simpliciter; that is, rape is often dealt with as a manifestation of the violation of another IHL fundamental guarantee. In this respect, a number of international tribunals have looked beyond the IHL–IHRL sources, and into national criminal law, in order to develop a definition of rape as a war crime, and thus as a self-contained, distinct, and separately identified violation of an IHL fundamental guarantee. This has not been without challenges—most particularly around the issue of whether it is coercion, or consent, or both that defines the circumstances. A very unsubtle generalization might be that the International Criminal Tribunal for Rwanda (ICTR) tended towards the former,[33] the International Criminal Tribunal for the former Yugoslavia (ICTY) tended towards the latter,[34] and that the Special Court for Sierra Leone and ICC appear to utilize both, noting that the ever-present threat of violence, and the coercive context of armed conflict in itself, can evidence non-consent.[35]

### 3. Scope

The final descriptive component useful in attempting to achieve a more holistic appreciation of the concept of IHL fundamental guarantees is that they are applicable in all armed conflict contexts—that is, across both non-international armed conflict (NIAC) and international armed conflict (IAC). To that end, they are universal and the substance of the rules does not differ between IAC and NIAC, as can be the case with other aspects of LOAC (eg the rules on maritime visit and search, which apply in IAC and in certain NIACs of belligerency status, but not across all NIAC types). Thus, the fundamental guarantee prohibiting rape has the same substantive content regardless of conflict type. The thresholds that are relevant to the application of the IHL fundamental guarantees are those between: (i) a situation below the threshold of Common Article 2 (that is, the situation is not an IAC); (ii) a situation that is below the lowest threshold for a NIAC—that is, Common Article 3; and (iii) formal belligerent occupation. Any situation below the relevant threshold for an armed conflict or formal belligerent occupation[36] is thus not governed de jure by the IHL fundamental guarantees precisely because IHL is de jure inapplicable; such situations are governed by IHRL alone. Thus it is the case that a single act—for example, torture—is at once definable in the context of an armed conflict as a breach of an IHL fundamental guarantee, a war crime, and perhaps also a crime against humanity if the systemic element is present; but at another time, outside of armed conflict, is definable as a breach of IHRL, and potentially (given the almost inevitable

---

[31] Shane Darcy, *Judges, Law and War: The Judicial Development of International Humanitarian Law* (CUP 2014) 178.

[32] *Prosecutor v Charles Taylor* (Trial Chamber II Judgment) SCSL-03-01-T-1283(18 May 2012) paras 1017–1207 (count 5); *Ntaganda 2nd Jurisdiction Appeal* decision (above n 20).

[33] *Prosecutor v Jean Paul Akayesu* (Judgment) ICTR-96-4-T (2 September 1998) paras 685–697.

[34] *Prosecutor v Dragoljub Kunarac, Radomir Kovac, and Zoran Vukovic* (Appeals Chamber Judgment) IT-96-23& IT-96-23/1-A (12 June 2002) paras 127–133.

[35] *Prosecutor v Issa Hassan Sesay, Morris Kallon, and Augustine Gbao* (Trial Chamber Judgment) SCSL-04-15-T (2 March 2009) paras 147–148.

[36] That is, a formal GCIV occupation where LOAC continues to apply, as opposed to the mixed provenance concept of 'transformative occupation', as set out so clearly by Adam Roberts, 'Transformative Military Occupation: Applying the Laws of War and Human Rights' (2006) 100 *AJIL* 580.

presence of the systematic element implied by the requirement for an official capacity element for torture in IHRL), also a crime against humanity.

A second point worth brief note in relation to the applicability of the fundamental guarantees across both IAC and NIAC is that it illustrates one of the very few situations within the corpus of LOAC where NIAC LOAC initially offered a level of detail that was then cross-referred back into IAC LOAC—the reverse of the standard practice. This is because for some time the 'minimal' guarantees within Common Article 3 had no single, concise, or as encompassing parallel elsewhere in the Geneva Conventions scheme, and thus were applied universally.[37] It has now been replicated and further evolved in Additional Protocols I (API) and II (APII).[38]

## B. Conclusion

The description of 'IHL fundamental guarantees' proffered by and employed within this chapter is thus as follows: that body of rules, equally applicable in both forms of armed conflict, that deals with the treatment (and its consequences) of civilians, and of combatants/civilians DPH/OAG who are *hors de combat* or otherwise under the control of an adversary belligerent party (and, in some cases, of their own party), when and whilst they remain under that control, and where no other more contextually specific rule of LOAC applies to the treatment or consequence in question.

## 3. The Procedural Fundamental Guarantee of Legality

The principle of legality[39]—nullum crimen sine lege—is described in the CIHL Study as follows:

No one may be accused or convicted of a criminal offence on account of any act or omission which did not constitute a criminal offence under national or international law at the

---

[37] *Prosecutor v Dusko Tadić* (Trial Chamber Judgment) IT-94-1-T (7 May 1997) para 607: 'For that reason, each of the victims of the acts ascribed to the accused in Section III of this Opinion and Judgment enjoy the protection of the prohibitions contained in Common Article 3, applicable as it is to all armed conflicts . . .'; see generally, Darcy (above n 31) 163–5.

[38] APII article 4; API article 75(2):

The following acts are and shall remain prohibited at any time and in any place whatsoever, whether committed by civilian or by military agents:

(a) violence to the life, health, or physical or mental well-being of persons, in particular:
  (i) murder;
  (ii) torture of all kinds, whether physical or mental;
  (iii) corporal punishment; and
  (iv) mutilation;
(b) outrages upon personal dignity, in particular humiliating and degrading treatment, enforced prostitution and any form of indecent assault;
(c) the taking of hostages;
(d) collective punishments; and
(e) threats to commit any of the foregoing acts.

[39] GCIII article 99; GCIV article 67; API article 75(4)(c); APII article 6(2)(c); International Covenant on Civil and Political Rights (adopted 16 December 1966, entered into force 23 March 1976) 999 UNTS 171 (ICCPR) article 15(1).

time it was committed; nor may a heavier penalty be imposed than that which was applicable at the time the criminal offence was committed.[40]

This principle, as both a procedural and substantive fundamental guarantee in IHL, is of long—albeit imprecise—provenance; as Laucci notes:

> The International Military Tribunal in Nuremberg for instance broadly relied on customary law as codified in The *Hague Regulations* of 1907. The same reasoning was applied by the ICTY Appeals Chamber in its decision of 2 October 1995 in the *Tadic case*[[41]] to extend the definition of war crimes under Article 3 of the ICTY Statute to non-international armed conflicts.[42]

At the ICTY, the court specifically recognized the risks inherent in determining if, the point at which, and in relation to what conduct, illegality in international law could be said to have coalesced into a clear indication of individual criminal responsibility. In the *Vasiljevic* case, the Court cited the progressive ambitions expressed in (inter alia) the *Aleksovski* and *Delalić* appeal judgments, but in a note of caution noted that:

> The principle of nullum crimen sine lege 'does not prevent a court from interpreting and clarifying the elements of a particular crime'. Nor does it preclude the progressive development of the law by the court. But under no circumstances may the court create new criminal offences after the act charged against an accused either by giving a definition to a crime which had none so far, thereby rendering it prosecutable and punishable, or by criminalising an act which had not until the present time been regarded as criminal.[43]

This principle has also long been applied by national courts when dealing with war crimes legislation. An example of the former risk—inadequate coalescence as a crime of individual criminal responsibility—is found in the seminal Australian High Court case of *Polyukovich v The Commonwealth* (1991).[44] One point at issue related to the validity of Australian legislation (the *War Crimes Act* 1945,[45] which had been 'almost entirely repealed and replaced' via 1989 amending legislation[46]). This Act made proscribed conduct (primarily in Europe) between 1 September 1939 and 8 May 1945—that is, prior to the coming into force of the Act—prosecutable under Australian law; the question was, on one reading, whether this amounted to a Bill of Attainder.[47] As Mr Justice Deane observed, 'it is basic to our penal jurisprudence that a person who has disobeyed no relevant law is not guilty of a crime', and thus 'the whole focus of a criminal trial is the ascertainment of whether it is established that the accused in fact committed a past act which constituted a criminal contravention of the requirements of a valid law which was applicable to the act at the time the act was done.'[48]

---

[40] CIHL rule 101.

[41] *Prosecutor v Tadić* (Appeals Chamber Decision on the Defence Motion for Interlocutory Appeal on Jurisdiction) IT-94-1-AR72 (2 October 1995) para 89.

[42] Laucci (above n 25) 203.

[43] *Prosecutor v Mitar Vasiljevic* (Trial Chamber Judgment) IT-98-32-T (29 November 2002) para 196.

[44] *Polyukovich v The Commonwealth* [1991] HCA 32.

[45] War Crimes Act 1945 (Commonwealth) www.legislation.gov.au/Details/C2010C00110.

[46] *Polyukovich v The Commonwealth* (above n 44) para 5 (Mason CJ).

[47] ibid paras 23–41 (Mason CJ), 27 (Deane J).

[48] ibid para 27 (Deane J).

The majority ultimately held that the Act was a valid exercise of the Commonwealth's external affairs power. However, for the purposes of legality in terms of retrospectivity, this is not the relevant finding. The inherent 'legality' question was eloquently expressed by Mr Justice Brennan, who ultimately dissented, finding that the offence as formulated in the Act did not reflect the offence as it existed in international law at the time, and thus the Act itself was invalid to this extent.[49] Consequently, Brennan J continued:

> [The] primary question on this branch of the case is whether the material relied on establishes that in 1989 there was either an obligation under customary international law or a matter of international concern that war criminals from the pre-1945 years be sought out and tried for their offences.[50]

He concluded that:

> ... international law not only refuses to countenance retrospective provisions in international criminal law; it condemns as offensive to human rights retrospective municipal criminal law imposing a punishment for crime unless the crime was a crime under international law at the time when the relevant act was done. It follows that there can be no international obligation to enact a municipal law to attach a penalty to past conduct unless that conduct, at the time when it was engaged in, was a crime under international law.[51]

Retrospectivity in the absence of an international law offence existing at the relevant time is thus a strong indicator of a breach of the IHL fundamental guarantee of legality.

A clear example of the second dilemma noted by the ICTY in the *Vasiljevic* case is the conviction of David Hicks—who came into US custody after having joined an adversary force in Afghanistan—on the charge of 'providing material support for terrorism' under the US Military Commissions Act 2006.[52] At issue was the question of whether this offence was known to LOAC, or to other international law applicable in that context, at the alleged time of Hicks' conduct—which was prior to the elucidation of the offence in the Military Commissions Act of 2006. In a subsequent appeal to the US Court of Military Commission Review, the conviction was vacated on the basis that he could not plead guilty (as he had) to an offence that was not a crime at the relevant time.[53]

---

[49]  ibid para 76 (Brennan J).

[50]  ibid paras 8, 26 (Brennan J).

[51]  ibid para 48.

[52]  Military Commissions Act of 2006 (US) 120 STAT 2617, section 950v(b)(25):

> Providing Material Support For Terrorism—'(A) Offense: Any person subject to this chapter who provides material support or resources, knowing or intending that they are to be used in preparation for, or in carrying out, an act of terrorism (as set forth in paragraph (24)), or who intentionally provides material support or resources to an international terrorist organization engaged in hostilities against the United States, knowing that such organization has engaged or engages in terrorism (as so set forth), shall be punished as a military commission under this chapter may direct.' '(B) Material Support Or Resources Defined: In this paragraph, the term "material support or resources" has the meaning given that term in section 2339A(b) of title 18.'

[53]  *David Hicks v United States of America* CMCR 13-004, 8–9, United States Court of Military Commission Review, 18 February 2015 citing, inter alia, the recent precedent of *Al Bahlul v United States of America*, 767 F.3d 1 (DC Cir 2014) 29.

## 4. Key Specific Fundamental Guarantees

### A. Humane Treatment

#### 1. In general

The CIHL Study describes 'humane treatment' as 'an overarching concept'.[54] As Laucci notes, 'what exactly constitutes "humane treatment" is not defined. The Study mentions different texts referring to "respect for dignity" and "prohibition of ill-treatment" as alternative formulations for "humane treatment".[55] As a matter of IHL treaty law and commentary, the general concept of dignity and humane treatment has a long provenance,[56] and is found in some form in each of the four Geneva Conventions and in API and APII.[57] It is also routinely found in human rights treaties,[58] and in the Rome Statute of the ICC.[59] The prohibition on inhumane treatment is also noted in many military manuals.[60] For example, the German *Law of Armed Conflict Manual* (2013) states that:

> Civilians not taking a direct part in hostilities must be respected and protected. They must be treated humanely in all circumstances and are entitled to respect for their persons, their honour, their family rights, their religious convictions and practices, and their manners and customs.[61]

The case law of a number of international tribunals also deals with cruel and inhumane treatment within armed conflict contexts. In the ICTY *Delacic* case—cited with approval in the *Aleksovski* appeal decision—the concept was held not to require a 'discriminatory intention or motive'.[62] The definition the Court ultimately adopted was that of:

---

[54]  CIHL 307–308 rule 87.

[55]  Laucci (above n 25) 195.

[56]  See the brief discussion in the CIHL (Vols I and II) with respect to rule 87.

[57]  See eg: Common Article 3; Geneva Convention (I) for the Amelioration of the Condition of the Wounded and Sick in the Armed Forces in the Field (adopted 12 August 1949, entered into force 21 October 1950) 75 UNTS 31 (GCI) article 12(1); Geneva Convention (II) for the Amelioration of the Condition of the Wounded, Sick, and Shipwrecked Members of Armed Forces at Sea (adopted 12 August 1949, entered into force 12 October 1949) 75 UNTS 85 (GCII) article 12(1); GCIII article 13 ('Prisoners of war must at all times be humanely treated ...'); GCIV articles 5 and 27 (article 27: 'Protected persons are entitled, in all circumstances, to respect for their persons, their honour, their family rights, their religious convictions and practices, and their manners and customs. They shall at all times be humanely treated, and shall be protected especially against all acts of violence or threats thereof and against insults and public curiosity ...'); API article 75(1) ('In so far as they are affected by a situation referred to in Article 1 of this Protocol, persons who are in the power of a Party to the conflict and who do not benefit from more favourable treatment under the Conventions or under this Protocol shall be treated humanely in all circumstances ...'); APII article 4(1).

[58]  See eg ICCPR article 10(1): 'All persons deprived of their liberty shall be treated with humanity and with respect for the inherent dignity of the human person.'

[59]  As a crime against humanity, Rome Statute of the International Criminal Court (adopted 17 July 1998, entered into force 1 July 2002) 2187 UNTS 3 (Rome Statute) article 7(i)(k): 'Other inhumane acts ... intentionally causing great suffering, or serious injury to body or to mental or physical health ...'; as a war crime, eg, article 8(2)(a)(ii) (international armed conflicts—'torture or inhuman treatment'), and article 8(2)(c)(i)–(ii) (non-international armed conflicts: 'violence to life and person ... cruel treatment and torture', 'committing outrages upon personal dignity, in particular humiliating and degrading treatment').

[60]  See the CIHL database for a comprehensive list from those manuals made available to the ICRC.

[61]  Bundesministerium der Verteidigung Joint Service Regulation (ZDv), 15/2, *Law of Armed Conflict Manual* (May 2013) para 504 (references excluded).

[62]  *Prosecutor v Zlatko Aleksovski* (Appeals Chamber Judgment) IT-95-14/1-A (24 March 2000) para 26.

... an intentional act or omission, that is an act which, judged objectively, is deliberate and not accidental, which causes serious mental or physical suffering or injury or constitutes a serious attack on human dignity ... Thus, inhuman treatment is intentional treatment which does not conform with the fundamental principle of humanity, and forms the umbrella under which the remainder of the listed 'grave breaches' in the Conventions fall. Hence, acts characterised in the Conventions and Commentaries as inhuman, or which are inconsistent with the principle of humanity, constitute examples of actions that can be characterised as inhuman treatment.[63]

In the *Taylor* case before the SCSL, cruel treatment was characterized in terms of examples: amputation, mutilation, assaults, and so on.[64] Other cases evince a similar approach—cruel treatment and inhumane treatment are not of fixed scope in the way that murder is, but rather are of the 'you will know it when you see it' species of offence. Hence forced trench digging (although this was characterized by the Court as 'a serious attack on human dignity' which caused 'serious mental—and depending on the circumstances physical—suffering or injury', thus straddling the permeable line between inhumane-as-cruel, and inhumane as an outrage on dignity),[65] incapacitation in a well (which similarly was described as both 'serious mental suffering and ... a serious attack on ... human dignity'),[66] and being kept in inhumane camp conditions[67] have also been cited as instances of cruel and inhuman treatment.

To this end, it is perhaps useful to attempt to point to conduct that is considered to have fallen below the cruel-as-inhumane threshold, so as to illustrate whether there is actually any meaningful line of demarcation between this more serious breach of an IHL fundamental guarantee, and breaches of the overlapping strata of IHL fundamental guarantees characterized as degrading treatment and outrages upon personal dignity. At paragraphs 64–65 of the ICC Prosecutor's article 53(1) Report in relation to the *Mavi Marmara* referral,

---

[63] *Prosecutor v Zejnil Delalić, Zdravko Mucić also known as 'Pavo', Hazim Delić, Esad Landzo also known as 'Zenga'* (Trial Chamber Judgment) IT-96-21-T, (16 November 1998) paras 543, 552.

[64] *Prosecutor v Taylor* (above n 32) paras 433–437, 1208–354 (counts 7 and 8 of the indictment).

[65] *Prosecutor v Tihomir Blaskic* (Appeals Chamber Judgment) IT-95-14-A (29 July 2004) paras 596–597:

The Appeals Chamber finds that the use of persons taking no active part in hostilities to prepare military fortifications for use in operations and against the forces with whom those persons identify or sympathise is a serious attack on human dignity and causes serious mental (and depending on the circumstances physical) suffering or injury. Any order to compel protected persons to dig trenches or to prepare other forms of military installations, in particular when such persons are ordered to do so against their own forces in an armed conflict, constitutes cruel treatment.

[66] *Prosecutor v Ramush Haradinaj, Idriz Balaj, and Lahi Brahimaj* (Appeals Chamber Judgment) IT-04-84-A (19 July 2010) paras 93–97:

his treatment caused him serious mental suffering and constituted a serious attack on his human dignity ... [his] wife was taken away to be interrogated at a headquarters of the KLA, which had a reputation for violence ... [he] suffered serious mental harm when he was incapacitated in the well and separated from his wife, who was now in the hands of armed KLA soldiers.

[67] *Delalić* (above n 63) para 558:

Given that, in the context of Article 3 of the Statute, cruel treatment carries the same meaning as inhuman treatment in the context of Article 2, this allegation of inhumane conditions is appropriately charged as cruel treatment. However, in light of the above discussion of these offences, the Trial Chamber is of the view that, while it is possible to categorise inhumane conditions within the offence of wilfully causing great suffering or serious injury to body or health under Article 2, it is more appropriately placed within the offence of inhuman treatment.

she listed a series of allegations that arose out of treatment of the people onboard by IDF personnel:[68]

> The statements and accounts of passengers indicate that such mistreatment included: overly tight handcuffing for extended periods (in some instances causing swelling, discoloration, and numbing in their hands and causing lingering problems after the incident); being beaten; being denied access to toilet facilities and medication (such as for diabetes, asthma, and heart conditions); being given only limited access to food and drink; being forced to remain kneeling on the decks, exposed to the sun (reportedly resulting in 13 passengers receiving first-degree burns) as well as continuous seawater spray and wind gusts from helicopters hovering nearby, for a period of several hours; being subjected to various physical and verbal harassment such as pushing, shoving, kicking, and threats and intimidation (including from dogs which reportedly also bit a few passengers); being blindfolded or having hoods put over their heads.
>
> As a result of the denial of access to bathrooms, some passengers reportedly soiled themselves, and in one described case, 'a kneeling passenger who tried to move away from urine coming down from his neighbour had his face pressed down into the puddle.' There is some information that those who were permitted to use toilet facilities were kept handcuffed and were watched.

This list of conduct and consequences thus provides a useful set of acts against which to measure the differing levels of characterization of conduct. For example, in relation to inhumane treatment, the Prosecutor ultimately concluded that:

> ... it does not appear that the mistreatment by the IDF amounts to infliction of 'severe' pain or suffering so as to fall within the intended scope of inhuman treatment under article 8(2)(a)(ii) ... Instead, considering the level of suffering and discomfort as well as humiliation caused to passengers, the mistreatment of the passengers on the *Mavi Marmara* by IDF soldiers, could rather amount to the war crime of outrages upon personal dignity, in particular humiliating and degrading treatment pursuant to article 8(2)(b)(xxi).[69]

However, as the examples noted above tend to indicate, the line between inhumane treatment that is cruel and that which is merely an outrage upon dignity is at best ambiguous.

### 2. Spectrum of proscribed conduct

Humane treatment, consequently, covers a wide range of individual crimes. At the lower end of the scale, as noted in section 2 ' "Fundamental Guarantees" within the Broader IHL/LOAC Scheme' above, are the prohibitions against corporal punishment,[70] and serious breaches of dignity.[71] In relation to the latter, this lower threshold was described in the *Katanga* case at the ICC thus:

---

[68] Office of the Prosecutor (ICC), *Situation on Registered Vessels of Comoros, Greece and Cambodia: Article 53(1) Report* (6 November 2014) (*Mavi Marmara Report*) paras 62–72, in relation to inhuman treatment pursuant to article 8(2)(a)(ii)-2, and committing outrages upon personal dignity, in particular humiliating and degrading treatment pursuant to article 8(2)(b)(xxi).

[69] ibid para 69.

[70] CIHL rule 91; GCIII article 87; GCIV article 32; API article 75(2)(a)(iii); APII article 4(2)(a).

[71] *Mavi Marmara Report* (above n 68) para 70:

The types of actions or omissions which could constitute a crime under article 8(2)(b)(xxi) were left undefined. As a result, the core element of this war crime is the humiliation, degradation, or violation of the person's dignity. In addition, the acts of humiliation, degradation or violation to the person's dignity must be committed with objectively sufficient gravity so as to be 'generally recognized as an outrage upon personal dignity'. Nevertheless, the jurisprudence of the ICTY provides that 'so long as the serious humiliation or degradation is real and serious,' there is no requirement that such suffering be lasting, or that it is 'necessary for the act to directly harm the physical or mental well-being of the victim'.[72]

At the other end of the scale, inhumane treatment also encompasses crimes that manifest as violence to life (murder,[73] torture[74] enforced disappearance[75]) and—in a variety of manifestations and characterizations—rape.[76] Of significance with respect to murder or willful killing (held to be, in almost every context, the same offence),[77] is the oft-cited maxim that the 'potential discrepancy between the provisions of HRL and IHL with respect to the right to life is rendered especially stark in situations in which the killings take place far from any conventional battlefield'.[78] However, as noted previously, it is vital that a battlefield killing—of a combatant within the bounds of LOAC, or of a civilian as permissible incidental injury/collateral damage as the result of a lawful attack—should not be assessed as a potential breach of the IHL fundamental guarantee prohibiting murder and willful killing. This is because in this narrow set of circumstances, the matter is de jure subject to more specialized rules of IHL, the application of which renders a different characterization of both the conduct and the result.

> The war crime of 'outrages upon personal dignity' requires the two following elements: (i) the perpetrator humiliated, degraded or otherwise violated the dignity of one or more persons; and (ii) the severity of the humiliation, degradation or other violation was of such a degree as to be generally recognized as an outrage upon personal dignity.

[72] *Prosecutor v Germain Katanga and Mathieu Ngudjolo Chui* (Pre-Trial Chamber Decision on the Confirmation of Charges) ICC-01/04-01/07 (30 September 2008) para 369.
[73] CIHL rule 89; Common Article 3; GCI article 50; GCII article 51; GCIII articles 13–14; GCIV article 147; API article 75(2)(a)(i); APII article 4(2)(a); ICCPR article 6(1); Turku Declaration article 8(1): 'Every human being has the inherent right to life. This right shall be protected by law. No one shall be arbitrarily deprived of his or her life ...'.
[74] CIHL rule 90 combines torture, cruel or inhuman treatment, and outrages upon personal dignity, and (as a subset of this latter) humiliating and degrading treatment, into a single rule; Common Article 3; GCI article 12; GCII article 12; GCIII articles 17, 87, and 89; GCIV article 32; API articles 75(2)(a)(ii); APII article 4(2)(a); ICCPR article 7.
[75] CIHL rule 98; Rome Statute article 7(2)(i):

> the arrest, detention or abduction of persons by, or with the authorization, support or acquiescence of, a State or a political organization, followed by refusal to acknowledge that deprivation of freedom or to give information on the fate or whereabouts of those persons, with the intention of removing them from the protection of the law for a prolonged period of time.

See generally, Balendra (above n 25) 2504:

> Enforced disappearances are not as such addressed by IHL treaties. However, they are closely connected to other forms of IHL violations, such as arbitrary deprivations of liberty, torture and other cruel treatments and murder, of which they may, under certain circumstances, constitute a consequence. The UN Declaration on Enforced Disappearance of 1992 specifically addresses the case of enforced disappearances, without defining it.

[76] CIHL rule 93; GCIII article 14; GCIV article 27; API article 75(2)(b); APII article 4(2)(e).
[77] See eg *Prosecutor v Tihomir Blaskic* (Trial Chamber Judgment) IT-95-14-T (3 March 2000) para 181.
[78] Balendra (above n 25) 2504.

### 3. Some current interpretive challenges

There is a range of challenges associated with distilling and applying this broad category of IHL fundamental guarantees; for illustrative purposes, however, it will suffice to briefly highlight only two. The first is that a single incident of conduct may simultaneously transgress a number of IHL fundamental guarantees. For example, the ICC *Elements of Crimes* defines torture as 'severe physical or mental pain or suffering' inflicted for the specific purpose of 'obtaining information or a confession, punishment, intimidation or coercion or for any reason based on discrimination of any kind'.[79] Indeed, inhumane treatment more generally can be differentiated from torture specifically by the absence of a specific purpose requirement.[80] This differentiation between cruel treatment and torture as hinging around the presence of a 'punishment, coercion, discrimination or intimidation' purpose has a long history in LOAC, having been clearly expressed (albeit as limited to 'extorting confessions') in the *Lieber Code*.[81] The European Court of Human Rights, the Inter-American Commission on Human Rights, and the ICTY (for example) have all found that rape can also be characterized as torture—both as a breach of a human right, and as a violation of an IHL fundamental guarantee when committed in the context of an armed conflict.[82]

This point raises a second ongoing challenge worth brief noting: that the content of a parallel or similarly named human right/IHL fundamental guarantee may differ as between IHL on the one hand, and IHRL on the other. The classic example is, again, torture.[83] The most authoritative IHRL definition of torture is that found in article 1 of the Convention against Torture 1984 (CAT):

---

[79]  ICC, *Elements of Crimes* (PrintPartners Ipskamp 2011) articles 8(2)(a)(ii)-1 and 8(2)(c)(i)-4.

[80]  See eg CIHL 317.

[81]  *Instructions for the Government of Armies of the United States in the Field*, General Orders No 100 (24 April 1863) article 16: 'Military necessity does not admit of cruelty—that is, the infliction of suffering for the sake of suffering or for revenge, nor of maiming or wounding except in fight, nor of torture to extort confessions . . .'.

[82]  *Aydin v Turkey* App No 571199616761866 (ECtHR, 25 September 1997) para 86; Inter-American Commission on Human Rights (IACommHR) *Fernando and Raquel Mejia v Peru* Case No 10.970 (1 March 1996) Report No 5/96, section V.B.2.3.a; *Delalić* (above n 63) paras 475–497:

> 494. In view of the above discussion, the Trial Chamber therefore finds that the elements of torture, for the purposes of applying Articles 2 and 3 of the Statute, may be enumerated as follows:
>  (i) There must be an act or omission that causes severe pain or suffering, whether mental or physical,
>  (ii) which is inflicted intentionally,
>  (iii) and for such purposes as obtaining information or a confession from the victim, or a third person, punishing the victim for an act he or she or a third person has committed or is suspected of having committed, intimidating or coercing the victim or a third person, or for any reason based on discrimination of any kind,
>  (iv) and such act or omission being committed by, or at the instigation of, or with the consent or acquiescence of, an official or other person acting in an official capacity.
> 495. The Trial Chamber considers the rape of any person to be a despicable act which strikes at the very core of human dignity and physical integrity. The condemnation and punishment of rape becomes all the more urgent where it is committed by, or at the instigation of, a public official, or with the consent or acquiescence of such an official. Rape causes severe pain and suffering, both physical and psychological. The psychological suffering of persons upon whom rape is inflicted may be exacerbated by social and cultural conditions and can be particularly acute and long lasting. Furthermore, it is difficult to envisage circumstances in which rape, by, or at the instigation of a public official, or with the consent or acquiescence of an official, could be considered as occurring for a purpose that does not, in some way, involve punishment, coercion, discrimination or intimidation. In the view of this Trial Chamber this is inherent in situations of armed conflict.
> 496. Accordingly, whenever rape and other forms of sexual violence meet the aforementioned criteria, then they shall constitute torture, in the same manner as any other acts that meet this criteria.

[83]  See generally CIHL rule 90 commentary, 317–18.

For the purposes of this Convention, the term 'torture' means any act by which severe pain or suffering, whether physical or mental, is intentionally inflicted on a person for such purposes as obtaining from him or a third person information or a confession, punishing him for an act he or a third person has committed or is suspected of having committed, or intimidating or coercing him or a third person, or for any reason based on discrimination of any kind, when such pain or suffering is inflicted by or at the instigation of or with the consent or acquiescence of a public official or other person acting in an official capacity. It does not include pain or suffering arising only from, inherent in or incidental to lawful sanctions.[84]

This definition—as is logical given the original state power–citizen victim focus of IHRL—requires an element of official capacity in respect of the perpetrator. However, the IHL fundamental guarantee in relation to torture does not contain this element. Although a number of early ICTY cases read this official capacity element into the offence insofar as it constituted a crime within ICTY jurisdiction,[85] in the 2002 *Kunarac* case appellate judgment, the ITCY Appeals Chamber engaged in a clarification exercise, noting that whilst torture for the purposes of the CAT required this element, torture as a more generally prohibited act under customary international law did not necessarily do so.[86] The Appeals Chamber approved 'the conclusions of the Trial Chamber identifying the crime of torture on the basis of three elements, these being respectively an intentional act, inflicting suffering, and the existence of a prohibited purpose'.[87] 'The public official requirement', consequently, 'is not a requirement under customary international law in relation to the criminal responsibility of an individual for torture outside of the framework of the *Torture Convention*.'[88] Thus the elements of the offence of torture as a breach of human rights—and perhaps also as a crime against humanity[89]—differ from torture as a violation of the relevant IHL fundamental guarantee.[90]

---

[84] Convention against Torture and Other Cruel, Inhuman or Degrading Treatment or Punishment (adopted 10 December 1984, entered into force 26 June 1987) 1465 UNTS 85.

[85] See eg *Akayesu* (above n 33) paras 593–594; *Prosecutor v Anton Furundzija* (Trial Judgment) IT-95-17/1-T (10 December 1998) paras 134–164; *Prosecutor v Anton Furundzija* (Appeal Chamber Judgment) IT-95-17/1-A (21 July 2000) para 111:

> The Trial Chamber correctly identified the following elements of the crime of torture in a situation of armed conflict: (i) … the infliction, by act or omission, of severe pain or suffering, whether physical or mental; in addition; (ii) this act or omission must be intentional; (iii) it must aim at obtaining information or a confession, or at punishing, intimidating, humiliating or coercing the victim or a third person, or at discriminating, on any ground, against the victim or a third person; (iv) it must be linked to an armed conflict; (v) at least one of the persons involved in the torture process must be a public official or must at any rate act in a non-private capacity, e.g., as a de facto organ of a State or any other authority-wielding entity.

[86] *Kunarac* (above n 34) paras 142–148.

[87] ibid para 134.

[88] ibid para 148; this now appears to be the accepted trajectory of ICTY jurisprudence—eg *Prosecutor v Miroslav Kvocka, Mlado Radic, Zoran Zigic, Dragoljub Prcac* (Appeals Chamber Judgment) IT-98-30/1-A (28 February 2005) paras 280–284.

[89] ICC, *Elements of Crimes* (above n 79) article 7(1)(f) does not specify this, but it is arguably implicit in the 'widespread or systematic attack on the civilian population' contextual requirement.

[90] See eg ICC *Elements of Crimes* (above n 79) article 8 (2)(a)(ii)-1, which has no 'official capacity' nexus or requirement; the offence does, however, require that the proscribed conduct be carried out in the context of (in this case) an IAC.

## B. Non-Detention-Based Restrictions on Freedom

Slavery and the slave trade,[91] and uncompensated or abusive forced labour,[92] must at the outset be distinguished from the compellable utilization of POWs as a labour force in certain industries (including, if they volunteer, in dangerous and unsafe industries), and for the purposes relating to the functioning of the POW camp[93] (for which POWs are entitled to remuneration[94]). Slavery of POWs and civilians was a common consequence of ancient warfare,[95] and continued as a routine practice in the early modern period—for example, after engagements between Ottoman and other European forces.[96] However, it was falling into disuse after the 1700s—although approximately 1000 British soldiers who had served in Bonnie Prince Charlie's forces during the 1745 uprising were sent to the American colonies as slaves (being traitors, not POWs).[97] Forced labour, however, is in some circumstances indistinguishable in effect from slavery, and remains a persistent source of breaches of IHL fundamental guarantees in one form or another.[98] 'Rape camps', such as those that existed during the 1991–1995 breakup of the Former Yugoslavia, along with sexual slavery as prosecuted in the SCSL and ICC, are an associated evil in a category of their own, combining the restrictions of slavery (or, if the 'ownership rights' component of slavery is not admitted, then at the very least forced labour) with the inhumane treatment attendant upon violence, torture, and rape.[99]

However, it is equally important to recall that violence is not a definitional component of slavery as a breach of the parallel IHL fundamental guarantee. In *US v Oswald Pohl and Others*, the US Military Tribunal sitting in Germany after the Second World War asserted that:

> Slavery may exist even without torture. Slaves may be well fed, well clothed, and comfortably housed, but they are still slaves if without lawful process they are deprived of their freedom by forceful restraint. We might eliminate all proof of ill-treatment, overlook the starvation,

---

[91] CIHL rule 94; APII article 4(2)(f); ICCPR article 8; Slavery Convention (adopted 25 September 1926, entered into force 9 March 1927) 60 LNTS 253; Supplementary Convention on the Abolition of Slavery, the Slave Trade, and Institutions and Practices Similar to Slavery (adopted 7 September 1956, entered into force 30 April 1957) 266 UNTS 3; Protocol to Prevent, Suppress and Punish Trafficking in Persons, Especially Women and Children, Supplementing the United Nations Convention against Transnational Organized Crime (adopted 15 November 2000, entered into force 25 December 2003) 2237 UNTS 319.

[92] CIHL rule 95; GCIII articles 49–68; GCIV articles 40, 51–52, 95–96 and 132–135.

[93] GCIII articles 49–57.

[94] ibid article 62: 'The rate shall be fixed by the said authorities, but shall at no time be less than one-fourth of one Swiss franc for a full working day ...'.

[95] See eg Gillespie (above n 3) Vol II, 112 (Ancient Greece).

[96] See eg: Noel Malcolm, *Agents of Empire: Knights, Corsairs, Jesuits and Spies in the Late Sixteenth-Century Mediterranean World* (OUP 2015) chapter 11, on the lucrative practice of hostage and POW slave ransoming and exchange that existed between the Ottoman Empire on one hand, and its routine adversaries—Spain, Venice, The Papacy, and the Holy Roman Empire—in the 1500s.

[97] Gillespie (above n 3) Vol I, 142.

[98] For example, German labour and concentration inmate 'Ausländereinsatz' policy during WWII: 'Nazi Germany created one of the largest forced labor systems in history: Over twenty million foreign civilian workers, concentration camp prisoners and prisoners of war from all of the occupied countries were required to perform forced labor in Germany in the course of the Second World War': Forced Labor 1939–1945: Memory and History Archive, 'Nazi Forced Labor: Background Information' www.zwangsarbeit-archiv.de/en/zwangsarbeit/zwangsarbeit/zwangsarbeit-2/index.html.

[99] See eg *Prosecution v Taylor* (above n 32) para 1028; for a summary of the ICTY's case law, see Matteo Fiori, 'The Foca "Rape Camps": A Dark Page Read through the ICTY's Jurisprudence' *Hague Justice Portal* (19 December 2007) www.haguejusticeportal.net/index.php?id=8712.

beatings, and other barbarous acts, but the admitted fact of slavery—compulsory uncompensated labour would still remain. There is no such thing as benevolent slavery. Involuntary servitude, even if tempered by humane treatment, is still slavery.[100]

*Pohl* was cited and updated in the ICTY *Kunarac* appeal judgment—albeit as a crime against humanity rather than as a war crime:

> The Appeals Chamber accepts the chief thesis of the Trial Chamber that the traditional concept of slavery, as defined in the 1926 Slavery Convention and often referred to as 'chattel slavery', has evolved to encompass various contemporary forms of slavery which are also based on the exercise of any or all of the powers attaching to the right of ownership. In the case of these various contemporary forms of slavery, the victim is not subject to the exercise of the more extreme rights of ownership associated with 'chattel slavery', but in all cases, as a result of the exercise of any or all of the powers attaching to the right of ownership, there is some destruction of the juridical personality; the destruction is greater in the case of 'chattel slavery' but the difference is one of degree. The Appeals Chamber considers that, at the time relevant to the alleged crimes, these contemporary forms of slavery formed part of enslavement as a crime against humanity under customary international law.[101]

This reasoning is arguably indicative of a trend towards collapsing the previously distinct concepts of slavery and uncompensated or inadequately compensated forced labour into a single concept, often by using the latter as an indicator of the former. This tendency is most evident in, for example, the *Krnojelac* case:

> To establish the allegation that detainees were forced to work and that the labour detainees performed constituted a form of enslavement, the Prosecution must establish that the Accused (or persons for whose actions he is criminally responsible) forced the detainees to work, that he (or they) exercised any or all of the powers attaching to the right of ownership over them, and that he (or they) exercised those powers intentionally.
> International humanitarian law does not prohibit all labour by protected persons in armed conflicts. Generally, the prohibition is against forced or involuntary labour. It is clear from the Tribunal's jurisprudence that 'the exaction of forced or compulsory labour or service' is an 'indication of enslavement', and a 'factor to be taken into consideration in determining whether enslavement was committed'.[102]

This trend is understandable, but perhaps unnecessary. The IHL fundamental guarantee against forced labour could readily cover the modern field, encompassing a spectrum of conduct in armed conflict that extends from enslavement (with its traditional requirement for the exercise of 'ownership rights') through to the 'indentured servitude' that characterizes much trafficking of workers. The differences may be akin to those between murder and wilful killing—situationally arguable, but for all practical effects negligible or even

---

[100] *US v Oswald Pohl and Others* (Judgement) (3 November 1947), reprinted in Trials of War Criminals before the Nuremberg Military Tribunals under Control Council Law No 10 (1997) Vol 5, 970.

[101] *Kunarac* (above n 34) para 117.

[102] *Prosecutor v Milorad Krnojelac* (Trial Chamber Judgment) IT-97-25-T (15 March 2002) paras 350–351, 358–359.

irrelevant. So long as differentiation is maintained between this—unlawful—category of slavery/forced labour, and those limited circumstances at the lower end of the scale in which adequately compensated forced labour of civilians, and forced labour of POWs, is retained, then clarity around the distinction should remain. To some extent this conundrum simply requires application of the same sort of symbiotic interpretive approach that attends differentiating wilful killing of a civilian (a breach of an IHL fundamental guarantee) and the (permissible) incidental killing of a civilian in a lawful targeting operation.

## 5. Conclusion

Justice O'Connor stated in the US Supreme Court case of *Hamdi* that 'it is during our most challenging and uncertain moments that ... we must preserve our commitment at home to the principles for which we fight abroad'.[103] Compliance with the IHL fundamental guarantees provides a sensitive and reliable barometer for this purpose. Informed as it is by IHL, IHRL, and practice, the concept of IHL fundamental guarantees both represents and embodies this general commitment through its broad-based ambit requirements—such as humane treatment and legality. Yet the concept also furnishes a detailed and interlocking rule set calibrated to foster practical attainment of this goal. Certainly, discrete elements of this rule set are still evolving—the increasing deployment of the war crime of rape as a response to the breach of an independent IHL fundamental guarantee, rather than as a crime indicative of the breach of some other IHL fundamental guarantee, still has some way to go. Similarly, some currently separate IHL fundamental guarantees may in the future consolidate around a single umbrella concept—as seems to be the trend with slavery, enslavement, and impermissible forms of forced labour. Additionally, the assertive independence that some courts and interpretive communities continue to display in ensuring focused differentiation, where required, between the substantive elements of an IHL fundamental guarantee on the one hand and its IHRL counterpart on the other—as with torture—also speaks well of the continuing dynamism and fitness for purpose of IHL fundamental guarantees as both concept and detailed rule set.

---

[103] *Hamdi v Rumsfeld* 542 US 507, 532 (2004).

# 7

# International Humanitarian Law and the Conduct of Hostilities

*Michael N Schmitt**

## 1. Introduction

This chapter examines the principles and rules of international humanitarian law (IHL) that govern the conduct of hostilities by states and other participants during an armed conflict. The term 'conduct of hostilities' refers to the application of force in the course of such conflicts.[1] In particular, it encompasses the various methods (tactics) and the means (weapons) that are used during the hostilities.

Those aspects of IHL that address the conduct of hostilities can best be understood by reference to a normative typology consisting of foundational principles, general principles, and rules. Foundational principles underpin the law, but are not themselves of direct applicability to the conduct of hostilities. States negotiate and adopt IHL treaties based on their assessment of the optimal balance between these foundational principles. They do so by conducting an auto-assessment of their national interests in the context of the particular IHL-related issue under consideration. Customary IHL likewise emerges from these foundational principles. Such law crystallizes when sufficient state practice and expressions of *opinio juris* exist for the emergence of a new IHL norm binding on all states. The relevant practice and expressions are the product of states' balancing of foundational principles consistent with their perceived national interests.

Foundational principles also underlie the interpretation and application of IHL. In cases in which the precise meaning of an IHL rule is unclear, or when its application in a particular circumstance is abstruse, states turn to these foundational principles, in addition to more doctrinal means of discerning international law, as a means of clarification in the circumstances. Although the process may be subliminal, states nevertheless inevitably consider these foundational principles in the process of ascertaining those interpretations and applications of IHL rules that best foster their particular interests.

Whereas foundational principles broadly inform IHL, general IHL principles are the sources of individual rules. They are the first product, in the form of binding 'hard law', to emerge from the process during which states balance the foundational principles. Although

* The views expressed are those of the author in his personal capacity and do not necessarily represent those of the US government.

[1] See also Sylvie-S Junod and Jean Pictet, 'Commentary on Protocol II', in Yves Sandoz, Christophe Swinarski, and Bruno Zimmermann (eds), *Commentary on the Additional Protocols of 8 June 1977 to the Geneva Conventions of 12 August 1949* (Martinus Nijhoff 1987) para 4788: '[h]ostilities have been defined as "acts of war that by their nature or purpose struck at the personnel and *materiel* of enemy armed forces"' (citations omitted) (AP Commentary).

prescriptive in nature, general principles are seldom applied directly during an armed conflict. Instead, they frame and inform the individual rules.

Rules are the instruments by which states, the sole generators of IHL, agree to limit their freedom of action, and that of other participants, during an armed conflict. They specifically delineate conduct that is unlawful and articulate the requirements with which participants in the conflict must comply when conducting hostilities. A violation of IHL is typically a breach of a particular rule.

This chapter is in three main parts. To place the remaining discussion in context, it begins with an introduction to the two foundational principles underlying the IHL applicable to the conduct of hostilities—military necessity and humanity. The chapter then turns to the content of this body of law, the general principles and their derivative rules. It concludes with a brief examination of certain new technologies warfare and highlights the key legal issues they raise with respect to the conduct of hostilities.

## 2. Foundational Principles

The foundational principles of military necessity and humanity undergird IHL in the sense that every IHL general principle and rule on the conduct of hostilities reflects a balancing by states of these foundational principles as they create, interpret, and apply individual operative norms.[2] States engage in hostilities because they have determined that doing so is in their national interest. Therefore, they must ensure that law does not impede their ability to engage in those hostilities that they deem militarily necessary to achieve such interests, which run the continuum from territorial conquest to self-defence. Yet, states also find limitations on the conduct of warfare to be in their interest, whether to protect their population and members of their armed forces from the excesses of war or out of a commitment to humanitarian values. Thus, states continuously struggle to find the optimal balance between these two oft-competing goods when adopting new law. The same dynamic takes place whenever states are faced with the prospect of having to interpret a particular rule or determine how an extant norm should be applied on the battlefield.

Military necessity is often misconstrued as a principal that justifies departure from an IHL rule when merited by the military exigencies of a situation. Historically, this notion was referred to as *Kreigraison*. Yet, *Kreigraison* began to be questioned by distinguished commentators soon after the turn of the twentieth century.[3] The International Military Tribunal at Nuremburg unambiguously rejected it in the aftermath of the Second World War.[4] Today, and despite occasional, unfortunate, counter-normative relapses,[5] *Kreigraison* has no place in the application of IHL.[6]

---

[2] For a discussion of the operation of IHL's foundational principles, see Michael N Schmitt, 'Military Necessity and Humanity in International Humanitarian Law: Preserving the Delicate Balance' (2010) 50 *Va J Int'l L* 795.

[3] Eg Elihu Root, 'Opening Address' (15th Annual Meeting of the American Society of International Law, Washington, 27 April 1921 (1921) 15 *ASIL PROC* 1, 3:'[e]ither the doctrine of Kriegsraison must be abandoned definitely and finally, or there is an end of international law, and in its place will be left a world without law'.

[4] *United States v Wilhelm List and others* (1949) 8 LRTWC 34 (19 February 1948) (*Hostage* case).

[5] Memorandum from Alberto R Gonzales, Counsel to the President, to George W Bush, President of the United States (25 January 2002): describing certain provisions of the Geneva Convention (IV) Relative to the Protection of Civilian Persons in Time of War (adopted 12 August 1949, entered into force 21 October 1953) 75 UNTS 287 (GCIV) as 'quaint'.

[6] See eg *Prosecutor v Fofana and Kondewa* (Appeals Chamber Judgment) SCSL-04-14-A (28 May 2008) para 247.

Instead, to the extent that military necessity justifies deviation from an IHL rule, the rule itself will expressly so indicate. For instance, the Fourth Geneva Convention of 1949 (GCIV) prohibits occupying powers from destroying certain property 'except where such destruction is rendered absolutely necessary by military operations'.[7] Similarly, Additional Protocol I of 1977 to the Geneva Conventions of 1949 (API) sometimes permits 'scorched earth' tactics in territory under a party's control, the use of enemy 'matériel and buildings of military units permanently assigned to civil defence organizations', and restrictions on civil defence and relief personnel in situations of 'imperative military necessity'.[8]

Military necessity is also occasionally misconstrued as a rule of IHL with direct application to the conduct of hostilities. By this approach, activities that have not been prohibited by either treaty or customary IHL are impermissible if they are unnecessary from a military perspective. The approach conflates foundational principles with rules. When IHL limits actions that are not sufficiently militarily advantageous to justify the resulting consequences, it specifically provides for such in the respective rule. The archetypal example is the rule of proportionality (see section 3.A.1.B *Proportionality* below), which prohibits attacks against valid military objectives when the attacks can be expected to cause excessive collateral damage (see section 3.A.1.B *Proportionality* below).

A second foundational principle, humanity, seeks to ensure that the effects of armed conflict on civilians, civilian objects, other protected persons and objects, and even combatants, is minimized. The aforementioned rule of proportionality is a paradigmatic expression of the principle since it bars militarily necessary attacks when their humanitarian consequences would be too egregious in the circumstances. Other examples include the requirement that medical facilities being misused for military purposes, and therefore qualifying as military objectives, be warned before being attacked;[9] the rule that wounded military personnel may not be attacked even when it is likely that they will be treated and returned to the battle;[10] and the prohibition on direct attacks against civilians or civilian property even if such attacks undercut the morale of the civilian population, thereby measurably enhancing the chances of victory.[11]

The inherent balancing of IHL's foundational principles is reflected in the famous Martens Clause. First included in the Hague Convention II of 1899,[12] article 1(2) of API

---

[7] GCIV article 53.

[8] Protocol Additional to the Geneva Conventions of 12 August 1949, and Relating to the Protection of Victims of International Armed Conflicts (adopted 8 June 1977, entered into force 7 December 1978) 1125 UNTS 3 (API) articles 54(5), 67(4), 62(1), and 71(3).

[9] Geneva Convention (I) for the Amelioration of the Condition of the Wounded and Sick in the Armed Forces in the Field (adopted 12 August 1949, entered into force 21 October 1950) 75 UNTS 31 (GCI) article 21; GCIV article 19; API article 13(1); Protocol Additional to the Geneva Conventions of 12 August 1949, and Relating to the Protection of Victims of Non-International Armed Conflicts (adopted 8 June 1977, entered into force 7 December 1978) 1125 UNTS 609 (APII) article 11(2); Jean-Marie Henckaerts and Louise Doswald-Beck (eds), *Customary International Humanitarian Law, Vol 1: Rules* (CUP 2005) (CIHL) 91–8, commentary to rule 28.

[10] Regulations Respecting the Laws and Customs of War on Land, annexed to Hague Convention (IV) Respecting the Laws and Customs of War on Land (adopted 18 October 1907; entered into force 26 January 1910) 187 CTS 227 (Hague Regulations) article 23(c); GCI article 3; Geneva Convention (II) for the Amelioration of the Condition of the Wounded, Sick, and Shipwrecked Members of Armed Forces at Sea (adopted 12 August 1949, entered into force 12 October 1949) 75 UNTS 85 (GCII) article 3; Geneva Convention (III) Relative to the Treatment of Prisoners of War (adopted 12 August 1949, entered into force 12 October 1950) 75 UNTS 135 (GCIII) article 3; API articles 40–41; APII article 4(1); CIHL 164, rule 47(b).

[11] See discussion below.

[12] Hague Convention (II) with Respect to the Laws and Customs of War on Land (adopted 29 July 1899; entered into force 4 September 1900) 187 CTS 429 (Hague Convention II) preamble. See also Hague Convention (IV) with Respect to the Laws and Customs of War on Land (adopted 18 October 1907; entered into force 26 January 1910) 205 CTS 227 (Hague Convention IV) preamble.

is its contemporary articulation: '[i]n cases not covered by this Protocol or by other international agreements, civilians and combatants remain under the protection and authority of the principles of international law derived from established custom, from the principles of humanity and from the dictates of public conscience'. The International Court of Justice (ICJ) has perceptively recognized that the Martens Clause captures IHL's balancing of military necessity and humanity. In its *Nuclear Weapons Advisory Opinion*, the Court noted that in conformity with the Martens Clause,

> ... humanitarian law, at a very early stage, prohibited certain types of weapons either because of their indiscriminate effect on combatants and civilians or because of the unnecessary suffering caused to combatants, that is to say, a harm greater than that unavoidable to achieve legitimate military objectives. If an envisaged use of weapons would not meet the requirements of humanitarian law, a threat to engage in such use would also be contrary to that law.[13]

It must be cautioned that the balance between the foundational principles can shift over time, with changes in the nature of conflict, the weapons used, and the interests of individual states and the international community. For instance, during the conflict in Afghanistan from 2001, a major debate surfaced over whether it was lawful to target the drug infrastructure that partly funded Taliban activities. Although it might previously have been agreed that such operations violated the rules against attacking civilians and civilian objects, the criticality of the funding to the Taliban's war effort caused some states to question their application in this circumstance. More recently, in the Syria conflict since 2012, coalition forces have been mounting airstrikes against Islamic State in Syria (ISIS) oil production and transportation assets, to undercut the group's financial base. Although such strikes are consistent with IHL when directed against oil being employed by the organization for its own military operations, it is not evident that oil-related targets qualify as military objectives when oil profits finance the group in a general sense. Nevertheless, there has been little criticism of the airstrikes by states that are not participating in them. It is unclear whether that silence reflects the near-universal contempt in which the group is held; whether it is a rational manifestation of the reality that ISIS is effectively countered by denying it critical financing; or whether it constitutes a normative signal that interpretation of the concept of military objective is evolving as groups like ISIS and Al Qaeda metastasize.

## 3. General Principles and Specific Rules

In the *Nuclear Weapons* case, the ICJ identified two of the three general principles of IHL informing the normative landscape governing the conduct of hostilities:

> The cardinal principles contained in the texts constituting the fabric of humanitarian law are the following. The first is aimed at the protection of the civilian population and civilian

---

[13] *Legality of the Threat of Use of Nuclear Weapons* (Advisory Opinion) [1996] ICJ Rep 66 (*Nuclear Weapons*) para 78.

objects and establishes the distinction between combatants and non-combatants; States must never make civilians the object of attack and must consequently never use weapons that are incapable of distinguishing between civilian and military targets. According to the second principle, it is prohibited to cause unnecessary suffering to combatants: it is accordingly prohibited to use weapons causing them such harm or uselessly aggravating their suffering. In application of that second principle, States do not have unlimited freedom of choice of means in the weapons they use.[14]

Both 'cardinal principles' embody the balancing of the foundational principles discussed above. The first—distinction—limits military operations by carving out, based on humanitarian concerns, categories of persons and objects that may not be attacked and with respect to which various precautions must be taken to avoid harming them. The second—unnecessary suffering—restricts certain forms of harm suffered by those who participate in the hostilities to that which is for the effective conduct of hostilities. Most IHL rules governing the conduct of hostilities, set forth below, derive from these two general principles. A third general principle—chivalry—also serves as a basis for specific rules.

Before turning to the rules, it must be noted that those that follow are meant to reflect customary international law in both non-international armed conflict (NIAC) and international armed conflict (IAC). Further, the discussion draws largely on API, which is the most comprehensive of the treaties dealing with the conduct of hostilities. Although the instrument does not bind non-party states like the US and Israel, most conduct-of-hostilities provisions contained therein are generally considered to reflect customary IHL norms. Where that is not the case, the deviation will be highlighted. Additionally, while the instrument is applicable only to IAC, there is wide consensus that most of its provisions with respect to the conduct of hostilities apply *mutatis mutandi* to NIAC, and bind non-state-organized armed groups participating in those conflicts.[15] Except as otherwise noted, the discussion will therefore generally adopt the stance taken by the International Committee of the Red Cross (ICRC) in its Customary International Humanitarian Law Study (CIHL Study) with respect to both the customary nature of the rules and their applicability in NIACs.

## A.  Distinction

Article 48 of API provides that:

> In order to ensure respect for and protection of the civilian population and civilian objects, the Parties to the conflict shall at all times distinguish between the civilian population and

---

[14] ibid para 78.
[15] *Prosecutor v Tadić* (Interlocutory Appeal on Jurisdiction) IT-94-1-AR72 (2 October 1995) para 127:

it cannot be denied that customary rules have developed to govern internal strife. These rules ... cover such areas as protection of civilians from hostilities, in particular from indiscriminate attacks, protection of civilian objects, in particular cultural property, protection of all those who do not (or no longer) take active part in hostilities, as well as prohibition of means of warfare proscribed in international armed conflicts and ban of certain methods of conducting hostilities.

combatants and between civilian objects and military objectives and accordingly shall direct their operations only against military objectives.

This articulation of the principle of distinction is universally accepted as an accurate reflection of the analogous customary IHL principle.[16] The principle is violated by conducting indiscriminate attacks, including direct attacks on unlawful targets. Additionally, when mounting attacks against lawful military objectives, an attacker must exercise constant care to ensure that harm to protected persons and objects is minimized.

Some dissonance exists, as is discussed below in section 1.B 'Proportionality', with regard to the precise scope of the terms appearing in article 48. For the purposes of this chapter, and except as otherwise apparent from the text, the term 'combatant' is used to broadly refer to those who are not civilians and therefore are usually subject to attack—members of the armed forces and organized armed groups, as well as civilians directly participating in hostilities. Additionally, although the term 'military objective' is defined in API with reference only to objects or locations that may be attacked, unless otherwise noted it will be used here in a wider sense to refer to lawful targets, including persons who may be attacked.[17]

## 1. Indiscriminate attacks
Indiscriminate attacks are those that fail to take adequate cognizance of the required distinction between lawful targets and persons and objects that enjoy protection under IHL. They are engaged in by employing either tactics or weapons that are indiscriminate.

## A. Indiscriminate tactics
The tactic of directly attacking a protected person or object is self-evidently indiscriminate and accordingly is absolutely prohibited.[18] ISIS attacks against elements of the Iraqi and Syrian population are paradigmatic. It is also indiscriminate to conduct an attack in a fashion that is 'of a nature to strike military objectives and civilians or civilian objects without distinction'.[19] This is most often done when an attacker fails to 'aim' at a military objective (as distinct from aiming at an unlawful one). Examples include simply releasing bombs over enemy territory or shelling a populated area, even when done in the hope of incidentally striking a military objective.

A more nuanced prohibition on indiscriminate attacks is that of treating 'as a single military objective a number of clearly separated and distinct military objectives located in a city, town, village or other area containing a similar concentration of civilians or civilian objects'.[20] It is sometimes mistakenly concluded that area targeting, including so-called 'carpet bombing', is consequently unlawful. However, an area attack is only prohibited when it is possible for the attacker to more discriminately mount the operation. Consider a situation in which military objectives are located in a populated area. If an attacker possesses the

---

[16] See also CIHL rules 1 and 7. For a non-API Party adoption of the principle, see US Department of Defense (DoD), Office of the General Counsel, *Law of War Manual* (December 2016) para 2.5.
[17] This is the approach taken by the International Committee of the Red Cross (ICRC). AP Commentary para 1207.
[18] API article 51(4)(a).
[19] ibid article 51(4)(c); CIHL rule 12(a).
[20] API article 51(5)(a); Protocol on Prohibitions or Restrictions on the Use of Mines, Booby-Traps and Other Devices as amended on 3 May 1996 (adopted 3 May 1996, entered into force 3 December 1998) 2048 UNTS 93 (CCW Amended Protocol II); CIHL rule 13.

means to conduct individual attacks against the targets, it must do so rather than targeting the entire zone in which they are located. This is most likely to be the case when the attacker fields precision munitions and advanced intelligence, surveillance, and reconnaissance (ISR) assets. Should the attacker not possess the capability to precisely locate and separately strike the targets, it may attack the entire area, but only consistent with the principle of proportionality and the requirement to take precautions in attack that are described below in section 1.H 'Precautions in attack'.

The principle of distinction is also the source of a number of additional rules regarding particular tactics. These include prohibitions or limitations on starvation, sieges, and reprisals against civilians, civilian objects, and other protected persons and objects. Some such methods of warfare are the subject of chapter 8 'Specifically Protected Persons and Objects'.

## B. Proportionality

The aforementioned forms of indiscriminate attack are relatively straightforward in terms of interpretation and application. More problematic is the rule of proportionality. By that rule, an attack is indiscriminate if it 'may be expected to cause incidental loss of civilian life, injury to civilians, damage to civilian objects, or a combination thereof, which would be excessive in relation to the concrete and direct military advantage anticipated'.[21] Of all the rules regarding the conduct of hostilities, it is the vaguest and, therefore, the most difficult to apply by those in the field or during *post factum* assessments of an attack's lawfulness.

To fully understand the rule, it is necessary to parse the text. First, an assessment of the proportionality of an attack is never to be made on the basis of the eventual results. Rather, as indicated by the terms 'expected' and 'anticipated', the evaluation must focus on the attacker's reasonable expectations with respect to collateral damage and military gain when planning, deciding on, or executing the attack. For any number of reasons, an attack may result in more civilian casualties and damage to civilian property, or less military gain, than the attacker believed was likely to eventuate. To take a simple example, when civilians have unexpectedly moved into the target area, or the target has departed the location, unbeknownst to the attacker, the attack will be assessed against the reasonableness of the attacker's *ex ante* understanding of the situation.

Second, the rule of proportionality is often misinterpreted as consisting of a balancing of expected collateral damage and anticipated military advantage. Such an approach ignores the fact that the rule only prohibits an attack when the expected collateral damage is 'excessive' relative to the anticipated military advantage. No accepted definition of the term 'excessive' exists, but it is clear that it does not involve a strict mathematical comparison. A useful definition is that set forth in the *Harvard Air and Missile Warfare Manual*. There, an international group of experts agreed that an attack results in excessive collateral damage 'when there is a significant imbalance between the military advantage anticipated, on the one hand, and the expected collateral damage to civilians and civilian objects, on the other'.[22] Operationally speaking, an attack causes excessive collateral damage when a

---

[21] API articles 51(5)(b), 57(2)(a)(ii), and 57(2)(b); CCW Amended Protocol II article 3(8)(c); CIHL rule 14; *Prosecutor v Galić* (Judgment) IT-98-29 (5 December 2003) paras 58–60; *Prosecutor v Kordić and Čerkez* (Judgment) IT-95-14/2-A (17 December 2004) para 52; *Prosecutor v Martić* (Judgment) IT-95-11 (12 June 2007) para 69.

[22] The Program on Humanitarian Policy and Conflict Research at Harvard University, *Manual on International Law Applicable to Air and Missile Warfare* (CUP 2009) (*AMW Manual*) 98 commentary to rule 14 para 7.

reasonable commander in same or similar circumstances would hesitate to launch it despite the anticipated military advantage his forces would attain.

'Excessive' should not to be equated with 'extensive'. The ICRC has averred that:

> The idea has also been put forward that even if they are very high, civilian losses and damages may be justified if the military advantage at stake is of great importance. This idea is contrary to the fundamental rules of the Protocol; in particular, it conflicts with Article 48 *(Basic rule)* and with paragraphs 1 and 2 of the present Article 51. The Protocol does not provide any justification for attacks which cause extensive civilian losses and damages. Incidental losses and damages should never be extensive.[23]

However, the assertion mischaracterizes the notion of excessiveness. It is not the degree of collateral damage that the rule of proportionality is meant to address, but rather the relationship between collateral damage and military advantage. This is the plain meaning of the rule and is borne out by state practice. There may be circumstances in which heavy civilian casualties are likely to result, but in which the military advantage that is anticipated is very high. Examples are a strike against a senior enemy leader, or one that would effectively neutralize enemy operations, for instance by targeting the oil reserves on which the enemy forces rely. Indeed, in its *Nuclear Weapon Advisory Opinion*, the ICJ was unwilling to express an opinion as to whether the use of nuclear weapons would be unlawful in situations where the survival of the state is at stake.[24] By the same token, an attack may violate the rule of proportionality when only slight collateral damage is expected if the anticipated military advantage is low enough. For example, it is arguably disproportionate to attack a single low-level soldier far from the battlefield when harm would befall even a few civilians.

It is sometimes questioned whether the collateral damage to be included in a proportionality analysis extends beyond that which is directly caused by the attack to indirect damage, sometimes referred to as reverberating or knock-on effects. By way of illustration, injury or damage caused by a weapon's blast or fragmentation effects are direct effects. If an attack on an electrical generating station results in denial of electricity to the civilian population, and the lack of electricity causes damage to civilian equipment or harm to individuals (as in the case of affecting heating during a severe winter), the results are indirect. The prevailing view is that all effects that are foreseeable by the attacker are included in the analysis.[25]

Collateral damage does not include such effects as fear, irritation, or inconvenience on the part of the civilian population. Nor would it necessarily extend to disruption of services unless such disruption, as in the case of electricity above, had tangible effects. This is clear from the textual reference to 'loss of civilian life, injury to civilians, or damage to civilian objects'.

Only advantages that are military in nature qualify for the purposes of the rule. Military advantage may result from the effect of an attack on the campaign and not just from the direct effects of the attack. Consider an attack that is a ruse intended to convince the enemy that the attacker's forces will strike somewhere other than the planned point of thrust for

---

[23] AP Commentary para 1980.

[24] *Nuclear Weapons* paras 96–97.

[25] See, eg, Michael N Schmitt (ed) *Tallinn Manual 2.0 on the International Law Applicable to Cyber Operations* (CUP 2017) commentary to rule 113 para 6 (*Tallinn Manual*).

the overall operation. The destruction of the target may have little military advantage in the direct sense, but it could prove invaluable in terms of tricking the enemy into orienting its forces in a disadvantageous manner. Military advantage is not, however, advantage that is purely political, psychological, or economic in nature. There must be some relatively direct nexus to military operations, whether those operations are those of the attacker or the enemy. In particular, an effect on the morale of the civilian population does not amount to military advantage in the proportionality sense. Take airstrikes against military objectives located in the enemy's capital. Although the fact that the strikes could be conducted with impunity may affect the enemy population's support for the conflict, only the destruction of the targets themselves, and the attendant military contribution to the attacker's campaign, qualify as military advantage.

As noted in the rule, only 'concrete and direct' military advantage is considered when making proportionality determinations. Although the phrase is somewhat vague, it is clear that the military advantage sought must be identifiable, clearly discernible, and 'relatively close[ly]' related to the attack. Advantages that are 'hardly perceptible and those which would only appear in the long term should be disregarded'.[26] No particular quantum of advantage need accrue to the attacker, but the advantage sought may not be speculative.

The rule of proportionality applies to all those who exercise a degree of control over an attack. In particular, it extends to attack planners, commanders who authorize the attack, and individuals who conduct the operation. For instance, a pilot executing an air attack is obliged to consider any facts that come to his or her attention that might affect proportionality, irrespective of whether the attack has been previously approved by the unit commander. The paradigmatic example is that of a pilot who upon arriving at the target area unexpectedly finds civilians in the vicinity of the intended strike. The pilot must factor those civilians into his proportionality calculations when deciding whether to carry out the mission. However, those who execute a strike may, in assessing proportionality, consider the fact that the mission was planned and approved by those with access to intelligence and other information that may be unavailable to them.

## C. Indiscriminate weapons

The prohibition on indiscriminate attacks includes those employing weapons that are inherently indiscriminate; that is, incapable of distinguishing lawful targets from those which protected by IHL.[27] A weapon can be indiscriminate in two ways. First, some weapons cannot be reliably aimed at a military objective. The classic example is the German V2 rocket used to target the UK during the Second World War. Although such rockets could generally be fired at large areas in the UK, their guidance system was so rudimentary that they were incapable of being aimed at distinct targets, even in situations in which there was a concentration of military objectives in a particular area. Similarly, during that conflict the Japanese used balloon-borne bombs against the US and Canada. Since they were dependent on air currents, the weapons were indiscriminate.

This prohibition applies to the weapon itself, not any particular use of it. For instance, during the 1991 Gulf War, Iraqi forces launched many Scud missiles. Although fairly imprecise, Scuds were capable of being directed at large military objectives, as illustrated by

---

[26] AP Commentary para 2209.
[27] API article 51(4); CIHL rule 12.

the successful use of them against the large US military installation at Dhahran.[28] Thus, they were not indiscriminate per se. Yet, the Iraqis sometimes used Scuds indiscriminately by firing them into population centres.[29] This illustrates the importance of distinguishing between weapons that are unlawful because there is no likely situation in which their use would be discriminate and weapons that are discriminate but used indiscriminately.

Note that the prohibition on indiscriminate weapons is temporally relative. As technology improves, normative expectations with respect to precision heighten. For example, air attacks during the Second World War regularly employed bombs that were, by contemporary standards, highly inaccurate and would be considered indiscriminate in light of the technology available today for aerial attacks. It is reasonable to believe that many of today's weapons will be considered indiscriminate in the future.

Weapons are also indiscriminate when, albeit sufficiently precise, they have effects are that are uncontrollable and therefore likely to harm the civilian population or civilian objects. Biological weapons that employ contagions that may be passed easily into the civilian population are indiscriminate on this basis because, although it is possible to direct them at combatants (for instance, by introducing them into a water supply or air-conditioning systems on a military installation), the attacker would be unable to limit their spread to civilians. Thus, they are unlawful even if their use had not otherwise been banned. Similarly, weapons releasing highly persistent airborne chemicals are indiscriminate given the likelihood that the chemicals would reach the civilian population by wind.

### D. Direct attacks against protected persons

As noted, attacks that are directed at civilians, civilian objects, and other protected persons and objects fall within the ambit of indiscriminate attacks. In this regard, the general principle of distinction set forth in article 48 of API has been operationalized in a number of specific rules.

Pursuant to article 51(2), which undeniably reflects customary law, '[t]he civilian population as such, as well as individual civilians, shall not be the object of attack.'[30] Although qualification as a civilian is the subject of chapter 5, it is useful to briefly summarize the concept here. API defines a civilian as 'any person who does not belong to one of the categories of persons referred to in Article 4A(1), (2), (3) and (6) of the [1949] Third [Geneva] Convention and in Article 43 of this Protocol.'[31] These categories refer respectively to members of the regular armed forces, including militia or volunteer corps like the reserves, that are part of the armed forces; members of a militia and other volunteer groups, including resistance movements, that belong to a party to the conflict and meet the conditions of being under responsible command, wearing attire or emblems that allow them to be distinguished from the civilian population, carrying their weapons openly, and, as a group, conducting their operations in accordance with IHL; members of the regular armed forces who

---

[28] US DoD, *Conduct of the Persian Gulf War: Final Report to Congress* (10 April 1992) 219.

[29] ibid 621–3.

[30] See also Geneva Conventions Common Article (CA) 3(1)(a); APII article 13(2); *Prosecutor v Kaing* (Judgment) ECCC-E188 (26 July 2010) paras 308–310; *Galić* (above n 21) para 19; *Prosecutor v Blaškić* (Appeal Judgment) IT-95-14-A (29 July 2004) paras 109–110; *Kordić* (above n 21) para 328; *Prosecutor v Strugar* (Judgment) IT- 01-42-T (31 January 2005) paras 220–221; Eritrea–Ethiopia Claims Commission, *Western Front, Aerial Bombardment and Related Claims,* Partial Award, Eritrea's Claims (19 December 2005) (*Western Front*) para 95; CIHL rule 1.

[31] API article 50(1).

have professed allegiance to a government or authority that is not recognized by the opposing party; and members of a *levée en masse*.[32] Article 43 of API provides that the armed forces 'consist of all organized armed forces, groups and units which are under a command responsible to that Party for the conduct of its subordinates, even if that Party is represented by a government or an authority not recognized by an adverse Party', but adds that such armed forces must be subject to a disciplinary system that enforces compliance with IHL. Taken together for the purposes of the conduct of hostilities, civilians are those individuals who are not members of a party's armed forces or an organized armed group.[33]

With regard to a NIAC, civilians are individuals who are not members of the state's security forces involved in the conflict, members of dissident armed forces that are in rebellion, or members of non-state armed groups engaged in the hostilities. Thus, in such conflicts, civilians are those persons who are not members of a group that is involved in the hostilities.

In light of the widespread appearance on contemporary battlefields of groups that are not affiliated with the armed forces of a party to the conflict, the ICRC sponsored a project between 2003 and 2008 to assess the phenomenon. The result was promulgation of its *Interpretive Guidance on the Notion of Direct Participation in Hostilities*.[34] Although the document has been the source of some controversy in other regards,[35] general agreement now exists with its conclusion that members of 'organized armed groups' are not to be considered civilians for targeting purposes.[36] Rather, they should be assimilated to members of the armed forces. Thus, direct targeting of their members is not barred by the prohibition on targeting civilians and any harm that befalls them during an attack against other lawful targets is not considered in either the proportionality analysis (section B 'Proportionality' above) or the requirement to take precautions in attack (section H 'Precautions in attack' below). Prominent examples of such groups include Al Qaeda, the Taliban, and ISIS.

Although consensus exists that organized armed groups may be targeted, a persistent controversy surrounds whether any members of the group continue to benefit from the prohibition on targeting civilians. There are two schools of thought. The ICRC has opined that only those members with a 'continuous combat function' are targetable.[37] Other members are treated as civilians with respect to the conduct of hostilities. This view is based in part on the argument that it is often difficult to distinguish members of an armed group

---

[32] A levée en masse consists of '[i]nhabitants of a non-occupied territory, who on the approach of the enemy spontaneously take up arms to resist the invading forces, without having had time to form themselves into regular armed units, provided they carry arms openly and respect the laws and customs of war': GCIII article 4(A)(6). See also Hague Regulations article 2.

[33] CIHL rule 5.

[34] ICRC, *Interpretive Guidance on the Notion of Direct Participation in Hostilities Under International Humanitarian Law* (ICRC 2009).

[35] See eg Kenneth Watkin, 'Opportunity Lost: Organized Armed Groups and the ICRC "Direct Participation in Hostilities" Interpretive Guidance' (2010) 42 *NYUJ Int'l Law & Pol'y* 641; Michael N Schmitt, 'Deconstructing Direct Participation in Hostilities: The Constitutive Elements' (2010) 42 *NYUJ Int'l Law & Pol'y* 697; William Boothby, ' "And for Such Time As": The Time Dimension to Direct Participation in Hostilities' (2010) 42 *NYUJ Int'l Law & Pol'y* 741; Hays Parks, 'Part IX of the ICRC "Direct Participation in Hostilities" Study: No Mandate, No Expertise, and Legally Incorrect' (2010) 42 *NYUJ Int'l Law & Pol'y* 769; Nils Melzer 'Keeping the Balance between Military Necessity and Humanity: A Response to Four Critiques of the ICRC's Interpretive Guidance on the Notion of Direct Participation in Hostilities' (2010) 42 *NYUJ Int'l Law & Pol'y* 831; Michael N Schmitt, 'The Interpretive Guidance on the Notion of Direct Participation in Hostilities: A Critical Analysis' (2010) 1 *NSJ* 5.

[36] ICRC, *Interpretive Guidance* (above n 34) 22.

[37] ibid 33–5: 'the decisive criterion for individual membership in an organized armed group is whether a person assumes a continuous function for the group involving his or her direct participation in hostilities'.

from the general population and that therefore it is sensible to extend targetability only to those who are directly involved in the hostilities.[38] The alternative view is that, like members of the armed forces, all members of an organized armed group may be attacked. From the perspective of those taking this approach, it is inconsistent for group members who do not perform a combat function to benefit from the protection from attack, while members of the armed forces such as military cooks do not.

There is one situation in which civilians may be directly attacked during both an IAC and a NIAC. API, article 53(3) and Additional Protocol II (APII), article 13(1), deprive civilians of protection from attack 'for such time' as they 'directly participate in hostilities'.[39] By extension, these provisions also exclude such persons from consideration in the proportionality analysis and precautions in attack requirements. It is generally accepted that both provisions generally mirror customary law.[40]

Direct participation by civilians must be distinguished from the notion of organized armed groups discussed above. Applicability of the rules regarding direct participation does not extend to members of such groups unless, by the ICRC approach, the member of the group does not perform a continuous combat function. Rather, they apply only to individuals lacking any direct affiliation with an organized group. For instance, a civilian who implants improvised explosive devices for a fee, as was common in Iraq, is a direct participant, whereas one who does so while a member of an organized group is targetable by virtue of membership in the group.

During the *Interpretive Guidance* deliberations, the ICRC suggested, and the majority of the experts agreed, that an act of direct participation consists of three cumulative constitutive elements. First, the act in question must be 'likely to adversely affect the military operations or military capacity of a party to an armed conflict or, alternatively, to inflict death, injury, or destruction on persons or objects protected against direct attack (threshold of harm)'.[41] Second, 'there must be a direct causal link between the act and the harm likely to result either from that act, or from a coordinated military operation of which that act constitutes an integral part (direct causation)'. Finally, 'the act must be specifically designed to directly cause the required threshold of harm in support of a party to the conflict and to the detriment of another (belligerent nexus)'.

Certain acts evidently qualify as direct participation in the hostilities. For example, a civilian who launches an attack is a direct participant, as is one who provides tactical-level intelligence by messaging enemy forces when military vehicles are entering an area where they may be attacked. Other acts are clearly not direct participation, despite the fact that they in some way foster the war effort. Civilians who cook for the armed group of which they are not members are, for instance, not direct participants, nor are civilian intelligence analysts operating at the strategic level.

Some cases remain unclear. A number of experts took the position that assembling an improvised explosive device (IED) satisfies the three criteria, whereas the ICRC is of the

---

[38] ibid 44–5.
[39] See also *Prosecutor v Abu Garda* (Decision on Confirmation of Charges) ICC-02/05-02/09 (8 February 2010) paras 78–82; *Prosecuctor v Milošević* (Judgment) IT-98-29/1-T (12 December 2007) para 947; *Kordić* (above n 21) para 51; *Prosecutor v Fofana and Kondewa* (Judgment) SCSL-04-14-J (2 August 2007) paras 134–135; *Prosecutor v Sesay and others* (Judgment) SCSL-04-15-T (2 March 2009) paras 86, 102–104; *Abella v Argentina* (*La Tablada* case), Inter-American Commission No 55/97 (18 November 1997) paras 177–178, 189, 328.
[40] CIHL rule 6.
[41] ICRC, *Interpretive Guidance* (above n 34) 46.

view that such activity is indirect because the second constitutive element is not met.[42] Similarly, as will be discussed, the ICRC asserted that voluntary human shields are not generally directly participating in hostilities, whereas a strong view was expressed by certain of the experts that doing so qualifies.[43]

A further point of contention surrounds the rules depriving civilians of protection for 'such time' as they directly participate in hostilities. The *Interpretive Guidance* states that the period includes 'measures preparatory to the execution of a specific act of direct participation in hostilities, as well as the deployment to and the return from the location of its execution'.[44] Recall the aforementioned case of the IED. A civilian engaging in such activity is directly participating as he prepares the device immediately prior to departing, during its transportation to the point where it is implanted, while he is implanting the device, and during travel home. Otherwise, as a civilian, he is immune from attack.

Some of the experts were of the view that this is an overly restrictive standard. By it, an individual may be engaged in a regular pattern of implanting IEDs, but nevertheless only be attackable as a matter of law during the cited period. This is problematic as intelligence may have identified the individual, but not know when he is next going to engage in the activity. If in a location where practically he cannot be detained, the ICRC's approach would in many cases effectively deprive his intended targets of any way to prevent an attack almost certain to occur. These experts argued that civilians who directly participate in the hostilities should be treated as engaging in a continuous course of conduct during which they are targetable.[45] Moreover, they urged that with respect to an individual act of direct participation, targetability extends as far upstream and downstream as a definitive causal link can be established.[46] Thus, an individual who builds and implants an IED is targetable from the point when he begins to plan the operation and acquire the necessary materials until such time as he desists in any further acts.

An issue of continuing controversy related to direct participation surrounds human shields.[47] Contemporary conflict has unfortunately witnessed many examples of this tactic. Clearly, the use of human shields is a violation of IHL.[48] The question is, however, how individuals who are shielding military objectives should be treated with respect to the prohibition on attacking civilians, as well as the rule of proportionality and requirement to take precautions in attack. There are numerous schools of thought. In order to outline them, it is necessary to distinguish between individuals who voluntarily shield military objectives and those who do so involuntarily, in the sense of being forced to remain at a location that is likely to be attacked.

General consensus exists that involuntary human shields are to be treated as civilians for the purposes of conduct of hostilities rules. Thus, they are immune from attack. Yet, there are three camps within this general consensus. Until recently, the US took a minority position on the matter. As noted in the original *Department of Defense* [DoD] *Law of War*

---

[42]   ibid 53–4 and n 123.
[43]   ibid 56–7 and n 141.
[44]   ibid 65–8.
[45]   ibid 71, 192.
[46]   This approach is reflected in Yoram Dinstein, *The Conduct of Hostilities Under the Law of International Armed Conflict* (2nd edn, CUP 2010) para 368. Professor Dinstein was a member of the expert group.
[47]   On this topic, see Michael N Schmitt, 'Human Shields in International Humanitarian law' (2009) 47 *Colum J Transnat'l L* 292.
[48]   GCIII article 23(1); GCIV article 28; API article 51(7); CIHL rule 97.

*Manual*: 'If the proportionality rule were interpreted to permit the use of human shields to prohibit attacks, such an interpretation would perversely encourage the use of human shields and allow violations by the defending force to increase the legal obligations on the attacking force.'[49]

The approach recognized that if involuntary human shields affect the proportionality analysis, the enemy can effectively gather enough of them in the target area so as to alter the proportionality analysis. This is because the target becomes immune from attack since the expected collateral damage is likely to be excessive relative to the anticipated value of striking the target. Therefore, all an attacker need do in shielding situations is to attempt to minimize the harm to them, consistent with the requirement to take precautions in attack.

A more nuanced, but also minority, approach is that adopted by the UK and reflected in its *Manual of the Law of Armed Conflict*. While taking the view that involuntary shields retain their status as civilians, the British *Manual* provides that 'the enemy's unlawful activity may be taken into account in considering whether the incidental loss or damage was proportionate to the military advantage expected.'[50] In other words, the value of the shields is somehow discounted when performing a proportionality analysis, although it is unclear how this would operate in practice. Again, the underlying logic is that the enemy should not be permitted to benefit from its unlawful behaviour, at least not to the extent that it would if the human shields were fully considered in the proportionality analysis. It is this approach that the US now appears to have embraced.[51]

The third approach, and that of the ICRC, is that involuntary human shields count fully in both the proportionality calculation and with regard to the requirement to take precautions in attack. Its proponents find no basis in any rule of IHL for relaxing the normative significance of their status as civilians. Moreover, they suggest that the previous approaches run counter to the object and purpose of IHL. Although reflecting a balancing of military advantage and humanitarian concerns, IHL generally does not seek a 'fair fight'. Rather, it strives to foster humanitarianism in the face of the reality of warfare. This purpose would be frustrated if belligerents were entitled to deprive civilians of the legal protections to which they are otherwise entitled in a situation to which those civilians have in no way contributed.

Voluntary human shields are an even more controversial matter. There are three views. The first is presumably reflected in the British *Manual* extract above, which does not distinguish involuntary from voluntary human shields; they count as civilians in the proportionality analysis, but their use by the enemy may be considered in making that calculus. By a second view, articulated in the *Interpretive Guidance*, voluntary human shields count fully as civilians in the proportionality analysis and precautions in attack requirements. The one exception is a situation in which 'civilians voluntarily and deliberately position ... themselves to create a physical obstacle to military operations'.[52] The ICRC notes that '[t]his scenario may become particularly relevant in ground operations, such as in urban environments, where civilians may attempt to give physical cover to fighting personnel supported by them or to inhibit the movement of opposing infantry troops'.[53] It goes on to argue that 'in operations involving more powerful weaponry, such as artillery or air attacks, the

---

[49] US DoD (above n 16) para 5.12.3.3.
[50] UK Ministry of Defense (MoD), *The Manual of the Law of Armed Conflict* (2004) para 5.22.1.
[51] US DoD (above n 16) para 5.12.3.4.
[52] ICRC, *Interpretive Guidance* (above n 34) 56.
[53] ibid.

presence of voluntary human shields often has no adverse impact on the capacity of the attacker to identify and destroy the shielded military objective'. Instead, the effect of civilians in the target area is to alter the proportionality analysis such that the rule of proportionality may preclude attack. The ICRC points out that this is solely a legal obstacle to direct attack and that therefore the behaviour does not amount to direct participation.[54]

A third view, which would seem to be that of the US, is that voluntary human shields qualify as direct participants in the hostilities. The December 2016 version of *DoD Law of War Manual*, notes that civilian human shields, 'provided they are not taking a direct part in hostilities', are to be considered civilians in the proportionality analysis.[55] This infers that voluntary shielding renders those engaging in it as direct participants who are not included in proportionality calculations or considered with respect to the taking of feasible precautions in attack. That said, the reality of contemporary warfare is that the presence of human shields, whether rendering an attack disproportionate or not, has great influence upon any decision to attack; after all, this is the very reason that the civilians voluntarily shield military objectives. It must be cautioned with respect to this view that if there is doubt as to whether the individual concerned is a voluntary or involuntary shield, the person must be considered to be the latter.[56]

### E. Direct attacks against protected objects

The principle of distinction has also been operationalized through a prohibition on attacking civilian objects. That prohibition, which undeniably reflects customary international law, is reflected in article 52(1) of API: '[c]ivilian objects shall not be the object of attack or of reprisals'.[57] The article defines civilian objects in the negative as those that are not 'military objectives', which requires resort to the definition of military objects found in article 52(2):

> ... objects which by their nature, location, purpose, or use, make an effective contribution to military action and whose total or partial destruction, capture or neutralization, in the circumstances ruling at the time, offers a definite military advantage.

It is universally agreed that this definition accurately restates customary international law.[58] Although the definition itself brooks no debate, its application does in certain circumstances and with respect to particular categories of objects.

To qualify as a military objective, and thus to lie beyond the prohibition on attacking civilian objects, an object must fall into one of the four enumerated categories. The term 'nature' refers to an object's 'inherent characteristic or attribute which contributes to military action'.[59] This category includes, for instance, weaponry, military equipment, and military

---

[54] ibid 57.
[55] US DoD (above n 16) para 5.12.3.4.
[56] API article 50(1); CIHL commentary to rule 6.
[57] See also CIHL rule 7; *Kaing* (above n 30) para 304; *Blaškić* (above n 30) paras 113–114; *Fofana and Kondewa* (above n 39) paras 116–117.
[58] CCW Protocol II article 2(4); CCW Amended Protocol II article 2(6); Protocol on Prohibitions or Restrictions on the Use of Incendiary Weapons (adopted 10 October 1980, entered into force 2 December 1983) 1342 UNTS 171 (CCW Protocol III); Second Protocol to the Hague Convention of 1954 for the Protection of Cultural Property in the Event of Armed Conflict (adopted 26 March 1999, entered into force 9 March 2004) 2253 UNTS 212 article 1(f) (Second Protocol 1999); *Galić* (above n 21) para 51; *Western Front* para 113; CIHL rule 8; US DoD (above n 16) para 5.6.3.
[59] *AMW Manual* commentary to rule 22(a) para 1. See also AP Commentary para 2020.

bases. An object becomes a military objective by 'purpose' once the enemy intends to use that object for military ends in the future.[60] There is no requirement that it be used militarily at the time; the sole condition is that the attacker reasonably concludes that the object is to be converted to military use. The classic cases are civilian transportation, such as trains or ships that have been designated for future military use, or facilities that are in the process of being converted, as in a civilian airfield at which military equipment is being installed to facilitate later use by combat aircraft. 'Location' denotes 'selected areas that have special importance to military operations'.[61] For instance, a force trying to stop the enemy's retreat may destroy or otherwise obstruct mountain passes in order to trap the enemy.

Other than objects that are military by nature, what were originally civilian objects are most likely to become military objectives through the 'use' criterion. 'Use' refers to the fact that the enemy is currently employing the object to further its operations or hinder its enemy's.[62] Contemporary examples include insurgents' use of apartments to store weapons, basements where IEDs are assembled, minarets or church steeples that serve as look-out posts, civilian vehicles that have been commandeered, and civilian communications networks on which enemy forces rely.

Any use for military ends, no matter how slight, transforms a civilian object into a military objective. Thus, an apartment used once for a meeting of insurgents is a military objective while the meeting takes place (and also by purpose once the decision is made to meet there again). So-called 'dual-use' objects that are used for both military and civilian purposes are military objectives even if their civilian use far outweighs that of the military use. For example, a civilian train transporting a few military personnel qualifies irrespective of what percentage of its passengers are civilian, as does a dual-use airfield that serves military aircraft, despite the fact that it is primarily devoted to civilian flight operations. Of course, in such cases, the proportionality rule may operate to preclude attack.

When a 'dual-use' object consists of clearly distinct parts, only that aspect being used for military purposes constitutes a military objective. Consider two apartment towers connected by a raised walkway. A weapons storage facility is located in one. Only that part of the building qualifies as a military objective. The remainder retains civilian object status; it may not be directly attacked and any damage to it will be factored into the proportionality analysis and the requirement to take precautions in attack.

A persistent debate in this regard relates to civilian apartment buildings in which only a single apartment is being used by the enemy.[63] The question is whether an attacker that has the precision weapons to allow it to strike that apartment must treat damage to other parts of the building as collateral damage. There are two views. By the first, the use converts the entire building into a military objective on the basis that it is an integral whole. Thus, at least as a matter of law, there is no need to consider expected collateral damage or to attempt to minimize harm to the parts of the building other than the apartment.

The other view takes the position that only the apartment qualifies as a military objective if the attacker's available weaponry (and other factors contributing to precision attack) permit limiting the strike to the apartment. The rest of the building is civilian in

---

[60] AP Commentary para 2022.

[61] *AMW Manual* commentary to rule 22(b). See also AP Commentary para 2021.

[62] AP Commentary para 2022.

[63] Michael N Schmitt and John Merriam, 'The Tyranny of Context: Israeli Targeting Practice in Legal Perspective' (2015) 37 *U Pa J Int'l L* 53, 120–1.

nature and therefore the rule of proportionality treats harm to it as collateral damage. The proponents of the view acknowledge it imposes relative obligations, but stress that the military necessity/humanitarian considerations balance discussed above such an interpretation.

While there is no threshold of use to qualify as a military objective, the object concerned may only be attacked for such time that it is so being used. This is an important caveat in contemporary warfare against non-state groups because insurgents often operate from among the civilian population and use civilian homes in which to hide or from which to operate. To avoid the ISR (intelligence, surveillance, reconnaissance) assets of advanced militaries, they are on the move constantly. In such circumstances, it is especially important for the attacker to have a reasonable basis for concluding that the place to be attacked is still being used at the time of the attack. In this regard, a civilian object that is repeatedly, although not constantly, used for military purposes comprises a military objective throughout the period of usage. For instance, an apartment serving as a safe house for insurgents does not cease to be a military objective because no one is using it on the night of the proposed strike. Similarly, civilian communications networks relied upon by the enemy for command-and-control purposes qualify as military objectives even though they may not be being used at the moment of attack.

The most persistent and significant debate regarding qualification as a military object surrounds the US view that so-called 'war-sustaining' objects are military objectives. There is consensus that 'war-fighting' objects, like weapons systems and command-and-control assets, qualify. Similarly, 'war-supporting' objects are military objectives. Such objects, as with a plant producing military equipment, directly support the war effort.

War-sustaining objects are 'economic objects of the enemy that indirectly but effectively support and sustain the enemy's war-fighting capability'.[64] A contemporary example is oil, the revenue from which finances a state's war effort. The US *DoD Law of War Manual* notes that '[a]lthough terms such as "war-fighting", "war-supporting", and "war-sustaining" are not explicitly reflected in the treaty definitions of military objective, the US has interpreted the military objective definition to include these concepts'.[65] This view has been an outlier among IHL experts.

The longstanding debate has heated up in recent conflicts. For instance, in 2008 NATO considered striking drug-related targets in Afghanistan because the Taliban relied on proceeds, often in the form of taxes or 'protection' levies on poppy growers, to fund its operations.[66] Eventually, NATO grounded its counter-drug campaign on legal bases other than qualification as military objectives. In 2015, the issue again surfaced when ISIS began using oil revenue from territory it controls as an important source of financing. Clearly, if ISIS uses the oil produced to fuel its combat operations, it qualifies as a military objective. But air campaigns have been mounted by a number of states against targets related to oil production and sale in an effort to deprive the group of funding for its campaign. It would be difficult to describe such targets as other than war-sustaining. This raises the question of whether states are rethinking how best to interpret the notion of military objectives in light

---

[64] United States Navy, United States Marine Corps, and United States Coast Guard, *The Commander's Handbook of the Law of Naval Operations* (2007) para 8.2.5.

[65] US DoD (above n 16) para 5.6.6. See also 10 USC section 950p(a)(1).

[66] See generally Michael N Schmitt, 'Targeting Narcoinsurgents in Afghanistan: The Limits of International Humanitarian Law' (2009) 12 *YIHL* 301–20.

of the difficulty of countering such groups and the ensuing shift in the balance between military necessity and humanitarian considerations.

Whether by nature, location, purpose, or use, qualification as a military objective requires satisfaction of two cumulative criteria. First, the object concerned must make an 'effective contribution' to the adversary's military action. Second, an attack on it must, in the circumstances, offer the attacker a 'definite military advantage'. An effective contribution is one that in fact contributes to the enemy's military action. The contribution need not be great, but the object must be of a kind that is militarily useful to the enemy in the circumstances. A definite military advantage is one that is more than 'potential or indeterminate',[67] although the advantage may manifest at the tactical or operational levels of war (that is, in battlefield operations or the campaign overall).[68]

The distinction between the two criteria is subtle but important. Effective contribution is about whether the object concerned helps the enemy militarily, whereas definite military advantage has to do with how its 'total or partial destruction, capture or neutralization' will benefit the attacker in the situation at hand. For instance, bridges that are crossed by the military during an armed conflict make an effective contribution to military action. However, if bridges far from the front are attacked in the waning days of the conflict as the enemy is retreating and obviously about to surrender, any purported military advantage to dropping them is somewhat speculative.

While most experts agree that the criteria are cumulative, disagreement exists over qualification as a military objective by nature. Some experts are of the view that the destruction, capture, or neutralization of any objects that fall into this category always offers a definite military advantage. In particular, because the 'fog and friction of war' make it difficult to predict outcomes, weakening enemy military capacity necessarily yields a definite military advantage. Troops in retreat, for instance, may be rallied; equipment located far from the field of battle may be transported there, and so forth. Other experts counter that the definite military advantage issue must nevertheless be considered in every case, even though the likely result may be that the attack will yield such an advantage. The example most commonly cited to illustrate the point is 'the Highway of Death' incident during the first Gulf War. Iraqi forces were in disarray and fleeing north to Baghdad when they were caught on an open highway by Coalition air forces. They were serially destroyed. At the time, many critics of the action suggested the war was essentially over and that the troops posed no threat. Those on the other side of the debate dismissed the criticism by noting that, as military forces, they were targetable until such time as they surrendered or were otherwise *hors de combat*.

### F. Doubt as to status

Whether a person or object considered for attack qualifies as a lawful target is often subject to a degree of doubt.[69] For instance, in many conflict zones civilians carry weapons not to

---

[67] AP Commentary para 2024.

[68] UK MoD (above n 53) para 5.33.5; UK, 'Additional Protocol Ratification Statement: Reservation' (28 January 1998) para. (i) ('UK Ratification Statement'); *AMW Manual* para 6 of commentary to rule 1(w); *Tallinn Manual* para 20 of commentary to rule 100.

[69] On the issue of doubt arising during targeting, see generally Michael N. Schmitt and Michael Schauss, 'Uncertainty in the Law of Targeting: Towards a Cognitive Framework' (2019) 10 *Harvard National Security Journal* 148–194.

take part in the hostilities, but rather to protect themselves, their families, and their property. Given the chronic failure of insurgents to properly identify themselves as fighters, this can create confusion for an attacker. Similarly, airborne ISR assets may identify a building that armed men of fighting age regularly enter and exit late at night. Or communications intelligence assets may have intercepted a phone conversation involving the leader of an insurgent group three hours before an attack can be mounted against a building from which the call has been made.

IHL provides for two presumptions in cases of doubt as to status. With respect to individuals, article 50(1) of API provides, '[i]n case of doubt whether a person is a civilian, that person shall be considered to be a civilian'.[70] Obviously, this standard cannot require absolute certainty, for doubt is a pervasive reality of warfare. To ensure it will not be interpreted in this manner, a number of states issued understandings when ratifying API to the effect that the presumption does not override a commander's duty to protect his forces.[71]

The point is that if a reasonable commander would hesitate to attack because of doubt as to whether an individual is a combatant, member of an organized armed group, or direct participant in hostilities, then the rule attaches. As noted by the ICRC:

... it is fair to conclude that when there is a situation of doubt, a careful assessment has to be made under the conditions and restraints governing a particular situation as to whether there are sufficient indications to warrant an attack. One cannot automatically attack anyone who might appear dubious.[72]

The presumption with regard to objects is analogous. Article 52(3) of API stipulates that:

[i]n case of doubt whether an object which is normally dedicated to civilian purposes, such as a place of worship, a house or other dwelling or a school, is being used to make an effective contribution to military actions, it shall be presumed not to be so used.

As with individuals, when an attacker is uncertain about the status of a potential target to such a degree that the attacker hesitates to attack in the circumstances, the attack may not go forward. Textually, this presumption attaches only to those objects normally dedicated to civilian purposes. Therefore, it would not apply to, for example, a civilian airfield which is capable of launching and recovering military aircraft and had occasionally done so during peacetime. Despite this limitation, the ICRC's cautionary warning that '[i]t cannot automatically be assumed that any object that appears dubious may be subject to lawful attack' is, as in the case of persons, a fair reflection of the rule's application in practice.[73]

Since the determination is to be made in light of the attendant circumstances, the requisite certainty can vary. For instance, if the target is of extremely high military advantage, the amount of doubt that would cause a reasonable attacker to hesitate, thereby activating the presumption, would be lower than in cases where the potential target appears to

---

[70]  See also *Galić* (above n 21) para 50; *Milošević* (above n 39) para 946.
[71]  See eg UK Ratification Statement para (h).
[72]  CIHL commentary to rule 6.
[73]  See also CCW Amended Protocol II article 3(8)(a); *Galić* (above n 21) para 51; CIHL commentary to rule 10.

be a low-level fighter. This again reflects the inherent balancing between military advantage and humanitarian considerations that permeates this body of law.

Although most experts believe the presumptions reflect customary international law, a position advocated by the ICRC, the US has contested that assertion in its *Law of War Manual*:

> Under customary international law, no legal presumption of civilian status exists for persons or objects, nor is there any rule inhibiting commanders or other military personnel from acting based on the information available to him or her in doubtful cases. Attacks, however, may not be directed against civilians or civilian objects based on merely hypothetical or speculative considerations regarding their possible current status as a military objective. In assessing whether a person or object that normally does not have any military purpose or use is a military objective, commanders and other decision-makers must make the decision in good faith based on the information available to them in light of the circumstances ruling at the time.[74]

The US position is based on concerns that the presumptions might create a bar too high to rebut when confronted with the realities of war. Moreover, the presumptions could 'encourage a defender to ignore its obligation to separate military objectives from civilians and civilian objects' and 'unprivileged belligerents may seek to take advantage of a legal presumption of civilian status'.[75] As a result, the US concludes that such presumptions 'likely would increase the risk of harm to the civilian population and tend to undermine respect for the law of war'.[76]

Perhaps the two sides are closer that might appear at first glance. First, the gap between the US view—that a determination as to targetability cannot be based on hypothetical or speculative considerations—and the ICRC's—that a party may not attack any person or object that appears dubious—is narrow. Second, applied in practice, most operators would apply the presumption anyway, if only to avoid the negative blow-back from civilian casualties that has come to haunt contemporary military operations. Third, the US acknowledges the legal requirement of an attacker to do all that is feasible to verify the target (see below). Therefore, refusal to accept the customary status of the presumptions does little to relieve US operations of any undue burden.

### G. *Special protections*
In addition to the rules regarding the protection of civilians and civilian objects, IHL contains a number of 'special protections' with respect to certain persons or objects. As to persons, they extend, inter alia, to members of the armed forces who are *hors de combat*; medical, religious, civil defence, and humanitarian relief personnel; civilian journalists; and peacekeeping personnel, unless they have become a party to the conflict.[77] Objects enjoying special protection include medical facilities and units; specially established areas for civilian protection and care of the wounded and sick; humanitarian relief facilities, supplies, and

---

[74] US DoD (above n 16) para 5.4.3.2.
[75] ibid.
[76] ibid.
[77] GCI articles 24–26; GCII article 36; API articles 15, 62, 67, 71(2), 79; APII article 9; CIHL rules 25, 27, 31, 33, 34.

transports; peacekeeping equipment and facilities; cultural property; works and installations containing dangerous forces, such as dams, dykes, and nuclear electrical generating stations (by treaty); the natural environment (by treaty); and objects indispensable to the survival of the civilian population.[78]

Special protections operate in one of three ways. First, they may extend protection to persons or objects that do not otherwise enjoy protected civilian or civilian object status. Military personnel who are *hors de combat* by virtue of wounds or surrender, as well as those who serve as chaplains or perform medical duties, exemplify this form of special protection. Second, special protection may simply serve to emphasize the protected status of certain especially vulnerable groups, such as civilian correspondents, that already enjoy protected civilian status. Finally, special protections may limit the right to take action against certain objects that have lost their protected civilian status, or have been placed at greater risk by the hostilities. Examples include the requirement to warn before attacking a medical facility that is being used for military purposes, and the API limits on attacking dams, dykes, and nuclear electrical generating stations. As special protections are the subject of chapter 8, they will not be examined further here.

## H. Precautions in attack

In addition to its various prohibitions, the principle of distinction is the basis for a requirement that 'in the conduct of military operations, constant care shall be taken to spare the civilian population, civilians and civilian objects'.[79] This general admonition is operationalized in a number of specific rules set forth in article 57 of API. A failure to take the requisite precautions in attack is itself an IHL violation, irrespective of the degree to which an attack otherwise comports with the principle of distinction.

With respect to precautions in attack, the military necessity/humanitarian considerations balancing is expressed in terms of feasibility.[80] In light of humanitarian considerations, an attacker must do everything feasible to avoid harm to protected persons and objects, but given military necessity it can be expected to do no more than is sensible in the circumstances.

Although undefined in API, feasibility is generally considered to consist of measures that are 'practicable or practically possible, taking into account all circumstances prevailing at the time, including humanitarian and military considerations'.[81] As noted in the ICRC *Commentary* to API, what is practicable or practically possible entails 'common sense and good faith'.[82] Feasibility is essentially a reasonableness standard that requires attackers to take those measures to avoid collateral damage that a reasonable attacker would in the same

---

[78] GCI articles 19, 20, 23; GCIV articles 14–15, 54–56, 59; API articles 12, 21–24, 53, 60, 69–70; APII articles 11–12, 16, 18(2); Convention on the Safety of the United Nations and Associated Personnel (adopted 9 December 1994, entered into force 15 January 1999) 2051 UNTS 363; Convention for the Protection of Cultural Property in the Event of Armed Conflict (adopted 14 May 1954, entered into force 7 August 1956) 249 UNTS 240; Second Protocol 1999; CIHL rules 28–29, 32–33, 35–36, 38, 42–45, 54.

[79] API article 57(1); Convention on Cluster Munitions (adopted 30 May 2008, entered into force 1 August 2010) 2688 UNTS 39, preamble; *Prosecutor v Kupreškić et al* (Judgment) IT-95-16-T (14 January 2000) para 524; CIHL rule 15.

[80] API articles 57(2)(a)(i)–(ii). The condition of feasibility is generally understood to apply to all of the precautionary requirements set forth in article 57.

[81] UK Ratification Statement para (b); CCW Protocol II article 3(4); CCW Protocol III article 1(5); CCW Amended Protocol II article 3(10); AP Commentary para 2198.

[82] AP Commentary para 2198.

or similar circumstances, in light of the information that is 'reasonably available at the relevant time and place'.[83]

A variety of factors may affect the reasonableness of precautionary measures. Looming large are military considerations. Thus, an attacker is entitled to consider such matters as the need for precision munitions at a later stage in the campaign, competing demands for ISR assets, and the risk to one's own forces when assessing the feasibility of a particular measure. In this latter regard, there is some debate in IHL circles over the extent to which an attacker must place its forces at risk from enemy defences when conducting an attack. Although this debate has not been resolved as a matter of law, most disciplined military forces accept the premise that it is reasonable to shoulder some degree of risk in order to avoid harming protected persons and objects. The question is where does the feasibility line lie between risk-free attacks and those which are suicidal? Additionally, at least one state takes the position that the 'cost' of the weaponry can be a factor in the feasibility determination, although no other state has taken the same position openly.[84]

The first of the specific precautions required by article 57 is that an attacker must 'do everything feasible to verify that the objectives to be attacked are neither civilians nor civilian objects ... [nor] subject to special protection'.[85] Modern technology has dramatically expanded the options for attackers in this regard. In particular, unmanned aircraft fitted with ISR capabilities, and real-time communications links to those involved in the targeting process, have contributed to greater transparency of the target area, and resultantly an enhanced ability to ensure the intended target is indeed a lawful one.

An attacker is also required to select means and method of attack that minimize 'incidental loss of civilian life, injury to civilians and damage to civilian objects'.[86] By this rule, if an attacker can use a different weapon that will lessen harm to civilians or civilians objects, such as one that is more precise or less destructive—without sacrificing military advantage, for instance because the probability of achieving the desired destructive effect drops—then that weapon must be employed if feasible in the circumstances. The same applies to tactics. As an example, the angle of aerial attack that is most likely to avoid collateral damage, because of the location of civilian objects relative to the aim-point, must be selected so long as it does not lower the likelihood of achieving the desired effect on the target or increase risk to the aircraft. Similarly, if a bridge may be attacked at night when the presence of civilians thereon is likely to be low, and the timing does not affect likely success, the first option must be selected.

The same approach is obligatory with respect to the selection of targets.[87] In many cases, an attacker can select from among an array of potential targets to achieve a desired effect. Consider an attack designed to disrupt command and control for a particular period by denying electricity to an enemy communications node. Potential targets include the electrical generating plant, related substation or, using carbon filament bombs, electricity lines. So long as an attack on each achieves the desired effect of interrupting the electricity during that period, and none of them presents a greater risk to an attacker, the attacker must select

---

[83]   UK Ratification Statement para (c). See also CCW Protocol III, US Understanding upon Ratification.
[84]   US DoD (above n 16) para 5.2.3.2.
[85]   API article 57(2)(a)(i); *Galić* (above n 21) para 58; CIHL rule 16.
[86]   API article 57(2)(a)(ii); CIHL rule 17. See also *Ergi v Turkey* App No 40/1993/435/514 (ECtHR, 28 July 1998) para 79.
[87]   API article 57(3); CIHL rule 21.

the option most likely to avoid causing collateral damage. It must be cautioned that some states reject the customary law status of the requirement, although that is a decidedly minority view.[88]

To foster protection of protected persons and objects, IHL requires attackers to provide advanced warning of an attack that may affect the civilian population, unless circumstances do not permit.[89] Significant state practice of warning exists. Warnings can be specific to a particular operation, as with the Israeli practices of phoning the residence of a home to be attacked, messaging individuals at risk, or using the 'roof-knocking' technique.[90] However, the 'if circumstances permit' caveat is central to the requirement because warnings can allow the defender to put defensive measures in place or enable individuals who are targeted to escape. In such cases, general warnings may suffice. As an example, coalition forces dropped thousands of leaflets over Iraq in 2003, before launching their campaign, warning the civilian population to avoid military sites. In some cases, the circumstances render warnings infeasible altogether and they need not be issued.

The requirement to take precautions in attack is a relative one. Some states, for example, have sophisticated systems for verifying targets, a robust catalogue of weaponry, and the ability to strike targets with impunity (despite enemy defences) by employing effective countermeasures. Others come to the battlefield with limited means to effectively minimize civilian harm. Since the issue is feasibility, it is possible that a failure to employ feasible precautions by one state would not constitute the same for another.

The measures set forth above are known as 'active' precautions. Their counterpart consists of 'passive' precautions from the effects of attack that are required of the defender. Passive precautions oblige defenders, to 'the maximum extent feasible', to:

> ... endeavor to remove the civilian population, individual civilians and civilian objects under their control from the vicinity of military objectives; avoid locating military objectives within or near densely populated areas; [and] take the other necessary precautions to protect the civilian population, individual civilians and civilian objects under their control against the dangers resulting from military operations.[91]

Pursuant to article 51(7) of API, the failure of a defender to comply with this obligation does not affect the attacker's obligation to take active precautions, nor does it alter the operation of the rule of proportionality.

However, recall that some states are of the view that an enemy's use of human shields, whether voluntary or not, excuses an attacker from having to take the shields into consideration when conducting the proportionality analysis. This position was taken on the basis that the enemy should not be entitled to benefit from its own violation of the law of armed conflict. Presumably, the same logic applies with respect to passive precautions, such that an attacker facing an enemy that has volitionally failed to comply with the requirement need not take the resultant collateral damage to civilians and civilian objects into consideration when assessing proportionality.

---

[88] US DoD (above n 16) para 5.11.7.1.
[89] API article 57(2)(c). See also Hague Regulations article 26; CIHL rule 20.
[90] Schmitt and Merriam (above n 63) 135–6.
[91] API article 58; *Kupreškić* (above n 79) paras 524–525; CIHL rules 22–24.

## B. Unnecessary Suffering

As noted, in its *Nuclear Weapons Advisory Opinion*, the ICJ labelled the principle of un-necessary suffering as one of the cardinal principles of IHL. The principle stretches back to the 1868 St Petersburg Declaration's prohibition on arms that 'uselessly aggravate the suffering of disabled men, or render their death inevitable'.[92] It was subsequently reflected, albeit employing different terminology, in the Hague Regulations of 1907.[93] Article 35(2) of API is the contemporary articulation of the principle: '[i]t is prohibited to employ weapons, projectiles and material and methods of warfare of a nature to cause superfluous injury or unnecessary suffering'.

Unnecessary suffering is a clear example of balancing the foundational principles of mili-tary necessity and humanitarian considerations, for it renders it unlawful to cause enemy combatants more suffering than is merited by one's military objectives. In other words, it acknowledges the need to cause suffering, even death, of enemy forces (military necessity), but countenances only such degree of suffering that is justified by the need to prevail on the battlefield (humanitarian considerations).

Like the other two IHL general principles, the principle of unnecessary suffering is re-flected in a number of derivative rules. These are discussed in chapter 11 'Weapons', which, in addition to further discussing the principle, deals with individual weapons restrictions and bans. A number of the rules analysed in chapter 10 'Methods of Warfare' on prohibited methods of warfare likewise find their roots in the principle of unnecessary suffering. These include the rules against declaring no quarter, attacking those who are *hors de combat*, and conducting reprisals against prisoners of war (POWs). Analysis of the principle is therefore deferred to those chapters. However, two points merit mention here.

First, the principle applies only to those individuals who may be lawfully targeted: mem-bers of the armed forces or other organized armed groups and individuals who are directly participating in hostilities. It does not extend to civilians and other protected persons, be-cause those individuals are immune from direct attack *ab initio*. Any harm to them is sub-ject to the aforementioned rules deriving from the principle of distinction.

Second, the legal issue is not the degree of suffering, but whether that suffering is logic-ally and unavoidably incidental to an attack involving the means or methods chosen. Thus, the notion of unnecessary suffering is not to be equated with severe suffering. For instance, some weapons can cause severe suffering, but that suffering nevertheless may be necessary in the circumstances. Consider the use of incendiary weapons. Even though the suffering that results from their use can be horrific, they are valuable weapons for such purposes as use against enemy personnel under armoured protection or in field fortifications. The fact that incendiary weapons do not run counter to the principle is reflected in the fact that states parties to Protocol III (on incendiary weapons) to the Convention on Certain Conventional Weapons have limited their use only in specified circumstances.[94] By the same token, there is no established floor of suffering to which the principle applies. For in-stance, combat knives with serrated edges are generally considered to cause unnecessary

---

[92] Declaration Renouncing the Use, in Time of War, of Explosive Projectiles under 400 Grammes Weight (St Petersburg Declaration) (29 November/11 December 1868) 138 Consol TS 297, 18 Martens Nouveau Recueil (ser 1) 474.

[93] Hague Regulations article 22: 'the right of belligerents to adopt means of injuring the enemy is not unlimited'.

[94] CCW Protocol III. See also CIHL rule 85

suffering, even though far less lethal or injurious than many weapons, because a person may be rendered *hors de combat* with a straight edged knife.[95]

## C. Chivalry

The third general principle of IHL bearing on the conduct of hostilities differs from the preceding two in that it is often both a reflection of the balancing of military necessity and humanity and an historical principle that finds its roots in the notion of fairness on the battlefield between honourable warriors.[96] Although chivalry may seem alien in conflicts with groups like ISIS or Boko Haram, its continued valence during armed conflict is evidenced by the fact that rules based in chivalry are often cited by states, intergovernmental organizations, non-governmental entities, and scholars when assessing compliance with IHL.

Violations of a number of chivalry rules have become appallingly commonplace in modern warfare, particularly by various organized armed groups facing states that enjoy conventional military superiority on the battlefield.[97] This is because the norms in question typically require an element of good faith on the part of the parties to the conflict. The expectation of good faith is susceptible to being perversely exploited by the asymmetrically disadvantaged party in order to offset its inferiority, by, for example, using ambulances to approach enemy forces or beheading prisoners to excite the emotions of potential recruits.

The most developed category of rules deriving from chivalry are those dealing with the treatment of POWs. Although rules governing the treatment of prisoners are of ancient lineage, the first modern codification occurred with the Geneva Convention of 1929.[98] In the aftermath of widespread prisoner abuse during the Second World War, the Third Geneva Convention of 1949 (GCIII), as well as API, were adopted to add greater prescriptive granularity to the subject. These rules and their customary international law counterparts are the subject of chapter 5 'Persons Covered by International Humanitarian Law: Main Categories'.

Also prominent among the rules stemming from the principle of chivalry is the prohibition of perfidy. Article 37 of API prohibits killing, injuring, or capturing enemy forces by feigning protected status,[99] although a number of states do not accept the reference to capture as reflecting customary international law.[100] Specifically cited as examples of perfidy in the article are feigning: an intent to negotiate or surrender, being wounded, enjoying civilian status, or having status as a member of the United Nations or of neutral states by using their signs, emblems or uniforms. Perfidy must be distinguished from ruses, which are military operations or other activities intended to mislead the enemy, but that do not in any way attempt to exploit feigned protected status to one's advantage.[101]

---

[95] CIHL commentary to rule 70.

[96] US DoD (above n 16) para 2.6. See generally, Tery Gill, 'Chivalry: A Principle of the Law of Armed Conflict?', in Mariëlle Matthee et al (eds), *Armed Conflict and International Law: In Search of the Human Face* (Asser 2013) 33–51.

[97] See eg Human Rights Watch, 'Ukraine: Insurgents Disrupt Medical Services' Human Rights Watch News (5 August 2014) www.hrw.org/news/2014/08/05/ukraine-insurgents-disrupt-medical-services.

[98] GCIII.

[99] See also CIHL rule 65.

[100] US DoD (above n 16) para 5.22.2.1.

[101] API article 37(2).

Misusing signs intended to signify protected status, as in the case of those that indicate civil defence facilities or the Red Cross, violates IHL, even when there is no intent to betray the confidence of the enemy in order to kill, capture, or wound.[102] Additionally, enemy uniforms or other enemy emblems may not be worn while conducting an attack. It should be noted that it is lawful to wear enemy uniforms at other times, such as while spying in enemy territory or during an attempt to escape capture. However, if captured in the enemy's uniform the individual concerned will not be entitled to POW status. Finally, chivalry is the source of the prohibition on compelling nationals of the enemy to take part in the operations of war directed against their own country.

## 4. New Technologies of Warfare

A number of new technologies have raised issues regarding the aforementioned IHL conduct-of-hostility rules. Prominent among these are remotely piloted aircraft (drones), autonomous weapon systems, and cyber technologies.[103] Full treatment of these and other emergent technologies is well beyond the scope of this chapter, and some aspects are dealt with in chapter 11 'Weapons'. Certain key issues merit mention here.

With respect to drones, consensus is slowly beginning to emerge that so long as the target is lawful and all feasible measures have been taken to assess proportionality and to avoid harm to protected persons and objects, such weapon systems do not present significant conduct-of-hostilities issues. Instead, controversy tends to focus on two issues. The first is whether an armed conflict, either international or non-international, exists during contemporary drone operations, such that IHL is the appropriate legal regime when conducting lethal drone operations, rather than international human rights law. Classification of armed conflict is dealt with in chapter 2.

Second, questions as to the geography of war, in particular the geographical reach of IHL beyond the immediate battlefield during an armed conflict, are particularly complex in light of the global reach of some drone operations.[104] In particular, there is an ongoing debate about the legality of crossing into another state's territory to conduct strikes that focuses on whether doing so violates the sovereignty of the state where the operations are being conducted, or constitutes a 'use of force' against that state in violation of article 2(4) of the UN Charter. These questions are beyond the scope of IHL. Even if the state conducting the operations is in violation of these norms, it and the 'injured' state must comply with the principles and rules set forth in this chapter if the situation amounts to an armed conflict.

Autonomous weapon systems are those that, for the sake of simplicity, can be described as weapon systems that identify, select, and engage targets without human interaction. They are colloquially known as 'man out of the loop systems', to distinguish them from 'man in

---

[102] CIHL rules 58–63.

[103] For a fuller treatment of the author's views on these technologies, see respectively, Michael N Schmitt, 'Unmanned Combat Aircraft Systems (Armed Drones) and International Humanitarian Law: Simplifying the Oft Benighted Debate' (2012) 30 *BU Int'l L J* 595; Michael N Schmitt and Jeffrey C Thurnher, '"Out of the Loop": Autonomous Weapon Systems and the Law of Armed Conflict' (2013) 4 *Harvard Nat Sec J* 231–81; Michael N Schmitt, 'Cyber Operations in the Jus in Bello: Key Issues' (2011) 87 *ILS* 89–110.

[104] Michael N Schmitt, 'Charting the Legal Geography of Non-International Armed Conflict' (2014) 90 *ILS* 1–19.

the loop' systems, in which a human is actively involved in the engagement, or 'man on the loop' systems that involve human monitoring of an engagement and the ability to take control should the need arise. There have been assertions that autonomous weapons systems are unlawful per se because they are incapable of complying with the principle of distinction. Since then, the debate has matured.[105] Whether a system may comply with IHL depends on its sensor capabilities, weapon, and the environment in which it is employed. Most analysis today is instead directed at identifying aspects of autonomy that may present difficulties with respect to the specific rules set forth in this chapter.

Especially problematic in this regard is the question of how such systems might comply with the rule of proportionality. As sensor technologies become increasingly accurate, they are likely to be able to provide sufficient information to distinguish lawful targets from those which are protected by IHL. Yet, it remains difficult to ascertain how an autonomous system could assess military advantage over time or distance. This is because combat can evolve so quickly and dramatically that what is highly militarily advantageous at one moment may not be an hour later. For instance, the military advantage of engaging enemy forces that are attacking your position is higher than doing the same with forces fleeing the battlefield after a major defeat. Some commentators have also pointed to the issue of accountability for autonomous systems should they engage in attacks that violate conduct-of-hostilities rules. Others reply that those who take the decision to employ the systems will be responsible for any foreseeable consequences, including violations of IHL, as they are with respect to other weapons and tactics.

Finally, the advent of cyber operations during armed conflict has raised a number of challenging IHL issues. With respect to the conduct of hostilities, two loom especially large. The first surrounds the meaning of the term 'attack'.[106] The definitional debate is of particular import because many of the prohibitions found in IHL are prohibitions on attack. For example, as discussed above, IHL prohibits 'attacks' on civilians and civilian objects, bars 'attacks' likely to result in excessive collateral damage, and requires the taking of precautions in 'attack'. These and other prohibitions, restrictions, and requirements do not come into play unless the cyber operation in question qualifies as an attack.

There is widespread agreement that any cyber operation causing injury or death to individuals, or damage or destruction of tangible property, qualifies as an attack. So too does one that causes such effects even though no damage or injury is suffered by the entity against which the cyber operation is actually directed (as in opening the flood doors of a dam, thereby killing persons downstream). Consensus also appears to be emerging that cyber operations causing permanent interference with the 'functionality' of cyber infrastructure, or equipment that depends on the infrastructure, amounts to an attack.[107] Whether a cyber operation not having consequences at these levels constitutes an attack for IHL, conduct-of-hostilities purposes remains an open question.[108]

---

[105] Human Rights Watch, 'Losing Humanity: The Case against Killer Robots' (2012) 30. But see Michael N Schmitt, 'Autonomous Weapon Systems: A Reply to the Critics' (2013) 4 *Harvard Nat Sec J* 1.

[106] API article 49: ' "Attacks" means acts of violence against the adversary, whether in offence or in defense.'

[107] *Tallinn Manual* para 20 of commentary to rule 92.

[108] Michael N Schmitt, 'Rewired Warfare: Rethinking the Law of Cyber Attack' (2014) 96 *IRRC* 189; ICRC, 'International Humanitarian Law and the Challenges of Contemporary Armed Conflicts', Official Working Document of the 32nd International Conference of the Red Cross and Red Crescent Doc 32IC/15/11 (December 2011) 41; Cordula Droege, 'Get Off My Cloud: Cyber Warfare, International Humanitarian Law, and the Protection of Civilians' (2012) 94 *IRRC* 533, 556–60.

The second controversy deals with whether data qualifies as an 'object', such that an operation that destroys or alters civilian data amounts to a prohibited attack on a civilian object. Additionally, the answer to this question will determine whether or not collateral harm to civilian data during a lawful cyber operation against a military objective must be considered in the proportionality analysis and the precautions in attack requirements. A majority of the International Group of Experts that prepared the humanitarian law aspects of *Tallinn Manual 2.0 on the International Law Applicable to Cyber Operations* concluded that, in the present state of the law, data is not an object. They did so on the basis that data 'neither falls within the "ordinary meaning" of the term object, nor comports with the explanation of it offered in the ICRC Additional Protocols Commentary'.[109] However, the conclusion has been questioned by some commentators.[110]

These two issues raise difficult questions of law that are likely to demand attention by the international community. The problem is that there does not appear to be an easy solution to either. Although it might appear appealing to altogether prohibit cyber operations directed against civilians and civilian objects, such a prophylactic ban would, for instance, rule out psychological operations by cyber means directed at the enemy's civilian population. Since such operations are generally accepted as lawful in the non-cyber context, for instance through broadcasting or the dropping of leaflets, it is unclear why they would be unlawful if conducted by cyber means. Similarly, it might appear excessive to permit cyber operations against civilian data on the basis that they do not constitute objects (unless, of course, the operation qualifies as an attack on the basis of its harmful effects on persons or objects). Much civilian data is essential to the normal functioning of civilian societies and it would seem contrary to the object and purpose of IHL to allow for such wide-ranging operations. However, if data qualifies as an object, the ability of states to conduct cyber operations will be dramatically affected, because they may not conduct cyber operations against civilian data. This is also because the rule of proportionality, and the requirement to take precautions, would prohibit many cyber operations against valid military targets due to the networking of civilian and military systems, and the fact that militaries around the world rely heavily on civilian systems to conduct their military operations. No resolution of either issue is on the horizon.[111]

These and other issues dealing with the application and interpretation of extant IHL norms to new technologies of warfare will inevitably be settled over time through state practice and *opinio juris*. They may also be resolved through adoption new treaty law, although this prospect is far less likely than contextual interpretation of existing general principles and rules. Indeed, IHL has repeatedly proven flexible enough to adapt contextually to the emergence of new technologies; this is worth recalling as the IHL community and states grapple with the confluence of such technologies and international law.

---

[109] *Tallinn Manual* para 6 of commentary to rule 100.

[110] Heather A Harrison Dinnis, 'The Nature of Objects: Targeting Networks and the Challenge of Defining Cyber Military Objectives' (2015) 48 *Isr Law Rev* 39; Kubo Macak, 'Military Objectives 2.0: The Case for Interpreting Computer Data as Objects under International Humanitarian Law' (2015) 48 *Isr Law Rev* 55. But see Michael N Schmitt, 'The Notion of 'Objects" during Cyber Operations: A Riposte in Defence of Interpretive Precision' (2015) 48 *Isr Law Rev* 81.

[111] For a proposed policy response to the issues of attack and data, see Michael N. Schmitt, 'Wired Warfare 3.0: Protecting the Civilian Population during Cyber Operations' (2019) 101(1) *IRRC* 333–355.

# 8

# Specifically Protected Persons and Objects

*Robin Geiß and Christophe Paulussen\**

## 1. Introduction

Probably the most fundamental rule in international humanitarian law (IHL) is that a distinction must be made between civilians and combatants and between civilian objects and military objectives (see also chapter 7 'International Humanitarian Law and the Conduct of Hostilities'). In addition to this general notion, certain categories of persons and objects receive specific protection, typically because they are seen as particularly vulnerable. These categories of specifically protected persons and objects are the focus of this chapter. The aim is to provide a tour d'horizon of the various categories. Some of them—namely the wounded and sick, as well as the protection accorded to cultural property—are addressed in detail in order to illustrate the legal mechanisms used to implement special protection; some are discussed cursorily, and others are mentioned only briefly, with the reader being directed to the relevant parts elsewhere in this book.

## 2. Historical Development

There are various documents pre-dating the 1949 Geneva Conventions and 1977 Additional Protocols containing provisions dealing with special protection. The oldest example, albeit on the national level, is the 1863 *Lieber Instructions* (better known as the *Lieber Code*), the first attempt to codify the laws of war (see also chapter 1 'History and Sources' in this book).[1] For instance, article 35 of the *Lieber Code*[2] states that '[c]lassical works of art, libraries, scientific collections, or precious instruments, such as astronomical telescopes, as well as hospitals, must be secured against all avoidable injury, even when they are contained

---

* The authors would like to thank Wim Zimmermann, intern at the TMC Asser Instituut, for his helpful assistance in the preparation of this chapter. Developments have been taken into account until July 2016.

[1] *Instructions for the Government of Armies of the United States in the Field*, General Orders No 100 (24 April 1863) (*Lieber Code*). The International Committee of the Red Cross (ICRC) notes about these instructions:

> Although they were binding only on the forces of the United States, they correspond to a great extend [*sic*] to the laws and customs of war existing at that time. The "Lieber Instructions" strongly influenced the further codification of the laws of war and the adoption of similar regulations by other states. They formed the origin of the project of an international convention on the laws of war presented to the Brussels Conference in 1874 and stimulated the adoption of the Hague Conventions on land warfare of 1899 and 1907 (www.icrc.org/ihl/INTRO/110).

[2] Susan Breau, 'Protected Persons and Objects', in Elizabeth Wilmshurst and Susan Breau (eds), *Perspectives on the ICRC Study on Customary International Humanitarian Law* (CUP 2007) 170.

in fortified places whilst besieged or bombarded'.[3] Also nowadays, special protection is offered to cultural property and hospitals; see below. Another example can be found in article 71 of the *Lieber Code*, which clarifies:

> Whoever intentionally inflicts additional wounds on an enemy already wholly disabled, or kills such an enemy, or who orders or encourages soldiers to do so, shall suffer death, if duly convicted, whether he belongs to the Army of the United States, or is an enemy captured after having committed his misdeed.[4]

This can be seen as an ancestor of modern provisions—such as article 41(1) Additional Protocol I (API)—which provide special protection to persons *hors de combat*. A third is article 79 of the *Lieber Code*, which stipulates that '[e]very captured wounded enemy shall be medically treated, according to the ability of the medical staff.' Indeed, the protection of the wounded and sick 'has been at the heart of humanitarian law since its modern inception'.[5] With respect to the international level, wounded and sick military personnel—and the medical staff assigned to their care—were the first category of 'protected persons' who benefitted from legal protection laid out in the 1864 First Geneva Convention, which was henceforth revised in 1906, 1929, 1949, and again in 1977, with the aim of gradually completing and adapting this legal regime of special protection to the changing nature of armed conflict.[6] For example, whereas initially the legal protections applied only to wounded and sick military personnel, API extended these protections also to wounded and sick civilians. Over time various other categories of persons and objects have been identified as being in need of special protection and specific regulation, and international treaty law as well as customary international law have developed accordingly. Thus, in addition to the legal protection granted to the wounded and sick, contemporary IHL specifically regulates religious personnel, medical units and transports, persons and objects displaying the distinctive emblem, humanitarian relief personnel and objects, personnel and objects involved in peacekeeping missions, journalists, women, children, missing persons, hospital and safety zones, cultural property, and the environment.

## 3. Categories of Persons and Objects

In the following pages, various categories of persons and objects receiving specific protection are addressed. The main categorization is naturally in categories of 'persons' (section A) and 'objects' (section B).

---

[3] *Lieber Code* www.icrc.org/ihl/INTRO/110.
[4] ibid article 71.
[5] Robin Geiss and Helen Durham, 'ICRC Commentary on Article 12 Geneva Convention'(GCI) (2016) para 1321 https://ihl-databases.icrc.org/applic/ihl/ihl.nsf/Comment.xsp?action=openDocument&documentId=CECD58D1E2A2AF30C1257F15004A7CB9.
[6] ibid.

# A. Categories of Persons

## 1. *Wounded and sick*

### A. *Definition*
The wounded and sick are specifically protected in both international armed conflicts (IACs) and non-international armed conflicts (NIACs). Legally speaking there is no difference between being either 'wounded' or 'sick'. The same legal protections apply. With regard to IACs—the same definition can, however, be used also for the purposes of NIACs[7]—article 8(a) API[8] defines 'wounded' and 'sick' as:

> … persons, whether military or civilian, who, because of trauma, disease or other physical or mental disorder or disability, are in need of medical assistance or care and who refrain from any act of hostility. These terms also cover maternity cases, new-born babies and other persons who may be in need of immediate medical assistance or care, such as the infirm or expectant mothers, and who refrain from any act of hostility.

It follows that unlike the colloquial understanding of the terms 'wounded' and 'sick', the legal definition requires the cumulative fulfilment of two distinct elements: a person must be in need of medical care and must refrain from any act of hostility.[9] As the listing in article 8(a) API makes clear, a person may be in medical need for a variety of reasons, without—in the strict sense—being wounded or sick (eg in the case of maternity cases).

### B. *Protection granted*
Various protections apply to the wounded and sick. The analysis below focuses on three central sets of obligations.

(i) **The obligation to respect and protect** The obligations to 'respect and protect' the wounded and sick can be found in various provisions.[10] These obligations are complementary. They entail that there is not only a *negative* obligation, hence that one must *abstain/refrain* from conduct harming the wounded and sick, that is sparing, not attacking the wounded and sick—an obligation of result ('to respect'), but also that there is a *positive* obligation, namely that one must *(pro)actively take measures* to ensure the protection of the wounded and sick, that is helping, supporting the wounded and sick—an obligation of

---

[7] Robin Geiss, 'ICRC Commentary on Common Article 3 GC I–IV' (2016) para 738 https://ihl-databases.icrc.org/applic/ihl/ihl.nsf/Comment.xsp?action=openDocument&documentId=59F6CDFA490736C1C1257F7D004BA0EC.

[8] Protocol Additional to the Geneva Conventions of 12 August 1949, and Relating to the Protection of Victims of International Armed Conflicts (adopted 8 June 1977, entered into force 7 December 1978) 1125 UNTS 3 (API).

[9] Geiss and Durham, 'Commentary on Article 12' (above n 5) para 1341.

[10] See eg Geneva Convention (I) for the Amelioration of the Condition of the Wounded and Sick in Armed Forces in the Field (adopted 12 August 1949, entered into force 21 October 1950) 75 UNTS 31 (GCI) article 12: 'Members of the armed forces and other persons mentioned in the following Article, who are wounded or sick, shall be respected and protected in all circumstances.' See also Geneva Convention (II) for the Amelioration of the Condition of Wounded, Sick and Shipwrecked Members of Armed Forces at Sea (adopted 12 August 1949, entered into force 21 October 1950) 75 UNTS 85 (GCII) article 12.

conduct ('to protect').[11] The various more detailed obligations applicable to the wounded and sick can be regarded as specifications of the general obligation to 'respect and protect'.

The complementary obligations to respect and protect—a phrase that first appeared in the 1906 Geneva Convention—are a recurrent feature of the legal regimes according special protection to different categories of persons and objects throughout the Geneva Conventions (GCs) and their Additional Protocols (APs). Thus, in Resolution 2286 the UN Security Council recalled the obligations 'to respect and protect, in situations of armed conflict, medical personnel and humanitarian personnel exclusively engaged in medical duties, their means of transport and equipment, and hospitals and other medical facilities, which must not be attacked'.[12]

**(ii) Humane treatment and medical care** In various provisions dealing with both IACs and NIACs, it is clarified that the wounded and sick shall be treated humanely and cared for by the party to the conflict in whose power they may be, without any adverse distinction founded on sex, race, nationality, religion, political opinions, or any other similar criteria.[13] In more detail:

> Any attempts upon their lives, or violence to their persons, shall be strictly prohibited; in particular, they shall not be murdered or exterminated, subjected to torture or to biological experiments; they shall not willfully be left without medical assistance and care, nor shall conditions exposing them to contagion or infection be created.[14]

Novak, referring to Pictet, has noted that '[w]hile the exact meaning of "humane treatment" depends on the respective context, it is at least considered as "a minimum to be reserved for the individual to enable him to lead an acceptable existence in as normal a manner as possible"'.[15] The obligation of humane treatment imposes an obligation of result. Treatment must never fall below this minimum standard. The obligation aims to protect the inherent human dignity of the wounded and sick and therefore 'pervades all aspects of treatment of the wounded and sick'.[16]

The obligation to provide medical care for the wounded and sick imposes an obligation of conduct; that is, it is an obligation of means that is to be carried out with due diligence. As such the obligation is context dependent. What exactly is required depends on what kind of medical care can reasonably be expected under the given circumstances of each case. Factors to be taken into consideration when assessing the required forms of medical

---

[11]   See also Gregor Novak, 'Wounded, Sick, and Shipwrecked', *Max Planck Encyclop Pub Intern'l L* (2013) http://opil.ouplaw.com/view/10.1093/law:epil/9780199231690/law-9780199231690-e448. For a more detailed analysis, see eg Geiss and Durham, 'Commentary on Article 12' (above n 5).

[12]   UN Security Council Resolution 2286 (3 May 2016) UN Doc S/RES/2286 para 8.

[13]   See eg GCI article 12. See for an (almost) identical version GCII article 12. cf also Geneva Convention (III) Relative to the Treatment of Prisoners of War (adopted 12 August 1949, entered into force 21 October 1950) 75 UNTS 135 (GCIII) article 3 (applicable to NIACs), Geneva Convention (IV) Relative to the Protection of Civilian Persons in Time of War (adopted 12 August 1949, entered into force 21 October 1950) 75 UNTS 287 (GCIV) article 16, API article 10, and Protocol Additional to the Geneva Conventions of 12 August 1949, and Relating to the Protection of Victims of Non-International Armed Conflicts (adopted 8 June 1977, entered into force 7 December 1978) 1125 UNTS 609 (APII) (applicable to NIACs).

[14]   See GCI article 12.

[15]   See Novak (above n 11).

[16]   Geiss and Durham, 'Commentary on Article 12' (above n 5) para 1373.

care include the type and severity of the medical condition, and the available medical expertise and resources, as well as the level of risk (eg if medical care is to be administered on the battlefield). As a general rule, the wounded and sick should receive the medical care required by their condition: severe injuries will require more than minor injuries and skilled medical personnel can be expected to do more than ordinary soldiers. Although no 'adverse' distinction is to be made, urgent medical reasons can in fact justify prioritization in the order of treatment to be administered.[17] Moreover, the law recognizes that sometimes a party may be compelled to abandon the wounded or sick to the enemy.[18] In such as case, and as far as military considerations permit, they must be left with a part of the party's medical personnel and material who can assist in their care.[19]

(iii) **Search, collect, and evacuate** Parties to both IACs and NIACs are also under an obligation to search for, collect, and evacuate the wounded and sick. These obligations are complementary and should be understood as a single obligation to carry out search-and-rescue activities whenever there is reason to believe that wounded and sick may be in the area. This is an obligation of conduct. As such it is relative and dependent on the circumstances of each particular case. The relevant point of reference is which kinds of measures and activities could reasonably be expected under the given circumstances.

### 2. *Shipwrecked*
Article 8(b) API defines 'shipwrecked' as 'persons, whether military or civilian, who are in peril at sea or in other waters as a result of misfortune affecting them or the vessel or aircraft carrying them and who refrain from any act of hostility'.[20] Similar to the status of the wounded and sick, the status of being shipwrecked requires the cumulative fulfilment of two distinct criteria, namely that of being in a perilous situation in a specific context and of abstaining from any act of hostility. The protective regime applicable to the shipwrecked in both IAC and NIAC is by and large identical to the regime applicable to the wounded and sick.

### 3. *Medical personnel and medical activities*
Article 8(c) API defines medical personnel as 'those persons assigned, by a Party to the conflict, exclusively to the medical purposes enumerated under sub-paragraph e)[21] or to the administration of medical units or to the operation or administration of medical transports. Such assignments may be either permanent or temporary.' This category includes:

i) [M]edical personnel of a Party to the conflict, whether military or civilian,[22] including those described in the First and Second Conventions, and those assigned to civil defence

---

[17] See GCI article 12.
[18] ibid article 12.
[19] ibid article 12.
[20] cf also GCII article 12.
[21] 'Namely the search for, collection, transportation, diagnosis or treatment—including first-aid treatment—of the wounded, sick and shipwrecked, or for the prevention of disease.' See also the category 'medical units' in section 3.B.1 below.
[22] Jean-Marie Henckaerts and Louise Doswald-Beck (eds), *Customary International Humanitarian Law, Volume I: Rules* (CUP 2005) (CIHL) 82: 'The term "military medical personnel" refers to medical personnel who are members of the armed forces. The term "civilian medical personnel" refers to medical personnel who are not members of the armed forces but who have been assigned by a party to the conflict exclusively to medical tasks.'

organizations; ii) medical personnel of national Red Cross (Red Crescent, Red Lion and Sun) Societies and other national voluntary aid societies duly recognized and authorized by a Party to the conflict [this includes the ICRC]; iii) medical personnel of medical units or medical transports described in Article 9, paragraph 2[23].[24]

Although APII does not contain a definition of medical personnel, the term, as used in NIACs, may be understood in the same sense as that defined in API.[25] The ICRC's Customary International Humanitarian Law Study (CIHL Study) explains that '[o]nly medical personnel assigned to medical duties by a party to the conflict enjoy protected status. Other persons performing medical duties ... are not medical personnel and as a result ... have no right to display the distinctive emblems'[26] (see also below).

The category of medical personnel is obviously highly inter-related to the category of wounded and sick (and shipwrecked) already discussed. For instance, article 24 GCI states that:

> Medical personnel exclusively engaged in the search for, or the collection, transport or treatment of the wounded or sick, or in the prevention of disease, staff exclusively engaged in the administration of medical units and establishments, as well as chaplains attached to the armed forces, shall be respected and protected in all circumstances.

In the same vein, the protection of medical personnel in NIACs can be retrieved from article 3 common to the GCs, which stipulates in its paragraph 2 that 'The wounded and sick shall be collected and cared for.' After all, if medical personnel cannot be protected in the first place to do their job, then the wounded and sick can also not be collected and cared for.[27] A more explicit protective provision—not only for medical, but also for religious personnel—can be found in article 9(1) APII.[28]

The special protection of medical personnel, whether military or civilian, is, however, not absolute, as is the case with so many of the categories under discussion in this chapter. Indeed, when they perpetrate, outside of their humanitarian function, acts harmful to the enemy, they lose their protection from direct attack.[29] Also here, it becomes clear that the protection of medical personnel 'is not a personal privilege but rather a corollary of the respect and protection due to the wounded and sick, who must be treated humanely in all

---

[23] This para states that:

[t]he relevant provisions of Articles 27 and 32 of the First Convention shall apply to permanent medical units and transports (other than hospital ships, to which Article 25 of the Second Convention applies) and their personnel made available to a Party to the conflict for humanitarian purposes: (a) by a neutral or other State which is not a Party to that conflict; (b) by a recognized and authorized aid society of such a State; (c) by an impartial international humanitarian organization.

[24] API article 8(c).
[25] CIHL 82.
[26] ibid 82.
[27] ibid 80.
[28] This para explains:

1. Medical and religious personnel shall be respected and protected and shall be granted all available help for the performance of their duties. They shall not be compelled to carry out tasks which are not compatible with their humanitarian mission. 2. In the performance of their duties medical personnel may not be required to give priority to any person except on medical grounds.

[29] CIHL 79.

circumstances'.[30] An act is considered harmful to the enemy when, for instance, medical teams are incorporated into combat units and their medical personnel bear arms and take a direct part in hostilities.[31] However, the mere caring for enemy wounded and sick military personnel or the sole wearing of enemy military uniforms is not considered to amount to a hostile act. In addition, medical personnel can be equipped with small arms to defend themselves or their patients and even their use, for that purpose, is allowed (see also section 3.B.1.B 'Hospital ships' below).[32]

When they are incorporated in the armed forces, medical personnel are not combatants, and thus cannot be taken as prisoners of war (POWs).[33] As a general rule, medical personnel shall be returned to the party to the conflict to whom they belong (article 30 GCI).

Even though the special protection for medical personnel seems obvious, in August 2014, Human Rights Watch (HRW) accused insurgents in eastern Ukraine of having 'threatened medical staff, stolen and destroyed medical equipment and hospital furniture, and compromised the ability of civilian patients to receive treatment'.[34] HRW also alleged that they had 'expropriated ambulances and used them to transport active fighters'.[35] Such attacks are clearly prohibited by IHL. Nevertheless, such attacks are on the increase and the UN Security Council recently felt the need to adopt a resolution in which it 'strongly condemns acts of violence, attacks and threats against the wounded and sick, medical personnel and humanitarian personnel' and the prevailing impunity for such violations of IHL.[36]

### 4. Religious personnel

Article 8(d) API defines religious personnel as:

> ... military or civilian persons, such as chaplains, who are exclusively engaged in the work of their ministry and attached: i) to the armed forces of a Party to the conflict; ii) to medical units or medical transports of a Party to the conflict; iii) to medical units or medical transports described in Article 9, paragraph 2[[37]]; or iv) to civil defence organizations of a Party to the conflict. The attachment of religious personnel may be either permanent or temporary, and the relevant provisions mentioned under subparagraph k)[[38]] apply to them.

The protection of religious personnel was mentioned in the previous category, section 3.A.3 'Medical personnel and medical activities', when discussing article 24 GCI (see the

---

[30] CIHL 84, referring to the Spanish LOAC (Law of Armed Conflict) Manual.

[31] CIHL 85.

[32] ibid 85.

[33] API article 43 para 2.

[34] Human Rights Watch, 'Ukraine: Insurgents Disrupt Medical Services' (5 August 2014) www.hrw.org/news/2014/08/05/ukraine-insurgents-disrupt-medical-services.

[35] ibid.

[36] UNSC Resolution 2286 paras 1 and 8.

[37] See n 23.

[38] This sub-para states:

> 'permanent medical personnel', 'permanent medical units' and 'permanent medical transports' mean those assigned exclusively to medical purposes for an indeterminate period. 'Temporary medical personnel', 'temporary medical units' and 'temporary medical transports' mean those devoted exclusively to medical purposes for limited periods during the whole of such periods. Unless otherwise specified, the terms 'medical personnel', 'medical units' and 'medical transports' cover both permanent and temporary categories.

reference to chaplains in that provision), as well as article 9(1) APII. Religious personnel, whether military or civilian, receive the same respect as medical personnel.[39] Although APII does not contain a definition of religious personnel, this term may be understood as applying in the same sense in NIACs.[40] When they are incorporated in the armed forces, religious personnel—just like medical personnel (see above)—are not combatants, and thus cannot be taken POWs.[41]

### 5. *Women*

The participation of women in armed conflict has grown significantly over time. As either combatants or civilians, women are subject to the general regulations. But in addition to these general protections, IHL also mentions women—whether as combatants or as civilians—specifically. This is done not because women are seen to be inherently (more) vulnerable but to emphasize that women have specific needs and may face specific physical and psychological risks in the context of armed conflicts 'including the increased risk of sexual violence'.[42]

Historically, armies even considered rape one of the legitimate spoils of war, although the atrocities in the former Yugoslavia and Rwanda led to recognition of sexual violence as an international crime, with the International Criminal Tribunal for Rwanda (ICTR) being the first international court to find an accused person—Jean-Paul Akayesu—guilty of rape as a crime of genocide in 1998.[43] Regardless of these positive steps, recent history teaches that sexual violence remains extremely problematic. For instance, the organization that calls itself Islamic State (IS) has admitted to and even 'justified' sex slavery.[44]

Returning to the rules of IHL and the two categories mentioned above: as to the first category (combatants), article 12 of both GCI and GCII explains that women shall be treated with all consideration due to their sex and article 14 of GCIII likewise stipulates that women shall be treated with all the regard due to their sex and shall in all cases benefit by treatment as favourable as that granted to men. More detailed provisions can be found in, for example, article 76 API, clarifying that '[w]omen shall be the object of special respect and shall be protected in particular against rape, forced prostitution and any other form of indecent assault,' and articles 97 and 108 GCIII, which explain that female POWs shall undergo their disciplinary punishment or be confined (after their sentence) in separate quarters and be

---

[39]   CIHL 595.

[40]   ibid 90.

[41]   API article 43(2).

[42]   See ICRC, 'Women and War: Women and Armed Conflicts and the Issue of Sexual Violence' (Report, Colloquium ICRC—EUISS, 30 September 2014) 5 www.icrc.org/en/download/file/8598/icrc_report_women_and_war.pdf. Geiss and Durham, 'Commentary on Article 12' (above n 5) para 1427.

[43]   See Outreach Programme on the Rwanda Genocide and the United Nations, 'Background Information on Sexual Violence used as a Tool of War' (March 2014) https://www.un.org/en/preventgenocide/rwanda/assets/pdf/Backgrounder%20Sexual%20Violence%202014.pdf.

[44]   See the ninth issue of IS' glossy magazine *Dabiq*, 'The Islamic State's (ISIS, ISIL) Magazine' *The Clarion Project* (10 September 2014) www.clarionproject.org/news/islamic-state-isis-isil-propaganda-magazine-dabiq#. See also Simon Tomlinson, 'ISIS "Rape Handbook" Reveals 15 Rules for Slaves' "Owners"—from Banning Sons and Fathers from Sharing the Same Woman to Outlawing Sex with a Mother and Daughter', *Daily Mail* (London, 29 December 2015) www.dailymail.co.uk/news/article-3377086/Islamic-State-ruling-ams-settle-sex-female-slaves.html, and Ludovica Iaccino, 'Isis Iraq News: Pregnant Women among 150 "Executed for Refusing to be Insurgents' Sex Slaves"' *International Business Times* (London, 17 December 2014) www.ibtimes.co.uk/isis-iraq-news-pregnant-women-among-150-executed-refusing-be-insurgents-sex-slaves-1479959.

supervised by women. However, if possible, families must stay together.[45] Such a rule is also applicable to internees in the context of NIACs.[46] Moreover, the dormitories[47] and hygienic conveniences[48] of female POWs shall be separated from those of male POWs, and there are also specific protective provisions on the execution of penalties.[49]

As to the second category (civilians), an example of special protection can be found in article 27 GCIV, which makes clear that women shall be especially protected against any attack on their honour, in particular against rape, enforced prostitution, or any form of indecent assault.[50] As with the first category (see above), women shall be confined in separate quarters and supervised by women,[51] but families must, if possible, be accommodated together.[52] As with the previous category (combatants), this rule is also valid in NIACs, for internees.[53] Moreover, women can only be searched by other women.[54] Finally, there are also specific protective provisions on non-repatriated persons[55] and accommodation and hygiene.[56]

In addition, it should be clarified that IHL has specific regulations for a special category of women, namely pregnant and nursing women, as well as mothers of dependent children. Examples can be found in article 16 GCIV (mentioned in section 3.A.1. 'Wounded and sick' above); in article 70(1) API (distribution of relief consignments); article 76(2) API, which explains that pregnant women and mothers having dependent infants who are arrested, detained, or interned for reasons related to the armed conflict, shall have their cases considered with the utmost priority; and article 76(3) API (death penalty).[57] That the death penalty shall not be carried out on pregnant women or mothers of young/dependent children can also be found in NIACs; see article 6(4) APII.

### 6. Children

Children are also a category of persons that are specifically mentioned—and protected— in IHL. The basis of the special protection for children in IHL is formed by their 'physical weakness and the importance of their preservation to future generations'.[58] Unfortunately and sadly, there are too many examples showing that special protection for this vulnerable group remains absolutely necessary. One can only think of the repugnant practices by IS, which is preparing an entire new generation of jihadi killers by training and brainwashing boys, the 'Cubs of the Caliphate', in how to manufacture bombs, fight in combat, and execute people.[59]

---

[45] See API article 75(5).

[46] See APII article 5(2)(a).

[47] See GCIII article 25.

[48] See ibid article 29.

[49] See ibid article 88.

[50] See for a comparable provision API article 76.

[51] See GCIV article 76. Also as regards disciplinary punishments, see GCIV article 124.

[52] See again (see also n 45) API article 75(5).

[53] See again (see also n 46) APII article 5(2)(a).

[54] See GCIV article 97.

[55] See ibid article 38.

[56] See ibid article 85.

[57] For other provisions, see eg ibid articles 17 (evacuation), 23 (consignment of medical supplies, food and clothing), 89 (food), 91V (medical attention), and 127 (conditions of transfer).

[58] See Jonathan Crowe and Kylie Weston-Scheuber, *Principles of International Humanitarian Law* (Edward Elgar 2013) 91.

[59] See eg Jessica Stern and J Berger, '"Raising Tomorrow's Mujahideen": The Horrific World of Isis's Child Soldiers' *The Guardian* (Sydney, 10 March 2015) www.theguardian.com/world/2015/mar/10/horror-of-isis-child-soldiers-state-of-terror

A few of the special protections that IHL has in place for children have already been mentioned, such as the provision on distribution of relief consignments (article 70 (1) API),[60] food (article 89 GCIV),[61] and with regard to the death penalty (article 6(4) APII).[62] Also the previously discussed category of 'mothers of dependent children' brings special protection, not only for those mothers, but obviously also for those dependent children. After all, executing a mother with dependent infants[63] will undoubtedly create many additional problems for the motherless children as well.[64]

A provision specifically dedicated to the protection of children is article 77(1) API, which states that '[c]hildren shall be the object of special respect and shall be protected against any form of indecent assault. The Parties to the conflict shall provide them with the care and aid they require, whether because of their age or for any other reason.' The same article also addresses recruitment and participation in hostilities (to be discussed in more detail below).[65] It clarifies, moreover, that arrested/detained/interned children shall be held in separate quarters (except where families are accommodated as family units)[66] and shall not be executed if at the time the offence was committed they had not attained the age of eighteen[67] (see also the rule for NIACs mentioned in section 3.A.5. 'Women' above).

In the context of NIACs, a broadly formulated protection can be found in article 4(3) of APII, which states that '[c]hildren shall be provided with the care and aid they require', followed by more specific rules on education,[68] family reunion,[69] recruitment and participation in hostilities (to be discussed in more detail below),[70] and evacuation.[71]

IHL has specific regulations for special categories of children, such as article 24 GCIV, which is aimed at children under fifteen, who are orphaned or are separated from their families as a result of the war. The same article also explains that the parties to the conflict 'shall, furthermore, endeavour to arrange for all children under twelve to be identified by the wearing of identity discs, or by some other means'. This is yet again an illustration of the fact that there exist various categories of children under IHL: children as such, young

and Rachel Bryson, 'This is Why Isis Uses Children Like the So-Called "Jihadi Junior" in their Propaganda Videos' *The Independent* (London, 4 January 2016) www.independent.co.uk/voices/this-is-why-isis-use-children-like-jihadi-junior-in-propaganda-videos-a6796191.html. See also the eighth issue of IS' glossy magazine *Dabiq*, glorifying its child soldier programme: *Dabiq*, 'The Islamic State's (ISIS, ISIL) Magazine' *The Clarion Project* (10 September 2014) www.clarionproject.org/news/islamic-state-isis-isil-propaganda-magazine-dabiq#.

[60] Which states that 'In the distribution of relief consignments, priority shall be given to those persons, such as children, expectant mothers, maternity cases and nursing mothers, who, under the Fourth Convention or under this Protocol, are to be accorded privileged treatment or special protection.'
[61] Which states that 'Expectant and nursing mothers and children under fifteen years of age, shall be given additional food, in proportion to their physiological needs.'
[62] Which states that 'The death penalty shall not be pronounced on persons who were under the age of eighteen years at the time of the offence and shall not be carried out on pregnant women or mothers of young children.' See also GCIV articles 17, 23, and 68 (see n 57).
[63] See API article 76(3).
[64] See also ibid article 76(2).
[65] ibid article 77(2)–(3).
[66] ibid article 77(4).
[67] ibid article 77(5).
[68] APII article 4(3)(a).
[69] ibid article 4(3)(b).
[70] ibid article 4(3)(c)–(d).
[71] ibid article 4(3)(e).

children, dependent children, children under twelve, children under fifteen,[72] as well as children under eighteen.[73]

This is also clearly visible in the regulations on child soldiers; the previously mentioned article 77(2) API clarifies that:

> The Parties to the conflict shall take all feasible measures in order that children who have not attained the age of fifteen years do not take a direct part in hostilities and, in particular, they shall refrain from recruiting them into their armed forces. In recruiting among those persons who have attained the age of fifteen years but who have not attained the age of eighteen years, the Parties to the conflict shall endeavour to give priority to those who are oldest.[74]

The rule that children under fifteen cannot be recruited in the armed forces or take (a direct) part in hostilities is also applicable in NIACs; see the previously mentioned article 4(3)(c) of APII. This minimum age of fifteen can, moreover, be found in the Statute of the International Criminal Court,[75] the Statute of the (now defunct) Special Court for Sierra Leone,[76] and the Convention on the Rights of the Child, which contains provisions from both international human rights law (IHRL) and IHL.[77] At the same time, there has been discussion about whether this minimum age should not be eighteen.[78] The CIHL Study therefore concludes that '[a]lthough there is not, as yet, a uniform practice with respect to the minimum age for recruitment, there is agreement that it should not be below 15 years of age'.[79]

Children must not be recruited into the armed forces or armed groups and must not be allowed to take part in hostilities. Regarding the question which kinds of activities would amount to such a participation in hostilities in the context of child soldiers, the ICC Trial Chamber in Lubanga held that:

> Those who participate actively in hostilities include a wide range of individuals, from those on the front line (who participate directly) through to the boys or girls who are involved in a myriad of roles that support the combatants ... The decisive factor in deciding, therefore, if an 'indirect' role is to be treated as active participation in hostilities is whether the

---

[72] See also GCIV article 38.

[73] See for the latter group for instance n 62 but also GCIV article 51 (on labour).

[74] Note that API article 77(3) explains that if 'children who have not attained the age of fifteen years take a direct part in hostilities and fall into the power of an adverse Party, they shall continue to benefit from the special protection accorded by this Article, whether or not they are prisoners of war'.

[75] Rome Statute of the International Criminal Court (adopted 17 July 1998, entered into force 1 July 2002) 2187 UNTS 3 (Rome Statute) article 8(2)(b)(xxvi)—for IACs—and (2)(e)(vii)—for NIACs. Note that the very first suspect of the ICC, Thomas Lubanga Dyilo, was found guilty, on 14 March 2012, of the war crimes of enlisting and conscripting of children under the age of fifteen years and using them to participate actively in hostilities. He was sentenced, on 10 July 2012, to a total of fourteen years' imprisonment. The verdict and sentence were confirmed by the ICC's Appeals Chamber on 1 December 2014.

[76] Statute of the Special Court of Sierra Leone (adopted 16 January 2002) article 4(c).

[77] Convention on the Rights of the Child (adopted 20 November 1989, entered into force 2 September 1990) 1577 UNTS 3 article 38(2)–(3). cf the Convention on the Rights of Persons with Disabilities (discussed below at text to n 83), which also contains elements of both IHL and IHRL.

[78] See CIHL 484–5.

[79] See ibid 485.

support provided by the child to the combatants exposed him or her to real danger as a potential target.[80]

## 7. Disabled persons

In armed conflict (as in natural disasters, for that matter), people with disabilities are often faced with severe obstacles when normal networks and support mechanism are disrupted.[81] IHL does not single out disabled persons as a specific category of protected persons, but nevertheless acknowledges their specific needs, with different treaty instruments containing provisions to ensure respect and protection for the disabled. These rules generally impose obligations on states regarding the medical treatment and physical protection of persons with disabilities.[82] The Convention on the Rights of Persons with Disabilities (CRPD),[83] while affirming many of the traditional IHL obligations regarding persons with disabilities, establishes a regime based on persons with disabilities as rights-bearing agents.[84]

Thus, while also imposing duties on states regarding the protection of persons with disabilities, the CRPD vests rights in individuals, who are capable of asserting, and to some extent, enforcing these rights.[85] It includes rights beyond physical security and health, such as the right to access to justice and equality before the law.[86] Furthermore, the CRPD recognizes disabilities as context-dependent problems; in armed conflicts, otherwise minor disabilities may become major impediments.[87] Therefore, article 11 of the CRPD requires states parties to take 'all necessary measures to ensure the protection and safety of persons with disabilities in situations of risk, including situations of armed conflict, humanitarian emergencies and the occurrence of natural disasters', essentially establishing that the rights in the Convention also apply in times of armed conflict.

## 8. Parachutists from aircraft in distress

On 24 November 2015, a Russian jet was downed by Turkish warplanes near the border with Turkey and Syria.[88] The pilot and navigator ejected but were fired upon by rebels from

---

[80] *Situation in the Democratic Republic of the Congo, In the Case of The Prosecutor v Thomas Lubanga Dyilo* (Case No ICC-01/04-01/06) ICC Trial Chamber 1, 'Judgment pursuant to Article 74 of the Statute' para 628 (emphasis added). Judge Benito in her separate and dissenting opinion argued in favour of an even broader interpretation of the notion 'to participate actively in hostilities'; see *The Prosecutor v Thomas Lubanga Dyilo*, 'Separate and Dissenting Opinion of Judge Odio Benito' para 15.

[81] See Naomi Hart, Mary Crock, Ron McCallum, and Ben Saul, 'Making Every Life Count: Ensuring Equality and Protection for Persons with Disabilities in Armed Conflicts' (2014) 40(1) *Mon LR* 148–9 www.monash.edu/__data/assets/pdf_file/0011/139835/mccallum.pdf.

[82] ibid 153. See eg GCIV article 30: 'Special facilities shall be afforded for the care to be given to the disabled, in particular to the blind, and for their rehabilitation, pending repatriation.' See also the already-mentioned API article 8(a), which explains that wounded and sick refer to *'persons, whether military or civilian, who, because of trauma, disease or other physical or mental disorder or disability, are in need of medical assistance or care* and who refrain from any act of hostility' (emphasis added).

[83] Convention on the Rights of Persons with Disabilities (adopted 13 December 2006, entered into force 3 May 2008) 2515 UNTS 3 (CRPD).

[84] Hart et al (above n 82) 153.

[85] ibid 156. This is based on a 'machinery of dialogue with states through progress reports and concluding observations and—under the CRPD Optional Protocol—individual complaints and investigations'.

[86] ibid 155.

[87] ibid 153.

[88] 'Turkey's Downing of Russian Warplane—What We Know' *BBC News* (London, 1 December 2015) www.bbc.com/news/world-middle-east-34912581.

Syria's ethnic Turkmen community as the two descended by parachute.[89] According to the rebels, one of them (the pilot) was dead when he landed on the ground.[90]

According to the CIHL Study, state practice establishes the rule—that making persons parachuting from an aircraft in distress the object of attack during their descent is prohibited—as a norm of customary international law applicable in both IACs and NIACs.[91] Persons bailing out of an aircraft in distress have been referred to as 'shipwrecked in the air'. They are considered *hors de combat* (see below) during their descent.

Article 42 API explains that the moment these persons reach the ground in territory controlled by an adverse party, they shall be given an opportunity to surrender before being made the object of attack, unless it is apparent that they are engaging in a hostile act,[92] and that airborne troops are not protected by the article.[93] With regard to NIACs, article 3 common to the GCs, while not specifically referring to parachutists, states more generally that persons *hors de combat*, 'by sickness, wounds, detention, *or any other cause*, shall in all circumstances be treated humanely'.[94] The CIHL Study (Rule 170) explains that:

> During the negotiation of the elements of war crimes against common Article 3 in the framework of the Statute of the International Criminal Court, the drafters understood that the term *hors de combat* should not be interpreted in a narrow sense, and made reference to Article 42 of Additional Protocol I.

### 9.  *Persons* hors de combat
In the CIHL Study, a person *hors de combat* is defined as:

> (a) anyone who is in the power of an adverse party; (b) anyone who is defenceless because of unconsciousness, shipwreck, wounds or sickness; or (c) anyone who clearly expresses an intention to surrender; provided he or she abstains from any hostile act and does not attempt to escape.[95]

According to the ICRC Study, state practice establishes the rule—that attacking persons who are recognized as *hors de combat* is prohibited—as a norm of customary international law, applicable in both IACs and NIACs.[96]

A clear example of persons that fall within the first category mentioned in the extract above are POWs, who are usually[97] members of the armed forces of one of the parties to

---

[89]  ibid.

[90]  ibid.

[91]  CIHL 170.

[92]  API article 42(2). As mentioned before, persons parachuting from an aircraft in distress have been called 'shipwrecked in the air', as shipwrecked are also considered *hors de combat*, but may swim ashore or be collected by a friendly ship and resume fighting. See CIHL 171.

[93]  API article 42(3). In the same way, and looking at shipwrecked in sea, these latter persons must be in distress, thus excluding 'combatants who are in the water because they are engaged in amphibious or underwater operations': Yoram Dinstein, *The Conduct of Hostilities under the Law of International Armed Conflict* (2nd edn CUP 2010) 161.

[94]  Emphasis added.

[95]  CIHL 164.

[96]  ibid 164.

[97]  GCIII—which is specifically designed to address the topic of POWs—also classifies other categories of persons who have the right to POW status or may be treated as POWs. See ICRC, 'Prisoners of War and Detainees

an IAC (the status of POW only applies in IACs) who fall into the hands of the adverse party. The topic of POWs is addressed in more detail in chapter 5 'Persons Covered by International Humanitarian Law: Main Categories'.

Several examples have already been mentioned of persons who would typically fall within the second category (b) mentioned above, such as the shipwrecked (including the shipwrecked in the air, namely persons bailing out from an aircraft in distress), and the wounded and sick.

As to persons clearly expressing an intention to surrender, in land warfare,[98] this can be done by laying down one's weapons and raising one's hands, or through the display of a white flag when emerging from one's position.[99] Under the Rome Statute, killing or wounding a combatant who, having laid down his arms or having no longer means of defence, has surrendered at discretion,[100] is considered a war crime.

### 10. Parlementaires

The French term *parlementaire* stands for 'a person belonging to a party to the conflict who has been authorized to enter into communication [*entrer en pourparlers* in the original French][101] with another party to the conflict'.[102] The main protective rule is that *parlementaires*, who need to be able to 'arrive at terms of surrender, effect a cease-fire, collect casualties from the battlefield, etc.' are inviolable.[103] However, commanders may take the necessary precautions to prevent the presence of a *parlementaire* from being prejudicial[104] and '[p]arlementaires taking advantage of their privileged position to commit an act contrary to international law and detrimental to the adversary lose their inviolability'.[105]

### 11. Persons displaying the distinctive emblem

The distinctive emblem refers to 'the distinctive emblem of the red cross, red crescent or red lion and sun on a white ground when used for the protection of medical units and transports, or medical and religious personnel, equipment or supplies'.[106] Since 2007, when the 2005 Additional Protocol III (APIII) entered in force, the new emblem—the red crystal—can also be used.[107] Persons entitled to wear the distinctive emblem, such as medical personnel,[108]

---

Protected under International humanitarian Law' (29 October 2010) www.icrc.org/eng/war-and-law/protected-persons/prisoners-war/overview-detainees-protected-persons.htm.

[98] Dinstein (above n 93) 161:

At sea, surrender generally requires that the vessel will haul down its flag and, in the case of a submarine, surface. But if the fighting takes place beyond-visual-range, these modes of surrender will not suffice. Radio communication will then become indispensable ... In the air, there is no accepted mode of surrender, even by a disabled aircraft within visual range, except through radio communication.

[99] CIHL 168.
[100] Rome Statute article 8(2)(b)(vi).
[101] See Dinstein (above n 93) 163.
[102] CIHL 228.
[103] ibid 229. For an example of a case where this rule was violated, see the (unlawful) detention of Mehmed Hajric, the mayor of Zepa, in late July 1995 by the forces of General Mladić.
[104] CIHL 231.
[105] ibid 232.
[106] API article 8(1).
[107] Protocol Additional to the Geneva Conventions of 12 August 1949, and Relating to the Adoption of an Additional Distinctive Emblem (adopted 8 December 2005, entered into force 14 January 2007) 2404 UNTS 261 (APIII).
[108] CIHL 80.

must not be attacked.[109] However, as mentioned earlier in section 3.A.3 'Medical personnel and medical activities', only medical personnel assigned to medical duties by a party to the conflict—and not other persons performing medical duties—can be qualified as medical personnel and have the right to display the distinctive emblem. Hence, *the symbols* used by organizations such as *Médecins Sans Frontières* do not benefit from international legal protection, 'although their work in favour of the victims of armed conflict must be respected. Upon recognition that they are providing care to the sick and wounded, NGOs are also to be respected.'[110]

Under the Rome Statute, intentionally directing attacks against buildings, material, medical units, and transport,[111] and personnel using the distinctive emblems of the GCs in conformity with international law constitutes a war crime in both IACs[112] and NIACs.[113] At the same time, making *improper* use of the distinctive emblem of the GCs, resulting in death or serious personal injury, also constitutes a war crime under the Rome Statute, albeit only in the context of IACs.[114]

## 12. Personnel involved in a peacekeeping mission

Directing an attack against personnel involved in a peacekeeping mission in accordance with the Charter of the United Nations, as long as they are entitled to the protection given to civilians under IHL, is prohibited—as a norm of customary international law applicable in both IACs and NIACs.[115] Hence, peacekeeping forces, even though they often consist of professional soldiers, are seen as civilians, with the same protection civilians enjoy.[116] Therefore, intentionally directing attacks against personnel in a peacekeeping mission, under the rule above, constitutes a war crime under the Rome Statute in both IACs[117] and NIACs.[118]

A clear distinction should, however, be made between peace*keeping* forces on the one hand and forces engaged in peace *enforcement* operations on the other. These latter are considered combatants bound to respect IHL, and do not enjoy the protection under the rule above.[119]

## 13. Civil defence personnel

Civil defence means:

> ... the performance of some or all of the undermentioned humanitarian tasks[[120]] intended to protect the civilian population against the dangers, and to help it to recover from the

---

[109] ibid 102.
[110] ibid 82 (referring to Canada's *Code of Conduct*).
[111] See also below under section B 'Categories of Objects'.
[112] Rome Statute article 8(2)(b)(xxiv).
[113] ibid article 8(2)(e)(ii).
[114] ibid article 8(2)(b)(vii).
[115] CIHL 112. See, however, Breau, who notes that very little state practice is outlined in the Study, and who concludes: 'this rule may be reflective of *developing* customary practice': Breau (above n 2) 183 (emphasis added).
[116] CIHL 112.
[117] Rome Statute article 8(2)(b)(iii).
[118] ibid article 8(2)(e)(iii).
[119] CIHL 114.
[120] These include warning, evacuation, rescue, medical services, including first aid, and religious assistance, firefighting, and assistance in the preservation of objects essential for survival. See API article 61(a).

immediate effects, of hostilities or disasters and also to provide the conditions necessary for its survival.[121]

The personnel of organizations involved in civil defence, in turn, refer to 'those persons assigned by a Party to the conflict exclusively to the performance of the tasks mentioned under sub-paragraph (a), including personnel assigned by the competent authority of that Party exclusively to the administration of these organizations'.[122]

Although it does not always happen,[123] civil defence personnel, as well as their organizations,[124] shall be respected and protected.[125] Hence, they must be able to perform their civil defence tasks except in case of imperative military necessity.[126]

Protection is also available to personnel of civilian civil defence organizations of neutral or other states not parties to the conflict which perform civil defence tasks in the territory of a party to the conflict, with the consent and under the control of that party.[127]

Also here, protection will cease once acts are committed by these persons, outside their proper tasks, which are harmful to the enemy (after due warning).[128] Some characteristics/situations will, however, *not* lead to loss of protection, including the fact that they may carry light individual weapons for the purpose of maintaining order of for self-defence.[129] The fact that some military personnel are attached to civilian civil defence organizations,[130] or that the performance of civil defence tasks may incidentally benefit military victims, particularly those who are *hors de combat*,[131] will also not lead to loss of protection.

Article 66(1) API explains that each party to the conflict shall endeavour to ensure that its civil defence organizations, their personnel, buildings, and *matériel*, are identifiable while they are exclusively devoted to the performance of civil defence tasks. This can be done through the display of the international distinctive sign of civil defence, which is an equilateral blue triangle on an orange ground.[132]

## 14. Journalists

There are two types of journalists in IHL; the first are war correspondents. But importantly not every journalist who reports from a conflict zone falls within this category.[133] Indeed, the category of 'war correspondents' refers to a specific group of journalists who accompany the armed forces without actually being members thereof[134] and who have received

---

[121] ibid article 61(a).
[122] ibid article 61(c).
[123] HRW, 'Fatal Strikes: Israel's Indiscriminate Attacks against Civilians in Lebanon' (2 August 2006) www.hrw. org/report/2006/08/02/fatal-strikes/israels-indiscriminate-attacks-against-civilians-lebanon.
[124] See API article 61(b).
[125] ibid article 62(1). This is also valid for 'civilians who, although not members of civilian civil defence organizations, respond to an appeal from the competent authorities and perform civil defence tasks under their control': ibid article 62(2).
[126] ibid article 62(1).
[127] ibid article 64.
[128] ibid article 65(1).
[129] ibid article 65(3).
[130] ibid article 65(2). See in more detail ibid article 67.
[131] ibid article 65(2).
[132] ibid article 66(4).
[133] Robin Geiss, 'The Protection of Journalists in Armed Conflicts' (2008) 51 *German YB Int'l L* 310.
[134] GCIII article 4(A)(4).

authorization from the armed forces which they accompany.[135] Although these war correspondents accredited to the armed forces enjoy POW status once captured by the enemy,[136] they are not combatants, but civilians.

The second type, to be found in article 79(1) API, '[j]ournalists engaged in dangerous professional missions in areas of armed conflict',[137] are also civilians. In fact, it has rightly been argued that this 'plainly non-innovative'[138] provision does not create a special status, but merely stresses 'that these journalists enjoy exactly the same protection as ordinary civilians who are placed in similar circumstances'.[139] An infamous example of the latter category is US journalist James Foley, who was tortured and beheaded by IS in August 2014.[140]

### 15. Displaced persons: refugees and IDPs

Civilians may be (forcibly) displaced for reasons related to an armed conflict, both within a national territory—as so-called internally displaced persons (IDPs)—and across an international border—as refugees.

From the humanitarian crisis in Syria alone, one can see the enormous numbers of people involved; as of April 2015, almost 4 million people had fled Syria, whereas as of July 2015, at least 7.6 million people were internally displaced in Syria itself.[141]

According to the ICRC CIHL Study, in IACs, parties may not deport or forcibly transfer the civilian population of an occupied territory, in whole or in part, unless the security of the civilians involved or imperative military reasons so demand.[142] A similar rule can be found in NIACs.[143] However, when such transfers and displacements take place, the necessary measures must be taken in terms of providing accommodation/shelter, hygiene, health, safety, and nutrition.[144]

Regarding the Syria conflict, Amnesty International has alleged that civilians in northern Syria under the de facto control of the Autonomous Administration are being subjected to serious abuses that include forced displacement.[145] The Autonomous Administration claimed that its forced displacement of civilians was not arbitrary because it was necessary on military grounds or for the security or protection of local residents (see the exception above), but Amnesty International asserted that there are cases where there was no such justification (but that civilians were displaced in retaliation for people's perceived sympathies with, or family ties to, suspected members of IS or other armed groups), leading it to conclude that war crimes had been committed.[146]

---

[135] ibid article 4(A)(4).
[136] ibid article 4(A)(4).
[137] API article 79(1).
[138] Dinstein (above n 93) 167.
[139] ibid.
[140] Rukmini Callimachi, 'The Horror before the Beheadings' *The New York Times* (New York, 25 October 2014)    www.nytimes.com/2014/10/26/world/middleeast/horror-before-the-beheadings-what-isis-hostages-endured-in-syria.html.
[141] Information retrieved from the website of the Internal Displacement Monitoring Centre, www.internal-displacement.org/.
[142] CIHL 457.
[143] ibid 457.
[144] GCIV article 49 and APII article 17.
[145] See Amnesty International, '"We Had Nowhere Else to Go": Forced Displacement and Demolitions in Northern Syria' (13 October 2015) 38 www.amnesty.org/en/documents/mde24/2503/2015/en.
[146] ibid 32.

## B. Categories of Objects

### 1. Medical units

Article 8(e) API defines medical units as:

> ... establishments and other units, whether military or civilian, organized for medical purposes, namely the search for, collection, transportation, diagnosis or treatment—including first-aid treatment—of the wounded, sick and shipwrecked, or for the prevention of disease. The term includes, for example, hospitals and other similar units, blood transfusion centres, preventive medicine centres and institutes, medical depots and the medical and pharmaceutical stores of such units. Medical units may be fixed or mobile, permanent or temporary.

They shall be respected and protected at all times and shall not be the object of attack,[147] but this protection is lost in case they are used to commit, outside their humanitarian duties/function, hostile acts/acts harmful to the enemy (after due warning),[148] language that is reminiscent of the category of medical personnel addressed above. Alas, the already-mentioned allegations of HRW towards the Ukrainian insurgents illustrate that protection of medical personnel and units in contemporary conflicts is not always respected.

### A. Medical units on land

The protection of medical units on land—such as hospitals—from attack can be found in article 19 GCI. This provision also clarifies that such units are, as far as possible, situated in such a manner that attacks against military objectives cannot imperil their safety.

### B. Hospital ships

Hospital ships are defined as 'ships built or equipped by the Powers specially and solely with a view to assisting the wounded, sick and shipwrecked, to treating them and to transporting them'.[149] These ships may in no circumstances be attacked or captured, but shall at all times be respected and protected.[150] One important condition for protection, though, is that their names and descriptions have been notified to the parties to the conflict ten days before those ships are employed.[151] Not only military hospital ships, but also hospital ships utilized by National Red Cross Societies, by officially recognized relief societies, or by private persons enjoy this protection, if the party to the conflict on which they depend has given them an official commission[152] and if the just-mentioned notification requirement has been complied with.[153]

Relief shall be afforded without distinction of nationality and the High Contracting Parties 'undertake' not to use these vessels for any military purpose.[154] The parties to the

---

[147] See eg GCI article 19, API article 12(1), and APII article 11(1).
[148] See eg GCI article 21, API article 13(1), and APII article 11(2).
[149] GCII article 22.
[150] ibid article 22.
[151] ibid article 22.
[152] ibid article 24.
[153] For hospital ships utilized by National Red Cross Societies, officially recognized relief societies, or private persons of neutral countries, see ibid article 25.
[154] ibid article 30.

conflict shall have the right to control and search the vessels and they can even be detained for a period not exceeding seven days from the time of interception, if the gravity of the circumstances so requires.[155]

As with the previous categories, protection for hospital ships shall cease when they are used to commit, outside their humanitarian duties, acts harmful to the enemy (after due warning has been given).[156] However, there are a few conditions which shall *not* deprive hospital ships of their protection, such as the fact that the crews are armed for the maintenance of order, for their own defence or that of the sick and wounded (see also the category of medical personnel in section 3.A.3 'Medical personnel and medical activities' above).[157]

In addition to the provisions from GCII, article 20 GCI stipulates that hospital ships entitled to the protection of GCII shall not be attacked from the land.

### C. Medical aircraft

Medical aircraft refers to any medical transports by air.[158] In principle, they must be respected and protected when performing their humanitarian functions.[159] In the context of API, this is even the case if there is no special agreement governing the flight.[160]

### 2. Medical transports

A subcategory of medical units is formed by medical transports, which article 8(g) API defines as 'any means of transportation, whether military or civilian, permanent or temporary, assigned exclusively to medical transportation[161] and under the control of a competent authority of a Party to the conflict'. Hence, *transportation* refers to the process, whereas the *transports* refer to the means; that is, to the objects which enable that process of transportation, such as for instance an ambulance.[162] The transports can be divided into medical transports by land (medical vehicles),[163] by water (medical ships and craft),[164] and by air (medical aircraft).[165]

Since medical transports are a subcategory of medical units, their protection is the same as mobile medical units.[166] Therefore, they arguably cannot be attacked or their passage arbitrarily obstructed.[167] However, just like medical units, they lose their protection if they are being used, outside their humanitarian function, to commit acts harmful to the enemy.[168] For instance, medical aircraft cannot carry equipment intended for the collection or transmission of intelligence.[169]

---

[155] ibid article 31.
[156] ibid article 34.
[157] ibid article 35.
[158] API article 8(j).
[159] CIHL 101.
[160] ibid 101.
[161] API article 8 also defines medical transportation (in its sub-paragraph (f)), namely as 'the conveyance by land, water or air of the wounded, sick, shipwrecked, medical personnel, religious personnel, medical equipment or medical supplies protected by the Conventions and by this Protocol'.
[162] ICRC, 'ICRC Appeal to All Involved in Violence in the Near East' (News Release 00/42, 21 November 2000).
[163] API article 8(h).
[164] ibid article 8(i).
[165] ibid article 8(j).
[166] GCI article 35.
[167] CIHL 101.
[168] ibid 91 and 102.
[169] ibid 102.

Although APII does not contain a definition of medical transports, this term may be understood as applying in the same sense in NIACs.[170]

### 3. Objects displaying the distinctive emblem

As with persons displaying the distinctive emblem (see section 3.A.11 'Persons displaying the distinctive emblem' above), under the Rome Statute, intentionally directing attacks against buildings, material, medical units, and transport using the distinctive emblems of the GCs in conformity with international law constitutes a war crime (in both IACs[171] and NIACs[172]). At the same time, making *improper* use of the distinctive emblem of the Geneva Conventions, resulting in death or serious personal injury, constitutes a war crime (but this time only in IACs[173]) under the Rome Statute as well.

It should be noted that the distinctive emblem as such does not confer protected status; it is merely used to better identify a group such as medical objects, which, because of their function, already receive special protection.[174] This also means that a failure to display the emblem does not mean, of itself, that an attack is justified, if the medical object is still recognized as such.[175]

### 4. Objects involved in a peacekeeping mission

As with personnel involved in a peacekeeping mission (see section 3.A.12 'Personnel involved in a peacekeeping mission' above), the CIHL Study finds that state practice establishes the rule—that directing an attack against objects involved in a peacekeeping mission in accordance with the Charter of the United Nations, as long as they are entitled to the protection given to civilian objects under international humanitarian law, is prohibited—as a norm of customary international law applicable in both IACs and NIACs.[176] Hence, objects in a peacekeeping operation are seen as civilian objects, which cannot be attacked.[177] Unfortunately, such attacks still happen on a regular base.[178]

Intentionally directing attacks against objects in a peacekeeping mission, under the rule above, constitutes a war crime under the Rome Statute in both IACs[179] and NIACs.[180]

### 5. Hospital and safety zones and neutralized zones

Article 23 GCI states that hospital zones and localities may be established in a party's own territory or, if needed, in occupied areas so as 'to protect the wounded and sick from the effects of war, as well as the personnel entrusted with the organization and administration of these zones and localities and with the care of the persons therein assembled'. A similar rule, but targeting another group (wounded, sick, and aged persons, children under fifteen, expectant mothers, and mothers of children under seven), and explicitly adding the term

---

[170]  ibid 100.
[171]  Rome Statute article 8(2)(b)(xxiv).
[172]  ibid article 8(2)(e)(ii).
[173]  ibid article 8(2)(b)(vii).
[174]  CIHL 104.
[175]  ibid 103–4.
[176]  ibid 112.
[177]  ibid 112.
[178]  See eg 'Mali: UN Condemns Attack which Killed Six Peacekeepers' *UN News Centre* (2 July 2015) www.un.org/apps/news/story.asp?NewsID=51331#.VrDgKlJ1w4A.
[179]  Rome Statute article 8(2)(b)(iii).
[180]  ibid article 8(2)(e)(iii).

'safety zones', can be found in article 14 GCIV. The next article of GCIV stipulates, moreover, that neutralized zones may be established for the same reason. The difference is that 'hospital and safety zones are meant to be far removed from military operations, whereas neutralized zones are intended for areas in which military operations are taking place'.[181]

Regardless, it is forbidden to attack a zone established to shelter the wounded, the sick, and civilians—whether a hospital and safety zone or a neutralized zone—from the effects of hostilities.[182] Obviously, this will be more of a challenge for neutralized zones, given their vicinity to the military operations.

## 6. Demilitarized zones

Yet another but somewhat related concept is that of 'demilitarized zones'. Such a zone 'is generally understood to be an area, agreed upon between the parties to the conflict, which cannot be occupied or used for military purposes by any party to the conflict'.[183] It is prohibited to direct an attack against a demilitarized zone.[184] The zone's special protection ceases if one of the parties commits a material breach of the agreement,[185] but the agreement 'may authorize the presence of peacekeeping forces or police personnel for the sole purpose of maintaining law and order without the zone losing its demilitarized character'.[186]

An infamous example is the 'Agreement on the Demilitarization of Srebrenica and Zepa Concluded between Lt Gen Ratko Mladic and Gen Sefer Halilovic on 8 May 1993 in the Presence of Lt Gen Philippe Morillon'.[187] As is known, this agreement was violated and Srebrenica was overrun by the Bosnian-Serb army led by Mladić in July 1995, leading to 'the worst crime on European soil since the Second World War',[188] namely the genocidal killing of more than 7,000 Bosnian Muslim men and boys.

## 7. Open towns and non-defended localities

Non-defended localities, a modern term for 'open towns',[189] are regulated in article 59 API. A non-defended locality may be declared by the appropriate authorities of a party to the conflict (hence unilaterally) at 'any inhabited place near or in a zone where armed forces are in contact which is open for occupation by an adverse Party'.[190] These localities cannot be attacked, by any means whatsoever,[191] if the conditions under paragraph 2 are fulfilled, namely:

(a) [A]ll combatants, as well as mobile weapons and mobile military equipment must have been evacuated; (b) no hostile use shall be made of fixed military installations or

---

[181] CIHL 119.
[182] ibid 119.
[183] ibid 120–1. A blueprint for such an agreement can be found in API article 60(3).
[184] CIHL 120.
[185] API article 60(7).
[186] CIHL 121.
[187] Agreement http://peacemaker.un.org/sites/peacemaker.un.org/files/BA_930508_DemilitarizationSrebrenicaZepo.pdf.
[188] '"May We All Learn and Act on the Lessons of Srebrenica" Says Secretary-General, in Message to Anniversary Ceremony' UN Press Release SG/SM/9993 (11 July 2005) https://www.un.org/press/en/2005/sgsm9993.doc.htm.
[189] Jean C Martin, 'Theatre of Operations', in Marc Weller, Alexia Solomou, and Jake W Rylatt (eds), The Oxford Handbook of the Use of Force in International Law (OUP 2015) 766.
[190] API article 59(2).
[191] ibid article 59(1).

establishments; (c) no acts of hostility shall be committed by the authorities or by the population; and (d) no activities in support of military operations shall be undertaken.[192]

The unilateral declaration must define and describe, as precisely as possible, the limits of the locality,[193] and this must also be done in case the parties to the conflict conclude an agreement on the establishment of a locality even if it does not fulfil the conditions of paragraph 2.[194]

The special protection under this provision is lost when the locality ceases to fulfil the conditions of paragraph 2 or when it ceases to fulfil the conditions of the above-mentioned agreement.[195] However, that does not mean that the locality will lose its general protection pursuant to other IHL rules.

## 8. Cultural property

A definition of cultural property can be found in article 1 of the 1954 Convention for the Protection of Cultural Property in the Event of Armed Conflict (1954 Convention),[196] where the term is defined as covering, irrespective of origin or ownership:

> (a) movable or immovable property of great importance to the cultural heritage of every people, such as monuments of architecture, art or history, whether religious or secular; archaeological sites; groups of buildings which, as a whole, are of historical or artistic interest; works of art; manuscripts, books and other objects of artistic, historical or archaeological interest; as well as scientific collections and important collections of books or archives or of reproductions of the property defined above; (b) buildings whose main and effective purpose is to preserve or exhibit the movable cultural property defined in sub-paragraph (a) such as museums, large libraries and depositories of archives, and refuges intended to shelter, in the event of armed conflict, the movable cultural property defined in sub-paragraph (a); (c) centres containing a large amount of cultural property as defined in sub-paragraphs (a) and (b), to be known as 'centres containing monuments'.

That cultural property should be protected has been eloquently clarified in the Preamble of the 1954 Convention, which states that 'damage to cultural property belonging to any people whatsoever means damage to the cultural heritage of all mankind, since each people makes its contribution to the culture of the world'.

Unfortunately though, cultural heritage has suffered great damage during recent armed conflicts, as may be exemplified by the destruction of the Buddhas of Bamiyan (Afghanistan) in 2001,[197] the 2012 attacks against historic monuments and buildings dedicated to

---

[192] ibid article 59(2).
[193] ibid article 59(4).
[194] ibid article 59(5).
[195] ibid article 59(7).
[196] Convention for the Protection of Cultural Property in the Event of Armed Conflict (adopted 14 May 1954, entered into force 7 August 1956) 249 UNTS 240 (1954 Convention).
[197] Ahmed Rashid, 'After 1,700 Years, Buddhas Fall to Taliban Dynamite', *The Telegraph* (London, 12 March 2001) www.telegraph.co.uk/news/worldnews/asia/afghanistan/1326063/After-1700-years-Buddhas-fall-to-Taliban-dynamite.html.

religion in Timbuktu (Mali),[198] and the 2015 piece-by-piece destruction of Palmyra (Syria).[199]

IHL makes clear that cultural property objects are civilian objects and as such enjoy general protection under IHL and must not be attacked unless (of course) they are subjected to military use, in which case they may become military objectives.[200] However, when not subjected to military use, they are entitled to special protection.[201]

## A. Before and after 1954

Already prior to the 1954 Convention, the protection of cultural property was stressed in several instruments. The very first provision discussed in this chapter, article 35 of the *Lieber Code*, is a good example in that respect. However, protective provisions can also be found back in, for example, regulations 27 and 56 of the 1899[202] and 1907[203] Hague Regulations (in the context of land warfare), in article 5 of Hague Convention (IX) of 1907[204] and article 4 of Hague Convention (XI) of 1907[205] (in the context of sea warfare), and in articles 25 and 26 of the 1923 Hague Rules of Air Warfare[206] (in the context of air warfare).[207] These protections were far from absolute, with formulations indicating that measures had to be taken 'as far as possible', and with protection not being valid for moveable property and for objects that were used for military purposes.[208]

The Pan-American Union's Roerich Pact of 1935[209] constituted the first international convention 'exclusively dedicated to the legal protection, in both war and peace, of certain cultural property',[210] with the movement based on the Roerich Pact (*Pax Cultura*) even sometimes called the 'Red Cross of Culture'.[211] The Pact is still in force for some (ten) American States.[212] Dinstein argues that on the one hand, the Pact has some clear flaws,

---

[198] Monica Mark, 'Malian Islamists Attack World Heritage Site Mosques in Timbuktu', *The Guardian* (Sydney, 2 July 2012) www.theguardian.com/world/2012/jul/02/mali-islamists-attack-world-heritage-mosques-timbuktu.

[199] Stuart Jeffries, 'Isis's Destruction of Palmyra: "The Heart has been Ripped Out of the City"', *The Guardian* (Sydney, 2 September 2015) www.theguardian.com/world/2015/sep/02/isis-destruction-of-palmyra-syria-heart-been-ripped-out-of-the-city.

[200] Dinstein (above n 93) 170.

[201] ibid.

[202] Convention (II) with Respect to the Laws and Customs of War on Land and Its Annex: Regulations concerning the Laws and Customs of War on Land (adopted 29 July 1899, entered into force 4 September 1900) 187 CTS 429 (Hague Convention II).

[203] Convention (IV) Respecting the Laws and Customs of War on Land and Its Annex: Regulations concerning the Laws and Customs of War on Land (adopted 18 October 1907, entered into force 26 January 1910) 187 CTS 227 (Hague Regulations).

[204] Convention (IX) concerning Bombardment by Naval Forces in Time of War (adopted 18 October 1907, entered into force 26 January 1910) 205 CTS 345 (Hague Convention IX).

[205] Convention (XI) Relative to certain Restrictions with regard to the Exercise of the Right of Capture in Naval War (adopted 18 October 1907, entered into force 26 January 1910) 205 CTS 367 (Hague Convention XI).

[206] Rules concerning the Control of Wireless Telegraphy in Time of War and Air Warfare (adopted 19 February 1923).

[207] For more information, see Dinstein (above n 93) 171–3.

[208] ibid.

[209] Treaty on the Protection of Artistic and Scientific Institutions and Historic Monuments (Roerich Pact) (adopted 15 April 1935, entered into force 26 August 1935) 167 UNTS 289.

[210] Roger O'Keefe, *The Protection of Cultural Property in Armed Conflict* (CUP 2006) 51.

[211] Friedrich T Schipper and Erich Frank, 'A Concise Legal History of the Protection of Cultural Property in the Event of Armed Conflict and a Comparative Analysis of the 1935 Roerich Pact and the 1954 Hague Convention in the Context of the Law of War' (2013) 9(1) *Archaeologies: J World Archaeol Congress* 17 http://link.springer.com/article/10.1007/s11759-013-9230-7.

[212] Dinstein (above n 93) 171–3.

including the fact that '[i]t does not concretize the scope of respect and protection enjoyed by cultural property. Specifically, it does not mention immunity from attack as such,[213] but that it also has some marked advantages over the 1954 Convention, such as the fact that '[i]t endows cultural property with protection that is not subject to considerations of imperative military necessity (although protection is lost when the monuments are used for military purposes)'.[214]

As a result of the horrors of the Second World War, the 1954 Convention for the Protection of Cultural Property in the Event of Armed Conflict, 'the first international treaty with a world-wide vocation focusing exclusively on the protection of cultural heritage in the event of armed conflict [IACs and NIACs]',[215] was adopted under the auspices of UNESCO, including a separate optional protocol (the First Protocol),[216] whose purpose it is to prevent the exportation of cultural property and to provide for the restitution of illegally exported objects.[217] At the time of writing this chapter, the Convention had 127, and the First Protocol 104, state parties.

As explained above, the 1954 Convention contains a definition (in fact the first)[218] of cultural property,[219] which seems very broad in that it protects 'movable or immovable property'—something which was not mentioned before.[220] However, at the same time, it only protects 'property *of great importance to the cultural heritage of every people*'.[221] Dinstein is right when he writes that this is quite subjective, there being no objective criteria to measure cultural importance (except in outstanding cases).[222] Also the phrase 'of every people' is puzzling, as it can mean both 'of all peoples jointly' or 'of each respective people'.[223] Preference should be given to the latter meaning.[224] Hence, '[t]he Convention ... has a universalist message that is worthy of emphasis, inasmuch as some Belligerent Parties are disposed to view the enemy's cultural property from a narrow ethnic or religious perspective, attempting to erase alien monuments and other memorabilia'.[225]

The general protective provision of the 1954 Convention can be found in its article 4(1) which stipulates:

> The High Contracting Parties undertake to respect cultural property situated within their own territory as well as within the territory of other High Contracting Parties by refraining

---

[213] ibid 174 (original footnote omitted).

[214] ibid.

[215] 'Convention for the Protection of Cultural Property in the Event of Armed Conflict' http://www.unesco.org/new/en/culture/themes/armed-conflict-and-heritage/convention-and-protocols/1954-hague-convention/.

[216] Protocol for the Protection of Cultural Property in the Event of Armed Conflict (adopted 14 May 1954, entered into force 7 August 1956) 249 UNTS 358 (First Protocol).

[217] First Protocol.

[218] Schipper and Frank (above n 211) 18.

[219] Which, by the way, may bear the distinctive emblem as described in 1954 Convention article 16(1) ('a shield, pointed below, per saltire blue and white (a shield consisting of a royal-blue square, one of the angles of which forms the point of the shield, and of a royal-blue triangle above the square, the space on either side being taken up by a white triangle)') so as to facilitate its recognition; see 1954 Convention article 6.

[220] Dinstein (above n 93) 174.

[221] Emphasis added.

[222] Dinstein (above n 93) 175.

[223] O'Keefe (above n 210) 103.

[224] ibid 104; Dinstein (above n 93) 175.

[225] Dinstein (above n 93) 175.

from any use of the property and its immediate surroundings or of the appliances in use for its protection for purposes which are likely to expose it to destruction or damage in the event of armed conflict; and by refraining from any act of hostility directed against such property.

Nevertheless, and as already mentioned above when discussing the advantage of the Roerich Pact of 1935, the Convention also allows for a waiver of these obligations, namely (and only) in cases where military necessity imperatively requires such a waiver.[226] Dinstein convincingly argues that:

> ... if imperative requirements of military necessity can trump the protection of cultural property, no real progress has been achieved since the days of the 'as far as possible' exhortation. After all, the value added of the adverb 'imperatively' is far from self-evident ... and the attacking force is prone to regard almost any military necessity as satisfying the requirement.[227]

In addition to the general protection under article 4, more specific protection can be found in article 8(1) of the 1954 Convention for certain cultural property, namely a limited number of refuges intended to shelter movable cultural property in the event of armed conflict, of centres containing monuments, and other immovable cultural property of very great importance. There are a few conditions though, namely that they are situated at an adequate distance from any important military objective constituting a vulnerable point and are not used for military purposes.[228] Also, it must be entered in the International Register of Cultural Property under Special Protection.[229]

Once these conditions are fulfilled, the special protection of article 9 1954 Convention applies (immunity from any act of hostility). However, also here, an exception is possible, namely (and only) 'in exceptional cases of unavoidable military necessity, and only for such time as that necessity continues'.[230] It has rightly been argued that even though the terms 'exceptional' and 'unavoidable' seem stricter than the word 'imperatively' from article 4 1954 Convention discussed above, 'the stark fact is that the status of special protection does not guarantee to any cultural property—not even of the greatest importance—full immunity from attack and destruction'.[231] Thus, the special protection regime of the 1954 Convention 'secures only marginally better safeguards'[232] than its general protection regime.

---

[226]  1954 Convention article 4(2).
[227]  Dinstein (above n 93) 176.
[228]  1954 Convention article 8(1).
[229]  ibid article 8(6). Schipper and Frank note about this register: 'To-date only a few properties have been added to the international register of cultural property under special protection, so that the practical value must not be estimated too high—the only site registered is the Vatican City, alongside eight shelters': Schipper and Frank (above n 211) 20. (The registered shelters, incidentally, are only to be found in Germany and the Netherlands.)
[230]  1954 Convention article 11(2).
[231]  Dinstein (above n 93) 177.
[232]  ibid.

*B. The Additional Protocols of 1977*

Both API and APII contain provisions relating to the protection of cultural property. The most notable examples are article 53 API[233] and article 16 APII.[234] Although they depart from the 1954 Convention through the non-acceptance of the military necessity exception, both provisions also clarify that they are '[w]ithout prejudice' to the provisions of the 1954 Convention, meaning that 'High Contracting Parties to both are not prevented from availing themselves of the waiver in respect of military necessity embodied in article 4(2) of the Convention.'[235]

However, O'Keefe argues that API remedies, at least in theory, three important reasons for the past destruction of cultural property in bombardment, namely through (i) prohibiting attacks on the civilian population and civilian objects; (ii) narrowing the definition of a military objective; and (iii) outlawing excessive incidental harm to the civilian population and civilian objects during attacks on military objectives.[236] As for APII, this Protocol constitutes 'an attenuated, impressionistic version of Protocol I'.[237] When explaining this correlation, between the protection of civilian objects and the protection of cultural property (a specific category of civilian objects), O'Keefe notes that:

> In terms of attack ... whereas other civilian objects may be targeted pursuant to article 52(2) [API[238]] on account of their nature, location, purpose *or use*, the practical effect of the additional protection afforded by article 53 is that historic monuments, works of art and places of worship which constitute the cultural spiritual heritage of peoples may be attacked *only on account of their use.*[239]

*C. 1999 Second Protocol to the Hague Convention*

Because of (i) the 'increased awareness regarding cultural property protection'[240] stemming from the APs; (ii) the fact that destruction of cultural monuments had become a tactic of war;[241] and (iii) the fact that 'military necessity' still left far too much discretion,[242] revision

---

[233]

Without prejudice to the provisions of the Hague Convention for the Protection of Cultural Property in the Event of Armed Conflict of 14 May 1954, and of other relevant international instruments, it is prohibited: (a) to commit any acts of hostility directed against the historic monuments, works of art or places of worship which constitute the cultural or spiritual heritage of peoples; (b) to use such objects in support of the military effort; (c) to make such objects the object of reprisals.

[234]

Without prejudice to the provisions of the Hague Convention for the Protection of Cultural Property in the Event of Armed Conflict of 14 May 1954, it is prohibited to commit any acts of hostility directed against historic monuments, works of art or places of worship which constitute the cultural or spiritual heritage of peoples, and to use them in support of the military effort.

(But see also API article 85(4)(d) for another example.)
[235] O'Keefe (above n 210) 202.
[236] ibid 203.
[237] ibid.
[238]

Attacks shall be limited strictly to military objectives. In so far as objects are concerned, military objectives are limited to those objects which by their nature, location, purpose or use make an effective contribution to military action and whose total or partial destruction, capture or neutralization, in the circumstances ruling at the time, offers a definite military advantage.

[239] O'Keefe (above n 210) 216 (emphasis added). See also Dinstein (above n 93) 181.
[240] Schipper and Frank (above n 211) 21.
[241] ibid.
[242] ibid.

of the 1954 Convention, which had failed to provide sufficient protection, was deemed necessary.[243] The 1999 Second Protocol[244] 'was intended to strengthen the existing regulations, and make their application more effective'.[245]

The 1999 Second Protocol, which incidentally applies to both IACs and NIACs, formally harmonized the 1954 Convention with API, 'by pronouncing that an attack against cultural property cannot be launched unless the site has been converted into a military objective'.[246] Moreover, it clarified the meaning of the waiver of article 4(2) 1954 Convention (imperative military necessity), by stating that it may only be invoked:

> ... to direct an act of hostility against cultural property when and for as long as: i. that cultural property has, by its function,[[247]] been made into a military objective; and ii. there is no feasible alternative available to obtain a similar military advantage to that offered by directing an act of hostility against that objective.[248]

In addition, the waiver may only be invoked to use cultural property for purposes which are likely to expose it to destruction or damage when and for as long as no choice is possible between such use of the cultural property and another feasible method for obtaining a similar military advantage.[249]

The 1999 Second Protocol also expands the system of precautions in attack,[250] and introduced a new system of enhanced protection for cultural property if:

> a. it is cultural heritage of the greatest importance for humanity; b. it is protected by adequate domestic legal and administrative measures recognizing its exceptional cultural and historic value and ensuring the highest level of protection; c. it is not used for military purposes or to shield military sites and a declaration has been made by the Party which has control over the cultural property, confirming that it will not be so used.[251]

If that is the case, and after placement under enhanced protection has been requested and approved,[252] immunity from attack is guaranteed,[253] although also here, there are a few exceptions, including if, and for as long as, the property has, by its use, become a military objective.[254] In that case, additional conditions apply before the property can be the object of attack.[255] As to the correlation between the 1954 Convention special protection regime and the enhanced protection system of the 1999 Second Protocol, article 4(b)

---

[243] ibid.

[244] Second Protocol to the Hague Convention of 1954 for the Protection of Cultural Property in the Event of Armed Conflict (adopted 26 March 1999, entered into force 9 March 2004) 2253 UNTS 172 (Second Protocol 1999).

[245] Schipper and Frank (above n 211) 21.

[246] Dinstein (above n 93) 183.

[247] Dinstein notes that '[t]he meaning of "function" is somewhat wider than use, although it should not be mixed up with either purpose of location': Dinstein (above n 93) 183.

[248] Second Protocol 1999 article 6(a).

[249] ibid article 6(b).

[250] ibid article 7.

[251] ibid article 10.

[252] ibid article 11.

[253] ibid article 12.

[254] ibid article 13(1)(b).

[255] ibid article 13(2).

of the latter instrument clarifies that where cultural property has been granted both special protection and enhanced protection, only the provisions of enhanced protection shall apply.

A final feature about the 1999 Second Protocol that needs to be mentioned is its increased focus on penal sanction, given that '[t]he process of the Convention's review revealed dissatisfaction with the penal sanction prescribed by article 28, a provision seen as too weak'.[256] For instance, the Protocol defines five serious violations, which will lead to individual criminal responsibility.[257]

To conclude the category of cultural property, and tying into the point about criminal responsibility and prosecution: to ensure respect for IHL, it is promising that the ICC has recently started a case against a suspect, Ahmad Al Faqi Al Mahdi, for war crimes of intentionally directing attacks against historic monuments and buildings dedicated to religion, including nine mausoleums and one mosque in Timbuktu, Mali, committed between about 30 June 2012 and 10 July 2012.[258] On 26 September 2015, Al Faqi Al Mahdi was transferred to The Hague.[259] Although Al Faqi Al Mahdi 'will not be the first accused in The Hague facing charges of destroying cultural property ... [i]t is the first time that war crimes against cultural heritage constitute the main charge of an international criminal proceeding'.[260]

## 4. Conclusion

From the discussions in this chapter, it becomes clear that IHL—in a generally sufficient, and oftentimes very detailed way—deals with the protection of certain persons and objects. However, current practice also shows that these categories continue to be vulnerable and that respect for the implementation of IHL is often lacking, with the repugnant practices of IS as the new nadir. In the words of Rachel Bryson: '[ISIS] is destroying the past, present and future in one; century-old historical artefacts are being obliterated, present day minorities are being wiped out, and the next generation is dispossessed of childhood and dropped headlong into a world of terror'.[261] Therefore, the enforcement of IHL, through the application of international criminal law, either at the national or international level, is of the utmost importance to show that conduct violating IHL will not be tolerated. An interesting and hopeful sign in that respect is the prosecution of Al Faqi Al Mahdi before the ICC.

However, when again looking at *the* conflict of our times, the conflict in Syria/Iraq, it is quite remarkable to see that almost all the prosecutions against (potential) Syria/Iraq travellers are based on terrorism, and not on IHL charges. One of the exceptions in this context is

---

[256] O'Keefe (above n 210) 274.
[257] Second Protocol 1999 article 15. For more information, see O'Keefe (above n 210) 274–88.
[258] Information retrieved from the ICC page dedicated to this case, https://www.icc-cpi.int/mali/al-mahdi.
[259] ibid.
[260] Marina Lostal, 'The First of Its Kind: The ICC Opens a Case against Ahmad Al Faqi Al Mahdi for the Destruction of Cultural Heritage in Mali' *Global Policy Forum* (2 October 2015) www.globalpolicy.org/home/163-general/52814-icc-opens-a-case-for-the-destruction-of-cultural-heritage-in-mali.html.
[261] Bryson (above n 59).

the Swedish case of Mouhannad Droubi, who was sentenced in February 2015 to five years' imprisonment for the war crime of attacking an enemy who was *hors de combat*, as well as of particularly grave assault.[262] Many more of such cases are needed to show, on a constant basis, that IHL must not be violated and to emphasize the special protection granted to protected persons and objects.

---

[262] See Christophe Paulussen and Eva Entenmann, 'National Responses in Select Western European Countries to the Foreign Fighter Phenomenon', in A de Guttry, F Capone, and C Paulussen (eds), *Foreign Fighters under International Law and Beyond* (Asser Press 2016) 419 (n 156).

# 9

# Protection of the Natural Environment

*Cymie R Payne*

## 1. Introduction

International Humanitarian Law (IHL) establishes limitations on warfare to protect the natural environment from extremely serious damage and to prevent unnecessary or wanton harm. IHL protection of the environment developed from the principle of protection of civilians, and it has similar motives and goals. This chapter describes a legal regime that is undergoing development. All three temporal branches of international law relating to armed conflict—the laws governing resort to armed force (*jus ad bellum*), the conduct of armed conflict (*jus in bello*, or IHL), and activities in the post-conflict period (*jus post bellum*)—address the natural environment. Protection of the environment in relation to land wars and the terrestrial environment is the most fully addressed, the marine environment less so. The International Law Commission (ILC) termed the overall topic 'Protection of the Environment in Relation to Armed Conflict' (PERAC).[1]

The central rules of IHL that are well accepted as customary law provide protection to aspects of the environment that can be considered public or private property, or that are essential to human survival. These aspects of PERAC are firmly rooted in the earliest law of war protections for drinking water, crops, and cultural elements, and in modern domestic environmental law and social norms. Yet protection of the environment during armed conflict as a specific legal obligation is a sufficiently recent international norm that its status as binding law has been more contested than early humanitarian commitments like neutrality of medical personnel. This reflects the tension between recognition of the importance of ecological integrity to peace and the interests of states in retaining freedom in their conduct of military operations. Environmental protection's status as customary international law has been challenged by those who take a restricted view of international commitments other than those made in treaties.[2] Some important military powers and some of the most active belligerents in recent years are not parties to all relevant treaties, so it is important to examine the extent to

---

[1] Three reports of the International Law Commission (ILC) provide a comprehensive review of the topic, including the comments on the reports by national legal advisers during Sixth Committee meetings. The ILC offered nine draft principles as a result of this study. ILC 'Report of the International Law Commission on the Work of Its Sixty-Sixth Session: Preliminary Report on the Protection of the Environment in Relation to Armed Conflicts' UN Doc A/CN.4/674 (30 May 2014); ILC 'Report of the International Law Commission on the Work of Its Sixty-Seventh Session: Second Report on the Protection of the Environment in Relation to Armed Conflicts' UN Doc A/CN.4/685 (28 May 2015); ILC, 'Report of the International Law Commission on the Work of Its Sixty-Eighth Session: Third Report on the Protection of the Environment in Relation to Armed Conflicts' UN Doc A/CN.4/700 (3 June 2016); ILC, Draft Principles A/CN.4/L.870/Rev.1 (26 July 2016); ILC Draft Principles A/CN.4/L.876 (3 August 2016).

[2] Michael P Scharf and Paul R Williams, *Shaping Foreign Policy in Times of Crisis: The Role of International Law and the State Department Legal Adviser* (CUP 2010) 56–8.

which the treaty norms are applied by all states and to evaluate the status of norms as customary international law.[3]

Notwithstanding this position, political and operational considerations—including respect for the norms of host countries and allies—may counsel adoption of rules that others hold as binding. Interoperability is an important consideration for allied military forces, which extends to law as well as technology.[4] Allies coordinate their approaches to international law, which sometimes means that a state agrees to apply treaty norms, although it is a non-party.[5]

It is also useful to remember that responsibility and liability can be incurred under international law obligations other than IHL, triggering the consequences of state responsibility.[6] Reparations bodies may apply a much more inclusive standard than IHL. For example, Iraq paid over US $5 billion for environmental damage, including damage from military fortifications, land and submarine mines, water pollution, and hazardous waste, as a result of the 1990–1991 Gulf War.[7] Uganda incurred liability for the consequences of its looting, pillage, and exploitation of the Democratic Republic of the Congo's natural resources, in violation of IHL.[8]

To understand and apply IHL in this context, it is necessary to understand what drives the evolution of these legal norms. Concern for the environment—whether environmental integrity as a whole, pollution threats to public health, or constituents like elephants, gorillas, or marshlands—is increasingly influential in the interpretation and application of legal rules. This is partly because we have a better scientifically based understanding of how environmental systems function; partly because we fill the environment more densely now—the human population grew from about 1.2 billion at the time of Francis Lieber's General Order No 100 to over 7 billion people today; partly because we now have technology that enables vast environmental destruction; and partly because military officers and citizens

---

[3] Hugh Thirlway, *The Sources of International Law* (OUP 2014); Catherine Redgwell and Jutta Brunnée, 'The Sources of International Environmental Law: Interactional Law', in Samantha Besson and Jean d'Aspremont (eds), *Oxford Handbook on the Sources of International Law* (OUP 2017) ch 22.

[4] See eg North Atlantic Treaty Organization (NATO), *Joint NATO Doctrine for Environmental Protection During NATO-Led Military Activities*, STANAG 7141, Edition 6 (15 May 2014).

[5] The give-and-take is reflected in a study of US practice: 'Even when the LOAC permits a given practice, U.S. policymakers may alter policies to reflect political or operational concerns. The resulting implementations, reflecting both legal and nonlegal factors, shape decisions on such matters as rules of engagement, targeting procedures, and the development of weapon systems.' Bryan Frederick and David E Johnson, *The Continued Evolution of US Law of Armed Conflict Implementation: Implications for the US Military* (RAND Corporation 2015) (*Law of War Manual*) iii, 83–84. See also Dale G Stephens, 'Coalition Warfare: Challenges and Opportunities' (2006) 82 ILS 245, 246; UK Ministry of Defence (MoD), *Joint Service Manual of the Law of Armed Conflict* (Joint Doctrine and Concepts Centre 2004) 1.13.2.

[6] See generally, Dinah Shelton and Isabelle Cutting, 'If You Break It, Do You Own It?' (2015) 6 *JIHLS* 1, 32, 39–44.

[7] UN Compensation Commission (UNCC) 'Report and Recommendations Made by the Panel of Commissioners concerning the Fifth Instalment of "F4" Claims' UN Doc S/AC.26/2005/10 (30 June 2005) paras 777, 784, approved by the Governing Council, Decision 248, UN Doc S/AC.26/Dec.248 (30 June 2005). For a comprehensive account, Cymie R Payne and Peter H Sand (eds), *Gulf War Reparations and the UN Compensation Commission: Environmental Liability* (OUP 2011).

[8] *Armed Activities on the Territory of the Congo (Democratic Republic of the Congo v Uganda)* (Judgment) [2005] ICJ Rep 168; Carl Bruch and Akiva Fishman, 'Institutionalizing Peacebuilding', in Payne and Sand (eds) 221 (above n 7). It is, however, notable that the case focused on conflict resources and other environmental impacts are not discussed, despite reports including severe impacts on the World Heritage site, Kahuzi Biega National Park, and its rare gorillas. International Alert, 'The Role of the Exploitation of Natural Resources in Fuelling and Prolonging Crises in the eastern DRC' (January 2010) para 15 www.international-alert.org/sites/default/files/publications/Natural_Resources_Jan_10.pdf.

have adopted an environmental protection ethic.[9] The rules governing armed forces are also influenced by changes in domestic law, which impose environmental accountability on military officers for their activities whether or not related to armed conflict.[10]

Since the primary purpose of IHL is to prevent unnecessary suffering, the rules call for difficult predictive decisions by legal advisers and planners. Tools to manage uncertainty about the potential environmental impacts of military activities include remote sensing, advanced scientific information, and the increasingly standard practice of environmental assessment. IHL rules are relevant for post-conflict accountability as well. Compensation commissions, transitional justice reviews, and war crimes trials will assess the extent of environmental damage, and the intent or knowledge of responsible parties. Military forces conduct their own reviews. The retrospective accounting will generally focus on actual damage, although in principle acting with the intent to cause harm or simply the knowledge that great environmental harm would be a likely outcome may be culpable even if no or only slight damage actually occurs.[11]

The effect of breach of IHL obligations may be criminal sanctions or reparations. Reparations may include satisfaction; a declaration of fault; restitution; or compensation. A new approach is taken in the revised version of the African Convention on the Conservation of Nature and Natural Resources article XV, paragraph 1d, which requires parties to restore and rehabilitate the damage. A similar focus on restoring the environment is found in the UNCC's Follow-up Programme.[12]

Section 2 of this chapter discusses the definition of 'environment' for the purposes of IHL. Section 3 'Damage to the Environment' turns to the application of the IHL principles of distinction, necessity, and proportionality, followed by section 4 'Environment as Weapon' on the customary and treaty law restricting the use of methods and means of warfare. Treatment of some kinds of environmentally damaging attacks as war crimes follows in section 5 'War Crimes'. The concept of solidarity and its application for environmental matters during armed conflict is next in section 6 'Protection of the Environment by Third Parties: Solidarity', followed by section 7 'Non-International Armed Conflict'. Finally, section 8 'Status of International Environmental Law and Domestic Law—Conflicts of Laws' addresses the treatment of international and domestic environmental law and problems of the *lex specialis* rules applicable to IHL, human rights, and international environmental law.

## 2. Definition of 'environment' in IHL

The intention of this section is to illustrate what we should identify as potentially protected environment. The lack of a commonly agreed definition of 'environment' in IHL should

---

[9] Ronald A DeMarco and John P Quinn, 'The Impact of War and Military Operations other than War on the Marine Environment: Policy Making on the Frontiers of Knowledge', in Richard J Grunawalt, John E King, and Ronald S McClain (eds), *Protection of the Environment During Armed Conflict* (Naval War College Press 1996) 87. ILC, 'Second Report on the Protection of the Environment in Relation to Armed Conflicts' (above n 1) paras 63, 64 (summaries of statements by states that operational law for their armed forces incorporates environmental rules).

[10] DeMarco and Quinn (above n 9). UNEP Environment Assembly, 'Protection of the Environment in Areas Affected by Armed Conflict' UN Doc UNEP/EA.2/L.16 (May 2016).

[11] Yoram Dinstein, 'Protection of the Environment in International Armed Conflict', in Joram A Frowein and Rüdiger Wolfrum (eds), *Max Planck Yearbook of United Nations Law* (Kluwer Law International 2001) 534.

[12] UNCC Governing Council Decision 258 UN Doc S/AC.26/Dec.258 (8 December 2005); Cymie R Payne, 'Oversight of Environmental Awards and Regional Environmental Cooperation', in Payne and Sand (eds) 105 (n 7).

not pose a serious problem.[13] An initial legal analysis of a planned activity should consider the effects that it may have in the relevant region on the 'environment' broadly defined, including soil, land, water, air, the living and non-living elements, and physical processes.[14] Relevant legal rules may apply to some or all of these aspects of the environment, as discussed below. The use of 'natural environment' rather than 'environment' was an artificial distinction of mainly academic interest and is not repeated here.[15] A broad definition is particularly important in this transitional period because developing norms are leading to broader coverage of environmental features than was common in the nineteenth and early twentieth centuries.

Modern warfare planning must take account of the traditional elements of the environment addressed by IHL—water, crops, extractive resources such as coal, and the land that is part of the urban fabric—as well as specially protected areas and the modern elements that are addressed by newer treaties, judicial decisions, and state practice—such as World Heritage sites, wildlife, and ecosystem services.[16] The latter aspects of environment were intended to be invoked by the expression 'natural environment', but it will generally be impossible and unnecessary to draw a distinction.[17] The International Court of Justice (ICJ) gave this eloquent description of environment in its *Legality of the Threat or Use of Nuclear Weapons* Advisory Opinion: 'the environment is not an abstraction but represents the living space, the quality of life and the very health of human beings, including generations unborn'.[18] This poetically captures the modern meaning,

[13] 'Conclusions by the Working Group of Experts on Liability and Compensation for Environmental Damage Arising from Military Activities', in Alexandre Timoshenko (ed), *Liability and Compensation for Environmental Damage: Compilation of Documents* (UNEP 1998) para 30; Jean de Preux, 'Article 35—Basic Rules', in Yves Sandoz, Christophe Swinarski, and Bruno Zimmerman (eds), *Commentary on the Additional Protocols of 8 June 1977 to the Geneva Conventions of 12 August 1949* (ICRC/Martinus Nijhoff 1987) (AP Commentary) 389, 410–20. NATO defines environment as 'the surroundings in which an organization operates, including air, water, land, natural resources, flora, fauna, humans, and their interrelations': NATO, agreed 31 October 2013.

[14] Cymie R Payne, 'The Norm of Environmental Integrity in Post-Conflict Legal Regimes', in Carsten Stahn, Jennifer S Easterday, and Jens Iverson (eds), *Jus Post Bellum: Mapping the Normative Foundations* (OUP 2014) 502.

[15] For example, 'environment' is used in UNGA Resolution 47/37 'Protection of the Environment in Times of Armed Conflict' (9 February 1993).

[16] NATO doctrine asks its members to consider the following characteristics of the environment that may be impacted by or have an impact on all phases of NATO-led missions: general environmental condition of the area; climate; water quality; air quality; natural and cultural resources; presence of endangered species and critical habitats; and presence of birds or bird migration routes. The doctrine also identifies common sources of pollution and provides guidelines to minimize it, and direction on planning exercises and operations to minimize environmental damage: NATO, *Joint NATO Doctrine for Environmental Protection* (above n 4). The UN Compensation Commission found that Iraq was liable for damage that included over 600 km of the Saudi Arabian coastline contaminated with oil whose toxicity will likely persist for decades more; in Kuwait, contaminated groundwater and desert ecology from the release of millions of barrels of oil when Iraqi forces detonated over 600 oil wells; construction of military fortifications, including ditches, berms, bunkers, trenches, and pits; the laying and clearance of mines; and in Iran, Jordan, and Turkey, damage to vegetation and water resources from hundreds of thousands of refugees and their livestock. UNCC, 'Report and Recommendations made by the Panel of Commissioners concerning the Second Instalment of "F4" Claims' UN Doc S/AC.26/2002/26 para 85, approved by the Governing Council Decision 171 UN Doc S/AC.26/Dec.171 (3 October 2002); UNCC, 'Report and Recommendations made by the Panel of Commissioners concerning the Third Instalment of "F4" Claims' UN Doc S/AC.26/2003/31 (18 December 2003) paras 61, 62, 64–74, 86–99, 106–111, 121–125, 134–138, 170–178, approved by the Governing Council Decision 212 UN Doc S/AC.26/Dec.212 (18 December 2003); UNCC, 'Report and Recommendations made by the Panel of Commissioners concerning Part One of the Fourth Instalment of "F4" Claims' UN Doc S/AC.26/2004/16 (9 December 2004) paras 68, 70–71, 105–108, approved by the Governing Council Decision 234 UN Doc S/AC.26/Dec.234 (9 December 2004).

[17] See eg de Preux (above n 13) 398.

[18] *Legality of the Threat or Use of Nuclear Weapons* (Advisory Opinion) [1996] ICJ Rep 226 (*Nuclear Weapons*) para 29.

which has advanced well beyond early military codes concerned with crops and drinking water.[19]

An example may be helpful. Imagine a hypothetical forest. It conceals enemy movements, and is therefore a military objective. There are people living in parts of the forest, and those areas are therefore civilian objects, private, and public property. The forest ecosystem includes a river that is kept pure by multiple interrelated living and non-living components, systems, and processes; the river is the sole drinking water supply for the forest peoples and for other humans downstream. The river is a civilian object. The forest ecosystem that provides the water and keeps it pure is therefore logically also a civilian object. The forest is, of course, a source of firewood and timber, which are useful, have commercial value, and which may be civilian objects or military objectives.[20]

## A.  Legal Categorization: Civilian or Military Object?

Discrimination between civilian objects and legitimate military objectives is a fundamental legal obligation; therefore, an adviser, planner, decision-maker, or executer needs to know into which legal category the natural environment falls. This is, however, a grey area. It has been said that although the principle of discrimination is 'a major part of the foundation on which the law of war is built, it is one of the least codified portions of that law'.[21] This is particularly true for the treatment of the environment as a civilian object. Some IHL rules apply to particular environments, leaving gaps or doubts about coverage. Environment that was not associated with humans as property or as a resource essential to human survival was, until the late twentieth century, simply not thought of at all. With the evolution of norms, the value of non-market resources, ecosystem services, and other instances of 'pure environment' is now acknowledged.

The environment is *ab initio* considered a civilian object. Like other civilian objects, some instances of environment can be converted to military objects. There is a limitation on the extent to which environment can be stripped of protection. That is, some environmental damage is prohibited even if the environment in question becomes a military objective, as discussed in greater detail below. Further, it is prohibited under all circumstances to destroy or disrupt ecosystem services that are indispensable to human survival.

Customary law, now codified in treaties, distinguishes military objects from property,[22] 'civilian objects', and 'objects indispensable to the survival of the civilian population', which

---

[19] *Instructions for the Government of Armies of the United States in the Field*, General Orders No 100 (24 April 1863) (*Lieber Code*); Ameur Zemmali, 'The Protection of Water in Times of Armed Conflict' (1995) 308 *IRRC* 550.

[20] The ILC debated whether exploitation of natural resources (such as timber) was directly related to the scope of PERAC. Among the arguments for including it, 'it was noted that the human rights implications caused by extraction and other actions relating to natural resources might be pertinent to address'. ILC, 'Third Report on the Protection of the Environment in Relation to Armed Conflicts' (above n 1) para 25.

[21] US DoD, 'Final Report to Congress on the Conduct of the Persian Gulf War' (1992) 31(3) *ILM* 612.

[22] *Lieber Code* articles 15–16; Regulations Annexed to the Hague Convention (IV) Respecting the Laws and Customs of War on Land and Its Annex: Regulation concerning the Laws and Customs of War on Land (adopted 18 October 1907, entered into force 26 January 1910) 187 CTS 227 (Hague Regulations) articles 23(g), 46, and 56; Geneva Convention (IV) Relative to the Protection of Civilian Persons in Time of War (adopted 12 August 1949, entered into force 21 October 1950) 75 UNTS 287 (GCIV) articles 33 and 53.

are protected.[23] These broad terms are traditionally understood to be applicable to certain instances of the environment. Additional Protocol I (API) specifies 'environment'.[24] The environment encompasses all four of these terms. For example, crops and water sources are public or private property, they are civilian objects, they are indispensable objects, and they are instances of environment. A rare species of wildlife might be considered by some to be public property and 'environment', and by others to be also a civilian object. A hydrological system that is integral to a water supply would be a civilian object, possibly public property, and clearly environment.[25]

Elements of the environment may become military objectives when they, 'by their nature, location, purpose or use make an effective contribution to military action and [when their] total or partial destruction, capture or neutralisation, in the circumstances ruling at the time, offers a definite military advantage'.[26] Where it is uncertain whether an object that is normally 'dedicated to civilian purposes' is making 'an effective contribution to military action', the presumption is that it is civilian.[27] Thus, the environment should generally be presumed to be civilian.[28]

Examples of objects indispensable to the survival of the civilian population are given in API article 54 as 'foodstuffs, agricultural areas for the production of foodstuffs, crops, livestock, drinking water installations and supplies and irrigation works'.

Turning to the hypothetical forest to illustrate these rules, the forest could be considered a civilian object, a military objective, or an indispensable object. The general rule is that the forest is a civilian object. The exception to the rule is that the forest may become a military objective if one side is using it for military purposes, such as concealment. But the parts of the forest that contribute to water supply, and therefore have sustenance value to the civilian population or the adverse party, could be analysed as indispensable objects. Damage to the forest cannot be analysed only in terms of harm to the trees, as loss of trees will cause changes in other systems, such as the quality and quantity of water resources; on the other hand, an endangered species or a sacred site might warrant particular attention.

## B. Marine Environment and Outer Space

IHL regarding the marine environment and outer space has particular features that stem from their (past) relative inaccessibility compared to land, therefore it must be clear when they are included in legal rules referencing 'environment'.[29] The IHL regime for space has

---

[23] Protocol Additional to the Geneva Conventions of 12 August 1949, and Relating to the Protection of Victims of International Armed Conflicts (adopted 8 June 1977, entered into force 7 December 1978) 1125 UNTS 3 (API) article 54, which is accepted as representing customary international law.

[24] de Preux (above n 13) 414.

[25] Grotius told the story of the King of Cappadocia, held liable for the chain of events unleashed by his action blocking a river, which burst its dam, which caused the Euphrates to flood. Hugo Grotius, *De jure belli ac pacis* (Carnegie Endowment for International Peace trans of 1646, 1925) Vol II, ch XVII, 434.

[26] API article 52. Previous efforts at a definition of 'military objective' failed.

[27] API article 52(3).

[28] ILC, 'Third Report on the Protection of the Environment in Relation to Armed Conflicts' (above n 1) para 28.

[29] The legal regime for Antarctica is similarly unique. The Antarctic Treaty, article 1(1), requires Antarctica to be 'used for peaceful purposes only'. The Antarctic Treaty (signed 1 December 1959, entered into force 23 June 1961) 402 UNTS 71.

been scarcely addressed.[30] Marine areas are divided into zones of national sovereignty (internal waters and territorial sea),[31] limited sovereignty (exclusive economic zone and extended continental shelf, if the coastal state has declared them)[32] and high seas;[33] the legal rules vary according to the type of resource and its location. Both the high seas and space pose special problems as areas beyond national jurisdiction (ABNJ): the concern that harm to these environments will affect neutral states or environmental resources that are the common heritage of humankind.[34] The law of these zones is in transition, rapidly shifting to ecosystem protection and resource management, from the bygone approach of freedom from regulation.[35]

As the setting for conflict, the military goal is likely to be sea denial and sea control.[36] The UN Convention on the Law of the Sea (UNCLOS) provides the definitional rules for the ocean zones noted above (which are also accepted as customary international law)[37] and its article 30 requires warships to 'comply with the laws and regulations of the coastal State concerning passage through the territorial sea'. The territorial principle applies as well to internal waters and archipelagic waters. Under UNCLOS, article 236, the convention's provisions regarding protection and preservation of the marine environment do not apply to 'any warship, naval auxiliary, other vessels or aircraft owned or operated by a State and used, for the time being, only on government non-commercial service', but some measure of environmental protection is provided by also requiring such vessels and aircraft to act in a manner consistent, so far as is reasonable and practicable, with the convention.[38]

As the subject of protection, particular aspects of the marine environment are not defined or described in the law of naval warfare. The marine environment includes life in the water column, on the seabed, and its subsoil; the living marine environment provides about half the oxygen humans need to breathe. Its physical processes are also essential to maintaining the Earth's climate. The *San Remo Manual on International Law Applicable to Armed Conflict at Sea* (*San Remo Manual*) protects 'the natural environment' without more precise definition, including it as an element of 'collateral damage'.[39]

[30] See Treaty on Principles Governing the Activities of States in the Exploration and Use of Outer Space, including the Moon and Other Celestial Bodies (signed 27 January 1967, entered into force 10 October 1967) 610 UNTS 205. The scope of the ENMOD Convention, discussed below, includes outer space.
[31] United Nations Convention on the Law of the Sea (adopted 10 December 1982, entered into force 16 November 1994) 1833 UNTS 3 (UNCLOS) articles 2–4 (territorial sea), 5–26 (baseline), 33 (contiguous zone), 46–49 (archipelagic waters), 50 (internal waters); Convention on the Territorial Sea and Contiguous Zone (adopted 29 April 1958, entered into force 10 September 1964) 516 UNTS 205, articles 1, 5.
[32] UNCLOS articles 55, 57 (exclusive economic zone), 76 (continental shelf).
[33] ibid article 86 (high seas); Tullio Treves, 'High Seas', Max Planck Encyclopedia of Public International Law (January 2010) www.mpepil.com
[34] Jutta Brunnée, 'Common Areas, Common Heritage and Common Concerns', in Daniel Bodansky, Jutta Brunnée, and Ellen Hey (eds), Oxford Handbook of International Environmental Law (OUP 2007) 557–64; Wolff Heintschel von Heinegg, 'The Law of Armed Conflict at Sea', in D Fleck (ed), The Handbook of International Humanitarian Law (3rd edn, OUP 2013) 474. Louise Doswald-Beck (ed), San Remo Manual on International Law Applicable to Armed Conflicts at Sea (CUP 1995) (San Remo Manual) rule 36.
[35] UNGA, 'Development of an International Legally Binding Instrument under the United Nations Convention on the Law of the Sea on the Conservation and Sustainable Use of Marine Biological Diversity of Areas Beyond National Jurisdiction' UN Doc A/RES/69/292 (6 July 2015).
[36] Heintschel von Heinegg (above n 34) 463; UNCLOS articles 88, 141, 279, and 301.
[37] For direct application see section 8 'Status of International Environmental Law and Domestic Law—Conflict of Laws' below.
[38] Thomas A Mensah, 'Environmental Damages under the Law of the Sea Convention', in Jay E. Austin and Carl E Bruch (eds), The Environmental Consequences of War (CUP 2000) 248–9.
[39] San Remo Manual rule 13(h). See also ILC, 'Second Report on the Protection of the Environment in Relation to Armed Conflicts' (above n 1) para 183.

More specifically, the *San Remo Manual* requires due regard for neutral coastal states' rights of exploitation and duties of protection regarding the economic resources of their exclusive economic zone, continental shelf, and marine environment, and rights of exploration and exploitation of the deep seabed on the high seas.[40] The kinds of marine environmental resources that are within the meaning of the *San Remo Manual* are fish populations, minerals, and marine ecosystems. The marine environment is included as part of the 'natural environment' under API article 35, and possibly under article 55.[41] While there is no authoritative interpretation to determine where the marine environment ends and the terrestrial environment begins, a conservative approach would be to consider as land the area landward of the lowest low tide.

## C. Protected Areas, Sensitive Areas

It has been recommended that especially valuable or sensitive environments should be identified for protection in order to mitigate the difficulty of discriminating between legitimate military objectives and protected objects and of applying the test of balancing military advantage with extent of harm to the environment. One study found that 'over 90% of the major armed conflicts between 1950 and 2000 occurred within countries containing biodiversity hotspots, and more than 80% took place directly within hotspot areas'.[42] According to the International Union for Conservation of Nature, 'roughly a tenth of the world's land surface is under some form of protected area'.[43] Some of these sites are declared as protected under domestic law; using this information would aid in identifying zones where military activity is likely to cause significant damage. Other sites are designated under international conventions, such as the United Nations Educational, Scientific and Cultural Organization (UNESCO) Convention for the Protection of the World Cultural and Natural Heritage (World Heritage Convention) and the Convention on Wetlands of International Importance (Ramsar Convention);[44] international law obligations apply to those, at least for parties to the relevant convention. There is no distinctive emblem to identify protected environmental sites such as those used for medical sites.[45]

Under the World Heritage Convention, state parties agreed that in order to protect 'natural heritage' they would not 'take any deliberate measures which might damage [property

---

[40] *San Remo Manual* rules 34, 35. Note that the high seas marine environment, other than the natural resources of 'the sea-bed and ocean floor, and the subsoil thereof' is not afforded protection.

[41] Erik V Koppe, *The Use of Nuclear Weapons and the Protection of the Environment during International Armed Conflict* (Rijksuniveriteit Groningen 2006) 136 ('the conclusion seems justified that both articles [35(3) and 55] do not only protect the "natural environment" on land, but also the marine environment and the atmosphere').

[42] Thor Hanson, Thomas M Brooks, Gustavo AB Da Fonseca, Michael Hoffmann, John F Lamoreux, Gary Machlis, Cristina G Mittermeier, Russell A Mittermeier, and John D Pilgrim, 'Warfare in Biodiversity Hotspots' (2009) 23 *Conserv Biol* 578, 578.

[43] International Union for the Conservation of Nature (IUCN), *Guidelines for Applying Protected Area Management Categories* (IUCN 2008).

[44] Convention on Wetlands of International Importance especially as Waterfowl Habitat (adopted 2 February 1971, entered into force 21 December 1975) 996 UNTS 245 (Ramsar Convention).

[45] Jean-Marie Henckaerts and Louise Doswald-Beck, *Customary International Humanitarian Law, Vol 1: Rules* (CUP 2005) (CIHL) rule 30 (Persons and Objects Displaying the Distinctive Emblem).

listed as world heritage] directly or indirectly' in Article 6(3). The Convention, article 2, defines natural heritage as:

> natural features consisting of physical and biological formations or groups of such formations, which are of outstanding universal value from the aesthetic or scientific point of view;

> geological and physiographical formations and precisely delineated areas which constitute the habitat of threatened species of animals and plants of outstanding universal value from the point of view of science or conservation;

> natural sites or precisely delineated natural areas of outstanding universal value from the point of view of science, conservation or natural beauty.[46]

It is also referred to as 'natural property … to whatever people it may belong'. Armed conflict is referenced as one of the threats that might lead to placing a site on the List of World Heritage in Danger.[47]

The *San Remo Manual*, rule 11, also provides a means of identifying sensitive and valuable environments. It states:

> The parties to the conflict are encouraged to agree that no hostile actions will be conducted in marine areas containing:
> (a)  rare or fragile ecosystems; or
> (b)  the habitat of depleted, threatened or endangered species or other forms of marine life.[48]

Similar protections have been extended to cultural objects and places of worship, and have been implemented in combat.[49] For example, the Hague Convention for the Protection of Cultural Property in the Event of Armed Conflict of 1954[50] was applied by the allies during the 1990–1991 Gulf War.[51] Some environmental sites hold important cultural and religious significance, but whether cultural protection should be considered as part of environmental protection is disputed.[52]

---

[46]  Convention concerning the Protection of the World Cultural and Natural Heritage (adopted 23 November 1972, entered into force 15 December 1979) 1037 UNTS 151 (World Heritage Convention).

[47]  Meyer discusses the various approaches to referencing armed conflict during the negotiations. Robert L Meyer, 'Travaux Preparatoires for the UNESCO World Heritage Convention' (1976) 2 *Earth LJ* 45, 52 reprinted in Peter H Sand (ed), *The History and Origin of International Environmental Law* (Elgar 2015); Britta Sjöstedt, 'The Role of Multilateral Environmental Agreements in Armed Conflict: Green-Keeping in Virunga Park—Applying the UNESCO World Heritage Convention in the Armed Conflict of the Democratic Republic of the Congo' (2013) 82 *Nordic J Int'l L* 129.

[48]  *San Remo Manual.*

[49]  See *Lieber Code* articles 34–36.

[50]  Convention for the Protection of Cultural Property in the Event of Armed Conflict with Regulations for the Execution of the Convention 1954, (adopted 14 May 1954, entered into force 7 August 1956) 249 UNTS 240 (1954 Convention).

[51]  US DoD, 'Conduct of the Persian Gulf War' (above n 21) 605–6.

[52]  ILC, 'Second Report on the Protection of the Environment in Relation to Armed Conflicts' (above n 1) para 24 (whether protection of cultural and natural heritage should be addressed as part of the PERAC topic was raised by ten states in 2014) and para 224 ('some members of the Commission suggested that cultural heritage should be included in the present report because to do otherwise would lead to inconsistencies. Most speakers, however, remained of the view that cultural heritage should be excluded').

In some cases, the customary rules found in the *Lieber Code* and the Hague Regulations, articles 46 and 56, may apply to protect environmental sites. Those rules protect private property and the property of municipalities and of institutions dedicated to religion, charity and education, the arts and sciences. It can certainly be imagined that sacred groves, research forests, and similar locations should be considered protected in the same way that a church or a research laboratory would be.

## 3. Damage to the Environment

Under customary international law, anticipated environmental damage must be proportional to the expected military advantage. At some very high level, environmental damage will never be justifiable. An explanation of this rule is that such severe damage will be disproportionate to any possible military advantage and it will have indiscriminate effect on combatants and non-combatants. Under customary international law, the principles of distinction, necessity, and proportionality apply to the environment.[53] These rules are codified in various treaties, as are more specific prohibitions. Further support is found in principle 24 of the Rio Declaration, which provides that: 'Warfare is inherently destructive of sustainable development. States shall therefore respect international law providing protection for the environment in times of armed conflict and cooperate in its further development, as necessary.'

## A. Applying the Principles of Distinction, Necessity, Proportionality

The application of the principles of distinction, necessity, and proportionality to the environment is generally accepted as customary international law.[54]

### 1. Principle of distinction: discrimination in attacks

When the environment is a civilian object, under the principle of distinction it may not be targeted unless it is militarily necessary.[55] The obligation to discriminate between civilian and military objects applies to both parties: attackers may not target civilian objects and defenders may not place military targets where civilian objects are located.

The principle that military and civilian personnel and objects must be distinguished is well-accepted customary international law.[56] The Convention on Certain Conventional Weapons (CCW), protocol III, article 2(4) illustrates the principle of distinction, prohibiting attacks on 'forests and other kinds of plant cover' unless they are 'used to cover, conceal or camouflage combatants or other military objectives, or are themselves military objectives.'[57]

---

[53] CIHL rule 43.

[54] ibid rule 43; ILC, Draft principle 9 (above n 1).

[55] CIHL rule 43; Dinstein (above n 11) 533 (the environment, 'once classified as a civilian object', may not be the object of an attack).

[56] See discussion at section 2.A 'Legal Categorization: Civilian or Military Object?' above.

[57] Convention on Prohibitions or Restrictions on the Use of Certain Conventional Weapons Which May be Deemed to be Excessively Injurious or to Have Indiscriminate Effects (adopted 10 October 1980, entered into force 2 December 1983) 1342 UNTS 162 (CCW).

Additional Protocol 1 to the Fourth Geneva Convention (API), article 48, states the basic customary rule:[58]

> In order to ensure respect for and protection of the civilian population and civilian objects, the Parties to the conflict shall at all times distinguish between the civilian population and combatants and between civilian objects and military objectives and accordingly shall direct their operations only against military objectives.

To implement the principle of distinction, those responsible for selection of targets and siting of military installations, personnel, and materiel should identify and account for areas identified as legally protected or especially sensitive and/or valuable environments. For example, during the 1990–1991 Gulf War, US target intelligence analysts compiled a 'joint no-fire target list' of ancient cultural monuments in Iraq and Kuwait.[59]

### 2. Principle of necessity

The prohibition of environmental damage not justified by military necessity is within the scope of several treaties and is now considered customary international law.[60] An absolute prohibition on extreme environmental damage, irrespective of whether it was associated with an act that was necessary to obtain a legal military aim, is considered by some to also be a rule of customary international law.[61]

The customary international law principle of necessity is codified in the Hague Regulations article 23:[62]

> In addition to the prohibitions provided by special Conventions, it is especially forbidden ... (g) To destroy or seize the enemy's property, unless such destruction or seizure be imperatively demanded by the necessities of war.

The Nuremburg Tribunal declared that by 1939, the Regulations 'were recognized by all civilized nations and were regarded as being declaratory of the laws and customs of war'.[63] The United Nations General Assembly invoked this principle to condemn as illegal 'environmental damage and depletion of natural resources, including the destruction of hundreds of oil-well heads and the release and waste of crude oil into the sea' caused by Iraq during the 1990–1991 Gulf War.[64] The ICJ also recognized that this customary international law principle applies to the environment, in its *Nuclear Weapons Advisory Opinion*, stating that 'Respect for the environment is one of the elements that

---

[58] While Dinstein reviewed arguments that API is customary international law, he suggested that it had not become so at the time of the ICJ's 1996 *Nuclear Weapons* advisory opinion, the ICJ having described it at para 31 as providing 'additional protection for the environment' for the states 'having subscribed to these provisions'. Dinstein (above n 11) 534. This may have changed now, twenty years later.

[59] US DoD, 'Conduct of the Persian Gulf War' (above n 21) 100.

[60] CIHL rule 43 (identifying support in military manuals, national legislation, and official statements); Dinstein (above n 11) 545.

[61] CIHL rule 45 but contested by Bellinger and Haynes, 'A US Government Response to the ICRC Study Customary International Humanitarian Law', (2007) 89(867) *IRRC*, 443, 455, 456.

[62] Hague Regulations article 23.

[63] 'Judgment of the Nuremberg International Military Tribunal 1946' (1947) 41 *AJIL* 172, 253–4.

[64] UNGA Resolution 47/37 (9 February 1993).

go to assessing whether an action is in conformity with the principles of necessity and proportionality.'[65]

Article 53 of the Fourth Geneva Convention (GCIV) provides that an occupying power may not destroy any property unless it is absolutely necessary for military operations.

Naval warfare is subject to an additional variant on the balancing of military advantage with protection of environmental resources. Belligerents conducting hostile actions in the exclusive economic zone or on the continental shelf of a neutral state are to have 'due regard' to the coastal state's rights and duties, regarding both economic resources of the exclusive economic zone and continental shelf that may be exploited, and the marine environment that must be protected and preserved.[66] A foreign state may lay mines in these zones if it judges that to be necessary, but it must notify the neutral coastal state.[67]

### 3. Principle that harm may not be disproportionate to military advantage

Excessive destruction is a violation of customary international law. Potential harm to the environment must be considered in planning and carrying out an action, and it is lawful only if the anticipated environmental damage is not excessive in relation to the expected military advantage.[68] This is a corollary of the principle of necessity.

Under article 147 of GCIV, the 'extensive destruction ... of property, not justified by military necessity and carried out unlawfully and wantonly' is a grave breach; grave breaches of GCIV are war crimes under the Rome Statute.

The *San Remo Manual*, rule 46(d) states that collateral damage, which the *Manual* defines to include the marine environment, that is excessive in relation to the anticipated concrete and direct military advantage is prohibited.

Proportionality balancing can be done for each target and for overall campaign objectives.[69] The International Criminal Tribunal for the Former Yugoslavia (ICTY) report on the NATO bombing campaign opined that 'in order to satisfy the requirement of proportionality, attacks against military targets which are known or can reasonably be assumed to cause grave environmental harm may need to confer a very substantial military advantage in order to be considered legitimate.'[70]

Both the importance of the anticipated military advantage and the extent, severity, and duration of the environmental harm are subjective and uncertain. This is the greatest weakness in the legal regime.[71] The attempt to provide clarity through

---

[65] *Nuclear Weapons* para 30. The ICJ referred to UNGA Resolution 47/37 as evidence of customary international law para 32.

[66] *San Remo Manual* rules 34, 35. This refers to coastal state rights and duties under UNCLOS. Note that the high seas marine environment, other than the natural resources of 'the sea-bed and ocean floor, and the subsoil thereof' is not afforded protection. ILC, 'Second Report on the Protection of the Environment in Relation to Armed Conflicts' (above n 1) para 184.

[67] *San Remo Manual* rule 35.

[68] Dinstein (above n 11) 523–49, 524.

[69] Discussed in section 6 'Protection of the Environment by Third Parties: Solidarity' below.

[70] International Criminal Tribunal for the Former Yugoslavia (ICTY), 'Final Report to the Prosecutor by the Committee Established to Review the NATO Bombing Campaign against the Federal Republic of Yugoslavia' (2000) 39 *ILM* 1257 para 22.

[71] The Nuremberg Tribunal's decision that the devastation of Finnmark, Norway under the orders of General Rendulic was justified by military necessity was criticized as a flawed example of balancing. Djamchid Momtaz, 'Le Recours à l'Arme Nucléaire et la Protection de l'Environnement: L'Apport de la Cour Internationale de Justice', in Laurence Boisson de Chazournes and Philippe Sands (eds), *International Law, the International Court of Justice and Nuclear Weapons* (CUP 1999) 365.

the provisions governing means and methods of warfare in API was not very successful.[72]

## B. Verification and Precautions

Planners, decision-makers, and executors of military actions must do everything feasible to verify that they do not target sites protected under applicable conventions, including protected environment.[73] More broadly, they must take all reasonable precautions to prevent excessive collateral damage to the environment, including through their choice of means and methods of attack.[74] When collateral damage is anticipated, they must not launch an attack that would cause excessive damage in relation to the military advantage expected.[75] If circumstances change, the decision to attack must be re-evaluated and the attack cancelled or suspended if it may cause such harm.[76] Defenders also have the obligation to protect civilian objects—including the environment—by not locating military objectives in zones that should be protected.[77]

These precautionary measures represent an affirmative duty, set out in API and the Conventional Weapons Convention, Protocols II, III, and V. They are the logical consequence of the principle of distinction; as such they may be considered customary law.[78] Some states support the principle that parties 'exercise reasonable precautions to minimize incidental or collateral injury to the civilian population or damage to civilian objects, consistent with mission accomplishment and allowable risk to the attacking forces' while rejecting API article 57 as customary international law.[79]

## C. Methods and Means: Weapons

Many states consider that customary international law prohibits the use of methods or means of warfare that are intended, or may be expected, to cause widespread, long-term, and severe damage to the environment.[80] France, the UK, and the US are persistent objectors to this provision.[81] The rule has been criticized by others as both too vague and too stringent.[82]

---

[72] Discussed in section 3.C 'Methods and Means: Weapons' below.

[73] API article 57(2)(a); ILC, Draft principle 9 (above n 1).

[74] API article 57(2)(a)(ii)(c). See also Protocol on Explosive Remnants of War to the Convention on Prohibitions or Restrictions on the Use of Certain Conventional Weapons Which May be Deemed to be Excessively Injurious or to Have Indiscriminate Effects (Protocol V) (adopted 28 November 2003, entered into force 12 November 2006) 2399 UNTS 100, article 5.

[75] API article 57(2)(a)(iii). The *San Remo Manual* rule 46(c) reiterates these requirements with regard to collateral damage, which the *Manual* defines to include the marine environment.

[76] API article 57(2)(b).

[77] ibid article 58(c); US DoD, *Law of War Manual* 186.

[78] Stefan Oeter, 'Methods and Means of Combat', in Dieter Fleck (ed) (n 34) 178–9.

[79] See eg US DoD, *Law of War Manual* 185–6, 188–92.

[80] CIHL rule 45. cf ICTY (above n 70) para 15 (equivocating about customary international law status of articles 35(3) and 55 of Additional Protocol I). *See also* ILC, Draft principle 8(1) (above n 1) ('Care shall be taken to protect the natural environment against widespread, long-term and severe damage.').

[81] See eg Bellinger and Haynes (above n 61) 457–8, 459.

[82] UNEP (Elizabeth Maruma Mrema, Carl Bruch, and Jordan Diamond, *Protecting the Environment during Armed Conflict: An Inventory and Analysis of International Law* (UNEP 2009) 4.

Methods and means of warfare are limited by several treaties, though only two—API and Protocol III of the 1980 Conventional Weapons agreement—have explicit strictures on harming the environment. API article 35 prohibits methods and means of warfare which are intended or may be expected to cause a high level of environmental damage:

> Article 35. Basic Rules. 1. In any armed conflict, the right of the Parties to the conflict to choose methods or means of warfare is not unlimited ... 3. It is prohibited to employ methods or means of warfare which are intended, or may be expected, to cause widespread, long-term and severe damage to the natural environment.[83]

This exact prohibition is repeated in the preamble to the 1980 Conventional Weapons Convention and its Protocols, which reiterate certain Geneva Convention protections for civilians.

Article 55 of API extends a more general duty of care to protect the environment:

> Protection of the Natural Environment.
> 1. Care shall be taken in warfare to protect the natural environment against widespread, long-term and severe damage. This protection includes a prohibition of the use of methods or means of warfare which are intended or may be expected to cause such damage to the natural environment and thereby to prejudice the health or survival of the population.[84]

It is the use of such methods or means that is prohibited, whether or not such damage actually occurs. While it might be difficult to prove intent, the foreseeability of a high level of environmental damage can provide an objective standard. Although in the past ignorance of foreseeable effects of many kinds of attacks might have been a defence, a higher level of constructive knowledge should be implied from improved reporting of the long-term environmental effects from World War 1 battlefields, the 1990–1991 Gulf War, and more recent conflicts.

The next paragraph, Article 55, paragraph 2, prohibits reprisals against the environment, with no qualifications. The threshold of widespread, long-term, and severe damage found in paragraph 1 and in article 35(3) is not included in paragraph 2.

The threshold requirement was included because the drafters of API recognized that some environmental damage would be inevitable during armed conflict. The negotiation report summarizes that the articles are intended to address 'such damage as would be likely to prejudice, over a long term, the continued survival of the civilian population or would risk causing it major health problems'.[85]

The threshold for damage is very high, but it is absolute: neither military necessity nor a proportionality balancing test apply in article 35(3) and article 55. Civilians and combatants

---

[83] API article 35.

[84] The report prepared for the ICTY in relation to claims of Yugoslavia against NATO forces for the 1999 Kosovo bombing observed that article 55 of API might be considered customary international law and thus applicable to non-parties. ICTY (above n 70) paras 14–25 (applying law of armed conflict principles of necessity and proportionality).

[85] *Official Record of the Diplomatic Conference on the Reaffirmation and Development of International Humanitarian Law Applicable in Armed Conflicts*, Vol 1 (1974–1977) 268–9 www.loc.gov/rr/frd/Military_Law/RC-dipl-conference-records.html.

are protected under both articles with language that is intentionally general and which does not specify only the civilian or non-combatant population.[86]

There is ambiguity as to whether widespread, long-term, and severe environmental damage from non-combat military activities such as oil spills from fuel depots falls within the scope of article 55. Modern military manuals, status-of-forces agreements, and domestic laws provide general and specific rules and procedures for managing environmentally hazardous activities.[87] When activities threaten a very high level of harm, they may fall within the scope of article 55.

A difficulty in applying the threshold test is that it asks military planners to predict environmental impacts, which will often be uncertain. Oil spill damage from the 1990–1991 Gulf War is an excellent example: several commentators opined that the damage would not be sufficiently long-term to meet the threshold.[88] However, evidence submitted to the UN Compensation Commission showed that impacts to the intertidal and seabed environments had persisted for over ten years after the conflict and were likely to continue for twenty or more years longer, causing widespread, long-term, and severe damage.[89] While no cases have yet interpreted articles 35 and 55, commentaries have also opined on their application to the NATO bombing of Kosovo,[90] the oil spill in Lebanon,[91] and environmental damage from the conflict between Eritrea and Ethiopia.[92] Lack of guidance on how to interpret the threshold for damage is one of the most serious gaps in this area of law.

API is generally held to apply at sea. The *San Remo Manual*, Rule 44, further provides that:

> Methods and means of warfare should be employed with due regard for the natural environment taking into account the relevant rules of international law. Damage to or destruction of the natural environment not justified by military necessity and carried out wantonly is prohibited.

This rule, to the extent that it represents customary international law, calls for a wider analysis of relevant international law in the particular circumstances and balancing of military requirements with the nature and extent of environmental damage. Marine pollution response vessels may not be attacked, according to rule 47(h) of the *Manual*; and under rule 136(g) they may not be captured if they are actually responding to pollution. No such provisions exist to protect terrestrial pollution response equipment.

---

[86]  ibid para 82.

[87]  See eg NATO, *Joint NATO Doctrine for Environmental Protection* (above n 4).

[88]  See eg UK MoD (above n 5) n 153.

[89]  UNCC, 'Report and Recommendations made by the Panel of Commissioners concerning the Third Instalment of "F4" Claims' (above n 16) para 177.

[90]  ICTY (above n 70) paras 14–25.

[91]  Serge Bronkhorst and Erik Koppe, *Lebanon Oil Spill Legal Assessment* (Institute for Environmental Security 2007).

[92]  Murphy, Kidane, and Snider discussed the potential for environmental damage claims for violations of *jus in bello*. Ethiopia claimed compensation for losses of gum Arabic and resin plants and damage to terraces in the Tigray region for a value of approximately US$1 billion and for loss of wildlife. It failed to provide evidence of harm beyond the claim forms, with no details and no supporting evidence, and the Commission rejected the claims on that basis; the wildlife claim was withdrawn. Sean D Murphy, Won Kidane, and Thomas R Snider, *Litigating War: Arbitration of Civil Injury by the Eritrea–Ethiopia Claims Commission* (OUP 2013) 146, 227–8. Agreement between the Government of the Federal Democratic Republic of Ethiopia and the State of Eritrea (Peace Agreement) (adopted 12 December 2000, entered into force 12 December 2000) 2138 UNTS 94.

There are specific weapons that are prohibited or whose use is restricted. Some states consider that the Hague law and Geneva law apply only to the use of conventional weapons. In their view, atomic, bacteriological, or chemical warfare is addressed elsewhere.[93] Other states consider that all arms are included.[94] Other important differences of position exist regarding the legality of use of nuclear weapons, which were not resolved by the ICJ in its advisory opinion on the *Threat or Use of Nuclear Weapons*.[95] The ICJ said that customary and conventional international law neither authorize nor prohibit the threat or use of nuclear weapons, and that the Court could not definitively conclude whether it would be lawful in response to an existential threat to a state, but that any such use must be compatible with the United Nations Charter and other relevant international law.[96] Otherwise, nuclear weapons are generally addressed through the extensive nuclear weapons regimes.[97] Several treaties establish nuclear-free zones, limiting the development and use of nuclear devices in the designated region.[98]

More recently, the use of depleted uranium (DU) for tank-armouring and anti-tank munitions has raised questions of legality.[99] While DU is used for its physical qualities, including high density and high melting point, and not its radiological properties, when used in conflict it can lead to toxic and, to a lesser degree, carcinogenic exposures. The extent to which DU leaves environmentally damaging remains is still being investigated.[100]

While other weapons treaties may have general application to protection of the environment, the Convention on Certain Conventional Weapons (CCW) has two Protocols of particular relevance to environmental protection.[101] They are: the restrictions on mines,

[93] For example, in the Convention on Prohibitions or Restrictions on the Use of Certain Conventional Weapons Which May be Deemed to be Excessively Injurious or to Have Indiscriminate Effects (with Protocols I, II, and III) (adopted 10 October 1980, entered into force 2 December 1983) 1342 UNTS 162, with Protocol II (mines, booby-traps and other devices and Protocol III (incendiary weapons); Protocol for the Prohibition of the Use in War of Asphyxiating, Poisonous or Other Gases and of Bacteriological Methods of Warfare (adopted 17 June 1925, entered into force 9 May 1926) 94 LNTS 65; Convention on the Prohibition of the Development, Production and Stockpiling of Bacteriological (Biological) and Toxin Weapons and on their Destruction (adopted 10 April 1972, entered into force 26 March 1975) 1015 UNTS 163.
[94] de Preux (above n 13) 411.
[95] *Nuclear Weapons* para 33.
[96] ibid para 105.
[97] de Preux (above n 13) 398 and n 39.
[98] Treaty for the Prohibition of Nuclear Weapons in Latin America and the Caribbean (Tlatelolco Treaty) (opened for signature 14 February 1967; entered into force 25 April 1969) reproduced in UN Doc A/6663 (23 February 1967); Treaty on the Southeast Asia Nuclear Weapon-Free Zone (Bangkok Treaty) (opened for signature 15 December 1995, entered into force 28 March 1997) 1981 UNTS 129; African Nuclear Weapon-Free-Zone Treaty (Pelindaba Treaty) (opened for signature 11 April 1996, entered into force 15 July 2009) 35 ILM 698; Treaty on a Nuclear-Weapon-Free Zone in Central Asia (opened for signature 8 September 2006, entered into force 21 March 2009) and its Protocol (ratified by China, France, Russian Federation, and UK; signed by United States); and The Antarctic Treaty (signed 1 December 1959, entered into force 23 June 1961) 402 UNTS 71.
[99] UNGA Resolutions 62/30 of December 2007 and 63/54 of January 2009 request the Secretary General to produce reports on the human health and environmental effects of the use of armaments and ammunitions containing depleted uranium. For an example of how DU use is assessed following conflict, see UNEP, *Lebanon: Post-Conflict Environmental Assessment* 149–52, 164–5 (2007) (no use of DU found in Lebanon). There is at this time no treaty addressing the use of DU. UNEP, *Protecting the Environment during Armed Conflict* (above n 82) 22; cf Ambassador Robert Wood, US Mission to the UN, Remarks at the 69th UNGA First Committee Cluster Five: Explanation of Vote before the Vote on L.43, Agenda Item 96(e) 'Effects of the use of armaments and ammunitions containing depleted uranium', 31 October 2014 (explaining position of France, UK, and US that DU does not pose a long-term health or environmental hazard).
[100] A Asic, A Kurtovic-Kozaric, and L Besir et al, 'Chemical Toxicity and Radioactivity of Depleted Uranium: The Evidence from In Vivo and In Vitro Studies' (2017) 156 *Envir Res* 665; World Health Organization—Department of Protection of the Human Environment, Depleted Uranium: Sources, Exposure and Health Effects, WHO/SDE/PHE/01.1 (2001).
[101] CCW.

booby-traps, and other devices (CCW Amended Protocol II);[102] and incendiary devices (CCW Protocol III).[103] Mines pose multiple environmental hazards. Protocol III article 2(3) specifically provides that:

> It is prohibited to make forests or other kinds of plant cover the object of attack by incendiary weapons except when such natural elements are used to cover, conceal or camouflage combatants or other military objectives, or are themselves military objectives.[104]

Cyber weapons that target the environment are governed by IHL rules.[105] Cyber warfare might, for example, disable the control system of critical infrastructure such as a nuclear power plant, dam, chemical plant, or a sewage system, resulting in a release of pollution.[106] Such an attack would be subject to the requirements of distinction, necessity, and proportionality, and the special rules of API and the Convention on the Prohibition of Military or Any Other Hostile Use of Environmental Modification Techniques (ENMOD) for the parties to those conventions.[107]

To consider how these rules might apply, assume that the army of state A is using our hypothetical forest for cover as it moves between its bases and it is staging attacks on state B from the forest. If there are ways for state B to obtain its military goals so that destroying all or part of the forest is not imperatively required—for example, observing the enemy using infrared imaging—state B is prohibited from destroying the forest by Hague Regulations article 23(g), if the forest is in state A and is therefore 'enemy property'. The same standard applies if state B is an occupier in state A, under GCIV article 53. Furthermore, under article 147, 'extensive destruction ... carried out unlawfully and wantonly' is a grave breach (see also section 5 'War Crimes' below).

State B might claim that deforestation is necessary to achieve its military goals, in which case the extent of the anticipated destruction must be limited to that which is necessary. Under customary international law, applicable to all states, the extent of damage to the forest must be in proportion to the military advantage sought: the ability to observe state A's activities. In making this evaluation, state B's planners must consider the environmental significance of the areas they intend to deforest. For example, the risk of polluting a water source or causing species extinction by targeting a protected area must be given more weight, and would likely not be justifiable by non-critical military goals. For parties to API, state B cannot make an intentional attack on the forest if the responsible actors expect it to have widespread, long-lasting, *and* severe environmental effects, even if their military objective requires that extent of destruction. Wherever the forest is located—in B's, A's, or another state's territory—this rule applies to all international conflicts. Not only are all kinds of weapons covered, but under API article 55, even a belligerent's accidental destruction of the forest may

---

[102] Protocol on Prohibitions or Restrictions on the Use of Mines, Booby-Traps and Other Devices as amended on 3 May 1996 (adopted 3 May 1996, entered into force 3 December 1998) 2048 UNTS 93 (CCW Amended Protocol II).

[103] Protocol on Prohibitions or Restrictions on the Use of Incendiary Weapons (adopted 10 October 1980, entered into force 2 December 1983) 1342 UNTS 171 (CCW Protocol III).

[104] CCW Protocol III article 2(3); Dinstein (above n 11) 537.

[105] Michael N Schmitt, 'Wired Warfare: Computer Network Attack and Jus in Bello' (2002) 846 *IRRC* 365, 374.

[106] Heather Harrison Dinniss, *Cyber War and Laws of War* (CUP 2012) 220–6.

[107] See section 4 'Environment as Weapon' below.

be illegal, if it causes widespread, long-lasting, *and* severe environmental effects where those effects are foreseeable.[108]

Further assume that the forest is providing cover for only a small number of troops, without great strategic importance, and remember that the forest also provides ecosystem services to the civilian population. In that case, state B's attack on the forest may be a violation of the fundamental IHL principle of proportionality, depending on how destructive it is under GCIV and customary international law. The forest is a military objective, but the terrible damage (which we have said is widespread, long-lasting, and severe) to civilian objects may be both indiscriminate and disproportionate to the military advantage anticipated. If the weapons used against the forest are incendiary weapons, Protocol III of the Conventional Weapons Convention applies. But it does not prohibit their use, since in this hypothetical, the forest is a military objective.

## D.  Remnants of War

A final step in fighting a war is cleaning up afterwards.[109] Explosive remnants of war combine the hazards of mines with the risk of toxic materials pollution of land, water, and sea.[110] Protocol V to the Convention on Certain Conventional Weapons, Explosive Remnants of War, article 4, requires parties to an armed conflict to record and keep information on their use and on the abandonment of explosive ordnance to the extent possible and as far as practicable—during the conflict. After hostilities end, article 3 commits its parties first to mark and then to clear, remove or destroy any explosive remnants of war in their territory.[111] All users of explosive ordnance must provide assistance, wherever feasible, for such efforts if they do not control the territory under article 1.[112] Cooperation between parties to Protocol V is expected under Article 2.[113]

## 4.  Environment as Weapon

All weapons are 'environment', shaped and harnessed into different forms, in the broadest, most literal sense, but certain uses of environment as a weapon are prohibited by specific treaty regimes. The Convention on the Prohibition of Military or Any Other Hostile Use of

---

[108]  Oeter (above n 78) 105, 117.

[109]  ILC, 'Third Report on the Protection of the Environment in Relation to Armed Conflicts' (above n 1) paras 239–265.

[110]  The ILC Special Rapporteur for PERAC called attention to the severity of this problem in her Third Report, particularly in the Baltic Sea and the Pacific Ocean, but noting that the Mediterranean, the Barents Sea, the Atlantic, and the Black Sea are also affected. ILC, 'Third Report on the Protection of the Environment in Relation to Armed Conflicts' (above n 1) paras 255–265.

[111]  While Protocol V was being negotiated, in 2002–2003, the UN Compensation Commission was reviewing environmental damage from the 1990–1991 Gulf War, including substantial harm from remnants of war. UNCC, 'Report and Recommendations made by the Panel of Commissioners concerning the Second Instalment of "F4" Claims' (above n 16) paras 80–117, approved by the Governing Council Decision 171 UN Doc S/AC.26/Dec.171 (3 October 2002); UNCC, 'Report and Recommendations made by the Panel of Commissioners concerning Part One of the Fourth Instalment of "F4" Claims (above n 16) paras 182–240.

[112]  Protocol V article 1.

[113]  See section 6 'Protection of the Environment by Third Parties: Solidarity' below.

Environmental Modification Techniques (ENMOD)[114] governs techniques that weaponize environmental forces. Chemical, bacteriological, and radiological weapons have their own treaty regimes. Use of dams, dykes, and nuclear power plants, referred to as 'works and installations containing dangerous forces'—where the dangerous forces are water and radiation—as weapons is addressed in API. To the extent that an attack, for example on a dam, is intended to release dangerous floodwaters in order to destroy what lies below the dam, API might apply. Customary international law and treaties that govern conventional methods and means of warfare, discussed in earlier sections, may also apply.

ENMOD prohibits deliberate manipulation of natural processes used as a weapon against other parties to the convention when such use has widespread, long-lasting, *or* severe environmental effects anywhere. ENMOD article 1(1) states:

> Each State Party to this Convention undertakes not to engage in military or any other hostile use of environmental modification techniques having widespread, long-lasting or severe effects as the means of destruction, damage or injury to any other State Party.

Parties also undertake not to 'assist, encourage or induce' any other state or international organization to do so, in article 1(2). Article 2 defines weaponization of the environment under ENMOD as any technique for changing the 'dynamics, composition or structure of the Earth ... or of outer space'. The Earth includes 'its biota [living things], lithosphere [the Earth's crust and upper mantle], hydrosphere [water] and atmosphere'.

ENMOD protects targets that could include 'cities, industries, agriculture, transportation and communications system and its natural resources and assets'[115] of states parties. In fact, the nature of the target is immaterial, but it must be another state party to ENMOD—whether hostile, ally, or neutral.[116] A number of uses of environmental modification are nonetheless allowed. Uses of environmental modification techniques that only affect one's own territory, the territory of a non-party, or areas beyond national jurisdiction are not prohibited by the treaty, nor are hostile uses that do not exceed any of the thresholds: severe, widespread, or long-lasting. Peaceful use of environmental modification techniques, consistent with other rules of international law, is specified as permissible in ENMOD article 3(1). Anthropogenic climate change may lead some states to consider geoengineering methods and technologies to deliberately manipulate the planetary environment at large scale to counteract warming.[117] Whether geoengineering intended to affect global warming could be regulated by ENMOD is a matter of current discussion.[118]

Exceeding any one of the three parameters (called 'the troika') of the threshold for environmental damage triggers the obligation, in contrast to API and the Rome Statute, where all three must be exceeded. Environmental damage exceeding the threshold and thereby

---

[114] Convention on the Prohibition of Military or Any Other Hostile Use of Environmental Modification Techniques (adopted 10 December 1976, entered into force 5 October 1978) 1108 UNTS 151 (ENMOD).

[115] UNGA, 'Report of the Conference of the Committee on Disarmament' (1976) GAOR 31st Session Supp No 27 (A/31/27) (vol I) para 333.

[116] Dinstein (above n 11) 529.

[117] Royal Society, *Geoengineering the Climate: Science, Governance and Uncertainty* (RS Policy document 10/09, Royal Society 2009); National Academy of Sciences, *Advancing the Science of Climate Change* (The National Academies Press 2010).

[118] Catherine Redgwell, 'Geoengineering the Climate: Technological Solutions to Mitigation—Failure or Continuing Carbon Addiction?' (2011) 2 *CCLR* 178, 182–3.

placing the environmental modification technique off-limits may occur anywhere; by the terms of the convention it is not restricted to the territory of state parties.

The meaning of the terms when used in ENMOD is defined as follows in the 'Understandings' that were included in the final report of the negotiating committee to the UN General Assembly:

(a) 'widespread': encompassing an area on the scale of several hundred square kilometres;
(b) 'long-lasting': lasting for a period of months, or approximately a season;
(c) 'severe': involving serious or significant disruption or harm to human life, natural and economic resources or other assets.[119]

What exactly constitutes prohibited environmental modification is unclear, and may be one reason this convention has never been invoked in a judicial context. Examples offered during the negotiations included: earthquakes; tsunamis; an upset in the ecological balance of a region; changes in weather patterns (clouds, precipitation, cyclones of various types, and tornadic storms); changes in climate patterns; changes in ocean currents; changes in the state of the ozone layer; and changes in the state of the ionosphere.[120] At the Second (and last) Review Conference of the Parties to ENMOD in 1992 the parties agreed to include herbicides that upset the ecological balance of a region within the scope of article 2.[121] The important change in position by the parties to include herbicide use suggests a shift to a broader prohibition on the use of any environmental modification expected to exceed the threshold.

Non-compliance with ENMOD is addressed first by consultation and cooperation, and may include the use of a Consultative Committee established by the convention.[122] A complaint may be made to the UN Security Council, and state parties undertake to cooperate with the Security Council's investigation of complaints. If the Security Council finds a party has been or is likely to be harmed by a breach of the convention, other parties will 'provide or support assistance'.

The distinction made between lesser damage and that which reaches the threshold of widespread, long-lasting, and severe does not have the same logic for ENMOD that it has for API and is another indicator of the parties' hesitancy to forego military options. API uses the threshold to distinguish regrettable but 'normal' environmental damage caused by armed conflict from unacceptable levels of damage, in light of the fact that the environment is everywhere and it would be impossible to absolutely ban any harm. However, ENMOD is a weapons treaty and absolutely banning the use of certain types of weapons, without a threshold, is the ordinary approach. The 1925 Geneva Protocol, which bans chemical and bacteriological weapons, does not set a threshold: they are banned absolutely.[123]

---

[119] UNGA (above n 115) 91.

[120] ibid 93. See also Telegram 1662 From the Mission in Geneva to the Department of State, Subject: CCD 691st Plenary Meeting, March 4, 1976, 574 Foreign Relations of the United States, 1969–1976, Vol E–14, Part 2.

[121] 'Final Document of the Second Review Conference of the Parties to the Convention on the Prohibition of Military or Any Other Hostile Use of Environmental Modification Techniques' UN Doc ENMOD/CONF.II/12 (Part II: Final Declaration) (22 September 1992) 12. The US used herbicides extensively against the North Vietnamese from 1962 until 1971.

[122] Compliance is addressed in ENMOD article 5.

[123] Protocol for the Prohibition of the Use in War of Asphyxiating, Poisonous or Other Gases, and of Bacteriological Methods of Warfare (adopted 17 June 1925, entered into force 9 May 1926) 94 LNTS 65.

Another form of using the environment as a weapon is an attack on installations that contain or control powerful natural forces.[124] Dams, dykes, and nuclear electrical generating stations may almost never be the object of an attack when it may lead to severe civilian losses due to flooding or radiation exposure, under API article 56.[125] This prohibition covers installations, and their defences, that are themselves military objectives, and extends to military objectives located where the attack might unleash the 'dangerous forces'. The exception is when the planned attack is the only feasible way to stop the facilities from being used in 'regular, significant and direct support of military operations'. Like medical facilities, these facilities may be marked with a special symbol—three bright orange circles in line—to make them easy to identify. Although it has been suggested that the requirement for defenders and attackers alike to take precautions might mean that a state would be obliged to drain the reservoir to avoid catastrophic flooding from a dam,[126] this would be not only impractical in many cases, but it would be likely to cause the very kind of environmental damage that other legal rules are intended to prevent. The suggestion itself points to the danger of focusing on narrow legal rules. The US is a persistent objector to customary law that may have formed in relation to this provision of API; however, the US has not attacked any facility covered by the provision since the Vietnam War.[127]

## 5. War Crimes

The criminalization of damage to the environment during armed conflict is a signal of its heightened seriousness for the international community.[128] Even if the likelihood of criminal prosecution appears low, describing certain acts as an environmental war crime has symbolic meaning.

Individuals and states may be prosecuted for committing war crimes. Prosecution can be the responsibility of an international court or a relevant domestic court. Modern trials for grave breaches of IHL and war crimes have been conducted by the International Criminal Court (ICC) and several ad hoc tribunals, including the Nuremberg Tribunal. The sources of law include customary international law; treaties and the statutes of international criminal tribunals; and domestic law.

Customary international law provides a basis for prosecution when a belligerent destroys or seizes the enemy's public or private property without military necessity.[129] Such behaviour may constitute a grave breach of IHL—behaviour that is illegal but that is not always criminal—in contrast with war crimes, which are simply criminal behaviour. For a judicial body, the applicability of a grave breach or a war crime will have different consequences and will depend on the circumstances of the case.[130] Some charges are subject to the defence

---

[124] See the discussion of cyber warfare above.

[125] Oeter (above n 78)M 217–21.

[126] ibid 221.

[127] Stephens (above n 5) 249–50.

[128] Michael Bothe, 'Criminal Responsibility for Environmental Damage in Times of Armed Conflict', in Richard J Grunawalt et al (eds) (above n 9) 473–8.

[129] Françoise J Hampson, 'Liability for War Crimes', in Peter Rowe (ed), *The Gulf War 1990-91 in International and National Law* (Routledge 1993) 254.

[130] Marko Divac Öberg, 'The Absorption of Grave Breaches into War Crimes Law' (2009) 91 *IRRC* 163, 164.

that the activities were defensive measures that satisfied the customary international law principles of necessity, distinction, and proportionality.

A number of acts, treated as either war crimes or grave breaches of the Hague and Geneva Conventions by the Nuremberg Tribunal, would have caused serious environmental damage integrally related to the purpose of the legal prohibition. Treated by the Tribunal as customary international law, they included the following:

- looting and destruction of agricultural products, minerals, and other natural resources, whether public or private property;[131]
- plunder of public and private property;[132]
- wanton destruction of cities, towns, and villages and devastation not justified by military necessity;[133]
- inundations not justified by military necessity;[134]
- the practice of 'total war' including 'methods of combat and of military occupation in direct conflict with the laws and customs of war, and the commission of crimes perpetrated on the field of battle during encounters with enemy armies ... and in occupied territories against the civilian population of such territories'.[135]

The Charter of the International Military Tribunal (Nuremberg Tribunal), article 6(b) gave the following definition:

War Crimes: namely, violations of the laws or customs of war. Such violations shall include, but not be limited to ... plunder of public or private property, wanton destruction of cities, towns or villages, or devastation not justified by military necessity[136]

The Indictment described minerals and crops being taken, including coal, iron ore, bauxite, wheat, and oats, as well as the complete destruction of cities.[137] It argued that, 'The result of this policy of plunder and destruction was to lay waste the land and cause utter desolation.'[138] The judgment reasoned that treaties, particularly the Hague and bilateral Agreements, established the illegality of plunder of public and private property and that custom and practice had punished violations as war crimes.[139]

The elements of a grave breach under the Hague Convention IV of 1907, Regulations, article 23(g), are:

In addition to the prohibitions provided by special Conventions, it is especially forbidden ... To destroy or seize the enemy's property, unless such destruction or seizure be imperatively demanded by the necessities of war.

---

[131] *Trial of the Major War Criminals before the International Military Tribunal*, Vol 1 (International Military Tribunal 1947) 55, 239–40, 297.
[132] ibid 281–2 (Göring convicted), 287 (Von Ribbentrop), 295 (Rosenberg), 297 (Frank), and 324–5 (Jodl).
[133] ibid 61.
[134] ibid 61.
[135] ibid 43 (Göring).
[136] ibid 11, 173–4.
[137] ibid 57, 58, 60.
[138] ibid 60.
[139] ibid 219–24.

Under GCIV article 147, the level of harm for the criminal standard of grave breach is higher:

> extensive destruction and appropriation of property, not justified by military necessity and carried out unlawfully and wantonly.[140]

Common Article 49/50/129/146 of the Geneva Conventions commits the parties to enact domestic legislation to enforce liability and sanctions.[141]

Iraq's destruction of oil wells in Kuwait has been called a grave breach of article 147.[142] Over 1 billion barrels of oil were released when Iraqi forces detonated more than 600 oil wells, contaminating groundwater and desert ecology.[143] Iraq's claim that the smoke from the fires was intended as a defensive manoeuvre was dismissed on the grounds that the same effect could have been achieved without destroying the well-heads, an action that resulted in months of continuous burning and spilling of oil.[144]

The Rome Statute considers intentional, serious violations of the environmental integrity norm a war crime, as well as destruction and plunder of civilian property.[145] So far, no other international criminal tribunal statute has done so. The Rome Statute defines war crimes for activities occurring after the ICC began working in 2002, when the state of the perpetrator is a member of the ICC. It extends the protections for environment from the traditional categories of civilian property and life-support system that were previously provided in IHL—in the words of the Nuremberg Indictment, 'devastation not justified by military necessity'—to the modern conception of the environment.

Relevant law for the ICC is its Statute, the *Elements of Crimes*, and, 'where appropriate, applicable treaties and the principles and rules of international law, including the established principles of the international law of armed conflict', general principles of law, and principles and rules of law as interpreted in its previous decisions.[146] War crimes specified in the Rome Statute that are or may be applicable to environmental damage are:

Article 8—War crimes
1. The Court shall have jurisdiction in respect of war crimes in particular when committed as part of a plan or policy or as part of a large-scale commission of such crimes.

---

[140] See also GCIV article 53.

[141] GCIV article 146.

[142] US DoD, 'Conduct of the Persian Gulf War' (above n 21) 710.

[143] UNCC, 'Report and Recommendations made by the Panel of Commissioners concerning the Third Instalment of "F4" Claims' (above n 16) paras 61, 86–99, 106–111, 121–125, 134–138.

[144] See also Rex J Zedalis, 'Burning of the Kuwaiti Oilfields and the Laws of War' (1991) 24(4) *Vand J Transnat'l L* 711, 738–9.

[145] Rome Statute of the International Criminal Court (opened for signature 17 July 1998, entered into force 1 July 2002) 2187 UNTS 90 (Rome Statute).

[146] Rome Statute article 21. ICC, *Assembly of States Parties to the Rome Statute of the International Criminal Court* (New York 3–10 September 2002) 1st Session (UN 2002) Part IIB. The *Elements of Crimes* adopted at the 2010 Review Conference are replicated from the ICC, *Review Conference of the Rome Statute of the International Criminal Court* (Kampala 31 May–11 June 2010) (ICC 2010) (*Elements of Crimes*).

2. For the purpose of this Statute, 'war crimes' means:
  (a) Grave breaches of the Geneva Conventions of 12 August 1949, namely, any of the following acts against persons or property protected under the provisions of the relevant Geneva Convention: …
    (iv) Extensive destruction and appropriation of property, not justified by military necessity and carried out unlawfully and wantonly …
  (b) Other serious violations of the laws and customs applicable in international armed conflict, within the established framework of international law, namely, any of the following acts: …
    (ii) Intentionally directing attacks against civilian objects, that is, objects which are not military objectives; …
    (iv) Intentionally launching an attack in the knowledge that such attack will cause incidental loss of life or injury to civilians or damage to civilian objects or widespread, long-term and severe damage to the natural environment which would be clearly excessive in relation to the concrete and direct overall military advantage anticipated …

For grave breaches under article 8(2)(a)(iv), the environment must be shown to be protected as public or private property under the Geneva Conventions.[147] A similar showing is required under article 8(2)(b)(ii), that the perpetrator intended that, and in fact that, the object of the attack was civilian objects, not military objectives.

Specifically intended to protect the environment, article 8(2)(b)(iv) sanctions an attack that is launched in the knowledge that it would cause particularly serious harm to the natural environment that would be disproportionate to the expected military advantage.[148] The environment in this case could be a military objective—the very high threshold offsets this wider scope. The relevant value judgment is the attacker's, based on the facts known to her at the time regarding the level of damage and the military advantage.[149] The attacker must therefore not launch an attack, knowing that it is the kind of attack that will cause environmental damage exceeding the threshold, unless the direct overall military advantage is of extraordinary importance.

These requirements are more stringent than API. First, the Statute requires intent to launch the attack and knowledge that it will cause the environmental damage, which is appropriately a more demanding *mens rea* than API, other treaty provisions, or customary international law that do not carry criminal sanctions; moreover, it is required by the Rome Statute article 30. The required intent and knowledge can be inferred from relevant facts and circumstances.[150] Second, the military advantage expected must be deficient when compared to the environmental damage. However, it may not be necessary for actual damage to occur.[151]

[147] *Elements of Crimes* 15–16.
[148] For a discussion of whether use of nuclear, chemical, and biological weapons is covered by the Rome Statute, see Ines Peterson, 'The Natural Environment in Times of Armed Conflict: A Concern for International War Crimes Law?' (2009) 22(2) *LJIL* 325, 336–7.
[149] *Elements of Crimes* 19.
[150] ibid 1.
[151] Peterson agrees with Dörmann that actual damage is not required. Peterson (above n 148) 14.

The threshold of damage—widespread, long-term, and severe—was adopted from a draft statute prepared for the ICC by the ILC, which borrowed from API. No judicial opinion has yet interpreted the three terms in either treaty; commentators differ on whether they should be understood to mean the same thing and whether they should be interpreted according to terms proposed during the API negotiations.[152] The serious, intentional environmental damage that was ordered by the Iraqi leadership during the 1990–1991 Gulf War did reach the level of harm for a war crime.[153] The oil spills Iraq could have claimed necessary in defending its destruction of Kuwaiti oil wells and creation of a massive oil spill in the Persian Gulf,[154] but on the facts the defence would have likely failed.[155] In another modern case, the Committee advising the ICTY Prosecutor decided that 'the environmental damage caused during the NATO bombing campaign does not reach the API threshold'.[156]

## 6. Protection of the Environment by Third Parties: Solidarity

Though not yet a formal part of IHL treaties, solidarity as an evolving legal principle is quite pertinent to the conduct of a state in taking steps to protect the environment during armed conflict. Solidarity is a concept rooted in Emer de Vattel's argument that states have a legitimate expectation that others will assist them when they are threatened with 'disaster and ruin', although its modern meaning and status in international law is much debated.[157] Currently, the actions of states that aid in responding to conflict-related disasters and environmental damage are considered voluntary, but are increasingly tinged with a sense of obligation.

Examples of this development include recent treaty terms, international commission decisions, and various international declarations. Parties to the CCW, Protocol V on Explosive Remnants of War agree to cooperate and assist each other by providing technical, financial, material, and human resources and by other means, under article 3(5).[158] During the 1990–1991 Gulf War:

> specific appeals for assistance in dealing with the environmental damage caused by Iraq's invasion and occupation of Kuwait were made by the United Nations General Assembly and by other organizations and bodies of the United Nations system as well as by the countries affected by environmental damage or threat of such damage resulting from Iraq's invasion and occupation of Kuwait.[159]

---

[152] ibid 330 (reviewing the debate and concluding that the terms in API and the Rome Statute must be interpreted independently, as is the case with the similar threshold in ENMOD).

[153] Although some commentators questioned this in the years immediately following the conflict, on the grounds that the harm was not going to persist for decades, environmental assessments undertaken from 2000 on showed that there was ongoing damage that would likely continue for a further twenty years or more. UNEP, *From Conflict to Peacebuilding: The Role of Natural Resources and the Environment* (UNEP 2009) 8.

[154] Mark Drumbl, 'Waging War Against the World: The Need to Move from War Crimes to Environmental Crimes' (1998) 22 *Fordham Intern'l LJ* 122, 126.

[155] Hampson (above n 129) 250–1, 259.

[156] ICTY (above n 70) paras 14–25.

[157] Rudiger Wolfrum and Chie Kojima (eds), *Solidarity: A Structural Principle of International Law* (Springer 2010).

[158] Protocol on Explosive Remnants of War (adopted 28 November 2003, entered into force 12 November 2006) 2399 UNTS 100 (CCW Protocol V).

[159] UNCC, 'Report and Recommendations made by the Panel of Commissioners Concerning the Second Instalment of "F4" Claims' (above n 16) paras 32–35, 34.

A number of international agreements and declarations recognize the obligation to provide assistance to respond to environmental emergencies. For example, principle 18 of the
Declaration of the United Nations Conference on Environment and Development (Rio
de Janeiro) 1992, provides that 'States shall immediately notify other States of any natural
disasters or other emergencies that are likely to produce sudden harmful effects on the environment of those States. Every effort shall be made by the international community to
help States so afflicted.'[160]

## 7. Non-International Armed Conflict

The majority of armed conflicts are not international; that is, they occur within the territory of a single state and the armed forces of no other state are engaged against the central government.[161] The ILC Special Rapporteur has written, 'it is clear that fundamental
principles, such as the principle of distinction and the principle of humanity (the dictates
of public conscience), reflect customary law and are applicable in all types of armed conflict'.[162] Customary international law protecting civilian objects continues to apply in non-
international armed conflict (NIAC).[163] Some international instruments state that some of
their terms apply to NIAC.[164] State practice fills the gap,[165] but it is exceedingly difficult to
obtain documentation.[166]

   Protocol II to the Geneva Conventions (APII), relating to the protections of victims of
non-international conflicts, does not refer directly to 'environment' but it does extend protection to cultural objects and objects indispensable to the survival of the civilian population and it prohibits attacks on installations containing dangerous forces, IHL measures
that are applicable to the environment as discussed above in section 6 'Protection of the
Environment by Third Parties: Solidarity'.[167] Frequently referenced in relation to NIAC,
the four Geneva Conventions of 1949 each include 'Common Article 3' which purports
to extend some of the core constraints on all parties to NIAC. It binds the parties to an internal conflict to provide humane treatment of persons not taking active part in hostilities,
the wounded, and the sick; to allow access to impartial humanitarian bodies; and to make

---

[160] UNGA, 'Report of the United Nations Conference on Environment and Development', Annex I: Rio
Declaration on Environment and Development (Rio de Janeiro, 3–14 June 1992) UN Doc A/CONF.151/26 (Vol I).
See also UNCLOS article 194.

[161] Michael N Schmitt, Charles HB Garraway, and Yoram Dinstein (eds), *The Manual on the Law of Non-
International Armed Conflict: With Commentary* (International Institute of Humanitarian Law 2006) definition
1.1.1 www.ihl.org/wp-content/uploads/2015/12/Manual-on-the-Law-of-NIAC.pdf.

[162] ILC, 'Second Report on the Protection of the Environment in Relation to Armed Conflicts' (above n 1) para 6.

[163] Schmitt et al (above n 161) 59.

[164] For example, Convention on Conventional Weapons (CCW); CCW Protocol III; Rome Statute 8(e);
Convention on the Prohibition of the Use, Stockpiling, Production and Transfer of Anti-Personnel Mines and
on their Destruction (adopted 18 September 1997, entered into force 1 March 1999) 2056 UNTS 211; CWC;
Convention for the Protection of Cultural Property in the Event of Armed Conflict (adopted 14 May 1954, entered
into force 7 August 1956) 249 UNTS 216; Second Protocol to the Hague Convention of 1954 for the protection of
Cultural Property in the Event of Armed Conflict (adopted 26 March 1999, entered into force 9 March 2004) 2253
UNTS 172 (Second Protocol 1999).

[165] Thirlway (above n 3) 185.

[166] ILC, 'Second Report on the Protection of the Environment in Relation to Armed Conflicts' (above n 1) para 8.

[167] Protocol Additional to the Geneva Conventions of 12 August 1949, and Relating to the Protection of Victims
of Non-International Armed Conflicts (adopted 8 June 1977; entered into force 7 December 1978) 1125 UNTS 609
(APII) articles 14–16.

special agreements to apply the other provisions of the Geneva Conventions. It makes no reference that directly applies to the environment, property, or civilian objects.

While it seems unlikely that belligerents in most cases will respect these legal rules,[168] the existence of the rules provides a guide for governments, the basis for sanctions to be imposed eventually, and a standard of behaviour for would-be leaders to observe if they wish to be admitted to the community of nations.

## 8. Status of International Environmental Law and Domestic Law—Conflict of Laws

There has been far less examination of choice of law in the environmental protection context than in the well-developed discussion of conflicts between relatively permissive rules of international humanitarian law and more restrictive human rights law.[169] At the minimum, some environmental treaty provisions are, by their terms, applicable during armed conflict; treaties and customary international environmental law rules that are silent on this point will sometimes be applicable as well. Domestic law—of an invading force, of a host nation, or of a neutral state—may also apply and are discussed briefly first.

Generally, host nation domestic law, including environmental law, applies with two significant exceptions. Where a foreign military enters another state with consent, specific agreements with the host nation can suspend application of some or all of the host's domestic law; these include status-of-forces agreements (SOFA) and stationing agreements. The second exception is the immunity provided for warlike acts done under military authority and in accordance with the law of war, committed when combatants are present in the host country.[170] And, of course, most nations implement their international humanitarian law commitments through their own domestic law. If a domestic law has extraterritorial effect, which depends on the specific law, and lacking an explicit statement suspending the law due to armed conflict, the law can be assumed to remain in effect.[171]

The general international law principle guiding the applicability of international environmental law is that *lex specialis*—special law—co-exists in parallel with non-conflicting law and takes precedence over more general rules of law that conflict.[172] A state of armed conflict does not automatically or necessarily suspend peacetime domestic and international law relating to the environment.[173] Some conventions expressly continue to apply; others allow parties to suspend the operation of the convention during conflict; others are silent.[174] Where two bodies of special rules, such as IHL and environmental law or human

[168] Geneva Call, a non-governmental organization, has compiled a collection of humanitarian commitments made by armed non-state actors (ANSAs) theirwords.org.
[169] ILC, 'Preliminary Report on the Protection of the Environment in Relation to Armed Conflicts' (above n 1) para 3.
[170] See, eg, US DoD, *Law of War Manual*, section 4.4.3.
[171] John P Quinn, Richard T Evans, and Michael J Boock, 'US Navy Development of Operational-Environmental Doctrine', in Austin and Bruch (eds) (n 38) 164–5.
[172] ILC, 'Third Report on the Protection of the Environment in Relation to Armed Conflicts' (above n 1) para 10.
[173] With respect to the continued vitality of treaties, see ILC, 'Draft Articles on the Effects of Armed Conflicts on Treaties, with Commentaries' in *Yearbook of the International Law Commission*, Vol II, Part 2 (ILC 2011) article 3.
[174] ibid articles 4, 6,

rights law, conflict, the traditional concept was that IHL controlled.[175] Where a general rule of IHL conflicts with a specific rule of an environmental treaty that is clearly intended to apply during armed conflict, the environmental treaty rule will control, for the parties to that treaty.

The easy case is where a treaty applicable to the belligerents includes an express statement. An example would be the World Heritage Convention, under which state parties agree not to take any deliberate measures that might directly or indirectly damage listed sites.[176] The fact that this convention provides a list of specific sites entitled to protection makes this operationally feasible. The International Watercourses Convention, article 29, 'serves as a reminder that there are rules of international law that protect international watercourses and related installations, facilities and other works during hostilities'.[177] This stakes out a general position that requires state parties to the Watercourses Convention to examine potentially relevant agreements with the understanding that they may continue to apply during armed conflict.

Other treaties are more ambiguous. For instance, several treaties for control of oil pollution at sea extend immunities to 'warships and other government ships operated for non-commercial purposes' as defined in the treaties,[178] but otherwise the conventions are held to continue to apply during conflict.[179]

The Law of the Sea is another *lex specialis*. It has both the force of a nearly unanimously subscribed treaty, UNCLOS, and status as customary international law. As seen in section 2.B. 'Marine Environment and Outer Space' above, UNCLOS establishes sovereign rights that are relevant to armed conflict. There remains ambiguity over the applicability of the Convention's protective measures in war time.[180] UNCLOS article 236 attempts to address the conflict:

> The provisions of this Convention regarding the protection and preservation of the marine environment do not apply to any warship, naval auxiliary, other vessels or aircraft owned or operated by a state and used, for the time being, only on government non-commercial service. However, each state shall ensure, by the adoption of appropriate measures not impairing operations or operational capabilities of such vessels or aircraft owned or operated by it, that such vessels or aircraft act in a manner consistent, so far as is reasonable and practicable, with this Convention.

The continuing development of international law in many specialized areas means that legal advisers will be obliged to regularly review the continuing application of the UN Charter,

---

[175] Christopher Greenwood, '*Jus ad Bellum* and *Jus in Bello* in the Advisory Opinion', in Laurence Boisson de Chazournes and Philippe Sand (eds), *International Law, the International Court of Justice and Nuclear Weapons* (CUP 1999) 252–3.

[176] See Section 2.C 'Protected Areas. Sensitive Areas'.

[177] Stephen McCaffrey, 'The UN Convention on the Law of the Non-Navigational Uses of International Watercourses: Prospects and Pitfalls', in Salman MA Salman and Laurence Boisson de Chazournes (eds), *International Watercourses: Enhancing Cooperation and Managing Conflict*, Technical Paper No 414 (World Bank1998) 25.

[178] UNCLOS articles 29–32; International Convention for the Prevention of Pollution from Ships (adopted 2 November 1973, entered into force 2 November 1983) 1340 UNTS 184 article 3(3).

[179] See UNEP, *Protecting the Environment During Armed Conflict* (above n 82) 35–7.

[180] Tullio Scovazzi, 'The Evolution of International Law of the Sea: New Issues, New Challenges' (2001) 286 *RCADI* 162; Heintschel von Heinegg (above n 34) 463.

international security law, IHL, international criminal law, human rights law, international environmental law, international economic law, and other bodies of international law.[181] These bodies of law must be taken into account as they may constitute: binding legal obligations; norms informing special rules effective during armed conflict as stated in the Law of Armed Conflict; international standards; non-binding norms; and guidelines and/or state practice, including practice integrated into rules of engagement, status-of-forces agreements, and military manuals, handbooks, and training guides.[182]

---

[181] US positions reflect this with regard to human rights. HRC 'Fourth Periodic Report of the United States of America to the United Nations Committee on Human Rights concerning the International Covenant on Civil and Political Rights' UN Doc CCPR/C/USA/4 (22 May 2012) para 506; US DoD, *Law of War Manual*.

[182] See eg NATO, Military Principles and Policies for Environmental Protection (MC 0469/1), October 2011; ILC 'Preliminary Report on the Protection of the Environment in Relation to Armed Conflicts' (above n 1) para 46.

# 10

# Methods of Warfare

*Gloria Gaggioli and Nils Melzer*

## 1. Introduction

Current world affairs are plagued by a plethora of conflicts, many of them marked by methods of warfare displaying a shocking disregard for the established principles of international humanitarian law (IHL). In some contexts, it seems that methods such as direct attacks against civilians and unarmed or wounded combatants, indiscriminate attacks, perfidious suicide-bombings, and the destruction and pillage of cultural objects have become commonplace, and it seems to have been forgotten that even wars have limits.

The so-called 'Hague Law', which regulates the use of means and methods of warfare so as to mitigate, as much as possible, the 'calamities of war',[1] is the oldest branch of IHL. Its basic tenet can be summarized in three fundamental maxims, namely: (i) that 'the only legitimate object which states should endeavour to accomplish during war is to weaken the military forces of the enemy';[2] and that therefore, in pursuing this aim, both (ii) 'the right of the Parties to the conflict to choose methods or means of warfare is not unlimited';[3] and (iii) '[t]he civilian population and individual civilians shall enjoy general protection against dangers arising from military operations'.[4]

The first maxim expresses the basic principle of military necessity, which limits the permissibility of means and methods of warfare to what is actually required for the achievement of a legitimate military purpose. The second maxim provides the basis for the prohibition of means and methods of warfare that are of a nature to cause superfluous injury or unnecessary suffering to combatants.[5] The third maxim concerns the principle of distinction,[6] which prohibits not only direct attacks against civilians and the civilian population, but also indiscriminate means and methods of warfare. Both the prohibition of unnecessary suffering and the principle of distinction are regarded as 'cardinal principles' of IHL by the International Court of Justice (ICJ)[7] and, in this basic form, are universally accepted as part of customary international law.[8]

---

[1]  Declaration Renouncing the Use, in Time of War, of Explosive Projectiles under 400 Grammes Weight, Saint Petersburg (29 November–11 December 1868) (St Petersburg Declaration).

[2]  ibid.

[3]  Protocol Additional to the Geneva Conventions of 12 August 1949, and Relating to the Protection of Victims of International Armed Conflicts (adopted 8 June 1977, entered into force 7 December 1978) (API) article 35(1). See also Regulations Annexed to the Hague Convention (IV) Respecting the Laws and Customs of War on Land and Its Annex: Regulation concerning the Laws and Customs of War on Land (18 October 1907, entered into force 26 January 1910) 187 CTS 227 (Hague Regulations) article 22.

[4]  API article 51(1).

[5]  Hague Regulations 1907 article 23(e); API article 35(2); Jean-Marie Henckaerts and Louise Doswald-Beck (eds), *Customary International Humanitarian Law* (CUP 2005) (CIHL) rule 70. See also St Petersburg Declaration.

[6]  API article 48; CIHL rule 1.

[7]  *Legality of the Threat or Use of Nuclear Weapons* (Advisory Opinion) [1996] ICJ Rep 266 (*Nuclear Weapons*) para 78.

[8]  CIHL rules 1 and 70.

Beyond the restatement of these fundamental maxims and principles, however, a more comprehensive discussion on methods of warfare gives rise to difficult questions. How should the notion of 'methods of warfare' be defined and, in particular, how should it be distinguished from the related notion of 'means of warfare'? Are the generic prohibitions of indiscriminate attacks and of superfluous injury/unnecessary suffering specific enough in terms of detail, and sufficiently broad in terms of scope, to regulate each and every method of warfare? What are the main methods of warfare that have been more specifically regulated in customary and treaty IHL? Are there differences as to how IHL regulates methods of warfare in international armed conflicts (IACs) and non-international armed conflicts (NIACs)?

Once these preliminary issues have been explored, the objective of this chapter is to outline the current state of the law regulating methods of warfare. For the purposes of the chapter, the rules of IHL regulating methods of warfare are distinguished according to their protective purpose, ie those aiming to protect civilians and the civilian population based on the principle of distinction[9] are discussed separately from those aiming to protect combatants based on the prohibition of unnecessary suffering or other principles of IHL. For each method of warfare, the questions analysed will be the following. When and how has the method been restricted or prohibited in customary or treaty law? Does recourse to the restricted/prohibited method of warfare give rise to individual criminal responsibility? Why has the method been restricted/prohibited (*ratio legis*)? What is the exact content and meaning of the restriction/prohibition? Are there open questions regarding the interpretation of the elements of the restriction/prohibition? Are there recent examples of contemporary practices and policies which may be relevant to the rule in question?

A concluding section summarizes our findings and attempts a cursory outlook as to the relevance of contemporary trends, such as the advent and seamless integration of new technologies into the arsenal, strategies, and tactics of armed and security forces throughout the world.

## 2. Defining and Regulating Methods of Warfare

### A. Defining Methods of Warfare

The notion of 'methods of warfare' is mentioned several times in Additional Protocol I (API) to the Geneva Conventions.[10] It is usually employed together with its twin notion 'means of warfare'. In Additional Protocol II (APII) dealing with NIACs, where states party to a treaty were hesitant to use the term 'warfare',[11] and on one occasion in

---

[9] Note: some of the methods used specifically against civilians are already dealt with under chapter 7 'International Humanitarian Law and the Conduct of Hostilities'. These will therefore be mentioned, but not necessarily much elaborated.

[10] The recent IHL provisions using the term methods of warfare: in API: Title of Part III, Section I; article 35(1–3) (Basic Rules); article 36 (New Weapons); article 51 (4(b)–(c) and 5(a)) (indiscriminate attacks); article 54(1) (starvation); article 55(1) (protection of the natural environment); and article 57(2)(a)(ii) (principle of precautions).

[11] The ICRC Commentary on Article 14 of the Protocol Additional to the Geneva Conventions of 12 August 1949, and Relating to the Protection of Victims of Non-International Armed Conflicts (adopted 8 June 1977, entered into force 7 December 1978) 1125 UNTS 609 (APII) specifies that the Conference 'considered inappropriate to refer to warfare in an instrument concerning non-international armed conflicts'. See Yves Sandoz, Chrisophe Swinarski, and Bruno Zimmerman (eds), *Commentary on the Additional Protocols of 8 June 1977 to the Geneva*

API,[12] treaty law also refers to 'methods of combat' instead. Generally, however, states preferred the term 'warfare' to that of 'combat', the latter having been proposed in the original draft text prepared by the International Committee of the Red Cross (ICRC), because they felt 'combat' might be construed more narrowly than 'warfare'.[13] For the purposes of the present analysis, both terms will be used synonymously.

In any event, neither the concept of 'methods of warfare' nor that of 'methods of combat' has been defined in treaty law and there was no attempt to do so in the discussions preceding the adoption of the Additional Protocols to the Geneva Conventions.[14] The Commentaries to the Additional Protocols simply state that while the term 'means' of warfare refers to weapons, the term 'methods' of warfare generally refers to the way in which weapons are used.[15] This distinction between 'means' and 'methods' of warfare is important because any weapon (means)—ie even lawful ones—can be used in an unlawful manner (method), whereas the use of weapons that have been prohibited because of their inherent characteristics is unlawful regardless of the manner in which they are being employed.[16] Nevertheless, the interpretation of the term 'methods of warfare' as proposed in the Commentaries is too restrictive, given that even methods not necessarily involving the use of a weapon, such as starvation,[17] improper use of emblems,[18] perfidy,[19] or denial of quarter[20] are either expressly described as 'methods of warfare' or as a 'method of combat', or are systematically included in Part III, Section I of API on 'Methods and Means of Warfare' (articles 35–42 API).[21]

A partly more convincing interpretation is proposed in the book *How does Law Protect in War?*, where methods of warfare are defined as: '(i) the way and manner in which the weapons are used; (ii) any specific, tactical or strategic, ways of conducting hostilities that are not particularly related to weapons and that are intended to overwhelm and weaken the adversary'.[22] This definition has the merit of highlighting that methods of warfare are more than just the manner in which weapons are used. It is less convincing in that it requires that methods of warfare must be 'intended to overwhelm and weaken the adversary'. This element seems to be overly restrictive, given that any hostile act, irrespective of its magnitude, intensity, or target, can employ a method of warfare subject to restrictions under IHL.

The notion of methods of warfare should be understood more accurately as referring to any particular manner of using weapons or of otherwise conducting hostilities, irrespective

---

*Conventions of 12 August 1949* (ICRC/Martinus Nijhoff 1987) (AP Commentary) para 4799. This point raises the question whether methods of warfare are supposed to be more restrictive in NIACs.

[12]  See API article 51(4)(b) and (c) using the terms 'methods of combat' as an element of the definition of 'indiscriminate attack'.
[13]  AP Commentary on API article 35 para 1401.
[14]  ibid on APII article 14 para 4799.
[15]  ibid on API article 35 para 1402; on API article 51 para 1957.
[16]  Nils Melzer, *International Humanitarian Law—A Comprehensive Introduction* (ICRC 2016) 104.
[17]  API article 54(1) AP and APII article 14.
[18]  ibid articles 38 and 39.
[19]  ibid article 37.
[20]  ibid article 40.
[21]  Not very helpful in this respect is the rather loose use of the term 'weapon' in the AP Commentary, which states that: 'Starvation is referred to here as a method of warfare, ie, a *weapon* to annihilate or weaken the population' (para 2090) or 'Starvation is prohibited as a method of combat, ie, when it is used as a *weapon* to destroy the civilian population' (para 4799)' (emphasis added).
[22]  Marco Sassòli, Antoine Bouvier, and Anee Quintin, *How Does Law Protect in War?* (ICRC 2011) 280.

of permissibility or appropriateness, and ranging from the use of emblems, flags, uniforms, and weapons or other equipment to the choice of targets for attack.

## B. Regulating Methods of Warfare

Methods of warfare are regulated, on the one hand, by general principles applicable to all military operations and, on the other hand, by special provisions governing a number of specific methods of warfare. This section focuses on general principles, more particularly on the principle of distinction and the prohibition of superfluous injury or unnecessary suffering.

The principle (or 'basic rule') of distinction has attained undisputed customary status in both IACs and NIACs.[23] It prohibits not only direct attacks against civilians, but also indiscriminate attacks as a method of warfare. While the prohibition of direct attacks against civilians is fairly straightforward and identical in both IACs and NIACs, the concept of indiscriminate attacks may require some further explanation. In essence, indiscriminate attacks strike military objectives, civilians, and civilian objects without distinction, either because they are not or cannot be directed at a specific military objective, or because their effects cannot be limited as required by IHL.[24]

Particularly devastating examples of indiscriminate attacks were the so-called 'carpet bombing' campaigns of the Second World War, in which entire areas containing both military objectives, civilians, and civilian objects were treated as a single military objective and attacked without distinction.[25] Another example of indiscriminate attacks are those which may be expected to cause incidental harm to civilians or civilian objects that would be excessive in relation to the concrete and direct military advantage anticipated and, therefore, violate the IHL principle of proportionality.[26] While the principle of proportionality is extremely important, its operationalization gives rise to challenging questions. When can incidental civilian damage be considered excessive? How does the value of a human life compare to that of a military objective? Should the safety of a belligerent's own forces be taken into account as part of the military advantage assessment? Should the lives of enemy combatants that are *hors de combat* be taken into account although the rule in API refers to civilians only?

Finally, it should be noted that intentionally attacking civilians or civilian objects, as well as wilfully launching an indiscriminate attack affecting the civilian population or civilian objects knowing that such attack will cause excessive loss of life or injury to civilians, or excessive damage to civilian objects, amounts to a war crime.[27]

The second general principle restricting methods of warfare is the prohibition of superfluous injury or unnecessary suffering. It is one of the rare principles, if not the only one, that protects combatants and other legitimate targets during the conduct of hostilities. Surprisingly, the prohibition of *methods* of warfare that cause superfluous injury

---

[23]  API article 48; CIHL rule 1.
[24]  API article 51 (4) and (5); CIHL rules 11–13.
[25]  Melzer, *Interntional Humanitarian Law* (above n 16) 86.
[26]  API article 51(5)(b).
[27]  ibid article 85(3)(a)–(b); Rome Statute of the International Criminal Court, 17 July 1998 (Rome Statute) article 8(2)(b)(i)(ii)(iv) and 8(2)(e)(i).

or unnecessary suffering was first introduced in API, whereas the 1868 Saint Petersburg Declaration and 1907 Hague Regulations only deal with *means*—but not with *methods*— of warfare causing superfluous injury or unnecessary suffering.[28] The prohibition now belongs to customary law which governs both IACs and NIACs, and the use of such methods is considered as amounting to a war crime in the Rome Statute.[29]

The key issue is to define 'superfluous' and 'unnecessary'.[30] In 1997, the Health Operations Division of the ICRC launched its *SIrUS Project*, which attempted to define what 'unnecessary suffering' means from a medical perspective.[31] According to the resulting study, a specific means or method of warfare should be considered as inflicting superfluous injury or unnecessary suffering if it: (i) would cause a specific disease, a specific abnormal physiological state, a specific abnormal psychological state, a specific and permanent disability, or specific disfigurement; or (ii) would imply a field mortality of more than 25 per cent or hospital mortality of more than 5 per cent; or (iii) would inflict grade 3 wounds as measured by the Red Cross wound classification; or (iv) would cause effects for which there is no well-recognized and proven treatment. However, this proposal failed to gather the support of states and, therefore, remained dead letter. The inevitability of serious permanent disability can nevertheless be regarded as a relevant factor, which was taken into account, most notably, for the prohibition of blinding laser weapons[32] and of antipersonnel landmines.[33]

Although treaty law does not define the meaning of the terms 'unnecessary' and 'superfluous', it can safely be said that the principle requires a balance between considerations of military necessity and of humanity.[34] As a minimum, the rule prohibits the infliction of suffering that has no military purpose.[35] The ICJ, in its Advisory Opinion on *Nuclear Weapons*, considered that inflicting superfluous injury or unnecessary suffering means to cause combatants 'harm greater than that unavoidable to achieve legitimate military objectives'.[36] In this conception of the principle, it is thus not so much the degree of the inflicted suffering that makes a means or method of warfare unlawful, but that the inflicted suffering exceeds the harm that is unavoidable—ie necessary—to achieve a legitimate military objective.[37]

---

[28]  CIHL commentary on rule 70.

[29]  Rome Statute article 8 (2)(b)(xx).

[30]  The St Petersburg Declaration also mentions arms rendering death inevitable, although this wording has unfortunately not been adopted by other IHL treaties. It is submitted that methods of warfare rendering death inevitable are equally prohibited.

[31]  Robin M Coupland (ed), *The SIrUS Project, Towards a Determination of Which Weapons Cause 'Superfluous Injury or Unnecessary Suffering'* (ICRC 1997).

[32]  Protocol (IV) on Blinding Laser Weapons (adopted 13 October 1995, entered into force 30 July 1998) 1380 UNTS 370 (CCW Protocol IV).

[33]  Convention on the Prohibition of the Use, Stockpiling, Production and Transfer of Anti-Personnel Mines and on their Destruction (18 September 1997) (so-called Ottawa Convention). See CIHL commentary on rule 70 and 86.

[34]  Melzer, *International Humanitarian Law* (above n 16) 110.

[35]  CIHL commentary on rule 70.

[36]  *Nuclear Weapons* para 78.

[37]  cf. in the context of the *Nuclear Weapons* Advisory Opinion requested by the WHO before the ICJ, see the letter dated 19 June 1995 from the Honorary Consul of Solomon Islands in London, together with written comments of the Government of Solomon Islands, para 4.6:

> The use of nuclear weapons necessarily causes 'superfluous injury' to its victims. ( ... ) Proponents of the legality of the use of nuclear weapons ( ... ) suggest that there is no unnecessary suffering where there exists a reasonable link between the military advantage gained and the damage caused to the enemy. (See eg United Kingdom ( ... ), Netherlands ( ... ), United States ( ... )). This approach disregards fundamental principles of humanitarian law. ( ... ) The concept of 'unnecessary suffering' does not depend on what a particular army judges to be good or bad in terms of military advantage, but on

When making this assessment, the availability of alternative—less harmful—means and methods of warfare must therefore be taken into account.[38]

However, as an argument for absolutely outlawing means and methods of warfare that may well be capable of delivering military advantage and even victory—such as poison, blinding laser weapons, and chemical weapons—the prohibition of unnecessary suffering and superfluous injury reflects not only considerations of military necessity, but also those of proportionality with respect to the harm inflicted on enemy combatants.[39] Thus, the fact that article 51(5)(b) of API focuses on the protection of the civilian population and does not consider the harm inflicted on able-bodied combatants does not mean that this particular provision exhaustively expresses all considerations of proportionality made in IHL governing the conduct of hostilities. Rather, these provisions of IHL (ie prohibition of unnecessary suffering and superfluous injury and the prohibition of disproportionate attacks) point towards an understanding of proportionality as a general principle of law that governs all resort to force and all causation of harm in any circumstances, including the harm inflicted on able-bodied enemy combatants during hostile conduct.

Based on the prohibition of superfluous injury or unnecessary suffering, certain weapons (ie *means of warfare*) have been prohibited, such as blinding laser weapons, expanding bullets, and weapons that injure by means of non-detectable fragments.[40] Even fewer examples come to mind concerning *methods of warfare* that cause superfluous injury or unnecessary suffering.[41] The denial of quarter is one of the few methods of warfare that indisputably inflicts unnecessary suffering because it excludes the possibility of weakening enemy forces by merely capturing or injuring—rather than killing—its combatants. Arguably, the denial or quarter was also applied to the scores of Iraqi soldiers needlessly being buried alive in their trenches by US forces in the early hours of the allied ground attack that ended the First Persian Gulf war.[42]

Although the principle of distinction and the prohibition of superfluous injury/unnecessary suffering are well established, it remains controversial whether or not they can directly prohibit specific means and methods of warfare without a more specific treaty provision or customary rule.[43] The predominant and more convincing view, which was also expressed by the ICJ in its *Nuclear Weapons* Advisory Opinion,[44] is that the prohibitions

---

an objective determination of the victims' injury. It is their suffering which is at issue, not the interest of obtaining military advantage.

[38] CIHL commentary on rule 70 and related practice. See, in particular, US, *Air Force Pamphlet* (1976) para 6-3(b)(1) and (2). See also UK, written statement submitted to the ICJ, *Nuclear Weapons* Advisory Opinion (16 June 1995) 50 para 3.64.

[39] See, for instance, in this sense: US, *Air Force Pamphlet* (1976), para 6-3(b)(1) and (2): 'This prohibition against unnecessary suffering is a concrete expression of the general principles of proportionality and humanity.'

[40] Melzer, *International Humanitarian Law* (above n 16) 110. For additional examples, see CIHL commentary on rule 70.

[41] See CIHL commentary on rule 70, which states that 'States articulating [the prohibition of methods of warfare that cause superfluous injury or unnecessary suffering] do not give any examples of methods of warfare that would be prohibited by virtue of this rule.'

[42] Robert Kolb, *Ius in bello: Le droit international des conflits armés, Précis* (Helbing and Lichtenhahn 2003) 139, para 311. For a newspaper article on this attack, see Eric Schmitt, 'U.S. Army Burried Iraki Soldiers Alive in Gulf War' *New York Times* (New York, 15 September 1991).

[43] For instance, France and Russia held in the context of the *Nuclear Weapons* Advisory Opinion before the ICJ that a weapon can be prohibited by virtue of one or the other of the said cardinal principles only if states prohibit the weapon by a treaty. See: Russian Federation, written statement submitted to the ICJ, *Nuclear Weapons* Advisory Opinion (19 June 1995) 12; French Republic, written statement submitted to the *Nuclear Weapons* Advisory Opinion (19 June 1995) 42.

[44] *Nuclear Weapons* para 95.

of indiscriminate attacks and of the means and methods causing superfluous injury or unnecessary suffering constitute generic and legally binding standards by which all means and methods of warfare have to be measured, even in the absence of specific treaty provisions or recognized customary rules relevant to the particular means or method in question.[45] In essence, therefore, the fact that a specific method of warfare is not prohibited or restricted by a specific treaty provision does not necessarily mean that this method is lawful. This conclusion receives further support in the longstanding customary principle expressed in the Martens Clause, according to which, where treaty law fails to provide a specific rule, 'both civilians and combatants remain under the protection and authority of the principles of international law derived from established custom, from the principles of humanity and from the dictates of public conscience'.[46]

A final general issue is whether there are any differences in the regulation of methods of warfare, which depend on whether the conflict is of international or non-international character. There are only a few treaty provisions applicable in NIACs that expressly address methods of warfare. While Common Article 3 focuses on the protection of persons *hors de combat*, it allows more specific conclusions as to the permissibility of methods of warfare, albeit only by implication. APII merely recognizes the duty to protect the civilian population against the dangers arising from military operations and prohibits a number of specifically mentioned methods of warfare such as starvation,[47] the denial of quarter,[48] and the recruitment of children into armed forces,[49] as well as deportations.[50] However, neither does the treaty contain a general prohibition on means and methods of warfare that are of a nature to cause superfluous injury or unnecessary suffering.

This omission should not be understood as an intended 'gap' in legal protection but, at least in the case of APII, as an incidental result of significant text cuts carried out on the original draft during the very late hours of negotiations, with the declared aim of producing a simplified text acceptable to states.[51] As 'cardinal principles' of customary international law, the principle of distinction, the prohibition of unnecessary suffering and superfluous injury, and the Martens Clause govern the lawfulness of methods of warfare in any armed conflict, including those of a non-international nature.[52] The Appeals Chamber of the International Criminal Tribunal for the former Yugoslavia (ICTY) asserted in the *Tadić* case that:

> [e]lementary considerations of humanity and common sense make it preposterous that the use by states of weapons prohibited in armed conflicts between themselves be allowed

---

[45] Melzer, *International Humanitarian Law* (above n 16) 110–11; Kolb (above n 42) 138–9, para 308; Sassòli et al (above n 22) 33–4; CIHL commentary on rules 70 and 71.

[46] API article 1(2). See also the preamble of APII for a shorter version of the Martens Clause and the preamble of the *Convention on Prohibitions or Restrictions on the Use of Certain Conventional Weapons Which May be Deemed to be Excessively Injurious or to Have Indiscriminate Effects,* Geneva (10 October 1980). For previous versions of the Martens Clause, see: Convention (II) with Respect to the Laws and Customs of War on Land (adopted 29 July 1899, entered into force 4 September 1900) 187 CTS 429 (Hague Convention II) preamble (§9); Convention (IV) Respecting the Laws and Customs of War on Land and Its Annex: Regulation concerning the Laws and Customs of War on Land (adopted 18 October 1907, entered into force 26 January 1910) 205 CTS 227 preamble (para 8); the four Geneva Conventions 1949 articles 63, 62, 142, and 158 respectively.

[47] APII article 14.

[48] ibid article 4(1).

[49] ibid article 4(3)(c).

[50] ibid article 17.

[51] CIHL commentary on rule 70.

[52] APII, preamble; CIHL rules 70 and 71.

when states try to put down rebellion by their own nationals on their own territory. What is inhumane, and consequently proscribed, in international wars cannot but be inhumane and inadmissible in civil strife.[53]

The same must hold true, mutatis *mutandis*, with respect to methods of warfare.

Indeed, methods of warfare that are prohibited in IACs based on legal principles expressing basic humanitarian considerations can be presumed to be equally prohibited in NIACs.

## 3. Methods of Warfare that Concern Primarily the Protection of Combatants

This section deals with prohibited/restricted methods of warfare which are primarily concerned with the protection of combatants; and more specifically, (i) the protection of persons *hors de combat*; (ii) the prohibition of denial of quarter; and (iii) the restriction of deception. Unless otherwise specified, the arguments made and the conclusions reached equally concern both IACs and NIACs. In the latter context, therefore, the term 'combatant' will be used in its functional sense, and as covering not only members of the armed forces of a belligerent state, but also members of organized non-state armed groups with a continuous combat function.[54]

### A.  Protection of Persons *hors de combat*

The protection of persons *hors de combat* against direct attack and abuse of power is a well-established rule of customary and treaty IHL.[55] The prohibition of direct attack against those *hors de combat* is explicitly recognized in both the 1907 Hague Regulations and in API.[56] Regarding NIACs, it is expressly recognized in article 3 common to the Geneva Conventions, which protects those taking no active part in the hostilities, including those placed '*hors de combat*', against violence to life and person and other forms of abuse. It has also been codified in article 4 of APII, albeit in slightly different words.[57] The prohibition is considered to constitute a customary rule applicable in both IACs and NIACs.[58] Wilfully making a person the object of attack in the knowledge that he or she is *hors de combat*, thus causing his or her death or serious injury to body or health, is a war crime.[59]

---

[53] *Prosecutor v Dusko Tadić a/k/a 'Dule'* (Decision on the Defence Motion for interlocutory Appeal on Jurisdiction, Appeals Chamber) IT-94-1-AR72 (2 October 1995) para 119.

[54] Nils Melzer, *Interpretive Guidance on the Notion of Direct Participation in Hostilities under International Humanitarian Law*, ICRCH DPH Guidance (ICRC 2009) 27.

[55] *Instructions for the Government of Armies of the United States in the Field*, General Orders No 100 (24 April 1863) (*Lieber Code*) article 71; *Project of an International Declaration concerning the Laws and Customs of War* (27 August 1874) (Brussels Declaration) article 13(c); Institute of International Law, *The Laws of War on Land* (Institute of International Law 9 September 1880) (*Oxford Manual*) article 9 (b).

[56] Hague Regulations article 23(c); API article 41(1).

[57] See in this sense CIHL commentary on rule 47.

[58] CIHL rule 47.

[59] See API article 85(3)(e). See also Rome Statute article 8 (2)(b)(vi). These provisions deal with IAs. It is submitted that it should also be considered a crime in NIACs.

The *ratio legis* for the protection of persons *hors de combat* is that persons *hors de combat* no longer pose a military threat and that, therefore, hostile acts against them could not be justified based on any reasonable balance between considerations of military necessity and humanity. Accurately understood, the reason for the protection granted by IHL is not that the killing of persons *hors de combat* could never offer a military advantage, but rather that absent of any hostile act on the part of those *hors de combat*, their killing would be regarded as inhumane or, more precisely, disproportionately harmful compared to the potential military benefit. Just like the prohibition on unnecessary suffering and superfluous injury, and probably at least in part a concretization of that rule, the *hors de combat* protection is based on generic considerations of necessity and proportionality. Arguably, the protection of those *hors de combat* could also be derived from a broad understanding of the principle of distinction as offering protection against attacks not only to civilians but also to combatants *hors de combat*.

A person is *hors de combat* if he or she is in the power of an adverse party, clearly expresses an intention to surrender, or is incapable of defending him- or herself because of unconsciousness, shipwreck, wounds, or sickness, and, in all those cases, abstains from any hostile act and does not attempt to escape.[60]

Persons are 'in the power' of a belligerent party not only when they are captured, but also when they are otherwise within the effective physical or material control of that party.[61] The ICRC Commentaries even argue that, in the context of an air strike, combatants might be 'in the power of' the air force operators if at some point they are at their mercy and thus defenceless.[62] A less extreme and, arguably, more convincing argument against attacking defenceless enemy forces that are unable to surrender could be made based on the absence of military necessity in conjunction with the imperatives of humanity.[63]

Persons can express their intention to surrender in various ways, depending on the circumstances. In land warfare, persons may commonly surrender by laying down their arms and by raising their hands or a white flag.[64] Regarding persons parachuting from aircraft in distress, attacks are prohibited for the duration of their descent.[65] Upon reaching the ground in territory controlled by an adverse party, they have to be given an opportunity to surrender before being attacked, unless it is apparent that they are engaging in a hostile act.[66] This protection does not apply to airborne troops, whose descent constitutes part of their hostile operations.[67]

What happens if a wounded or surrendering soldier on the battlefield resumes fighting or tries to escape? According to the ICRC Commentaries, force can be used against such a soldier but only as a last resort and after a warning appropriate in the circumstances.[68] The legal

[60] API article 41(1) and (2); CIHL rule 47.
[61] AP Commentary paras 1611–1617.
[62] ibid para 1612.
[63] See also, most notably, Melzer, *Interpretive Guidance* (above n 54) section IX, 77–82.
[64] AP Commentary paras 1618–1619. See also CIHL commentary on rule 47.
[65] API article 42(1); CIHL rule 48.
[66] ibid article 42(2).
[67] ibid article 42(3).
[68] AP Commentary on API article 41 para 1613:

> From the moment that combatants have fallen 'into the hands' of the adversary, the applicability of the Third Convention can no longer be contested. They are prisoners of war and should never be maltreated, but should always be treated humanely. If they make an attempt to escape or commit any

reasoning leading to such an assertion is far from clear, however. Article 41 of the API does not seem to support these restrictions. It merely states that a person enjoys the protection of persons *hors de combat* provided that he/she abstains from any hostile act and does not attempt to escape. This would logically mean that the protection of persons *hors de combat* ceases as soon as they commit a hostile act or attempt to escape, and therefore, they become subject to direct attacks under the hostilities paradigm.[69] On the one hand, it seems clear that once a person *hors de combat* has been taken into custody, any force used in response to a hostile act or attempted escape must be absolutely necessary to prevent said act or escape and strictly proportionate to the danger resulting from such action. Accordingly, the Third Geneva Convention provides that the 'use of weapons against prisoners of war (POWs), especially against those who are escaping or attempting to escape, shall constitute an extreme measure, which shall always be preceded by warnings appropriate to the circumstances'.[70] On the other hand, persons who are prima facie *hors de combat*, but who attempt an escape or engage in hostile acts *before* being taken into custody can hardly benefit from a restricted use of force regime comparable to that applicable to POWs. In such a situation, engaging in hostile acts would generally amount to feigning surrender or other protected status with the intent of attacking the enemy by surprise. Both variants would amount to prohibited combat by resort to perfidy and would not justify any restriction of the normal targeting regime.

When enemies have been captured 'under unusual conditions of combat which prevent their evacuation', API expressly requires that 'they shall be released and all feasible precautions shall be taken to ensure their safety'.[71] Thus, if enemy combatants indicate an intention to surrender or otherwise become *hors de combat*, they must be captured or, if their evacuation is not possible, released. Although this rule might seem difficult to comply with, in particular in the context of small-scale operations in enemy territory, treaty law makes it unequivocally clear that, even in unusual combat conditions, *hors de combat* protection remains absolute and non-derogable.[72]

## B.  Prohibition of Denial of Quarter

Another longstanding rule that is related to the protection of persons *hors de combat* is the prohibition of denial of quarter.[73] It is explicitly recognized in the 1907 Hague Regulations and in API (IACs),[74] as well as in article 4 of APII (NIACs).[75] Moreover, this rule is considered customary law[76] and its violation amounts to a war

---

hostile act, the use of arms against them is once more permitted within the conditions prescribed in the Third Convention. The same applies a fortiori for adversaries who benefit only from the safeguard of Article 41 without being recognized as prisoners of war. In fact, the proviso at the end of the present paragraph specifically provides it.

[69]  Melzer, *International Humanitarian Law* (above n 16)106.
[70]  Geneva Convention (III) Relative to the Treatment of Prisoners of War (adopted 12 August 1949, entered into force 21 October 1950) 75 UNTS 135 (GCIII) article 42. See also AP Commentary para 1613 and n 17.
[71]  API article 41 (3).
[72]  Melzer, *International Humanitarian Law* (above n 16) 107.
[73]  *Lieber Code* article 60; Brussels Declaration article 13(d); *Oxford Manual* article 9(b).
[74]  Hague Regulations article 23(d); API article 40.
[75]  APII article 4(1).
[76]  CHIL rule 46.

crime[77] in both IACs and NIACs. The *ratio legis* for the prohibition of denial of quarter is comparable to that of the *hors de combat* protection, albeit without any aspects of the principle of distinction. As stated in section 2 'Defining and Regulating Methods of Warfare' above, it is a derivate of the prohibition of superfluous injury or unnecessary suffering and a codified expression of the maxim that the purpose of military hostilities in warfare is not to kill combatants but to defeat the enemy, even if this requires the killing of combatants.[78] The prohibition of denial of quarter, too, balances the potential military advantage of leaving no survivors against the requirements of humanity and, deciding in favour of the latter, expresses generic considerations not only of military necessity but also of proportionality.

According to the rule, '[i]t is prohibited to order that there shall be no survivors, to threaten an adversary therewith or to conduct hostilities on this basis'.[79] The prohibition of denial of quarter also makes it illegal to deliberately refuse or render impossible an enemy's surrender or to put to death those who are *hors de combat*.

Given that persons *hors de combat* are already protected, the added value of the prohibition of denial of quarter lies in: (i) the prohibition of threatening or ordering that there shall be no survivors; and (ii) the restraints this imposes on hostile conduct, namely in the prohibition of hostile conduct on the basis that there shall be no survivors.[80]

The prohibition of threatening or ordering that there shall be no survivors primarily concerns military commanders, given that they are in a position to issue such threats or orders.[81] It is rare in international law that the mere threat of committing a violation is prohibited in itself, the other two examples being the prohibition of 'the threat or use of force in international relations'[82] and the IHL prohibition to threaten to attack the civilian population with the primary purpose of spreading terror.[83] The most likely rationale for outlawing the mere threat of a prohibited conduct is to avoid the escalatory effect of such threats. Thus, threatening the enemy with a general refusal to accept his surrender could potentially incite the threatened opponent to discard the principles of IHL and to resort to any lawful or unlawful means or method of warfare to overcome his enemy.

The prohibition of conducting hostilities on the basis that there shall be no survivors essentially requires that an adversary endeavouring to surrender must be given the opportunity to do so as circumstances reasonably permit.[84] On the one hand, therefore, methods calculated to completely exterminate opposing forces would be in breach of this rule.[85] Surprise attacks or employing means and methods of warfare that are incapable of taking prisoners, on the other hand, do not necessarily amount to denial of quarter. In air warfare, for instance, it may not always be feasible to accept surrender. Nevertheless, a policy or practice of conducting 'follow-up strikes' or 'double strikes'—ie 'attacks that occur after

---

[77] Rome Statute article 8(2)(b)(xii) (for IACs) and Rome Statute article 8(2)(e)(x) (for NIACs).

[78] See also the St Petersburg Declaration, which prohibited the use of explosive projectiles, which 'uselessly aggravate the sufferings of disabled men, or render their death inevitable'.

[79] API article 40. See also Hague Regulations article 23(d) and CIHL rule 46.

[80] AP Commentary para 1598. Article 23(c) of the Hague Regulations prohibits the killing and wounding of a combatant *hors de combat* separately from the denial of quarter.

[81] CIHL commentary on rule 46.

[82] Charter of the United Nations (26 June 1945) article 2(4).

[83] API article 51(2).

[84] Melzer, *International Humanitarian Law* (above n 16) 107.

[85] ibid.

a first one and that may intentionally or incidentally kill wounded persons as well as rescuers'[86]—would be unlawful both under the prohibition of killing persons *hors de combat*
and other protected persons and under the prohibited method of denial of quarter. It is
also unclear whether conducting warfare exclusively through means and methods of warfare that are incapable of taking prisoners—for example, drone strikes—would be permissible under the prohibition of conducting hostilities on the basis that there shall be no
survivors.

## C. Deception

### 1. The prohibition of perfidy or treachery

The Hague Regulations of 1907 already prohibited to 'kill or wound treacherously individuals belonging to the hostile nation or army'.[87] API broadens this rule by prohibiting the
use of perfidy to kill, injure, or capture an adversary.[88] Although Common Article 3 to the
Geneva Conventions and APII do not contain a similar provision, the prohibition of perfidious killing, injury, and capture is considered customary IHL in both IACs and NIACs.[89]
Under the ICC Statute, 'killing or wounding treacherously' an adversary—but not perfidious capture—constitutes a war crime in both IACs and NIACs.[90]

According to the rule, perfidy denotes 'acts inviting the confidence of an adversary to
lead him to believe that he is entitled to, or is obliged to accord, protection under the rules
of international law applicable in armed conflict, with intent to betray that confidence'.[91]
Relevant examples would include the feigning: (i) of surrender; (ii) of an intent to negotiate under a flag of truce; (iii) of incapacitation by wounds or sickness; (iv) of civilian,
non-combatant status; and (v) of protected status by the use of the signs, emblems, or
uniforms of the United Nations, of neutral or other non-belligerent states, or of the protective emblem of the red cross, red crescent, or red crystal. It should be noted that IHL
does not prohibit perfidy per se, but only the killing, injuring, or capturing of an adversary by resort to perfidy. The resort to perfidy for other purposes, such as intelligence
gathering or sabotage, is not covered by the prohibition of perfidy, but may be subject to
other restrictions, such as the prohibition on misuse of emblems, signs, and uniforms.[92]
Moreover, the prohibition of perfidy does not prohibit ruses of war, ie 'acts which are intended to mislead an adversary or to induce him to act recklessly but which infringe no

---

[86] 'Double strikes' or 'follow-up strikes' are 'attacks that occur after a first one and that may intentionally or incidentally kill wounded persons as well as rescuers': Raymond Ouigou Savadogo and Julia Grignon, 'Attacks against
Wounded, Sick, Shipwrecked and Medical Personnel, as Well as the Challenges Posed by 'Follow Up Strikes',
in Stephane Kolanowski (ed.), *Proc Bruges Coll, Vulnerabilities in Armed Conflicts: Selected Issues*, 14th Bruges
Colloquium, 17–18 October 2013, No 44, Autumn 2014, 12.
[87] Hague Regulations article 23(b). For earlier prohibitions, see *Lieber Code* article 101; Brussels Declaration
article 13 (b); *Oxford Manual* article 8(b).
[88] API article 37.
[89] CIHL rule 65.
[90] Rome Statute article 8(2)(b)(xi) (for IACs); Rome Statute, article 8(2)(e)(ix) (for NIACs). See also API article
85(3)(f).
[91] API article 37.
[92] See below, section 3.C.2 'Misuse of emblems, signs, and uniforms'.

rule of international law applicable in armed conflict and which are not perfidious because they do not invite the confidence of an adversary with respect to protection under that law'.[93] Examples of permissible ruses include the use of camouflage, decoys, mock operations, and misinformation.[94] Mere intelligence gathering by undercover units disguised as civilians also does not amount to prohibited perfidy.[95] If captured, such personnel would lose their POW status and, therefore, could be prosecuted as spies under the domestic legislation of the capturing state.

Thus, the *ratio legis* of the prohibition of perfidy or treachery is to safeguard the good faith of the belligerents as far as it concerns their duty to afford, or their own entitlement to, protection under IHL. Indeed, any uncertainty on the part of belligerents as to the reliability and truthfulness of behaviour or circumstances affording civilians or opposing combatants protection under IHL would seriously jeopardize their respect for the principle of distinction.

## 2. Misuse of emblems, signs, and uniforms

IHL not only prohibits the use of perfidy to kill, injure, or capture an adversary, but also more generally the misuse of recognized distinctive emblems and emblems of nationality. In particular, it is prohibited to make improper use of emblems, signs, or signals provided for in IHL, such as the distinctive emblem of the red cross, red crescent, or red crystal, or to deliberately misuse other internationally recognized protective emblems, signs, or signals, including the flag of truce, the protective emblem of cultural property (downward-pointed square blue shield on white ground), the distinctive signs of civil defence (orange triangle on blue ground), installations containing dangerous forces (three orange circles), and the distinctive emblem of the United Nations.[96] IHL also prohibits the use of the flags or military emblems, insignia, or uniforms of neutral or non-belligerent states in an armed conflict, whereas those of adverse parties can be used as a ruse of war, except during direct hostile contact with the enemy, namely while engaging in attacks or in order to shield, favour, protect, or impede military operations.[97] Under the ICC Statute, 'Making improper use of a flag of truce, of the flag or of the military insignia and uniform of the enemy or of the United Nations, as well as of the distinctive emblems of the Geneva Conventions' amounts to a war crime in IACs when it results in death or serious personal injury.[98]

A well-known example of a violation of this prohibition was the use of the Red Cross emblem by a Colombian military intelligence team in a hostage rescue mission that freed fifteen hostages from the hands of the Revolutionary Armed Forces of Colombia (FARC) rebels in July 2008.[99] This misuse was subsequently condemned by the ICRC.[100]

---

[93]  API article 37.
[94]  ibid. See also CIHL rule 57.
[95]  Melzer, *International Humanitarian Law* (above n 16) 109.
[96]  API article 38; APII article 12; CIHL rules 59–61.
[97]  API article 39; CIHL rules 62 and 63.
[98]  Rome Statute article 8(2)(b)(vii).
[99]  Karl Penhaul, 'Uribe: Betancourt Rescuers Used Red Cross', *CNN* (16 July 2008) http://edition.cnn.com/2008/WORLD/americas/07/16/colombia.cross/index.html.
[100]  ibid.

## 4. Methods of Warfare Primarily Affecting the Civilian Population and Civilian Objects

Prohibited methods of warfare are numerous. Many of them have been discussed in other chapters of this book and do not need to be elaborated on here.[101] This section focuses on three methods of warfare giving rise to particularly thorny legal issues: starvation, reprisals, and destruction and seizure of property.

### A.  Starvation

Modern IHL prohibits the starvation of civilians as a method of warfare, ie deliberately depriving [them] of food.[102] Derived from the principle of distinction, this rule appears for the first time in both Additional Protocols of 1977[103] and, today, is considered customary law in both IACs and NIACs.[104] The Rome Statute provides that 'intentionally using starvation of civilians as a method of warfare' is a war crime in IACs.[105] Under domestic criminal law, individuals have also been convicted for the crime of starvation in the context of NIACs.[106]

A corollary to the prohibition of starvation of civilians, IHL also prohibits the attack, destruction, removal, or rendering of useless objects indispensable to the survival of the civilian population (eg foodstuffs, agricultural areas, crops, livestock, drinking water, and irrigation systems) for the specific purpose of denying them for their sustenance value to the civilian population or to the adverse party, whether in order to starve out civilians, to cause them to move away, or for any other motive.[107] These prohibitions do not apply when the objects in question are used as sustenance solely for the opposing armed forces, or otherwise in direct support of military action, unless action taken against them may be expected to starve the civilian population or force its movement.[108] Arbitrarily denying humanitarian access in favour of civilians in need, or arbitrarily restricting the freedom of movement of humanitarian relief personnel will also constitute violations of the prohibition of starvation.[109]

Although sieges, naval blockades, and embargoes have been condemned by the international community,[110] they are not prohibited, even if they cause starvation, as long as the

---

[101] The prohibition of direct attacks against civilians and civilian objects, the prohibition of indiscriminate attacks, and the prohibition of human shields are dealt with in chapter 7 'International Humanitarian Law and the Conduct of Hostilities'. The prohibition of methods causing widespread, long-term, and severe damage to, or involving the hostile manipulation of, the natural environment is dealt with in chapter 9 'Protection of the Natural Environment'. The prohibition of acts or threats of violence with the primary purpose of spreading terror among civilians as well as hostage taking is dealt with in chapter 17 'International Humanitarian Law and International Human Rights Law'.

[102] See generally, Dapo Akande and Emanuela-Chiara Gillard, 'Conflict-induced Food Insecurity and the War Crime of Starvation of Civilians as a Method of Warfare: The Underlying Rules of International Humanitarian Law' (2019) 17 JICJ 753.

[103] API article 54(1); APII article 14.

[104] CIHL rule 53.

[105] Rome Statute article 8(2)(b)(xxv).

[106] See eg Croatia, District Court of Zadar, *Perišić and others* (Judgment) (24 April 1997).

[107] API article 54 (2); CIHL rule 54.

[108] API article 54 (3).

[109] See CIHL rules 55 and 56. On access to humanitarian relief, see also chapter 13 'Occupation' in this book.

[110] See eg UN General Assembly Resolutions 48/88 (1993), 49/10 (1994), and 49/196 (1994); UN Commission on Human Rights Resolutions 1994/74 (1994) para 9 and 1995/76 (1995) para 10.

purpose is to achieve a military objective and not to starve the civilian population.[111] At the same time, the prohibition of starvation implies that the besieging party must either allow the inhabitants to leave the besieged area or permit the free passage of humanitarian relief supplies.[112]

For example, in the context of the Gaza blockade, which led to harsh humanitarian consequences and 'food insecurity', the issue of starvation has been discussed by several commissions of inquiry. Although these discussions did not reach the same conclusions regarding the lawfulness of the blockade (in terms of proportionality and on whether it amounted to collective punishment), none concluded that the blockade amounted to a violation of the prohibition of starvation as a method of warfare.[113] The reason for this was that the starvation of the civilian population was not the 'sole'[114] and not even the 'main' purpose[115] of the blockade. This does not, however, relieve the blockading party from their obligation to take into account, when assessing the proportionality of incidental harm, any starvation which may be expected to result as an unwanted consequence resulting from the blockade.[116]

## B. Reprisals

Belligerent reprisals are forcible countermeasures. They cover any 'action that would otherwise be unlawful but that in exceptional cases is considered lawful under international law when used as an enforcement measure in reaction to unlawful acts of an adversary'.[117] Traditionally, reprisals were regarded as a method of enforcement of IHL.[118] Modern IHL, however, prohibits many types of reprisals without outlawing them altogether.

More specifically, the 1949 Geneva Conventions prohibit reprisals against protected persons and objects in the power of the enemy. Thus, reprisals are prohibited against the

---

[111] See CIHL commentary on rule 53. See also France: Ministère de la Défense, *Manuel de Droit des Conflits Armés*, Direction des affaires juridiques, Sous-direction du droit international humanitaire et du droit européen (Bureau du droit des conflits armés 2001) 33; New Zealand: New Zealand Defence Forces, *Interim Law of Armed Conflict Manual*, DM 112 (New Zealand Defence Forces 1992) para 504(2) n 9; Louise Doswald-Beck (ed), *San Remo Manual on International Law Applicable to Armed Conflicts at Sea* (CUP 1995) (adopted 1994, reproduced 1995) No 309 IRRC 583 (*San Remo Manual*) para 102(a).

[112] CIHL commentary on rules 53 and 55. See also Israel: Military Advocate, *Laws of War in the Battlefield: Manual on the Laws of War* (Military Advocate General Headquarters 1998) 59: the prohibition of starvation 'clearly implies that the city's inhabitants must be allowed to leave the city during a siege'.

[113] See notably Human Rights Council, *Report of the International Fact-Finding Mission to Investigate Violations of International Law, Including International Humanitarian and Human Rights Law, Resulting from the Israeli Attacks on the Flotilla of Ships Carrying Humanitarian Assistance*, UN Doc A/HRC/15/21 (27 September 2010) (it found that the blockade was not proportionate and constituted collective punishment); *Report of the Secretary-General's Panel of Inquiry on the 31 May 2010 Flotilla Incident* (July 2011) (UN Appointed Palmer Commission) (it found that the blockade was lawful). *The Public Commission Appointed to Examine the Maritime Incident of 31 May 2010*, Part One (January 2011) (Turkel Commission's Report) (it found that the blockade was lawful).

[114] See *San Remo Manual* para 102(a), which is often considered as restating customary law.

[115] See >Humanitarian Policy and Conflict Research at Harvard University (HPCR), 'The Commentary on the Humanitarian Policy and Conflict Research (HPCR) Manual on International Law Applicable to Air and Missile Warfare' (March 2010) 296 article 157(a) http://ihlresearch.org/amw/Commentary%20on%20the%20HPCR%20 Manual.pdf. This Manual proposed amending the wording of article 102(a) of the *San Remo Manual* in order to prohibit the imposition of a naval blockade not only if starvation of the civilian population is its 'sole' but also its 'main' purpose.

[116] In this sense, Turkel Commission's Report para 75.

[117] CIHL commentary on rule 145.

[118] See eg Emerich de Vattel, *The Law of Nations, or the Principles of Natural Law* (1797) para 342 http://files.libertyfund.org/files/2246/Vattel_1519_LFeBk.pdf.

wounded, sick, and shipwrecked, POWs and civilians,[119] as well as against the property of civilians in the hands of an adverse party to the conflict or an occupying power[120] and against medical objects.[121]

API further prohibits attacks in reprisals directed against civilians,[122] civilian objects,[123] historic monuments, works of art or places of worship that constitute the cultural or spiritual heritage of peoples,[124] against objects indispensable to the survival of the civilian population,[125] against the natural environment,[126] and against works and installations containing dangerous forces, namely dams, dykes, and nuclear electrical generating stations.[127] Cultural property 'of great importance to the cultural heritage of a people' is also protected against 'any act directed by way of reprisals' in the Hague Convention for the Protection of Cultural Property.[128]

As these provisions make clear, reprisals against military objectives (be they persons or objects) are not prohibited. To be lawful, however, they must fulfil a number of conditions:[129] They must:

(1) respond to a prior serious of IHL violations (no 'anticipatory/preventive' reprisal);
(2) aim to induce the adversary to stop such violations (no punishment or revenge);
(3) be carried out as a last resort, when no more lawful measures are available and after prior warning has been given;
(4) be proportionate to the prior violation;
(5) be authorized at the highest political or military level;
(6) be terminated as soon as the adversary complies with the law.

This means, for example, that a belligerent victim of an IHL violation (eg the enemy uses chemical weapons), might decide, as a last resort, to use the same prohibited weapons against enemy soldiers in a proportionate way. Although this is disturbing from a humanitarian perspective, this is the current state of the law.

Surprisingly, in the case of the prohibition of reprisals, treaty and customary law do not necessarily match. While it is uncontroversial that the prohibition of reprisals against protected persons and objects in enemy's hands (Geneva Law) is

---

[119] Geneval Convention (I) for the Amelioration of the Condition of the Wounded and Sick in Armed Forces in the Field (adopted 12 August 1949, entered into force 21 October 1950) 75 UNTS 31 (GCI) article 46; General Convention (II) for the Amelioration of the Condition of Wounded, Sick and Shipwrecked Members of Armed Forces at Sea (adopted 12 August 1949, entered into force 12 October 1949) 75 UNTS 85 (GCII) article 47; GCIII article 13(3); Geneva Convention (IV) Relative to the Protection of Civilian Persons in Time of War (12 August 1949, entered into force 21 October 1950) 75 UNTS 287 (GCIV) article 33.
[120] GCIV article 33.
[121] GCI article 46; GC II art 47.
[122] API article 51(6).
[123] ibid article 52.
[124] ibid article 53.
[125] ibid article 54.
[126] ibid article 55.
[127] ibid article 56.
[128] Convention for the Protection of Cultural Property in the Event of Armed Conflict (adopted 14 May 1954, entered into force 7 August 1956) 249 UNTS 240 (1954 Convention) article 4 (4).
[129] CIHL commentary on rule 145 (and further references therein). For relevant jurisprudence, see eg Special Arbitral Tribunal, *Naulilaa* case (Decision) (31 July 1928) 1026–7; *Nuclear Weapons* para 46; *Kupreškić* case (ICTY Judgment) (14 January 2000), para 535; *Martić* case (ICTY Trial Judgment) (2007) paras 465–467.

customary,[130] the same is not true for reprisals against persons and objects in the conduct of hostilities (Hague Law).[131]

The rule prohibiting reprisals against civilians in API was regarded as a novelty when it was adopted and several states made reservations to it.[132] State practice has substantially evolved since then,[133] although rarely states maintain that reprisals against civilians in the conduct of hostilities might be lawful in exceptional circumstances.[134] According to the ICRC Customary IHL Study:

> [I]t is difficult to conclude that there has yet crystallized a customary rule specifically prohibiting reprisals against civilians during the conduct of hostilities. Nevertheless, it is also difficult to assert that a right to resort to such reprisals continues to exist on the strength of the practice of only a limited number of states, some of which is also ambiguous. Hence, there appears, at a minimum, to exist a trend in favour of prohibiting such reprisals.[135]

This very cautious approach contradicted earlier ICTY jurisprudence. In its review of the indictment in the *Martić* case in 1996 and in its judgment in the *Kupreškić* case in 2000, the ICTY found that customary law prohibits reprisals against civilians in combat situations in all types of armed conflicts.[136] It invoked several arguments, some of which were more convincing than others. It first referred to IHL provisions prohibiting reprisals. While assuming that articles 51 (paragraph 6) and 52 (paragraph 1) of API were not declaratory of customary law, it contended that they have subsequently been transformed into general rules of international law under the pressure of the principle of humanity and the dictates of public conscience (Martens Clause) and under the influence of human rights law.[137] It pointed to the customary obligation to 'respect and ensure respect' for IHL 'in all circumstances',[138] even when the behaviour of the other party might be considered wrongful.[139] It argued that Common Article 3, which belongs to customary law and is applicable in all

---

[130] The ICJ even considered that massacres of civilians as a form of reprisal during the Second World War were clearly serious violations of the law of armed conflict applicable at the time. See *Jurisdictional Immunities of the State (Germany v Italy; Greece intervening)* (Judgment) (3 February 2012) para 52.

[131] CIHL commentary on rules 146 and 147.

[132] ibid commentary on rule 146. For reservations, see eg UK, Reservations and Declarations made upon ratification of the 1977 Additional Protocol I (28 January 1998) para (m). See also the more ambiguous reservations/ declarations of Egypt (9 October 1992) para 3; France (11 April 2001) para 11; Germany (26 May 1997) 167 para 137; and Italy (27 February 1986) para 10 https://ihl-databases.icrc.org/applic/ihl/ihl.nsf/states.xsp?xp_viewstates=XPages_NORMstatesParties&xp_treatySelected=470.

[133] For instance, Egypt, France, and Germany have since considered that reprisals against civilians in the conduct of hostilities is prohibited. See: Egypt, *Written statement submitted to the ICJ, Nuclear Weapons* (Advisory Opinion) (20 June 1995) para 46; France, Ministère de la Défense (above n 111) 85; Germany, Bundesministerium der Verteidigung, *Druckschrift Einsatz n 03, Humanitäres Völkerrecht in bewaffneten Konflikten—Handbuch*, DSK SF009320187, RII3 (Bundesministerium der Verteidigung 2006) 4.

[134] See eg US Department of Defense (DoD), *Law of War Manual* (Department of Defense June 2015, updated December 2016) 1115–16 para 18.18.3.4. See also (more narrowly) Italy, Ufficio Adestramento e Regolamenti, *Manuale di diritto umanitario, Intro and Vol I, Usi e Convenzione di Guerra*, SMD—G-014, Stato Maggiore della Difesa, I Reparto (Ufficio Adestramento e Regolamenti 1991) paras 23 and 25.

[135] CIHL commentary on rule 146. See also rule 147.

[136] *Martić* (Review of the Indictment) (8 March 1996) paras 15–17; *Kupreškić* (above n 129) paras 527–531.

[137] *Kupreškić* (above n 129) paras 527 and 529.

[138] Common Article 1 to the 1949 Geneva Convention; API article 1(1).

[139] *Martić* (Review of the Indictment) (above n 136) para 15.

types of armed conflicts,[140] 'prohibits any reprisals in non-international armed conflicts with respect to the expressly prohibited acts as well as any other reprisal incompatible with the absolute requirement of humane treatment'.[141] It insinuated that reprisals are a form of collective punishment, which is prohibited under both treaty and customary law.[142] It also referred to non-binding documents, such as Resolution 2675 (1970) of the UN General Assembly,[143] providing that 'civilian populations, or individual members thereof, should not be the object of reprisals'.[144] This has been confirmed—albeit much less clearly and forcefully—in the later Trial Judgment of the *Martić* case, when the ICTY stated that 're-prisals must be exercised, to the extent possible, in keeping with the principle of the pro-tection of the civilian population in armed conflict and the general prohibition of targeting civilians'.[145] The International Criminal Court (ICC) agreed with the ICTY that 'no circum-stances would legitimize an attack against civilians even if it were a response proportionate to a similar violation perpetrated by the other party'.[146]

As for the prohibition of reprisals against civilian objects during the conduct of hostil-ities, practice seems even less clear.[147] In the aforementioned *Martić* case (Trial and Appeal Judgment), the ICTY examined whether the shelling of Zagreb could be considered a lawful reprisal as argued by the Defence.[148] Although it was found that this shelling was illegal because the conditions justifying reprisals had not been met (no ultima ratio, no warning), it implicitly recognized the possibility of lawful reprisals against civilian objects irrespective of the type of armed conflict.[149]

In recent state practice, not many belligerents invoked reprisals to justify IHL violations in IACs.[150] A major exception is to be found in the context of the Iran–Iraq War (1980–1988) when both belligerent states invoked reprisals to justify attacks against cities belonging to the adversary.[151] The international community vigorously condemned these justifications.[152]

---

[140] *Case concerning Military and Paramilitary Activities in and against Nicaragua (Nicaragua v United States of America)* (Judgment) (27 June 1986) para 219.

[141] Sentence quoted in the *Kupreškić* case (above n 129) para 534. This quotation must be attributed to the International Law Commission. See the Commission's comments on the former Article 14 of the 2nd Part of the Draft Articles in *Yearbook of the International Law Commission*, Vol 2, Part 2 (1995) A/CN.4/SER.A/1995/Add.1 (Part 2) (State responsibility) 72 para 18. For more information on Common Article 3 and the prohibition of reprisals, see below.

[142] *Martić* (Review of the Indictment) (above n 136) para 16. *Kupreškić* (above n 129) para 528. On the cus-tomary prohibition of collective punishment, see CIHL rule 103.

[143] UN General Assembly Resolution 2675 (XXV) (9 December 1970).

[144] *Martić* (Review of the Indictment) (above n 136) para 16; *Kupreškić* (above n 129) para 532.

[145] *Martić* (ICTY Trial Judgment) (above n 129) para 467. Although the armed conflict was probably non-international at the time, the ICTY did not classify the situation considering that '[w]hen an accused is charged with violation of Article 3 of the Statute, it is immaterial whether the armed conflict was international or non-international in nature' (para 42).

[146] *Mbarushimana*, ICC (Decision on the Confirmation of Charges) (16 December 2011) para 143 (quoting the ICTY's *Martić* decision of 8 March 1996). (Note that the case concerns a NIAC, but the ICC considers that reprisals against civilians are always prohibited irrespective of the type of armed conflict). See further below on NIACs.

[147] CIHL commentary on rule 147.

[148] *Martić* (ICTY Trial Judgment) (above n 129) paras 464–468 and (Appeal Judgment) (2008) paras 263–267.

[149] *Martić* (ICTY Trial Judgment) (above n 129) para 468.

[150] CIHL commentary on rule 145.

[151] Iraq, Letter dated 2 May 1983 to the UN Secretary General, UN Doc S/15743 (4 May 1983); Iraq, Letter dated 18 February 1987 to the UN Secretary General, UN Doc S/18704 (18 February 1987); Islamic Republic of Iran, Letter dated 2 February 1987 to the UN Secretary General, UN Doc S/18648 (2 February 1987); Islamic Republic of Iran, Letter dated 24 February 1987 to the UN Secretary General, UN Doc S/18721 (25 February 1987); Islamic Republic of Iran, Minister of Foreign Affairs, Letter dated 27 February 1987 to the UN Secretary General, UN Doc S/18728 (27 February 1987); Islamic Republic of Iran, Letter dated 24 June 1987 to the UN Secretary General, UN Doc S/18945 (24 June 1987).

[152] See UN Secretary General, Message dated 9 June 1984 to the Presidents of the Islamic Republic of Iran and the Republic of Iraq, UN Doc S/16611 (11 June 1984); UN Security Council, Statement by the President, UN Doc

Regarding NIACs, applicable IHL treaty provisions do not refer to the concept of reprisals at all. However, Common Article 3 and Common Article 4 of APII specify that persons taking no active part in hostilities shall 'in all circumstances' be treated humanely and that acts such as violence to life and person, collective punishment, hostage taking, and outrages upon personal dignity shall remain prohibited 'at any time and in any place whatsoever'. APII contains similar additional absolute prohibitions.[153] The ICRC and the ICTY, as well as numerous commentators, have interpreted these provisions as implying that reprisals involving the prohibited acts are also prohibited.[154]

What is more controversial is whether all other types of reprisal are equally prohibited in NIACs. According to the ICRC, the concept of belligerent reprisals 'has never materialized in non-international armed conflicts', as it originates from state practice dating back to the nineteenth and early twentieth centuries and pertaining to IACs exclusively.[155] The *travaux préparatoires* of APII somehow support this argument. Suggestions made at the time to prohibit certain reprisals in APII (as in API) were rejected because, for many states, the very concept of belligerent reprisals had no place in NIACs.[156] The international community has also often condemned reprisals in the context of NIACs.[157] The ICRC therefore considers that customary law prohibits reprisals altogether in the context of NIACs.[158]

This view is not shared by everyone. The ICTY has considered that reprisals are possible if they fulfil stringent conditions and are as far as possible in keeping with the prohibition of targeting civilians.[159] Most authors seem to hold the view that belligerent reprisals might be applicable in NIAC, but be subject to stringent conditions (whose legal basis varies depending on authors).[160] For instance, Cassese maintained that 'there is no logical obstacle' to prevent the use of reprisals by parties to a NIAC as a means to enforce APII, except for those provisions that demand obedience 'in all circumstances' or 'at any time and in any place whatsoever'.[161] This possibility for lawful reprisals would be subject to stringent conditions derived from the object and purpose of APII and

S/PV.2798 (16 March 1988) 2; ICRC, Press Release No 1479: 'Iran–Iraq War: ICRC Appeals to Belligerents' (15 December 1983); ICRC, Press Release No 1489: 'Bombing of Iraqi and Iranian Cities' (7 June 1984).

[153] See APII article 7 (humane treatment of wounded, sick and shipwrecked in all circumstances), article 10(1) (no punishment for having carried out medical activities compatible with medical ethics under no circumstances), article 11 (respect and protection of medical units and transports at all times unless they are used to commit hostile acts), and article 12 (respect of the distinctive emblem in all circumstances). See also Antonio Cassese, 'The Status of Rebels under the 1977 Geneva Protocol on Non-International Armed Conflicts' (1981) 30 *ICLQ* 434.
[154] ICRC, *Commentary on the First Geneva Convention: Convention (I) for the Amelioration of the Condition of the Wounded and Sick in Armed Forces in the Field* (2nd edn, ICRC 2016) (ICRC Commentary 2016) commentary on Common Article 3, para 905; AP Commentary para 4530; Michael Bothe, Karl Josef Partsch, and Waldemar A Solf (eds), *New Rules for Victims of Armed Conflicts* (Martinus Nijhoff 2013) 731; Cassese (above n 153) 435. See also: *Martić* (Review of the Indictment) (above n 136) para 16; *Kupreškić* (above n 129) para 534; cf Veronika Bilkova, 'Belligerent Reprisals in Non-International Armed Conflicts' (2014) 63 *ICLQ* 155–7.
[155] See ICRC Commentary 2016, Common Article 3, para 905; CIHL rule 148.
[156] CIHL commentary on rule 148.
[157] See eg UNGA Resolutions 48/152 (20 December 1993) para 8 and 49/207 (23 December 1994) para 9.
[158] CIHL rule 148.
[159] *Martić* (ICTY Trial Judgment) (above note 129).
[160] For a careful review of existing literature on the topic, see Bilkova (above n 154) 31–65.
[161] Cassese (above n 153) 433–4.

conforming with the general requirements governing countermeasures under general international law. As Bilkova aptly puts it:

> Views on belligerent reprisals in NIAC are divided in both the case law and the literature. There is disagreement whether the institution applies in NIAC at all. Opinions range from a clear *yes* by the ICTY, through a hesitant *probably* by some scholars, to a reluctant *no* by the ICRC and other scholars.

However, instances where belligerent parties officially referred to belligerent reprisals to justify IHL violations in NIACs have not been identified.[162]

In practice, it appears that most of the time reprisals were useless and counterproductive. Even the US *Law of War Manual* (2015–2016), which boldly contends that 'reprisals are generally permissible under customary international law',[163] recognizes that, in practice, 'reprisals frequently lead only to further unwanted escalation of the conflict by an adversary or a vicious cycle of counter-reprisals'.[164] As such, reprisals are probably one of the most ineffective and dangerous means of enforcing IHL. It therefore may legitimately be asked whether belligerent reprisals can still be considered to strike a fair balance between the principles of military necessity and humanity. Can they ever respect the 'principles of humanity and the dictates of public conscience' as set forth in the Martens Clause? Are they not the remainder of an obsolete concept of reciprocity in respect of IHL, which threatens the very humanitarian purpose of that body of law? It is striking that the International Law Commission's Articles on State Responsibility provide that countermeasures 'shall not affect ... b) obligations for the protection of fundamental human rights; c) obligations of a humanitarian character prohibiting reprisals; d) other obligations under peremptory norms of general international law'.[165] Insofar as the prohibition of arbitrary killings as well as of cruel inhuman, and degrading treatment are fundamental human rights, whose peremptory character has often been recognized, the continued relevance of belligerent reprisals jeopardizing those rights is questionable. At the very least, it is to be hoped that state practice will continue to develop, *de lege ferenda*, towards the complete prohibition of reprisals.

## C. Destruction and Seizure of Property

Article 23(g) of the 1907 Hague Regulations provides that it is prohibited 'to destroy or seize the enemy's property, unless such destruction or seizure be imperatively demanded by the necessities of war'.[166] Under the 1949 Geneva Conventions, 'extensive destruction

---

[162] See ICRC Commentary 2016 on Common Article 3, para 905; Bilkova (above n 154) 49.

[163] US DoD (above n 134) 1096.

[164] ibid) 1099. See also Australia, Australian Defence Force, *Manual on Law of Armed Conflict*, Operations Series, ADFP 37, Interim edn (Australian Defence Force Publications 1994) para 1310; Kenya, School of Military Police, *Law of Armed Conflict, Military Basic Course (ORS)* Précis No 4 (School of Military Police 1997) 4; Sweden, Swedish Ministry of Defence, *International Humanitarian Law in Armed Conflict, with Reference to the Swedish Total Defence System* (Swedish Ministry of Defence 1991) section 3.5, 89; UK, Ministry of Defence, *The Law of Armed Conflict*, D/DAT/13/35/66, Army Code 71130 (rev edn, Ministry of Defence 1981) section 4, 17.

[165] International Law Commission, *Draft Articles on Responsibility of States for Internationally Wrongful Acts* (2001) article 50.

[166] This rule can also be found in older documents, such as the *Lieber Code* articles 15–16 and the Brussels Declaration article 13(g).

and appropriation of property, not justified by military necessity and carried out unlawfully and wantonly' is a grave breach of the Geneva Conventions.[167] This provision only concerns property that is 'protected' by the Geneva Conventions, such as fixed medical establishments and mobile medical units,[168] hospital ships,[169] medical transports, including medical aircraft,[170] or objects and property in occupied territory.[171] Article 53 of the Fourth Geneva Convention generally protects 'real or personal property belonging individually to private persons of an occupied belligerent state or to other public authorities'.[172] The term 'destruction' is not defined under IHL, but it has been understood as setting fire to a protected object, attacking it, or otherwise seriously damaging it.[173] The destruction does not need to be committed within the context of military action, but it must be closely related to the hostilities.[174] The 'appropriation' of protected property can also be defined broadly and does not require a formal transfer of property title.[175] It covers the 'taking, obtaining or withholding of property, theft, requisition, plunder, spoliation and pillage'.[176] Pillage is a form of unlawful appropriation for private or personal use, which is also prohibited in separate IHL provisions.[177] Although the provision reads 'destruction *and* appropriation', it is clear that the drafters' intent was to criminalize the two acts separately rather than only cumulatively.[178]

To constitute a grave breach the destruction or appropriation must be (i) extensive; (ii) not justified by military necessity; (iii) carried out unlawfully; and (iv) wantonly.

First, the extent of the destruction/appropriation must be assessed on a case-by-case basis.[179] Usually, this criterion will be fulfilled when there is repeated unlawful destruction or appropriation, as made clear by the French translation of 'extensive' that is 'executées sur grande échelle'. In exceptional cases, though, a single act, such as the destruction of a hospital, may suffice.[180] We can conclude that the extensive character of the criminalized acts might be either a quantitative criterion (number of destructions/appropriations) or a qualitative criterion (importance of the object's value).[181] Less numerous/serious forms of

---

[167] GCI article 50; GCII article 51; GCIV article 147. See also Rome Statute article 8(2)(b)(xiii).

[168] GCI articles 19, 33, and 34; GCII articles 11 and 23; and GCIV article 18.

[169] GCI article 20; GCII articles 22 and 24.

[170] GCI articles 35 and 36; GCII articles 38 and 39; GCIV article 22.

[171] *Kordić and Čerkez* (ICTY Judgment) (26 February 2001) para 341.

[172] GCIV article 53 only applies to occupied territories as defined in the Hague Regulations article 42. Article 23(g) of the Hague Regulations is thus wider in scope. The destruction of property situated on enemy territory may nevertheless be considered a war crime (but not a grave breach). See *Kordić and Čerkez* (above n 171) paras 335–341 and 347.

[173] ICRC Commentary 2016 para 3009.

[174] *Hadžihasanović* (ICTY Judgment) (15 March 2006) para 46.

[175] ICRC Commentary 2016 para 3011.

[176] ibid.

[177] For the specific provisions on pillage, see: Hague Regulations articles 28 and 47; GCIV article 33(2); APII article 4(2)(g). On the customary character of the prohibition of pillage, see: CIHL rule 52. See also ICC, *Review Conference of the Rome Statute of the International Criminal Court* (Kampala 31 May–11 June 2010) (ICC 2010) ('Elements of Crimes'), which specify that pillage is done 'for private or personal use' (Rome Statute article 8(2)(b)(xvi) and (e)(v)).

[178] ICRC Commentary 2016 para 3008. See also the Rome Statute, which has reformulated the crime in the following manner: 'destroying or seizing the enemy's property unless such destruction or seizure be imperatively demanded by the necessities of war' (Rome Statute article 8(2)(b)(xiii) and article 8(2)(e)(xii)).

[179] ICRC Commentary 2016 para 3014; *Blaškić* (ICTY Trial Judgment) (3 March 2000) para 157.

[180] Ibid. See also *Brđanin* (ICTY Trial Judgment) (1 September 2004) para 587; *Prosecutor v Naletilić and Martinović* (Trial Chamber Judgment) (*Naletilić* case) (31 March 2003) para 576; *Prlić* (ICTY Trial Judgment) (29 May 2013) para 126.

[181] See, in this sense, *Hadžihasanović* (above n 174) para 43.

destruction/appropriation are still prohibited and might still amount to war crimes, but not to grave breaches.[182]

Second, destruction/appropriation must not be justified by military necessity. While contemporary IHL does not permit invoking military necessity to justify violations of IHL, the principle is still operational where the relevant treaty norm contains a derogatory clause in favour of military necessity.[183] Thus, where IHL expressly permits the destruction/appropriation of civilian property, the scope and extent of such destruction/appropriation is limited by considerations of military necessity. Except for interpretative purposes, this criterion does not have much normative value.

Third, the destruction/appropriation must be unlawful 'under the specific standards pertaining to the primary obligations' of IHL.[184] For instance, the destruction by an occupying power of a private house is unlawful, except where such destruction is rendered absolutely necessary by military operations as specified in the relevant provision.[185] Similarly, the appropriation of the property belonging to aid societies is unlawful except in case of urgent necessity, and only after the welfare of the wounded and sick has been ensured.[186]

Finally, the destruction/appropriation must be committed 'wantonly'. This mental element has been understood as prohibiting not only the intentional commission of the criminalized act but also recklessness.[187]

Several accused individuals were found guilty by the ICTY for unlawful destruction and appropriation of property.[188] For instance, in the *Blaškić* case, the accused was found guilty of a grave breach of the Geneva Conventions for extensive destruction of Bosnian Muslim dwellings, buildings, businesses, private property, and livestock between January 1993 and September 1993.[189]

Although Common Article 3 and APII do not address the aforementioned issue as such, the prohibition of destroying or seizing the enemy's property unless such destruction or seizure be imperatively demanded by the necessities of war has been considered as customary law for both IACs and NIACs.[190] It has also been criminalized in the ICC Statute for Non-International Armed Conflicts.[191]

Regarding occupied territories, additional specific rules apply and complement the general prohibition of unlawful destruction/appropriation of property discussed above. They are essentially stated in the 1907 Hague Regulations.[192] The legal framework differs

---

[182] ibid para 44; ICRC Commentary 2016 para 3015.

[183] ICRC Commentary 2016 para 3013. See also Nils Melzer, *Targeted Killing under International Law* (OUP 2008) 280–2 (and additional references therein).

[184] ICRC Commentary 2016 para 3015.

[185] GCIV article 53.

[186] GCI article 34(2).

[187] ICRC Commentary 2016 para 3016. See also See *Brđanin* (above n 180) para 589; *Naletilić* case (above n 180) para 577(iv) and n 1440; *Kordić and Čerkez* (above n 172) para 341(iii); and *Prlić* (above n 181) paras 127 and 131.

[188] *Blaškić* (above n 180); *Kordić and Čerkez* (above n 171); *Naletilić* case (above n 180).

[189] *Blaškić* (above n 180).

[190] See CIHL rule 50; *Hadžihasanović*, ICTY (Decision on Motions for Acquittal Pursuant to Rule 98 *bis* of the Rules of Procedure and Evidence) (27 September 2004) para 104.

[191] Rome Statute article 8(2)(e)(xii).

[192] In ICJ, *Legal Consequences of the Construction of a Wall in the Occupied Palestinian Territory* (Advisory Opinion) (9 July 2004) (*Palestinian Wall* case) para 124, the ICJ considered that article 23(g) of the Hague Regulations was not pertinent regarding the situation in the West Bank, since this article is located in section II dedicated to 'hostilities'. Pertinent rules were found thus exclusively in section III dedicated to occupation (see articles 46 and 52).

depending on the type of property. *Movable public property* which may be used for military operations, such as cash, arms, or means of transport, may be confiscated, or in other words, taken without compensation.[193] There is an exception to this rule: the property of municipalities and of institutions dedicated to religion, charity and education, the arts and sciences, including historic monuments and works of art and science, cannot be seized, destroyed, or wilfully damaged.[194] *Immovable public property,* such as public buildings, real estate, forests, and agricultural estates, may not be confiscated by the occupying power. The latter must administer these properties according to the rules of usufruct and safeguard their capital.[195] *Private property* must be respected (and therefore not destroyed) and cannot be confiscated.[196] However, private property that may be used as war material—such as telecommunication and radio equipment, cars, arms, munitions, etc—may be seized, but must be restored and compensated for after the war.[197] Requisitions in kind and services may also be carried out provided that: (i) they are done for the needs of the army of occupation; (ii) they are in proportion to the resources of the country; (iii) they do not involve obliging civilians to take part in military operations against their own country; (iv) they are requested by the military commander in charge of the region; and (v) contributions in kind must as far as possible be paid for in cash as soon as possible.[198] The aforementioned rules are considered as customary law for situations of belligerent occupation.[199] There are no equivalent rules for NIACs.[200] The issue must therefore be analysed under domestic law.[201]

Regarding related judicial practice, two examples can be provided. In the *Palestinian Wall* Advisory Opinion, the ICJ found—without much elaboration—that the construction of the wall had led to the destruction or requisition of private Palestinian properties in a manner that was not consonant with articles 43, 46, and 52 of the 1907 Hague Regulations, and with article 53 of the Fourth Geneva Convention.[202] Furthermore, the Eritrea–Ethiopia Claims Commission considered that Ethiopia, as an occupying power in Tserona Town in 2000–2001, had violated articles 43, 46, and 47 of the 1907 Hague Regulations when it 'permitted'—or rather did not prevent—the unlawful looting and 'stripping' (ie demolition) of buildings.[203] The commission argued that this was the case regardless of whether these acts had been committed by Ethiopian military personnel or by civilians.[204]

Finally, for the sake of completeness, it should be recalled that the general rules on the conduct of hostilities, including the basic principle of distinction, are also relevant to determine which objects are protected from direct attacks and therefore from being destroyed. This point will not be elaborated upon here as it has already been extensively discussed elsewhere.[205]

---

[193] Hague Regulations article 53(1).
[194] ibid article 56.
[195] ibid article 55.
[196] ibid article 46.
[197] ibid article 53.
[198] ibid article 52.
[199] CIHL rule 51.
[200] ibid.
[201] ibid.
[202] See ICJ (n 192) paras 124, 126, 132, and 135.
[203] Eritrea–Ethiopia Claims Commission, *Central Front, Eritrea's Claim, Partial Award* (28 April 2004) para 67.
[204] ibid.
[205] See chapter 7 'International Humanitarian Law and the Conduct of Hostilities' in this book.

## 5. Conclusion

The right of belligerents to choose methods of warfare, ie any particular manner of using weapons or of otherwise conducting hostilities, remains both limited and strictly regulated under IHL. The belligerents are governed by general principles applicable to all military operations, most notably the principles of distinction and the prohibition of superfluous injury or unnecessary suffering, both of which have undisputed customary status in both IACs and NIACs.

By virtue of these principles, numerous specific methods of warfare have been prohibited/restricted by IHL treaty provisions. The rationale underlying the restriction or prohibition of certain methods of warfare can be either to protect combatants from superfluous injury or unnecessary suffering, or to protect civilians against the effects of the hostilities. Examples for the first category, protecting primarily combatants, include the prohibition of attacking persons *hors de combat,* the prohibition of denial of quarter, and the restriction on the use of deception. Examples for the second category primarily protecting the civilian population and civilian objects include the prohibition of starvation, reprisals, and destruction and seizure of property as methods of warfare.

Although IHL provisions regulating methods of warfare are much scarcer in treaties applicable to NIAC rather than IAC, this difference can often be compensated by taking into account customary law. Normally, a resort to prohibited methods of warfare not only entails state responsibility but also individual criminal responsibility. Thus, individuals have been prosecuted both at the national and the international level for having resorted to prohibited/restricted methods of warfare.

While this view may still be disputed by some states, the fact that a specific method of warfare is not prohibited or restricted by a specific treaty provision does not necessarily mean that this method is lawful. On the contrary, any method of warfare that has not been subject to specific treaty regulation can also be restricted or prohibited based on the principles of distinction and the prohibition on superfluous injury or unnecessary suffering.

In practice, the legality of new methods of warfare must continuously be examined in light of these and other relevant legal principles, even if they are not (or not yet) prohibited by specific treaty provisions. Article 36 of API provides that:

[i]n the study, development, acquisition or adoption of a new weapon, means or method of warfare, a High Contracting Party is under an obligation to determine whether its employment would, in some or all circumstances, be prohibited by this Protocol or by any other rule of international law applicable to the High Contracting Party.

This obligation also applies to states which are not parties to API because they are legally responsible for ensuring that they do not use prohibited weapons or use lawful weapons in a manner that is prohibited.[206]

Article 36 of API implies that when developing new weapon systems (*means of warfare*), belligerent parties must ensure that they do not endanger compliance with existing

---

[206] Melzer, *International Humanitarian Law* (above n 16) 122. Arguably, this duty can also be derived from the Martens Clause, which is considered to be customary law: Melzer, *International Humanitarian Law* (above n 16) 123.

prohibitions/restrictions in terms of *methods of warfare*. For instance, when developing increasingly autonomous weapons systems, states must ensure that they will be capable of being used in compliance with the prohibition of indiscriminate attacks, with the prohibition of attacking persons *hors de combat*, or with the prohibition of denial of quarter. Hypothetically, if soldiers were to be replaced by robots exclusively capable of killing, but not capturing, enemy combatants, this would likely raise serious issues under the prohibition of denial of quarter. In addition, new 'methods', such as human enhancement (eg chemical 'hardening' of soldiers or resort to nano-technologies to render troops invisible) might give rise to new legal challenges, such as whether these methods unduly affect the physical/mental integrity of belligerents' own forces; an issue traditionally not governed by IHL, given its focus on ensuring minimal protection to the enemy. In light of the speed of technological evolution and the unlimited inventiveness of the human mind, however, it may safely be assumed that ensuring the compliance of new methods of warfare with longstanding and fundamental principles of IHL will give rise to considerable challenges both in law and in practice.

# 11
# Weapons

*Stuart Casey-Maslen*

## 1. Introduction

Weapons are integral to the use of force but there is no accepted definition of what constitutes a weapon under international law.[1] It seems clear, though, that the notion is broader than 'arms', which are factory-produced weapons, especially when destined for the military market. It is not restricted to devices that cause harm by means of kinetic energy, such as a bullet fired from a gun, as damage to the body can also be effected by heat, sound, electricity, bacteria, poison, or electromagnetic energy.[2] The notion of a weapon would thus encompass a dual-use item, such as a knife, and adapted devices such as improvised explosive devices (IEDs) or a 'dirty bomb', where radioactive material is associated with conventional explosives. The term could also be applied to the use of the internet in a cyber-attack wherein computer code is 'weaponized', for instance, in viruses or worms.[3]

International humanitarian law (IHL) has traditionally focused on prohibiting or restricting the *use* of weapons, whether under its Geneva law or Hague law branches (see chapter 7 'International Humanitarian Law and the Conduct of Hostilities'), while disarmament law addressed their manufacture and supply. Beginning in the late nineteenth century, IHL instruments prohibited the use of, among others, exploding bullets;[4] asphyxiating or deleterious gases;[5] expanding 'dum-dum' bullets;[6] chemical and bacteriological methods of warfare;[7] and modification of the environment;[8] while two protocols adopted in 1980

---

[1] A United States (US) Department of Defense Working Group reportedly suggested a definition of 'all arms, munitions, materiel, instruments, mechanisms or devices that have an intended effect of injuring, damaging, destroying or disabling personnel or property'. Cited in International Committee of the Red Cross (ICRC), *A Guide to the Legal Review of New Weapons, Means and Methods of Warfare: Measures to Implement Article 36 of Additional Protocol I of 1977* (ICRC 2007) 8 n 17. Within the context of international humanitarian law (IHL), a weapon has been defined by one British military lawyer as connoting 'an offensive capability that can be applied to a military object or enemy combatant'. Justin McClelland, 'The Review of Weapons in Accordance with Article 36 of Additional Protocol I' (2003) 85 *IRRC* 397, 404.

[2] See proposed definition in Stuart Casey-Maslen (ed), *Weapons under International Human Rights Law* (CUP 2014), xx.

[3] See David P Fidler, 'Cyberattacks and international human rights law', in Casey-Maslen, *Weapons under International Human Rights Law* (above n 2) 303.

[4] Declaration Renouncing the Use, in Time of War, of Explosive Projectiles under 400 Grammes Weight (adopted 11 December 1868) (1868) 138 CTS 297.

[5] Declaration concerning the Prohibition of the Use of Projectiles Diffusing Asphyxiating Gases (adopted 29 July 1899, entered into force 4 September 1900) 187 CTS 453 (Hague IV, 2).

[6] Declaration on the Use of Bullets Which Expand or Flatten Easily in the Human Body (adopted 29 July 1899, entered into force 4 September 1900) 187 CTS 459 (Hague IV, 3).

[7] Protocol for the Prohibition of the Use in War of Asphyxiating, Poisonous or Other Gases, and of Bacteriological Methods of Warfare (signed 17 June 1925, entered into force 8 February 1928) 94 LNTS 65 (1925 Geneva Protocol).

[8] Convention on the Prohibition of Military or Any Hostile Use of Environmental Modification Techniques (adopted 18 May 1977 UNGA Resolution 31/72, entered into force 10 December 1976) 1108 UNTS 151.

under the Convention on Certain Conventional Weapons (CCW)[9] respectively restrict the use of landmines[10] and incendiary weapons.[11]

In contrast, in 1971 the Biological and Toxin Weapons Convention (BWC)[12] prohibited states parties 'to develop, produce, stockpile or otherwise acquire or retain' biological weapons, but not their use.[13] This was despite the fact that the prohibition of biological weapons was based on the 1925 Geneva Protocol to which more than twenty states had made reservations,[14] effectively limiting the prohibition to one of 'no first use'.

The clear distinction that once existed in the regulation of weapons under international law was first overridden in the 1992 Chemical Weapons Convention (CWC),[15] which prohibited, in a single instrument. the development, production, stockpiling, transfer, and use of chemical weapons.[16] Then in 1995 the CCW Protocol IV on Blinding Laser Weapons,[17] an IHL treaty adopted within the United Nations (UN), prohibited not only the use but also the transfer of weapons designed to blind.

In tandem with negotiations to tackle the threat from anti-personnel mines, which led to the conclusion of Amended Protocol II in 1996,[18] states had come to understand that merely regulating use without constraining supply was often ineffective. The adoption of the 1997 Anti-Personnel Mine Ban Convention (APMBC)[19] and then, a decade later, the 2008 Convention on Cluster Munitions (CCM)[20] has confirmed a new trend that international weapons treaties follow the approach taken in the 1992 CWC and prohibit not only the use, but also the development, production, stockpiling, and transfer of specific weapons. Despite this evolution in international law, however, most general IHL norms pertain only to use, as section 2 describes.

[9] The formal title is the Convention on Prohibitions or Restrictions on the Use of Certain Conventional Weapons Which May Be Deemed to Be Excessively Injurious or to Have Indiscriminate Effects (adopted 10 October 1980, entered into force 2 December 1983) 1342 UNTS 137 (CCW).

[10] Protocol (II) on Prohibitions or Restrictions on the Use of Mines, Booby-Traps and Other Devices (adopted 10 October 1980, entered into force 2 December 1983) 1342 UNTS 168 (CCW Protocol II), annexed to the CCW. As discussed below, the Protocol was amended in 1996 and a new instrument adopted by state parties to the CCW.

[11] Protocol (III) on Prohibitions or Restrictions on the Use of Incendiary Weapons (adopted 10 October 1980, entered into force 2 December 1983) 1342 UNTS 171 (CCW Protocol III), annexed to the CCW.

[12] Convention on the Prohibition of the Development, Production and Stockpiling of Bacteriological (Biological) and Toxin Weapons and on their Destruction (opened for signature 10 April 1972, entered into force 25 March 1975) 1015 UNTS 163.

[13] Use is mentioned in the preamble, with reference to the 1925 Geneva Protocol. Subsequently, however, state parties have included in the declarations of review conferences the statement that a prohibition on use is inherent in the other prohibitions set out in article I.

[14] 1925 Geneva Protocol.

[15] Convention on the Prohibition of the Development, Production, Stockpiling and Use of Chemical Weapons and on Their Destruction (adopted 13 January 1993, entered in force 29 April 1997) 1974 UNTS 45 (CWC).

[16] Its primary obligations in article I were still of a purely disarmament nature: 'never under any circumstances... (a) To develop, produce, otherwise acquire, stockpile or retain chemical weapons, or transfer, directly or indirectly, chemical weapons to anyone'. But sub-para (b) contained an explicit and unequivocal prohibition on use of chemical weapons.

[17] Protocol (IV) on Blinding Laser Weapons (adopted 13 October 1995, entered into force 30 July 1998) 1380 UNTS 370 (CCW Protocol IV), annexed to the CCW.

[18] CCW Protocol II (as amended 3 May 1996). The amended Protocol also prohibits the transfer of weapons whose use is outlawed therein.

[19] Convention on the Prohibition of the Use, Stockpiling, Production and Transfer of Anti-Personnel Mines and on their Destruction (adopted 18 September 1997, entered into force 1 March 1999) 2056 UNTS 211 (APMBC).

[20] Convention on Cluster Munitions (adopted 30 May 2008, entered into force 1 August 2010) 2688 UNTS 30 (CCM).

## 2. General Principles and Rules Governing Use of Weapons

A general IHL principle holds that the right of parties to an armed conflict 'to choose methods or means of warfare is not unlimited'.[21] This means that parties to an armed conflict are restricted by applicable treaty and customary rules in the weapons they may lawfully use as well as in the way they may lawfully use them. Furthermore, according to the International Committee of the Red Cross (ICRC), '[m]ilitary necessity cannot justify any derogation from rules which are drafted in a peremptory manner'.[22] The general principle is believed to be part of customary international law[23] and applies to situations of both international armed conflict (IAC) and non-international armed conflict (NIAC).

If, however, a weapon is not per se illegal, its use in armed conflict is always subject to the rule of distinction. This fundamental IHL rule holds that parties to a conflict must direct attacks only against lawful military objectives (military personnel or objects of concrete military value) and never against the civilian population, individual civilians, or civilian objects. According to the ICRC's Customary International Humanitarian Law Study (CIHL Study), the rule, which applies in all armed conflicts, is formulated as follows:

> The parties to the conflict must at all times distinguish between civilians and combatants. Attacks may only be directed against combatants. Attacks must not be directed against civilians.
>
> The parties to the conflict must at all times distinguish between civilian objects and military objectives. Attacks may only be directed against military objectives. Attacks must not be directed against civilian objects.[24]

Civilians are persons who are not members of the armed forces, while the civilian population comprises all persons who are civilians.[25] Civilian objects are defined as any objects that are not military objectives, while:

> In so far as objects are concerned, military objectives are limited to those objects which by their nature, location, purpose or use make an effective contribution to military action and whose partial or total destruction, capture or neutralization, in the circumstances ruling at the time, offers a definite military advantage.[26]

---

[21] Protocol Additional to the Geneva Conventions of 12 August 1949, and Relating to the Protection of Victims of International Armed Conflicts (adopted 8 June 1977, entered into force 7 December 1978) 1125 UNTS 3 (API) article 35(1).

[22] Yves Sandoz, Christophe Swinarski, and Bruno Zimmerman (eds), *Commentary on the Additional Protocols of 8 June 1977 to the Geneva Conventions of 12 August 1949* (ICRC/Martinus Nijhoff 1987) 1405 (AP Commentary).

[23] According to the US Department of the Navy, for example, 'it is a fundamental tenet of the law of armed conflict that the right of nations engaged in an armed conflict to choose methods or means of warfare is not unlimited'. US Department of the Navy, *The Commander's Handbook on the Law of Naval Operations*, NWP 1-14M (US Department of the Navy 2007) para 9.1. In *Legality of the Threat of Use of Nuclear Weapons* (Advisory Opinion) [1996] ICJ Rep 226 (*Nuclear Weapons*) 266 para 78, the International Court of Justice (ICJ) affirmed that states 'do not have unlimited freedom of choice of means in the weapons they use', though the Court incorrectly limited the principle to the rule prohibiting use of weapons that cause unnecessary suffering to combatants.

[24] Jean-Marie Henckaerts and Louise Doswald-Beck (eds), *Customary International Humanitarian Law, Vol 1: Rules* (CUP 2005) (CIHL) rule 1: 'The Principle of Distinction between Civilians and Combatants' and rule 7: 'The Principle of Distinction between Civilian Objects and Military Objectives'.

[25] CIHL rule 5: 'Definition of Civilians'.

[26] ibid rule 8: 'Definition of Military Objectives'.

The content and application of the rule are explained in detail in chapter 7 'International Humanitarian Law and the Conduct of Hostilities', while the implications for the illegality of an 'indiscriminate' weapon are discussed in section 3 'General Prohibitions on Use of Weapons' below.

Even if a weapon is targeted at a lawful military objective, the circumstances of its use must still respect the rule of proportionality in attack. According to the CIHL Study, an attack will be unlawful where it is expected to cause incidental civilian harm—deaths or injuries, destruction or damage to civilian objects, or a combination thereof—that is 'excessive' compared to the military advantage anticipated.[27] Proportionality thus has 'nothing to do with injury to combatants or damage to military objectives'.[28] Moreover, the assessment of likely civilian harm is made by the attacker in advance of the attack: it is not an *ex post facto* analysis based on the extent of any civilian casualties which are actually inflicted.

In its application to means of warfare, the rule of proportionality does not render any given weapon inherently unlawful, as its application and the assessment of legality are always context dependent. It is therefore incorrect to refer to a 'disproportionate' weapon. Controversially, the ICRC has asserted that the rule 'does not provide any justification for attacks which cause extensive civilian losses and damages. Incidental losses and damages should never be extensive.'[29] It is by no means certain that this is the state of the law. As Yoram Dinstein has observed, the rule is a balancing act: the greater the anticipated military advantage, the greater the extent of foreseeable civilian harm that may not be unlawful.[30]

Complementary to the rules on distinction and proportionality in attack is the rule of precautions in attack. According to the ICRC's formulation of this customary IHL rule, which is similarly deemed to apply in all armed conflicts: '[a]ll feasible precautions must be taken to avoid, and in any event to minimize, incidental loss of civilian life, injury to civilians and damage to civilian objects'.[31] This has particular implications for the choice of weapons as well as the decision when and how to use them in any attack. It is correct to assert that the current state of the law is not yet such as to oblige parties to a conflict to use precision-guided ('smart') munitions in populated areas.[32] But as the UK has observed, the rule of precautions in attack amounts to an obligation to select the weapons and tactics 'which will cause the least incidental damage commensurate with military success'.[33]

It is sometimes argued that the Martens Clause has an influence on the use of weapons under IHL.[34] Indeed, no less an authority than the International Court of Justice (ICJ) affirmed in its 1996 *Nuclear Weapons* Advisory Opinion that the Martens Clause 'has proved to be an effective means of addressing the rapid evolution of military technology'.[35]

---

[27] The ICRC has expressed the customary IHL rule as follows: 'Launching an attack which may be expected to cause incidental loss of civilian life, injury to civilians, damage to civilian objects, or a combination thereof, which would be excessive in relation to the concrete and direct military advantage anticipated, is prohibited.'

[28] Yoram Dinstein, *The Conduct of Hostilities under the Law of International Armed Conflict* (2nd edn, CUP 2010) 129.

[29] AP Commentary para 1980.

[30] Dinstein (above n 28) 131.

[31] CIHL rule 15: 'Principle of Precautions in Attack'.

[32] Dinstein (above n 28) 142–3.

[33] UK Ministry of Defence (MoD), *Manual of the Law of Armed Conflict* (OUP 2004) para 5.32.4.

[34] A version of the Martens Clause is included in API article 1(2) and the CCW preamble. According to the Martens Clause, in cases not covered by treaty, 'civilians and combatants remain under the protection and authority of the principles of international law derived from established custom, from the principles of humanity and from the dictates of public conscience'.

[35] *Nuclear Weapons* para 78.

The Court did not provide any evidence of how this has been the case and the assertion is not persuasive. The use of weapons in the conduct of hostilities is systematically regulated by the IHL rules described both above and in section 3 'General Prohibitions on Use of Weapons' below. Where a specific weapon is deemed to cause excessive civilian harm or inflict cruel wounds, whether generally or on a wide scale, efforts have been made to prohibit or restrict it by treaty negotiation.

## 3. General Prohibitions on Use of Weapons

### A. Inherently Indiscriminate Weapons

In addition to restricting the use of weapons in all military operations, whether offensive or defensive in nature,[36] the rule of distinction means that any weapon that is 'incapable of distinguishing between civilian and military targets' is unlawful. The ICJ described this as a 'cardinal' principle in its 1996 *Nuclear Weapons* Advisory Opinion.[37] In 2005, the CIHL Study concluded that: '[t]he use of weapons which are by nature indiscriminate is prohibited'.[38] According to the ICRC, the rule is a customary norm applicable in all armed conflicts.[39]

The UK's 2004 *Manual on the Law of Armed Conflict* describes the applicable rule as comprising two alternative tests: if a weapon cannot be targeted against a specific military objective (for instance, because it has a rudimentary guidance system), or if its effects cannot be limited to a military objective in accordance with IHL, it is an indiscriminate weapon.[40] While this understanding is not generally contentious, the application of the rule to specific weapons is. In its discussion of the customary rule, the ICRC cites a number of conventional weapons and weapons of mass destruction that have been alleged to be of an indiscriminate nature but observes that there is 'insufficient consensus … to conclude that, under customary international law, they all violate the rule prohibiting the use of indiscriminate weapons'.[41]

Although the precise parameters for what is an inherently indiscriminate weapon are not clear, the strongest argument for a weapon in modern use that cannot be targeted sufficiently accurately is probably a first generation 'Scud' missile. This Soviet missile, the R-11, which was manufactured during the Cold War from 1959 to 1984, was intended to strike targets in Western Europe. Early Scuds, whose gyroscopes and electronics dated back to the 1950s, were notoriously inaccurate. In general, it was expected that half of the missiles fired at a single target would miss by more than one kilometre.[42]

---

[36] See API article 49(1) ('Definition of attacks and scope of application'): ' "Attacks" means acts of violence against the adversary, whether in offence or in defence.'

[37] *Nuclear Weapons* para 78. The Court's formulation is unfortunate, given that it implies there are civilian 'targets'. A better formulation would have been 'incapable of distinguishing between civilians and civilian objects and military objectives'.

[38] CIHL rule 71: 'Weapons That Are by Nature Indiscriminate'.

[39] ibid rule 71. See also William H Boothby, *Weapons and the Law of Armed Conflict* (OUP 2009) 82.

[40] UK MoD (above n 33) para 6.4: '[i]t is prohibited to employ weapons which cannot be directed at a specific military objective or the effects of which cannot be limited as required by Additional Protocol I and consequently are of a nature to strike military objectives and civilians or civilian objects without distinction'.

[41] CIHL rule 71: 'Weapons That Are by Nature Indiscriminate'.

[42] See Stuart Casey-Maslen, 'The Use of Nuclear Weapons under Rules Governing the Conduct of Hostilities', in Gro Nystuen et al (eds), *Nuclear Weapons under International Law* (CUP 2014) 100.

Another weapon that has frequently been cited as 'indiscriminate' is the landmine. Here it is the fact that the weapon is activated by the victim that is at the heart of the argument. An anti-personnel mine cannot distinguish between the footfall of a soldier or that of a civilian: either will detonate the weapon. This would tend to suggest that its effects are indiscriminate. The flaw in the argument, though, is that placing anti-personnel mines in a marked and fenced area, and especially one that is patrolled by military personnel, can effectively ensure that the victims of any explosion are predominantly military and not civilian. That this is rarely the case in practice justifies their prohibition by treaty but not the assertion that they are inherently indiscriminate weapons. Moreover, any state that accepts otherwise must surely accept that the use of an anti-vehicle mine is similarly unlawful, yet there is scant evidence of such *opinio juris*.

The US Air Force's *1976 Manual on International Law* cites biological weapons as a 'universally agreed illustration of … an indiscriminate weapon', observing that the uncontrollable effects from such weapons 'may include injury to the civilian population of other states as well as injury to an enemy's civilian population'.[43] These uncontrolled effects exist not only spatially but also over time. The same often applies to poison; as the ICRC has observed, 'poison is unlawful in itself, as would be any weapon which would, by its very nature, be so imprecise that it would inevitably cause indiscriminate damage'.[44]

## B. Weapons Causing Superfluous Injury

One of the very few rules that protect combatants while they are fighting is the prohibition on weapons that are of a nature to cause superfluous injury or unnecessary suffering. The origins of the rule can be traced back to the first modern treaty law prohibition on a conventional weapon, the 1868 Saint Petersburg Declaration on Explosive Bullets.[45] The Declaration observed that the only 'legitimate object' which states should endeavour to accomplish through warfare is 'to weaken the military forces of the enemy' and that this objective 'would be exceeded by the employment of arms which uselessly aggravate the sufferings of disabled men, or render their death inevitable'.[46]

In 1899, the regulations on land warfare annexed to Hague Convention II stipulated that 'it is especially prohibited … [t]o employ arms, projectiles, or material of a nature to cause superfluous injury'.[47] Today, the rule prohibiting the use of weapons causing superfluous injury is a customary IHL norm applicable to all parties to any armed conflict.[48] In its Advisory Opinion on the Legality of the Threat or Use of Nuclear Weapons, the ICJ defined unnecessary suffering as 'a harm greater than that unavoidable to achieve legitimate military objectives'.[49] Its application to specific weapons is, though, frequently contested.

---

[43]   US Department of the Air Force, 'International Law—The Conduct of Armed Hostilities and Air Operations' Air Force Pamphlet 110–31 (19 November 1976) 6–3.

[44]   AP Commentary para 1402.

[45]   Declaration Renouncing the Use, in Time of War, of Explosive Projectiles under 400 Grammes Weight (adopted 11 December 1868, entered into force 11 December 1868) 138 CTS 297.

[46]   ibid.

[47]   Regulations Annexed to the Hague Convention (IV) Respecting the Laws and Customs of War on Land and Its Annex: Regulation concerning the Laws and Customs of War on Land (18 October 1907, entered into force 26 January 1910) 187 CTS 227 (Hague Regulations) article 23(e).

[48]   CIHL rule 70: 'Weapons of a Nature to Cause Superfluous Injury or Unnecessary Suffering'.

[49]   *Nuclear Weapons* para 78.

For instance, it is not settled whether to kill or seriously injure combatants by deliberately burning them out in the open (using napalm or a flamethrower), to deliberately blind them (using a laser), or to kill them slowly through the irremediable effects of radiation (using a nuclear weapon) is a violation per se of the customary rule. The ICRC has asserted that the following are unlawful as a result of the rule:

- Explosive bullets and projectiles filled with glass;
- Bullets which easily expand or flatten in the human body;
- Poison and poisoned weapons, as well as any substance intended to aggravate a wound;
- Asphyxiating or deleterious gases; and
- Bayonets with a serrated edge and lances with barbed heads.[50]

It further notes that 'hunting shotguns are the object of some controversy, depending on the nature of the ammunition and its effect on a soft target'.[51]

## 4. Prohibitions and Restrictions on the Use of Specific Weapons

In addition to the general treaty and customary prohibitions on use of weapons, certain conventional weapons and weapons of mass destruction have been outlawed by specific treaties. Conventional arms are understood in the negative to encompass all arms other than weapons of mass destruction.[52] Weapons of mass destruction have been defined by the US Department of Defense as 'chemical, biological, radiological, or nuclear weapons capable of a high order of destruction or causing mass casualties'.[53] This definition implies, for instance, that chemical agents that do not generally inflict mass casualties (such as riot control agents) are not weapons 'of mass destruction' and should therefore be considered as conventional arms. The scope and main provisions of the treaty prohibitions are summarized below.

## A. Conventional Weapons and Ammunition

### 1. Anti-personnel mines
In 1996, an Amended Protocol II was adopted by states parties to the CCW,[54] in reaction to the 'epidemic' of landmine injuries occurring in many developing nations even long after the end of armed conflict.[55] The Protocol prohibits the use or transfer of anti-personnel

---

[50] AP Commentary 1419.

[51] ibid.

[52] See eg US Department of Defense (DoD), *DoD Dictionary of Military and Associated Terms* (DoD as amended 31 October 2009) 122.

[53] But not 'the means of transporting or propelling the weapon where such means is a separable and divisible part from the weapon'. US Department of Defense (DoD), *DoD Dictionary of Military and Associated Terms* (DoD as amended November 2019). This and previous editions of the *DoD Dictionary* no longer include a definition of the term 'conventional arms'.

[54] CCW Protocol II (as amended 3 May 1996).

[55] See eg Robin M Coupland and Remi Russbach, 'Victims of Antipersonnel Mines: What is Being Done?' (1994) 1 *Medicine & Global Survival* 18.

mines that are deemed undetectable,[56] and/or are remotely delivered (eg by artillery or aircraft) but which fail to meet the technical specifications for self-destruction and self-deactivation (outlined in a technical annex).[57]

On 3 May 1996, at the closing assembly of the diplomatic conference that adopted the Protocol, Canada announced that, given the number of states already favouring an out-right prohibition on anti-personnel mines (more than forty at the time), it would host a meeting of like-minded states in Ottawa to discuss how to achieve a total ban. This meeting, held in early October 1996, saw the genesis of a fast-tracked negotiation of a comprehensive prohibition of anti-personnel mines, known as the Ottawa Process. The process resulted in the adoption in Oslo in September 1997 of the Anti-Personnel Mine Ban Convention (APMBC).

The agreement was based primarily on text adapted from the 1992 Chemical Weapons Convention. Article 1 prohibits all use, as well as development, production, acquisition, stockpiling, retention, and transfer of anti-personnel mines. Assisting, encouraging, or inducing prohibited activities is also unlawful. Each state is allowed up to four years after becoming party to the treaty to destroy all stocks[58] (aside from the 'minimum number ab-solutely necessary' for the 'development of and training in mine detection, mine clearance, or mine destruction techniques').[59] It requires clearance of anti-personnel mines in mined areas within ten years (although it allows affected states to seek and obtain extensions of up to ten years at a time to this deadline from the other states parties; to date, several dozen have done so).

The APMBC calls for donor support for risk education and victim assistance, but does not explicitly require a state to assist its own mine victims. A verification and compliance mechanism has been included, which allows the possibility of non-consensual fact-finding (however remote the likelihood of this occurring in practice).[60] Annual meetings of states parties are complemented by five-yearly review conferences; the latest (the fourth) was held in Oslo, Norway, in November 2019. No reservations are allowed to the treaty's provisions.[61]

## 2. Cluster munitions

A few years after the adoption of the APMBC, another group of weapons came under increasing international scrutiny: cluster munitions.[62] These weapons contain multiple submunitions, within a container or dispenser, that are dropped or ejected and then dis-perse over a wide area.[63] They were originally developed with a view to targeting personnel

---

[56] All anti-personnel mines produced after 1 January 1997 must 'incorporate in their construction a material or device that enables the mine to be detected by commonly-available technical mine detection equipment and provides a response signal equivalent to a signal from 8 grammes or more of iron in a single coherent mass'. CCW Protocol II, technical annex sub-para 2(a).

[57] No more than one in ten activated mines may fail to self-destruct within thirty days after emplacement, and each mine shall have a back-up self-deactivation feature with the result that, in combination with the self-destruction mechanism, 'no more than one in one thousand activated mines will function as a mine 120 days after emplacement'. CCW Protocol II, technical annex sub-para 3(a).

[58] APMBC article 4.

[59] ibid article 3(1).

[60] ibid article 8.

[61] ibid article 19.

[62] See eg ICRC, *Cluster Bombs and Landmines in Kosovo: Explosive Remnants of War* (2001) https://www.icrc.org/en/doc/assets/files/other/icrc_002_0780.pdf.

[63] The term 'bombie' was used in south-east Asia to describe the hundreds of millions of submunitions dropped by the US during the Vietnam War.

and/or materiel: during the Cold War, NATO powers saw them as a way to stop Warsaw Pact tank divisions advancing through West Germany in the event of war between the East and the West. As with other air-dropped ordnance, though, the munitions would frequently not detonate as intended upon impact with the ground but were all too often killing civilians, sometimes long after the end of conflicts, in a similar way to mines.[64]

Norway was the catalyst for the treaty prohibition. The Oslo Process, launched at a gathering of states and non-governmental organizations (NGOs) in the Norwegian capital in February 2007, culminated in the adoption on 30 May 2008 of the Convention on Cluster Munitions (CCM) at a diplomatic conference in Dublin. The basis for the treaty was the APMBC and the core prohibitions in the CCM, set out in article 1 of the CCM, are to all intents and purposes the same as in the APMBC. Reservations are not possible to any of the provisions.

Stockpiling is still clearly prohibited but with a longer period of time allowed for destruction than in the APMBC (eight years after entry into force for each state party)[65] and, in contrast to the APMBC, the CCM includes the possibility of seeking extensions (for up to four years at a time).[66] Unexploded and abandoned submunitions, known collectively as 'cluster munition remnants', must be cleared by each affected state party, with ten years again the primary deadline, but with the possibility of seeking extensions of up to only five, not ten, years at a time.[67]

An article is dedicated to victim assistance (article 5), which imposes clear duties on each state party 'with respect to cluster munition victims in areas under its jurisdiction or control'.[68] A streamlined verification and compliance provision is incorporated (article 8). As with the APMBC, annual meetings of states parties are complemented by five-yearly review conferences, the first of which took place in Dubrovnik, Croatia, in September 2015.[69]

The CCM differs materially from the APMBC though. In particular, the prohibition on assisting, encouraging, or inducing 'in any way, anyone to engage in any activity prohibited to a State Party' contained in article 1(c) of the APMBC was materially softened in the CCM. The words 'in any way' were deleted and a new provision in article 21(3) expressly allows states parties, their military personnel or nationals, to 'engage in military cooperation and operations' with states not party 'that might engage in activities prohibited' for a state party. A state party may not, though, itself use cluster munitions or 'expressly request the

[64] The distinction being that mines are victim activated by design whereas unexploded submunitions are victim activated by failure (for instance, of the detonation mechanism).

[65] Of all but the 'minimum number absolutely necessary' for 'the development of and training in cluster munition and explosive submunition detection, clearance or destruction techniques, or for the development of cluster munition counter-measures': CCM article 3(6).

[66] CCM article 3. It subsequently appears that fears of the time and cost involved in stockpile destruction were unfounded, though in 2019 Cluster Munition Monitor reported that Guinea-Bissau did not meet its stockpile destruction deadline of 1 May 2019 and has been in violation of the convention since then while Bulgaria submitted a request to extend its stockpile destruction deadline by another 18 months, until 1 April 2021, the first State Party to make such a request. See *Cluster Munition Monitor 2019* (Cluster Munition Coalition) (2019) 2 http://the-monitor.org/media/3047840/Cluster-Munition-Monitor-2019_online.pdf.

[67] CCM article 4. Where, after a state has become party to the CCM there is new use by another state on its territory, clearance and destruction of any resultant cluster munition remnants 'must be completed as soon as possible but not later than ten years after the end of the active hostilities during which such cluster munitions became cluster munition remnants': ibid article 4(1)(a).

[68] ibid article 5(1).

[69] The second review conference of the CCM was taking place in Lausanne in November 2020.

use of cluster munitions in cases where the choice of munitions used is within its exclusive control'.[70]

### 3. Blinding laser weapons

Under article 1 of CCW Protocol IV it is 'prohibited to employ laser weapons specifically designed, as their sole combat function or as one of their combat functions, to cause permanent blindness to unenhanced vision, that is to the naked eye or to the eye with corrective eyesight devices'. The negotiation of the Protocol was motivated by the development of laser rifles that could blind instantly at a distance of several kilometres; this included the marketing of a hand-held blinding laser rifle by China. As noted in section 1 'Introduction' above, a prohibition on transfer was also included in the Protocol.[71] The argument advanced by a small number of states, notably the US, that it would be more humane to blind combatants than to kill them was thus not accepted. In 2001, a US commentator claimed that the Protocol 'does not conclude that blinding laser weapons cause unnecessary suffering or superfluous injury'.[72] In December 2015, *China's People's Liberation Army Daily* announced that Chinese soldiers were equipped with laser guns to counter technology such as unmanned aerial systems (drones) or the thermal imagers of tanks.[73] China is a state party to CCW Protocol IV.

### 4. Exploding bullets

The 1868 Saint Petersburg Declaration on Explosive Bullets, referred to in section 3 'General Prohibitions on Use of Weapons' above, outlawed the use among states parties' armed forces 'of any projectile of a weight below 400 grammes, which is either explosive or charged with fulminating or inflammable substances'. The Declaration represents the first modern treaty prohibiting the use of a specific weapon during war. Five years previously, the Russian military had invented a bullet that exploded on contact with hard substances and whose primary military utility was to blow up ammunition wagons. In 1867, however, the bullet was modified so it would explode on contact with a soft substance, which would have meant that its use against the body would render the victim almost certain to be killed. According to the ICRC, under customary IHL: '[t]he anti-personnel use of bullets which explode within the human body is prohibited'.[74] This rule applies in all armed conflicts.

### 5. Expanding bullets

Expanding bullets are those which 'expand or flatten easily in the human body, such as bullets with a hard envelope which does not entirely cover the core or is pierced with incisions'.[75] In the early 1890s, concerned that their new .303' calibre rifle ammunition was ineffective in 'stopping' attacking tribesmen, British troops began filing down the tip of the round in the field to reveal the bullet's lead core. This caused the bullet to expand when it entered the human body, inflicting significantly greater wounds than its unadapted original. This

---

[70]  CCM article 23(4)(c)–(d).

[71]  CCW Protocol IV article 1.

[72]  Donna M Verchio, 'Just Say No! The SIrUS Project: Well-Intentioned, but Unnecessary and Superfluous' (2001) 51 *AFL Rev* 183.

[73]  Jeffrey Lin and Peter Singer, 'Chinese Soldiers Have Laser Guns: Be Careful, You'll Burn Someone's Eyes Out', *Popular Science* (7 January 2016) www.popsci.com/chinese-soldiers-have-laser-guns.

[74]  CIHL rule 78: 'Exploding Bullets'.

[75]  Hague IV, 3.

improvised soft-point round[76] became known as the 'Dum Dum' bullet, so called after the factory at Dum Dum near Calcutta that manufactured it in the mid-1890s. Subsequently, a hollow-point bullet[77] with similar terminal ballistics effects was produced at the Woolwich ordnance factory in the late 1890s.[78]

In general, use of expanding bullets by armed forces in the conduct of hostilities is not only a serious violation of IHL, it is also, when it occurs with the requisite *mens rea*, a war crime.[79] It should, though, be noted that expanding bullets are permissible for use in law enforcement operations, meaning that a soldier of one state may not use expanding bullets against a soldier of another state during an armed conflict but a police officer may lawfully use expanding ammunition against one of his state's own citizens.[80] This is one of the very few instances when IHL does not allow a weapon that is permissible (albeit under far more restrictive circumstances) under the law of law enforcement.

## 6. Incendiary weapons

CCW Protocol III prohibited only certain uses of incendiary weapons. Efforts by some states in the 1970s to ban outright the use of incendiary weapons, particularly napalm, following extensive use by the US in the war in Indochina, were unsuccessful. The Protocol prohibited direct attacks on civilians or attacks that would be expected to have disproportionate effects (consonant with the general rule on proportionality in attack described in section 2 'General Principles and Rules Governing Use of Weapons' above).[81] Upon its ratification of the Protocol in 2009, the US included a reservation whereby it retained 'the right to use incendiary weapons against military objectives located in concentrations of civilians where it is judged that such use would cause fewer casualties and/or less collateral damage than alternative weapons'.[82] It pledged that, in so doing, it would take 'all feasible precautions with a view to limiting the incendiary effects to the military objective and to avoiding, and in any event to minimizing, incidental loss of civilian life, injury to civilians and damage to civilian objects'.[83]

The ICRC acknowledged in its commentary of 1977 Additional Protocol I (API) that none of the rules in CCW Protocol III explicitly protects combatants against incendiary weapons such as flame-throwers or napalm. It observed, however, that 'it is generally

---

[76] A soft-point bullet is one whose metal jacket is cut back at the nose to reveal the lead core.

[77] A hollow-point bullet is a semi-jacketed bullet, the nose of which has a cavity.

[78] Open-tip-match rounds, which have been used by US forces in Afghanistan, have a small aperture in the nose. This is the result of the manufacturing process, during which the core is poured in through the aperture. It is intended to improve the bullet's accuracy as it was originally developed for match competition.

[79] The Rome Statute of the International Criminal Court (adopted 17 July 1998, entered into force 1 July 2002) 2187 UNTS 90 (Rome Statute) gave the International Criminal Court (ICC) possible jurisdiction over the war crime, in IAC, of '[e]mploying bullets which expand or flatten easily in the human body, such as bullets with a hard envelope which does not entirely cover the core or is pierced with incisions': Rome Statute article 8(2)(b)(xix). An amendment to the Rome Statute adopted by states parties in 2010 extends the jurisdiction of the ICC to the use of expanding bullets in NIACs (that is, a situation in which one or more states is/are engaged in regular and intense armed violence against an organized armed group): Rome Statute (as amended) article 8(2)(e)(xv). The US is not a party to the Rome Statute and may lay claim to persistent objector status to the customary prohibition on use of expanding ammunition.

[80] Given that law enforcement operations are often conducted in public places, and that expanding ammunition is believed to significantly reduce the risk of over-penetration and possibly also of ricochet, the danger of innocent bystanders being harmed when police officers open fire must be reduced to a minimum.

[81] CCW Protocol III article 2.

[82] See CCW 'Declarations and Reservations' 6–14, 8. A significant number of states have objected to the US's reservation to Protocol III, notably Austria, Belgium, Cyprus, Denmark, Finland, France, Germany, Greece, Ireland, Netherlands, Norway, Poland, Portugal, Spain, Sweden, Switzerland, and the United Kingdom.

[83] See CCW 'Declarations and Reservations' 6–14, 8.

admitted that these weapons should not be used in such a way that they will cause unnecessary suffering ... which means that in particular they should not be used against individuals without cover'.[84] In its CIHL Study published in 2005, the ICRC affirmed that a rule existed whereby the 'anti-personnel use of incendiary weapons is prohibited, unless it is not feasible to use a less harmful weapon to render a person hors de combat'.[85] It further claimed that it was 'reasonable to conclude that the rule is applicable in non-international armed conflicts'.[86] Whether the proposed rule is indeed black-letter law is not settled.

### 7. Anti-vehicle mines

Anti-vehicle mines are specifically governed by the 1980 Protocol II and 1996 Amended Protocol II to the CCW. In fact, the provisions add little to the general customary IHL rules that govern all weapons. Article 6(3) of Amended Protocol II prohibits the use of remotely delivered anti-vehicle mines 'unless, to the extent feasible', they have an 'effective self-destruction or self-neutralization mechanism' and 'a back-up self-deactivation feature', which will operate when the mine 'no longer serves the military purpose for which it was placed in position'. Subsequent efforts to impose stricter rules on the use of anti-vehicle mines have run into strong opposition, particularly from China and Russia.

## B.  Weapons of Mass Destruction

### 1. Chemical weapons

The use in warfare of asphyxiating and poisonous gases, such as chlorine or sulphur mustard, was first prohibited in the Hague Declaration (IV, 2) of 29 July 1899. In 1925, however, following their widespread use against combatants during the First World War, a new protocol was negotiated at a conference held in Geneva under the auspices of the League of Nations.[87] The preamble to the 1925 Geneva Protocol noted the intention of states parties to ensure that the prohibition of the use of 'asphyxiating, poisonous or other gases, and of all analogous liquids materials or devices' would become 'universally accepted as a part of International Law, binding alike the conscience and the practice of nations'.[88] However, as noted above, subsequent reservations by more than twenty states parties effectively reduced the Protocol to only a ban on first use.

It took a further sixty-seven years to transform that prohibition on use into a comprehensive disarmament treaty prohibiting all use of chemical weapons in the conduct of hostilities. Thus, the development, production, stockpiling, transfer, and use of chemical weapons are generally prohibited under the 1992 CWC, and their use as a method of warfare in armed conflict is prohibited under customary international law. Use of chemical weapons is also a war crime for which potential jurisdiction is given to the ICC through the prohibition of 'Employing asphyxiating, poisonous or other gases, and all analogous liquids, materials or devices'.[89] While the use of riot control agents such as tear gas is specifically prohibited as

[84] AP Commentary 390 para 1424.
[85] CIHL rule 85: 'The Use of Incendiary Weapons against Combatants'.
[86] ibid.
[87] 1925 Geneva Protocol.
[88] ibid.
[89] ICC Statute articles 8(2)(b)(xviii) and 8(2)(e)(xiv).

a method of warfare, the CWC admits an exception for their use for law enforcement, 'including domestic riot control'.[90]

Oversight of the implementation of the Convention was tasked to the Organisation for the Prohibition of Chemical Weapons (OPCW), specially created by the CWC for the purpose. Despite the OPCW's involvement in Syria, though, following that state's accession to the CWC in October 2013, chemical weapons have been used on many occasions during the different armed conflicts that were ongoing as of writing. In March 2016, it was claimed that some 1,500 people had been killed by chemical attacks during the five years of armed conflict. The report by the Syrian–American Medical Society documented 161 chemical attacks in Syria on the basis of testimony from doctors operating in the areas that had borne the brunt of chemical attacks, leading to the deaths of 1,491 people and injuries to 14,581 others. More than one-third of the attacks used chlorine gas.[91]

### 2. Biological weapons

Biological weapons potentially comprise viruses such as smallpox and bacteria such as anthrax. The development, production, stockpiling, and transfer of biological weapons are generally prohibited under the 1972 Biological and Toxin Weapons Convention (BTWC) and their use as a method of warfare in armed conflict is prohibited under customary international law.[92] The 1925 Geneva Protocol explicitly extended the prohibition on use of chemical weapons to the use of bacteriological methods of warfare. Use of biological weapons is also a war crime, even though it was not specifically included in the Rome Statute.[93] As of writing, no verification system exists with respect to biological weapons, though a protocol to the BTWC has been proposed by a number of authorities.[94]

## 5. Disarmament-Type Prohibitions

In addition to the disarmament treaties that prohibit production, stockpiling, and transfer of weapons discussed above, a number of provisions across a range of international instruments impose obligations or disarmament-type prohibitions linked to compliance with IHL during armed conflict. Here two key norms are considered, the first of which concerns the duty to conduct a legal review prior to procurement, and the second of which regards a prohibition on transfer when war crimes would be committed, or a prohibition on export where an 'overriding' risk exists of their being used to commit or facilitate a serious violation of IHL.

---

[90] CWC articles 1(5) and 2(9).

[91] See eg Kareem Shaheen, 'Almost 1,500 Killed in Chemical Weapons Attacks in Syria', *The Guardian* (Beirut, 14 March 2016) www.theguardian.com/world/2016/mar/14/syria-chemical-weapons-attacks-almost-1500-killed-report-united-nations.

[92] CIHL rule 73: 'Biological Weapons'.

[93] Although the ICRC customary IHL Study does not make it explicit, it is stated that the use of prohibited weapons is a war crime, which unquestionably includes biological weapons. ICRC Customary IHL, 'Rule 156 ("Definition of War Crimes"), "List of War Crimes"' https://ihl-databases.icrc.org/customary-ihl/eng/docs/v1_rul_rule156.

[94] See Natalino Ronzitti, 'Aspetti Giuridici del Progetto di Zona Priva di Armi di Distruzione di Massa in Medio Oriente', in Natalino Ronzitti (ed), *Una Zona Priva di Armi di Distruzione di Massa in Medio Oriente: Problemi Aperti* (Istituto Affari Internazionali 2012) 43. See also 'Civil Society Preparations for the 7th BWC Review Conference 2011' (*BioWeapons Prevention Project*) www.bwpp.org/revcon-verification.html.

## A. Review Prior to Procurement

Article 36 of API requires that states parties conduct legal reviews prior to procurement or adoption of a new weapon. The aim of the review is to determine whether the weapon's use would inevitably, or only in certain circumstances, be prohibited by the Protocol or any other applicable rule of international law.[95] Such law could be disarmament law or international human rights law (IHRL) in addition to IHL, and could be a customary rule or a treaty obligation.

The requirement for a review of legality of weapons under international law prior to the 'development, acquisition or adoption' of a weapon was not, though, included in the rules identified by the ICRC in its study of customary IHL. However, it has since been asserted that the obligation is not only treaty-based, but also one of customary law.[96] Indeed, it is hard to understand how a state could lawfully deploy a new weapon without conducting at least some form of legal assessment.

## B. Transfer Prohibitions Linked to IHL

The Arms Trade Treaty (ATT) was adopted on 2 April 2013 by the UN General Assembly,[97] after consensus-based negotiations in a specially convened diplomatic conference were blocked by opposition from Iran, the Democratic People's Republic of Korea, and Syria. The ATT entered into force on 24 December 2014, and aims to contribute to international and regional peace, security, and stability; reduce human suffering; and promote responsible action in the international trade in conventional arms.

Article 6(3) of the ATT prohibits the transfer of conventional arms within the scope of the treaty when a state party 'has knowledge at the time of authorization' that the weapons or associated ammunition 'would be used in the commission of' certain war crimes, including grave breaches of the 1949 Geneva Conventions and 'attacks directed against civilian objects or civilians protected as such'.[98] While the notion of grave breaches only applies in IACs, the reference to attacks against civilians or civilian objects applies to all armed conflicts. Where a transferring state is party to other IHL agreements in which war crimes are 'defined', the relevant war crimes will also be covered by the provision.

If a proposed export of weapons or associated ammunition is not prohibited under article 6, it will be prohibited under article 7, where the requisite risk assessment[99] determines

---

[95] According to API article 36:

> [i]n the study, development, acquisition or adoption of a new weapon, means or method of warfare, a High Contracting Party is under an obligation to determine whether its employment would, in some or all circumstances, be prohibited by this Protocol or by any other rule of international law applicable to the High Contracting Party.

[96] See Michael N Schmitt, 'Autonomous Weapon Systems and International Humanitarian Law: A Reply to the Critics' (2013) *Harv Nat'l Secur J Featur* http://harvardnsj.org/2013/02/autonomous-weapon-systems-and-international-humanitarian-law-a-reply-to-the-critics; see also William H Boothby, *Conflict Law: The Influence of New Weapons Technology, Human Rights and Emerging Actors* (Asser Press 2014) 170–1.

[97] Arms Trade Treaty (adopted 2 April 2013 by A/RES/67/234b, entered into force 24 December 2014) UN Doc A/CONF.217/2013/L.3 (ATT). The ATT was adopted by 154 votes to 3, with twenty-three states abstaining.

[98] For a detailed discussion of this provision, see Andrew Clapham, 'Commentary on Article 6(3)', in Stuart Casey-Maslen et al, *The Arms Trade Treaty, A Commentary* (OUP 2016) para 6.153ff.

[99] See ATT article 7(1).

that there is an 'overriding' risk that it would be used to commit or facilitate a serious violation of IHL. A serious violation encompasses all IHL rules that form the basis of a war crime and also includes conduct that is not itself criminalized, for example where isolated instances of unlawful conduct are nevertheless of a serious nature; where conduct takes on a serious nature because of its systematic repetition or the circumstances; and where there are 'global' violations, for instance where a situation, territory, or category of persons or objects is withdrawn from the application of IHL.[100]

## 6. Conclusion: Regulation on the Horizon

In the future, IHL will need to apply additional restrictions to specific means or methods of warfare. As of writing, there are a number of challenging regulatory issues in the area of weapons law, including fully autonomous weapons, cyber weapons, and nuclear weapons, as well as the use of conventional weapons in space. Fully autonomous weapons—robots that determine what or whom to target and when to fire, without reference to a human operator—are already available to armed forces. Discussions on lethal autonomous weapons systems were first held in May 2014 under the auspices of the CCW though little substantive progress towards the prohibition that many NGOs are seeking has so far been achieved.[101] Indeed, in October 2015 the ICRC had encouraged states to 'now turn their attention to fixing limits on autonomy in the critical functions of weapon systems, to ensure that they can be used in accordance with IHL and within the bounds of what is acceptable under the dictates of public conscience'.[102]

A little-referenced provision in the 2008 CCM presages future regulation of autonomous weapons. Article 2(2)(c) of the CCM excludes from the definition of a cluster munition (for the purposes of the treaty) a munition that contains fewer than ten submunitions where each submunition weighs more than 4 kilogrammes, is designed to detect and engage a single target object, and is equipped with an electronic self-destruction mechanism and an electronic self-deactivating feature. This is a form of fully autonomous weapon.[103]

There is no treaty specifically regulating cyber warfare. As Michael Schmitt explains, the international legal aspects of cyber operations in armed conflict were first discussed in some detail in the late 1990s but the issue gained a far higher profile from the extensive Russian cyber operations against Estonia in 2007 and against Georgia during a war in 2008, as well as the targeting of the Iranian nuclear facilities with the Stuxnet worm in 2010.[104] The *Tallinn Manual on the International Law Applicable to Cyber Warfare* was written by an 'International Group of Experts' at the invitation of the North Atlantic Treaty Organization (NATO) Cooperative Cyber Defence Centre of Excellence (CCDCOE), an international

---

[100] See Clapham and Casey-Maslen (above n 98) para 7.44ff (citing AP Commentary para 3592).

[101] See, eg, 'Ban Support Grows, Process Goes Slow', *Campaign to Stop Killer Robots* (15 April 2016) www.stopkillerrobots.org.

[102] ICRC, 'Weapons: ICRC Statement to the United Nations, 2015'. Statement to the UNGA First Committee (70th Session) (15 October 2015) (ICRC Weapons Statement).

[103] See eg Textron Systems, 'Textron Systems' BLU-108 Submunition is Successful in Weaponized UAV Demonstration', 13 September 2004 https://investor.textron.com/news/news-releases/press-release-details/2004/Textron-Systems-BLU-108-Submunition-is-Successful-in-Weaponized-UAV-Demonstration/default.aspx.

[104] Michael N Schmitt, 'Introduction', in Michael N Schmitt (ed), *Tallinn Manual on the International Law Applicable to Cyber Warfare* (CUP 2013) 1–2.

military organization based in the Estonian capital.[105] This soft-law document, which took three years to complete, identified seventy 'black-letter rules' applicable to cyber warfare during situations of armed conflict.[106]

After many years without substantive progress, a treaty outlawing nuclear weapons was adopted by the United Nations in 2017.[107] On 7 July 2017, 122 states a UN conference 'to negotiate a legally binding instrument to prohibit nuclear weapons, leading towards their total elimination' agreed on the text of the Treaty to Prohibit Nuclear Weapons. The nine nuclear-armed states boycotted the negotiations. As of writing, 34 states had adhered to the Treaty, whose entry into force will be triggered once 50 have done so. This will not directly affect the conduct of the nuclear-armed states, but will dent a little further the notion that these weapons could ever be used lawfully.

Finally, the issue of weapons in space is also receiving renewed attention after the range of treaties adopted in the 1960s and 1970s, such as the 1967 Outer Space Treaty[108] and the 1979 Moon Treaty.[109] In its address to the UN General Assembly's First Committee in October 2015, the ICRC raised concerns over the 'weaponization' of outer space:

> While the Outer Space Treaty clearly prohibits the placement of weapons of mass destruction in orbit, it does not expressly apply such prohibition to other weapons, although virtually all States support the prevention of an arms race in outer space. What is certain is that any hostile use of outer space in armed conflict—that is, any use of means and methods of warfare in, from, to or through outer space—must comply with IHL, in particular its rules of distinction, proportionality and precautions in attack. It is important to stress that, by asserting that IHL applies to outer space warfare, the ICRC is in no way condoning the weaponization of outer space, which recurring resolutions of the General Assembly have sought to prevent. The point is that warfare in outer space would not occur in a legal vacuum.[110]

In a conference on space security convened by the UN Institute for Disarmament Research (UNIDIR) in 2014, one expert, Professor Li Juqian of the China University of Political Science and Law, suggested that new treaty law would be needed to address the fast-paced evolution of space weaponry and related technologies.[111]

---

[105] North Atlantic Treaty Organization (NATO) Cooperative Cyber Defence Centre of Excellence (CCDOE), 'Tallinn Manual' (CCDCOE) https://www.peacepalacelibrary.nl/ebooks/files/356296245.pdf.

[106] Six further rules confirm that cyber warfare is indeed subject to IHL and set out in which circumstances this would be the case.

[107] Treaty on the Non-Proliferation of Nuclear Weapons (opened for signature 1 July 1968, entered into force 5 March 1970) 729 UNTS 161 (NPT) article 6 obliges states parties to 'pursue negotiations in good faith on effective measures relating to cessation of the nuclear arms race at an early date and to nuclear disarmament, and on a Treaty on general and complete disarmament under strict and effective international control'.

[108] Treaty on Principles Governing the Activities of States in the Exploration and Use of Outer Space, including the Moon and Other Celestial Bodies (adopted 19 December 1966, entered into force 10 October 1967) 610 UNTS 205.

[109] Agreement Governing the Activities of States on the Moon and Other Celestial Bodies (adopted 5 December 1979, entered into force 11 July 1984) 1363 UNTS 3.

[110] ICRC Weapons Statement.

[111] United Nations Institute for Disarmament Research (UNIDIR), *UNIDIR Space Security 2014 Conference: The Evolving Space Security Regime: Implementation, Compliance, and New Initiatives* 7 www.unidir.org/files/publications/pdfs/space-security-2014-en-614.pdf.

# 12

# Detention in Armed Conflict

*Jelena Pejic**

## 1. Introduction

Deprivation of liberty—detention—is a regular occurrence in armed conflict. Along with the conduct of hostilities it is one of the ways in which a belligerent attempts to weaken—and ultimately defeat—an adversary. Detention is regulated by a large number of provisions of international humanitarian law (IHL), the underlying and overarching purpose of which is to ensure the humane treatment of persons deprived of liberty. Apart from the relevant IHL treaty provisions,[1] some of which will be mentioned in this chapter, rules on various aspects of detention in armed conflict are also found in customary IHL, domestic law, and human rights law. The chapter focuses on IHL rules on detention related to armed conflict without elaborating on the relationship between IHL and other legal frameworks, except where it highlights the specificity of particular IHL norms.

Similar to other submissions in this book, the chapter cannot identify or respond to all of the open issues related to the topic. Its purpose, within the space available, is to outline some of the main principles and rules governing certain aspects of detention and to flag a few points of controversy. The following issues are briefly addressed: treatment and conditions of detention; procedural safeguards in internment; fair trial rights; and the transfer of detainees. A few remarks looking towards the future are offered in conclusion.

Before turning to the substantive law, several points of a preliminary nature are useful. IHL rules govern only detention related to an armed conflict. Where a deprivation of liberty is not related to an armed conflict, even if it takes places within it, IHL provisions are not applicable. The term 'detention/deprivation of liberty' in this chapter is always intended to mean 'detention/deprivation of liberty in relation to an armed conflict', but the full phrase is not repeated each time.

The treaties of IHL do not expressly include the term 'arbitrary' detention. It is nevertheless generally accepted, and it is a rule of customary IHL, that arbitrary detention is prohibited.[2] This proscription, like most other norms of customary law, is necessarily general in nature and does not provide specific guidance that would allow an assessment of when a deprivation of liberty in armed conflict may be deemed arbitrary. This will depend on a careful examination of the facts and on the proper application of the relevant law to the facts in any given case.

---

* The views expressed are the author's alone and do not necessarily reflect those of the International Committee of the Red Cross (ICRC).

[1] The 'IHL treaties' collectively referred to here and elsewhere in the chapter are the four Geneva Conventions for the protection of victims of war of 1949 and their two Additional Protocols of 1977.

[2] See Jean-Marie Henckaerts and Louise Doswald-Beck (eds), *Customary International Humanitarian Law, Vol 1: Rules* (CUP 2005) (CIHL) rule 99.

IHL treaties contain the terms 'capture', 'arrest', 'detention', and 'internment' to denote deprivation of liberty related to armed conflict, but do not define them, and occasionally use them in an interchangeable manner. The omission of definition(s) of the relevant terms is not only of conceptual interest, but can give rise to uncertainty with regard to the extent of legal protections owed in a given situation. By way of example, IHL treaties do not specifically establish when 'detention' becomes 'internment' in either international armed conflict (IAC) or non-international armed conflict (NIAC), thus triggering the application of the specific provisions making up this detention regime. Given the occasional reluctance of states to recognize that their detention operations include internment, particularly in situations of NIAC with an extra-territorial element (see section 2 'Procedural Safeguards in Internment' below), it appears that an answer to this query is needed.

Detention by non-state armed groups (NSAGs) that are party to NIAC is not as common as detention by states, but, when it does occur, it poses more questions of a legal, policy, and practical nature than detention carried out by states. Challenges arise not only because of the general paucity of IHL rules governing certain aspects of deprivation of liberty in NIACs—discussed in section 2 'Procedural Safeguards in Internment' below—but also because of the great variety of NSAGs and the circumstances in which they operate. A key issue is the feasibility for NSAGs to apply some of the relevant IHL rules on detention. The NIAC-related sections on detention that follow should thus be read keeping in mind that the manner in which certain provisions will be applied will inevitably depend on the context.

## 2. Treatment and Conditions of Detention

### A. Treatment

As noted in section 1 'Introduction', the principle of humane treatment underlies all IHL provisions on detention. While IHL encapsulates a balance between the principles of military necessity and humanity, it is obvious, and may be said to be beyond discussion, that there can be no justification of military necessity by a belligerent for inhumane behaviour towards a person, or persons, whom it has in its power. Humane treatment is explicitly reflected in key provisions of IHL treaties and cannot be modified by reference to the exigencies of military necessity.[3]

With respect to prisoners of war (POWs) in IAC, the Third Geneva Convention (GCIII), inter alia, states that:

> Prisoners of war must at all times be humanely treated. Any unlawful act or omission by
> the Detaining Power causing death or seriously endangering the health of a prisoner of
> war in its custody is prohibited, and will be regarded as a serious breach of the present

---

[3] In this context, see White House, *Memorandum on the Humane Treatment of al Qaeda and Taliban Detainees* (7 February 2002) para 5 www.pegc.us/archive/White_House/bush_memo_20020207_ed.pdf, which incorrectly provided for such a modification.

Convention. In particular, no prisoner of war may be subjected to physical mutilation or to medical or scientific experiments of any kind which are not justified by the medical, dental or hospital treatment of the prisoner concerned and carried out in his interest. Likewise, prisoners of war must at all times be protected, particularly against acts of violence or intimidation and against insults and public curiosity.[4]

The treaty further provides that POWs are 'entitled in all circumstances to respect for their persons and their honour', and that 'Women shall be treated with all the regard due to their sex and shall in all cases benefit by treatment as favourable as that granted to men.'[5]

In order to underline responsibility for the implementation of these provisions, GCIII expressly stipulates that POWs 'are in the hands of the enemy Power, but not of the in-dividuals or military units who have captured them. Irrespective of the individual re-sponsibilities that may exist, the Detaining Power is responsible for the treatment given them.'[6] Prohibited acts that will give rise to individual criminal responsibility, within a regime of universal jurisdiction, are outlined in the Convention's grave breaches provisions.[7]

The Fourth Geneva Convention (GCIV) on the protection of civilians, also applicable to IAC, contains similar and even more detailed prescriptions. It provides, inter alia, that per-sons protected by this treaty, including detained civilians, are:

[E]ntitled, in all circumstances, to respect for their persons, their honour, their family rights, their religious convictions and practices, and their manners and customs. They shall at all times be humanely treated, and shall be protected especially against all acts of violence or threats thereof and against insults and public curiosity. Women shall be especially protected against any attack on their honour, in particular against rape, enforced prostitution, or any form of indecent assault.[8]

The treaty prohibits the parties from taking any measure which would:

[C]ause the physical suffering or extermination of protected persons in their hands. This prohibition applies not only to murder, torture, corporal punishment, mutilation and medical or scientific experiments not necessitated by the medical treatment of a protected

---

[4]  Geneva Convention (III) Relative to the Treatment of Prisoners of War (adopted 12 August 1949, entered into force 21 October 1950) 75 UNTS 135 (GCIII) article 13.

[5]  ibid article 14. The Convention also includes a 'no adverse distinction' clause, in article 16. The concept of no adverse distinction, which is the IHL equivalent of the human rights prohibition on discrimination, is applicable to both IACs and NIACs. Apart from the prohibition of discrimination on the non-exhaustive grounds listed, it also implies that in certain circumstances, and depending on the special needs of certain groups of persons, preferential treatment may, and indeed must, be granted. For example, priority in medical care given to wounded or sick per-sons may depend on the seriousness of their condition.

[6]  ibid article 12.

[7]  ibid articles 129 and 130. See also the Rome Statute of the International Criminal Court (adopted 17 July 1998, entered into force 1 July 2002) 2187 UNTS 3 (Rome Statute) art 8(2)(a) and (b) www.icc-cpi.int/nr/rdonlyres/ea9aeff7-5752-4f84-be94-0a655eb30e16/0/rome_statute_english.pdf.

[8]  Geneva Convention (IV) Relative to the Protection of Civilian Persons in the Time of War (adopted 12 August 1949, entered into force 21 October 1950) 75 UNTS 287 (GCIV) article 27. Obviously, the formulation of the last sentence reflects the era in which it was drafted and would not be thus worded today. The Convention also includes a 'no adverse distinction' clause, in article 27.

person, but also to any other measures of brutality whether applied by civilian or military agents.[9]

The treaty also states that 'no protected person may be punished for an offence he or she has not personally committed' and that 'collective penalties and likewise all measures of intimidation or of terrorism are prohibited'.[10]

Similar to GCIII, GCIV stresses that the party in whose hands protected persons may be 'is responsible for the treatment accorded to them by its agents, irrespective of any individual responsibility which may be incurred'.[11] Prohibited acts which will give rise to individual criminal responsibility, within a regime of universal jurisdiction, are outlined in the Convention's grave breaches provisions.[12]

In the context of the rules on treatment, it is sometimes said that GCIII protects POWs from coercive interrogation in a way that GCIV does not protect detained civilians. This interpretation is based on the provisions of GCIII according to which POWs, when questioned, are bound to give 'only' their 'surname, first names and rank, date of birth, and army, regimental, personal or serial number, or failing this, equivalent information'.[13] It is submitted that there is no justification for this view. The fact that POWs are not bound upon questioning to provide the adversary with information of potential intelligence value, and may not be forced in any way to do so (see section 3 'Procedural Safeguards in Internment' below), is a logical consequence of the drafters intending to avoid giving a possible military advantage to the capturing side. What is overlooked is that both Conventions, albeit in different wording, essentially prohibit the same behaviour. According to GCIII:

No physical or mental torture, nor any other form of coercion, may be inflicted on prisoners of war to secure from them information of any kind whatever. Prisoners of war who refuse to answer may not be threatened, insulted, or exposed to any unpleasant or disadvantageous treatment of any kind.[14]

Pursuant to GCIV:

'No physical or moral coercion shall be exercised against protected persons, in particular to obtain information from them or from third parties.'[15]

Additional Protocol I to the Geneva Conventions (API) further reinforces the centrality of the principle of humane treatment. Its 'Fundamental Guarantees'[16] provisions are meant to serve as a legal safety net, covering any person, including those who may be detained in

---

[9]  ibid article 32.
[10]  ibid article 33.
[11]  ibid article 29.
[12]  ibid articles 147 and 146. See also Rome Statute articles 8(2)(a) and (b).
[13]  GCIII article 17.
[14]  ibid.
[15]  GCIV article 31.
[16]  Protocol Additional to the Geneva Conventions of 12 August 1949 and Relating to the Protection of Victims of International Armed Conflicts (Protocol I) (adopted 8 June 1977, entered into force 7 December 1978) 1125 UNTS 3 (API) article 75.

relation to an IAC, who does not already benefit from more favourable treatment under the Geneva Conventions. Article 75 of the Protocol provides that such persons 'shall be treated humanely in all circumstances and shall enjoy, as a minimum, the protection provided by this article without any adverse distinction'.[17] It also lists specific acts that are prohibited 'at any time and in any place whatsoever, whether committed by civilian or by military agents'.[18]

While IHL treaty provisions governing detention in NIACs are generally far less developed than those relative to IACs, this does not apply to the principle of humane treatment and its elaboration in either Common Article 3 of the four Geneva Conventions or Additional Protocol II to the Geneva Conventions (APII). Half of Common Article 3, which also covers detainees, is devoted to the obligation of humane treatment and the list of specific acts that are prohibited 'at any time and in any place whatsoever' are:

a) violence to life and person, in particular murder of all kinds, mutilation, cruel treatment and torture;

b) taking of hostages;

c) outrages upon personal dignity, in particular humiliating and degrading treatment;

d) the passing of sentences and the carrying out of executions without previous judgment pronounced by a regularly constituted court, affording all the judicial guarantees which are recognized as indispensable by civilized peoples.[19]

The proscriptions of Common Article 3 with regard to treatment have been supplemented by customary IHL, as reflected in the ICRC's 2005 Study on customary IHL (CIHL).[20]

For its part, APII stipulates that, inter alia, the persons covered, including those whose 'liberty has been restricted', are 'entitled to respect for their person, honour and convictions and religious practices' and that they shall 'in all circumstances be treated humanely, without any adverse distinction'.[21] It contains a longer enumeration of prohibited acts than that in Common Article 3.[22]

---

[17] ibid article 75(1). The full wording of the 'no adverse distinction' clause has been omitted here.

[18] ibid article 75(2). The prohibited acts are:

a) violence to the life, health, or physical or mental well-being of persons, in particular: i) murder; ii) torture of all kinds, whether physical or mental; iii) corporal punishment; and iv) mutilation; b) outrages upon personal dignity, in particular humiliating and degrading treatment, enforced prostitution and any form of indecent assault; c) the taking of hostages; d) collective punishments; and e) threats to commit any of the foregoing acts.

[19] Geneva Conventions Common Article 3(1). The last sentence would obviously be differently worded nowadays and was, in fact, rephrased in the corresponding text of the Rome Statute: '... all judicial guarantees which are generally recognized as indispensable'. See Rome Statute, article 8(2)(c)(iv).

[20] CIHL 'Fundamental Guarantees', section V(1).

[21] Protocol Additional to the Geneva Conventions of 12 August 1949, and Relating to the Protection of Victims of Non-International Armed Conflicts (Protocol II) (adopted 8 June 1977, entered into force 7 December 1978) 1125 UNTS 609 (APII) article 4(1) and (2).

[22] ibid article 4(2) prohibits the following acts against, inter alia, detainees:

'at any time and in any place whatsoever': 'a) violence to the life, health and physical or mental well-being of persons, in particular murder as well as cruel treatment such as torture, mutilation or any form of corporal punishment; b) collective punishments; c) taking of hostages; d) acts of terrorism; e) outrages upon personal dignity, in particular humiliating and degrading treatment, rape, enforced prostitution and any form of indecent assault; f) slavery and the slave trade in all their forms; g) pillage; h) threats to commit any of the foregoing acts'.

## B. Conditions of Detention

The principle of humane treatment is expressed in the prohibited acts outlined above, but must also be observed with respect to the conditions of detention. Persons deprived of liberty are in a position of vulnerability because the preservation of their physical and mental health, and of their very life, depends on the detaining authority. In this context, humane treatment means that such authority must provide an adequate response to both the physical needs (accommodation, food, clothing, hygiene, medical attention, etc), and the psychological needs (family contacts, relations with the outside world, religious and other activities, etc), of persons detained.

GCIII and GCIV include a detailed set of provisions on conditions of detention for POWs and civilians, and elaborate a range of other aspects of the respective internment regimes. The number of provisions is such that justice cannot be done to them here.[23] What should be noted is that internment is a non-punitive form of detention which is designed, with very few exceptions,[24] to allow detainees to live in a communal setting,[25] and to have contacts with the outside world, including with members of their families.[26]

Common Article 3 does not include any provisions on conditions of detention in NIACs. APII rectifies this somewhat for situations in which it is applicable, by means of provisions which are to be applied 'as a minimum' with regard to persons deprived of liberty for reasons related to the armed conflict, 'whether they are interned or detained'.[27] The Protocol thus provides that such persons shall, 'to the same extent as the local civilian population, be provided with food and drinking water and be afforded safeguards as regards health and hygiene and protection against the rigours of the climate and the dangers of the armed conflict'.[28] They shall be 'allowed to receive individual or collective relief' and to 'practise their religion and, if requested and appropriate, to receive spiritual assistance from persons, such as chaplains, performing religious functions'.[29]

The Protocol also specifies that those responsible for internment or detention shall also, 'within the limits of their capabilities',[30] ensure that: except where families are housed together, women are held in quarters separated from those of men and are under the immediate supervision of women; that persons deprived of liberty shall be allowed to send and receive letters and cards; that places of internment and detention shall not be located close to the combat zone; and that the persons involved shall have the benefit of medical examinations.[31] APII likewise stipulates that the physical or mental health and integrity of persons deprived of liberty shall not be endangered by any unjustified act or omission, and that it is prohibited to subject such persons to any medical procedure which is not indicated by their state of health and is not consistent with the generally accepted medical standards applied to free persons under similar medical circumstances.[32]

---

[23] API has very few provisions which may be deemed to specifically regulate conditions of detention in IAC.
[24] See eg in the case of disciplinary or penal sanctions.
[25] See eg GCIII articles 21, 22, 25 and GCIV, articles 82, 83, 85.
[26] See eg GCIII, articles 70, 71, and 72; GCIV articles 106, 107, and 108. Civilian internees are also allowed family visits (article 116).
[27] APII article 5(1).
[28] ibid article 5(1)(b).
[29] ibid article 5(1)(c) and (d).
[30] ibid article 5(2).
[31] See ibid article 5(2)(a)–(d).
[32] See ibid article 5(e).

While customary IHL rules have to some extent filled the gap as regards conditions of detention in NIACs,[33] it remains a fact that IHL lacks a sufficiently detailed catalogue of norms on conditions of detention in this type of armed conflict.

Provided below, in keeping with the purpose of this chapter, is an enumeration of a number of basic rules that could serve as a guide to assessing the lawfulness of conditions of detention in NIACs.[34] The list is drawn from rules of customary IHL, specific provisions of IHL treaties, provisions of human rights 'soft law' on detention,[35] and best practices. The rules are by no means exhaustive and do not purport to define the parameters of humane conditions of detention.

### 1. Dignity and respect
Detention regimes for particular detainee populations should take due account of the customs and social relations of the communities to which the detainees belong. Detention regimes and conditions of detention must be adapted to a detainee's age, sex, and health status.

### 2. Safety
No detainee may at any time be sent to, or detained in areas where s/he may be exposed to the dangers of the combat zone, nor may his or her presence be used to render certain points or areas immune from military operations. Detainees must benefit from all available protective systems, such as shelters against aerial bombardment. Detainees are under the protection of the detaining authority. Detainees must be protected from other inmates or from external attacks that may be directed against them.

### 3. Food and drinking water
Detainees must be provided with adequate food and drinking water; consideration shall also be given to the detainees' customary diet, with expectant and nursing mothers and children being given additional food.

### 4. Hygiene and clothing
Detainees must be provided with adequate clothing to preserve their dignity and be protected from the adverse effects of the climate and/or be allowed to keep their own clothing. They shall be provided with the means to maintain personal hygiene, as well as to wash and dry their clothes. Access to sanitary facilities must be available to detainees at all times and organized in a way that ensures respect for dignity.

### 5. Personal belongings
Pillage of the personal belongings of detainees is prohibited.

---

[33] CIHL rules 118–127.

[34] The list, with slight modifications to the one above, was first published in Jelena Pejic, 'The Protective Scope of Common Article 3: More than Meets the Eye' (2011) 93(881) *IRRC* 28 www.icrc.org/fre/assets/files/review/2011/irrc-881-pejic.pdf.

[35] See eg The UN Standard Minimum Rules for the Treatment of Prisoners (the Nelson Mandela Rules), UNGA Resolution 70/175 (8 January 2016) and the Body of Principles for the Protection of All Persons under Any Form of Detention or Imprisonment, UNGA Resolution 43/173 (9 December 1988).

### 6. Accommodation
Detainees must be provided with adequate accommodation; sleeping and living accommodation shall meet all the requirements of health, with due regard being paid to climatic conditions.

### 7. Medical care
Detainees must be provided with adequate medical care, in keeping with recognized medical ethics and principles; patients should be provided with all relevant information concerning their condition, the course of their treatment, and the medication prescribed for them. Every patient must be free to refuse treatment or any other intervention.

### 8. Humanitarian relief
Detainees must be allowed to receive individual or collective relief.

### 9. Religion
The personal convictions and religious practices of detainees must be respected.

### 10. Open air and exercise
Detainees must have sufficient access to the open air daily, in order to practice suitable exercise if they so wish.

### 11. Women
Women must be held in quarters separate from those of men, except where families are accommodated as family units. Women must be under the immediate supervision of women and benefit from treatment and facilities appropriate to their specific needs.

### 12. Minors
Children under eighteen years of age must be held in quarters separate from those of adults, except where families are accommodated as family units.

### 13. Work and recruitment
No detainee shall be forced/requested to take part in military operations, directly or indirectly, or to contribute through his/her work to the war effort. Detainees must, if made to work, have the benefit of working conditions and safeguards similar to those enjoyed by the local civilian population.

### 14. Family contact
Detainees must, subject to reasonable conditions, be allowed to be in contact with their family, through correspondence, visits, or other means of communication available.

### 15. Discipline and punishment
Disciplinary proceedings must be clearly established for defined disciplinary offences and be limited in time. No more restriction than is necessary to maintain order and security in the place of detention shall be applied. In no circumstances may disciplinary measures be inhuman, degrading, or harmful to the mental and physical health and integrity of the detainees. Account must, inter alia, be taken of a detainee's age, sex, and state of health.

Punishment may be imposed only on detainees personally responsible for disciplinary offence(s) and must be limited in time. Solitary confinement is an exceptional and temporary disciplinary measure of last resort. Instruments of restraint such as shackles, chains, and handcuffs may be used only in exceptional circumstances and may never be applied as punishment.

### 16. Records
The personal details of detainees must be properly recorded.

### 17. Public curiosity
Detainees may not be exposed deliberately or through negligence to public curiosity or to insults or condemnation on the part of the public.

### 18. Death
In case of death, the family of the deceased detainee must be informed of the circumstances and causes of death. Deceased detainees must be handed over to their next of kin as soon as practicable. Where handover to family is not practicable, the body must be temporarily interred according to the rites and traditions of the community to which the deceased belonged; the grave must be respected, and marked in such a way that it can always be recognized.

### 19. Complaint mechanism
A complaint process must be clearly established. Detainees must be allowed to present to the detaining authority any complaint on treatment or conditions of detention, or express any specific needs they may have.

### 20. Foreigners
Foreign nationals must be allowed to inform the diplomatic and consular representatives of the state to which they belong of their detention. Such information may also be conveyed through intermediaries such as the ICRC.

### 21. Oversight
Independent monitoring bodies, such as the ICRC, must be given access to all detainees in order to monitor treatment and conditions of detention and perform other tasks of a purely humanitarian nature.

## 3. Procedural Safeguards in Internment

In armed conflict, 'internment' denotes the non-criminal detention of a person based on the serious threat that his or her activity poses to the security of the detaining authority in relation to the conflict.[36] It is with respect to the regulation of the grounds and process for

---

[36] See Yves Sandoz, Christophe Swinarski, and Bruno Zimmermann (eds), *Commentary on the Additional Protocols of 8 June 1977 to the Geneva Conventions of 12 August 1949, and relating to the Protection of Victims of International Armed Conflicts (Protocol I)* (ICRC/Martinus Nijhoff 1987) 875 (para 3063) (with regards to article 75(3)) ('AP Commentary').

internment that dissimilarities emerge between IHL applicable in IACs and NIACs, and between IHL and the corresponding rules of human rights law. This is one of the areas in which the question of the interplay between the two branches of international law arises, and has triggered controversy, due to divergences between the relevant provisions.

Outside armed conflict, deprivation of liberty should, in the great majority of cases, occur because a person is suspected of having committed a criminal offence. Additionally, in guaranteeing the right to liberty of person, the International Covenant on Civil and Political Rights (ICCPR)[37] and equivalent provisions of regional human rights treaties[38] provide that anyone detained, for whatever reason, has the right to judicial review of the lawfulness of his or her detention[39] (also known in some legal systems as the right to *habeas corpus*). While this right is not explicitly included as non-derogable in the ICCPR,[40] it is being increasingly viewed as such.[41]

Situations of armed conflict often constitute a different reality from peacetime, as a result of which IHL incorporates different rules related to non-criminal detention for security reasons to those of human rights law. International human rights bodies and regional courts seem to have accepted that IHL provides the appropriate procedural framework for internment in IACs,[42] but have either not yet pronounced on or have taken another view with respect to internment in NIACs.[43]

The focus of this section of the chapter is on the group of rules related to internment in armed conflict, their rationale, and relevant procedural safeguards.

## A. IAC

In IAC, which may include situations of occupation, IHL permits the internment of POWs and, under certain conditions, of civilians.

---

[37] International Covenant on Civil and Political Rights (adopted 16 December 1966, entered into force 23 March 1976) 999 UNTS 171(ICCPR).

[38] European Convention for the Protection of Human Rights and Fundamental Freedoms (European Convention on Human Rights, as amended) (ECHR) article 5(4); American Convention on Human Rights (Pact of San José, Costa Rica) (adopted 22 November 1969, entered into force 18 July 1978) 1144 UNTS 123 article 7(6); African Charter on Human and People's Rights (adopted 27 June 1981, entered into force 21 October 1986) (1982) 21 ILM 58 (African Charter) article 6.

[39] ICCPR article 9(4).

[40] See ibid article 4(2), which does not include article 9 in the list of non-derogable rights. Article 5(4) ECHR is also not among the non-derogable rights under article 15 of that treaty. Under the jurisprudence of the Inter-American Court of Human Rights, the right to habeas corpus is itself non-derogable in order to protect non-derogable rights (see *Habeas Corpus in Emergency Situations* (Advisory Opinion) OC-8/87, Inter-American Court of Human Rights Series A No 8 (30 January 1987); *Judicial Guarantees in States of Emergency* (Advisory Opinion) OC-9/87, Inter-American Court of Human Rights Series A No 9 (6 October 1987)). The African Charter is silent on the issue of derogation.

[41] United Nations Human Rights Committee, 'General Comment No. 35, Article 9 (Liberty and security of person)' UN Doc CCPR/C/GC/35 (16 December 2014) (HRC GC 35) paras 15, 45, and 66. The paras suggest that there can be no derogation from the right to judicial review in NIAC. The General Comment does not, unfortunately, make any mention of NIAC with an extraterritorial element (see further below), where the issue has proven to pose an actual legal and practical challenge.

[42] See HRC GC 35, paras 64 and 66, and *Case of Hassan v The United Kingdom* App No 29750/09 (ECtHR, 16 September 2014), paras103–107. In the view of this contributor, IHL rules on procedural safeguards in internment in IAC are the *lex specialis* to human rights law, an approach not adopted in HRC GC 35 or by the European Court of Human Rights (ECtHR).

[43] At the time of writing, the ECtHR has not heard a case related to procedural safeguards in NIAC. As already noted, HRC GC 35 essentially rejects any specificity of detention in NIAC.

### 1. POW internment

POWs[44] include combatants captured by the adverse party in an international armed conflict. As a term of art, 'combatant' denotes a legal status that, as such, exists only in this type of conflict. Under IHL rules on the conduct of hostilities, a combatant is a member of the armed forces of a party to an international armed conflict who has 'the right to participate directly in hostilities'.[45] This means that he or she may use force against (ie target and kill or injure) other persons taking a direct part in hostilities, and attack military objectives. Because such activity is obviously prejudicial to the security of the adverse party, the GCIII provides that a detaining state 'may subject prisoners of war to internment'.[46]

In case of doubt about the entitlement to POW status of a captured belligerent, article 5 of the GCIII provides that such person shall be protected by the Convention until his or her status has been determined by a competent tribunal.[47] This provision is sometimes understood as requiring judicial review, which is not the case. Article 5 tribunals are meant to operate in or near the zone of combat; they only determine status, and no other issue.[48]

It is generally uncontroversial that GCIII provides a sufficient legal basis for POW internment and that an additional domestic law basis is not required. The detaining state is not obliged to provide review, judicial or other, of the lawfulness of POW internment as long as active hostilities are ongoing,[49] because POWs are *ipso facto* considered to pose a security threat. POW internment must end, and POWs must be released, without delay after the cessation of active hostilities,[50] unless they are subject to criminal proceedings or are serving a criminal sentence.[51] They may also be released earlier on medical grounds[52] or on their own cognizance.[53] Unjustifiable delay in the repatriation of POWs after the cessation of active hostilities is a grave breach of API.[54]

### 2. Internment of civilians

Under GCIV, internment—and assigned residence—are the most severe 'measures of control'[55] that may be taken by a state with respect to civilians whose activity is deemed to pose a serious threat to its security. It is undisputed that the direct participation of civilians in hostilities falls into that category, as do other acts that meet the same threshold.[56] Civilians who take a direct part in hostilities are colloquially called 'unprivileged belligerents' (or incorrectly referred to as 'unlawful combatants').

---

[44]  GCIII article 4.
[45]  API article 43(2). This excludes medical and religious personnel.
[46]  GCIII article 21.
[47]  ibid article 5(2).
[48]  See AP Commentary to article 45(1) of API, on the nature of a 'competent tribunal' under GCIII article 5, para 1745.
[49]  Judicial review under the domestic law of the detaining state could be sought to obtain the release of a POW who is detained despite the end of active hostilities.
[50]  GCIII article 118(1).
[51]  ibid article 119(5).
[52]  ibid articles 109(1) and 110.
[53]  ibid article 21(2).
[54]  API article 85(4)(b).
[55]  GCIV articles 27, 41, and 78.
[56]  Examples of activities that are not direct participation in hostilities but would constitute a serious security threat are general financing or general intelligence gathering, recruitment for military operations, etc.

GCIV provides different standards in terms of permissible grounds for internment depending on whether an internee is detained in a state party's own territory ('if the security of the Detaining Power makes it absolutely necessary')[57] or is held in occupied territory ('imperative reasons of security').[58] It has been suggested that the difference in wording only indicates that internment in occupied territory should in practice be more exceptional than in the territory of a party to the conflict.[59]

The internment review process in the two IAC scenarios would also appear to differ somewhat. In a state party's own territory internment review is to be carried out by an 'appropriate court or administrative board',[60] while in occupied territory GCIV refers to a 'regular procedure' that is to be administered by a 'competent body'.[61] Despite these and other textual differences, the rules are in essence the same. A person interned in IAC has the right to submit a request for review of the decision on internment (to challenge it), the review must be expeditiously[62] conducted either by a court or an administrative board, and periodic review is thereafter to be automatic, on a six-monthly basis.[63] GCIV is silent on the issue of legal assistance.

It is sometimes queried why IHL provides procedural safeguards to civilians interned in IAC, and not to POWs. The simple answer is that, in reality, there is far less certainty as to the threat that a captured enemy civilian actually poses than is the case with a combatant who is, after all, a member of the adversary's armed forces. In contemporary warfare civilians are, for example, often detained not only in direct combat, but also on the basis of intelligence information suggesting that they represent a security threat. The purpose of the review process is to enable a determination of whether such information is reliable and whether the person's activity meets the high legal standard that would justify internment and its duration.

Civilian internment must cease as soon as the reasons which necessitated it no longer exist.[64] It must in any event end 'as soon as possible after the close of hostilities'.[65] Unjustifiable delay in the repatriation of civilians is also a grave breach of API.[66]

There is some debate among experts whether, on its own, GCIV constitutes a sufficient legal basis for the internment of civilians in IAC or whether it must be accompanied by domestic law of a statutory nature (legislation). It is not clear why this question is posed only in relation to the GCIV and not the GCIII, for there is no reason to conclude that the treaties differ in the legal authority provided. It is submitted that GCIV constitutes a sufficient legal basis for internment, which means that states do not have to enact additional domestic legislation to provide for a legal basis.[67]

---

[57] GCIV article 42(1).

[58] ibid article 78(1).

[59] Jean Pictet (ed), *Commentary: Geneva Convention IV Relative to the Protection of Civilian Persons in Time of War* (ICRC 1958) 367.

[60] GCIV article 43.

[61] ibid article 78(2).

[62] ibid articles 43(1) and 78(2).

[63] ibid articles 43(1) and 78(2). See also Pictet (above n 59) 261, 368–9.

[64] GCIV article 132(1) and API article 75(3).

[65] GCIV articles 46(1) and 133(1). Judicial review under the domestic law of the detaining state could be sought to obtain the release of a civilian who is detained despite the close of hostilities.

[66] API article 85(4)(b).

[67] But regulations elaborating on the internment review process would in practice be necessary.

## B. NIAC

IHL does not contain rules on procedural safeguards for persons interned in NIAC, in which, it should be recalled, there is no POW or protected person status within the meaning of GCIII and GCIV, respectively. Common Article 3 does not explicitly provide a legal basis for detention and is silent on the possible grounds for and process in internment, even though this form of detention is practiced by both states and NSAGs. APII explicitly mentions 'internment',[68] thus confirming that this type of deprivation of liberty is inherent to NIAC, but likewise does not incorporate an explicit legal basis, grounds, or process. The lack of sufficient IHL rules on these issues has generated a range of views on how the gap may be filled.

### 1. Legal basis for internment

According to one view, the legal basis for internment must be explicit, as it is for example in the GCIV; in its absence IHL cannot be interpreted to implicitly provide it.[69] Pursuant to this position, only domestic law, limited by human rights law (which does not contain an explicit legal basis for any type of detention), can provide the requisite legal authority for internment in NIAC. According to another view, to which this contributor subscribes, IHL should be interpreted as containing an inherent power to intern.

Several cogent reasons may be advanced,[70] but only one will be briefly mentioned here. It is a fact that, unless IHL is interpreted as incorporating such an inherent power, the deprivation of liberty by NSAGs would be completely outside of any legal authority. Domestic law does not allow NSAGs to detain and moreover, states may criminalize all acts including detention by the non-state party in a NIAC. The lack of a stand-alone legal authority for detention under human rights law has been noted at the start of this section, but this body of norms also does not bind NSAGs de iure. Given that IHL does bind them,[71] it is not logical to claim that NSAGs are legally obliged to implement the specific provisions of Common Article 3 and APII (some of which explicitly regulate treatment and conditions in internment as outlined above), but also that IHL does not even provide an inherent power for deprivation of liberty to begin with.

The controversy over legal basis may in any event be said to be somewhat of a 'red herring' in the case of a 'traditional' NIAC, occurring in the territory of a state between its armed forces and one or more NSAGs. Regardless of a possible separate basis to intern under IHL, states will in practice be guided by their domestic law authority, informed by their human rights obligations, and the relevant norms of IHL, in determining the legal framework—including grounds and process—for the possible internment of persons whose activity

---

[68] APII articles 5 and 6.

[69] A good overview of this and other positions is provided for in *Abd Ali Hameed Al-Waheed (Appellant) v Ministry of Defence (Respondent)* and *Serdar Mohammed (Respondent) v Ministry of Defence (Appellant)* [2017] UKSC 1 and [2017] UKSC 2. https://www.supremecourt.uk/cases/docs/uksc-2014-0219-judgment.pdf, accessed 18 March 2020.

[70] For a review see Kubo Macak, 'A Needle in a Haystack? Locating the Legal Basis for Detention in Non-International Armed Conflict' (2015) *45 Isr YB HR* (forthcoming) http://ssrn.com/abstract=2559220, and Ezequiel Heffes, 'Detentions by Armed Opposition Groups in Non-International Armed Conflicts: Towards a New Characterization of International Humanitarian Law' (2015) 20(2) *JC & SL* 229.

[71] See eg Sandesh Sivakumaran, *The Law of Non-International Armed Conflict* (OUP 2012) 236–42.

presents a serious security threat. This will require a careful examination of the interplay between national law and the applicable international legal regimes.

Identifying the legal framework governing internment is more complex in NIACs with an extraterritorial element, ie those in which the armed forces of one or more states, or of an international or regional organization, fight alongside the armed forces of a host state, in its territory, against one or more organized NSAG. Several legal issues, which cannot be expounded on here, will arise.[72] It is submitted that, along with the recognition of an inherent power to intern in NIAC, a practically feasible legal approach[73] would be to require that the grounds and process for internment in this scenario be specifically provided for in one of the following ways: first, an international agreement concluded between an assisting state(s), or international or regional forces, and the host state; second, in the domestic law of the host state or, in exceptional circumstances, of the assisting state(s); third, in the Standard Operating Procedures or other equivalent document of the assisting states(s), or of international or regional forces, which must be of a legally binding nature.[74] The aim of the legal 'package' suggested above would be to prevent arbitrary detention by intervening forces in situations of extraterritorial NIAC.

In this context it should be recalled that a UN Security Council Resolution adopted under Chapter VII of the UN Charter may also provide a legal basis for internment in an 'extraterritorial NIAC'. Legal experts differ as to whether such a resolution must expressly authorize internment or whether the standard formula of authorization—to use 'all necessary means' (to accomplish a mission)—is sufficient. Such resolutions, however, do not elaborate on the grounds and process for internment. It is submitted that, in such a case, these will still need to be specified in one of the ways outlined above.[75]

## 2. Grounds and process for internment

As already mentioned, IHL applicable in NIAC does not specify permissible grounds for internment. The ICRC has relied on 'imperative reasons of security' as the legal standard that should inform internment decisions in NIAC.[76]

The exact meaning of 'imperative reasons of security' has not been sufficiently elaborated in international or domestic law to enable a determination of the specific type of conduct that would meet that threshold. As noted in the Commentary to GCIV:

> It did not seem possible to define the expression 'security of the State' in a more concrete fashion. It is thus left very largely to Governments to decide the measure of activity prejudicial to the internal or external security of the State which justifies internment or assigned residence.[77]

---

[72] Eg the uncertain extraterritorial reach of domestic law, and questions related to the application of human rights law in NIACs with an extraterritorial element. The extent of the extraterritorial reach of human rights obligations is evolving (and remains disputed by some states), and the issue of whether assisting states must derogate from their human rights obligations in order to intern persons abroad is unresolved in practice (as already mentioned, no state has done so to date).

[73] This approach is believed to be feasible given the current unwillingness of states to further develop IHL governing NIACs by means of binding norms, including those regulating various aspects of detention such as grounds and process for internment.

[74] This is the proposal made by the ICRC, 'Internment in Armed Conflict: Basic Rules and Challenges', Opinion Paper, November 2014, 8 (ICRC Paper on Internment).

[75] ibid.

[76] Pejic (above n 34) 28–31.

[77] GCIV Commentary 257.

The Commentary nevertheless adds that, '[i]n any case such measures can be ordered for real and imperative reasons of security, their exceptional character must be preserved'.[78]

While states are thus left a margin of appreciation in deciding on the specific activity deemed to represent a serious security threat, there are pointers in terms of what activity would or would not meet that standard. It is uncontroversial that direct participation in hostilities is an activity that would meet the imperative reasons of security standard.[79] Conversely, internment cannot be resorted to for the sole purpose of interrogation or intelligence gathering, unless the person in question is deemed to represent a serious security threat based on his or her own activity. Internment may also not be resorted to in order to punish a person for past activity, or to act as a general deterrent to the future activity of another person.

As a general matter, internment should not be used in lieu of criminal prosecution in individual cases when criminal process is in fact feasible. It must in any event be recognized that the imperative reasons of security standard is high, and a careful evaluation of whether it has been met must take place in relation to each person detained.

The absence of IHL rules on the process for internment has proven to be a significant legal—and protection—issue, particularly in NIACs with an extraterritorial element. It prompted the ICRC to attempt to fill the gap by means of institutional guidelines issued in 2005, entitled 'Procedural Principles and Safeguards for Internment/Administrative Detention[80] in Armed Conflict and Other Situations of Violence'[81] (Guidelines). The 'rules' are based on law and policy,[82] and are meant to be implemented in a manner that takes into account the specific circumstances at hand. They are briefly discussed here as there is currently no other elaboration of this particular subject matter which could be applied in NIAC.[83]

The Guidelines provide that a person must, among other things, be informed promptly, in a language he or she understands, of the reasons for internment. An internee likewise has the right to challenge, with the least possible delay, the lawfulness of his or her internment, and the review of lawfulness must be carried out by an independent and impartial body. Where internment review is administrative rather than judicial in nature, ensuring the requisite independence and impartiality of the review body will require particular attention. Assistance of counsel should be provided whenever feasible, but other modalities to ensure expert legal assistance may be considered as well.

The right to periodical review of the lawfulness of continued internment is also provided for in the Guidelines. It obliges the detaining authority to ascertain whether the internee

---

[78]  ibid 368.

[79]  The question here is what constitutes direct participation in hostilities, an issue outside the scope of this chapter. See eg Nlis Melzer, 'Interpretive Guidance on the Notion of Direct Participation in Hostilities under IHL' (ICRC 2009) www.icrc.org/eng/assets/files/other/icrc-002-0990.pdf.

[80]  The terms 'internment' and 'administrative detention' are used interchangeably in the guidance. It encompasses, in addition to armed conflict, other situations of violence, as the ICRC has observed in practice that non-criminal detention for security reasons is a common occurrence in peacetime practice as well.

[81]  The institutional position is entitled: 'Procedural Principles and Safeguards for Internment/Administrative Detention in Armed Conflict and Other Situations of Violence'. It was published as Annex 1 to an ICRC Report, ICRC, 'International Humanitarian Law and the Challenges of Contemporary Armed Conflicts' (30th International Conference of the Red Cross and Red Crescent) (2007) www.icrc.org/eng/assets/files/other/icrc_002_0892.pdf.

[82]  The purpose of the commentary is only to provide an overview of the various legal sources, primarily IHL, but also human rights law, on the basis of which the 'rules' were formulated.

[83]  The guidance does not cover POW detention, outlined above.

continues to pose an imperative threat to security and to order release if that is not the case. It should be noted that the longer internment lasts, the greater the burden on the detaining authority to show that the concerned person remains an imperative threat to security. The safeguards that apply to initial review are also to be applied at periodical review.

IHL in NIAC is silent as regards the outer temporal limit of internment. It is, however, widely accepted that this form of detention is to cease, as a matter of IHL, at the end of the armed conflict in relation to which a person was interned. The end of a NIAC is a factual matter that is determined on a case-by-case basis.[84]

## 4. Transfer of Detainees

The transfer among states of persons deprived of liberty has emerged as one of the key legal and practical challenges linked to detention in armed conflict. The legal debate has focused on the meaning and scope of the principle of *non-refoulement*, while the principal challenge in practice has arisen in NIAC with an extraterritorial element. The question is: are assisting states, or international or regional forces, who may be detaining persons in the territory of a host state, allowed to hand them over to the authorities of the latter and, if so, under what circumstances?

By way of reminder, the principle of *non-refoulement* prohibits a state from transferring a person to another state if there are substantial grounds to believe that he or she runs a real risk of being subjected to certain violations of fundamental rights. These include, in particular, torture or other cruel, inhuman, or degrading treatment or punishment, arbitrary deprivation of life, and persecution on account of race, religion, nationality, membership of a particular social group, or political opinion. According to some views, an even broader list could be drawn up.[85]

*Non-refoulement* is found, with variations in scope, in IHL, human rights law,[86] and refugee law,[87] and is also contained in a number of extradition treaties.[88] The exact coverage

---

[84] See ICRC, 'Report on International Humanitarian Law and the Challenges of Contemporary Armed Conflicts' (32nd International Conference of the Red Cross and the Red Crescent) (ICRC October 2015) 7–8 and 10–11 http://reliefweb.int/sites/reliefweb.int/files/resources/32ic-report-on-ihl-and-challenges-of-armed-conflicts.pdf.

[85] See International Commission of Jurists, 'The ICJ Declaration on Upholding Human Rights and the Rule of Law in Combating Terrorism' (adopted 28 August 2004) (Belin Declaration) www.unhcr.org/refworld/docid/41dec1f94.html. Pursuant to Principle 10 on *non-refoulement*:

> States may not expel, return, transfer or extradite, a person suspected or convicted of acts of terrorism to a state where there is a real risk that the person would be subjected to a serious violation of human rights, including torture or cruel, inhuman or degrading treatment or punishment, enforced disappearance, extrajudicial execution, or a manifestly unfair trial; or be subject to the death penalty.

[86] In human rights law, *non-refoulement* is expressly provided for in the Convention against Torture pursuant to which: 'No State Party shall expel, return ("refouler") or extradite a person to another State where there are substantial grounds for believing that he would be in danger of being subjected to torture.' The Convention also states that: 'For the purpose of determining whether there are such grounds, the competent authorities shall take into account all relevant considerations including, where applicable, the existence in the State concerned of a consistent pattern of gross, flagrant or mass violations of human rights.' See UN Office of the United Nations High Commissioner for Human Rights, Convention against Torture and Other Cruel, Inhuman or Degrading Treatment or Punishment (adopted 10 December 1984, entered into force 26 June 1987) 1465 UNTS 85 article 3(1) and (2).

[87] Persecution as a ground for *non-refoulement* is provided for in international refugee law. See 1951 Convention Relating to the Status of Refugees (adopted 28 July 1951, entered into force 22 April 1954) 189 UNTS 150 article 33.

[88] The operation of the principle of *non-refoulement* under human rights law and refugee law or under extradition treaties is beyond the scope of this chapter and will not be further discussed.

of the principle and the violations that must be taken into account will depend on the spe-cific norms applicable in a given context, ie on the relevant treaties and customary law.

The Geneva Conventions do not mention the term *non-refoulement* as such, but incorp-orate specific substantive provisions to that effect for situations of IAC. Pursuant to GCIII and GCIV, POWs and civilians may only be transferred by the detaining state to a state that is a party to the respective Convention, and after it has 'satisfied itself' of the 'will-ingness and ability' of such transferee state to apply the Convention.[89] The Conventions also provide that the transferring state must take corrective measures or request the return of POWs, or civilians, if it determines that the receiving state fails to fulfil its obligations under the treaty.[90] GCIV also stipulates that a protected person may 'in no circumstances' be transferred to a country where he or she may have reason to fear persecution for his or her political opinions or religious beliefs.[91]

There are no IHL norms on *non-refoulement* in NIAC. However, as discussed above, a party to such an armed conflict is bound by Common Article 3 in all circumstances. It may be argued that it would contravene the provisions of this article if a party were to transfer a person in its power to another party if there are substantial grounds to believe that he or she runs a real risk of being tortured or otherwise ill-treated, or arbitrarily deprived of life. Put differently, similar to IHL in IAC—which prohibits the circumvention of safeguards owed to protected persons by means of handover to a non-compliant party—IHL applicable in NIAC should also not be side-stepped by the transfer of detainees to a party that will not respect its Common Article 3 obligations.

The issue of whether the principle of *non-refoulement* applies only where a transferred person crosses an international border, or may also apply to transfers between states within the same country, remains unsettled.[92] While this question has not yet been conclusively decided as a matter of international law, protection concerns leave no doubt that the latter interpretation should be preferred. This view is not meant to suggest a lack of awareness of the very real practical problems posed by the implementation of the principle of *non-refoulement* to transfers within the territory of a (host) state. Depending on the circum-stances, feasible solutions may include: prolongation of detention by the state of custody; transfer to a third state; transfer to select places of detention within the host state in which there is no risk of violations; monitoring of the treatment of transferred detainees in host state facilities; or joint administration of places of detention in the host state for the purpose of enabling individual follow-up of transferees. It should be noted that due to the narrow range of rights protected, observance of the principle of *non-refoulement* is not likely to im-pede the transfer of thousands of persons in practice; rather, it will stand in the way of the transfer of specific individuals who face a real risk.

One of the most contentious issues related to the transfer of detainees concerns the procedural safeguards that should precede a transfer decision.[93] While neither treaty nor

---

[89]  GCIII article 12(2); GCIV article 45(2).
[90]  GCIII article 12(3); GCIV article 45(3).
[91]  GCIV article 45(4).
[92]  This is the position of human rights bodies. See eg Committee against Torture, 'Conclusions and Recommendations: United Kingdom of Great Britain and Northern Ireland —Dependent Territories' UN Doc CAT/C/CR/33/3 (10 December 2004) para 5(e); Human Rights Committee, 'Concluding Observations: United States of America' UN Doc CCPR/C/USA/CO/3/Rev.1 (18 December 2006) para 16.
[93]  Another such issue is the reliance by a sending state on 'diplomatic assurances'. In order to comply with their obligations under the principle of *non-refoulement*, sending states have increasingly resorted to transfer agree-ments under which the receiving state provides assurances that a transferred person will be treated in accordance

customary IHL—or human rights law—provide for procedural safeguards that must be applied before transfer, an obligation to provide them may be derived from the general international law principle that a person whose rights may be, or have been, violated has the right to an effective remedy.[94] In the context of *non-refoulement*, this may be interpreted to mean that a process should be put in place enabling the review of a transfer decision if and when the person involved alleges a real risk of abuse in the receiving state. A number of procedural safeguards may be envisaged, such as: (i) timely information to the concerned person of the intended transfer; (ii) the opportunity for the person concerned to express fears he or she may have about the transfer and to challenge the transfer before a body that is independent of the one that took the transfer decision; (iii) the possibility for the person in question to make representations before the review body in order to explain the reasons he or she would be at risk in the receiving state; and (iv) suspension of transfer during the review because of the irreversible harm that would be caused if the person was transferred. Where possible, the person should also have legal assistance.

The process outlined above has been followed in practice by states in cases of expulsions, extraditions, deportations, or other measures of removal of individuals from their territory. Typically, the remedy is before national courts. The phenomenon of transfers linked to NIACs with an extraterritorial element is, however, relatively new and obviously involves different circumstances. State practice has therefore, not surprisingly, been conflicting. In this context, it should be borne in mind that a review of transfer need not be exclusively judicial in nature. As with procedural safeguards in internment, the key issue is whether the remedy is effective, ie whether the concerned person has a meaningful chance to obtain an independent and impartial decision to prevent a transfer that would be contrary to the principle of *non-refoulement*.

It may be concluded that while the law and policy are a work in progress, it is clear that transfers between states occurring outside of the transferring state's territory require urgent practical responses at the international level. Workable solutions need to be devised that would address the material limitations of states or of international or regional organizations participating in extraterritorial operations, and their obligation to protect transferees from torture and ill-treatment or arbitrary deprivation of life.

## 5. Fair Trial Rights

Fair trial rights, referred to as 'judicial guarantees', are a prominent feature of IHL in both IAC and NIAC. The aim is to ensure that any proceedings undertaken against a person on suspicion of having committed a criminal offence related to the conflict meet the internationally agreed standards of due process. The latter serve to safeguard the fundamental rights of criminal suspects which, it should be recognized, may be particularly under

---

with international standards. While it is uncontroversial that such assurances do not, per se, relieve a sending state of its *non-refoulement* obligations, there are different views as to whether assurances may ever be resorted to. Some believe they cannot, while others focus on the conditions that must accompany them.

[94] In human rights law, this is articulated in ICCPR article 2(3). In the context of IACs, due also to the ICRC's efforts, a practice has developed allowing POWs to express fear of repatriation to their state of origin and to not be repatriated if the circumstances point to a danger of a violation of their fundamental rights upon return.

pressure in situations of armed conflict when emotions run high and an urge for revenge against the adversary can arise.

GCIII and GCIV both include detailed provisions on criminal proceedings against POWs[95] or civilians[96] who may be subject to trial in an IAC, and include specific judicial guarantees. The catalogue is updated and expanded in API which, as already mentioned, constitutes a safety net in terms of fundamental guarantees.[97] Denial of the right to a fair trial to POWs or civilians is a grave breach of GCIII[98] and GCIV[99] respectively, and is also a listed as a grave breach in API.[100] As regards NIACs, the passing of sentences without a trial that affords 'all the judicial guarantees which are recognized as indispensable' is one of the specific prohibitions of Common Article 3.[101] APII likewise provides a list of fair trial rights.[102] In this context it should be noted that the relevant articles of the two Additional Protocols were fashioned largely according to the fair trial guarantees of the ICCPR.[103] However, the right to a fair trial may not be derogated from in situations of armed conflict under IHL, even though the ICCPR appears to allow it.[104] The right to a fair trial is also a norm of customary IHL, applicable in both IACs and NIACs.[105]

Given the undisputed nature of judicial guarantees under IHL, and the relative similarity of its catalogue of rights with that in human rights law (which has been extensively interpreted in the jurisprudence), this chapter does not list or summarize the individual guarantees. It is perhaps more useful to very briefly highlight two broader issues related to criminal proceedings linked to an armed conflict under IHL.

The first is the difference, in IAC, between the criminal offences for which POWs and civilians may be tried. As noted in section 3 'Procedural Safeguards in Internment' above, POWs are essentially combatants captured by the adverse party in an IAC. Combatants are members of the armed forces of a party to an IAC who have the explicit right under IHL and domestic law to participate directly in hostilities. As a result, POWs may not be prosecuted by the detaining state for lawful acts of violence committed in the course of hostilities (known as 'combatant privilege'). Their immunity from criminal prosecution under the domestic law of the captor does not, however, extend to violations of IHL, in particular grave breaches of the Geneva Conventions or API and other war crimes,[106] or for criminal acts committed after capture.[107] GCIII obliges the detaining state to procedurally treat POWs suspected of having committed a criminal offence as it would members of its own forces. The general rule is that a POW can be validly sentenced only if the sentence has been pronounced 'by the same courts according to the same procedure as in the case of members of the armed forces of the Detaining Power'.[108]

---

[95]  See GCIII articles 82–88 and 99–108.
[96]  See GCIV articles 64–76 and 126.
[97]  API article 75(4).
[98]  GCIII article 130.
[99]  GCIV article 147.
[100]  API article 85(4)(e).
[101]  CA3(1)(d).
[102]  APII article 6.
[103]  See ICCPR article 14.
[104]  See ibid article 4(2).
[105]  See CIHL rule 100.
[106]  See Rome Statute article 8(1) and (2).
[107]  See GCIII article 93. POWs may be tried for other crimes under international law which they may have committed, such as genocide or crimes against humanity.
[108]  ibid article 102. The Convention also specifically stipulates that a POW 'shall be tried only by a military court, unless the existing laws of the Detaining Power expressly permit the civil courts to try a member of the armed

Civilians do not enjoy the 'combatant privilege'. Whether in IAC or NIAC, civilians who take a direct part in hostilities can be prosecuted by the detaining state for the very fact of having taken up arms, and all acts of violence committed during such participation, as well as for other offences related to the armed conflict that may be penalized under the domestic law of the captor. This includes grave breaches of the Geneva Conventions or API and other war crimes.[109] It should be noted, however, that civilian direct participation in hostilities is not a violation of IHL and is not a war crime per se under either treaty or customary IHL.[110]

The second issue that merits highlighting is the death penalty. It is sometimes said that IHL provides for the death penalty, which is not the case. This body of norms establishes a certain number of substantive offences under international law and obliges states to adopt domestic legislation that would enable their prosecution and punishment. It does not, however, incorporate specific penalties, and it thus does not allow or disallow capital punishment, which is the purview of regulation at the national level. The aim of IHL provisions on the death penalty, where it is foreseen in domestic law, is to ensure that certain persons are protected against it and that safeguards exist with respect to its possible implementation.

Pursuant to API, parties to an IAC shall endeavour to avoid the pronouncement of the death penalty on pregnant women or mothers having dependent infants, for an offence related to the armed conflict. It stipulates that the death penalty shall not be executed on such women.[111] In addition, capital punishment for a conflict-related offence shall not be executed on persons below the age of eighteen years at the time of commission of the offence.[112] APII contains similar provisions in situations of NIAC: '[t]he death penalty shall not be pronounced on persons who were under the age of eighteen years at the time of the offence and shall not be carried out on pregnant women or mothers of young children'.[113]

GCIII and GCIV incorporate additional specific safeguards with respect to the death penalty that is imposed on POWs or civilians, respectively, related to: information about offences that carry the death penalty and a prohibition to impose such a penalty on other acts thereafter;[114] notification of its pronouncement to the Protecting Power;[115] and an obligatory minimum six-month moratorium on its execution where it is pronounced.[116]

---

forces of the Detaining Power in respect of the particular offence alleged to have been committed by the prisoner of war' (ibid article 84(1)). It also provides that POWs "may not be sentenced by the military authorities and courts of the Detaining Power to any penalties except those provided for in respect of members of the armed forces of the said Power who have committed the same acts' (ibid article 87(1)).

[109] In addition to war crimes, civilians may likewise be tried for other crimes under international law which they may have committed, such as genocide or crimes against humanity.
[110] See eg the list of War Crimes under article 8 of the Rome Statute.
[111] API article 76(3).
[112] ibid article 77(5).
[113] APII article 6(4).
[114] GCIII article 100(1) and (2); GCIV article 68(2).
[115] GCIII article 107(2); GCIV article 71(2).
[116] GCIII article 101; GCIV article 75(2). Under the latter treaty, the six-month suspension may be reduced in 'individual cases in circumstances of grave emergency involving an organized threat to the security of' the detaining State or its forces, provided that the Protecting Power is notified and given an opportunity to make representations to the competent authorities (GCIV article 75(3)).

# 6. Conclusion

An obvious conclusion that may be drawn from any review of IHL rules on detention is that deprivation of liberty is far more comprehensively regulated in situations of IAC than NIAC. Common Article 3 of the four Geneva Conventions and APII provide key protections for detainees, but these are limited in both scope and specificity compared to those provided in IAC by the Geneva Conventions and API. In addition, debate and disagreement continue over the applicability and adequacy of human rights law, the precise contours of customary IHL, and how international law can reach the behaviour of non-state parties to an armed conflict. Given that NIAC is significantly more prevalent than IAC, and that new scenarios of NIAC have emerged over the past decade-and-a-half, an effort to fill the IHL gaps would appear necessary.

While steps to this effect have been taken by some states at the domestic level in the form of legal and policy guidance,[117] and on one occasion by a group of interested states,[118] they remain fragmented and insufficient. In this context, it should be noted that the ICRC was mandated by the International Conference of the Red Cross and Red Crescent in 2011 to pursue research and consultation with states and other relevant actors to identify and propose a range of options—and recommendations—in order to ensure that IHL remains practical and relevant in providing legal protection to persons deprived of liberty.[119] The results of the ensuing four-year consultation process, the focus of which was detention in NIAC, were submitted to the 2015 International Conference of the Red Cross and Red Crescent in the form of a comprehensive concluding report.[120] A corresponding resolution was likewise adopted by Conference members,[121] paving the way for a new phase of deliberations among states on this issue but, unfortunately, these proved unsuccessful. No further substantive exchanges were held within the process as states were unable to agree on the procedure that should govern discussions going forward. A very brief progress report was thus submitted to the 2019 International Conference of the Red Cross and Red Crescent.[122] This outcome can only be called disappointing. It must be hoped that if and when the international political climate improves a way will be found for states to again focus on the vitally important issue of strengthening IHL protection for persons deprived of their liberty.

[117] See eg UK Ministry of Defence (MoD), 'Joint Doctrine Publication 1-10: Captured Persons (CPERS)' (3rd edn, January 2015) www.gov.uk/government/uploads/system/uploads/attachment_data/file/455589/20150920-JDP_1_10_Ed_3_Ch_1_Secured.pdf.

[118] See eg 'The Copenhagen Process on the Handling of Detainees in International Military Operations: Principles and Guidelines' (19 October 2012) http://um.dk/en/~/media/UM/English-site/Documents/Politics-and-diplomacy/Copenhagen%20Process%20Principles%20and%20Guidelines.pdf.

[119] See ICRC, 'Resolution 1 "Strengthening Legal Protection for Victims of Armed Conflicts"' (31st International Conference of the Red Cross and Red Crescent (December 2011) www.icrc.org/eng/resources/documents/resolution/31-international-conference-resolution-1-2011.htm.

[120] See ICRC, 'Concluding Report on Strengthening International Humanitarian Law Protecting Persons Deprived of Their Liberty' (32nd International Conference of the Red Cross and Red Crescent (October 2015) http://rcrcconference.org/wp-content/uploads/sites/3/2015/04/32IC-Concluding-report-on-persons-deprived-of-their-liberty_EN.pdf.

[121] See ICRC, 'Resolution on Strengthening International Humanitarian Law Protecting Persons Deprived of Their Liberty' (32nd International Conference of the Red Cross and Red Crescent (December 2015) http://rcrcconference.org/wp-content/uploads/sites/3/2015/04/32IC-AR-Persons-deprived-of-liberty_EN.pdf.

[122] Please see the link for the cover page of the report in order to complete the reference https://rcrcconference.org/app/uploads/2019/10/33IC-Deprived-of-liberty_EN.pdf

# 13

# Occupation

*Sylvain Vité\**

## 1. Introduction

Since the beginning of human history, force has been used to subdue enemy powers and impose authority upon foreign populations. While this phenomenon has always attracted the interest of scholars and political authorities, formal regulation of war through the adoption of multilateral treaties started in the second half of the nineteenth century and has never stopped since then. Different issues have been addressed, covering all aspects of war, including its legality, the conduct of hostilities, the treatment afforded to the wounded, sick, and shipwrecked, the fate of enemy prisoners, and the fate of civilians.

In this framework, attention has also been paid to 'occupation'.[1] Occupation refers to this particular phase in international armed conflict (IAC) where a belligerent has overpowered the adverse party and taken control of enemy territories, but the final outcome of the war has not yet been decided. Occupation is thus a transition phase between the end of active hostilities and formal conclusion of the conflict. It is a period where foreign armed forces (the Occupying Power) are responsible for the administration of territories belonging to the defeated state. During this transitory period towards peace, international law seeks to ensure that the rights of the territorial state are not infringed and that local populations are protected against any risk of abuse by potentially hostile authorities.

Following the Second World War, the notion and law of occupation largely ceased to draw international attention. For about five decades, this issue was barely discussed, except in relation to the Palestinian territories under Israeli control. This tendency, however, has dramatically changed. Following a number of international crises, including the invasion of Kuwait (1990), the international administrations in Kosovo and East Timor (1999), and the interventions in Afghanistan (2001) and Iraq (2003), the scope and implications of the law of occupation have generated renewed interest among both scholars[2] and international institutions.

This chapter provides an introduction to the law of occupation. It opens with a short discussion of the legal origin, or sources, of this legal framework. While relevant rules mainly

---

\* At the time of writing this chapter, the author was Lecturer at Bilkent University (Ankara) and he is now Legal Adviser at the International Committee of the Red Cross. The views expressed in the chapter reflect the author's opinion and not necessarily those of these institutions.

[1] For a presentation on the historical development of the law of occupation, see Robert Kolb and Sylvain Vité, *Le droit de L'Occupation Militaire: Perspectives Historiques et Enjeux Juridiques Actuels* (Bruylant 2009) 5–58; Eyal Benvenisti, *The International Law of Occupation* (2nd edn, OUP 2012) 20–42.

[2] Among numerous examples, see Yoram Dinstein, *The International Law of Belligerent Occupation* (CUP 2009) 303; Yutaka Arai-Takahashi, *The Law of Occupation, Continuity and Change of International Humanitarian Law, and Its Interaction with International Human Rights Law* (Martinus Nijhoff 2009) 758; Kolb and Vité (above n 1) 482; Benvenisti (above n 1) 383; Hans-Peter Gasser and Knt Dörmann, 'Protection of the Civilian Population', in Dieter Fleck (ed) *The Handbook of International Humanitarian Law* (OUP 2013) 231–320.

fall under international humanitarian law (IHL), it is recognized today that human rights law is also applicable during occupation. This contribution also addresses the scope of the law of occupation. It explains the meaning of occupation, as it is defined in international law, and highlights a number of questions that are currently being debated. Finally, the bulk of this chapter deals with the substance of the law of occupation. An overview of the main principles and rules is presented.

## 2. The Law of Occupation: Sources

The law of occupation is a particular branch of IHL. Relevant rules may be considered as *lex specialis*, meaning that they have been specifically tailored to address the challenges and needs resulting from occupation. In addition, since international human rights law applies both in time of peace and armed conflict, it is also relevant in occupied territories. The contemporary law governing occupation is thus a combination of rules pertaining to IHL and human rights law. The interplay between these two legal frameworks, however, is not completely clear. It raises a number of questions that have been discussed mainly in recent years and that, to a certain extent, still remain open.[3]

## A. International Humanitarian Law

The law of occupation has evolved over time. It is composed today of a certain number of treaties that have shaped progressively both the notion of occupation and the rules applicable to it. The first relevant multilateral treaty still in force today is the fourth Hague Convention on the Laws and Customs of War, adopted in 1907, and its annexed Regulations.[4] More particularly, section III of the Hague Regulations (articles 42–56) specifically applies to occupation, as it deals with 'military authority over the territory of the hostile State'.[5] This Convention was ratified by only thirty-seven states, but has been recognized as expressing customary international law,[6] and as such its norms are binding upon all states.

Rules of IHL governing occupation were later augmented with the adoption of the four Geneva Conventions in 1949. These Conventions apply to all cases of declared war or any other armed conflict occurring between states, including occupation.[7] They also clarify that their scope of application extends to 'all cases of partial or total occupation of the territory of a High Contracting Party, even if the said occupation meets with no armed resistance'.[8]

---

[3] See chapter 17 'International Humanitarian Law and International Human Rights Law' in this book.
[4] Hague Convention (IV) Respecting the Laws and Customs of War on Land and Its Annex: Regulation concerning the Laws and Customs of War on Land (adopted 18 October 1907, entered into force 26 January 1910) 187 CTS 227 (Hague Regulations).
[5] Hague Regulations section III (marginal title).
[6] This was confirmed by the Nuremberg Military Tribunal in Judgment of the Nuremberg International Military Tribunal 1946 (1947) 41 AJIL172, 248–9; and more recently by the International Court of Justice in *Legal Consequences of the Construction of a Wall in the Occupied Palestinian Territory* (Advisory Opinion) [2004] ICJ Rep 136 (*Palestinian Wall* case) para 89.
[7] Geneva Conventions Common Article 2(1). See ICRC, *Commentary on the First Geneva Convention* (2nd edn, ICRC 2016) (ICRC Commentary 2016) paras 285–7.
[8] Common Article 2(2).

These Conventions have been universally accepted (ratified). All states have formally committed to respect and ensure respect for them.[9] Provisions especially related to occupation may be found in the fourth Geneva Convention on the Protection of Civilian Persons in Time of War (GCIV).[10]

GCIV does not replace the Hague Regulations, but provides supplementary rules.[11] Although the provisions of these two instruments largely overlap, those in the Hague Regulations remain applicable.[12] Thus, in order to have full understanding of the international law governing occupation, it is essential to take both instruments into consideration.[13] To a lesser extent, other more recent treaties of IHL also provide complementary rules.[14]

## B.  International Human Rights Law

Even if the issue is still a source of controversy,[15] there is little question today that international human rights law is applicable to situations covered by IHL, that is, armed conflicts, including occupation. This position has been confirmed by a wealth of international and domestic practice.[16] With regard to occupation, the International Court of Justice (ICJ) explicitly declared that states remain bound by international human rights instruments even when acting outside of their own territory, and stressed that this was valid 'particularly in occupied territories'.[17] The ICJ applied this position to the occupied Palestinian territory, and to the deployment of Ugandan armed forces in the Democratic Republic of Congo.[18] The United Kingdom has also recognized that 'an occupying power is ... responsible for ensuring respect for applicable human rights standards in the occupied territory'[19] and further clarified that '[w]here the occupying power is a party to the European Convention on

---

[9]  ibid 1.

[10]  Most provisions of the Geneva Convention (IV) Relative to the Protection of Civilian Persons in Time of War (adopted 12 August 1949, entered into force 21 October 1950) 75 UNTS 287 (GCIV) apply to occupation, with the exception of article 3 (armed conflicts not of an international character) and articles 35–46 (aliens in the territory of a Party to the conflict).

[11]  GCIV article 154; ICRC Commentary 2016 para 296.

[12]  Jean S Pictet (ed), *Commentary IV, Geneva Convention Relative to the Protection of Civilians Persons in Time of War* (ICRC 1958) 620.

[13]  Tristan Ferraro (ed), *Occupation and Other Forms of Administration of Territory*, Expert Meeting Report (ICRC 2012) 58.

[14]  See Protocol Additional to the Geneva Conventions of 12 August 1949, and Relating to the Protection of Victims of International Armed Conflicts (adopted 8 June 1977, entered into force 7 December 1978) 1125 UNTS 3 (API) article 1(3); Hague Convention for the Protection of Cultural Property in the Event of Armed Conflict (adopted 1 May 1954, entered into force 6 August 1956) 249 UNTS 240 article 5.

[15]  Michael J Dennis, 'Application of Human Rights Treaties Extraterritorially in Times of Armed Conflict and Military Occupation' (2005) 99(1) *AJIL* 119–41.

[16]  See chapter 17 'International Humanitarian Law and International Human Rights Law' in this book. See also, with specific references to occupation, Cordula Droege 'Elective Affinities? Human Rights and Humanitarian Law' (2008) 90 *IRRC* 503; Noam Lubell, 'Human Rights Obligations in Military Occupation' (2012) 94 *IRRC* 317; Sylvain Vité, 'The Interrelation of the Law of Occupation and Economic, Social and Cultural Rights: the Examples of Food, Health and Property' (2008) 90 *IRRC* 629.

[17]  *Case concerning Armed Activities on the Territory of the Congo (Democratic Republic of the Congo v Uganda)* (Judgment) [2005] ICJ Rep 215 (*Armed Activities* case) para 216.

[18]  *Palestinian Wall* case para 106; *Armed Activities* case para 216. For a contrary position, see US Department of Defense (DoD), *Law of War Manual* (2015) para 11.1.2.6.

[19]  UK Ministry of Defence (MoD), *The Joint Service Manual on the Law of Armed Conflict* JSP 383 (2004) para 11.19.

Human Rights, the standards of that Convention may, depending on the circumstances, be applicable in the occupied territories'.[20]

Various legal arguments have been proposed to support this view. It has been put forward, for instance, that IHL as such foresees the application of human rights law in time of occupation. This is a logical consequence of article 43 of the Hague Regulations, which requires the Occupying Power to take all feasible measures 'to restore, and ensure, as far as possible, public order and safety, while respecting, unless absolutely prevented, the laws in force in the country'.[21] It may also be recalled that Additional Protocol I (API) explicitly recognizes that some of its provisions applicable in times of occupation are complementary not only to rules of GCIV, but also to 'other applicable rules of international law relating to *the protection of fundamental human rights* during international armed conflict'.[22] Conversely, it has also been argued that human rights law is applicable, regardless of relevant rules of IHL, as soon as a state exercises sufficient territorial control abroad, including in case of occupation.[23] Territorial control in itself is enough to trigger the applicability of human rights instruments, even when such control is exercised beyond national borders. In addition, even those who do not accept this argument agree that the Occupying Power is bound by local laws implementing the occupied state's international human rights obligations.[24]

While recognition of the applicability of human rights law in times of occupation is supported by solid international practice, the concrete implications of this evolution still raise a number of questions that remain open for discussion. One of the current, most debated questions relates to the interplay between human rights law and IHL, as rules from each of these legal frameworks are concurrently applicable in situations of occupation and overlap to a certain extent. Addressing this issue in relation to the Palestinian occupied territory, the ICJ confirmed that both of these branches of international law were applicable in this case, but also declared that it would take IHL into consideration as '*lex specialis*'.[25] The exact meaning of this statement, however, is not clear and has aroused different interpretations. Some have argued that the rules of IHL must prevail as a matter of principle. Under this understanding, human rights law should apply only when it offers greater protection, or in case IHL is unclear or contains lacuna.[26] Others would rather consider that IHL and human rights law are complementary and as such are not exclusive, but 'influence and reinforce each other mutually'.[27] In accordance with this interpretation, one of these legal frameworks should prevail over the other, pursuant to the principle of '*lex specialis*', only when two particular rules dealing with the same issue contradict each other.[28]

---

[20]  ibid.

[21]  *Armed Activities* case para 178.

[22]  API article 72 (emphasis added). See Yves Sandoz, Christophe Swinarski, and Bruno Zimmerman (eds), *Commentary on the Additional Protocols of 8 June 1977 to the Geneva Conventions of 12 August 1949* (ICRC/Martinus Nijhoff 1987 (AP Commentary) para 2927 confirming that article 72 refers here to 'the various instruments relating to human rights'.

[23]  For an analysis of this particular question, including controversial issues and international practice, see Lubell (above n 16).

[24]  US DoD (above n 18) para 11.1.2.6.

[25]  *Palestinian Wall* case para 106. While reproducing a similar statement in the *Armed Activities* case, the ICJ did not reiterate this reference to the principle of '*lex specialis*'. It is not clear, however, whether this omission was deliberate, and therefore whether it indicates a change in the ICJ's approach to this question: para 216.

[26]  Gasser and Dörmann (above n 2) 265.

[27]  Droege (above n 16) 521. This approach is supported notably by the United Nations Human Rights Committee 'General Comment 31' UN Doc CCPR/C/21/Rev.1/Add.13 (2004) para 11.

[28]  Droege (above n 16) 522–4. On the '*lex specialis*' issue, see also Dinstein (above n 2) 85–8.

## 3. The Law of Occupation: Scope

Identifying the scope of application of the law of occupation requires a clear understanding of the notion of occupation. This is essential to determine in which situations vulnerable persons may claim protection under this legal framework. While this notion was defined initially in the Hague Regulations, and later clarified in the Geneva Conventions and through international practice, the extent to which relevant rules are applicable in practice is not always clear. Discussions in this regard have recently focused on the criteria that should be used to identify the beginning and end of occupation.

## A. Definition of Occupation

Pursuant to article 42 of the Hague Regulations,[29] 'territory is considered occupied when it is actually placed under the authority of the hostile army'.[30] This provision is usually considered as providing the core definition of the notion of occupation.

Article 42 shows that this notion relies on factual criteria.[31] There is occupation in a given situation as soon as the conditions in article 42 are 'actually' realized. As such, the existence of an occupation does not suppose formal acceptance by the parties to the conflict or recognition by other states. It does not depend on a subjective assessment of the situation, but is based on objective elements. This was confirmed in international jurisprudence and state practice on a number of occasions. The US Military Tribunal at Nuremberg, for instance, clearly stated that 'whether an invasion has developed into an occupation is *a question of fact*'.[32] The exclusiveness of the factual criteria in the notion of occupation also means that the origin or causes of the conflict, as well as the motivations of the parties involved in it, are not relevant. The US Military Tribunal at Nuremberg also recalled in this regard that '[i]nternational law makes no distinction between a lawful and unlawful occupant in dealing with the respective duties of occupant and population in occupied territories'.[33]

Another fundamental characteristic of the notion of occupation is that it concerns military operations abroad and supposes interstate confrontation. The Hague Regulations govern 'war on land', meaning armed conflict between opposing sovereign entities. Section III of this instrument, which governs occupation, confirms that it applies to '[m]ilitary authority over the territory of the hostile *State*'.[34] Similarly, the Geneva Conventions characterize occupation as a form of armed conflict between 'High Contracting Parties', meaning between states.[35]

The above implies that the notion of occupation does not cover non-international armed conflicts (NIACs).[36] In those situations, the re-establishment of authority by government

---

[29] See Adam Roberts, 'What is a Military Occupation?' (1984) 55 *BYBIL* 249.

[30] Hague Regulations article 42(1).

[31] US DoD (above n 18) para 11.2.1. See Gasser and Dörmann (above n 2) 269; Tristan Ferraro, 'Determining the Beginning and End of an Occupation under International Humanitarian Law' (2012) *IRRC* 134–6.

[32] *United States v Wilhelm List and others* (1949) 8 LRTWC 34 (19 February 1948) (*Hostage* case) (emphasis added). See also *Armed Activities* case para 173; *Prosecutor v Naletilić and Martinović* (Trial Chamber Judgment) IT-98-34 (31 March 2003) para 211 (*Naletilić* case).

[33] *Hostage* case 59.

[34] Emphasis added.

[35] Common Article 2.

[36] US DoD (above n 18) para 11.1.3.3. See Gasser and Dörmann (above n 2) 267.

armed forces over national territory following temporary loss of effective control does not trigger the applicability of the law of occupation. In this case, domestic law and other rules of international law, including human rights law, will apply. Similarly, territorial control exercised by non-state armed groups (NSAGs) may not be legally classified as occupation. In these situations, these groups are bound by rules of IHL governing NIACs, namely Common Article 3 of the four Geneva Conventions, Additional Protocol II (APII) of 1977 when applicable, and relevant customary international law.

Finally, it may be inferred from article 42 that the notion of occupation entails basically two conditions: (i) a foreign power is in a position to exercise effective control over a territory, which does not belong to it (the territory is placed 'under its authority'); and (ii) the intervention has not been approved by the legitimate sovereign (territorial control is exercised by a 'hostile army'). While this understanding is generally accepted, the interpretation and practical consequences of each of the two constitutive elements have raised doctrinal debate.

## 1. Effective territorial control

A first question relates to the level of territorial control required to trigger the application of the law of occupation. A number of provisions support the view that this level is relatively high. Article 42 of the Hague Regulations states that '[t]he occupation extends only to the territory where such authority *has been established and can be exercised*'.[37] This suggests that the situation in the territory must be relatively stable and that the new authorities are sufficiently organized to be able to meet their responsibilities under international law. This requirement is also implicit in a number of provisions of the Hague Regulations and GCIV. Stability and organization are indeed necessary preconditions, for instance, to ensure the availability of food, to maintain medical and hospital establishments, or to ensure, more generally, proper administration of the occupied territory.[38]

Article 43 of the Hague Regulations expresses the same idea by stating that an occupation exists where '[t]he authority of the legitimate power [has] in fact *passed into the hands of the occupant*'.[39] The ICJ has recalled in this regard that occupation is characterized by a shift of power. In the *Armed Activities* case, when contemplating whether the armed forces of Uganda were to be considered as an Occupying Power in the Democratic Republic of the Congo, the ICJ declared that it would need to be demonstrated that these forces 'were not only stationed in particular locations but also that they had substituted their own authority for that of the Congolese Government'.[40] In other words, the ICJ considered that there is 'effective control', and thus occupation, when (i) the ousted government is no longer in a position of exercising its authority; and (ii) the foreign troops have substituted their own authority for that of the government.[41]

This rather strict understanding of the notion of 'effective control', however, does not mean that the notion of occupation is incompatible with some forms of disturbance

---

[37] Hague Regulations article 42(2) (emphasis added).

[38] Ferraro, 'Determining the Beginning and End of an Occupation under International Humanitarian Law' (above n 31) 143.

[39] Emphasis added.

[40] *Armed Activities* case para 173. The ICTY has also proposed in this regard some indicators that may be used in order to assess whether this shift of power has actually occurred in a given situation: see *Naletilić* case para 217.

[41] See also UK MoD (above n 19) para 3; US DoD (above n 18) para 11.2.2.2.

or armed violence in the country. The International Criminal Tribunal for the former Yugoslavia (ICTY) recalled in this regard that 'sporadic local resistance, even successful, does not affect the reality of occupation'.[42] To a certain extent, the law of occupation does take into consideration this concern. It indicates that the Occupying Power has the obligation to ensure law and order in the territory.[43] In most cases, this requires law enforcement measures governed by human rights standards. However, in situations involving high-intensity confrontations against organized armed groups, rules of IHL governing the conduct of hostilities may also become applicable.[44]

## 2. Lack of consent

The law of occupation aims to preserve the rights of the territorial sovereign and to protect local populations against risks of abuse by foreign forces. These risks are particularly acute when the presence of foreign forces is not agreed to by local authorities. This is why lack of consent to this presence is a fundamental characteristic of the notion of occupation. Article 42 of the Hague Regulations specifies in this regard that there is occupation when the territory is under the authority of a '*hostile* army'.[45] These situations are traditionally called 'belligerent occupation'.[46] In other words, the notion of occupation implies imposition of effective control 'by coercive, military, means'.[47]

The Geneva Conventions, while reiterating this original approach, have also clarified the scope of the notion of occupation.[48] They apply to 'all cases of partial or total occupation of the territory of a High Contracting Party', thus referring to the conceptual framework of the Hague Regulations, but also specifying that this must be the case 'even if the said occupation meets with no armed resistance'.[49] Thus the existence of an occupation does not necessarily suppose active hostilities on the ground.[50] Absence of reaction to the deployment of foreign troops on national territory does not imply consent. If such consent is not explicitly given by the local government, the troops will be considered as an Occupying Power.[51] Conversely, when foreign forces enter a country upon the invitation or with the agreement of the local government, their presence may not be considered as 'hostile', and therefore the specific legal protections under the law of occupation do not apply. These situations are usually characterized as 'pacific occupation'[52] and are governed by other legal frameworks, including human rights law.

In practice, it may be extremely difficult to assess whether consent to the presence of foreign armed forces is genuine and valid. History shows numerous examples of states manipulating 'puppet governments' abroad in order to impose, under fictitious agreements, control over foreign territories. Under general international law, consent must be given by

---

[42] *Naletilić* case para 217. See also UK MoD (above n 19) para 11.7.1.
[43] Hague Regulations article 43.
[44] See Dinstein (above n 2) 99–101. For further details, see below section 3.B.1 'Beginning of occupation'.
[45] Emphasis added.
[46] See eg Michael Bothe, 'Occupation, Belligerent', in *Encyclopedia of Public International Law, Vol 3* (Elsevier 1997) 763–6.
[47] Ferraro, 'Determining the Beginning and End of an Occupation under International Humanitarian Law' (above n 31) 152.
[48] Common Article 2.
[49] ibid.
[50] ICRC Commentary 2016 para 288.
[51] Ferraro, *Occupation and Other Forms of Administration of Territory* (above n 13) 21.
[52] See Bothe, 'Occupation, Belligerent' (above n 46) 766–8.

authorities entitled to express themselves on behalf of the state,[53] and must not be obtained under duress, that is, by the threat or use of force in violation of international principles and rules.[54]

## B. Beginning and End of Occupation

The notion of occupation, as defined by the Hague Regulations and clarified by the Geneva Conventions, provides the legal concepts necessary to determine the beginning and end of occupation. There may be an occupation in a given situation only when the two components of this notion—namely effective territorial control and lack of consent—are fulfilled. Conversely, an existing occupation comes to an end when one of these components does not exist anymore.[55] In other words, 'the criteria for establishing the end of an occupation should mirror the ones used to determine its beginning'.[56] However, this logical approach raises a number of practical questions.[57]

### 1. Beginning of occupation

As to the beginning of occupation, it has been debated what should be the minimum level of control required to trigger the application of the relevant legal framework. This question is especially sensitive in relation to the invasion phase of the armed conflict, during which the forces of one party have entered a foreign country but have not yet been able to impose stable authority over any part of the territory. In this scenario, the civilians concerned may not be in a position to claim protection under the law of occupation, since the minimum requirement of territorial control is not realized.

In these situations, the ICRC has proposed a flexible approach. In order to guarantee minimum protection to civilians at risk, it has advocated that some rules of GCIV governing occupied territories should apply as soon as foreign troops are in contact with local populations, even though the minimum level of control required for the existence of an 'occupation' has not been reached.[58] In other words, the ICRC suggests that the notion of occupation in GCIV has a 'wider meaning' than it has in the Hague Regulations, and thus the former has a broader scope of application than the latter.[59]

This position finds some support in international practice. ICTY has considered, for instance, that rules providing individual protection under the law of occupation should apply each time that a person comes within the power of foreign troops, even though these

---

[53] Vienna Convention on the Law of Treaties (adopted 23 May 1969, entered into force 27 January 1980) 1155 UNTS 33 (VCLT) article 7.

[54] ibid article 52. See further Kolb and Vité (above n 1) 152–5; Ferraro, *Occupation and Other Forms of Administration of Territory* (above n 13) 20–3.

[55] US DoD (above n 18) para 11.3.1.

[56] Ferraro, *Occupation and Other Forms of Administration of Territory* (above n 13) 28; Gasser and Dörmann (above n 2) 274.

[57] For a detailed analysis on the beginning and end of occupation, see Vaios Koutroulis, *Le Début et la Fin de L'Application du Droit de L'Occupation* (Pedone 2010).

[58] Pictet (above n 12) 60–1.

[59] ibid 61. This approach was more recently reaffirmed by the ICRC, *International Humanitarian Law and the Challenges of Contemporary Armed Conflicts* (ICRC 2011) 27. In this sense, see also Marco Sassòli, 'A Plea in Defence of Pictet and the Inhabitants of Territories under Invasion: The Case for the Applicability of the Fourth Geneva Convention during the Invasion Phase' (2012) 94 *IRRC* 42.

troops do not exercise effective control over the concerned area.[60] 'Otherwise', explained the Tribunal, 'civilians would be left, during an intermediate period, with less protection than that attached to them once occupation is established'.[61]

This approach, however, has been criticized by a number of governments and experts on the basis of the plain meaning of the two components of the notion of occupation.[62] As expressed by the US Military Tribunal at Nuremberg:

> The term invasion implies a military operation while an occupation indicates the exercise of governmental authority to the exclusion of the established government. This presupposes the destruction of organised resistance and the establishment of an administration to preserve law and order. To the extent that the occupants' control is maintained and that of the civil government eliminated, the area will be said to be occupied.[63]

Supporters of a strict interpretation also consider that nothing in GCIV nor subsequent practice indicates that rules governing occupation in this Convention have a different scope of application than under section III of the Hague Regulations.[64]

## 2. End of occupation

The end of occupation may occur following two main scenarios. First, the Occupying Power may lose control over the territory. This usually happens through the withdrawal of its troops, either on a voluntary basis, or forced by local resistance. Second, the occupation may also come to an end when these troops, while remaining in the country, are not considered as 'hostile' anymore, but are authorized to stay by the local authorities.[65] It is generally agreed, for instance, that the occupation of Iraq was terminated in June 2004 following a process determined by mutual consent between the local authorities (the Iraqi Governing Council) and the temporary administrative structure established by the Occupying Powers (the Coalition Provisional Authority). The UN Security Council adopted a resolution endorsing this process and the transfer of governmental responsibilities. It also recognized the creation of 'a sovereign Interim Government of Iraq' and proclaimed the end of the occupation, despite the continuing presence of foreign armies on Iraqi territory.[66]

In practice, however, termination of occupation by consent may not be obvious. In those situations where local authorities do not enjoy sufficient autonomy from the Occupying Power, the validity of the process of giving consent risks being challenged. In such cases, the process may also be contrary to article 47 of GCIV, which provides that protected persons

---

[60]  *Naletilić* case paras 219–22.

[61]  ibid para 221. In the meeting of experts organized by the ICRC in 2012, most participants (but not all) supported this view, arguing that 'such a broad interpretation of the concept of occupation, one that would include the invasion phase, was necessary in order to avoid protection gaps, and was the only legal construction that would ensure that the basic needs of the civilian population were met': Ferraro, *Occupation and Other Forms of Administration of Territory* (above n 13) 25. For a contrary view on this question, see ibid 25–6.

[62]  US DoD (above n 18) para 11.1.3.1.

[63]  *Hostage* case 55–6.

[64]  Marten Zwanenburg, 'Challenging the Pictet Theory' (2012) 94 *IRRC* 30–6.

[65]  For further details on the end of occupation, see Roberts, 'What is a Military Occupation?' (above n 29) 257–60.

[66]  UNSC Resolution 1546 UN Doc S/RES/1546 (8 June 2004) paras 1–2. For a detailed analysis of this case, see Adam Roberts, 'The End of Occupation: Iraq 2004' (2005) 54(1) *ICLQ* 27–48. See also Knut Dörmann and Laurent Colassis, 'International Humanitarian Law in the Iraq Conflict' (2004) 47 *German YB Int'l L* 293–342.

must not be deprived of the benefits of the Convention 'by any change introduced, as the result of the occupation of a territory, into the institutions or government of the said territory,
nor by any agreement concluded between the authorities of the occupied territories and the
Occupying Power ...'. This is why it is crucial that consent to foreign presence be genuine
and given by effective local authorities.

While in principle the end of occupation must be determined on the basis of the same
criteria as those used for its beginning, GCIV contains an exception to this purely logical
approach. When occupying forces remain in the country more than one year after the 'general close of military operations', the Convention ceases to apply except for a number of
explicitly listed provisions.[67] These provisions include, for instance, those related to the
treatment of individuals, such as the obligation to respect honour, family rights, and religious convictions, as well as the prohibition of murder and torture.[68] Concerning states
that are parties to API, however, this rule does not apply. For these states, relevant provisions of GCIV and API remain applicable until the termination of occupation. In this
case, the symmetrical interpretation of the beginning and end of occupation is followed.
However, API introduces one exception 'for those persons whose final release, repatriation
or re-establishment takes place [after the occupation]'.[69] These persons must indeed benefit
from relevant protections until their personal situation is solved, even after the formal end
of occupation.[70]

## C. Selected Issues

Even though occupation was defined in article 42 of the Hague Regulations, and further
clarified through subsequent legal developments, the exact scope of this notion remains,
to a certain extent, subject to controversy due to new uncertainties arising in practice. As
Adam Roberts points out, 'the core meaning of the term is obvious enough; but as usually
happens with abstract concepts, its frontiers are less clear'.[71] Two scenarios have been particularly debated: (i) territorial control exercised by a state from abroad, that is, without
military presence on the ground; and (ii) territorial control exercised by international
organizations.

### 1. Territorial control without presence on the ground

This issue was especially discussed in relation to the situation of the Gaza Strip following
the total withdrawal of Israeli armed forces in September 2005, after almost forty years of
continuous presence and control in this area. This operation was part of a 'Disengagement
Plan' adopted by the Israeli government on 6 June 2004 and endorsed by Parliament on
25 October of that same year.[72] By virtue of that plan, the authorities' intention was to put
an end to their responsibilities vis-à-vis the people living in the Gaza Strip.[73] Should it

---

[67] GCIV article 6(2).
[68] ibid article 6(3).
[69] API article 3(b)
[70] ibid.
[71] Roberts, 'What is a Military Occupation?' (above n 29) 249.
[72] Israeli Prime Minister's Office, Cabinet Resolution Regarding the Disengagement Plan: Addendum A—
Revised Disengagement Plan—Main Principles (6 June 2004).
[73] ibid.

therefore be concluded that those measures marked the end of the occupation of the terri-tory? In other words, was the physical withdrawal of the Israeli forces enough to admit that effective territorial control characteristic of occupation did not exist any longer?

Some observers have answered that question in the negative. They have recalled that Israel retains substantial authority over the Gaza Strip, although its troops are no longer physically deployed in that area.[74] The Disengagement Plan clearly stated that Israel was to continue to exercise control over the borders of that territory, as well as over its air space and coastal region.[75] Moreover, these observers have also stressed that Israel has the advantage of being able to enter Palestinian territory at any time in order to maintain public order. This power is made greater by the small size of the territory of Gaza and the military means available. As provided by article 42(2) of the Hague Regulations, there is occupation when the authority of the hostile army 'has been established and *can be exercised*'. This wording could be interpreted as meaning that potential authority would suffice as evidence of the reality of occupation. These views were shared, for instance, by the UN Secretary General, who declared that 'the actions of IDF [Israeli Defense Forces] in respect of Gaza have clearly demonstrated that modern technology allows an occupying Power to effectively control a territory even without a military presence'.[76] According to this position, occupation of the Gaza Strip would therefore not have ceased with the withdrawal of troops in 2005, as Israel could be said to continue to exercise from a distance a power equivalent to the 'effective con-trol' required under the law of occupation.[77]

Other experts, however, consider that a closer study of the treaty texts shows that the ability of an occupier to impose its effective control cannot be separated from its physical presence in the territory concerned.[78] While article 42 of the Hague Regulations accepts that occupation exists when the adversary's authority 'can be exercised', it makes it clear that that authority must first be 'established'. It thus forges an inseparable link between the estab-lishment of authority, implying the deployment of a presence on the ground, and the ability to extend that authority to the entire territory concerned. Moreover, as explained, effective control becomes apparent as a result of a substitution of powers. Obviously, this threshold of application cannot be achieved if the foreign forces are located outside the region in ques-tion. Supporters of this position also argue that it is impossible to conceive of the imple-mentation of most of the rules of occupation unless there is a presence in the territory. It is impossible, for instance, to ensure public order and civil life in a territory, as required by article 43 of the Hague Regulations, from outside.[79] It would thus be paradoxical to require a state to fulfil its international obligations if it is unable to do so because it is not present in

---

[74] See UNGA, 'Note by the Secretary-General: Situation of Human Rights in the Palestinian Territories Occupied since 1967' UN Doc A /61/470 (2006) para 6. See also UNHCR, 'Report of the Special Rapporteur on the Situation of Human Rights in the Palestinian Territories Occupied by Israel since 1967' UN Doc E/CN.4/2006/29 (2006) para 6ff.

[75] Israeli Prime Minister's Office (above n 72), ch 1.

[76] UNGA (above n 74) para 7. See also UNHCR, 'Report of the Special Rapporteur on the Situation of Human Rights in the Palestinian Territories Occupied by Israel since 1967' (above n 74).

[77] This argumentation is also supported by the ICRC, which refers to it as the 'functional approach' to the ap-plication of the law of occupation: 'International Humanitarian Law and the Challenges of Contemporary Armed Conflict' (32nd International Conference of the Red Cross and Red Crescent, Geneva, October 2015) 12.

[78] See Yuval Shany, 'Faraway, So Close: The Legal Status of Gaza after Israel's Disengagement' (2006) *Hebrew University of Jerusalem Intn'l Law Forum Research Paper 12-06*, 19 http://papers.ssrn.com/sol3/papers. cfm?abstract_id=923151. See also Roberts, 'What is a Military Occupation?' (above n 29) 300.

[79] Other examples include GCIV articles 55–56, 59.

the area concerned. Such an interpretation would run counter to the basic tenets of the law of occupation.

## 2. Territorial control by international organizations

The increasing development of military operations by international organizations, especially by the United Nations, has raised questions and triggered controversies about the legal framework applicable to such operations. When armed forces under the command of these organizations are deployed in a territory, which in some cases may involve vast administrative power, the question arises as to whether and under what conditions their presence may amount to an occupation, and therefore whether the law of occupation is binding upon them.[80]

While a detailed analysis of this question goes beyond the scope of this chapter,[81] suffice it to say that some observers have answered the question in the negative. Stressing the differences between states and international organizations, they have argued that the latter should not be assimilated to Occupying Powers when engaged in military operations. They consider that such operations do not defend the interests of a particular state, but rather seek to implement mandates received from the international community. As such, they are not based on conflicting interests, which is the characteristic of occupation, but tend to promote cooperation to secure peace and protect local populations.[82]

These views, however, are not generally supported. It is widely accepted today among scholars that the law of occupation may apply under certain circumstances to international operations.[83] The reason is that the existence of an occupation, as explained previously, does not depend on political motivations, but rather on criteria that must be assessed objectively. If these criteria, namely effective territorial control and lack of consent, are met, then the law of occupation must apply, whether the troops deployed on the ground are under the command of a state or an international organization.

However, this conclusion does not mean that all specific rules concerned are relevant in this context. These rules were developed with state structure in mind, at a time when occupation by international organizations was not an issue. Article 49 of GCIV, for instance, mentions the 'territory' or the 'civilian population' of the Occupying Power. Obviously, these notions do not apply to international organizations.

## 4. The Law of Occupation: Contents

The international legal regime governing occupation is based on three fundamental principles that are illustrated and made more precise through a number of specific rules. While

---

[80] See Ferraro, *Occupation and Other Forms of Administration of Territory* (above n 13) 33: [s]ome experts also pointed out that certain UN missions entailed the exercise of functions and powers over a territory that could be compared to those assigned to an occupant under occupation law: they cited the UN's operations in Cyprus, Cambodia, Eastern Slavonia, East Timor, Kosovo and the Congo (in the 1960s).

[81] For a more detailed overview of this debate, see Benvenisti (above n 1) 62–6.

[82] See eg Daphna Shraga, 'The UN as an Actor Bound by International Humanitarian Law', in Luigi Condorelli, Anne-Marie La Rosa, and Sylvie Scherrer (eds), *The United Nations and International Humanitarian Law* (Pedone 1996) 326–8.

[83] See eg Roberts, 'What is a Military Occupation?' (above n 29) 289–91; Ferraro, *Occupation and Other Forms of Administration of Territory* (above n 13) 33–4; ICRC Commentary 2016 paras 333–336.

this section proposes a broad overview of this framework, it also provides a more specific analysis of certain issues that have been of particular interest in recent practice.

## A. Overview: Fundamental Principles

The three fundamental principles upon which the law of occupation is based require the Occupying Powers to (i) restore and ensure public order and civil life in the occupied territory; (ii) respect the local legal system; and (iii) respect and protect the individuals and property under its control.[84]

### 1. Obligation to restore and ensure public order and civil life

Although expressing distinct obligations, the first two principles are in fact closely connected. They are both included in the same sentence of article 43 of the Hague Regulations, which provides that the Occupying Power 'shall take all the measures in his power to restore, and ensure, as far as possible, public order and safety, while respecting, unless absolutely prevented, the laws in force in the country'. This provision, which 'broadly define[s] the occupant's scope of authority',[85] lays down the basis of the Occupying Power's responsibilities in the administration of the occupied territory and establishes the legal framework in which such responsibilities are to be implemented.[86] This provision is thus central in the law of occupation and is part of customary international law.[87]

The first part of this dual rule, namely the obligation 'to restore, and ensure, as far as possible, public order and safety', entails vast responsibilities. Contrary to what a plain reading of this text may suggest, the obligation incumbent on the Occupying Power is not limited to law-and-order functions. The original, authentic French version of article 43 makes clear that this obligation extends to measures necessary to restore and ensure 'civil life' more generally.[88] This is further confirmed by more specific rules of the law of occupation addressing various aspects of territorial administration. These are not limited to security concerns and criminal matters,[89] but also include broader concerns, such as medical care, education, food, clothing, and housing.[90] In other words, the purpose of these provisions is 'to protect the civilian population in an occupied territory from a meaningful decline in orderly life'.[91]

It may not, however, always be possible for an Occupying Power to fully achieve the results expected under article 43. Specific circumstances, including the military situation on the ground, may affect its capacity to comply with this provision. This is why article 43 allows some flexibility in this regard in order to take into account practical constraints.

---

[84]  US DoD (above n 18) para 11.5.

[85]  Ferraro, *Occupation and Other Forms of Administration of Territory* (above n 13) 56.

[86]  On this provision, see Marco Sassòli, 'Legislation and Maintenance of Public Order and Civil Life by Occupying Powers' (2005) 16 *EJIL* 661–94; M Bothe, 'The Administration of Occupied Territory', in Andrew Clapham, Paolo Gaeta, and Marco Sassòli (eds), *The 1949 Geneva Conventions: A Commentary* (OUP 2015) 1455.

[87]  *Palestinian Wall* case para 89.

[88]  The French version of article 43 provides that the Occupying Power has an obligation 'de rétablir et d'assurer l'ordre et la *vie publics*' (which may be translated as 'to restore and ensure public order and *civil life*' (emphasis added)). See Dinstein (above n 2) 91.

[89]  GCIV articles 64–75, 78–135.

[90]  See further ibid articles 29, 47–135.

[91]  Dinstein (above n 2) 92. Michael Bothe also suggests that these provisions, taken as a whole, entail a 'duty of good governance': Bothe, 'The Administration of Occupied Territory' (above n 86) 1467.

It stresses that the Occupant's obligation to ensure proper administration of the territory extends only to measures that are 'in his power', and further indicates that this obligation must be implemented 'as far as possible'. Article 43 does not create an obligation of results, but rather seeks to ensure that the Occupying Power will use all available means to restore and ensure public order and civil life under the prevailing circumstances in each situation.

### 2. Obligation to respect the domestic legal system

As explained, occupation is de facto control over a territory. It does not confer sovereignty upon the Occupying Power,[92] but consists of a transitory period during which foreign forces assume the responsibility of administering the territory while long-term solutions are being sought. This situation is meant to be temporary.[93] It follows from this that the law of occupation tends to preserve the legal system in place. It prohibits the Occupying Power from undertaking changes in the domestic law of the occupied country, except under strict conditions and for determined purposes. Article 43 of the Hague Regulations expresses this rule by providing that the Occupying Power must respect the laws in force in the country 'unless absolutely prevented' from doing so. While seeking to maintain legal stability in the occupied territory, this provision does not completely exclude modifications under exceptional circumstances.

The concrete implications of this obligation, however, are not always clear. Military operations abroad whose main objective is to introduce fundamental changes in the institutional and political system of the occupied territory (so-called 'transformative occupations') are prohibited.[94] It is, however, debated in which circumstances an Occupying Power is indeed 'absolutely prevented' from respecting the laws in force in the country, and whether it may therefore adopt derogative measures.

One clear limitation in this regard may be found in article 47 of GCIV. As already mentioned, this article prohibits, among other things, changes in local institutions or governmental structures that would result in the suppression of individual protections recognized by the Convention. Apart from this, modifications in domestic law are not prohibited in an absolute manner. Such modifications may even be necessary in certain circumstances to meet legitimate purposes. Article 47 guarantees that individual protections are not annihilated through institutional transformations, but does not prohibit these transformations as a matter of principle.[95]

Modification of the legal framework may be necessary to implement the obligation, under article 43 of the Hague Regulations, to 'restore, and ensure, as far as possible, public order and safety'. Especially in case of prolonged occupation, it may be necessary to adapt local legislations to evolving social needs.[96] This obligation, however, as general and vague as it is, does not help much to determine the exact extent of the legislative latitude conferred on the Occupying Power. In practice, it has been interpreted by concerned authorities

---

[92] See *Affaire de la Dette Publique Ottomane* (Sentence) (18 April 1925) I Recueil des Sentences Arbitrales 555. API also makes clear that '[n]either the occupation of a territory nor the application of the Conventions and this Protocol shall affect the legal status of the territory in question': article 4. See also UK MoD (above n 19) para 11.9.

[93] UK MoD (above n 19) para 11.9.

[94] Gasser and Dörmann (above n 2) 275.

[95] Pictet (above n 12) 274.

[96] Dinstein (above n 2) 116–20.

sometimes extensively, in order to support important legislative powers, and sometimes restrictively, in order to justify limited involvement in the administration of the territory.[97]

To a certain extent, however, article 64 of GCIV helps in resolving this uncertainty. The second paragraph of this article is usually recognized as providing details that may be used to clarify the meaning and implications of article 43 of the Hague Regulations.[98] This paragraph establishes that the Occupying Power may derogate from its obligation to respect the laws in force in the occupied territory for three purposes, namely (i) to fulfil its obligations under GCIV, which is usually interpreted today more broadly as also including other relevant instruments of IHL and human rights law;[99] (ii) to 'maintain the orderly government of the territory'; and (iii) to ensure its own security.[100] It is admitted, for instance, that the Occupying Power may decide to suspend local laws concerning conscription, freedom of public assembly, or the bearing of arms.[101] The Occupying Power may also have to legislate to implement policies on child welfare, labour, food, and public health.

This list of three exceptions is exclusive,[102] meaning that no other reason may be used to justify changes in the domestic legal order. The legislative room for manoeuvre granted to the Occupying Power is thus circumscribed, even though it is broad enough to allow necessary adaptations to the needs and challenges resulting from the administration of the occupied territory. In addition, concerned authorities must exercise restraint in using this power. Article 64 authorizes only those transformations that are 'essential' to one of the three mentioned purposes.[103] It thus confirms that legislative status quo must be the prevailing rule in occupied territories, while changing local laws should remain the exception.

## 3. Obligation to respect and protect individuals and property

The third fundamental principle of the law of occupation, which requires the Occupying Power to respect and protect individuals and property in the occupied territory, is directly connected to the two previous ones. The ICJ has confirmed that the two obligations formulated in article 43 of the Hague Regulations comprise 'the duty to secure respect for the applicable rules of international human rights law and international humanitarian law, to protect the inhabitants of the occupied territory against acts of violence, and not to tolerate such violence by any third party'.[104] This principle is far reaching, as, according to the Court, it obliges the Occupying Power to prevent abuses that may be perpetrated not only by its own forces, but also by other actors. The Court also considers that this principle covers potential violations of both IHL and human rights law, thus stressing the complementary nature of these legal frameworks in this context.

More specific rules of IHL, illustrating and detailing this principle,[105] provide for instance that protected persons in occupied territories are entitled to respect for their persons, honour, family rights, and religious convictions and practices.[106] They must be treated

---

[97] Benvenisti (above n 1) 78.
[98] Pictet (above n 12) 335.
[99] Gasser and Dörmann (above n 2) 284; Sassòli, 'Legislation and Maintenance' (above n 86) 675–8.
[100] GCIV article 64(2). See also ibid article 27(4): 'the Parties to the conflict may take such measures of control and security in regard to protected persons as may be necessary as a result of the war'.
[101] See UK MoD (above n 19) para 11.25.
[102] Pictet (above n 12) 337.
[103] GCIV article 64(2).
[104] *Armed Activities* case para 178.
[105] For a detailed presentation of these rules, see Dinstein (above n 2) 146–237.
[106] GCIV article 27(1).

humanely 'at all times',[107] which includes protection against all forms of violence and prohibition of murder, torture, or corporal punishment.[108] These rules also require special treatment for certain categories of persons, such as women, children, workers, or internees.[109] They also guarantee respect for public and private property,[110] and determine strict conditions under which such property may be seized, requisitioned, or used.[111]

IHL governing occupation also seeks to guarantee that the basic needs of the local population are satisfied. The Occupying Power has the obligation, to the fullest extent of its available means, to ensure the provision of food, medical supplies, clothing, bedding, housing, and 'other supplies essential to the survival' of the population.[112] If the Occupying Power is not in a position to comply with this obligation, it must accept relief operations undertaken by other states or by humanitarian organizations.[113]

It is also important to note, in terms of individual protection, that IHL pays particular attention to risks related to movements of populations in situations of occupation. It strictly prohibits forcible transfers and deportations of protected persons to the territory of the Occupying Power or to any other state.[114] Evacuations abroad may be allowed only if 'the security of the population or imperative military reasons so demand', and only if these evacuations cannot be avoided for 'material reasons' and are temporary.[115] Conversely, under no circumstances may the population of the Occupying Power be transferred into the occupied territory.[116]

These are a few examples of legal protections in times of occupation under IHL. As mentioned, applicable instruments of human rights provide essential complementary protections in terms of civil and political rights and economic, social, and cultural rights.[117]

## B. Selected Issues

While the three fundamental principles of the law of occupation are well established, their concrete implications have raised a number of questions. Particular areas of interest include the use of force in the maintenance of law and order, the application of security measures to civilians, and the protection and use of property and resources.

### 1. Use of force
Quite surprisingly, IHL does not provide clear guidance as to when and how force, including potentially lethal force, may be used in occupied territories. While article 43 of the

---

[107] ibid.

[108] ibid article 27(1); Hague Regulations article 46. For concrete implications of the obligation of humane treatment, see also GCIV articles 27–34; API article 75.

[109] See GCIV articles 27(2), 50, 51–52, 79–135.

[110] Hague Regulations article 46.

[111] See below, section 4.B.3 'Property and resources'.

[112] GCIV article 55(1); API article 69. With regard to medical care, health, and hygiene, see also GCIV article 56(1) and API article 14(1).

[113] GCIV article 59; API articles 69–71.

[114] GCIV article 49(1).

[115] ibid article 49(2).

[116] ibid article 49(6).

[117] See eg International Covenant on Civil and Political Rights (adopted 16 December 1966, entered into force 23 March 1976) 999 UNTS 171 (ICCPR); International Convention on the Rights of the Child (adopted 20 November 1989, entered into force 2 September 1990) 1577 UNTS 3.

Hague Regulations requires the Occupying Power to guarantee public security and order in areas under its effective control, it does not further specify the rules that must be followed when implementing this obligation. The question is important, because depending on the circumstances the Occupying Power may be confronted with different challenges calling for distinct responses. In some cases, it may have to use police powers, when, for instance, it has to fight against criminality or quell social unrest. In other cases, military means of action may be more adequate when it is engaged in high-intensity violence against organized armed groups.

This distinction is crucial as each scenario requires the application of specific rules that may result in quite different results as to when and how force may be used. The rules governing law enforcement have been developed and detailed in human rights law, in relation to the right to life.[118] They basically provide that lethal force may only be used in very limited circumstances and under strict conditions. Under this legal framework, the use of potentially lethal force is allowed only to achieve a number of essential and narrowly defined objectives, and when less extreme means are insufficient to achieve these objectives.[119] In any event, intentional lethal use of firearms is permissible only when 'strictly unavoidable in order to protect life'.[120] Conversely, the rules applicable to conduct of hostilities in armed conflict are based on IHL. They recognize that some categories of persons may be lawfully targeted in such situations. In IAC, these persons include enemy combatants and civilians taking a direct part in hostilities. With regard to these persons, the Occupying Power enjoys more leeway in using force than it would under the law enforcement model.[121]

Distinction between these two forms of armed violence is, however, not always clear-cut in practice. In times of occupation, it may be difficult to draw a clear line between situations requiring law enforcement measures and those amounting to hostilities. It may happen that both situations overlap in the same context or that a police operation evolves into high-intensity fighting against organized groups, and vice versa.[122] Thus uncertainty may arise as to the identification of the legal regime applicable in such scenarios.[123] Nuanced approaches are therefore necessary when determining relevant rules governing the use of force in occupied territories, taking into account a number of factors such as the degree of control exercised by the Occupying Power over a given area and the origin and the nature of armed violence in a given situation.[124] It is also important that security forces be prepared to meet this challenge. They must be able to apply both legal models, and to switch from one to the other each time that the circumstances so require. As such, they must be trained and instructed accordingly.

---

[118] See ICCPR article 6.

[119] Basic Principles on the Use of Force and Firearms by Law Enforcement Officials (adopted by the Eighth United Nations Congress on the Prevention of Crime and the Treatment of Offenders, Havana, Cuba, 27 August to 7 September 1990) principle 9.

[120] ibid.

[121] Ferraro, *Occupation and Other Forms of Administration of Territory* (above n 13) 109.

[122] Kenneth Watkin, 'Use of Force during Occupation: Law Enforcement and Conduct of Hostilities' (2012) 94 *IRRC* 311.

[123] Ferraro *Occupation and Other Forms of Administration of Territory* (above n 13) 110.

[124] Examples and an analysis of such a nuanced approach to the use of force are available in Watkin (above n 122) 311–14.

## 2. Security measures: internment and assigned residence
Complying with the obligation to maintain law and order may be an extremely challenging task in time of occupation. Even though the Occupying Power is able to impose and maintain its authority in the territory under its control, it may be confronted by forms of instability and violence that may require resorting to exceptional means of action. IHL takes this into account by authorizing the Occupying Power to adopt 'safety measures'. These measures have no penal character, meaning that they are not aimed at sanctioning persons having infringed criminal rules, but constitute means of controlling individuals who might pose a serious threat to public security in particularly unstable situations. They may include, 'at the most', assigned residence or internment.[125]

However, as such measures constitute important limitations on the right to liberty, they must only be used in very exceptional circumstances, that is, only if they may be considered as absolutely necessary for 'imperative reasons of security'.[126] They must be applied only as a last resort—that is, only if other means of control involving less serious restrictions on personal liberty have proved ineffective—and they must be temporary. Persons arrested, detained, or interned for actions related to the conflict must be released 'with the minimum delay possible and in any event as soon as the circumstances justifying [the deprivation of liberty] have ceased to exist'.[127]

The exceptional character of internment or assigned residence also requires the adoption and implementation of procedural safeguards. These measures must be based on a 'regular procedure',[128] which must include the right to appeal and the right to 'periodical review, if possible every six months, by a competent body set up by the [Occupying Power]'.[129]

GCIV also contains a detailed set of provisions concerning the treatment and welfare of the internees, as well as the administration of internment facilities. This includes rules concerning food, clothing, and accommodation; hygiene and medical care; practice of religion; intellectual and physical activities; personal property and financial resources; camp administration and discipline; relations with the exterior; transfer; and end of internment.[130]

## 3. Property and resources
IHL protects property and resources in occupied territories[131] against potential risks of abuse by the occupying forces. However, it also recognizes that the administration of these territories involves expenses that may not be entirely covered at the Occupying Power's own expenses. Thus a fair balance must be found between the legitimate use of local property and resources and practices amounting to unlawful appropriation of public and private goods.

As a bottom line, the law of occupation prohibits pillage.[132] It also provides that private property must be respected; it may not be confiscated.[133] This, however, does not preclude the Occupying Power from collecting taxes, dues, and tolls. In this case, it must proceed, as

---

[125] GCIV article 78(1).
[126] ibid article 78(1).
[127] API article 75(3).
[128] GCIV article 78(2).
[129] ibid article 78(2).
[130] ibid articles 79–135.
[131] Dinstein (above n 2) 195–237.
[132] Hague Regulations article 47.
[133] ibid article 46.

much as possible, in accordance with the existing legislation of the occupied territory and must use the revenue thus obtained for the one specific purpose of covering the expenses of the administration of the territory.[134] Additional contributions may also be levied if all these expenses are not met or if the maintenance and proper working of the army of occupation so require.[135] However, taxes and other contributions may not be used for other purposes, such as the economic development of the Occupying Power or its general war effort.[136]

In addition to financial revenues, and subject to certain conditions and limitations, the Occupying Power may also demand contributions in kind and services ('requisitions') from municipalities or inhabitants to meet the needs of the army of occupation.[137] It may also compel protected persons to work for the welfare of the local population.[138] Requisitions, however, are not unlimited. For instance, they may not apply to food and medical supplies, unless 'the requirements of the civilian population have been taken into account'.[139] Civilian hospitals may be requisitioned, but only temporarily and in cases of urgent necessity. In this case, the care and treatment of the patients and proper attendance of the civilian population must be ensured.[140] Contributions in kind must be compensated[141] and compulsory work must be remunerated by a fair wage.[142]

The Occupying Power is also allowed to take possession of all movable government property that may be used for military operations, such as cash, means of transport, weapons, and food supplies.[143] These may be taken without compensation. Subject to certain exceptions, other goods, such as communication and transport appliances and munitions of war, including those belonging to private individuals, may be seized, but must be restored and compensated once the conflict has ended.[144]

With respect to immovable government property, such as public buildings, real estate, forests, and agricultural estates, the regime of usufruct is applicable. The Occupying Power is allowed to use the products coming from the exploitation of these properties to cover the expenses of the administration of the occupied territory and to ensure the welfare of the local population,[145] but it must safeguard their capital.[146]

Finally, some categories of public property enjoy special protection, and as such must be treated as private property. These include goods belonging to municipalities, as well as to institutions dedicated to religion, charity, education, and the arts and sciences. It is prohibited to seize, destroy, or wilfully damage such property.[147]

---

[134] ibid article 48.
[135] ibid article 49. These contributions must be based on a written order and must be collected under the responsibility of a commander-in-chief, following local laws as much as possible: ibid article 51.
[136] UK MoD (above n 19) para 11.31; Gasser and Dörmann (above n 2) 290.
[137] Hague Regulations article 52(1).
[138] These persons must be over eighteen and may also be used to work 'for the public utility services, or for the feeding, sheltering, clothing, transportation or health of the population of the occupied country': GCIV article 51(2).
[139] ibid article 55(2).
[140] ibid article 57(1).
[141] Hague Regulations article 52(3).
[142] GCIV article 51(3).
[143] Hague Regulations article 53(1).
[144] ibid article 53(2).
[145] Gasser and Dörmann (above n 2) 292.
[146] Hague Regulations article 55.
[147] ibid article 56.

## 5. Conclusion

The international law governing occupation has constantly evolved since the adoption of the Hague Regulations. With the entry into force of GCIV in 1949, essential and detailed provisions for the protection and welfare of the concerned populations were added to the earlier legal framework. More recently, recognition of the applicability of human rights law in situations of occupation has also greatly contributed to strengthening and complementing the existing rules, even though this development has raised a number of questions that remain to be solved. As a result of this evolution, the international law governing occupation today provides a very comprehensive set of rules that address most of the challenges facing Occupying Powers and meet the needs of persons under their control. In addition, to a large extent, these rules are part of customary international law, and as such are universally binding on states.

While the contents of international law governing occupation is globally satisfactory, important uncertainties remain as to the conditions and scope of its application. It may be very difficult in a given situation to clearly identify whether the two components of the notion of occupation—namely the effective territorial control and a lack of consent by the local sovereign authorities—are actually realized. Debates about the beginning and end of occupation, territorial control without military presence on the ground, or the nature of international military interventions are illustrations of these problems. In addition, political reluctance to recognize the existence of an occupation may also block the application of the relevant legal framework, thus depriving concerned populations of crucial protections.

# 14

# Humanitarian Relief Operations

*Eve Massingham and Kelisiana Thynne*

## 1. Introduction: Humanitarian Relief Operations in Armed Conflict

The main tenet of international humanitarian law (IHL) is that human suffering should be limited, even in an environment where causing death and injury is, to a certain extent, legitimate. In amongst the violence and death that characterizes armed conflict in all its forms, humanitarian relief operations seek to assuage the suffering by providing protection and assistance to persons who are affected by the armed conflict. Humanitarian relief actors not only promote IHL to the parties to a conflict, but they also provide protection and assistance to victims (both combatant and civilian) of a conflict. States have the primary responsibility to provide humanitarian assistance to their citizens,[1] to provide them with protection,[2] and to respect and ensure respect for IHL.[3] Non-state armed groups (NSAGs) engaged in armed conflict also have a responsibility to uphold IHL and provide assistance to people in the territory which they control.[4] However, where the state or armed group is not able to provide such assistance, humanitarian relief actors and organizations can fill the gap. Therefore, like combatants, civilians, and other protected persons, humanitarian relief personnel have specific protections, obligations, and requirements under IHL.

Humanitarian relief organizations play a special role in the conflict environment.[5] Being able to provide protection and assistance in the midst of conflict, and to give that assistance impartially and with the consent of all parties to the conflict, requires particular modes

---

[1] See eg Swiss Federal Department of Foreign Affairs (Swiss FDFA), *Humanitarian Access in Situations of Armed Conflict: Handbook on the International Normative Framework*, Version 2 (FDFA, December 2014) 11.

[2] See eg United Nations General Assembly (UNGA), '2005 World Summit Outcome' UN Doc A/RES/60/1 (24 October 2005) para 138.

[3] Geneva Convention (I) for the Amelioration of the Condition of the Wounded and Sick in the Armed Forces in the Field (adopted 12 August 1949, entered into force 21 October 1950) 75 UNTS 31 (GCI); Geneva Convention (II) for the Amelioration of the Condition of the Wounded, Sick and Shipwrecked Members of Armed Forces at Sea (adopted 12 August 1949, entered into force 12 October 1949) 75 UNTS 85 (GCII); Geneva Convention (III) Relative to the Treatment of Prisoners of War (adopted 12 August 1949, entered into force 12 October 1950) 75 UNTS 135 (GCIII); Geneva Convention (IV) Relative to the Protection of Civilian Persons in Time of War (adopted 12 August 1949, entered into force 21 October 1953) 75 UNTS 287 (GCIV); Protocol Additional to the Geneva Conventions of 12 August 1949, and relating to the Protection of Victims of International Armed Conflicts, 8 June 1977 (entered into force 7 December 1978) 1125 UNTS 3 (API); Protocol additional to the Geneva Conventions of 12 August 1949, and relating to the Adoption of an Additional Distinctive Emblem (adopted 8 December 2005, entered into force 14 January 2007) 2404 UNTS 19 (APIII) Geneva Conventions Common Article 1. For further reading see ICRC, *Commentary on the First Geneva Convention: Convention (I) for the Amelioration of the Condition of the Wounded and Sick in Armed Forces in the Field*, 2nd edition, 2016; Eve Massingham and Annabel McConnachie, *Ensuring Respect for International Humanitarian Law: State Responses to Common Article 1* (Routledge, forthcoming 2020).

[4] IHL applies to all parties to a conflict. See eg Françoise Bouchet-Saulnier, 'Consent to Humanitarian Access: An Obligation Triggered by Territorial Control, not States' Rights' (2014) 96 *IRRC* 207, 210.

[5] Such organizations also play an important role during times of emergency or disaster; however, the IHL framework that is the subject of this chapter only applies during armed conflict.

of operating. Humanitarian relief in armed conflict has a specific definition and humanitarian relief organizations have specific limited mandates. This chapter gives a brief history of humanitarian relief organizations, and addresses what constitutes a humanitarian relief organization for the purposes of IHL. It outlines the legal framework which regulates humanitarian relief organizations and operations in armed conflicts, including the rights, roles, and responsibilities of humanitarian relief organizations in armed conflict. It also notes the obligations on the parties to an armed conflict to protect humanitarian relief personnel and objects and discusses the emblems of protection under IHL. The chapter concludes by considering some current challenges to the legal framework governing the humanitarian relief space.

## 2. History of Humanitarian Relief Organizations under IHL

### A. The First Geneva Convention and Humanitarian Relief

During wars from the 1700s to the 1800s in Europe, it was common practice for military generals to agree on where their medical posts would be located, so that wounded and sick soldiers could be tended to in protected locations near the battlefield.[6] The medical staff were provided from and paid by the military corps. This practice was abandoned after the French Revolution, where medical staff were not seen as important and had fewer protections.[7] In the mid-1800s, nurses such as Florence Nightingale and Clara Barton started campaigns for the reinforcement of military medical services and organized medical care and relief for the wounded in the Crimean and American civil wars, respectively.[8] Henry Dunant, the Swiss businessman who came across the Battle of Solferino in 1859, also provided some first aid to wounded soldiers. It was his account of his experiences, in the book *A Memory of Solferino*, that started a movement towards the creation of more permanent relief organizations and the legal protections for humanitarian efforts enshrined in today's Geneva Conventions. At the time, mostly soldiers were being wounded on the battlefield, not civilians, and humanitarian relief personnel would generally assist the military with these traditional medical tasks.

Dunant argued that everyone needed to be prepared in peacetime for wartime and, to that end, argued that relief societies should be set up to provide assistance to both sides of the conflict: '[t]hey would not wait for hostilities to start before establishing relations with the military authorities because the authorities would then be too busy fighting the war to discuss other matters'.[9] From 1863 onwards these relief societies became what we now know as Red Cross and Red Crescent Societies, as well as the founding organization, the International Committee of the Red Cross (ICRC).

---

[6] François Bugnion, 'Birth of an Idea: The Founding of the International Committee of the Red Cross and of the International Red Cross and Red Crescent Movement: From Solferino to the Original Geneva Convention (1859–1864)' (2012) 94 *IRRC* 1312.

[7] ibid.

[8] Vincent Bernard, 'Editorial: The Quest for Humanity 150 Years of International Humanitarian Law and Action' (2012) 94 *IRRC* 1195, 1198; Daniel Palmieri, 'An Institution Standing the Test of Time? A Review of 150 Years of the History of the International Committee of the Red Cross' (2012) 94 *IRRC* 1273, 1276.

[9] Bugnion (above n 6) 1313.

While relief prior to 1863 entailed first aid and medical treatment, at Solferino Henry Dunant also wrote letters to the families of dying men. His actions of hearing and recording the last words of soldiers and sending them to their families is a key function of the Red Cross Red Crescent Movement today and part of the legal framework applicable to armed conflict.[10] He also, unusually, persuaded the French army to release Austrian doctors and nurses from prison so they could continue to perform their functions[11]—the first act in what we might now call protection work.

The first Geneva Convention of 1864, which resulted from Dunant lobbying European leaders for greater protection for the wounded, strengthened this aim, by providing protection to military hospitals and ambulances and those staffing the hospitals (administrative staff as well as nurses and doctors). The limitation was that military medical facilities had protection from attack only for the time during which they continued to treat the wounded and sick, and as long as they remained neutral.[12] They also had to treat the sick and wounded from all sides to the conflict.[13] The Convention set up the basis for future relief operations to be humanitarian in purpose and neutral in execution. It even went further than previous military medical practice and recognized that civilians might also engage in relief activities. Article 5 states that:

> Inhabitants of the country who bring help to the wounded shall be respected and shall remain free. Generals of the belligerent Powers shall make it their duty to notify the inhabitants of the appeal made to their humanity, and of the neutrality which humane conduct will confer.[14]

The states negotiating the first Geneva Convention recognized that if a person is to be truly humanitarian in function, they would also need to treat all sides equally and without reference to their nationality or for which party they fought.

## B.  The Geneva Conventions of 1949 and Humanitarian Relief

The modern-day battlefield has necessitated a change in the IHL paradigm. The Geneva Conventions of 1949 continue to provide protection for military hospitals, and staff, facilities, military hospitals, and medical staff continue to be protected from attack.[15] However, nowadays, caring for those not (or no longer) taking part in the fighting encompasses a broader range of activities, and the victims of armed conflict are no longer almost exclusively military personnel. Civilians are also very much in need of medical care and humanitarian relief due to their being so devastatingly impacted by the conduct of warfare.

---

[10]  See eg GCIV articles 25–26; GCIII article 71 regarding correspondence for prisoners of war.

[11]  Bugnion (above n 6) 1304. See also GCIII article 33, noting that medical personnel are not considered prisoners of war (POWs) when captured, but rather are retained personnel and shall be able to exercise their medical functions.

[12]  1864 first Geneva Convention article 1.

[13]  ibid article 6.

[14]  ibid article 5.

[15]  GCI article 19.

Humanitarian relief encompasses medical care, to civilians as well as military personnel. Medical care comes under the broader banner of assistance, which also includes water and sanitation programmes, food relief, provision of non-food items, and agricultural support. Humanitarian relief also includes protection work—ensuring that individuals are respected and maintain their dignity, that their lives and health are protected, and that their suffering is alleviated.[16] This involves not only placing the needs of the individuals affected by conflict at the core of whatever relief is provided, but also speaking to authorities and reminding them of their obligations under IHL in relation to the population. Since the 1864 Convention, states have continued to develop the legal framework applicable to those providing this humanitarian relief. The key characteristics of humanitarian actors and the legal framework applicable to them today—the Geneva Conventions of 1949—will now be discussed.

## 3. Key Characteristics of Humanitarian Organizations under IHL

Humanitarian relief organizations are more prevalent nowadays than they have ever been;[17] indeed since the 1990s, the number of aid workers in conflicts has expanded considerably.[18] The types of role they undertake has also expanded—humanitarian assistance can mean work from short-term emergency assistance to protection, and from capacity building to post-conflict stabilization and reconstruction.[19] However, it is not so much the types of work that they engage in that defines such organizations as humanitarian relief organizations for the purposes of IHL, but rather how they engage in those activities.

As noted in section 2 'History of Humanitarian Relief Organizations under IHL', the early development of IHL relating to medical care was based on the idea that such care was being provided by medical staff that were neutral; that is, medical staff treated the wounded and sick from all parties to the conflict. Today the concept of neutrality is understood as being slightly more nuanced and as distinct from the principles of non-discrimination and impartiality. The Fundamental Principles of the International Red Cross Red Crescent Movement provide clarity on this point.[20] As an impartial organization, the Movement as a whole (encompassing all Red Cross and Red Crescent societies, the ICRC, and the International Federation of Red Cross and Red Crescent Societies):

> ... makes no discrimination as to nationality, race, religious beliefs, class or political opinions. It endeavours to relieve the suffering of individuals, being guided solely by their needs, and to give priority to the most urgent cases of distress.[21]

---

[16] ICRC, 'Professional Standards for Protection Work' (ICRC 2013) www.icrc.org/eng/assets/files/other/icrc-002-0999.pdf.

[17] Vincent Bernard, 'Editorial: The Future of Humanitarian Action' (2011) 93 *IRRC* 891, 893.

[18] Abby Stoddard, Adele Harmer, and Katherine Haver, *Providing Aid in Insecure Environments: Trends in Policy and Operations*, HPG Report 23 (Overseas Development Institute, September 2006) 11.

[19] Swiss FDFA, *Handbook on the International Normative Framework* (above n 1) 13.

[20] See also Laura Hammond, 'Neutrality and Impartiality', in Roger MacGinty and Jenny Peterson (eds), *The Routledge Companion to Humanitarian Action* (Routledge 2015).

[21] The Fundamental Principles proclaimed by the 20th International Conference of the Red Cross, Vienna, 1965. This is the revised text contained in the ICRC, 'Statutes of the International Red Cross and Red Crescent Movement, adopted by the 25th International Conference of the Red Cross, Geneva 1986' (31 October 1986) www.icrc.org/eng/resources/documents/red-cross-crescent-movement/fundamental-principles-movement-1986-10-31.htm.

As a neutral organization:

> In order to continue to enjoy the confidence of all, the Movement may not take sides in hostilities or engage at any time in controversies of a political, racial, religious or ideological nature.[22]

The Geneva Conventions of 1949 do not require humanitarian relief organizations to be neutral.[23] Indeed the 2016 Commentary to GCI notes, 'In the context of humanitarian activities, "neutrality" refers to the attitude to be adopted towards the Parties to the armed conflict.'[24] Rather, GCI requires 'impartial humanitarian organization[s]'[25] to provide 'humanitarian activities … subject to the consent of the Parties to the conflict concerned, … for the protection of wounded and sick, medical personnel and chaplains, and for their relief'[26] and for 'the protection of civilian persons'.[27] As such, the key characteristic of the IHL framework relating to humanitarian relief organizations is that they are impartial in the delivery of their humanitarian relief.

Despite the lack of reference to neutrality in the Geneva Conventions of 1949, humanitarian relief organizations in armed conflict are often better able to access victims of the conflict and provide them with humanitarian assistance if they adhere to neutrality, as well as impartiality and humanity.[28] As the ICRC Professional Standards for Protection state:

> The principle of humanity—that all people must be treated humanely in all circumstances— remains fundamental to effective protection work, placing the individual at risk at the centre of protection efforts … The principle of impartiality aims to ensure that a protection activity addresses the specific and most urgent protection needs of affected communities and individuals. It thus requires that humanitarian … actors define the protection activities to be undertaken in their area of responsibility, following an assessment of needs using objective criteria.[29]

The ICRC is specifically mentioned as a type of humanitarian relief organization which can provide humanitarian assistance under the Geneva Conventions, but not as the only humanitarian relief organization.[30] The ICRC had already been created at the time of the first Geneva Convention of 1864, and indeed assisted in convening the meeting and drafting the text of the Convention (and all subsequent Geneva Conventions). It was officially recognized in the 1864 Convention as a neutral, impartial, independent humanitarian organization, able to provide assistance during armed conflict.

One of the ICRC's primary initial roles was to assist in establishing National Red Cross and Red Crescent societies,[31] which are also recognized in the Geneva Conventions of

---

[22] ICRC, 'Statutes of the International Red Cross and Red Crescent Movement, adopted by the 25th International Conference of the Red Cross, Geneva 1986' (above n 21).

[23] Jean Pictet (ed), *Commentary to the Geneva Conventions of 1949* (ICRC 1952), commentary to GCI article 9.

[24] ICRC, *Commentary on the First Geneva Convention: Convention (I) for the Amelioration of the Condition of the Wounded and Sick in Armed Forces in the Field* (2nd edn, 2016) para 1164 https://ihl-databases.icrc.org/ihl/full/ GCI-commentary (ICRC Commentary 2016).

[25] GCI article 9; GCII article 9; GCIII article 9; GCIV article 10.

[26] GCI article 9; GCII article 9; GCIII article 9.

[27] GCIV article 10.

[28] ICRC Commentary 2016.

[29] ICRC, 'Professional Standards for Protection Work' (above n 16) 22.

[30] GCI article 9; GCII article 9; GCIII article 9; GCIV article 10.

[31] Bugnion (above n 6) 1318.

1949.[32] National Red Cross and Red Crescent societies may provide assistance to the medical personnel of the armed forces,[33] and can provide humanitarian assistance to civilians.[34] All members of the Red Cross and Red Crescent Movement adhere to the seven fundamental principles of humanity, neutrality, impartiality, independence, voluntary service, unity, and universality.[35] The 1952 Commentaries to the Geneva Conventions note that often it is difficult for National Societies to be perceived as neutral and able to act for both sides of a conflict, given the necessary ties they must have with their governments (known as 'auxiliary status'),[36] but this does not often prevent them being able to fulfil the requirements of an impartial relief organization for the purposes of the Conventions.

Non-governmental organizations can also be impartial humanitarian relief organizations. Save the Children (co-founded by the ICRC in 1919),[37] Médecins sans Frontières (founded in 1971 by former ICRC employees),[38] Oxfam (founded in 1942 during the Second World War) and World Vision (a faith-based, but still impartial, organization, founded in 1950) are all examples. United Nations agencies, such as the UN High Commissioner for Refugees (UNHCR) or the UN Children's Fund (UNICEF) are humanitarian organizations in that they provide humanitarian assistance to victims of armed conflict. While they can be associated with the political nature of the UN's security and peacekeeping roles, and can rarely be neutral,[39] they can often fulfil the role of a humanitarian relief organization for the purposes of IHL.

State-based institutions providing aid and even humanitarian assistance can rarely meet the requirements of humanity and impartiality where they belong to a party to the conflict. Regional organizations can coordinate humanitarian relief, such as the Association of South East Asian Nations in Myanmar during Cyclone Nargis in 2008 (where there was also an ongoing armed conflict), but they are politicized by national interests.[40] Foreign national provincial reconstruction teams in Afghanistan and Iraq have done development work in conflicts that is similar to humanitarian work,[41] as have regular military forces in these conflicts, but their aim is more to 'win hearts and minds' and counter insurgencies than to genuinely assist the humanitarian needs of the local population.[42] Similarly, most faith-based organizations and human rights organizations, while seeking justice for victims of conflict and providing humanitarian assistance, often have different goals than purely providing humanitarian assistance to the victims of armed conflict.[43] This is not to criticize

---

[32]  GCI article 26; GCIV articles 30 and 65.

[33]  GCI article 26.

[34]  GCIV article 30.

[35]  Proclaimed in 1965 by the 20th International Conference of the Red Cross and Red Crescent and included in ICRC, 'Statutes of the International Red Cross and Red Crescent Movement, adopted by the 25th International Conference of the Red Cross, Geneva 1986' (above n 21).

[36]  Pictet (above n 23) commentary to GCIV article 30.

[37]  Palmieri (above n 8) 1273, 1280.

[38]  See eg Rony Brauman, 'Médecins Sans Frontières and the ICRC: Matters of Principle' (2012) 94 *IRRC* 1523, 1524.

[39]  Kate Mackintosh, 'Beyond the Red Cross: The Protection of Independent Humanitarian Organisations and their Staff in International Humanitarian Law' (2007) 89 *IRRC* 113, 124.

[40]  Randolph Kent, 'Planning from the Future: An Emerging Agenda' (2011) 93 *IRRC* 939, 954.

[41]  Mackintosh (above n 39) 126.

[42]  Jamie A Williamson, 'Using Humanitarian Aid to "Win Hearts and Minds": A Costly Failure?' (2011) 93 *IRRC* 1035, 1037, 1040; Fiona Terry, 'The International Committee of the Red Cross in Afghanistan: Reasserting the Neutrality of Humanitarian Action' (2011) 93 *IRRC* 173, 173.

[43]  Elizabeth Ferris, 'Faith-Based and Secular Humanitarian Organisations' (2005) 87 *IRRC* 311, 316, 319, 320.

any of these actors, but to demonstrate how they do not fall within the category of impartial humanitarian relief organizations under IHL.

Ultimately it depends on why a so-called humanitarian relief organization is acting and how it performs its tasks that determines whether IHL will accord it the relevant protections, rights, and obligations as a humanitarian relief organization. While the Geneva Conventions do not talk about neutrality, it has been described as the 'guiding principle of humanitarian action' for humanitarian relief organizations.[44] As emphasized by the first Geneva Convention of 1864, to be purely humanitarian requires an element of neutrality—the goal is to provide humanitarian assistance to victims of an armed conflict and this often means not taking sides, having a dialogue with all parties to the conflict, having access to all areas, and being able to provide impartial assistance to victims on both sides.[45] Often such humanitarian assistance can lead to stabilization, a reduction of violence, and peace, but it is not the aim of a humanitarian organization to ensure that end point—as long as victims are provided relief impartially, they have met their objectives. In terms of impartiality, '[t]he degree and urgency of the need should ... be taken into consideration when distributing relief'.[46] Any humanitarian relief must be provided to people who most need the assistance, without consideration of nationality, ethnicity, race, religion, or other criteria, on the basis of an on-the-ground assessment. Finally, in order to be a humanitarian relief organization for the purposes of IHL, organizations should actually be present during the conflict, providing assistance as the conflict continues.

## 4. IHL Frameworks of Humanitarian Relief Operations

### A. Source and Scope of Responsibility

As noted in section 1 'Introduction: Humanitarian Relief Operations in Armed Conflict', the international legal framework of humanitarian relief operations is underpinned by the fundamental principle of international law that states have primary responsibility for ensuring the protection of affected civilian populations under their control.[47] This responsibility is drawn from the principle of state sovereignty and other legal frameworks, including international human rights law,[48] which make it clear that states have responsibilities for their population's access to primary health care, essential foods, and basic shelter.[49] However, as pointed out by Bouchet-Saulnier, the IHL regime slightly modifies this general principle. In relation armed conflict the responsibility is placed not solely on states, but rather on the 'Parties to the conflict'.[50] This is in recognition that it may actually be non-state actors who

---

[44] Terry (above n 42) 176.

[45] Claudia McGoldrick, 'The Future of Humanitarian Action: An ICRC Perspective' (2011) 93 *IRRC* 965, 984.

[46] Pictet (above n 23) commentary to GCIV article 10.

[47] See eg UNSC Resolution 1674 UN Doc S/RES/1674 (28 April 2006); see also Emanuela-Chiara Gillard, 'The Law Regulating Cross-Border Relief Operations' (2013) 95 *IRRC* 351, 355; ICRC, 'ICRC Q&A and Lexicon on Humanitarian Access' (2014) 96 *IRRC* 359, 365–6.

[48] Which does not cease to apply in times of armed conflict: *Legal Consequences of the Construction of a Wall in the Occupied Palestinian Territory* (Advisory Opinion) [2004] ICJ Rep 136 para 106 (*Palestinian Wall* case).

[49] See eg Felix Schwendimann, 'The Legal Framework of Humanitarian Access in Armed Conflict' (2011) 93 *IRRC* 993, 1003–04; UNCHR, 'Guiding Principles on Internal Displacement' UN Doc E/CN/4/1998/Add.2 (11 February 1998).

[50] API article 70(2).

have control of territory and therefore assume the obligations to protect the civilian popula-tion.[51] This is also reflected in recent debates on the application of human rights principles to non-state actors in conflict, particularly those who control territory.[52]

As such, parties to a conflict assume obligations under IHL towards affected civilian populations under their control. The scope of these obligations is outlined in the Geneva Conventions of 1949 and their Additional Protocols of 1977. IHL specifically notes that, in international armed conflict (IAC), civilian populations have rights in relation to care of the wounded, sick, infirm, and expectant mothers.[53] Further, civilian populations have rights to access medical and hospital stores (particularly for those under the age of fifteen, expectant mothers, and maternity cases), essential foodstuffs, and clothing.[54] This is by virtue of the corollary of the requirement to allow access to essential items for their survival by civilian populations, and in accordance with basic principles of international human rights law.[55] Moreover, it is a war crime to deprive the civilian population of items essential to their sur-vival.[56] Civilians also have the right to family news[57] and, where possible, reunification of dispersed families.[58] Additionally, for orphans under fifteen years of age it is a requirement that 'their maintenance, the exercise of their religion and their education are facilitated'.[59]

In situations of occupation the duty of the occupying power to ensure that the civilian population has access to food and medical supplies is clearly articulated.[60] Article 55 of GCIV provides that if such stores are inadequate, the occupying power is required to bring them in. Article 69(1) of API extends this obligation to require the occupying power to also ensure the provision of 'clothing, bedding, means of shelter, other supplies essential to the survival of the civilian population of the occupied territory and objects necessary for reli-gious worship'.[61]

Although no specific provisions exist in APII regarding the nature of parties' obli-gations to the civilian population in non-international armed conflict (NIAC), as with IAC, the deprivation of access to food and medicine to affected civilians populations may constitute a war crime.[62] As such, a corollary of this obligation must be the obligation on

---

[51] Bouchet-Saulnier (above n 4). See also at 211 that this terminology has been adopted by the UNSC Resolutions, which call on 'all Parties to the conflict'.

[52] See eg Tilman Rodenhäuser, 'Human Rights Obligations of Non-State Armed Groups in Other Situations of Violence: The Syria Example' (2012) 3 JIHLS 263; Eve Massingham and Kelisiana Thynne, 'Promoting Access to Health Care in "Other Situations of Violence": Time to Reignite the Debate on International Regulation' (2014) 5 JIHLS 105, 122.

[53] GCIV article 16.

[54] ibid article 23.

[55] Such as the 'right of everyone to an adequate standard of living for himself and his family, including adequate food, clothing and housing', under International Covenant on Civil and Political Rights (adopted 16 December 1966, entered into force 23 March 1976) 999 UNTS 171 (ICCPR) article 11.

[56] Rome Statute of the International Criminal Court (opened for signature 17 July 1998, entered into force 1 July 2002) 2187 UNTS 90 (Rome Statute) article 8(2)(b)(xxv).

[57] GCIV article 25.

[58] ibid article 26.

[59] ibid article 24.

[60] Although note the proviso on this obligation in relation to the capacity of the state, namely that the obliga-tion is one to be fulfilled to the 'fullest extent of the means available to [the Occupying Power]'. See Pictet (above n 23) 310.

[61] API article 69(1).

[62] Rome Statute, article 8(2)(c)(i); see further, ICRC Commentary 2016 620, particularly citing ICTY, *Prosecutor v. Mile Mrksic Miroslav Radic Veselin*, ICTY (Trial Judgement) Case No.: IT-95-13/1-T, 27 September 2007, para 517, where the Chamber held that 'the failure to provide adequate medicine and medical treatment would consti-tute the offence of "cruel treatment" if, in the special circumstances, it causes serious mental or physical suffering'. See also, Jean-Marie Henckaerts and Louise Doswald-Beck (eds), *Customary International Humanitarian Law, Vol 1: Rules* (CUP 2005) (CIHL) rule 55.

parties to the conflict to provide affected civilian populations with food and medicine.[63] Further, as the wounded and sick must be collected and cared for in an armed conflict, regardless of its nature, pursuant to Common Article 3, a corollary of this obligation must be the obligation of the parties to provide medical supplies to affected civilian populations.

Humanitarian relief operations clearly become necessary when a party to a conflict is failing to provide adequately for the population under their control in relation to the above-mentioned criteria. The Geneva Conventions of 1949 provide that third-party states[64] and/or the ICRC or any other impartial humanitarian organization[65] may offer their services to assist the population.

## B. Basic Rules: The Relief Operations of Humanitarian Organizations

IHL provides for the right of impartial humanitarian actors, where the needs of the civilian population are not being adequately met, to offer their services to assist those affected by armed conflict, subject to the consent of the parties. This applies both in times of IAC (including occupation) and NIAC. In IAC (including occupation) this right to offer their services belongs to the ICRC 'or any other impartial humanitarian organization'.[66] In relation to medical personnel, the 'staff of National Red Cross Societies and that of other Voluntary Aid Societies, duly recognized and authorized by their Governments' may assist the military medical services.[67] In NIAC Common Article 3 recognizes the right of an impartial humanitarian body, such as the ICRC, to offer its services to the parties to the conflict. In NIAC's additionally covered by APII, this right is also specifically extended to allow those relief societies located within a state, such as the national Red Cross and Red Crescent Societies, to offer their services to assist the civilian population.[68] Although specifically mentioned in the Geneva Conventions, the ICRC and Red Cross Red Crescent Movement 'do not have a monopoly on humanitarian activities, and there are other organizations capable of providing effective assistance',[69] subject to the criteria of impartiality and acceptance by the parties to the conflict.

The purpose of relief operations is to address protection concerns for the civilian population. The provisions of GCIV and API and II provide for the free passage of essential relief supplies, including medical stores, essential foodstuffs, clothing, and 'tonics intended for children under fifteen, expectant mothers and maternity cases'.[70] They also provide for

---

[63] See further ICRC Commentary 2016, para 767.

[64] This is a component of the obligation to respect and ensure respect for IHL under Common Article 1 to the Geneva Conventions, which has been described as going 'beyond an entitlement for third States to take steps to ensure respect for IHL. It establishes not only a right to take action, but also an international legal obligation to do so': Knut Dörmann and José Serralvo, 'Common Article 1 to the Geneva Conventions and the Obligation to Prevent International Humanitarian Law Violations' *IRRC First View Articles* (CUP, 30 January 2015) 3, 17.

[65] See eg GCIV article 10.

[66] GCI article 9; GCII article 9; GCIII article 9; GCIV article 10, 59; API article 70(1).

[67] GCI article 26.

[68] Protocol Additional to the Geneva Conventions of 12 August 1949, and relating to the Protection of Victims of Non-International Armed Conflicts, 8 June 1977, 1125 UNTS 609 (entered into force 7 December 1978) 1125 UNTS 3 (APII) article 18(1).

[69] Yves Sandoz, Christophe Swinarski, and Bruno Zimmerman (eds), *Commentary on the Additional Protocols of 8 June 1977 to the Geneva Conventions of 12 August 1949* (Martinus Nijhoff 1987) (AP Commentary) 1477.

[70] GCIV article 23; API article 70(1). See also GCIV article 55 regarding situations of occupation.

the fulfilment of basic needs in situations of occupation (clothing, bedding, shelter, and other supplies essential to the survival of the civilian population[71]), and the entry of exclusively humanitarian and impartial relief supplies where civilians are suffering undue hardship in NIAC.[72]

In IAC, the parties to the conflict 'shall allow and facilitate the rapid and unimpeded passage of all relief consignments, equipment and personnel'.[73] Although these consignments may be searched, they must not be delayed or diverted.[74] The parties shall protect these consignments and facilitate their rapid distribution.[75] The parties shall also 'encourage and facilitate effective international coordination of . . . relief activities'.[76]

In situations of occupation, occupying powers 'shall agree to relief schemes on behalf of the said population, and shall facilitate them by all the means at . . . [their] disposal'.[77] In NIAC, the obligation to facilitate such activities is not specified, but is implied from article 18 of APII. The obligation to facilitate relief operations in both IAC and NIAC is contained in customary IHL.[78]

The organization carrying out the relief operation must comply with certain conditions, including providing relief in an impartial manner—that is, in determining who is to receive the aid, the organization must do so without reference to any consideration other than humanitarian need. It must also ensure that the assistance only goes to the beneficiaries and is not diverted for purposes other than for which it is intended. Humanitarian relief operations must further be conducted in accordance with domestic legal frameworks. Limitations may also be placed on the number of humanitarian organizations which are able to provide the services.[79]

## C. Consent

The consent of the party to the conflict that controls the territory where the relief operation is to be conducted must be sought before it can be carried out. This is because IHL, in balancing military necessity and humanity, does not grant an unfettered right to humanitarian access; rather it grants, to impartial humanitarian organizations, the right to offer their services.[80]

The issue regarding from whom consent is required for humanitarian relief operations to be conducted depends on the nature of the conflict. The 'consent of the Parties to the conflict concerned' is required in IAC (including occupation).[81] The consent of the state

---

[71] API article 69.
[72] APII article 18.
[73] GCI article 23; GCII article 59(3); GCIII article 61(3); GCIV articles 70(2), 70(3).
[74] API article 70(3). Note the exception of 'cases of urgent necessity in the interests of the civilian population concerned'.
[75] ibid article 70(4).
[76] ibid article 70(5).
[77] GCIV article 59.
[78] ICRC, 'Study on Customary International Humanitarian Law: A Contribution to the Understanding and Respect for the Rule of Law in Armed Conflict' (2005) 87 IRRC 175, 203 (Customary Rule 55).
[79] GCIV article 142.
[80] See ICRC, 'Q&A and Lexicon on Humanitarian Access' (above n 47) 368.
[81] GCI article 9; GCII article 9; GCIII article 9; GCIV articles 10, 59; API article 70(1).

on whose territory the armed conflict is taking place is required to deliver relief activities in NIAC.[82]

However, while consent must be sought, consent cannot be refused arbitrarily.[83] This means that where a party to a conflict is not able or willing to adequately meet the needs of the population under its control it must consent to offers by impartial humanitarian organizations.[84] Acceptable grounds for refusal would only be:

- if there was no need—for example during occupation the population was not 'inadequately supplied'[85] or in NIAC there was no 'undue hardship';[86]
- because the assistance provider is not impartial and the relief operations are not carried out without distinction;[87] or
- for reasons of imperative military necessity. While it is not clear exactly what constitutes imperative military necessity it can certainly be argued that this could only prevent consent being given for a period of time rather than indefinitely. For example, in respect of ICRC visits to detainees as authorized by GCIII, reasons of imperative military necessity can only limit such visits 'as an exceptional and temporary measure'.[88]

Gillard notes that other valid reasons for the refusal of consent may include suspected unneutral behaviour, foreign relief personnel hampering military operations, or the existence of ongoing combat operations.[89] The ICRC, in its 2016 Commentary to GCI, goes as far as suggesting that the issue of consent is effectively void nowadays. This is because article 23 of GCIV requires states 'to allow and facilitate the rapid and unimpeded passage of relief consignments, equipment and personnel destined for the civilian population, even that of an opposing Party'. If states were to refuse consent to humanitarian relief organizations from providing this service, they would be in breach of this article, 'and thus render the consent given by the Parties to the conflict void'.[90]

## D.  Protections Offered by IHL to Humanitarian Relief Personnel and Objects

IHL protects those who are not, or who are no longer, taking part in hostilities. As was discussed in earlier chapters, IHL divides personnel and objects into two distinct

---

[82]  See ICRC, 'Q&A and Lexicon on Humanitarian Access' (above n 47) 369–70, which notes that as a matter of practicality the consent of the parties concerned would also be sought by the ICRC before carrying out its humanitarian activities.

[83]  See further Dietrich Schindler, 'Humanitarian Assistance, Humanitarian Interference and International Law', in Ronald Macdonald (ed), *Essays in Honour of Wang Tieya* (Martinus Nijhoff 1994) 689, 696–7; UNSC Resolution 668 UN Doc S/RES/668 (20 September 1990) and UNGA Resolution 45/170 UN Doc A/RES/45/170 (18 December 1990) condemned the refusal of humanitarian assistance by Iraq, from both humanitarian organizations, and in the case of the General Assembly Resolution, from the Government of Kuwait.

[84]  See further ICRC Commentary 2016 para 1173.

[85]  GCIV article 59.

[86]  APII article 18(2).

[87]  GCI article 9; GCII article 9; GCIII article 9; GCIV articles 10, 59; API article 70(1).

[88]  GC III article 126.

[89]  Gillard (above n 47) 360.

[90]  ICRC Commentary 2016 para 1168.

categories—military and civilian. Specifically, civilians are all persons who are not military (as defined by article 4A of GCIII) and civilian objects are those objects which do not 'by their nature, location, purpose or use make an effective contribution to the military action.'[91] Humanitarian relief personnel and objects are therefore protected by the provisions of IHL that protect civilians, including protection against the 'dangers arising from military operations'.[92]

However, IHL also provides specific protection for humanitarian relief personnel and supplies in both IAC and NIAC.[93] Personnel participating in such relief activities shall be respected and protected[94] and '[o]nly in case of imperative military necessity may ... [their] activities ... be limited or their movements temporarily restricted'.[95] Parties to the conflict must in no way divert relief consignments or delay them.[96]

Attached to these protection rights are a number of obligations. Relief personnel 'shall be subject to the approval of the Party in whose territory they will carry out their duties'[97] and must not 'exceed the terms of their mission'.[98]

In order to protect humanitarian workers, the Rome Statue of the International Criminal Court details as a war crime:

> ... intentionally directing attacks against personnel, installations, material, units or vehicles involved in a humanitarian assistance or peacekeeping mission in accordance with the Charter of the United Nations, as long as they are entitled to the protection given to civilians or civilian objects under the international law of armed conflict.[99]

Additionally, there is a specific treaty related to the safety of UN personnel.[100] Article 7(1) of the treaty notes that 'United Nations and associated personnel, their equipment and premises shall not be made the object of attack or of any action that prevents them from discharging their mandate'. A number of Security Council resolutions also call for greater respect for the protections for UN and humanitarian relief personnel. For example, UN Security Council resolution 1502 on the Protection of United Nations Personnel, Associated Personnel and Humanitarian Personnel in Conflict Zones:

> *Urges* all those concerned as set forth in international humanitarian law, including the Geneva Conventions and the Hague Regulations, to allow full unimpeded access by humanitarian personnel to all people in need of assistance, and to make available, as far as possible, all necessary facilities for their operations, and to promote the safety, security and

[91]  API article 52(2).
[92]  ibid article 51(1).
[93]  ibid article 71(2); CIHL rules 31–32.
[94]  API article 71(2).
[95]  ibid article 71(3).
[96]  ibid article 70(3)(c).
[97]  ibid article 71(1).
[98]  ibid article 71(4).
[99]  Rome Statute article 8(2)(b)(iii).
[100]  Convention on the Safety of United Nations and Associated Personnel (opened for signature 15 December 1994, entered into force 15 January 1999) 2051 UNTS 363.

freedom of movement of humanitarian personnel and United Nations and its associated personnel and their assets.[101]

## 1. The emblems of protection

An important aspect of the IHL framework relating to humanitarian activities is the distinctive emblems of the Geneva Conventions. The Red Cross, Red Crescent, and red crystal emblems[102] are protected by IHL for use by military medical personnel and equipment employed in the medical service[103] so as to indicate their protected status and to ensure that persons who are 'out of the fight' are respected and protected. Military medical services are entitled to this special protected status on the basis of their role as impartial medical providers. Military medical personnel are required by IHL (as well as by their medical ethics) to treat the wounded or sick 'without any adverse distinction founded on sex, race, nationality, religion, political opinions, or any other similar criteria'.[104] In line with medical ethics, the Geneva Conventions require that '[o]nly urgent medical reasons will authorize priority in the order of treatment to be administered'.[105]

The use of the emblems indicates the impartial nature of these medical personnel. These emblems are not to be used, either in peace time or war time, except for the purpose of indicating or protecting medical units and establishments and personnel protected by GCI and GCII.[106] The only exceptions to this are for the ICRC (permitted at all times to use the Red Cross emblem) and national Red Cross or Red Crescent societies, as agreed by their governments (and in accordance with domestic legislation). The national societies are permitted to use these emblems to indicate their services (although such use of the emblems must be 'comparatively small in size' and 'cannot be considered as conferring the protection of the Convention').[107]

The protection of the medical mission in armed conflict is a fundamental aspect of IHL. These rules are not always respected and the ICRC notes that this lack of respect is becoming more prevalent.[108] An ICRC project on 'Health Care in Danger' aims to raise awareness about violence against health care but also to propose some 'operational strategies' and 'encourage decision-makers to take action to prevent violence against health care'.[109] The findings of the project include some very practical recommendations,[110] including on the protection of the emblems under law and practice. The recommendations highlight the importance of respect for the legal framework for both military medical personnel and medical relief supplies.

---

[101]   UNSC Resolution 1502 UN Doc S/RES/1502 (26 August 2003).
[102]   GCI chapter VII; APIII.
[103]   See eg GCI article 39; APII article 12.
[104]   GCI article 12.
[105]   ibid article 12; Note also the UNSC Resolution 2139 UN Doc S/RES/2139 (22 February 2014) in relation to Syria which 'demands that all parties respect the principle of medical neutrality ... and *recalls* that under international humanitarian law, the wounded and sick must receive, to the fullest extent practicable, and with the least possible delay, medical care and attention required by their condition ...'.
[106]   GCI article 44.
[107]   ibid article 44.
[108]   See eg ICRC, 'Q&A: Health Care in Danger: In Conversation with Pierre Gentile' (2013) 95 *IRRC* 341, 341.
[109]   ICRC, *Violent Incidents Affecting the Delivery of Health Care: Health Care in Danger: January 2012 to December 2014* (ICRC 2015) 1.
[110]   See further, ICRC 'Q&A: Health Care in Danger' (above n 108) 345.

## 5. Challenges for Humanitarian Relief

Many areas of IHL have been the subject of some discussion about their compatibility with modern-day armed conflict.[111] However in the main, the IHL framework is able to be applied to these challenges, by relying on a principled approach rather than unchangeable provisions,[112] and in light of its universally agreed status. However, new laws applicable to a variety of IHL-related themes, such as weapons, cyber warfare or the very nature of conflict and who is a party to such conflicts, continue to be developed. Expanded legal frameworks to address challenges will be important in the future, such as giving greater consideration to how characteristics such as gender or disability affect both access to and needs from humanitarian relief operations. Both these areas are currently the focus of some attention from the international community, including the International Red Cross and Red Crescent Movement.[113] It is clear that three main themes emerge in considering challenges to the humanitarian relief operations legal framework. These will now be discussed.

### A. Maintaining Neutrality and Impartiality

In the mid-1990s, humanitarian relief organizations faced many challenges. The organizations were unable to prevent atrocities in Rwanda and the Balkans and in some cases were unable to provide assistance to the victims of the atrocities, often as a result of poor planning and lack of common understanding and standards.[114] Common standards were subsequently drawn up, including the SPHERE Standards,[115] the ICRC Professional Standards for Protection,[116] and more recently the Core Humanitarian Standards, which have been incorporated into the SPHERE Project. These standards clarified the roles of different actors in providing humanitarian assistance in conflict and set minimum standards that should be met in providing water, health, sanitation, shelter, food, and protection. The standards have

---

[111] See eg ICRC, 'Report on International Humanitarian Law and the Challenges of Contemporary Armed Conflicts', 32nd International Conference of the Red Cross and Red Crescent, Geneva 8–10 December 2015 https://www.icrc.org/en/document/international-humanitarian-law-and-challenges-contemporary-armed-conflicts.

[112] In the sense that IHL prohibits acts that are indiscriminate and disproportionate and/or cause unnecessary suffering, rather than seeking to list the circumstances of all prohibited acts.

[113] For example, numerous references are made to gender in ICRC, 'Resolutions of the Council of Delegates of the International Red Cross and Red Crescent Movement' (31st International Conference of the Red Cross and Red Crescent, Geneva 28 November–1 December 2011) www.icrc.org/eng/assets/files/publications/icrc-002-1130.pdf. Resolution 9 of the 2013 Council of Delegates of the International Red Cross and Red Crescent Movement concerns promoting disability inclusion within the Movement: ICRC, 'Resolutions of the Council of Delegates of the International Red Cross and Red Crescent Movement' (Sydney, November 2013), Resolution 9 www.icrc.org/eng/assets/files/publications/icrc-002-1140.pdf. Additionally, at the 2017 Council of Delegates Meeting of the International Red Cross and Red Crescent Movement a resolution was passed calling on the Movement itself to take concrete steps to improve gender equality in its own leadership: ICRC, *Reinforcing Gender Equality and Equal Opportunities in the Leadership and Work of the International Red Cross and Red Crescent Movement* 'Resolutions of the Council of Delegates of the International Red Cross and Red Crescent Movement' (Turkey, November 2017) Resolution 12.

[114] Michael Barnett and Peter Walker, 'Regime Change for Humanitarian Aid: How to Make Relief More Accountable' [2015] July/August *Foreign Aff* 130, 132.

[115] Sphere Project, *Sphere Handbook: Humanitarian Charter and Minimum Standards in Humanitarian Response* (3rd edn, Sphere Project 2011); see also Peter Walker, 'Victims of Natural Disaster and the Right to Humanitarian Assistance: A Practitioner's View' (1998) 325 *IRRC* 611.

[116] ICRC, 'Professional Standards for Protection Work' (above n 16).

in general ensured that organizations understand each other, and coordinate and conduct themselves better in conflicts and in disaster response.

After 2001, humanitarian relief organizations faced challenges with acceptance and access. Some humanitarian relief organizations accepted the new paradigm of the need for counter-insurgency against terrorists and were implicated in what has been called 'the unholy alliance between development and counter-terrorism'.[117] They were often being instrumentalized in what the parties to the conflict wanted to achieve, which was a potential cause for a rise in attacks on humanitarian relief personnel.[118] Once the perception existed that they were no longer simply there for humanitarian reasons they lost their neutrality, which was difficult for them to win back. This arguably also had an effect on all humanitarian relief organizations during the early 2000s.[119] The ICRC had a challenge to redefine its neutrality in the war in Afghanistan and to demonstrate its purely humanitarian functions before it would be accepted again by all parties to the conflict.[120]

In 2009 Switzerland launched an initiative to develop practical resources to assist humanitarian relief organizations in gaining access for humanitarian purposes in armed conflict. The resulting *Handbook* and *Manual* seek to demonstrate how actors can remain neutral, and have humanity as their goal and impartiality as their means of operating, to ensure access to victims of a conflict.[121] In some ways these are also guides for states to recognize that humanitarian relief organizations should be allowed to do their job unhindered by political associations.

Setting modes of humanitarian action assists organizations in maintaining credibility, acceptance, and access, and ensures that they can continue to meet the requirements to be an impartial humanitarian relief organization. The ICRC, for example, maintains strict neutrality and attempts to demonstrate and uphold this by engaging in confidential dialogue with each party to the conflict. The decision to fully demonstrate neutrality and not speak out[122] means that the ICRC is often one of the only humanitarian relief organizations which can operate in some conflicts. This is because speaking out sometimes means that organizations will be asked to leave the country, and then there will be little humanitarian relief available to victims of a conflict. However, in many instances, actors in the conflict get frustrated by the silence. Tellingly, the Legal Advisor to George Bush, John Bellinger, said that he wished ICRC had spoken publicly about the legal framework for detention in the war in Afghanistan.[123] A Guantanamo inmate, Sami El-haj, likewise said that the ICRC should have spoken about what legal protections should apply under the Geneva Conventions in that war.[124] The ICRC took the unusual step in Gaza in 2014 of issuing a press release to both sides, saying that it could not do more in the conflict, urging the parties to let it undertake

---

[117] McGoldrick (above n 45) 972.
[118] Stoddard et al (above n 18) 23.
[119] Williamson (above n 42) 1037, 1046.
[120] Terry (above n 42) 173.
[121] Swiss FDFA, *Humanitarian Access in Situations of Armed Conflict: Practitioners' Manual*, Version 2 (FDFA, December 2014); Swiss FDFA, *Handbook on the International Normative Framework* (above n 1).
[122] In rare cases where other methods have been tried and there are still serious violations of IHL, ICRC will denounce—publicly make a statement that one or both parties to a conflict are violating IHL. This is an unusual step for ICRC and it generally means that serious violations of IHL are occurring, and that humanitarian relief is not able to reach the intended beneficiaries.
[123] John B Bellinger III, 'Observations on the 150th Anniversary of the ICRC' (2012) 94 *IRRC* 1223, 1226.
[124] Sami El-haj, 'A Guantanamo Detainee's Perspective' (2012) 94 *IRRC* 1229, 1231.

what it could do in that difficult environment, and even went as far as asking politicians to end the war.[125]

## B.  Compliance with the Law and Denial of Access by Non-State Actors

Reflective of the violent situation of armed conflict, the legal framework of protection of humanitarian assistance is not always able to be fully utilized by relevant actors. Schwendimann notes that the international legal framework is a 'tool' and 'an important basis for seeking agreement on access'.[126] In this respect these legal provisions are not a panacea. Kalshoven has noted that, '[t]he serious shortcomings of the entire system of international humanitarian assistance … come to light every day'.[127] Humanitarian relief organizations which fulfil the Geneva Conventions' requirements of being impartial, such as the ICRC, must continually work with states and non-state actors to educate them about their mandate and the legal frameworks. This will instil confidence in the state and non-state actors about the validity of their relief operations, such that they can access affected populations in armed conflict.

It is inevitably more challenging to install this confidence in non-state actors and this is a particular challenge of modern humanitarian relief operations, given the prevalence of NIAC. As Hofman points out, there are three key reasons for this. First, the non-state actors, although bound by IHL, were not present at the negotiating table when the rules of IHL were adopted. Second, states are not keen on support for these groups, and indeed in some jurisdictions the provision of aid to such groups is criminalized.[128] Third, without support for civilian infrastructure the delivery of aid is very difficult. A legal framework response to this challenge is unlikely to ever be fully effective. Rather, non-state actors must be convinced to 'maintain a dialogue' and will only do so 'if they believe the organization they are talking to does not have a role in the political and military strategies in support of the state they oppose'.[129]

There are many examples of the denial of access to humanitarian organizations which have resulted in human suffering. While IHL 'does not explicitly regulate the consequence of an unlawful denial of consent',[130] it is clear that in certain circumstances doing

[125] Jacques de Maio, 'No Wonder Gazans are Angry. The Red Cross Can't Protect Them' (ICRC, 25 July 2014) www.icrc.org/eng/resources/documents/article/editorial/07-24-gaza-israel-palestine-maio.htm.

[126] Schwendimann (above n 49) 993, 995–6.

[127] Frits Kalshoven, 'Assistance to the Victims of Armed Conflict and Other Disasters', in Frits Kalshoven (ed) *Assisting the Victims of Armed Conflict and Other Disasters* (Martinus Nijhoff 1989) 24.

[128] See eg a discussion of Australian counter-terrorism laws in Phoebe Wynn-Pope, Yvette Zegenhagen, and Fauve Kurnadi, 'Legislating against Humanitarian Principles: A Case Study on the Humanitarian Implications of Australian Counterterrorism Legislation' (2016) 97 *IRRC* 897(8), 235. It is clear that counter-terrorism legislation has also become a key challenge for humanitarian relief operations as a number of humanitarian relief activities could be encompassed in broad definitions of assistance or material support to terrorists. Such provisions place a heavy burden on humanitarian organizations and their staff to try and prove that their activities are compliant with IHL and that the legislation itself must be read in compliance with IHL. It also places a heavy burden on the communities in designated areas who will suffer the effects of conflict more because humanitarian assistance will not be able to be delivered. Some States in implementing these and other international instruments have provided for humanitarian exemptions, but in each context humanitarian organizations must remind States that seek to enact new legislation about the need for humanitarian exemptions to facilitate their work. Saul, in chapter 18 of this volume, especially at part 4, discusses this in more detail.

[129] Michiel Hofman, 'Non State Armed Groups and Aid Organisations', in Roger MacGinty and Jenny Peterson (eds) *The Routledge Companion to Humanitarian Action* (Routledge 2015) 324.

[130] ICRC, 'Q&A and Lexicon on Humanitarian Access' (above n 47) 370.

so constitutes a violation of IHL. The Commentary to the Additional Protocols to the Geneva Conventions notes that an example of this would be where the refusal to consent to relief operations results in the starvation of the civilian population.[131] The UN Security Council has also noted that arbitrary denial of humanitarian access can constitute a violation of IHL.[132]

In response to a lack of access, humanitarian relief organizations can call on the parties to the conflict to respect IHL and humanitarian principles and allow humanitarian assistance—as, for example, has often occurred in the Syrian conflict.[133] They can also provide support to relief operations that have been consented to by the parties. The structure of the International Red Cross and Red Crescent Movement is particularly valuable in cases where access is being denied to humanitarian relief personnel and objects coming from outside. This is because the existence of a national Red Cross or Red Crescent Society in almost every country in the world (there are currently 190 recognized national societies, and some that are still being formed) gives the ICRC a permanent partner in every country. The ICRC can work with the relevant national society to strengthen its capacity to respond to the humanitarian needs on the ground.

The international community, through the UN Security Council, also has a number of options. The UN Security Council can call on parties to the conflict to allow the delivery of humanitarian relief supplies.[134] The UN Security Council can deem the lack of access to humanitarian supplies a threat to international peace and security and deem it appropriate to use military force to facilitate the delivery of humanitarian supplies to affected populations.[135] The creation by the UN Security Council of monitoring mechanisms at border posts to get aid into Syria is another approach that effectively rendered the consent question mute.[136]

Third states, by virtue of the obligation to respect and ensure respect for IHL pursuant to Common Article 1 of the Geneva Conventions, have obligations to ensure humanitarian relief operations are facilitated. A state in conflict cannot protest that a third state is acting unlawfully by interfering, through lawful measures, to ensure respect for IHL.[137] The delivery of humanitarian relief operations is not unlawful interference in the affairs of

---

[131] AP Commentary (above n 69) 820.

[132] '[W]hile *condemning* all cases of denial of humanitarian access and *recalling* that arbitrary denial of humanitarian access and depriving civilians of objects indispensable to their survival, including wilfully impeding relief supply and access, can constitute a violation of international humanitarian law': UNSC Resolution 2139 UN Doc S/RES/2139 (22 February 2014).

[133] See eg *Médecins Sans Frontières* (MSF), 'Syria: Humanitarian Assistance in Deadlock' (7 March 2013) www. msf.org/article/syria-humanitarian-assistance-deadlock; ICRC, 'Syria: A People Ignored, a Land Destroyed' (14 September 2015) www.icrc.org/en/document/syria-people-ignored-land-destroyed.

[134] See eg UNSC Resolution 794 (1992), which demanded 'that all parties, movements and factions in Somalia take all measures necessary to facilitate the efforts of the United Nations, its specialized agencies and humanitarian organizations to provide urgent humanitarian assistance to the affected population in Somalia' and more recently UNSC Resolution 2139(2014), which demanded 'that all parties, in particular the Syrian authorities, promptly allow rapid, safe and unhindered humanitarian access for United Nations humanitarian agencies and their implementing partners, including across conflict lines and across borders, in order to ensure that humanitarian assistance reaches people in need through the most direct routes'.

[135] UN Charter Article 42. Dapo Akande and Emanuela-Chiara Gillard, *Oxford Guidance on the Law Relating to Humanitarian Relief Operations in Situations of Armed Conflict*, (United Nations Office for the Coordination of Humanitarian Affairs, 2016), 19 articulate that indeed Security Council resolutions on this theme may eventually lead to the use of force.

[136] UNSC Resolution 2165(2014). See further Akande and Gillard (above n 135) 18–19. The right of UN humanitarian agencies and their implementing partners to cross conflict lines and boarders as set out in this resolution has been renewed on a regular basis by the UN, most recently in UNSC Res 2449 (2018).

[137] *Military and Paramilitary Activities in and against Nicaragua (Nicaragua v United States of America)*, (Merits) [1986] ICJ Rep 14, 388–9; Paolo Benvenuti, 'Ensuring Observance of International Humanitarian

a state and must not be refused arbitrarily.[138] Where consent is arbitrarily refused, and IHL is consequently violated because, for example, civilians are starving or not getting access to medical supplies, then a third state can deliver humanitarian relief operations and the host state cannot legally object.[139] Further, article 64 of API to the Geneva Conventions, relating to civilian civil defence organizations of neutral or other states, requires that the parties to the conflict receiving assistance under this provision 'should facilitate international cooperation'.

Finally, the IHL framework regarding humanitarian relief operations is supplemented by a broader discourse which involves UN entities such as the UN Office for the Coordination of Humanitarian Affairs, associated documents such as the Guiding Principles on Internal Displacement[140] and the Guiding Principles on the Right to Humanitarian Assistance,[141] and concepts such as the Responsibility to Protect.[142] As such, outside the IHL legal framework, there may be other avenues to be utilized as tools to persuade parties to a conflict to accept relief operations. For example, Akande and Gillard conclude that while ordinarily any humanitarian relief operation conducted without state consent is a violation of sovereignty and territorial integrity, a binding Security Council decision can render such operation lawful and 'exceptionally, state or international organization may conduct temporary humanitarian relief operations to bring life-saving supplies to a people in extreme need, when no alternatives exists'.[143]

## C. Accountability to Beneficiaries and Social Media

One issue which is becoming an increasing challenge for humanitarian relief organizations is accountability to those to whom they give relief. Persons receiving humanitarian relief have sometimes been seen as just victims of a conflict, without the resources to help themselves or assess the situation. Humanitarian relief organizations need to understand the strengths of these populations and the specific needs of the population if they are to adequately do their work. Previously victims could not hold humanitarians accountable if they did insufficient or inadequate work.[144] Nowadays beneficiaries are often connected to technology. They understand what they need and are able to communicate those needs through technology.[145] Yves Daccord, Director General of the ICRC, has suggested that the ICRC and other actors will need to be more accountable as they will be rated on social

Law: Function, Extent and Limits of the Obligations of Third States to Ensure Respect for IHL' [1992] Int'l Inst Hum L YB 1989–90 27, 33.

[138] Birgit Kessler, 'The Duty to "Ensure Respect" under Common Article 1 of the Geneva Conventions: Its Implications on International and Non-International Armed Conflicts' (2001) 44 German YB Int'l L 498, 502.

[139] See ibid; see eg GCIV article 23; Benvenuti (above note 137).

[140] Guiding Principles on Internal Displacement, E/CN.4/1998/53/Add.1, February 11 (New York: United Nations).

[141] 'Guiding Principles on the Right to Humanitarian Assistance' (1993) 33(297) IRRC 519–525.

[142] International Commission on State Sovereignty, The Responsibility to Protect (International Development Research Centre, 2001); UNGA, '2005 World Summit Outcome' (above n 2).

[143] Akande and Gillard (above n 135) 61.

[144] Barnett and Walker (above n 114) 131.

[145] ibid 141.

media for their performance. In the age of Twitter, beneficiaries may be able to 'critique' the humanitarian response.[146]

Similarly, social media can assist victims to demonstrate where their needs are and assist humanitarian relief organizations in responding to those needs. Crowdsourcing platforms such as Ushadidi enable people affected by conflict and disasters to post where the problems are. Ushahidi itself was established in the wake of the Kenyan elections in 2008, where mobile phone text messages (SMS), emails, and mainstream media were monitored to give a picture of where the violence was taking place and how intense it was.[147] Such data collection can be useful for humanitarian relief organizations, but can also pose additional challenges. Humanitarian relief organizations need to do their own assessments of the needs on the ground, talking to those affected by conflict, in order to uphold their impartiality. To demonstrate their neutrality through their fundamentally humanitarian work, humanitarian organizations must also rely on confidential dialogue with the parties to ensure access is not interrupted. The desire for information, social media, and other platforms such as WikiLeaks, puts that confidentiality, and consequently the access to victims of conflict, in jeopardy and impedes humanitarian relief operations in a conflict.[148]

## 6. Conclusion

From, at least, the mid-1800s to today, humanitarian relief organizations have been providing protection and assistance in armed conflicts. Legal frameworks have been developed to ensure that civilians and combatants, whether taking part in hostilities or not, have access to humanitarian relief. The legal frameworks also protect organizations with a purely humanitarian purpose and an impartial approach, and protect humanitarian relief objects against diversion, misuse, and attack. Such legal frameworks have a significant role to play in the creation of norms and best practice in relation to particular conduct. While these frameworks are respectful of state sovereignty, they do require states to cooperate in the interests of humanitarian need, and as is the case with much of IHL, compliance with those legal frameworks remains a challenge.

A lack of understanding of what humanitarian relief organizations actually do, and of their necessary impartiality, leads to increasing attacks on humanitarian relief personnel and a denial of assistance to victims of conflict, thereby increasing humanitarian suffering. Indeed, adhering to that fundamental neutrality and impartiality also remains a challenge for humanitarian relief organizations today, with increased pressure from donors, victims, and state and non-state actors who would otherwise give consent to their work. Sadly, deliberate attacks on humanitarian workers, and in particular health-care workers, are also an increasingly common feature of armed conflict today.

---

[146] Chatman House, 'Interview: Yves Daccord' 70(5) *The World Today* (October 2014) www.chathamhouse.org/publication/twt/interview-yves-daccord.

[147] Patrick Meier, 'New Information Technologies and Their Impact on the Humanitarian Sector' (2011) 93 *IRRC* 1239, 1242.

[148] McGoldrick (above n 45) 978.

The future of the legal frameworks on humanitarian relief operations will no doubt include further guides and standards addressed to all stakeholders.[149] However, it is the continuing education about the legal and moral imperatives of protecting humanitarian relief actors and resources that will always be most valuable, given the longstanding existence in law of the most fundamental of protections for those suffering the effects of war and those seeking to assist them.

---

[149] The 2016 *Oxford Guidance on the Law Relating to Humanitarian Relief Operations in Situations of Armed Conflict*, commissioned by the United Nations Office for the Coordination of Humanitarian Affairs (Akande and Gillard (above n 136)) being the most recent of them.

# 15

# War Crimes

*Robert Cryer*

## 1. Introduction

Rather like in the way that the law of theft and fraud is a set of crimes that intersect, but are narrower than the civil law of property, the law of war crimes is a criminalized subset of violations of International Humanitarian Law (IHL).[1] Hence the law here is parasitic on a violation of IHL.[2] Although this chapter will return to the precise relationship between the two areas of law, it suffices for this moment to say that whilst every war crime is a violation of IHL, the converse is not the case.

There have been prosecutions for war crimes throughout history,[3] however the bases have evolved across the years. In the Chivalric era, it was often on the basis of Chivalric codes which were enforceable across what were, at the time, functionally states.[4] By the eighteenth century though, war crime charges were brought on the basis of domestic military codes. Although states could bring charges against enemy nationals, it was perhaps not clear at the time whether this was on the basis of individual liability under international law, or an exceptional additional domestic jurisdictional ground largely based on passive personality (ie nationality of the victim) if the crimes were not committed on the territory of the prosecuting state.[5]

By the end of the First World War, the majority view was probably that liability was based directly on international law,[6] although the matter was not beyond contention.[7] There were still doubts in some quarters even in the Second World War,[8] but the Nuremberg International Military Tribunal had no truck with such arguments. It famously pronounced that:

---

[1] Michael Bothe, 'War Crimes', in Antonio Cassese, John RWD Jones, and Paolo Gaeta (eds), *The Rome Statute of the International Criminal Court* (OUP 2002) 381.

[2] As such, the law of war crimes, in spite of considerable convergence between the two types of law, retains the distinction between international armed conflicts (IACs) and non-international armed conflicts (NIACs). See eg Sonja Boelaert-Suominen, 'The Yugoslavia Tribunal and the Common Core of Humanitarian Law Applicable to All Armed Conflicts' (2000) 13 *Leiden JIL* 19.

[3] See generally, Timothy LH McCormack, 'From Sun Tzu to the Sixth Committee: The Evolution of an International Criminal Law Regime', in Timothy LH McCormack and Gerry J Simpson (eds), *The Law of War Crimes: National and International Approaches* (Martinus Nijhoff 1997) 31.

[4] Maurice H Keen, *The Laws of War in the Late Middle Ages* (Keegan Paul 1965).

[5] On the bases of jurisdiction here, see Robert Cryer, Håkan Friman, Darryl Robinson, and Elizabeth Wilmshurst, *An Introduction to International Criminal Law and Procedure* (4th edn, CUP 2019) ch 3.

[6] 'Report of the Commission on the Responsibility of the Authors of the War and Enforcement' (1920) 14 AJIL 95, 122.

[7] The American and Japanese members dissented from this position: ibid 146 (US), 152 (Japan).

[8] Manfred Lachs, *War Crimes: An Attempt to Define the Issues* (Stevens and Sons 1944); George Manner, 'The Legal Nature and Punishment of Criminal Acts of Violence Contrary to the Laws of War' (1943) 37 *AJIL* 407.

crimes against international law are committed by men, not abstract entities, and only by punishing individuals who commit such crimes can the provisions of international law be enforced ... individuals have international duties which transcend the national obligations of obedience imposed by the individual state.[9]

It said, with reference to war crimes:

the crimes defined by Article 6, section (b) [i.e the provision that covered such offences] were already recognized as war crimes under international law. They were covered by Articles 46, 50, 52 and 56 of the Hague Convention of 1907 and Articles 2, 3, 4, 46 and 51 of the Geneva Convention of 1929. That violation of these provisions constituted crimes for which the guilty individuals were punishable is too well settled to admit argument.[10]

The position was usefully summed up by the Special Tribunal for Lebanon, which said that:

[War crimes were] originally born at the domestic level: States began to prosecute and punish members of the enemy military (then gradually also of their own military) who had performed acts that were termed either as criminal offences perpetrated in time of war (killing of innocent civilians, wanton destruction of private property, serious ill-treatment of prisoners of war, and so on), or as breaches of the laws and customs of war. Gradually this domestic practice received international sanction, first through the Versailles Treaty (1919) and the following trials before the German Supreme Court at Leipzig (1921), then through the London Agreement of 1945 and the trials at Nuremberg. Thus, the domestic criminalisation of breaches of international humanitarian law led to the international criminalisation of those breaches and the formation of rules of customary international law authorising or even imposing their punishment.

The nature of the law of war crimes thus necessitates an investigation into its sources.

## 2. The Sources of War Crimes Law

The sources of war crimes law are the same as those of IHL, which further are those of public international law more generally; in other words treaty law, customary law, general principles of law, and as subsidiary means of identifying the law, judicial decisions, and the writings of the most highly qualified publicists.[11] It is also important to note the role of national law in this regard, which may be both over and under-inclusive. Nonetheless, for many domestic courts that will be the predominant law (although it may be subject to

---

[9] Nuremberg International Military Tribunal, 'Judgment and Sentence' (1947) 41 *AJIL* 171, 221.
[10] ibid.
[11] See generally Dapo Akande, 'The Sources of International Criminal Law', in Antonio Cassese et al (eds), *The Oxford Companion to International Criminal Justice* (OUP 2009) 41.

oversight by, inter alia, human rights bodies or, in relevant circumstances, the International Criminal Court).[12]

As is the case in other areas of international law, in spite of their notionally subsidiary role, large developments in the law of war crimes have come through the decisions of courts and tribunals,[13] but there have been times when states have rejected some cases outright.[14] This is not always for nefarious reasons. There are times when the reasoning of international tribunals is unconvincing, and the dissents are more persuasive,[15] which can undermine their authority. That said, national courts often seem unwilling or unable to understand or apply IHL either, perhaps to a greater degree.[16]

Still, the law of war crimes has contributed greatly to IHL.[17] Even so, there are some notes of caution that ought to be made. The first is that war crimes are not just part of IHL, they are part of international criminal law, and the two have different principles of interpretation. Perhaps most important is the *nullum crimen sine lege* (no crime without pre-existing law) principle.[18] This mandates a very careful approach to interpreting war crimes. For example, article 22 of the Rome Statute of the International Criminal Court reads, 'The definition of a crime shall be strictly construed and shall not be extended by analogy. In cases of ambiguity the definition shall be interpreted in favour of the person being investigated, prosecuted or convicted.'[19] This does not apply to state responsibility for violations of IHL, where the more general principles of treaty interpretation are favoured instead (although they are also relevant for war crimes too).

In spite of this, there have been some criticisms of the international criminal tribunals (the International Criminal Tribunal for the former Yugoslavia (ICTY) in particular), for taking the humanitarian side of humanitarian law and elevating it over the other side of IHL, namely military necessity.[20] Others celebrate what they call the 'humanization' of humanitarian law, in particular by the ad hoc Tribunals.[21] This may be more a conflict of different cultures in the face of interpretation between military practitioners and others,[22] one which is sometimes rather antagonistic, and is, more generally, an issue in IHL.[23]

---

[12] For useful discussion, see Alexandra Huneeus, 'International Criminal Law by Other Means: The Quasi-Criminal Jurisdiction of the Human Rights Courts' (2013) 107 *AJIL* 1.

[13] Shane Darcy, *Judges, Law and War: The Judicial Development of International Humanitarian Law* (CUP 2014) 25–38 is quite rightly, sanguine, to a point.

[14] UK Ministry of Defence (MoD), *Manual of the Law of Armed Conflict* (OUP 2004) 421.

[15] *Prosecutor v Gotovina and Markač* (Judgment) ICTY-06-90-A (16 November 2012). See Janine N Clarke 'Courting Controversy: The ICTY's Acquittal of Croatian Generals Gotovina and Markač' (2013) 11 *JICJ* 399.

[16] Sharon Weill, *The Role of National Courts in Applying International Humanitarian Law* (OUP 2014).

[17] Christopher J Greenwood, 'The Development of International Humanitarian Law by the International Criminal Tribunal for the Former Yugoslavia' (1998) 2 *Max Planck YB UN L* 97; Darcy (above n 13); Robert Cryer, 'Of Custom, Treaties, Scholars and the Gavel: The Impact of the International Criminal Tribunals on the ICRC Customary Law Study' (2006) 11 *JCSL* 239.

[18] See eg Kenneth Gallant, *The Principle of Legality in International and Comparative Law* (CUP 2009).

[19] On which see Bruce Broomhall, 'Article 22', in Otto Triffterer and Kai Ambos (eds), *Commentary on the Rome Statute of the International Court* (3rd edn, Hart 2015) 949.

[20] Michael Schmitt, 'Military Necessity and Humanity in International Humanitarian Law: Preserving the Delicate Balance' (2010) 50 *Vir J Int'l L* 795.

[21] See eg Theodor Meron, 'The Humanization of International Humanitarian Law' (2000) 94 *AJIL* 239.

[22] David Luban, 'Military Necessity and the Cultures of Military Law' (2013) 26 *Leiden JIL* 315.

[23] Robert Cryer, 'The ICRC and Direct Participation in Hostilities: See a Little Light', in Robin Geiß (ed), *The International Red Cross and Red Crescent Movement at 150: Developing and Clarifying International Humanitarian Law* (CUP 2017) 113.

## A. The Types of War Crime

The law on war crimes is complicated by the knot that forms the term war crimes itself and is far from easy to unpick.[24] As noted above it seems that not every violation of IHL can a priori be considered a war crime.[25] The issue is also tangled up with the question of the jurisdiction of states, international criminal courts and tribunals, as well as the sources of IHL itself.

As a starting point though, the classic (although not uncontroversial) statement of the conditions for a violation of IHL to be considered a war crime was given by the ICTY in its foundational *Tadić* decision. The Appeals Chamber argued that there were four such (cumulative) conditions:

  i. the violation must constitute an infringement of a rule of international humanitarian law;
  ii. the rule must be customary in nature or, if it belongs to treaty law, the required conditions must be met;
  iii. the violation must be 'serious', that is to say, it must constitute a breach of a rule protecting important values, and the breach must involve grave consequences for the victim; and
  iv. the violation must entail, under customary or conventional law, the individual criminal responsibility of the person breaching the rule.[26]

The authority for these propositions becomes more controversial as they move from (i) to (iv), and all have certain issues of interpretation that are complex.[27] Probably the clearest example of violations of IHL that fulfil all of these criteria are grave breaches of the Geneva Conventions, defined (in a parsing of the Conventions themselves) in the Rome Statute of the International Criminal Court, as being:

> ... any of the following acts against persons or property protected under the provisions of the relevant Geneva Convention:
> (i) Willful killing;
> (ii) Torture or inhuman treatment, including biological experiments;
> (iii) Willfully causing great suffering, or serious injury to body or health;
> (iv) Extensive destruction and appropriation of property, not justified by military necessity and carried out unlawfully and wantonly;
> (v) Compelling a prisoner of war or other protected person to serve in the forces of a hostile Power;

---

[24] Charles Garraway, 'War Crimes', in Elizabeth Wilmshurst and Susan Breau (eds), *Perspectives on the ICRC Study on Customary Humanitarian Law* (CUP 2007) 377.

[25] Fausto Pocar, 'The Criminalization of the Violations of International Humanitarian Law from Nuremberg to the Rome Statute', in Fausto Pocar, Marco Pedrazzi, and Micaela Frulli (eds), *War Crimes and the Conduct of Hostilities: Challenges to Adjudication and Investigation* (Edward Elgar 2013) 3.

[26] *Prosecutor v Tadić* (Decision on Interlocutory Appeal on Jurisdiction) ICTY-94-1-AR72 (2 October 1995) para 94. For more detailed discussion see Robert Cryer, 'Individual Liability for Violations of the Law of Armed Conflict', in Rain Liivjoa and Timothy LH McCormack (eds), *The Routledge Handbook on the Law of Armed Conflict* (Routledge 2016) 538, 540–6.

[27] See Cryer, ibid.

  (vi)  Willfully depriving a prisoner of war or other protected person of the rights of fair and
        regular trial;
 (vii)  Unlawful deportation or transfer or unlawful confinement;
(viii)  Taking of hostages.[28]

For these offences, states are required to criminalize them on the basis of universal jurisdiction (ie irrespective of where they have occurred), and seek out, extradite, or prosecute
anyone (at least in their territories, or territories over which they have authority) who is
suspected of such offences.[29]

It ought to be said, though, that if a violation of IHL does not fulfil the criteria that international law requires, it is still within the rights of a state to criminalize it domestically, subject
to the usual principles of criminal jurisdiction that international law provides for.[30] It will not,
however, be a war crime for the purposes of individual liability under international law. Things
are rendered further complicated by the fact that there may be things, owing to the operation
of treaty law, that may be war crimes for the purposes of states parties to certain treaties, but
where they are not reflective of custom for non-parties. Certain aspects of Additional Protocol
I may be at issue here,[31] and also some weapons conventions, such as the Ottawa Convention
on Anti-Personnel Landmines and the Cluster Munitions Convention, neither of which can
be taken as customary per se.[32] It might be thought that these are more akin to arms control
treaties than IHL regimes, but the line between the two is porous, to say the least.


### 3.  Defining War Crimes: Substance and Jurisdiction


A further issue is that the existence of a war crime in treaty-based or customary international law is not the same as an international criminal tribunal having jurisdiction to
prosecute it. Whilst the Nuremberg and Tokyo International Military Tribunals had the
authority to prosecute an open-ended list of war crimes pursuant to articles 6(b) and 5(b)
of their respective Statutes, owing to the nature of the conduct of the defendants, there was
little that was prosecuted pursuant to those provisions that would not have traditionally
been thought of as war crimes, a point that was not seriously contested by the defence in
those proceedings.[33] The ICTY, in addition to the right to prosecute grave breaches of the

---

[28]  On which, see Paolo Gaeta, 'Grave Breaches of the Geneva Conventions', in Andrew Clapham, Paolo Gaeta,
and Marco Sassòli (eds), *The 1949 Geneva Conventions: A Commentary* (OUP 2015) 615; Markus D Öberg, 'The
Absorption of Grave Breaches into War Crimes Law' (2009) 91 *IRRC* 163, 163; Horst Fischer, 'Grave Breaches of
the 1949 Geneva Conventions', in Gabrielle Kirk-McDonald and Olivia Swaak-Goldman (eds), *Substantive and
Procedural Aspects of International Criminal Law* (Kluwer 2000) 65, 70, 71.

[29]  Fischer (above n 28).

[30]  Pocar (above n 25).

[31]  Where there are obligations to domestically criminalize such violations (Protocol Additional to the Geneva
Conventions of 12 August 1949, and Relating to the Protection of Victims of International Armed Conflicts
(adopted 8 June 1977, entered into force 7 December 1978) 1125 UNTS 3 (API) article 85). On the customary
status of Additional Protocol I, see eg Christopher Greenwood, 'Customary Status of the 1977 Geneva Protocols',
in Astrid JM Delissen and Gerard J Tanja (eds), *Humanitarian Law of Armed Conflict: Challenges Ahead* (Nijhoff
1991) 93, albeit things may have moved on since then, see eg Jean-Marie Henckaerts and Louise Doswald-Beck,
*Customary International Humanitarian Law* (CUP 2005) (CIHL).

[32]  William A Boothby, *Weapons and the Law of Armed Conflict* (OUP 2009) chs 11, 15.

[33]  Nuremburg International Military Tribunal (above n 9).

Geneva Conventions pursuant to article 2 of its Statute, also had an open-ended provision on war crimes (article 3) which that Tribunal interpreted as granting it the right to prosecute violations of any applicable IHL in the relevant conflict, so long as it was customary, or brought into force by agreement between the parties.[34] This led the ICTY to engage in detailed, and at times transformative discussions of what, in particular, customary law provided for.[35]

With respect to the International Criminal Tribunal for Rwanda (ICTR), it was given a closed list of violations of IHL, perhaps as at the time (1994) it was doubted by many whether the law of war crimes applied to non-international armed conflicts (NIACs).[36] The position is now settled though: whilst the substantive law is not identical (tracing the distinction between the two types of conflict), there is criminal liability for certain violations of IHL in NIACs.[37]

One of the most modern (and broadly ratified) sets of war crimes can be found in the Rome Statute of the International Criminal Court, and owing to this, it deserves to be quoted in full in spite of its length. Despite its detailed nature, it ought not to be taken as a comprehensive codification of the law of war crimes: it is not.[38] Nonetheless, it is the definition that has been incorporated into many domestic criminal laws,[39] and is a baseline for the law on this point.[40] War crimes are covered by article 8 of the Rome Statute. This reads, in a slightly redacted form:[41]

1. The Court shall have jurisdiction in respect of war crimes in particular when committed as part of a plan or policy or as part of a large-scale commission of such crimes.
2. a. [grave breaches of the Geneva Conventions, as set out above]
   b. Other serious violations of the laws and customs applicable in international armed conflict, within the established framework of international law, namely, any of the following acts:
      i. Intentionally directing attacks against the civilian population as such or against individual civilians not taking direct part in hostilities;

[34] *Tadić* (above n 26) paras 87–93. See Christopher Greenwood, 'International Humanitarian Law and the *Tadić* Case' (1996) 7 *EJIL* 265.
[35] UK MoD (above n 14).
[36] Peter Rowe, 'Liability for War Crimes in a Non-International Armed Conflict' (1995) 34 *Revue de Droit Militaire et de Droit de la Guerre* 149.
[37] ibid.
[38] See generally, William Schabas, *The International Criminal Court: A Commentary on the Rome Statute* (2nd edn, OUP 2016) 213–319.
[39] This is often so they may take advantage of the complementarity provisions of the Rome Statute, which provides that the International Criminal Court is not capable of intervening if a State is willing or able to prosecute such offences itself, on which see Rome Statute of the International Criminal Court (adopted 17 July 1998, entered into force 1 July 2002) 2187 UNTS 3 (Rome Statute) articles 17–19 and Carsten Stahn and Mohammed el Zeidy (eds), *The International Criminal Court and Complementarity* (CUP 2012).
[40] Although other states have gone beyond this to update their criminal codes to include all of the war crimes which they feel ought to be criminalized domestically; see eg David A Blumenthal, 'Australian Implementation of the Rome Statute of the International Criminal Court', in David A Blumenthal and Timothy LH McCormack (eds), *The Legacy of Nuremberg: Civilising Influence or Institutionalised Vengeance* (Martinus Nijhoff 2008) 283; William A Schabas, 'Canadian Legislation for Implementing the Rome Statute' (2000) 3 *YBIHL* 337.
[41] And needs to be read alongside the ICC, *Elements of Crimes* (PrintPartners Ipskamp 2011) (*Elements of Crimes*) adopted by the Assembly of States party to the Statute, which, but by virtue of article 9 of the Rome Statute, are to guide the Court in its interpretation of the crimes (see Erkin Gadriov and Roger Clark, 'Article 9', in Triffterer and Ambos (eds) (above n 19) 619).

ii. Intentionally directing attacks against civilian objects, that is, objects which are not military objectives;

iii. Intentionally directing attacks against personnel, installations, material, units or vehicles involved in a humanitarian assistance or peacekeeping mission in accordance with the Charter of the United Nations, as long as they are entitled to the protection given to civilians or civilian objects under the international law of armed conflict;

iv. Intentionally launching an attack in the knowledge that such attack will cause incidental loss of life or injury to civilians or damage to civilian objects or widespread, long-term and severe damage to the natural environment which would be clearly excessive in relation to the concrete and direct overall military advantage anticipated;

v. Attacking or bombarding, by whatever means, towns, villages, dwellings or buildings which are undefended and which are not military objectives;

vi. Killing or wounding a combatant who, having laid down his arms or having no longer means of defence, has surrendered at discretion;

vii. Making improper use of a flag of truce, of the flag or of the military insignia and uniform of the enemy or of the United Nations, as well as of the distinctive emblems of the Geneva Conventions, resulting in death or serious personal injury;

viii. The transfer, directly or indirectly, by the Occupying Power of parts of its own civilian population into the territory it occupies, or the deportation or transfer of all or parts of the population of the occupied territory within or outside this territory;

ix. Intentionally directing attacks against buildings dedicated to religion, education, art, science or charitable purposes, historic monuments, hospitals and places where the sick and wounded are collected, provided they are not military objectives;

x. Subjecting persons who are in the power of an adverse party to physical mutilation or to medical or scientific experiments of any kind which are neither justified by the medical, dental or hospital treatment of the person concerned nor carried out in his or her interest, and which cause death to or seriously endanger the health of such person or persons;

xi. Killing or wounding treacherously individuals belonging to the hostile nation or army;

xii. Declaring that no quarter will be given;

xiii. Destroying or seizing the enemy's property unless such destruction or seizure be imperatively demanded by the necessities of war;

xiv. Declaring abolished, suspended or inadmissible in a court of law the rights and actions of the nationals of the hostile party;

xv. Compelling the nationals of the hostile party to take part in the operations of war directed against their own country, even if they were in the belligerent's service before the commencement of the war;

xvi. Pillaging a town or place, even when taken by assault;

xvii. Employing poison or poisoned weapons;

xviii. Employing asphyxiating, poisonous or other gases, and all analogous liquids, materials or devices;

xix. Employing bullets which expand or flatten easily in the human body, such as bullets with a hard envelope which does not entirely cover the core or is pierced with incisions;

xx. Employing weapons, projectiles and material and methods of warfare which are of a nature to cause superfluous injury or unnecessary suffering or which are inherently indiscriminate in violation of the international law of armed conflict, provided that such weapons, projectiles and material and methods of warfare are the subject of a comprehensive prohibition and are included in an annex to this Statute, by an amendment in accordance with the relevant provisions set forth in articles 121 and 123;

xxi. Committing outrages upon personal dignity, in particular humiliating and degrading treatment;

xxii. Committing rape, sexual slavery, enforced prostitution, forced pregnancy, as defined in article 7, paragraph 2 (f), enforced sterilization, or any other form of sexual violence also constituting a grave breach of the Geneva Conventions;

xxiii. Utilizing the presence of a civilian or other protected person to render certain points, areas or military forces immune from military operations;

xxiv. Intentionally directing attacks against buildings, material, medical units and transport, and personnel using the distinctive emblems of the Geneva Conventions in conformity with international law;

xxv. Intentionally using starvation of civilians as a method of warfare by depriving them of objects indispensable to their survival, including willfully impeding relief supplies as provided for under the Geneva Conventions;

xxvi. Conscripting or enlisting children under the age of fifteen years into the national armed forces or using them to participate actively in hostilities.

Article 8(2)(c) of the Rome Statute separately lists war crimes in NIACs:

c. In the case of an armed conflict not of an international character, serious violations of article 3 common to the four Geneva Conventions of 12 August 1949, namely, any of the following acts committed against persons taking no active part in the hostilities, including members of armed forces who have laid down their arms and those placed *hors de combat* by sickness, wounds, detention or any other cause:

i. Violence to life and person, in particular murder of all kinds, mutilation, cruel treatment and torture;

ii. Committing outrages upon personal dignity, in particular humiliating and degrading treatment;

iii. Taking of hostages;

iv. The passing of sentences and the carrying out of executions without previous judgement pronounced by a regularly constituted court, affording all judicial guarantees which are generally recognized as indispensable.

d. Paragraph 2 (c) applies to armed conflicts not of an international character and thus does not apply to situations of internal disturbances and tensions, such as riots, isolated and sporadic acts of violence or other acts of a similar nature.

   e. Other serious violations of the laws and customs applicable in armed conflicts not of an international character, within the established framework of international law, namely, any of the following acts:

      i. Intentionally directing attacks against the civilian population as such or against individual civilians not taking direct part in hostilities.

      ii. Intentionally directing attacks against buildings, material, medical units and transport, and personnel using the distinctive emblems of the Geneva Conventions in conformity with international law;

      iii. Intentionally directing attacks against personnel, installations, material, units or vehicles involved in a humanitarian assistance or peacekeeping mission in accordance with the Charter of the United Nations, as long as they are entitled to the protection given to civilians or civilian objects under the international law of armed conflict;

      iv. Intentionally directing attacks against buildings dedicated to religion, education, art, science or charitable purposes, historic monuments, hospitals and places where the sick and wounded are collected, provided they are not military objectives;

      v. Pillaging a town or place, even when taken by assault;

      vi. Committing rape, sexual slavery, enforced prostitution, forced pregnancy, as defined in article 7, paragraph 2 (f), enforced sterilization, and any other form of sexual violence also constituting a serious violation of article 3 common to the four Geneva Conventions;

      vii. Conscripting or enlisting children under the age of fifteen years into armed forces or groups or using them to participate actively in hostilities;

      viii. Ordering the displacement of the civilian population for reasons related to the conflict, unless the security of the civilians involved or imperative military reasons so demand;

      ix. Killing or wounding treacherously a combatant adversary;

      x. Declaring that no quarter will be given;

      xi. Subjecting persons who are in the power of another party to the conflict to physical mutilation or to medical or scientific experiments of any kind which are neither justified by the medical, dental or hospital treatment of the person concerned nor carried out in his or her interest, and which cause death to or seriously endanger the health of such person or persons;

      xii. Destroying or seizing the property of an adversary unless such destruction or seizure be imperatively demanded by the necessities of the conflict.

   f. Paragraph 2 (e) applies to armed conflicts not of an international character and thus does not apply to situations of internal disturbances and tensions, such as riots, isolated and sporadic acts of violence or other acts of a similar nature. It applies to armed conflicts that take place in the territory of a state when there is protracted armed conflict between governmental authorities and organized armed groups or between such groups.

3. Nothing in paragraph 2 (c) and (e) shall affect the responsibility of a Government to maintain or re-establish law and order in the state or to defend the unity and territorial integrity of the state, by all legitimate means.

## A. The Rome Definition

There is no space here to discuss the details of this definition,[42] and it is better to refer to the chapters on the relevant IHL norms herein than recapitulate discussion. However, certain things can be highlighted. The first of these is that article 8(1) was a compromise provision between states that only wanted the International Criminal Court (ICC) to get involved with very high-level offences, so suggested that there be a jurisdictional limit on the ICC such that it could not deal with 'small fry' or isolated offences (irrespective of the possible duties on states to do so), and those that were utterly opposed to such a limit. As such, article 8(1) is a careful compromise that is framed as guidance to the Prosecutor, rather than a jurisdictional limit.[43]

Looking first to international armed conflicts (IACs), as mentioned above, in addition to violations of the Grave Breaches provisions of the 1949 Geneva Conventions (but not Additional Protocol I—Protocol II having no analogous provision anyway), the ICC has jurisdiction over various other violations of the law applicable to IACs 'within the established framework of international law'. This provides for a *renvoi* to the relevant IHL norms, reaffirming the parasitic nature of the law of war crimes on IHL.[44] Hence the interpretation of IHL is at the least what the law of war crimes cannot go beyond. This said, certain provisions of the Rome Statute may be narrower than the relevant IHL norms—article 8(2)(b)(iv) may be amongst these.[45] And indeed some clear prohibitions, such as those of biological weapons, are simply missing.[46] This is owing (again), to the fact that the Rome Statute is a negotiated document, and some uncomfortable compromises were reached.[47] Hence it is important to reiterate that the Rome Statute definition is not the alpha and omega of the law of war crimes, as states may have further obligations in relation to conduct, criminalization, and prosecution that do not find their basis there. This is part of the reason that article 10 of the Rome Statute provides that 'Nothing in this Part shall be interpreted as limiting or prejudicing in any way existing or developing rules of international law for purposes other than this Statute.'[48]

The law relating to NIAC is, in many ways, a pared down version of the provisions relating to international armed conflict. There are some notable omissions, such as any provision on collateral damage, but also, as the Statute was originally drafted, any weapons offences. This was an omission at least partially rectified by the 2010 amendments adopted (although not directly brought into force) that same year, which made the same weapons

---

[42] The discussion of war crimes in the Rome Statute (not even more generally), takes up just shy of 300 pages in the standard commentary on the Rome Statute, see 'Article 8' in Triffterer and Ambos, above note 19 295–580.

[43] Schabas, *The International Criminal Court* (above n 38) 225–8.

[44] See above n 2.

[45] Robert Cryer, *Prosecuting International Crimes: Selectivity and the International Criminal Law Regime* (CUP 2005) 272–3.

[46] Aspects of this may be remedied if the amendments that were adopted by the Assembly of States Parties in 2017, to include such weapons, as well as some of those covered by the 1980 Conventional Weapons Convention, such as those that injure by non-detectable fragments, blinding laser weapons, and see, C.N.116.2018, C.N.125.2018, and C.N.126.2018. However they are not in force. Some other provisions proved controversial, for political reasons, so eg the provision on the transfer of population into occupied territory was considered by some to be directed at Israel, see ibid 273–4.

[47] ibid chs 5–6.

[48] On which, see Otto Triffterer and Alexander Heinze, 'Article 10', in Triffterer and Ambos (eds) (above n 19) 644.

offences applicable in IACs applicable to NIACs.[49] For its parties, this is now in force. But there is also customary law applicable that is not referable to the Rome Statute. The extent to which it is applicable in a domestic legal order would depend on the constitutional arrangements of the relevant state, but for such customary war crimes it would not violate the principle of non-retrospectivity to introduce *ex post facto* legislation to deal with them, as they were already criminal under international law.[50]

## 4. Individual Criminal Responsibility

When it comes to war crimes, the substantive law is only part of the story. Although domestically we may see the primary perpetrator as the most responsible (depending on our legal traditions), in international criminal law the position tends to be reversed (although not always). In international criminal law, the further away from the direct perpetrator someone gets, the greater the responsibility often becomes.[51] The principles of liability are largely (although not comprehensively) set out in the Rome Statute, article 25 of which states:

1. The Court shall have jurisdiction over natural persons pursuant to this Statute.
2. A person who commits a crime within the jurisdiction of the Court shall be individually responsible and liable for punishment in accordance with this Statute.
3. In accordance with this Statute, a person shall be criminally responsible and liable for punishment for a crime within the jurisdiction of the Court if that person:
   a. Commits such a crime, whether as an individual, jointly with another or through another person, regardless of whether that other person is criminally responsible;
   b. Orders, solicits or induces the commission of such a crime which in fact occurs or is attempted;
   c. For the purpose of facilitating the commission of such a crime, aids, abets or otherwise assists in its commission or its attempted commission, including providing the means for its commission;
   d. In any other way contributes to the commission or attempted commission of such a crime by a group of persons acting with a common purpose. Such contribution shall be intentional and shall either:
      (i) Be made with the aim of furthering the criminal activity or criminal purpose of the group, where such activity or purpose involves the commission of a crime within the jurisdiction of the Court; or
      (ii) Be made in the knowledge of the intention of the group to commit the crime;
   e. In respect of the crime of genocide, directly and publicly incites others to commit genocide;
   f. Attempts to commit such a crime by taking action that commences its execution by means of a substantial step, but the crime does not occur because of

---

[49] Amendments to Article 8 of the Rome Statute (adopted 10 June 2010) RC/Res.5; Amal Amaluddin and Phillippa Webb, 'Expanding Jurisdiction over War Crimes under Article 8 of the ICC Statute' (2010) 8 *JICJ* 1219.

[50] *Vasiliaukas v Lithuania* (Application No 35343/05) (ECtHR Judgment of 20 October 2015) paras 165–69.

[51] See William Schabas, 'Enforcing Individual Criminal Responsibility in International Criminal Law: Prosecuting the Accomplices' (2001) 843 *IRRC* 439.

circumstances independent of the person's intentions. However, a person who abandons the effort to commit the crime or otherwise prevents the completion of the crime shall not be liable for punishment under this Statute for the attempt to commit that crime if that person completely and voluntarily gave up the criminal purpose.

4. No provision in this Statute relating to individual criminal responsibility shall affect the responsibility of states under international law.

Many of these principles of liability will be familiar to domestic criminal lawyers. There are lengthier treatments of the details of them elsewhere.[52] Perhaps what is notable is that the ICC has used article 25(2)(a) to develop a theory of co-perpetration, including what is known as indirect co-perpetration, which, drawing on theories of criminal law from Germany, provides for liability of those who are part of a group or system that violates international criminal law.[53] It is questionable whether such a principle is part of customary international law (although for the ICC, as a matter of treaty law, article 25 as interpreted by the Court is the controllling law).[54]

The ICTY, on the other hand, has asserted that customary international law recognizes a concept of perpetration through being a part of joint criminal enterprise, which includes where someone is part of such an enterprise and foresees the possibility of offences occurring. Suffice to say that it is controversial, both as to the extent to which it is firmly established in customary law, and also as to whether it is consistent with the principles of criminal law, as intentional offences can be committed by what in the common law world would be considered recklessness.[55] Article 25(3)(d) reflects an analogous concept, but requires that the person knows that the relevant crime will be committed.[56]

Furthermore, when it comes to assistance to a crime, probably narrower than customary international law[57] the Rome Statute requires that an accomplice engages in their conduct with the purpose of assisting or encouraging a crime. The customary law on this point though is controversial too, especially with respect to those who are physically distant, and the jurisprudence with respect to whether any assistance being required to be 'specifically directed' to helping or encouraging the primary offence is a little mixed.[58] The balance of authorities are against such a requirement.[59]

---

[52] See eg Elies van Sliedregt, *Individual Criminal Responsibility in International Criminal Law* (OUP 2012); Cryer et al (above n 5) ch 15.

[53] See 'Symposium' (2011) 9 *JICJ* 85–226, especially Thomas Weigend, 'Perpetration through an Organization: The Unexpected Career of a German Legal Concept' (2011) 9 *JICJ* 91.

[54] *Prosecutor v Stakić* (Judgment), IT-97-25-A (2006) para 62, and Schabas, *The International Criminal Court* (above n 38) 579–82.

[55] For a useful overview, see Elies van Sliedregt, *The Criminal Responsibility of Individuals for Violations of International Humanitarian Law* (Martinus Nijhoff 2003) 94–110. See also 'Symposium and Anthology' (2007) 5 *JICJ* 67–244. On the overlaps, see Stefano Manacorda and Chantel Meloni, 'Indirect Perpetration versus Joint Criminal Enterprise: Concurring Approaches in the Practice of International Criminal Law' (2011) 9 *JICJ* 159.

[56] See eg *Prosecutor v Mbarushimana* (Decision on the Confirmation of Charges) ICC-01/04.01/10 (16 December 2011) paras 288–289.

[57] See *Prosecutor v Tadić* (Judgment), ICTY-94-1-A (15 July 1999) para 229.

[58] Leila N Sadat, 'Can the ICTY *Šainović* and *Perišić* Cases be Reconciled?' (2014) 108 *AJIL* 475.

[59] ibid.

## A.  Command Responsibility

For war crimes, as with other international crimes, international criminal law has a principle of liability that is relatively unknown in domestic law. This is the principle of command responsibility, which is the liability of superiors for crimes committed by their subordinates. The customary law on point is the subject of considerable disagreement, both as to the ambit of the principle and the nature of the responsibility, the two aspects of which are interlinked.[60] It finds its modern basis in post-war jurisprudence,[61] but its most recent treaty formulation is article 28 of the Rome Statute.[62] This reads:

> In addition to other grounds of criminal responsibility under this Statute for crimes within the jurisdiction of the Court:
> a. A military commander or person effectively acting as a military commander shall be criminally responsible for crimes within the jurisdiction of the Court committed by forces under his or her effective command and control, or effective authority and control as the case may be, as a result of his or her failure to exercise control properly over such forces, where:
>   i. That military commander or person either knew or, owing to the circumstances at the time, should have known that the forces were committing or about to commit such crimes; and
>   ii. That military commander or person failed to take all necessary and reasonable measures within his or her power to prevent or repress their commission or to submit the matter to the competent authorities for investigation and prosecution.
> b. With respect to superior and subordinate relationships not described in paragraph (a), a superior shall be criminally responsible for crimes within the jurisdiction of the Court committed by subordinates under his or her effective authority and control, as a result of his or her failure to exercise control properly over such subordinates, where:
>   i. The superior either knew, or consciously disregarded information which clearly indicated, that the subordinates were committing or about to commit such crimes;
>   ii. The crimes concerned activities that were within the effective responsibility and control of the superior; and
>   iii. The superior failed to take all necessary and reasonable measures within his or her power to prevent or repress their commission or to submit the matter to the competent authorities for investigation and prosecution.

The requirements for this form of liability have been usefully parsed by the ICTY, who asserted that there are, as a matter of customary law, three requirements: first, there is a superior/subordinate relationship; second, there is a 'mental element'; and third, a failure to take reasonable measures to prevent or punish violations of international criminal law.[63] The Rome Statute adds the requirement that the violations must occur as a result of a failure to exercise

[60] See generally, Guénaël Mettraux, *The Law of Command Responsibility* (OUP 2009); and van Sliedregt (above n 55) ch 8; see specifically Christopher Greenwood, 'Command Responsibility and the *Hadžihasanović* Decision' (2004) 2 *JICJ* 598.
[61] William Hays Parks, 'Command Responsibility for War Crimes' (1973) 62 *Military L Rev* 1, 1–20.
[62] It is also contained in API articles 86 and 87.
[63] *Prosecutor v Delalić* (Judgment) IT-96-21 (16 November 1998) para 344.

control over those subordinates. This, in other words, requires an element of causation, which is controversial as a matter of custom, and has been a matter of considerable debate, both judicially and academically, especially with respect to a failure to punish offences.[64]

In terms of the requirements, the condition that there be effective control is not always simple, in particular when non-state actors are at issue, as there may not be a formal structure involved.[65] In practice, this has proved difficult, although not impossible, to prove.[66] When it comes to the mental element, the ICTY has said that what is required is that, as a matter of customary law:

> [A superior] … may possess the *mens rea* for command responsibility where: (1) he had actual knowledge, established through direct or circumstantial evidence, that his subordinates were committing or about to commit crimes … or (2) where he had in his possession information of a nature, which at the least, would put him on notice of the risk of such offences by indicating the need for additional investigation in order to ascertain whether such crimes were committed or were about to be committed by his subordinates.[67]

This is not beyond controversy,[68] and is different to the standards set out in the Rome Statute. Notably, the Rome Statute adopts different mental elements for military and civilian superiors, a distinction not known to customary law.[69] With respect to superior responsibility, the ICC has determined that, for military superiors, the standard is essentially one of negligence.[70] The standard for civilian superiors has yet to be pronounced upon, but the ICC has expressed its separation from the ad hoc Tribunals' jurisprudence on this point.[71] It is likely that with regard to civilian superiors, the standard applicable before the ICC is practically the same as constructive knowledge.[72]

Looking to the action that needs to be taken to fulfil the duties that are imposed by the international law of command responsibility, the ICTY has said that what is required is what:

> can be taken within the competence of a commander as evidenced by the degree of effective control he wielded over his subordinates … What constitutes such measures is not a matter of substantive law but of evidence.[73]

Hence the level of activity required is linked to the level of control the superior has.

In relation to the duty to prevent and punish (which are separate). the ICC has said that it:

> 'depend[s] on the degree of effective control over the conduct of subordinates at the time a superior is expected to act'; (2) measures must be taken to prevent planning

[64] Cryer et al (above n 5) 390–2.
[65] See Sandesh Sivakumaran, 'Command Responsibility in Irregular Groups' (2012) 10 *JICJ* 1129.
[66] ibid 386–8; *Prosecutor v Bemba Gombo* (Decision Pursuant to Article 61(7)(a) and (b) of the Rome Statute) ICC-01/05-01/08 (15 June 2009) paras 414–416.
[67] *Bemba Gombo* (above n 66) paras 223–241.
[68] Mettraux (above n 60) ch 10.
[69] van Sliedregt (above n 55) 191–2.
[70] *Bemba Gombo* (above n 66) 429.
[71] ibid 434
[72] Mettraux (above n 60) 194–6.
[73] *Prosecutor v Blaškić* (Judgment) IT-95-14 (29 July 2004 72. See eg Kai Ambos, *Treatise on International Criminal Law Volume I: Foundations and General Part* (OUP 2013) 217–20.

of preparation of crimes, not simply their execution; (3) 'the more grievous and/or imminent the potential crimes of subordinates appear to be, the more attentive and quicker the superior is expected to react'; and (4) a superior is not 'obliged to do the impossible'.[74]

The duty is thus to do what is possible. It is a duty of conduct rather than result. Not least, it ought to be noted that the duty to punish can be fulfilled by submitting the matter to the relevant prosecutorial authorities, as article 28 makes clear.

## B.  Grounds for Excluding Criminal Responsibility

Although less discussed, perhaps as a result of some discomfort with dealing with the issue,[75] there are defences to war crimes. The clearest of the definitions of such general defences is provided in the Rome Statute. Articles 31–32 provide that:

Article 31 ... 1. In addition to other grounds for excluding criminal responsibility provided for in this Statute, a person shall not be criminally responsible if, at the time of that person's conduct:

(a) The person suffers from a mental disease or defect that destroys that person's capacity to appreciate the unlawfulness or nature of his or her conduct, or capacity to control his or her conduct to conform to the requirements of law;

(b) The person is in a state of intoxication that destroys that person's capacity to appreciate the unlawfulness or nature of his or her conduct, or capacity to control his or her conduct to conform to the requirements of law, unless the person has become voluntarily intoxicated under such circumstances that the person knew, or disregarded the risk, that, as a result of the intoxication, he or she was likely to engage in conduct constituting a crime within the jurisdiction of the Court;

(c) The person acts reasonably to defend himself or herself or another person or, in the case of war crimes, property which is essential for the survival of the person or another person or property which is essential for accomplishing a military mission, against an imminent and unlawful use of force in a manner proportionate to the degree of danger to the person or the other person or property protected. The fact that the person was involved in a defensive operation conducted by forces shall not in itself constitute a ground for excluding criminal responsibility under this subparagraph;

(d) The conduct which is alleged to constitute a crime within the jurisdiction of the Court has been caused by duress resulting from a threat of imminent death or of continuing or imminent serious bodily harm against that person or another person, and the person acts necessarily and reasonably to avoid this threat, provided that the person

---

[74] *Prosecutor v Orić* (Judgment) IT-03-68 (30 June 2006) para 329.

[75] Albin Eser, 'Defences in War Crimes Trials', in Yoram Dinstein and Mala Tabory (eds), *War Crimes in International Law* (Martinus Nijhoff 1996) 251. On the issues mentioned here see generally Cryer et al (above n 5) ch 16.

    does not intend to cause a greater harm than the one sought to be avoided. Such a
    threat may either be:
     (i)  Made by other persons; or
     (ii)  Constituted by other circumstances beyond that person's control.

2.  The Court shall determine the applicability of the grounds for excluding criminal responsibility provided for in this Statute to the case before it.

3.  At trial, the Court may consider a ground for excluding criminal responsibility other
than those referred to in paragraph 1 where such a ground is derived from applicable
law as set forth in article 21. The procedures relating to the consideration of such a
ground shall be provided for in the Rules of Procedure and Evidence.

    Article 32 Mistake of fact or mistake of law 1. A mistake of fact shall be a ground
for excluding criminal responsibility only if it negates the mental element required by
the crime.

2.  A mistake of law as to whether a particular type of conduct is a crime within the jurisdiction of the Court shall not be a ground for excluding criminal responsibility.
A mistake of law may, however, be a ground for excluding criminal responsibility if it
negates the mental element required by such a crime, or as provided for in article 33.

Most of these will also be recognizable to domestic criminal lawyers, although the definitions are, as with all aspects of the Rome Statute, the outcome of compromises that do not
reflect any one domestic approach. They include both justifications (such as self-defence),
excuses (such as duress), and what may be called failure of proof defences (such as mental
incapacity).[76] The extent to which some of them reflect customary law is not necessarily
clear.[77]

Rather like principles of liability, especially command responsibility, when it comes to
defences, international criminal law has some specific provisions.[78] The most important
of these is superior orders.[79] Such a defence was excluded in the Statutes of the Nuremberg
and Tokyo International Military Tribunals, as well as of those of the ICTY and ICTR.[80]
The Rome Statute, however, reinstates a limited form of the defence, in article 33, which
provides:

1.  The fact that a crime within the jurisdiction of the Court has been committed by a person
pursuant to an order of a Government or of a superior, whether military or civilian, shall
not relieve that person of criminal responsibility unless:

---

[76]  Ambos (above n 73) 304–7.

[77]  See eg *Prosecutor v Erdemović* (Judgment) IT-96-22-A (7 October1997). Belgium considers the provision on
self-defence of property to be contrary to *jus cogens*.

[78]  Pursuant to article 31(3) of the Rome Statute, other, customary defences, perhaps including (in limited circumstances, reprisals, insofar as they are not banned under the law of armed conflict, may also be applicable.

[79]  The classic study remains Yoram Dinstein, *The Defence of Superior Orders in International Criminal Law*
(OUP 2012).

[80]  Charter of the International Military Tribunal, annex to the London Agreement on the Prosecution and
Punishment of the Major War Criminals of the European Axis Powers 82 UNTS 279, article 8. Article 6 of the
Tokyo IMT Charter is largely the same: see Special Proclamation: Establishment of an International Military
Tribunal for the Far East (19 January 1946) TIAS No1589. See also Updated Statute of the International Criminal
tribunal for the Former Yugoslavia (adopted 25 May 1993, as amended 7 July 2009 by resolution 1877) article 7(4);
Statute of the International Criminal Tribunal for Rwanda (adopted 8 November 1994, as amended 13 October
2006 by resolution 1717) article 6(4).

  a. The person was under a legal obligation to obey orders of the Government or the superior in question;
  b. The person did not know that the order was unlawful; and
  c. The order was not manifestly unlawful.
2. For the purposes of this article, orders to commit genocide or crimes against humanity are manifestly unlawful.

The customary status of this provision is controversial,[81] and its ambit is not entirely clear.[82] In particular, what is 'manifestly' unlawful, and to whom, is a matter of considerable difficulty.[83] It is also the case that that subparagraph 2 is not easy to interpret, as, although the intention was to limit the defence to war crimes, rather than other offences, orders tend to engage in conduct, rather than being easily reduced to the categories of international crimes *in abstracto*.[84] The ICC has yet to pronounce on the provision.

## 5. State Responsibility for War Crimes

Responsibility for war crimes is not limited to individual liability (although, as will be seen, there are obligations in this regard).[85] States have responsibility to prevent and punish war crimes.[86] Looking to the duties of parties to an armed conflict, it is important to note that liability for war crimes between individuals and states is parallel.[87] Neither excludes the other. There is liability for violations of IHL (which all war crimes are), but of course, there is the necessity of attributability to the state. For the actions of the armed forces, as state actors, they naturally entail state responsibility.[88] For non-state actors the issue is more complex, as their actions are not always referable to a state.[89]

The positive duties of states with respect to preventing and punishing war crimes are surprisingly similar. With respect to IACs, all states are obliged, pursuant to the Grave Breaches provisions of the Geneva Conventions, to domestically criminalize such violations, and seek out and either extradite or prosecute those violations.[90]

---

[81] Paolo Gaeta, 'The Defence of Superior Orders: The Statute of the International Criminal Court Versus Customary International Law' (1999) 10 *EJIL* 172; *cf* Charles Garraway, 'Superior Orders and the International Criminal Court: Justice Delivered or Justice Denied?' (1999) 836 *IRRC* 785.

[82] See further Robert Cryer, 'Superior Orders in the International Criminal Court', in Richard Burchill, Nigel White, and Justin Morris (eds), *International Conflict and Security Law* (CUP 2005) 49.

[83] ibid 61–3.

[84] Cryer (above n 5).

[85] See generally Hans-Peter Gasser, 'Ensuring Respect for the Geneva Conventions and Protocols: The Role of Third States and the United Nations', in Hazel Fox and Michael A Meyer, *Armed Conflict and the New Law: Vol II: Effecting Compliance* (BIICL 1993) 15.

[86] See Silja Voleki, 'Implementation and Enforcement of International Humanitarian Law', in Dieter Fleck, (ed), *The Handbook of International Humanitarian Law* (3rd edn, OUP 2013) 647.

[87] André Nollkaemper, 'Concurrence between Individual Responsibility and State Responsibility in International Law' (2003) 52 *ICLQ* 615.

[88] International Law Commission, 'Draft Articles on the Responsibility of States for Internationally Wrongful Acts' (ILC 2001) ch II.

[89] The conditions upon which the actions of rebels may be attributable to third states is a matter of some controversy; see eg ibid articles 8 and 47–49.

[90] Articles 50, 51, 130, and 147 of the four Geneva Conventions 1949. See Symposium, 'The Grave Breaches Regime in the Geneva Conventions: A Reassessment Sixty Years On' (2007) 7 *JICJ* 4 653–877; and Paolo Gaeta, 'The Interplay between the Geneva Conventions and International Criminal Law', in Clapham et al (above n 28) 737.

The situation is different for NIACs, although human rights obligations are relevant here.[91]

The fundamental obligation that lies upon states, whether parties to a conflict or not, is contained in Common Article 1 of the 1949 Geneva Conventions, which provides that, 'The High Contracting Parties undertake to respect and to ensure respect for the present Convention in all circumstances.[92] This requires both prophylactic, and *ex post facto* measures. The former are to be preferred.

The duty in Common Article 1 was, in its initial conception, related to the duties in peacetime, such as dissemination rather than anything else, but gradually as time went on, it became used by states as an entry into issuing diplomatic protests about violations of IHL in conflicts to which they were not parties. However, these were by no means always forthcoming, not least as states were concerned that saying anything could be interpreted as taking sides in the conflict, and therefore often keep silent.

The ICJ, has taken a very broad approach to Common Article 1 in the *Palestinian Wall Advisory Opinion*, and 'piggy-backed' this to their discussion of the *erga omnes* nature of many, if not most, rules of IHL.[93] In this opinion it noted that:

> It follows from that provision that every State party to that Convention, whether or not it is a party to a specific conflict, is under an obligation to ensure that the requirements of the instruments in question are complied with ... [and] ... In addition, all the States parties to the Geneva Convention relative to the Protection of Civilian Persons in Time of War of 12 August 1949 are under an obligation, while respecting the United Nations Charter and international law, to ensure compliance by Israel with international humanitarian law as embodied in that Convention.[94]

Perhaps unsurprisingly, this was not beyond controversy within the Court. Hence, for example, Judge Koojimans questioned the extent to which Common Article 1 imposed obligations on parties that were not part of the relevant armed conflict.[95] Judge Higgins, on the other hand, thought that the obligation not to recognize the situation did not rely on the concept of *erga omnes* obligations but the Common Article 1 requirement that states should attempt to ensure compliance. She also noted that 'the Court has, in subparagraph (3)(D) of the *dispositif*, carefully indicated that any such action should be in conformity with the Charter and international law'.[96] This is probably the best interpretation of the nature of the obligation as it is currently seen by states.[97] Reprisals that violate the *jus ad bellum*, are certainly not permitted.

---

[91]  *Velasquez-Rodriguez v Honduras*, IACtHR Series C No 4 (29 July 1988); *McCann v UK* (1995) 21 EHRR 67, para 161.

[92]  On which see Robin Geiß, 'The Obligation to Respect and Ensure Respect for the Geneva Conventions', in Clapham et al (above n 28) 111 ; Frits Kalshoven, 'The Undertaking to Respect and Ensure Respect in All Circumstances: From Tiny Seed to Ripening Fruit' (1999) 2 *YBIHL* 3; Carlo Focarelli, 'Common Article 1 of the 1949 Geneva Conventions: A Soap Bubble?' (2010) 21 *EJIL* 125.

[93]  *Legal Consequences of the Construction of a Wall in the Occupied Palestinian Territories* (Advisory Opinion) [2004] ICJ Rep 36 para 157.

[94]  ibid paras 158–159.

[95]  ibid Separate Opinion of Judge Koojimans paras 46–50.

[96]  ibid Separate Opinion of Judge Higgins para 39.

[97]  ibid.

In terms of state obligations relating to creating (domestic) individual liability, criminalization is required by the Geneva Conventions for grave breaches of their provisions. Hence, article 49 of Geneva Convention I of 1949 provides that:

The High Contracting Parties undertake to enact any legislation necessary to provide effective penal sanctions for persons committing, or ordering to be committed, any of the grave breaches of the present Convention . . .

Each High Contracting Party shall be under the obligation to search for persons alleged to have committed, or to have ordered to be committed, such grave breaches, and shall bring such persons, regardless of their nationality, before its own courts. It may also, if it prefers, and in accordance with the provisions of its own legislation, hand such persons over for trial to another High Contracting Party concerned, provided such High Contracting Party has made out a 'prima facie' case. Each High Contracting Party shall take measures necessary for the suppression of all acts contrary to the provisions of the present Convention other than the grave breaches defined in the following Article . . .[98]

Added to this, article 52 of the same convention provides that:

At the request of a Party to the conflict, an enquiry shall be instituted, in a manner to be decided between the interested Parties, concerning any alleged violation of the Convention. If agreement has not been reached concerning the procedure for the enquiry, the Parties should agree on the choice of an umpire who will decide upon the procedure to be followed. Once the violation has been established, the Parties to the conflict shall put an end to it and shall repress it with the least possible delay.

That said, this latter provision (and, to a large extent the former) has not been implemented in practice, in large part because states are often unwilling to prosecute their own nationals for war crimes.[99]

Criminal law is not the only, nor even the best, measure for supressing violations of IHL. Hence the Geneva Conventions, in Common Article 47/48/127/144, create an obligation on States to disseminate IHL, and train people in its use:

The High Contracting Parties undertake, in time of peace as in time of war, to disseminate the text of the present Convention as widely as possible in their respective countries, and, in particular, to include the study thereof in their programmes of military and, if possible, civil instruction, so that the principles thereof may become known to the entire population, in particular to the armed fighting forces, the medical personnel and the chaplains.

Additional Protocol I, Article 83, says, essentially the same thing.[100]

[98] On which, see Elizabeth Miles Sturza 'Dissemination of the Geneva Conventions', in Clapham et al (above n 28) 597.

[99] Timothy McCormack, 'Their Atrocities and Our Misdemeanours: the Reticence of States to Try their "Own Nationals" for International Crimes', in Phillippe Sands and Matthew Lattimer (eds), *Justice for Crimes against Humanity* (Hart 2003) 107.

[100] See Michael Bothe, Karl Josef Partsch, and Waldemar A Solf, *New Rules for Victims of Armed Conflict* (Martinus Nijhoff 182) 501–4.

There is sense in this, not least in that it is something of a stretch to say that people ought to be held to standards of which they were entirely, and reasonably, unaware. However, there are limits to this too, not least the fact that during armed conflicts, nationalistic considerations tend to dominate. Further, states have not always been assiduous in implementing this obligation. And where they have, this has not necessarily led to compliance with the law.[101]

One of the most important mechanisms of implementation is the integration of legal advisors into the military decision-making system. This is required by article 82 of Additional Protocol I of 1977, which reads:

> The High Contracting Parties at all times, and the Parties to the conflict in time of armed conflict, shall ensure that legal advisers are available, when necessary, to advise military commanders at the appropriate level on the application of the Conventions and this Protocol and on the appropriate instruction to be given to the armed forces on this subject.[102]

This is extremely important, as although there may be differences of opinion on the interpretation of IHL,[103] well-trained military lawyers can provide important advice on IHL, and can prevent possible violations at the outset.

## 6. Conclusion

The law of war crimes is a controversial one, not least as states cannot be certain that their nationals will not commit them. Young soldiers in stressful situations, and who are highly armed, may well end up violating IHL (as well as their superiors), and thus be responsible for war crimes. This is not inappropriate, but leads to worry in states about their possible liability, both political and legal. This, in addition to nationalist sentiment that often accompanies armed conflicts, often makes the circumstances surrounding prosecution difficult. Whilst the deterrent effect of prosecutions is not clear,[104] there are important retributive reasons for prosecuting war crimes, and, in addition, criminal law is only one means of enforcing IHL.

---

[101] Yugoslavia was frequently feted for its work in this area prior to its dissolution, in a series of conflicts notable for the violations of IHL, which led to the creation of the ICTY.

[102] Bothe et al (above n 100) 498–50.

[103] Meron (above n 21).

[104] For a modern discussion, see Mark Kersten, *Justice in Conflict: The Effects of the International Criminal Court's Intervention on Ending Wards and Building Peace* (OUP 2016).

# 16

# Implementation of International Humanitarian Law

*David Turns*

## 1. Introduction

It is something of a truism to say that legal rules are not worth the paper they are written on if they are not enforced. In the second decade of the twenty-first century there is a striking contrast between the apparent inability—or unwillingness—of the world's nations to properly implement and enforce the rules of international humanitarian law ('IHL') and the manifold methods by which such implementation and enforcement may be achieved. On one level this might be viewed as resulting in part from, on the one hand, the accelerated development of the law itself since 1945, and on the other, from the very high levels of media and public interest in the conduct of the various actors in situations of armed conflict. This interest is spurred on by the omnipresence of social media and ever-increasing round-the-clock media scrutiny of military operations, particularly where (as is almost invariably the case, to a greater or lesser extent) these involve civilian casualties; but it is also the case that the law itself provides for its own implementation and enforcement in a multiplicity of ways. These arise under IHL itself and also under various other specific legal regimes within the broad framework of public international law; they address the duties and liabilities of States and also of individuals; they are judicial and quasi-judicial in nature, and also political; and they require action at the national, as well as at the regional and universal, levels. Usually, the action that is required to give effect to these various legal mechanisms is comparatively clear and straightforward. In theory, therefore, one might be forgiven for assuming that the implementation of IHL should be a matter of no great controversy.

And yet, four brief vignettes of recent topical situations suffice to illustrate the difficulties that are encountered in practice when states, international organizations, and non-governmental organizations (NGOs) seek to do nothing more than secure greater observance of this body of law to which, after all, every sovereign state in the world is at least formally and voluntarily committed to.

- Following the United Nations High Commissioner for Human Rights' recommendation for the establishment of 'prompt, thorough, effective, independent and impartial investigations into … alleged violations of international humanitarian law' committed by both sides in the Yemeni Civil War,[1] the Netherlands sponsored a draft resolution in the Human Rights Council (HRC) which would have mandated a UN mission to

---

[1] United Nations Human Rights Council (UNHRC), 'Situation of Human Rights in Yemen: Report of the United Nations High Commissioner for Human Rights' UN Doc A/HRC/30/31 (7 September 2015) para 91.

Yemen in order to establish facts and document violations by both the Houthi forces currently in control in Sana'a and the Saudi-led regional coalition that has been intervening in support of the internationally recognized government in Aden since March 2015.[2] However, in the face of intense Saudi pressure and open hostility on the part of other Arab members of the coalition, as well as conspicuous lack of support from various other countries in the HRC, including the US and the UK, the Dutch draft—negotiations on which had also been boycotted by the Yemeni Government in the HRC—was withdrawn[3] and a much weaker Arab-drafted resolution, calling merely for 'technical assistance' to support a domestic investigative committee in Yemen and the reporting already taking place, was adopted by consensus.[4] A Group of International and Regional Eminent Experts on Yemen appointed by the HRC has reported on 'patterns of continued violations by all parties to the conflict', but to date no action has been taken to end the impunity noted in the Experts' report.[5]

- On 3 October 2015, a US Special Forces airstrike provided by way of close air support in response to a request from Afghan National Army personnel on the ground in Kunduz in northern Afghanistan, which had recently been retaken by Taliban fighters, hit a hospital operated by the humanitarian organization *Médecins Sans Frontières* (MSF), killing thirty civilians (MSF staff and patients) and wounding thirty-seven more.[6] An internal US military investigation's findings were summarized in the following terms: 'the approximate cause of this tragedy was a direct result of avoidable human error compounded by process and equipment failures … some of the US individuals involved did not follow the rules of engagement. With regard to … proportionality … the actions of the aircrew and the Special Operations Forces were not appropriate to the threats that they faced.[7] Although sixteen US military personnel were suspended and other investigations were undertaken by the North Atlantic Treaty Organization (NATO) Command in Afghanistan and the Afghan national authorities, nobody has been charged with any offences in relation to the incident and the lack of any reference to possible criminal investigations was criticized by the NGO Human Rights Watch (HRW)[8] as well as by MSF itself.[9]

- Although the Agreement on the Victims of the Conflict[10] reached between the Colombian Government and the rebel *Fuerzas Armadas Revolucionarias de*

[2] UNHRC, 'Draft Resolution: Situation of Human Rights in Yemen' UN Doc A/HRC/30/L.4/Rev.1 (30 September 2015) para 13.

[3] Human Rights Watch (HRW), 'UN: Rights Council Fails Yemeni Civilians', *Human Rights Watch* (2 October 2015) www.hrw.org/news/2015/10/02/un-rights-council-fails-yemeni-civilians.

[4] HRC Resolution 30/18 UN Doc A/HRC/RES/30/18 (12 October 2015).

[5] Report of the Group of Eminent International and Regional Experts as submitted to the United Nations High Commissioner for Human Rights, UN Doc A/HRC/42/17 (9 August 2019).

[6] US Senate Committee on Armed Services, 'Hearing to Receive Testimony on the Situation in Afghanistan', Statement of General John F Campbell, Stenographic Transcript (6 October 2015) 14 www.armed-services.senate.gov/imo/media/doc/15-76%20-%2010-6-15.pdf.

[7] Brigadier General Wilson Shoffner, quote in 'Department of Defense Press Briefing by General Campbell via Teleconference from Afghanistan', News Transcript, US Department of Defense (25 November 2015) https://www.defense.gov/Newsroom/Transcripts/Transcript/Article/631359/department-of-defense-press-briefing-by-general-campbell-via-teleconference-fro/fro.

[8] 'Letter from HRW to Secretary of Defense Ashton Carter' (17 December 2015) www.hrw.org/sites/default/files/supporting_resources/hrw_letter_to_sec_def_carter_on_msf_strike.pdf.

[9] See Françoise Bouchet-Saulnier and Jonathan Whittall, 'An Environment Conducive to Mistakes? Lessons Learnt from the Attack on the Médecins Sans Frontières Hospital in Kunduz, Afghanistan' (2018) 100 *IRRC* 337.

[10] Acuerdo sobre las Víctimas del Conflicto: 'Sistema Integral de Verdad, Justicia, Reparación y No Repetición', incluyendo la Jurisidcción Especial para la Paz; y Compromiso sobre Derechos Humanos (5 December 2015)

*Colombia—Ejército del Pueblo* (usually referred to as 'FARC') makes provision for a new 'Special Jurisdiction for Peace' to consist of a Peace Tribunal and Judicial Panels to determine which cases of grave violations of human rights and IHL committed in the Colombian Civil War can go to trial, the sanctions provided for have likewise been criticized for 'not reflect[ing] accepted standards of appropriate punishment for grave violations and mak[ing] it virtually impossible that Colombia will meet its binding obligations under international law to ensure accountability for crimes against humanity and war crimes.[11]

- As a mandated outcome of the 31st International Conference of the Red Cross and Red Crescent in 2012, the International Committee of the Red Cross (ICRC) and the Swiss Government initiated a consultation process with states in order to identify and propose possible ways of strengthening legal protection for victims of armed conflicts by 'exploring ways of enhancing and ensuring the effectiveness of mechanisms of compliance' with IHL.[12] In particular, it was proposed to institute a regular Meeting of States, which would serve primarily as a non-politicized forum for states 'to examine IHL issues of common concern based on dialogue and cooperation' and to carry out activities (such as the sharing of best practices and technical expertise, to be agreed by participating states) related to the implementation of IHL, in order to strengthen respect for the law.[13] The proposed mechanism, therefore, was conceived as something entirely non-partisan and unthreatening to states' sovereignty. Nevertheless, after four consultative meetings convened by Switzerland and the ICRC with the participation of a total of ninety-one states, it proved impossible to reach a multilateral agreement on even this relatively harmless proposal;[14] instead, all that could be agreed upon was to launch a four-year inter-governmental process to discuss further the methods of enhancing the implementation of IHL, with a view to reporting back to the next Conference.[15]

This chapter takes a holistic view of the implementation of IHL as including all the various tools which may be used to render IHL effective in practice, whether they are used primarily before a situation of armed conflict arises, or during or after such a situation, whether they invoke the civil responsibility of the state or the criminal responsibility of individuals, and whether they fall to be implemented in a national or international

---

http://legal.legis.com.co/document/Index?obra=legcol&document=legcol_ee52f558022d4ec8bc714555c034519e (only in Spanish).

[11] HRW, 'Human Rights Watch Analysis of Colombia–FARC Agreement' (21 December 2015) www.hrw.org/news/2015/12/21/human-rights-watch-analysis-colombia-farc-agreement#_edn1.

[12] International Committee of the Red Cross (ICRC), 'Strengthening Compliance with International Humanitarian Law: Draft Resolution and Concluding Report', 32nd International Conference of the Red Cross and Red Crescent, 32IC/15/19.2 (Geneva, 8–10 December 2015, 32IC/15/19.2) 7 http://rcrcconference.org/wp-content/uploads/sites/3/2015/10/32IC-DR-and-concluding-report-on-Strengthening-Compliance-with-IHL_EN.pdf.

[13] ibid 19.

[14] ICRC, 'No Agreement by States on Mechanism to Strengthen Compliance with Rules of War' (10 December 2015) www.icrc.org/en/document/no-agreement-states-mechanism-strengthen-compliance-rules-war.

[15] ICRC, 'Resolution 2: Strengthening Compliance with International Humanitarian Law', 32nd International Conference of the Red Cross and Red Crescent, 32IC/15/R2 (Geneva 8–10 December 2015) http://rcrcconference.org/wp-content/uploads/sites/3/2015/04/32IC-AR-Compliance_EN.pdf. See also Jelena Pejic, 'Strengthening Compliance with IHL: The ICRC-Swiss Initiative' (2016) 98 *IRRC* 315.

context. Enforcement of IHL, though arguably susceptible of treatment as a separate topic discrete from implementation as such, is here subsumed within the same framework as it is a logical and necessary consequence of IHL implementation. Starting with a brief review of the evolution and development of national and international implementation mechanisms for the laws of war during the era of modern warfare from the early seventeenth century to the aftermath of the Second World War, the chapter sets out the contemporary legal framework provided by treaty instruments and recognized as customary international law before examining specific state obligations relating to pre-conflict preventive measures, the supervision of conduct and repression of violations during conflict, and the subsequent enforcement of IHL by judicial, quasi-judicial, and non-judicial means. Finally, the chapter considers the increasingly important role played by non-state actors (NSAs), such as NGOs, civil society, and the media, in monitoring and advocacy on IHL issues.

## 2. The Historical Context

Early attempts at the enforcement of the laws of war appeared through the prism of punishing those who were judged guilty of violating that body of rules. Although the notion of having rules of law in war (*jus in bello*) is probably about as old as organized warfare itself, and concepts of honour and chivalry in ancient and mediaeval warfare were historically adjudicated in various forums,[16] it was not until the advent of mass citizen-armies organized by nation-states as a public activity in the course of the seventeenth century that something resembling systematic national implementation of the laws of war began to take place. Even then, these were couched in terms of domestic military law and the extension of national criminal offences to cover military discipline, rather than international law as such; among the earliest known examples are the Articles of War promulgated for the Swedish army in the Thirty Years' War (1618–1648).[17] In England the source of disciplinary enforcement for the Army was the royal prerogative, under which King Charles I promulgated 'Lawes and Articles of Warre' (building on ad hoc mediaeval precedents dating back to Plantagenet times) in 1625—these were reissued in 1629 and 1639;[18] their substantive essence, along with the constitutional authority to issue them, began to be transferred to a statutory footing with the adoption of the first Mutiny Act in 1689. Discipline in the Royal Navy was covered by statute for the first time shortly after the Restoration of King Charles II.[19] These early articles of national military law provided, naturally, for the trial and punishment of soldiers and sailors accused of breaches of service discipline; but they also enacted a variety of offences amounting to crimes under the civil law, which under modern

---

[16] For a general overview, see Leslie C Green, *The Contemporary Law of Armed Conflict* (3rd edn, Manchester UP 2008) 26–32; also Robert C Stacey, 'The Age of Chivalry', in Michael Howard, George J Andreopoulos, and Mark R Shulman (eds), *The Laws of War: Constraints on Warfare in the Western World* (Yale UP 1994) 27, 31.

[17] See Kenneth Ögren, 'Humanitarian Law in the Articles of War decreed in 1621 by King Gustavus II Adolphus of Sweden' (1996) 36 *IRRC* 438.

[18] See Charles M Clode, *The Military Forces of the Crown: Their Administration and Government*, Vol 1 (John Murray 1869) 18, 429 (annexed Illustration (VI)).

[19] Charles II, 1661, 'An Act for the Establishing [of] Articles and Orders for the Regulating and Better Government of His Majesties Navies Ships of Warr and Forces by Sea', in John Raithby (ed), *Statutes of the Realm: Vol 5, 1628–1680* (first published 1819) 311.

IHL could be characterized as war crimes or crimes against humanity. Nevertheless, the actual effectiveness of such purely national and disciplinary codes for the protection of the civilian population—in later times to become one of the main aspects of IHL—in the early modern period of warfare has been questioned.[20]

While the jurisdiction of a State to conduct trials of *its own* soldiers for violations of national service law has never been disputed, as it is an obvious aspect of criminal jurisdiction over a states' own nationals, it is not clear exactly when it became definitively accepted that a state could legitimately assert such enforcement jurisdiction in respect of *enemy soldiers* (ie foreign nationals) who, after capture, were accused of violating the laws and customs of war. Early modern writers on international law suggested that persons who violated the laws of war, by analogy with pirates, were to be considered mere *banditti* or brigands, and could be subjected to punishment by whichever authority's hands they fell into.[21] The main examples in early modern practice derive largely from the US— the first systematic institutional mechanism for punishing what would today be called war crimes appeared in the Mexican–American War (1846–1848), when Major General Winfield Scott's *General Orders No 20* instituted military commissions for the trial and punishment of 'atrocious crimes' whether committed by civilians or military persons, Mexicans or Americans, namely: '[m]urder, premeditated murder, injuries or mutilation, rape, assaults and malicious beatings; robbery, larceny, desecration of Churches, cemeteries or houses, and religious buildings; and the destruction of public or private property that was not ordered by a superior officer'.[22] The first clear enunciation of the notion of prosecuting enemy soldiers for 'violation of the laws of war' appears in the orders issued at the behest of the US Army's department commander in Missouri, Major General Henry Halleck, in respect of guerrilla warfare against irregular Confederate forces during the American Civil War (1861–1865):

> …a soldier duly enrolled and authorized to act in a military capacity in the enemy's service is not according to the code military individually responsible for the taking of human life in battle, siege, &c., while at the same time he is held individually responsible for any act which he may commit in violation of the laws of war. Thus he cannot be punished by a military tribunal for committing acts of hostility which are authorized by the laws of war but if he has committed murder, robbery, theft, arson, &c., the fact of his being a prisoner of war does not exempt him from trial by a military tribunal.[23]

This power to enforce the laws of war by prosecuting one's own or the enemy's soldiers for violations was clearly generally acknowledged by the late nineteenth century,[24] and was to

---

[20]  See eg Markus Meumann, 'Civilians, the French Army and Military Justice during the Reign of Louis XIV, circa 1640–1715', in Erica Charters, Eve Rosenhaft, and Hannah Smith (eds), *Civilians and War in Europe, 1618–1815* (Liverpool UP 2014) 100.

[21]  See eg Emmerich de Vattel, *Le Droit des Gens* (1758) Liv III, Chap XV para 226.

[22]  Cuartel General del Egercito, 'Ordenes Generales—No 20' (Tampico, 19 February 1847) English translation https://scholarship.rice.edu/jsp/xml/1911/27562/3/aa00208tr.tei.html. For discussion, see John F Witt, *Lincoln's Code: The Laws of War in American History* (Free Press 2012) 118–32; Louis Fisher, 'Military Tribunals: Historical Patterns and Lessons', US Congressional Research Service Report RL32458 (9 July 2004) 11–14.

[23]  Department of Missouri, 'General Orders No 1' (Saint Louis, 1 January 1862) in US War Department, *The War of the Rebellion: A Compilation of the Official Records of the Union and Confederate Armies, Series II, Vol 1* (Government Printing Office 1894) 249.

[24]  Institute of International Law, *Manual of the Laws of War on Land* (Oxford 1880) Part III.

be reasserted as a result of the wholesale atrocities committed during both World Wars.[25] As noted by authorities at the time, however, it was not always possible for a belligerent to secure custody of an accused in order to bring him to trial; and if the state of his nationality refused or otherwise failed to investigate and prosecute him,[26] a standard recourse for the injured state was to have resort to the right of belligerent reprisal, whereby a belligerent would engage temporarily in proportionate illegal conduct with a view to inducing the enemy to desist from his own unlawful behaviour.[27]

Aside from enforcement by means of criminal sanctions, the concept of specifically implementing parts of the laws of war by the enactment of regulations and legislation appears to have entered the lexicon of international conventions only with the adoption of the first Geneva Convention in 1864; initially this was conceived of as being a matter which was delegated to military commanders in the field, who would act in accordance with the instructions promulgated by their governments.[28] Subsequent iterations of the Geneva Convention in the early twentieth century repeated that injunction and also required signatories to 'take the necessary steps to acquaint their troops ... with the provisions of this convention and to make them known to the people at large'[29] and also to introduce 'such measures as may be necessary' to prevent the unauthorized use of the protected emblem of the Red Cross and to repress 'individual acts of robbery and ill treatment of the sick and wounded of the armies, as well as to punish ... the wrongful use of the flag and brassard of the Red Cross'.[30] These requirements pointed the way forward to the post-1945 emphasis on enactment of penal sanctions in domestic legislation and on dissemination of the Geneva Conventions, as discussed further in section 4 'The Geneva Conventions and Their Additional Protocols' below.

On a more general level, in the pre-1945 era, the only other specific provision for giving effect to the laws of war was to be found in the Hague Convention's adoption of the general rule of state responsibility for unlawful acts by state organs: 'A belligerent party which violates the provisions of the [annexed] Regulations shall, if the case demands, be liable to pay compensation. It shall be responsible for all acts committed by persons forming part of its armed forces.'[31] This, however, was and is a general doctrine of public international

---

[25] See James W Garner, 'Punishment of Offenders against the Laws and Customs of War' (1920) 14 *AJIL* 70; Hersch Lauterpacht, 'The Law of Nations and the Punishment of War Crimes' (1944) 21 *BYBIL* 58; Willard B Cowles, 'Universality of Jurisdiction over War Crimes' (1945) 33 *CLR* 177.

[26] For centuries it was the custom for commanders on the battlefield to communicate directly with each other under a flag of truce, usually via *parlementaires*, for a variety of purposes, including bringing each other's attention to alleged violations of the laws of war: see Green (above n 16) 113–16. As direct governmental control of armed forces increased and technology developed, such communications could be addressed by a commander directly to the enemy government or indirectly between the belligerent governments, via the good offices of a neutral state: see eg correspondence between the British Commander-in-Chief in South Africa and the Afrikaner State Presidents concerning reported abuse of the white flag on the battlefield during the Second Boer War, *Telegrams from Field-Marshal Lord Roberts to the Secretary of State for War* (Cd 122, 1900).

[27] See William Winthrop, *Military Law and Precedents* (2nd edn, Government Printing Office 1920) 796–9; Shane Darcy, 'The Evolution of the Law of Belligerent Reprisals' (2003) 175 *Mil L Rev* 184.

[28] Geneva Convention for the Amelioration of the Condition of the Wounded in Armies in the Field (signed 22 August 1864, entered into force 22 June 1865) 129 CTS 361 article 8.

[29] Geneva Convention for the Amelioration of the Condition of the Wounded and Sick in Armies in the Field (adopted 6 July 1906, entered into force 9 August 1907) 202 CTS 144 articles 25–26.

[30] ibid articles 27–28.

[31] Hague Convention (IV) Respecting the Laws and Customs of War on Land (adopted 18 October 1907, entered into force 26 January 1910) 205 CTS 277 (Hague Convention IV) article 3.

law and is in no way peculiar to the laws of war; neither can it be said to constitute a rule of enforcement per se, perhaps even less so a rule for specific implementation of the law. Although it was used against Germany by the victorious Allied Powers in the infamous reparations clauses of the peace settlement after the First World War,[32] in historical terms and notwithstanding the settled rules of international law this represented something of an aberration: in the aftermath of the Second World War the emphasis returned very firmly to criminal sanctions and the prosecution of accused war criminals.[33] Both Germany and Japan as occupied territories after 1945 saw the creation of military tribunals—the Nuremberg and Tokyo Trials, respectively, for the trial of major war criminals, and a myriad of national tribunals, in both the occupied states and their erstwhile enemies, for the trial of so-called minor war criminals. But these were ad hoc expedients adopted by the victors exclusively against their defeated enemies in a situation of *debellatio*; systemic reliance upon mechanisms of national implementation of IHL would not come until the adoption of the updated Geneva Conventions in 1949.

## 3. The Contemporary Framework

### A. Generalities

Broadly speaking, the contemporary implementation of IHL in the holistic sense alluded to in the introduction to this chapter may be achieved in some seven different ways.[34] It is difficult to gauge the relative impact and effectiveness of these methods, as they are quite different from each other: some consist of implementation *stricto sensu*, others are more in the nature of prevention and/or punishment, while yet others are not strictly speaking legal in nature. Nevertheless, for the purposes of summarizing them here, they may be enumerated in approximately the following generalized order of impact and effect:

(1) belligerent reprisals;
(2) state responsibility;
(3) dissemination and instruction;
(4) command responsibility;
(5) national implementation;
(6) criminal prosecution;
(7) external scrutiny/pressure.

For the purposes of this chapter, these aspects of implementation are considered by reference to a temporal framework: those that exist under general public international law are

---

[32] Treaty of Peace between the Allied and Associated Powers and Germany (adopted 28 June 1919, entered into force 10 January 1920) 225 CTS 188 (Versailles Treaty) part VIII: Reparation.

[33] After World War I the Treaty of Versailles had deferred such matters to German national jurisdiction: see Mahmoud Cherif Bassiouni, 'World War I: "The War to End All Wars" and the Birth of a Handicapped International Criminal Justice System' (2002) 30 *Denv J Intl L & Pol'y* 244, 281–85.

[34] For an outline, see David Turns, 'The Law of Armed Conflict (International Humanitarian Law)', in Malcolm D Evans (ed), *International Law* (5th edn, OUP 2018) 840.

dealt with first, followed by obligations of prevention that arise before armed conflicts, then securing compliance during armed conflict, then enforcement—which usually, though not invariably, occurs in the aftermath of armed conflict. This is followed by some discussion of non-judicial methods that are nevertheless established by law; methods of scrutiny that are primarily political or diplomatic, or that arise as a result of media or social pressure, are considered last. It should be borne in mind that there is some inevitable overlap between some of the methods to be considered, such that neither the categorization nor the methodology of their analysis is perfect.

The implementation of IHL treaties since the end of the Second World War has become relatively systematized and has tended to follow a set pattern, depending on the type of treaty in question, all under the *chapeau* of the general doctrine of state responsibility in public international law, as noted in section 2 'The Historical Context' above. The 1949 Geneva Conventions and their 1977/2005 Additional Protocols have specific inbuilt mechanisms for their own dissemination, implementation, and enforcement. The majority of the other IHL treaties adopted post-1945 are concerned with the prohibition or restriction of various types of weaponry, which generally fall to be implemented by means of the creation of specific criminal offences in the national laws of states parties to those treaties.

## B.  Belligerent Reprisals

Historically, in the absence of international institutions and a rule-of-law-based system of international governance, belligerent reprisals, as a means of self-help, were one of the main ways in which a state could attempt to secure greater compliance with the law by its enemies. Although the theoretical possibility of belligerent reprisals remains in the law today, the likelihood of their being used in contemporary armed conflicts has been increasingly attenuated by the progressive interdiction of whole categories of persons as legitimate targets for reprisal action in successive treaties of modern IHL. Thus, for example, reprisals against the civilian population and the natural environment are both now flatly prohibited.[35] The idea of belligerent reprisals is to compel cessation of violations by the adverse party in an armed conflict by resort to a proportionate action that is itself illegal. Unfortunately, they often achieve precisely the opposite effect, producing a downward spiral of retaliation and counter-retaliation which undermines the law rather than enhances it, as seen in incidents of reciprocal shackling of prisoners of war (POWs) by the UK, Canada, and Germany during the Second World War, ostensibly in reaction to attempts by POWs to escape from captivity and subsequent 'mutinies' in POW camps.[36] Generally, the use of belligerent reprisals in the twenty-first century—if it is even seriously contemplated—will in many countries be circumscribed by stringent conditions and subject to political approval at the highest level of government.[37]

---

[35]  Protocol Additional to the Geneva Conventions of 12 August 1949, and Relating to the Protection of Victims of International Armed Conflicts (adopted 8 June 1977, entered into force 7 December 1978) 1125 UNTS 3 (API) articles 51(6) and 55(2), respectively.

[36]  See Jonathan F Vance, 'Men in Manacles: The Shackling of Prisoners of War, 1942–1943' (1995) 59 *J Mil Hist* 483.

[37]  Eg UK Ministry of Defence (MoD), *The Manual of the Law of Armed Conflict* (OUP 2004) paras 16.16–16.19.

## C.  State Responsibility

In the modern era states have continued to present civil claims for monetary or other satisfaction against each other, based on allegations that IHL was violated by members of the
regular state armed forces; that is, by individuals or units belonging to an organ of the state.[38]
Such claims generally involve an element of international arbitration in order to be adjudicated. Following the conclusion of the Gulf War, a United Nations Claims Commission
(UNCC) was established as a subsidiary organ of the Security Council in order to process
claims for compensation in respect of losses and damage resulting directly from the Iraqi
occupation of Kuwait in 1990–1991,[39] To date the UNCC has paid out some $47.8 billion
in compensation awards, with about $4.6 billion (awarded for production and sales losses
resulting from the destruction of Kuwaiti oil fields) still outstanding.[40] The Algiers Peace
Agreement, which terminated the 1998–2000 armed conflict between Ethiopia and Eritrea,
created a Claims Commission under the auspices of the Permanent Court of Arbitration to
adjudicate:

> all claims for loss, damage or injury by one Government against the other, and by
> nationals ... of one party against the Government of the other party or entities owned
> or controlled by the other party that are (a) related to the conflict ... and (b) result from
> violations of international humanitarian law ...[41]

Sitting between 2004 and 2009, the Eritrea–Ethiopia Claims Commission delivered a total
of seventeen Awards, of which all but three relate to alleged violations of IHL, in response to
eight claims submitted by Ethiopia and thirty-two submitted by Eritrea.[42]

Similarly, the United Nations (and other international or regional organizations, if appropriate) may consider the attribution of responsibility for damage and loss suffered by the
organization itself and its employees in the course of military operations, as was done for
instance in respect of incidents of such damage and loss suffered by various UN specialized
agencies during the 2008–2009 conflict between Israel and Hamas in the Gaza Strip.[43] On
that occasion damage worth in excess of $11 million was attributed to actions by the Israel

---

[38] Draft Articles on Responsibility of States for Internationally Wrongful Acts article 4 in *Yearbook of the
International Law Commission 2001, Vol II* UN Doc A/CN.4/SER.A/2001/Add.1 (Part 2) (UN 2001) 30. The generic modern restatement of state responsibility for violations of IHL is contained in API article 91.

[39] UN Security Council (UNSC) Resolution 687 UN Doc S/RES/687 (8 April 1991) para 18. Resolution 687 declared, inter alia, that Iraq was 'liable under international law for any direct loss, damage, including environmental
damage and the depletion of natural resources, or injury to foreign Governments, nationals and corporations,
as a result of Iraq's unlawful invasion and occupation of Kuwait': ibid para16. Note the broad similarity of language and intent between this provision and articles 231–233 of the Versailles Treaty, which affirmed Germany's
liability based on its aggression in 1914 and established a Reparation Commission to consider claims made against
Germany in respect of the First World War.

[40] For details of the UNCC's work since 1991, see www.uncc.ch.

[41] UNSC, 'Agreement between the Government of the State of Eritrea and the Government of the Federal
Democratic Republic of Ethiopia: Identical letters dated 12 December 2000 from the Permanent Representative of
Algeria to the United Nations addressed to the Secretary-General and the President of the Security Council' UN
Doc A/55/686-S/2000/1183 (13 December 2000) annex, article 5(1).

[42] For details, see https://pca-cpa.org/en/cases/71/.

[43] UNSC, 'Summary by the Secretary-General of the report of the United Nations Headquarters Board of
Inquiry into certain incidents in the Gaza Strip between 27 December 2008 and 19 January 2009' UN Doc A/63/
855-S/2009/250 (15 May 2009).

Defence Forces, with a provisional estimate of some \$29,000 worth of damage being laid at the door of a Palestinian armed faction, most likely to have been Hamas.[44]

## 4. The Geneva Conventions and Their Additional Protocols

It is appropriate to deal with the generalities of the 1949 Geneva Conventions and the 1977 Additional Protocols thereto separately within the framework of the contemporary law, as they have their own particular implementation scheme. The Conventions' starting point is that, 'The High Contracting Parties undertake to respect and to ensure respect for the present Convention[s] *in all circumstances*', an injunction which is repeated *verbatim* in the first Protocol (but not the second).[45] It is therefore immediately apparent that there are certain provisions which fall to be implemented during peacetime as well as in situations of armed conflict—these will be discussed in section D 'Non-Judicial Mechanisms of Implementation' below.

Insofar as implementation during situations of armed conflict is concerned, the practice prior to 1949 had generally been to make a state's application of its treaty obligations dependent on reciprocity and to include them among the final provisions of each treaty, as expressed in the following typical formulation: 'The provisions of the present Convention do not apply except between contracting Powers, and then only if all the belligerents are parties to the Convention.'[46] Although this approach persisted in the interwar period's sole adopted treaty regulating the conduct of hostilities,[47] the updated Geneva Conventions adopted in 1929 introduced the 'in all circumstances' rule and modified for the first time the 'all-participation clause' by stipulating that, 'if one of the belligerents is not a party to the Convention, its provisions shall, nevertheless, remain binding as between the belligerents who are parties thereto'.[48] This new wording did not alter the technical possibility that the Conventions would remain legally inapplicable in cases where one belligerent was, but its opponent was not, a party to the Conventions; nevertheless, the introduction of the 'in all circumstances' language created a potentially inconsistent obligation. The effect could be seen in Germany's refusal to apply the Geneva Conventions on the Eastern Front during the

---

[44]  ibid paras 94–95.

[45]  Geneva Convention (I) for the Amelioration of the Condition of the Wounded and Sick in the Armed Forces in the Field (adopted 12 August 1949, entered into force 21 October 1950) 75 UNTS 31 (GCI); Geneva Convention (II) for the Amelioration of the Condition of the Wounded, Sick and Shipwrecked Members of Armed Forces at Sea (adopted 12 August 1949, entered into force 12 October 1949) 75 UNTS 85 (GCII); Geneva Convention (III) Relative to the Treatment of Prisoners of War (adopted 12 August 1949, entered into force 12 October 1950) 75 UNTS 135 (GCIII); Geneva Convention (IV) Relative to the Protection of Civilian Persons in Time of War (adopted 12 August 1949, entered into force 21 October 1953) 75 UNTS 287 (GCIV); Geneva Conventions Common Article 1 (emphasis added); API article 1.

[46]  Hague Convention (V) Respecting the Rights and Duties of Neutral Powers and Persons in Case of War on Land (adopted 18 October 1907, entered into force 26 January 1910) 205 CTS 299 (Hague Convention V) article 20. An identical provision was inserted in each of the other conventions adopted at the 2nd Hague Peace Conference, except for Conventions (I)–(III), which are not properly speaking part of the *jus in bello*.

[47]  Namely, the Protocol for the Prohibition of the Use in War of Asphyxiating, Poisonous or Other Gases, and of Bacteriological Methods of Warfare (signed 17 June 1925, entered into force 8 February 1928) 94 LNTS 65, the High Contracting Parties to which agreed 'to be bound as between themselves'.

[48]  Convention Relative to the Treatment of Prisoners of War (adopted 27 July 1929, entered into force 19 June 1931) 118 LNTS 343, article 82. The equivalent provision in article 25 of the contemporaneous Convention for the Amelioration of the Condition of the Wounded and Sick in Armies in the Field (above n 29) contained minor variations in wording but was substantively identical.

Second World War on the basis that the Soviet Union was not a party to those instruments, although those deemed responsible for the resulting ill-treatment of Soviet prisoners of war were subsequently condemned as war criminals.[49]

There has been a shift in emphasis since the Second World War away from all-participation clauses to a more universalist approach, as well as placing these provisions at the very start of the substantive contents of the modern instruments, rather than burying them among procedural provisions at the end of the documents. These can be attributed to a desire to strengthen the imperative encapsulated by the maxim *pacta sunt servanda*: the inclusion of the phrase 'in all circumstances' stresses that the treaties are to be applied even outside the parameters of the situations to which they pertain—namely, armed conflicts—by taking in peacetime the preventive actions, to be discussed in 4.A 'Pre-Conflict: Obligations of Prevention' below. Notwithstanding the importance attached to the treaty texts, it is worth recalling that the International Court of Justice (ICJ) has stated that, '[the obligation in Common Article 1] does not derive only from the Conventions themselves, but from the general principles of humanitarian law to which the Conventions merely give specific expression'.[50]

Given the vagueness of the wording in Common Article 1, the question may well be asked: vis-à-vis from whom a state is to 'ensure respect'. Obviously it must ensure respect by its own regular armed forces, and also by irregular forces whose conduct is attributable to it.[51] Ensuring respect by *other states*, in the sense of influencing them in the context of general friendly relations, or pursuant to a specific alliance, or at the 'hard end' of joint military operations in a multinational coalition, wherein different nations may not necessarily all be parties to the same IHL treaties, can be surprisingly problematic.[52] Differences between allied nations in respect of legal obligations, or even of bona fide interpretation of legal provisions—as in, for example, detailed aspects of the definition of military objectives under article 52(2) of API—do not give rise to any doctrinal controversy in this respect. More difficult, however, are situations where individual states may reasonably be expected to use their influence on friends and allies to induce the latter to comply with IHL in the conduct of their military operations. Diplomatic and economic policies may eclipse humanitarian concerns, as attested by the British Government's 2016 response to criticism in respect of its arms sales to Saudi Arabia in light of the latter's extremely destructive campaign in Yemen.[53] Occasionally a multilateral attempt is made pursuant to a treaty,[54]

---

[49] International Military Tribunal (IMT), *Trial of the Major War Criminals before the International Military Tribunal: Nuremberg, 14 November 1945–1 October 1946, Vol XXII* (IMT 1948) 472, 474–5.

[50] *Military and Paramilitary Activities in and against Nicaragua (Nicaragua v United States of America)*, (Merits) [1986] ICJ Rep 14 para 220.

[51] ibid paras 115–116.

[52] This may be the case, especially in relation to API and some of the treaties prohibiting or restricting the use of specific weapons.

[53] Despite extensive evidence gathered by the UN and various NGOs of IHL violations committed in Yemen in the course of Saudi operations, and sharp criticism within Parliament, the British Government's response has been to either contest that such violations are occurring, or insist that they are best investigated by the Saudis' own internal procedures rather than by impartial international mechanisms. For details of alleged IHL violations in Yemen, see UNSC, 'Final Report of the Panel of Experts on Yemen established pursuant to Security Council Resolution 2140 (2014)' UN Doc S/2016/73 (26 January 2016) paras 123–142; for domestic British criticism and Government responses, see House of Commons International Development Committee, *Crisis in Yemen: Fourth Report of Session 2015–16*, HC532 (House of Commons, 4 May 2016) paras 39–73, annex 2 and appendices 1–4.

[54] See eg the Swiss-convened Conference of High Contracting Parties to the Fourth Geneva Convention, which resulted in a Declaration (dated 5 December 2001) calling inter alia upon 'all parties, [whether] directly involved in the conflict or not, to respect and to ensure respect for the Geneva Conventions in all circumstances ...'. For the full text of the Declaration, see https://unispal.un.org/DPA/DPR/unispal.nsf/0/8FC4F064B9BE5BAD852

or within the forum of an international organization to exert pressure upon a perceived delinquent state in order to induce it to comply with its obligations under IHL.[55] However, this often seems to achieve little other than to push the target state into a defensive and un-cooperative position of reflexive denial.[56] Arguably the most credible attempts to 'ensure respect' for IHL on the part of other states are evinced by international court decisions,[57] and diplomatic responses thereto,[58] but such cases are rare indeed. As for the notion that a state should ensure respect for IHL on the part of NSAs, this will plainly be a dead letter insofar as opposition NSAs on the state's own territory are concerned, but it would be a reasonable expectation that a state should prevail upon NSAs over which it has effective control, whether within its own borders or elsewhere, to conduct their operations in accordance with IHL.[59]

## A. Pre-Conflict: Obligations of Prevention

Although the most publicly visible form of IHL implementation is post-conflict enforce-ment by means of criminal proceedings for the punishment of violations, and it is through that prism that the consciousness of IHL has largely become embedded in the general population in many countries, actually modern IHL mandates various measures to be taken by states in advance of any armed conflict breaking out with a view to avoiding or minim-izing the risk of future violations. Broadly, these may be broken down into those measures that are of a general, ongoing nature and those that entail specific one-off actions. While compliance with these obligations of prevention is not, in and of itself, a panacea for IHL violations, and they are only addressed to states as opposed to NSAs, it is arguably the case that effective implementation of these measures assists in the development of a culture of compliance with the law, as well as mitigating the opportunities for future violations.

---

56C1400722951. For an overview of the process, which reconvened in 2014 and resulted in another Declaration, see Pierre-Yves Fux and Mirko Zambelli, 'Mise en Œuvre de la Quatrième Convention de Genève dans les Territoires Palestiniens Occupés: Historique d'un Processus Multilateral (1997–2001)' (2002) 84 *IRRC* 661; also Matthias Lanz, Emilie Max, and Oliver Hoehne, 'The Conference of High Contracting Parties to the Fourth Geneva Convention of 17 December 2014 and the Duty to Ensure Respect for International Humanitarian Law' (2014) 96 *IRRC* 1115 (including the text of the 2014 Declaration at 1128–30).

[55] See eg the Tenth Emergency Special Session of the UN General Assembly (UNGA) (first convened in 1997 and periodically resumed on several occasions since, most recently in 2009), which is concerned specifically with 'Illegal Israeli actions in occupied East Jerusalem and the rest of the Occupied Palestinian Territory'. A typical early resolution:

> [r]ecommends to the States that are High Contracting Parties to the Geneva Convention relative to the Protection of Civilian Persons in Time of War to take measures, on a national or regional level, in fulfilment of their obligations under article 1 of the Convention, to ensure respect by Israel, the occupying Power, of the Convention (UNGA Resolution ES-10/2 UN Doc A/RES/ES-10/2 (25 April 1997) para 8).

[56] See eg UNGA, 'Statement by Ambassador Gabriela Shalev, Permanent Representative of Israel, Tenth Emergency Special Session (resumed)' (15 January 2009) https://www.un.org/press/en/2009/ga10807.doc.htm.
[57] See eg *Legal Consequences of the Construction of a Wall in the Occupied Palestinian Territory* (Advisory Opinion) [2004] ICJ Rep 136 (*Palestinian Wall* case), in which the Court found that certain obligations arising under IHL were obligations *erga omnes* (at para 155), and emphasized the corresponding obligation arising under article 1 of GCIV (at para 158).
[58] See eg UNGA Resolution ES-10/15 UN Doc A/RES/ES-10/15 (2 August 2004) paras 1, 7.
[59] See David Turns, 'Implementation and Compliance', in Elizabeth Wilmshurst and Susan Breau (eds), *Perspectives on the ICRC Study on Customary International Humanitarian Law* (CUP 2007) 354, 359–60, 372–3.

## 1. General measures

Each of the 1949 Geneva Conventions contains a whole chapter or part headed 'Execution of the Convention'.[60] This is equally the case for API,[61] though not for APII, whose sole provision for implementation is the requirement that, 'This Protocol shall be disseminated as widely as possible.'[62] The central requirement is a dual one, of *dissemination* and *instruction*: states undertake to propagate the text of the Conventions 'as widely as possible in their respective countries' so that 'the entire population' may become aware of their principles.[63] This is to be achieved by educating the civilian population at large, as well as the members of armed forces, in the principles and rules of IHL. As to the civilian population, the subject may be included in the curriculum of universities and even (in some countries) schools, and there is a myriad of programmes such as moot court competitions, simulations, subject-specific projects, and voluntary youth instruction, all designed to foster an interest in and awareness of IHL.[64] Inevitably, however, this method of implementation is somewhat uneven, depending as it does on the availability of staff expertise and educational resources: even in a country like the UK, for example, IHL as a discrete subject is comprehensively taught at little more than a handful out of approximately 100 university-level law schools, and there is no evidence of any government initiatives to promote the dissemination of IHL among the general population in the UK, although the British Red Cross does encourage the teaching of aspects of IHL in schools.[65]

A crucial part of the dissemination of IHL is the education and training of armed forces, which is expressly mandated by the provisions discussed above. This is primarily the responsibility of the military legal advisory services, which now exist in virtually all states around the world: for example, in the British Army, such instruction is delivered via the medium of the Mandatory Annual Training Tests (MATTs), which must be taken by all active and reserve soldiers; currently MATT 7 is designated as covering Operational Law, including the Law of Armed Conflict. Specific pre-operational deployment training in IHL is provided by officers of the Army Legal Services (ALS) Operational Law Branch, based in the Land Warfare Centre at Warminster. For officers, pre-commission instruction in IHL is provided by the Department of Defence and International Affairs at the Royal Military Academy Sandhurst, and opportunities exist for subsequent academic study to Masters

---

[60]  GCI ch VIII; GCII ch VII; GCIII pt VI; GCIV pt IV.

[61]  API pt V.

[62]  Protocol Additional to the Geneva Conventions of 12 August 1949, and Relating to the Protection of Victims of Non-International Armed Conflicts (adopted 8 June 1977, entered into force 7 December 1978) 1125 UNTS 609 (APII) article 19.

[63]  GCI article 47; GCII article 48; GCIII article 127; GCIV article 144; API article 83(1). The GCIII and GCIV articles include particular requirements for personnel with responsibilities for, respectively, prisoners of war and protected persons (ie civilians in occupied territory) to be 'specially instructed' as to those Conventions' provisions; these requirements are amalgamated in API article 83(2). Other modern IHL treaties also include the requirement of dissemination, while limiting it to armed forces: eg Convention on Prohibitions or Restrictions on the Use of Certain Conventional Weapons Which May Be Deemed to Be Excessively Injurious or to Have Indiscriminate Effects (adopted 10 October 1980, entered into force 2 December 1983) (1980) 19 ILM 1523 (CCW) article 6.

[64]  Among many such initiatives worldwide, prominent examples include the Jean-Pictet Competition http://concourspictet.org/indexen.html, the Martens Moot Court Competition on IHL, and the Israeli Alma National IHL Competition for Students www.alma-ihl.org/ihl-competition. Most such projects are organized by, or at least with the support of, the ICRC at national, regional, and/or international level; for an example of the organization's approach to IHL civil education, see Luisa Vierucci, 'Promoting the Teaching of International Humanitarian Law in Universities: The ICRC's Experience in Central Asia' (2001) 83 *IRRC* 155 (and other articles in the same thematic issue).

[65]  See British Red Cross, 'Teaching Resources' www.redcross.org.uk/What-we-do/Teaching-resources.

and Doctoral level at various higher education institutions. IHL is expressly included on the staff courses of many states' staff colleges, such as the Joint Services Combined Staff College at the UK Defence Academy, the Italian Centre for Defence Higher Studies, and the Sri Lankan Defence Services Command and Staff College. Similar programmes of legal instruction, which may or may not include university-level programmes of study, exist in armed forces as diverse as those of Uruguay, Algeria, and Indonesia: the pattern is now genuinely quite universal.

A further layer of education in IHL for armed forces is provided by API, which requires states to maintain an establishment of legal officers, 'to advise military commanders at the appropriate level ... on the appropriate instruction to be given to the armed forces on this subject'.[66] In some states, such as Canada or the Republic of Ireland, military legal advisers are tri-service; in others, such as the US and the UK, the various services that make up the armed forces maintain their own completely separate legal advisory services.[67] While these military legal services provide education and training in IHL for the rest of the armed forces, they also themselves often receive such training from academic providers; for example, in the UK, ALS officers currently attend academic courses in international law (including IHL) at the University of Nottingham, while Royal Navy lawyers attend the University of Oxford; Royal Air Force Legal Officers have in recent years attended academic courses provided by the University of Bristol and by Cranfield University at the UK Defence Academy. On an international level, remarkable work in IHL education for military officers (both lawyers and operators) has for many years been done by the International Institute of Humanitarian Law at San Remo (Italy),[68] as well as on a more geo-politically restricted basis by such institutions as the NATO School at Oberammergau (Germany),[69] and the Asia Pacific Centre for Military Law (Australia).[70] Operationally, military legal advisers fulfil a critical role by advising the commanders to whose staff they are attached about a wide range of legal issues, including the application of IHL in—for instance—the selection of targets for attack and the precautions to be observed in planning and executing such attacks, and the classification and treatment of battlefield detainees.[71]

Although the mandating of legal advisers for armed forces in international treaty law since 1977 has given added impetus to the production and status of modern military law manuals, the precedents for such documents, as outlined in section 2 'The Historical Context' above, go back several centuries.[72] Such manuals fulfil a number of functions, all of them equally important in the legal regulatory framework of state armed forces.[73] They may

---

[66]  API article 82.

[67]  For example each of the US services—Army, Navy, Air Force, Marine Corps, and Coast Guard—has its own separate Judge Advocate General's Corps.

[68]  See International Institute of Humanitarian Law www.iihl.org.

[69]  See NATO School Oberammergau www.natoschool.nato.int.

[70]  See Asia Pacific Centre for Military Law http://apcml.org.

[71]  See US Department of Defense, 'Final Report to Congress on the Conduct of the Persian Gulf War, Appendix O—The Role of the Law of War' (1992) 31 ILM 615, 617.

[72]  Indeed, although ALS (to take the UK, and more specifically England, as an example) dates in its modern form only from 1948, it traces its genesis back to the authority of the mediaeval offices of Earl Marshal and Advocate of the Army—the origin of the modern term 'court-martial', signifying a military court, derives from the Court of the Marshal (or 'Marshal's Court'), which was instituted by King Henry VIII in 1521 and was itself based on a much older institution.

[73]  See Hans-Peter Gasser, 'Military Manuals, Legal Advisers and the First Additional Protocol of 1977', in Nobuo Hayashi (ed), National Military Manuals on the Law of Armed Conflict (2nd edn, Forum for International Criminal and Humanitarian Law 2010) 55.

provide evidence of states' views as to the scope, ambit, and interpretation of rules of IHL, and the normative status thereof in customary international law.[74] Ultimately their most practical purpose in terms of the implementation of IHL is that they tell soldiers what the law is and according to what legal standard their actions in armed conflict will be judged.[75] Such manuals may be published exclusively in official format,[76] or they may be made separately available as an academic publication.[77] One innovative approach is to publish them with extensive academic commentary.[78] However precisely they are publicized, these military manuals—and the Rules of Engagement that are based on them—are a crucial aspect of the dissemination of IHL to armed forces.

### 2. Specific measures

Various treaties that make up the corpus of codified IHL impose requirements for state parties to undertake specific measures of implementation: principally, these are the requirements in the Geneva Conventions and API (along with many of the weaponry treaties) to enact certain criminal offences into states' national legal systems with a view to securing compulsory enforcement jurisdiction, and the promulgation of protective measures in respect of particular objects, areas or persons. While these measures may be taken at any time, it is obviously best, with an eye to the prevention of violations, for them to be taken at an early stage before any armed conflict breaks out.

The mandatory repression of grave breaches of the Geneva Conventions and of API requires states 'to enact any legislation necessary to provide effective penal sanctions' for their commission,[79] a jurisdiction which is then enforced according to the principle of *aut dedere aut judicare*—whereby states are under a legal obligation to search for alleged perpetrators and either place them on trial in their own courts or extradite them to any other state that wishes to do so.[80] In the large majority of states the implementation of this obligation has necessarily entailed the passage of special legislation creating new criminal offences and providing for extradition arrangements, as exemplified by the UK's Geneva Conventions

---

[74] See David Turns, 'Military Manuals and the Customary Law of Armed Conflict', in Hayashi (above n 73) 65. In this context they are cited by courts in both international and national jurisdictions: see eg the Israeli High Court of Justice's references to the UK's military manual in *Public Committee against Torture in Israel v Government of Israel* (2006) 46 ILM 375.

[75] Charles Garraway, 'Military Manuals, Operational Law and the Regulatory Framework of the Armed Forces', in Hayashi (above n 73) 45.

[76] See eg France Ministry of Defence, *Manuel de Droit des Conflits Armés* (2012 edn) https://www.defense.gouv.fr/sga/le-sga-en-action/droit-et-defense/droit-des-conflits-armes/droit-des-conflits-armes ; US Department of Defense (DoD), *Department of Defense Law of War Manual* (June 2015) (Updated December 2016) https://dod.defense.gov/Portals/1/Documents/pubs/DoD%20Law%20of%20War%20Manual%20-%20June%202015%20Updated%20Dec%202016.pdf?ver=2016-12-13-172036-190 .

[77] See eg UK Ministry of Defence (MoD), *The Joint Service Manual of the Law of Armed Conflict* (JSP 383) www.gov.uk/government/uploads/system/uploads/attachment_data/file/27874/JSP3832004Edition.pdf, and its book format (MoD (above n 35)).

[78] The German *Bundeswehr's ZDv 15/2—Humanitäres Völkerrecht in bewaffneten Konflikten* (1992) has been published in English with extensive academic commentary as Dieter Fleck (ed), *The Handbook of International Humanitarian Law* (3rd edn, OUP 2013).

[79] GCI article 49; GCII article 50; GCIII article 129; GCIV article 146. These provisions are then referred back to in a consolidating clause in API article 85(1). The Protocol also provides for mutual assistance between states parties in criminal matters connected with grave breaches: API article 88.

[80] As to the generalities of *aut dedere aut judicare*, see *Questions Relating to the Obligation to Prosecute or Extradite (Belgium v Senegal)* (Merits) [2012] ICJ Rep 422, Separate Opinion of Judge Yusuf at paras 18–22; ILC, 'The Obligation to Extradite or Prosecute (*aut dedere aut judicare*): Final Report of the International Law Commission', submitted to the UNGA by the ILC in 'Report of the International Law Commission on the Work of its 66th Session' UN Doc A/69/10 (1 May–6 June and 7 July–8 August 2014) para 65.

Act 1957 and Geneva Conventions (Amendment) Act 1995.[81] This process was given added impetus for many states in the years following the entry into force of the 1998 Rome Statute of the International Criminal Court, because of the need to implement the principle of complementarity of jurisdiction contained therein.[82] In addition to the punishment of grave breaches as war crimes, there is also specific provision for the penal repression by special legislation of any abuse of the various distinctive emblems of the Red Cross.[83] Various other IHL treaties, notably those that prohibit the use of specified types of weaponry, similarly contain obligations to criminalize in national law the conduct that is prohibited by treaty.[84]

Perhaps less obvious than the measures relating to penal repression by the creation of criminal offences in national law are various treaty provisions requiring specific practical actions by state authorities. These are generally of an unspectacular, often technical, nature: for example, there is an obligation 'to prepare in time of peace for the safeguarding of cultural property situated within their own territory against the foreseeable effects of an armed conflict, by taking such measures as [the High Contracting Parties] consider appropriate'.[85] States may conclude agreements as to the designation of demilitarized zones, with the aim of protecting an area and its civilian population against military operations,[86] although the ICRC has conceded somewhat enigmatically that, 'it is unlikely that two or more States will agree in advance to keep one or more zones clear of military operations in the event of a conflict breaking out between them: this seems, at least, a rather theoretical point'.[87] Although the rationale for the existence of the possibility in peacetime is thus not very clear, nevertheless it exists on the face of the law.

As military history has amply demonstrated, particularly since the Industrial Revolution, one of the most significant peacetime activities by states to have a direct bearing on armed conflict is the development of new weaponry. In light of the rules of IHL prohibiting the employment of weapons that are indiscriminate or that cause superfluous injury and unnecessary suffering, a precautionary requirement was introduced into the law in 1977:

> In the study, development, acquisition or adoption of a new weapon, means or method of warfare, a High Contracting Party is under an obligation to determine whether its

---

[81] See David Turns, 'Prosecuting Violations of International Humanitarian Law: The Legal Position in the United Kingdom' (1999) 4 *JACL* 1.

[82] See David Turns, 'Aspects of National Implementation of the Rome Statute: The United Kingdom and Selected Other States', in Dominic McGoldrick, Peter Rowe, and Eric Donnelly (eds), *The Permanent International Criminal Court—Legal and Policy Issues* (Hart Publishing 2004) 337.

[83] GCI article 54; GCII article 45; Protocol Additional to the Geneva Conventions of 12 August 1949, and Relating to the Adoption of an Additional Distinctive Emblem (adopted 8 December 2005, entered into force 14 January 2007) 2404 UNTS 261 (APIII) article 6(1).

[84] Eg CCW Amended Protocol II (1996) 35 ILM 1206 article 14.

[85] Convention for the Protection of Cultural Property in the Event of Armed Conflict (adopted 14 May 1954, entered into force 7 August 1956) 249 UNTS 240 (1954 Convention) article 3. This Convention also entails dissemination in terms virtually identical to those of the Geneva Conventions (ibid article 25); the production of quarterly reports to the Director General of the UN Educational, Scientific and Cultural Organisation 'concerning any measures being taken, prepared or contemplated' in fulfilment of the Convention (ibid article 26(2)); and the enactment of penal or disciplinary sanctions in domestic criminal law for violations of the Convention (ibid article 28). See further the Second Protocol to the Hague Convention of 1954 for the Protection of Cultural Property in the Event of Armed Conflict (adopted 26 March 1999, entered into force 9 March 2004) 2253 UNTS 172 articles 5, 11, 15–21.

[86] API article 60(2).

[87] Yves Sandoz, Christophe Swinarski, and Bruno Zimmermann (eds), *Commentary on the Additional Protocols of 8 June 1977 to the Geneva Conventions of 12 August 1949* (ICRC/Martinus Nijhoff 1987) (AP Commentary) para 2308.

employment would, in some or all circumstances, be prohibited by [API] or by any other rule of international law applicable ...[88]

While the precise methodologies, as well as the detailed substance, of these weapons reviews are classified by the states concerned for inevitable reasons of national security—and only a handful of High Contracting Parties to the Protocol are known to conduct them at all—an important recent move to greater openness in this context is the institution in 2015 of an annual Weapons Review Forum, convened on behalf of the UK MoD by the Development, Concepts and Doctrine Centre (DCDC) in the UK Defence Academy at Shrivenham. This initiative brought together state representatives, defence industry and procurement teams, academics, the ICRC and other NGOs to compare their practices and learn from each other's experiences.[89]

## B. Compliance during Armed Conflict

It is hardly necessary to state that the ideal position to attain is one of full compliance with the rules of IHL during actual situations of armed conflict, since those are the situations in which IHL applies. It is a tragedy for the law and perceptions thereof that in contemporary armed conflicts such compliance is usually conspicuous by its absence. All too often, insurgent NSAs that display scant respect for the law, and indeed have little incentive to comply with it, are pitted against state armed forces that persist in regarding the former as 'terrorists' and show correspondingly little inclination to give them the benefit of the law. Arguably there has not been a generally 'clean' armed conflict, in which both sides were scrupulous in their adherence as far as circumstances permitted to the letter and spirit of the law and where there were very few (if any) accusations of war crimes, since the Falklands War between Argentina and the UK in 1982. However, the picture is not irredeemably gloomy: for a variety of reasons, NSAs can and do engage with IHL, and accept and apply its principles.[90] Although it has never been used successfully, a mechanism exists in API whereby, as a consequence of the extended definition of international armed conflicts to include those 'in which peoples are fighting against colonial domination and against racist régimes in the exercise of their right of self-determination',[91] an authority representing such a people may make a unilateral declaration undertaking to apply the Geneva Conventions and the Protocol.[92] In reality, such putative declarations have been stymied by the relevant states' obfuscations due precisely to their unwillingness to accept the extended scope of application of API.[93]

---

[88] API article 36. For discussion, see Justin McClelland, 'The Review of Weapons in Accordance with Article 36 of Additional Protocol I' (2003) 85 *IRRC* 397; Kathleen Lawand, *A Guide to the Legal Review of New Weapons, Means and Methods of Warfare: Measures to Implement Article 36 of Additional Protocol I of 1977* (ICRC 2006).

[89] See MoD, 'UK Weapons Reviews' (Development, Concepts and Doctrine Centre) www.gov.uk/government/uploads/system/uploads/attachment_data/file/507319/20160308-UK_weapon_reviews.pdf.

[90] For general discussion, see Olivier Bangerter, 'Reasons Why Armed Groups Choose to Respect International Humanitarian Law or Not' (2011) 93 *IRRC* 353.

[91] API article 1(4).

[92] ibid article 96(3).

[93] For discussion of the UK's reservation to API in respect of articles 1(4) and 96(3) prompted by the situation in Northern Ireland, and the failure of the Palestine Liberation Organization to have its 1989 declaration accepted in relation to its struggle against Israel, see Turns, 'The Law of Armed Conflict' (above n 32).

This notwithstanding, it is possible for NSAs to signal their willingness to comply with IHL by both unilateral actions—such as accepting engagement with the ICRC, issuing internal codes of conduct and enforcing discipline,[94] making Deeds of Commitment,[95] and entering into special bilateral or multilateral agreements such as Memoranda of Understanding.[96]

Within regular organized armed forces, the principal mechanisms for securing compliance with IHL are the enforcement of military discipline and the doctrine of command responsibility. Armed forces are required to be subject to 'an internal disciplinary system which, *inter alia*, shall enforce compliance with the rules of international law applicable in armed conflict'.[97] This in turn relies on the commander's discharge of his responsibility to supervise his subordinates. Although command responsibility as a modern legal doctrine was created in less than ideal circumstances, and applied in a way that would surely be thrown out of court instantly today,[98] it is now mandated by IHL in the form of the requirement that commanders take all feasible measures to prevent or repress violations of the law committed by troops under their command, provided that they know or have information which should enable them to conclude in the circumstances at the time that such violations are being committed or going to be committed.[99] This is a form of liability based on omission, rather than commission; it is self-evident that a commander who actually orders his troops to commit a violation will be guilty as a principal of that crime. The Protocol places commanders under a positive duty to ensure that troops under their command are aware of their obligations under IHL, to prevent and suppress violations of the law by those troops, and to report such violations to the authorities and initiate disciplinary or penal action as required.[100] Although the language of the Protocol is couched exclusively in terms of military commanders, the latest form of the doctrine as enshrined in the 1998 Rome Statute of the International Criminal Court extends the concept to 'a person effectively acting as a military commander' and to persons not in traditional military-type superior–subordinate relationships, but where the superior has 'effective authority and control' over the subordinate.[101]

[94] See eg ICRC, 'A Collection of Codes of Conduct Issued by Armed Groups' (2011) 93 *IRRC* 483 (examples from China, the Philippines, Colombia, Uganda, Sierra Leone, and Libya).
[95] See Pascal Bongard and Jonathan Somer, 'Monitoring Armed Non-State Actor Compliance with Humanitarian Norms: A Look at International Mechanisms and the Geneva Call *Deed of Commitment*' (2011) 93 *IRRC* 673.
[96] For a useful overview of the typology of such commitments, see Sandesh Sivakumaran, 'Lessons for the Law of Armed Conflict from Commitments of Armed Groups: Identification of Legitimate Targets and Prisoners of War' (2011) 93 *IRRC* 463 at 465–9.
[97] API article 43(1). The internal disciplinary system of armed forces will typically be enforced by military police or provost-marshals, with investigations of cases where crimes appear to have been committed and subsequent prosecution in courts-martial or civilian courts, as appropriate. The military legal and disciplinary system in the UK is provided for in the regulations promulgated for each service (eg *The Queen's Regulations for the Army 1975* www.gov.uk/government/uploads/system/uploads/attachment_data/file/433769/QR_Army.pdf, with similar but separate regulations existing for the Royal Navy and the Royal Air Force) and the tri-service Armed Forces Act 2006.
[98] For an overview of the doctrine, see Guénaël Mettraux, *The Law of Command Responsibility* (OUP 2009).
[99] API article 86(2).
[100] ibid article 87.
[101] Rome Statute of the International Criminal Court (adopted 17 July 1998, entered into force 1 July 2002) 2187 UNTS 3 (Rome Statute) article 28.

## C. Post-Conflict Enforcement: Criminal Justice Mechanisms

The modern consciousness of IHL and its effective implementation has been developed through the prism of criminal justice: essentially this has meant the prosecution of persons alleged to have committed violations of the law in armed conflicts, as an outgrowth of the disciplinary powers of the commander discussed above. Until the advent of truly international criminal tribunals in the twentieth century, this justice was always dispensed by national criminal courts, which retained a nationality-based jurisdiction to prosecute soldiers of their own side who were accused of violating the laws of war,[102] and simultaneously asserted what came to be recognized as a universal jurisdiction likewise to prosecute soldiers of the adverse party after capture.[103] The nationality-based jurisdiction over own soldiers—the notion that military troops in effect carry the criminal law of their own country with them, wherever in the world they are deployed—remains an integral part of military law in all states to this day,[104] and has given rise to some of the most famous war crimes prosecutions of modern times, like those of Lieutenant William Calley for the massacre of civilians at My Lai during the Vietnam War,[105] and Sergeant Alexander Blackman for the murder of a wounded Taliban insurgent in Afghanistan.[106]

Putting aside the International Military Tribunals convened by the Allied Powers' occupation authorities in Germany and Japan after the Second World War, the first genuinely international tribunals for the prosecution of serious violations of IHL were established by the UN Security Council pursuant to its Chapter VII powers in the early 1990s.[107] They have since been followed by other ad hoc international or 'internationalized' tribunals,[108] generally established by special treaty agreements between the UN and the individual states concerned, but the most important progress was made by the adoption of the Rome Statute of the International Criminal Court ('ICC') in 1998. The ICC has been in existence since 2002 and has heard such pioneering cases in the enforcement of IHL as those involving the recruitment and use of child soldiers[109] and directing attacks against cultural property during armed conflict.[110] In addition, the Statute's articles providing for ICC jurisdiction over war crimes and crimes against humanity may to a considerable extent be viewed as a de facto codification of those crimes for the modern era. Although the primary jurisdiction to punish war crimes remains that of individual states according to their national legislation,

---

[102] For an early modern Anglo-Australian example, see the case of Lieutenants Harry Morant, Peter Handcock, and George Witton of the Bushveldt Carbineers, court-martialled and executed for the murder of prisoners of war during the Second Boer War: *The Brisbane Courier* (24 May 1902).

[103] For an early American example, see *Trial of Henry Wirz* (1865), US House of Representatives, 40th Congress, 2nd Session, Ex Doc No 23.

[104] This jurisdiction is based exclusively on national legislation. For instance, in the UK it is currently provided for by the International Criminal Court Act 2001, pt 5 (Offences under domestic law) and the Armed Forces Act 2006; in the US, by the Uniform Code of Military Justice (1950) 10 USC paras 802, 805, 877–934.

[105] *United States v William L Calley, Jr* (US Court of Military Appeals, 21 December 1973) 22 USCMA 534.

[106] *Reg v Blackman* (UK Courts Martial Appeal Court) [2014] EWCA Crim 1029 (22 May 2014).

[107] The International Criminal Tribunal for the Former Yugoslavia, established by UNSC Resolution 827 UN Doc S/RES/827 (25 May 1993); the International Criminal Tribunal for Rwanda, established by UNSC Resolution 955 UN Doc S/RES/955 (8 November 1994).

[108] For instance, the Special Court for Sierra Leone (established in 2000) and the Special Court for Kosovo.

[109] *The Prosecutor v Thomas Lubanga Dyilo* (Judgment) ICC-01/04-01/06, T Ch I (14 March 2012).

[110] *The Prosecutor v Ahmad Al Faqi Al Mahdi* (Decision on the Confirmation of Charges) ICC-01/12-01/15, Pre-Trial Ch I (24 March 2016).

the importance of having a permanent international court to punish the most serious violations of IHL can hardly be overstated in terms of the law's enforcement.


## D.  Non-Judicial Mechanisms of Implementation

Finally, a variety of mechanisms that do not involve judicial investigations, prosecutions,
or other legal sanctions fall to be considered under this generic heading. Although they are
mostly quite different from one another, they have in common that they generally seek to
obtain compliance with IHL by the exertion of external pressure and public scrutiny, as well
as unofficial monitoring and advocacy of issues related to violations of the law in armed
conflicts. For the purposes of discussion in this context, it is expedient broadly to divide
them into two types: those that are mandated by IHL itself, and those that are not.

### 1.  Mechanisms mandated by IHL

The four Geneva Conventions and API all contain provisions for the designation of
Protecting Powers to represent belligerent states' interests vis-à-vis their adverse parties
in situations of international armed conflict.[111] By this system, neutral states voluntarily
undertake to safeguard the supervision and implementation of IHL as between belligerents, who have no direct formal mutual diplomatic relations due to the existence of a state
of armed conflict between them. This is not to be confused with the more generic diplomatic protection of interests, whose protagonists are also often referred to as Protecting (or
Protective) Powers, but whose operation is not confined to situations of armed conflict.[112]
The system under IHL had its genesis in the late nineteenth century—it has been traced
in its modern form specifically to the Franco-Prussian War (1870–1871), when the US
Minister in Paris arranged the evacuation of citizens of the North German Confederation
from French territory—and was entirely a creature of customary law until its incorporation
into the codified framework of the Geneva Conventions.[113] Protecting Powers can fulfil a
valuable role in securing the protection of POWs by visiting camps and monitoring trials of
POWs and civilians of the adverse party and in making representations to the relevant belligerent concerning general compliance with IHL. Unfortunately, the system of Protecting
Powers has largely fallen into disuse in modern armed conflicts, principally because the
designation of a Protecting Power must be agreed by the adverse party. In most recent
armed conflicts such mutual agreement has not often been forthcoming, since it has been
difficult to find a neutral state maintaining equally good diplomatic relations with both parties to the conflict. The Falklands War (1982) was the last in which neither side objected to
the other's nominee.[114]

   Although one practical response to the decreasing use of Protecting Powers has been
to have recourse to the good offices of the ICRC, actually the role of the ICRC in securing

---

[111]  GCI, GCII, and GCIII article 8; GCIV article 9; API article 5.

[112]  Current examples are the Swiss diplomatic representation of American and Saudi interests in Iran and of
Russian interests in Georgia, and the Swedish representation of American, Australian, and Canadian interests in
North Korea.

[113]  See Howard S Levie, 'Prisoners of War and the Protecting Power' (1961) 55 *AJIL* 374.

[114]  Switzerland acted for the UK, while Brazil acted for Argentina. See ICRC, *Commentary on the First Geneva
Convention: Convention (I) for the Amelioration of the Condition of the Wounded and Sick in Armed Forces in the
Field* (2nd edn, ICRC 2016) paras 1115–1119.

compliance with IHL is clearly mandated in the law that has evolved since the first Geneva Convention in 1864. The ICRC has the right under treaty law to offer its impartial services in place of a Protecting Power, if none is designated,[115] and to visit and interview POWs,[116] and other protected persons,[117] as well as assisting in the institution and recognition of hospital and safety zones,[118] and various other specific humanitarian tasks on the battlefield. The organization also communicates regularly with the parties to armed conflicts with its observations and concerns as to their compliance—or lack thereof—with IHL; normally these communications are not published, in order to preserve the confidence of the belligerents as to the ICRC's neutrality and impartiality and discreetly to encourage compliance with IHL rather than pointing an accusatory finger, but on some rare occasions the organization has famously been moved to go public with its criticisms.[119] The ICRC Advisory Service on IHL, made up of expert legal advisers, assists states with the national implementation of IHL; through its network of Regional and National Delegations and delegates to armed forces and non-state armed groups (NSAGs), the organization maintains a strong global presence and is indefatigable in its advocacy of respect for IHL.

A further mechanism for monitoring compliance is available in the form of the International Humanitarian Fact-Finding Commission ('IHFFC'). This body was created in 1977,[120] and became operational in 1992, with a mandate impartially to investigate alleged violations of IHL and confidentially establish facts in cases of mutual allegations and denials of responsibility.[121] With seventy-six states having accepted its competence in accordance with the Protocol—although the Russian Federation notably withdrew its acceptance in 2019—in theory the IHFFC should be a prime tool for the enforcement of the law, except for the fact that the consent of both belligerent states or other parties to the conflict is required; it also has no powers of enforcement, but can simply issue confidential reports. To date the Commission has been used only once, to lead an independent forensic investigation in Luhansk province in Eastern Ukraine in 2017—a remarkable testimony to the reluctance of states, commented upon in the Introduction to this chapter, to submit their military actions to any kind of impartial authoritative scrutiny.

## 5. Conclusion: Other Mechanisms

In a world of twenty-four-hour rolling international news coverage, it is inevitable that situations of armed conflict should attract a great deal of attention from the media. The phenomenon often referred to as 'the CNN effect', while decidedly modern in terminology, arguably dates back in its earliest form to the horrified public fascination stimulated by photographs taken in the aftermath of the fighting on the great battlefields of the American

---

[115] GCI article 10. This has been the case, for instance, in respect of Russia and Georgia since their brief conflict over South Ossetia and Abkhazia in 2008.

[116] GCIII article 126.

[117] GCIV article 143.

[118] ibid article 14.

[119] See eg ICRC, 'Iran/Iraq Memoranda of 7 May 1983 and 10 February 1984' (Case Study, 12 January 2012) https://casebook.icrc.org/case-study/icrc-iraniraq-memoranda.

[120] API article 90.

[121] For further details of the IHFFC's mandate and work, see IHFFC, www.ihffc.org/index.asp?Language=EN&page=home.

Civil War (1861–1865).[122] Today, images of the atrocities of war are beamed into the living rooms and onto the smartphones of millions around the world on an almost daily basis. Users of social media are quick to vent their fury in apparently spontaneous reaction to missile strikes that have the effect, whether desired by the attacker or not, of harming the civilian population. In this kind of febrile environment it is not surprising that a multiplicity of non-governmental and civil society organizations thrive on bringing external scrutiny and pressure to bear on governments to account for the conduct of their armed forces in conflict: Amnesty International, Human Rights Watch, B'Tselem, MSF, and a myriad of other similar organizations serve to monitor violations and demand accountability in accordance with the law. While this advocacy has had the beneficial effect of helping to raise the profile of IHL and its application in armed conflicts, it has perhaps inevitably led to a backlash in some governmental and military quarters, where the term 'lawfare' has acquired increasing (and pejorative) currency.[123] In a British context especially, it has come to be used to decry the increasing involvement of European human rights organs as a tool for hampering military operations.[124] The growing tendency to apply the standards of civilian life to military operations in human rights complaints has also been condemned as the 'judicialisation of war'.[125]

The growing significance of interpretations of IHL by human rights bodies is also evidenced by the increasing tendency of such organs as the UN Human Rights Council to mandate commissions of inquiry, fact-finding missions, and other such bodies to report on situations where violations are alleged to have occurred.[126] Although these reports again have the effect of bringing discussions of IHL more into the public domain, the atmosphere is often openly inquisitorial, with the investigated state tending to withhold or restrict cooperation, resulting in an often blatantly one-sided report. Sometimes the mandate, too, is criticized for being one-sided in its focus on violations by state armed forces as opposed to NSAs. Discussion of such reports is all too often excessively politicized, with no discernible achievement other than to foreclose rational and balanced discussion of the substantive issues of IHL.

---

[122] One of the best-known examples is TH O'Sullivan's 'The Harvest of Death', depicting the bloated and contorted bodies of Federal soldiers killed at the Battle of Gettysburg in 1863.

[123] 'Lawfare' has been defined as, 'the strategy of using—or misusing—law as a substitute for traditional military means to achieve and operational objective': Charles J Dunlap, 'Lawfare Today: A Perspective' (Winter 2008) *Yale J Int'l Affairs* 146, 146.

[124] See Richard Ekins, Jonathan Morgan, and Tom Tugendhat, *Clearing the Fog of Law—Saving Our Armed Forces from Defeat by Judicial Diktat* (Policy Exchange 2015).

[125] The phrase was coined by Lord Hope in *Smith and Others v Ministry of Defence* [2013] UKSC 41, [2013] 2 WLR 27; see also Richard Scorer, 'The Judicialisation of War?' (2013) 163(7571) *NLJ*.

[126] See eg UN Human Rights Council (HRC), 'Report of the Commission of Inquiry on Lebanon pursuant to Human Rights Council Resolution S-2/1' UN Doc A/HRC/3/2 (23 November 2006); UNHRC 'Report of the United Nations Fact-Finding Mission on the Gaza Conflict' UN Doc A/HRC/12/48 (15 September 2009); UN, 'Report of the Secretary-General's Panel of Experts on Accountability in Sri Lanka' (31 March 2011) https://www.securitycouncilreport.org/atf/cf/%7B65BFCF9B-6D27-4E9C-8CD3-CF6E4FF96FF9%7D/POC%20Rep%20 on%20Account%20in%20Sri%20Lanka.pdf.

# 17

# International Humanitarian Law and International Human Rights Law

*Marco Sassòli**

## 1. Introduction

While international human rights law (IHRL), unlike international humanitarian law (IHL), was not founded specifically to protect people affected by armed conflicts, both branches of international law apply simultaneously during such conflicts. This raises the question of how they interrelate and also how possible contradictions between them can be resolved. After summarizing the traditional differences between the two branches, the chapter then determines when both branches apply simultaneously. Only then can the main question discussed in this chapter be approached: what law applies if, on a particular issue, the two branches contradict each other or otherwise lead to divergent results. Finally, the chapter briefly discusses whether the use of enforcement mechanisms created within one branch can help enforce the norms of the other.

## 2. Traditional Differences

Traditionally, analysts have stressed just how different IHL and IHRL are.[1] The former developed to regulate international armed conflicts (IACs), and therefore a comparison inevitably takes, as its starting point, the law applicable to such conflicts. Most contemporary armed conflicts, however, are not of an international character (and represent situations where the differences mentioned hereafter are less important).

IHL is one of the oldest branches of international law, while it has only been since the Second World War that international law has concerned itself with the protection of the human rights of all individuals who find themselves under the jurisdiction of a state. Despite all political correctness reigning in international fora, controversies about universality affect IHRL far more than IHL. On the other hand, because of the philosophical axiom driving IHRL, and as it applies to everyone everywhere, it has a much greater impact on public opinion and international politics than IHL. This is because IHL is applicable only in armed conflicts, which are themselves to be avoided in our era, where the use of force

* I would like to warmly thank Ms. Yvette Issar, LL.M., then research assistant and doctoral candidate at the University of Geneva, for her research, for her useful and challenging comments and for having revised this text, which has been written in 2016 and only very slightly updated in 2019.

[1] See for an extreme view Henri Meyrowitz, 'Le droit de la guerre et les droits de l'homme' (1972) 88(5) *Rev Droit Pen Mil & Droit Guerre* 1059.

in international relations has been outlawed. In reality, IHL is therefore increasingly influenced by human rights-like thinking.

While IHL applies only in armed conflicts, IHRL was primarily conceived for peacetime situations, although it also applies in times of armed conflict (see below part 3.A 'Material Scope of Armed Conflict'). The protection IHL offers individuals has not been expressed, as in IHRL, in terms of subjective rights of persons: rather, it results from objective rules of behaviour for states, armed groups, and (through them) individuals.

IACs are necessarily regulated by international law and all rules of IHL are conceived as applying universally. On the other hand, regional rules and mechanisms feature greatly in IHRL, and even today human rights are still seen as being governed mainly by national (constitutional) law. IHRL only provides for a framework and minimum requirements for domestic rules. As human rights cannot be protected and regulated solely by international rules, IHRL requires domestic legislation to guarantee the protected rights. Conversely, a number of issues arising in armed conflicts (eg the treatment of prisoners of war (POWs) or the conduct of hostilities) are exclusively regulated by IHL and do not necessarily require domestic law regulation, nor a legal basis in domestic law.

Both branches of international law are today largely codified. IHL, however, is codified in a broadly coherent international system of binding universal instruments, of which the more recent or specific clarify their relationship to the older or more general treaties. IHRL, conversely, is codified in an impressive number of instruments—both universal and regional, and binding and exhortatory, with some encompassing the whole range of human rights, others dealing with specific rights, and yet others focusing only on implementation. These instruments emerge, develop, are implemented and die in a relatively organic, uncoordinated manner.

As for their beneficiaries, IHRL requires that all human beings benefit equally from its protection, while the traditional approach of IHL, consistent with its development as inter-state law, has essentially been to protect enemy nationals. To protect them when they are in the power of a belligerent party, the IHL of IACs therefore defines a category of 'protected persons', which consists basically of enemy nationals who enjoy its full protection.[2] Those who are not 'protected persons' do benefit from a growing number of protective rules, which are particularly significant in non-international armed conflicts (NIACs), but which do not offer the full protection foreseen for 'protected persons'. When it comes to protection against (the effects of) hostilities, IHL is based upon the fundamental distinction between civilians and combatants, a distinction irrelevant for IHRL. The latter only admits differences in protection based upon the conduct of the individual in question, not upon their status. More generally, and beyond that between civilians and combatants, many other distinctions influence the determination of applicable IHL rules. Such distinctions play no role in IHRL, where, on the contrary, the principle of equality features prominently.

When it comes to protected rights, if rules of IHL are translated into rights and these are compared with those enshrined in IHRL, it becomes apparent that IHRL covers

---

[2]  See Geneva Convention (III) Relative to the Treatment of Prisoners of War (adopted 12 August 1949, entered into force 21 October 1950) 75 UNTS 135 (GCIII) article 4; Geneva Convention (IV) Relative to the Protection of Civilian Persons in Time of War (adopted 12 August 1949, entered into force 21 October 1950) 75 UNTS 287 (GCIV) article 4.

virtually all issues of human existence, most of which are not regulated by IHL (eg freedom of opinion, freedom of association, the right to social security, and so on). In armed conflicts, IHL only covers some human rights: those that are particularly endangered by armed conflicts[3] and are not, as such, incompatible with the very nature of armed conflicts.[4] Under IHL, these few rights are protected through much more detailed regulations that are better adapted to the specific problems arising in armed conflicts than the articulation of the same rights under IHRL, where they are formulated in a much more general, abstract manner.[5] In addition, IHL regulates some problems of vital import for protection in armed conflicts, which cannot meaningfully be translated into human rights (eg who may participate in hostilities, who may use the emblem of the red cross/red crescent, etc).

Ever since it was first codified, IHL has protected civil and political rights;[6] economic, social, and cultural rights;[7] and collective or group rights.[8] It has never distinguished between rules imposing a positive obligation on the state and those requiring the state to abstain from certain conduct. The positive obligation to collect and care for the wounded and sick is, for example, one of the oldest rules of modern, codified IHL,[9] which has always contained obligations not only to respect, but also to protect persons (including from the acts of private actors).[10]

When comparing their substantive rules, the differences between IHL and IHRL should not be over-emphasized. Both branches have the same aim—to ensure the respect for the lives and dignity of human beings—and the conduct or result required by both branches is the same on most issues. This convergence in substantive protection is even growing, in particular because the IHL applicable to NIACs (the most frequently occurring type) is increasingly influenced by IHRL and its implementation mechanisms. During armed conflicts, both branches prohibit the killing of civilians and detainees, torture, rape, and the taking of hostages. They both require the collection of and care for wounded and sick, humane treatment of detainees, and the respect of judicial guarantees in any trial. Simply, one of the two branches provides more detailed regulations, depending on the given situation. Their substantive rules actually differ significantly only in two respects: on the use of force against persons who are legitimate targets under IHL and on the admissible reasons, legal basis, and necessary procedural guarantees for interning enemies.

---

[3] Such as the rights to life, health, and personal freedom.

[4] For instance, the right to peace is by definition violated in armed conflicts and cannot be protected by IHL. The exercise of the right to self-determination through the use of force is one of the situations to which IHL of IACs applies, but that right cannot be protected by IHL.

[5] Thus the detailed precautionary measures in attack mentioned in Protocol Additional to the Geneva Conventions of 12 August 1949, and Relating to the Protection of Victims of Non-International Armed Conflicts (adopted 8 June 1977, entered into force 7 December 1978) 1125 UNTS 609 (API) article 57 translate the right to life and physical integrity of civilians into detailed rules of behaviour for those who conduct hostilities.

[6] Thus API article 41 protects the right to life of those who are *hors de combat*.

[7] Thus Geneva Convention (I) for the Amelioration of the Condition of the Wounded and Sick in Armed Forces in the Field (adopted 12 August 1949, entered into force 21 October 1950) 75 UNTS 31 (GCI) article 12 protects the right to health of wounded soldiers.

[8] Thus API articles 55–56 protect the right to a healthy environment.

[9] See currently GCI article 12 and Geneva Conventions Common Article 3(2).

[10] See GCI article 12; Geneva Convention (II) for the Amelioration of the Condition of Wounded, Sick and Shipwrecked Members of Armed Forces at Sea (adopted 12 August 1949, entered into force 12 October 1949) 75 UNTS 85 (GCII) article 13(2); GCIV article 27.

As explained in chapter 7 'International Humanitarian Law and the Conduct of Hostilities' in this book, under IHL rules on the conduct of hostilities, the use of deadly force against combatants and civilians directly participating in hostilities is considered legitimate. Under IHRL, use of lethal force is admissible only in extreme situations, after warnings and the attempt to arrest the target have been exhausted (where feasible). Under IHRL, the proportionality evaluation takes the right to life of the targeted individual into account. In addition, under IHRL each violent death must give rise to an inquiry, while the obligation is limited to special cases under IHL: deaths of POWs or civilian internees and cases of suspected war crimes. This makes it particularly important to determine the applicable rules in two types of situations. The first is where the dividing line between peace and armed conflict is blurred, for example at the lower threshold of violence sufficient for the law of NIACs to apply, or along the continuum between peacekeeping and peace enforcement operations. The second situation is where IHRL governs certain conduct even in armed conflicts, for example in law enforcement operations in NIACs or in occupied territories in IACs.[11]

Chapter 12 'Detention in Armed Conflict' in this book discusses the admissibility of detaining enemies. Under IHL of IACs, combatants may be detained as POWs until the end of active hostilities without judicial control, and civilians may be detained for imperative security reasons upon individual determination by a body, which must not necessarily be a fully independent and impartial tribunal in the sense of IHRL. Under IHRL instruments, admissible reasons for depriving anyone of their liberty are explicitly or implicitly limited. Furthermore, a domestic legal basis must exist for detention, and detailed procedural guarantees apply.

Particularly because of the two differences discussed above, it is crucial to determine the relationship between IHL and IHRL where they differ on substance. This is the main focus of this chapter. First however, we must clarify when these regimes apply. Indeed, if only one branch applies, the question of compatibility does not arise and contradiction is impossible. Hopefully, there exists no situation in which neither of the two branches applies, although this has been argued frequently in recent years.

## 3. When Do Both Branches Apply Simultaneously?

The first line of defence adopted by states wishing to disregard the substantive rules of IHL or IHRL is to claim that they do not apply. In some cases, the same objections are levelled to dispute the applicability of both branches. Examples include the arguments that neither branch binds international organizations (and that the conduct in question is only attributable to an international organization), or that UN Security Council resolutions prevail over obligations under both branches. Such objections are not of interest for this chapter. Most objections, however, concern only one branch, or apply differently in the case of the two branches. They are discussed below.

---

[11] International Committee of the Red Cross (ICRC), 'The Use of Force in Armed Conflicts: Interplay between the Conduct of Hostilities and Law Enforcement Paradigms, Expert Meeting Report' (ICRC 2013) iii, 6, 14, 16, 59.

## A. Material Scope of Application

IHL only applies to armed conflicts and its treaty rules sharply distinguish between IACs and NIACs, although the alleged customary rules (deduced from official practice) converge for both types of conflicts.[12] Controversies about whether a situation constitutes an IAC, a NIAC, or whether it is not an armed conflict at all (see chapter 2 'Classification of Armed Conflicts' in this book) obviously have implications for whether the IHRL answer to a certain question can at all be contradicted by the IHL answer. In addition, it is controversial how many rules of IHL of IACs equally apply *qua* customary law to NIACs, which in turn determines whether or not IHL and IHRL may at all contradict each other on a certain issue arising in a NIAC. Due to the increasing convergence of IHL of IACs and NIACs, there is an inevitable, but in my view highly questionable[13] tendency in scholarly writings, jurisprudence, and the views of most states to consider that the relationship between IHL and IHRL is the same in both kinds of conflicts.

IHRL protects human beings in all situations. Its applicability during armed conflicts has been re-affirmed time and time again by the UN Security Council, the International Court of Justice (ICJ), regional human rights courts, the UN General Assembly, and the UN Human Rights Council (and its predecessor) and its Special Procedures.[14]

## B. Possibility of Derogations

The European Convention on Human Rights (ECHR) contains a clause permitting a state to, '[i]n time of war or other public emergency threatening the life of the nation', take measures derogating from some of the rights protected by the Convention, but only 'to the extent strictly required by the exigencies of the situation, provided that such measures are not inconsistent with ... other obligations under international law'.[15] Moreover, the derogating state must inform the Council of Europe of the measures taken and provide justification. At least for IACs, the European Court of Human Rights (ECtHR) considers that an explicit derogation is not necessary.[16] However, some 'core human rights' are non-derogable. They include the right to life as well as prohibitions against torture, slavery, and the application of retroactive criminal laws. Other IHRL instruments contain similar provisions for situations threatening the life of the nation, but their lists of non-derogable rights are more extensive.[17]

---

[12] See Jean-Marie Henckaerts and Louise Doswald-Beck, *Customary International Humanitarian Law, Volume 1: Rules* (CUP 2005) (CIHL).

[13] See Marco Sassòli, 'The Convergence of the International Humanitarian Law of Non-International and of International Armed Conflicts: Dark Side of a Good Idea', in Giovanni Biaggini, Oliver Diggelmann, and Christine Kaufmann (eds), *Polis und Kosmopolis: Festschrift für Daniel Thürer* (Nomos 2015) 678.

[14] See, for a comprehensive overview, Cordula Droege, 'The Interplay between International Humanitarian Law and International Human Rights Law in Situations of Armed Conflict' (2007) 40 *Isr L Rev* 310, 314–17, 320–24.

[15] Convention for the Protection of Human Rights and Fundamental Freedoms (adopted 4 November 1950, entered into force 3 September 1953, 213 UNTS 222 (ECHR) article 15.

[16] *Hassan v UK* App No 29750/09 (ECtHR, 16 September 2014) paras 99–103.

[17] See International Covenant on Civil and Political Rights (adopted 16 December 1966, entered into force 23 March 1976) 999 UNTS 171 (ICCPR) article 4; American Convention on Human Rights (adopted 22 November 1969, entered into force 18 July 1978) 1144 UNTS 143 (ACHR) article 27.

Armed conflicts certainly constitute a situation 'threatening the life of the nation'. In my view, this must be equally true when a NIAC is conducted extraterritorially, without really threatening the life of the intervening state, as long as the life of the host state is threatened. The reference to 'other obligations' ensures that IHL constitutes, in armed conflicts, the minimum threshold below which derogations of human rights law may not extend. In addition, even where a derogation is admissible, arguably human rights bodies (and national courts) may verify in every individual case whether it is proportionate to the threat, namely that it is 'strictly required by the exigencies of the situation'.

IHL was made for armed conflicts, which are, by definition, situations of necessity. Derogations from IHL based on a state of necessity are therefore not permitted, except where specifically foreseen by an IHL rule.[18] One of those rules is article 5 of Geneva Convention IV (GCIV), which allows for derogations. On their own territories, states may thus limit the rights of protected persons who are 'definitely suspected of or engaged in activities hostile to the security of the State', if the exercise of those rights would be 'prejudicial to the security of such State'. In occupied territories, the same provision permits states to limit the communication rights set out in GCIV in the case of a protected person 'detained as a spy or saboteur, or as a person under definite suspicion of activity hostile to the security of the Occupying Power'. The rights to humane treatment and fair trial are, however, reserved. Independently of the relationship between IHL and IHRL when both apply, any derogation of rights protected by IHL that is not admissible under this provision would also be inadmissible under IHRL, because of the latter's requirement that derogations be compatible with 'other international obligations'.

## C. Geographical Scope of Application

The controversies about the geographical scope of application of IHL are discussed in chapter 3 'The Temporal ad Geographic Reach of International Humanitarian Law' in this book, but they have a particular impact on whether IHL and IHRL must be reconciled concerning a given problem.

The issue of whether IHRL applies extraterritorially is even more controversial than IHL's extraterritorial application. Most regional human rights conventions clearly indicate that the states parties must secure the rights listed in those conventions for everyone within their jurisdiction.[19] This includes in occupied territory.[20] At the universal level, however, according to the text of the International Covenant on Civil and Political Rights (ICCPR), a Party undertakes 'to respect and to ensure to all individuals within its territory *and* subject to its jurisdiction the rights recognized in the present Covenant . . .'.[21] This wording and the negotiating history lean towards understanding territory and jurisdiction as cumulative conditions under the ICCPR.[22] Therefore several states, such as the US and Israel, deny

---

[18] ILC, *Draft Articles on Responsibility of States for Internationally Wrongful Acts* UN Doc A/56/10 (November 2001), *Commentary*, article 25, [19], and [21]. The ICJ left this question open: *Legal Consequences of the Construction of a Wall in the Occupied Palestinian Territories* (Advisory Opinion) [2004] ICJ Rep 136 (*Palestinian Wall* case) para 140.

[19] ACHR article 1; ECHR article 1.

[20] *Loizidou v Turkey* ECHR 1996-VI 2216 para 56; *Cyprus v Turkey* ECHR 2001-IV para 77.

[21] ICCPR article 2(1) (emphasis added).

[22] See Michael J Dennis, 'Application of Human Rights Treaties Extraterritorially in Times of Armed Conflict and Military Occupation' (2005) 99 *AJIL* 119, 123–4.

that the ICCPR is applicable extraterritorially. The ICJ,[23] the United Nations Human Rights Committee (UNHRC),[24] and other states[25] are, however, of the opinion that the ICCPR applies in occupied territory. Indeed, from a teleological point of view, it is the occupying power rather than the territorial state that can actually violate or protect the rights of individuals in such cases. However, a limitation of the extraterritorial application of certain rights, in particular of economic, social, and cultural rights, results from the limited legislative powers of occupying powers under the law of occupation.[26]

If IHRL applies extraterritorially, the next question that arises is when a person can be considered to be under a state's jurisdiction. The jurisprudence of human rights bodies is evolving and not always coherent, but it now clearly suggests that not only territorial control, but also control over persons (such as those detained), is sufficient to constitute jurisdiction.[27] Some isolated cases go even further, and certain authors go as far as to conclude that a person is under the jurisdiction of a state as soon as the latter can affect their rights.[28] One solution to this question lies in adopting a functional approach, requiring a different degree of territorial/personal control for every right protected or even for every obligation resulting from a right (eg positive and negative obligations).[29] Such a 'sliding scale' approach would reconcile the object and purpose of human rights—to protect everyone—with both the need not to bind states by guarantees they cannot deliver outside territory they fully control (in particular, obligations to protect and to fulfil) and concerns about the sovereignty of the territorial state. The latter interest may be encroached upon by foreign forces present with the state's consent, if the former protect and fulfil human rights with respect to the general population and not only in relation to their own conduct.

### D. IHL Only Applies to Conduct That Has a Nexus with an Armed Conflict

Even during an armed conflict and on territory controlled by a party, conduct is only governed by IHL if it has a nexus to the armed conflict.[30] The nexus concept has been developed mainly in the context of international criminal jurisprudence (through the requirement that a war crime has a nexus to the conflict),[31] but the nexus required for the applicability

---

[23] *Palestinian Wall* case, paras 107–112; *Armed Activities on the Territory of the Congo (Dem Rep Congo v Uganda)* (Merits) [2005] ICJ Rep 168 (*Armed Activities* case), paras 216–217.

[24] UN Human Rights Committee (UNHRC), 'Concluding Observations of the Human Rights Committee: Israel' UN Doc CCPR/C/79/Add.93 (18 August 1998) para 10; UNHRC, 'General Comment No 31 [80], The Nature of the General Legal Obligation on States Parties to the Covenant' UN Doc CCPR/C/21/Rev.1/Add.13 (General Comment No 31) (26 May 2004) para 10.

[25] UK Ministry of Defence (MoD), *The Manual of the Law of Armed Conflict* (OUP 2004) 282.

[26] The ICJ held in the *Palestinian Wall* case, para 112 that an occupying power was only bound by economic social and cultural rights '[i]n the exercise of the powers available to it on this basis', but had in addition 'an obligation not to raise any obstacle to the exercise of such rights in those fields' where it had no jurisdiction.

[27] *Hassan* (above n 16) paras 75–76. A comprehensive overview may be found in *Al Skeini v UK* App No 55721/07 (ECtHR, 7 July 2011) paras 130–42.

[28] Noam Lubell, *Extraterritorial Use of Force against Non-State Actors* (OUP 2010) 220–4.

[29] See John Cerone, 'Human Dignity in the Line of Fire: The Application of International Human Rights Law During Armed Conflict, Occupation, and Peace Operations' (2006) 39 *Vand J Transnat'l L* 1447, 1494–507; Ralph Wilde, 'Triggering State Obligations Extraterritorially: The Spatial Test in Certain Human Rights Treaties', in Roberta Arnold and Noëlle Quénivet (eds), *International Humanitarian Law and Human Rights: Towards a New Merger in International Law* (Martinus Nijhoff 2008) 144–52.

[30] *Prosecutor v Tadić* (Judgment) ICTY-94-1 (7 May 1997) paras 573–575.

[31] See Guénaël Mettraux, *International Crimes and the Ad Hoc Tribunals* (OUP 2005) 38–61.

of IHL rules (which may or may not be the same) remains largely underexplored. The type and degree of nexus required would likely differ for different rules of IHL. In any case, if certain conduct has no nexus with the conflict, it can only be governed by IHRL (if attributable to a state or, possibly, an armed group). No contradiction with IHL is possible in such cases.

## E. Addressees

### 1. Armed non-state actors

Most participants in the most frequent armed conflicts today, which are not of an international character, are armed non-state actors (ANSAs). The latter are directly addressed by both treaty and customary IHL. On the other hand, IHRL is traditionally held to bind only states. Only very few scholars advocated that entities other than the state—and ANSAs more problematically—had IHRL obligations.[32] While it remains a minority view, the claim has gained traction in recent years. It is also reflected in the terminology employed by international organs, which previously referred to human rights 'abuses' committed by ANSAs, but now increasingly refer to human rights 'violations'.[33] The Office of the UN High Commissioner for Human Rights has recently stated that '[i]t is increasingly considered that *under certain circumstances* non-state actors can also be bound by international human rights law and can assume, voluntarily or not, obligations to respect, protect and fulfill human rights'.[34] Even the most state-centric body, the UN Security Council, refers to ANSAs in a manner that suggests that the latter have human rights obligations.[35] One treaty that is seen by many as an IHRL instrument—the Optional Protocol on Children in Armed Conflict—arguably also directly addresses ANSAs.[36]

However, it is not very clear precisely what 'circumstances' need to be present for IHRL obligations to attach to armed groups. The practice of certain international bodies suggests

[32] August Reinisch, 'The Changing International Legal Framework for Dealing with Non-State Actors', in Philip Alston (ed), *Non-State Actors and Human Rights* (OUP 2005) 38, referred to a 'radical conceptual change in the way we use and think about human rights' and 'a new awareness of the need to protect human rights, beyond the classic paradigm of the powerful state against the weak individual, to include protection against increasingly powerful non-state actors'. See also Daragh Murray, *Human Rights Obligations of Non-State Armed Groups* (Hart 2016); Katharine Fortin, *The Accountability of Armed Groups under Human Rights Law* (OUP 2017); Andrew Clapham, *Human Rights Obligations of Non-State Actors* (OUP 2006); Andrea Bianchi, 'Globalization of Human Rights: The Role of Non-state Actors', in Gunther Teubner (ed), *Global Law Without a State* (Dartmouth 1997); Tilman Rodenhäuser, *Organizing Rebellion, Non-State Armed Groups under International Humanitarian Law, Human Rights Law and International Criminal Law* (OUP 2018) 115–212,
[33] The term 'abuse' was preferred for armed groups, as the traditional view held that strictly speaking armed groups could not 'violate' human rights. For an endorsement of the traditional approach by an eminent human rights defender, see Nigel S Rodley, 'Can Armed Opposition Groups Violate Human Rights Standards?', in Kathleen Mahoney and Paul Mahoney (eds) *Human Rights in the Twenty-First Century* (Kluwer 1993) 297.
[34] Office of the High Commissioner for Human Rights (OHCR), *International Legal Protection of Human Rights in Armed Conflicts* (United Nations 2011) 24 (emphasis added).
[35] See Aristoteles Constantinides, 'Human Rights Obligations and Accountability of Armed Opposition Groups: The Practice of the UN Security Council' (2010) 4 *HR&ILD* 89.
[36] See Seura Yun, 'Breaking Imaginary Barriers: Obligations of Armed Non-State Actors under General Human Rights Law—the Case of the Optional Protocol to the Convention on the Rights of the Child' [2014] *JIHLS* 213, saying that Optional Protocol to the Convention on the Rights of the Child on the Involvement of Children in Armed Conflict (adopted 25 May 2000, entered into force 12 February 2002) 2171 UNTS 227 article 4(1), prescribing that armed groups 'should' not engage in certain conduct, was meant to create full legal obligations. The African Union Convention for the Protection and Assistance of Internally Displaced Persons in Africa (adopted 22 October 2009; entered into force 6 December 2012) (2010) 49 ILM 83, article 7(1) also addresses armed groups.

that armed groups that are de facto authorities are bound by IHRL, due to their control of territory and the governmental functions they exercise therein.[37] One scholar has argued that this is the result of the recent debate on states' extraterritorial human rights obligations.[38] Shrouded in similar uncertainty is the question of exactly *which* IHRL norms may bind ANSAs.[39] In any case, many of them have to be reformulated to become meaningful for armed groups.[40] Under one view, the more territorial control a group has and/or the more governmental functions it exercises, the more IHRL obligations attach to it.[41] It has, understandably, been easier for states to accept that armed groups may be bound by 'negative' obligations to *refrain* from particular conduct (such as, eg, recruiting children into their armed forces)[42] than by 'positive' obligations (such as, eg, the provision of education and health care in territories under their control), as the latter are functions considered to be proper to government.[43]

If one accepts that ANSAs are bound by the positive obligations in IHRL, it remains to be delimited exactly which norms they are bound to uphold. Are they bound only by positive obligations on issues that—to use IHL terminology—have a 'nexus' with the armed conflict? Or do those obligations stretch to cover all of the everyday rights of persons under their control? In order to respect certain positive obligations, such as that to provide a fair trial, may an armed group legislate, or is it expected to implement the laws of the state whose territory it has taken over (similar to what an occupying power is supposed to do under GCIV)?

## 2. *Individuals*

At least those rules of IHL the violation of which constitutes a war crime apply to every act committed with a nexus to the conflict,[44] even if the perpetrator does not belong to any party to the conflict and acts outside any structure of authority. Many claim that even beyond war crimes some IHL rules bind individuals, because the parties to a treaty so intended, because the treaties are self-executing, or because (it is claimed) all rules of customary IHL are binding upon individuals.[45] Violations of some IHRL rules are also criminalized as international crimes and therefore bind individuals.

For the remaining rules, as discussed above in section 3.E.1 'Armed non-state actors' dealing with armed groups, different theories have been put forward to support claims that IHRL binds all those who exercise governmental authority, or even every organ of society.

---

[37]  See Constantinides (above n 35) 101–3.

[38]  Yaël Ronen, 'Human Rights Obligations of Territorial Non-State Actors' (2013) 46 *Cornell ILJ* 21, 25–7.

[39]  ibid 22; Jonathan Somer, 'Education and Armed Non-State Actors: Towards a Comprehensive Agenda' (Background Paper for the PEIC/Geneva Call Workshop, PEIC 2015), 26.

[40]  Ronen (above n 38) 30–1: 'The existing human rights catalogue is, by definition, a catalogue of human rights in state–individual relations. An international human rights catalogue tailored for other relationships, namely between individuals and actors other than states, might well differ from the one currently prevailing.' See also Murray (above n 32) 172–202, proposing a gradated application of IHRL obligations to NSAGs, and 205–71, testing such approach with respect to the right to prosecution, detention, and the right to health.

[41]  See Ronen (above n 38); Fortin (above n 32) 240–84, and Murray (above n 32) 120–54.

[42]  See UNSC, 'Report of the Secretary-General on Children and Armed Conflict' UN Doc S/2002/1299 (2002) para 3; UNHRC, 'Annual Report of the Special Representative of the Secretary-General for Children and Armed Conflict, Radhika Coomaraswamy' UN Doc A/HRC/15/58 (2010) para 16.

[43]  Somer (above n 39) 26.

[44]  *Prosecutor v Tadić* (Decision on the Defence Motion on Jurisdiction) ICTY-94-1 (2 October 1995) para 70; *Prosecutor v Akayesu* (Judgment) ICTR-96-4-A, A Ch (1 June 2001) paras 425–446.

[45]  See Lindsey Cameron and Vincent Chetail, *Privatizing War, Private Military and Security Companies under Public International Law* (CUP 2013) 350–82, with further references.

Some instruments also prescribe duties for individuals.[46] In addition, states not only have an obligation to respect human rights, but also to protect the rights of individuals under their jurisdiction against other individuals.[47] This must be implemented, inter alia, through legislative measures that are, by definition, binding upon individuals. In addition, some states have provided victims of IHRL violations access to tort claims against those responsible.[48] States have attempted to specify international legal obligations and best practices for private military and security companies working in conflict areas (whose employees are, obviously, individuals), many of which are based upon IHRL.[49] Finally, companies have more or less voluntarily accepted codes of conduct[50] that are often based upon IHL and IHRL provisions, translated to reflect the specificities of private companies.[51]

## 4. How to Deal with Divergences if Both Branches Apply?

When both IHL and IHRL apply and lead to divergent results, the nature of the relationship between them is a controversial matter, regarding both the terminology used to reflect the relationship and the practical outcomes of it. At the centre of these controversies is the *lex specialis* principle, increasingly contested in scholarly writings. Some preliminary issues that blur the debate must first be discussed. I then suggest solutions, which I derive from a correct understanding of the *lex specialis* principle, but which do not differ greatly from solutions found by those who reject the term.

### A. The Traditional Starting Point: the *Lex Specialis* Principle

Traditionally, the problems of application and interpretation caused by the overlapping of IHL and IHRL are resolved by invoking the maxim *lex specialis derogat legi generali*, namely the more special rule prevails over the more general rule, discussed further below. The ICJ has considered that '[t]he test of what is an arbitrary deprivation of life ... falls to be determined by the applicable *lex specialis*, namely, the law applicable in armed conflict which

---

[46] Universal Declaration of Human Rights (adopted 10 December 1948) UNGA Resolution 217 A(III) (UDHR) article 29; African Charter on Human and Peoples' Rights (adopted 27 June 1981, entered into force 21 October 1986) 1520 UNTS 217 articles 27, 28.

[47] See eg *Mahmut Kaya v Turkey, Merits, App No 22535/93*, ECHR 2000-III, Judgment of 28 March 2000, especially [85]–[101].

[48] See the US Alien Torts Claims Act 28 USC para 1350.

[49] See 'Montreux Document on Pertinent International Legal Obligations and Good Practices of States Related to Operations of Private Military and Security Companies during Armed Conflicts, 17 September 2008' (Swiss Department of Foreign Affairs and ICRC).

[50] See eg Organisation for Economic Co-Operation and Development (OECD), *OECD Guidelines for Multinational Enterprises* (2000 rev, OECD 2008); 'Voluntary Principles for Security and Human Rights' www.voluntaryprinciples.org; 'The International Code of Conduct for Private Security Service Providers (ICoC)' (9 November 2010) http://icoca.ch/sites/all/themes/icoca/assets/icoc_english3.pdf.

[51] See also generally on human rights obligations of business companies United Nations, *Guiding Principles on Business and Human Rights: Implementing the United Nations 'Protect, Respect and Remedy' Framework* (HR/PUB/11/04) (UN 2011). See also specifically on private military and security companies Lindsey Cameron, 'Private Military Companies: Their Status under International Humanitarian Law and Its Impact on their Regulation' (2006) 863 *IRRC* 574, 595–6, and Nicki Boldt, 'Outsourcing War: Private Military Companies and International Humanitarian Law' (2004) 47 *German YB Int'l L* 502, at 529, on private military companies' self-imposed codes of conduct.

is designed to regulate the conduct of hostilities.'[52] The Inter-American Commission on Human Rights, for its part, has affirmed that:

> ... in a situation of armed conflict, the test for assessing the observance of a particular right [protected by the American Declaration of the Rights and Duties of Man 1948], may, under given circumstances, be distinct from that applicable in a time of peace. For that reason, the standard to be applied must be deduced by reference to the applicable *lex specialis*.[53]

As for the UNHRC, it writes that 'more specific rules of international humanitarian law may be specially relevant for the purposes of the interpretation of Covenant rights'.[54] Depending on how the *lex specialis* principle is understood, the Committee's statement can be considered as supporting the principle. The International Law Commission has also used *lex specialis* to discuss the relationship between IHL and IHRL in the Report of its Study Group on the Fragmentation of International Law.[55]

## B. Alternatives to the *Lex Specialis* Principle

The ECtHR has avoided using the term '*lex specialis*', but has recently finally accepted that human rights guarantees 'should be accommodated, as far as possible' within applicable provisions of IHL treaties.[56] In scholarly writings, the employment of the *lex specialis* principle to discuss the relationship between IHL and IHRL is increasingly contested.[57] Although scholars invariably point out that the ICJ dropped the term in the latest relevant case,[58] the ICJ did not provide any suggestions for alternative ways that contradictions between the two branches could be resolved.

Some of the critics want to apply IHL and IHRL cumulatively.[59] They may indeed base their views upon what international tribunals actually do and upon a textual reading of most resolutions of the Security Council.[60] However, in practice, this would mean IHRL

---

[52] *Legality of the Threat of Use of Nuclear Weapons* (Advisory Opinion) [1996] ICJ Rep 66 (*Nuclear Weapons*), para 25.

[53] *Coard v United States*, Case No 10.951, Report No 109/99, IACommHR (29 September 1999) paras 38–44; see also Inter-American Commission of Human Rights (IACommHR), 'Detainees in Guantánamo Bay, Cuba (Request for Precautionary Measures)' (2002) 41 *ILM* 532.

[54] General Comment No 31 (above n 24), para 11.

[55] International Law Commission (ILC), 'Fragmentation of International Law: Difficulties Arising from the Diversification and Expansion of International Law, Report of the Study Group of the International Law Commission' UN Doc A/CN.4/L.682 (1 May–9 June and 3 July–11 August 2006, finalized by Martti Koskenniemi) paras 104–105.

[56] *Hassan* (above n 16), para 104.

[57] Nancie Prud'homme, 'Lex Specialis: Oversimplifying A More Complex and Multifaceted Relationship?' (2007) 40 *ILR* 356, 378–86; Gerd Oberleitner, *Human Rights in Armed Conflict: Law, Practice, Policy* (CUP 2015) 88, 95, 99, 103–4; Marko Milanović, 'Norm Conflicts, International Humanitarian Law, and Human Rights Law', in Orna Ben-Naftali (ed), *International Humanitarian Law and International Human Rights Law* (OUP 2011) 98, 115, 116, 124; Françoise Hampson and Noam Lubell, 'Amicus Curiae Brief Submitted to the ECtHR in *Hassan v UK*' (Human Rights Centre University of Essex 2014) 18 www.essex.ac.uk/hrc/documents/practice/amicus-curae.pdf.

[58] *Armed Activities* case para 216.

[59] Walter Kälin, *Human Rights in Times of Occupation: The Case of Kuwait* (Stämpfli 1994) 27.

[60] Gloria Gaggioli, *L'influence mutuelle entre les Droits de l'Homme et le droit international humanitaire à la lumière du droit à la vie* (Pedone 2013) 39–40.

completely overriding IHL on crucial issues like the admissible degree of the use of force and the admissible reasons of detention, because states would always have to respect the more demanding and restrictive standards of IHRL to comply with their international obligations (unless, of course, they derogate from their IHRL obligations). This leads to unrealistic results that are not even suggested by proponents of this approach (eg under the ECHR POWs could not be interned or combatants could only be attacked if they presented an immediate threat to human life).

Others seek to solve possible contradictions through systemic integration or interpretation, taking other applicable rules of international law into account, as prescribed by article 31(3)(c) of the Vienna Convention on the Law of Treaties 1969.[61] This is indeed what the ECtHR claimed to do when it 'accommodated' the requirements of article 5 of the ECHR within IHL.[62] However, it is not possible to add—to a list of five exhaustively enumerated reasons justifying a deprivation of liberty in article 5 of the ECHR—a *sixth* admissible reason, and consider this addition an 'interpretation' of the original five reasons. This case can only be solved by letting the IHL provisions prevail as *lex specialis* (while admittedly for other human rights instruments, the same result can be achieved by merely interpreting the term 'arbitrary' in the prohibitions on deprivations of life and personal liberty in light of the applicable IHL).

Still other scholars suggest a flexible set of variables, depending on the case to be decided. They want to find the solution on a spectrum between, on the one hand, situations where IHRL is only breached if IHL is breached and, on the other hand, situations in which the two branches have to be blended, rather than necessarily taking a uniform approach to the interaction across the board.[63] It may indeed be the case that in actual practice the relationship between IHL and IHRL varies depending on the subject matter or rules in question. This may be an intellectually correct description of what human rights organs and decision makers do, but it is too sophisticated an approach to be applied in practice by a soldier who has to decide in split seconds whether to target under IHL, or to issue a warning and attempt arrest under IHRL. It opens the door to abuse, subjectivity, and manipulation.

Finally, some go one step further and seek, in some cases, to abandon, at least for international law, the pretence that the legal order provides only one solution—and therefore I would add *any solution*. They prefer to solve the few real conflicts through the political process.[64] This is, in my view, a surrender of law as a distinct science. The grand delusion of law, but at the same time the essence of the rule of law, is that decision-makers apply norms, including when they contradict other norms, according to legal rules and *not* according to policy preferences.

[61] Jean D'Aspremont and Elodie Tranchez, 'The Quest for a Non-Conflictual Coexistence of International Human Rights Law and Humanitarian Law: Which Role for the Lex Specialis Principle?', in Robert Kolb and Gloria Gaggioli (eds), *Research Handbook on Human Rights and Humanitarian Law* (Elgar 2013) 235–8, with further references.

[62] *Hassan* (above n 16) para 104.

[63] Hampson and Lubell (above n 57), paras 26–30. Their approach seems to develop the 'theory of harmonization' suggested by Prud'homme (above n 57) 386–93.

[64] Milanović, 'Norm Conflicts' (above n 57) 98, 124.

## C. Factors Blurring the Debate on What Prevails When IHL and IHRL Contradict Each Other

Debates on what applies when IHL and IHRL differ are often confused by unresolved controversies about questions that have nothing to do with the relationship between IHL and IHRL, but rather involve uncertainties pertaining either to one or the other of the two branches, to definitions and terminology, or to the understanding of what the term *lex specialis* means.

### 1. What is a contradiction?

First, one needs to clarify when two rules may be considered to lead to different solutions.[65] The most restrictive understanding is that two rules only differ if one prescribes certain conduct that the other rule prohibits (all other divergences requiring merely systemic interpretation of rules in conformity with the rest of international law).[66] If this is correct, the only contradiction between IHL and IHRL I am aware of is that between the prohibition on bringing civilians before military courts under the jurisprudence of the ECtHR[67] and the obligation of an occupying power to try civilians for security offences *only* before its military courts[68] under IHL applicable in military occupation (the establishment of civilian courts by an occupying power being tantamount to annexation).

A broader understanding of contradictions would also cover *potential* conflicts, namely situations in which IHL does not prohibit or—according to many—even authorizes conduct prohibited by IHRL (eg, interning enemy combatants without any individual procedure to determine the legality of such internment).[69] Although below I will explain my doubts as to whether many IHL rules actually authorize conduct, it remains that I prefer this wider understanding of contradictions. Moreover, I suggest applying the *lex specialis* principle equally when a rule of either branch provides additional details as compared to the other. I admit, however, that such cases may simply be solved by systemic interpretation or integration.

### 2. Does IHL provide for authorizations?

If IHL does provides for authorizations, such authorizations may either contradict prohibitions foreseen in IHRL or provide the legal basis required by IHRL for legitimate limitations on human rights. In a discussion of the relationship between IHL and IHRL, it is therefore necessary to enquire whether IHL contains such authorizations.

When Henry Dunant initiated the codification of modern IHL after the battle of Solferino, it was seen as requiring states (and, later, armed groups) to do certain things—for

[65] See, for what follows, Joost Pauwelyn, *Conflict of Norms in Public International Law, How WTO Law Relates to other Rules of International Law* (CUP 2004) 164–200.
[66] Wilfred Jenks, 'Conflict of Law-Making Treaties' (1953) 30 *BYIL* 401, 426; Wolfram Karl, 'Conflicts between Treaties', in Rudolf Bernhardt (ed), *Encyclopedia of Public International Law, Vol VII* (North-Holland 1984) 468; Hans Kelsen, *Reine Rechtslehre* (2nd edn, Verlag Franz Deuticke 1960) 209; Gabrielle Marceau, 'Conflicts of Norms and Conflicts of Jurisdiction: The Relationship between the WTO Agreement and MEAs and other Treaties' (2001) 35 *JWT* 1081, 1084.
[67] *Cyprus v Turkey* (above n 20) paras 354–59.
[68] GCIV article 66.
[69] Koskenniemi (above n 55) paras 24–25; Gaggioli (above n 60) 51; Anja Lindroos, 'Addressing Norm Conflicts in a Fragmented System: The Doctrine of Lex Specialis' (2005) 74 *Nordic J Int'l L* 27, 46; Pauwelyn (above n 65) 167–70.

example, to collect and care for the wounded and sick—and as prohibiting other things—for instance, attacks on medical personnel. All existing treaty IHL may still be read in this sense. Some states, in particular the US since the beginning of its 'war on terror', increasingly argue, however, that IHL equally provides authorization for certain conduct. The question of whether states need authorization under international law at all or whether it is sufficient that they do not violate legal prohibitions has haunted international law since the famous *Lotus* case before the Permanent Court of International Justice in 1927.[70] In the field of IHL, the famous Martens Clause of 1899 adds complexity to this debate, according to which:

> ... in cases not included in the Regulations ... populations and belligerents remain under the protection and empire of the principles of international law, as they result from the usages established between civilized nations, from the laws of humanity, and the requirements of the public conscience.[71]

This fundamental challenge for the theory of international (humanitarian) law is over-shadowed by a very practical requirement of IHRL. Interferences in human rights, in particular in the rights to life and personal freedom, must have a legal basis.[72]

For IACs, it is difficult to deny that IHL contains certain authorizations. Many consider that combatant privilege implies a 'right to kill' enemy combatants.[73] Article 43(2) of API indeed states that 'combatants ... have the right to participate directly in hostilities'. Concerning the deprivation of personal freedom of POWs, the case is even clearer. Article 21 of GCIII states: '[t]he Detaining Power may subject prisoners of war to internment'. No state has legislated to provide a legal basis for interning POWs or to provide for any procedure for deciding to intern them, which would be required by most domestic laws and IHRL, if IHL itself did not authorize, and constitute a sufficient legal basis for, the internment of POWs without any individual assessment.

Treaty IHL of NIACs does not contain any similar explicit rules that could be seen as authorizing deliberate killings or detention without trial. Admittedly, neither does it prohibit detention without trial or targeting members of armed groups (except if they have laid down their arms). For such issues not regulated by an IHL rule as the *lex specialis*, one would therefore normally have to look to the IHRL rule, which allows deliberate killings only if they are absolutely necessary to protect human life (or to quell a riot),[74] and internment only where there is a legal basis and the possibility to challenge the detention's lawfulness before a court.[75] However, if the IHL of IACs was applied by analogy or *qua* customary law to NIACs, targeted killings of suspected associates of Al Qaeda would be authorized (as

---

[70]   *SS Lotus (France v Turkey)* (Judgment) PCIJ Series A No 10 para 53.

[71]   Preamble of Hague Convention (II) with Respect to the Laws and Customs of War on Land and its annex: Regulations concerning the Laws and Customs of War on Land (adopted 29 July 1899; entered into force 4 September 1900) 187 CTS 429 (Hague Convention II).

[72]   See eg ICCPR articles 6 and 9(1); Human Rights Committee (HRC), 'General Comment No. 36 on Article 6 of the International Covenant on Civil and Political Rights, on the Right to Life' CCPR/C/GC/36 (30 October 2018) paras 11 and 13 https://tbinternet.ohchr.org/Treaties/CCPR/Shared%20Documents/1_Global/CCPR_C_GC_36_8785_E.pdf; HRC, 'General Comment No. 35—Article 9 (Liberty and Security of Person) CCPR/C/GC/35 (16 December 2014) para 11.

[73]   Yoram Dinstein, *The Conduct of Hostilities under the Law of International Armed Conflict* (2nd edn, CUP 2010) 33.

[74]   See eg ECHR article 2.

[75]   See eg ibid article 5.

the Obama Administration argued). Similarly, the internment of members of armed groups based upon the 'laws of war' and in the absence of individual determination would be authorized (as the Bush Administration initially argued for those held in Guantánamo).[76]

In December 2015, states adopted, by consensus, a resolution entitled 'Strengthening international humanitarian law protecting persons deprived of their liberty' which, however, recognized in a preambular paragraph that 'under international humanitarian law (IHL) States [but, interestingly, not armed groups] have in all forms of armed conflicts ... the power to detain'.[77] This would mean that IHL, which was intended to protect those affected by armed conflicts, has become a justification for denying persons detained by states in NIACs protections under IHRL and domestic legislation. I have serious doubts as to whether any human rights body or domestic judge would recognize such an inherent authorization to detain in NIACs as a sufficient legal basis for depriving persons of their freedom. I doubt even more that such alleged IHL authorization may, as *lex specialis,* dispense with *habeas corpus* guarantees under IHRL. For the time being, UK courts share both doubts.[78] The possible legal reasons to justify such authorization—an analogy to IHL of IACs (which is very different in this respect), or an alleged customary rule (which fortunately lacks sufficiently widespread state practice)—are, in my view, very weak.

### 3. Controversies concerning the meaning and applicability of the lex specialis principle

The meaning of the *lex specialis* principle and its field of application are controversial even among those who use this terminology. Some claim it applies only to contradictions between rules of the same treaty or the same branch of international law.[79] I have myself expressed doubt as to whether the principle can resolve contradictions between customary rules, if these are—as they should traditionally be—derived from state practice and *opinio juris* (however, I admitted that the *lex specialis* principle may be used when customary rules are derived from written texts).[80]

The relationship between the *lex posterior* principle (namely that the later rule prevails over the earlier rule) and the *lex specialis* principle is not without controversy either. In my view, the *lex specialis* principle is only meaningful if it prevails over the *lex posterior* principle.[81] In any case, for regimes such as IHL and IHRL, which are constantly developed by

---

[76] Marco Sassòli, 'The International Legal Framework for Fighting Terrorists According to the Bush and Obama Administrations: Same or Different, Correct of Incorrect' (2011) *Proceedings of the 104th Annual Meeting of the ASIL* 277.

[77] See Resolution 1, 'Strengthening International Humanitarian Law Protecting Persons Deprived of their Liberty', 32nd International Conference of the Red Cross and the Red Crescent 32IC/15/R1 (10 December 2015) para 1.

[78] *Serdar Mohammed v Ministry of Defence* (2 May 2014) [2014] EWHC 1369 (QB), confirmed by the UK Court of Appeal, Civil Division, *Serdar Mohammed v Secretary of State for Defence* (30 June 2015) [2015] EWCA Civ 843, [2016] 2 WLR 247; and UN Working Group on Arbitrary Detention 'Report: United Nations Basic Principles and Guidelines on remedies and procedures on the right of anyone deprived of their liberty to bring proceedings before a court' UN Doc A/HRC/30/37 (6 July 2015) annex paras 31 and 96. The UK Supreme Court left this question open in *Abd Ali Hameed Al Waheed v Ministry of Defence and Serdar Mohammed v Ministry of Defence* (17 January 2017) [2017] UKSC 1 and [2017] UKSC 2 paras 14, 16, 44, 61, 133.

[79] Oberleitner (above n 57) 89; Prud'homme (above n 57) 379–80; D'Aspremont and Tranchez (above n 61) 229–30.

[80] Marco Sassòli, 'The Role of Human Rights and International Humanitarian Law in New Types of Armed Conflicts' in Ben-Naftali (ed) (above n 57) 34, 72.

[81] Thus also Marko Milanovic, 'The Lost Origins of Lex Specialis: Rethinking the Relationship between Human Rights and International Humanitarian Law', in Jens D Ohlin (ed), *Theoretical Boundaries of Armed Conflict and Human Rights* (CUP 2016) 111.

new treaties, soft law, state practice, and jurisprudence, it would be difficult to determine the *lex posterior*. Some use the *lex specialis* principle only to avoid norm conflicts through interpretation and not to solve norm conflicts.[82] However, a strict distinction between norm conflict avoidance and norm conflict resolution is artificial, especially in international law.

Finally, and most importantly, the very meaning of the principle, in particular when applied to the relationship between IHL and IHRL, is controversial. Some hold that it concerns the relationship between two branches of law.[83] They conclude that in armed conflicts, IHL always prevails. For some persons, who could be called 'absolute IHL supremacists', any silence in IHL is qualified and means no rule of international law regulates the respective conduct or issue. This approach, in effect, denies that IHRL applies to armed conflicts.

Others, whom I would label 'moderate IHL supremacists', admit that issues not regulated by IHL (such as freedom of opinion or the press, or the right to form trade unions) remain governed by IHRL in an armed conflict (except if the state concerned derogates from the respective right). However, they contend that as soon as any regulation by IHL exists, it must prevail as *lex specialis*, at least in the case of a genuine norm conflict that cannot be avoided by suitably interpreting the rules of both branches.[84]

A third approach borrows from IHRL the rule of interpretation according to which, in case of contradiction between IHRL rules, the most protective prevails.[85] This view neglects that the object and purpose of IHL is not only to offer the best possible protection to individuals, but also to find a balance between humanity and military necessity. These 'protection supremacists', in fact, adopt a cumulative approach to the relationship between the two branches, which results, in practice, in IHRL (which, in theory, prescribes more far-reaching prohibitions and other obligations) prevailing on any issue regulated by both branches. They forget that unrealistic rules do not offer any protection in practice and undermine the willingness of parties, and individual fighters, to comply with any rules of international law in an armed conflict.

What remains is a probably majoritarian view that I would label 'the common contact surface area' (between each of the norms and the facts of the case)[86] approach, which seeks to determine the *lex specialis* in every case of application, based upon logic and the overall systemic purposes of international law. I will detail this approach and explain why it leads to the same results as those reached by most scholars who criticize use of the *lex specialis* principle to describe the relationship between IHL and IHRL.

---

[82] Oberleitner (above n 57) 99; D'Aspremont and Tranchez (above n 61) 234; (if at all) Milanovic, 'The Lost Origins of Lex Specialis' (above n 81) 27–9.

[83] This was the approach of the US under the Bush Administration (see 'Response of the US to the Request for Precautionary Measures on Behalf of the Detainees in Guantánamo Bay, Cuba', reprinted in (2002) 41 *ILM* 1015, 1020–1); UN Human Rights Committee 'Comments by the Government of the United States of America on the concluding observations of the Human Rights Committee' UN Doc CCPR/C/USA/CO/3/Rev.1/Add.112 (10 October 2007) para 12, and sometimes of Israel (Second Periodic Report of Israel UN Doc CCPR/C/ISR/2001/2 (4 December 2001) para 8) and Russia (*Georgia v Russia (II)* App No 38263/08 (ECtHR, 13 December 2011) para 69).

[84] Heike Krieger, 'A Conflict of Norms: The Relationship between Humanitarian Law and Human Rights Law in the ICRC Customary Law Study' (2006) 11 *JC & SL* 265, 272; Cordula Droege, 'Elective Affinities? Human Rights and Humanitarian Law' (2008) *IRRC* 501, 524.

[85] See Gloria Gaggioli and Robert Kolb, 'A Right to Life in Armed Conflicts? The Contribution of the European Court of Human Rights' (2007) 37 *Isr YB HR* 115, 122, and *Juan Carlos Abella v Argentina* (Case No 11.137) Inter-American Commission of Human Rights (1997) paras 164–165, contradicting how it actually dealt with the case and later explained the *lex specialis* principle (*Abella* ibid paras 166–170, 176–189).

[86] These terms were first used by Mary Ellen Walker, LLM Student at the Geneva Academy of International Humanitarian Law and Human Rights in my 2007–2008 IHL course.

## D. Suggested: A Nuanced and Case-by-Case Determination of the *Lex Specialis*

I have tried elsewhere to explore what the *lex specialis* principle means in general, and concerning IHL and IHRL in particular.[87] In my view, the principle does not indicate an inherent quality of one branch of law. It is not because IHL applies to and was designed for armed conflicts that it always constitutes the *lex specialis*.[88] In an armed conflict, IHL constitutes the *lex specialis* on certain questions, whereas IHRL is *lex specialis* on others.[89] This is, however, largely a question of terminology. One would reach the same practical results by considering that some issues are governed by IHL as *lex specialis*, and others by IHRL as the *lex generalis* (as long as one admits that the *lex generalis* may prevail even on issues on which the *lex specialis* contains a rule).

I do not believe the principle determines, once and for all, the relationship between two rules. Rather, it determines which rule prevails over another in a particular situation.[90] Each case must be analysed individually.[91] Several factors must be weighed to determine which rule, in relation to a certain problem, is special. Specialty, in the logical sense, implies that the norm that applies to a certain set of facts must give way to the norm that applies to that same set of facts as well as to an additional fact that is present in a given situation. Between two applicable rules, the one which has the larger 'common contact surface area' with the facts of the problems at hand applies. It is the norm with the more precise or narrower material and/or personal scope of application that prevails.[92] Precision requires that the norm addressing a problem explicitly prevails over the one that treats it implicitly, one that provides more details prevails over another's generality,[93] and a more restrictive norm prevails over one that covers a problem fully but in a less exacting manner.[94]

A less formal (and less objective) factor that permits determination of the *lex specialis* is the conformity of the solution to the systemic objectives of the law.[95] Characterizing this solution as '*lex specialis*' perhaps constitutes misuse of language. The systemic order of international law is a normative postulate founded upon value judgments.[96] In particular when formal standards do not indicate a clear result, this teleological criterion must weigh in, even though it creates space for subjective value judgments.[97]

---

[87] Marco Sassòli, 'Le Droit International Humanitaire, une Lex Specialis par Rapport aux Droits Humains?', in Andreas Auer et al (eds), *Les Droits de l'Homme et la Constitution, Etudes en l'Honneur du Professeur Giorgio Malinverni* (Schulthess 2007) 375.

[88] Oberleitner (above n 57) 97.

[89] ibid 95, 101–3; Milanovic, 'Norm Conflicts' (above n 57) 116; Noam Lubell, 'Challenges in Applying Human Rights Law to Armed Conflict' (2005) 87 *IRRC* 737, 752.

[90] Koskenniemi (above n 55) para 112; Krieger (above n 84) 269, 271; Philip Alston, Jason Morgan-Foster, and William Abresch, 'The Competence of the UN Human Rights Council and Its Special Procedures in Relation to Armed Conflicts: Extrajudicial Executions in the "War on Terror"' (2008) 19 *EJIL* 183, 192; ILC, *Report of the International Law Commission on the Work of its 56th Session*' UN Doc A/59/10 (3 May–4 June, 5 July–6 August 2004) para 304; Gaggioli (above n 60) 56–8, provides an example.

[91] Lindroos (above n 69) 42.

[92] Norberto Bobbio, 'Des Critères pour Résoudre les Antinomies', in C Perelman (ed), *Les Antinomies en Droit: Études* (Bruylant 1965) 244.

[93] See eg Seyed-Ali Sadat-Akhavi, *Methods of Resolving Conflicts between Treaties* (Martinus Nijhoff 2003) 124.

[94] See eg the ECtHR concerning the relationship between ECHR articles 13 and 5(4), *Brannigan and McBride v UK* (1993) Series A No 258, 57 para 76.

[95] Koskenniemi (above n 55), para 107.

[96] Krieger (above n 84) 280.

[97] Bobbio (above n 92) 240–1. See also Jenks (above n 66) 401, 450.

In my view, most who apply both branches (which is not the case for some IHRL mechanisms) apply the 'common contact area' approach, even if they do not call this operation the determination of the *lex specialis*, but systemic integration or interpretation. To call this mere interpretation is, in my view, abusive if one branch contains no term that could be interpreted by taking the other branch into account, and also when it comes to the application of concurrent customary rules. The practical results of my approach are very similar, but hopefully more predictable, than those derived from situating an issue on a spectrum according to a flexible set of variables.[98]

To reject the *lex specialis* principle because its applicability and meaning are controversial[99] is as justifiable as rejecting the right to self-defence in the *jus ad bellum* or the precautionary principle in international environmental law, because their meanings are subject to many controversies. The almost allergic reaction of some to the term *lex specialis* is, in my view, caused by a fear of being seen to be among the ranks of the absolute or moderate IHL supremacists (who use this term), or, more practically, as supporting drone attacks against suspected Al Qaeda operatives or indefinite detention in Guantánamo. In reality, those attacks and detentions are justified by the US and its supporters by a combination of interpretations about the geographical scope of IHL and its validity as a source of authorization, as well as broad conceptions concerning NIACs, legitimate targets of attacks, and enemy combatants.

In practice, for IACs, IHL is generally the more specific regime and corresponds to the overall normative purpose of international law. The situation in occupied territories is more nuanced. In particular when it comes to the use of force, the *lex specialis* has to be determined according to whether certain conduct is part of a law enforcement operation or a military operation, simply because IHL of military occupation does not contain detailed rules on how an occupying power may (indeed, must) restore and maintain law and order.[100]

In NIACs, the determination of the *lex specialis* is more difficult for several reasons. First, IHL rules applicable in such conflicts are often determined by analogy to those applicable to IACs (an operation often disguised as the search for customary law). Historically, the push in favour of such analogies originated in humanitarian attempts to carry definitions, prohibitions, and prescriptions over to the realm of NIACs, but today, the analogies are also made with respect to 'authorizations'. Second, if IHL protections in NIACs are mainly situated in customary law, the question arises whether customary IHL of NIACs and customary IHRL in NIACs exist separately, or whether, based upon practice and *opinio juris,* only one rule of customary law rule applicable to a certain problem can exist (and no *lex specialis* determination is therefore necessary).

Third, it is unclear whether the more limited regulatory density of IHL of NIACs necessarily makes IHRL, as interpreted and developed by judicial bodies and soft law, the *lex specialis*. Furthermore, does the *lex specialis* change each time either a human rights body

---

[98] For details of the practical consequences I derive from my understanding of the *lex specialis* principle, see Sassòli, 'The Role of Human Rights' (above n 80) 72–8, 84–6, and 92–3.

[99] Prud'homme (above n 57) 381–3; Milanovic, 'Norm Conflicts' (above n 57) 98 and 124; more nuanced, Andrew Clapham, 'The Complex Relationship between the Geneva Conventions and International Human Rights Law', in Andrew Clapham, Paola Gaeta, and Marco Sassòli (eds), *The 1949 Geneva Conventions, A Commentary* (OUP 2015) 729.

[100] ICRC, *Expert Meeting, Occupation and Other Forms of Administration of Foreign Territory* (ICRC 2012) 109–30.

clarifies IHRL or an international criminal tribunal clarifies IHL? Fourth, if armed groups are only bound by IHL, but governments also by IHRL, both sides do not have to fight according to the same rules, because the government would, in some circumstances, have to apply the more protective *lex specialis* IHRL, while the armed group the less protective IHL. In my view, this is acceptable, because the equality of belligerents is a principle of IHL and not of IHRL.[101] The same question arises even if it is held that armed groups are bound by IHRL, because the rules of the latter for armed groups are not the same as for states.[102]

Fifth, this problem of asymmetry also exists in the opposite sense, privileging governments, as neither IHL nor IHRL prohibit a state from prosecuting rebels who committed acts of hostility against government soldiers or military objectives. Even those who claim that rebels may legislate will find it difficult to argue that such legislation binds government soldiers when they are not under rebel control. Sixth, even persons who are not under the control of a state are protected by IHRL vis-à-vis that state if they find themselves on its territory.[103] It may nevertheless be that the determination of which obligation constitutes the *lex specialis* for the state must be different for persons who are under the control of an armed group than for those who are not.

Despite all this, as mentioned in section 2 'Traditional Differences' above, even in NIACs both branches lead to the same results on most issues. It is only on the admissibility of attacks against and internment of rebel fighters that IHL leads to different and clearly less protective results than IHRL (at least according to the majority of commentators, who applies to NIACs the same rules as IACs by analogy or *qua* customary law). Possible solutions are discussed in chapters 7 'International Humanitarian Law and the Conduct of Hostilities' and 11 'Weapons' in this volume, and I have explained my opinion elsewhere.[104]

## 5. Implementation of the Rules of One Branch by the Mechanisms of the Other Branch

Apart from the general implementation mechanisms of public international law, to which both branches belong, each branch has its own distinct enforcement mechanisms. They are applied by distinct epistemic communities, which have a tendency to persist in their traditional approaches even when dealing with the other branch. In addition, transparency and democratic control play a greater role for IHRL, while criminalization of certain violations and enforcement through (international) criminal tribunals have recently played a much greater role for IHL. This leads to distinct challenges for evidence gathering and standards of proof. At least traditionally, and putting the international criminal law aspect aside, investigations and international and domestic judicial processes play a greater rule for IHRL. In contrast, the approach of the IHL implementation mechanism par excellence—the ICRC—is focused on practical results for war victims, action in the field, access, dialogue, cooperation with parties, and confidentiality. Nevertheless, on both sides of the divide, the implementing mechanisms of one branch increasingly take the other branch into account.

---

[101] See Marco Sassòli, 'Taking Armed Groups Seriously: Ways to Improve their Compliance with International Humanitarian Law' (2010) 1 *JIHLS* 5, 20.
[102] Murray (above n 32) 178; Fortin (above n 32) 160–70.
[103] *Ilascu and others v Moldova and Russian Federation* ECHR 2004-VII para 333.
[104] See Sassòli, 'The Role of Human Rights' (above 80) 78–93.

## A.  Human Rights Mechanisms Increasingly Refer to and Enforce IHL

As states reject new mechanisms dealing with violations of IHL during armed conflict,[105] it is not astonishing that victims, non-governmental organizations (NGOs), and states turn to a variety of IHRL mechanisms—some of which lead to binding decisions and can be triggered by individual victims of IHRL violations—to enforce respect for IHL. For this purpose, claimants have to couch IHL violations in IHRL language, which is not particularly arduous given the increasing convergence of the substantive rules of both branches, as demonstrated above. UN Charter-based mechanisms have historically labelled IHL as 'human rights in armed conflicts'[106] and in its Universal Periodic Review of the human rights performance of all states the UN Human Rights Council is entrusted, 'given the complementary and mutually interrelated nature of international human rights law and international humanitarian law, ... [with taking] into account applicable international humanitarian law'.[107]

Regional and universal IHRL treaty bodies may base their references to IHL on a variety of reasons. They must verify that derogations are compatible with IHL.[108] In line with this, the ECHR considers the right to life as non-derogable, except for 'lawful acts of war'.[109] IHL defines what is lawful in 'war'. It may also be considered to specify what action may be 'lawfully taken for the purpose of quelling insurrection',[110] in which case a derogation is not even necessary under the ECHR in a NIAC. More broadly, many terms in IHL treaties, such as the prohibitions of 'arbitrary' killings and detention, may and must be interpreted taking other applicable rules of international law into account, which include, in armed conflicts, those of IHL. Finally, as explained in section 4 'How to Deal with Divergences if Both Branches Apply' above, most IHRL treaty bodies take IHL into account as the *lex specialis*, and recently even the ECtHR, which was for a long time reluctant to apply IHL, has decided that it must 'accommodate' the ECHR with respect to applicable IHL.

As long as states refuse to accept efficient IHL enforcement mechanisms, the turn to IHRL mechanisms is inevitable. It is nevertheless not without risks. The epistemic IHRL community is distinct from the IHL community. As explained, there are fundamental differences in structure, approach, and values between IHL and IHRL. Judges and members of other IHRL bodies are often not familiar with IHL and with the practical problems its implementation raises, particularly from a military perspective. Therefore, decisions by IHRL bodies that declare they have taken IHL into account contribute as much to the substantive fragmentation of international law as if they had based their decisions, even in armed conflicts, exclusively on IHRL. Finally, as violations of IHL are much more widely criminalized as war crimes, the finding of an IHRL violation in an armed conflict may be based upon

---

[105]  See the refusal of states to agree, after eight years of extensive consultations on a new mechanism proposed by the ICRC and Switzerland to strengthen compliance with IHL: 33rd International Conference of the Red Cross and the Red Crescent, ICRC and Switzerland, 'Factual Report on the Proceedings of the Intergovernmental Process on Strengthening Respect for IHL', Document 33IC/19/9.2 https://rcrcconference.org/app/uploads/2019/10/33IC-IHL-Compliance-factual-report-_en.pdf.

[106]  See, UNGA Resolution 2444 (XXIII) (19 December 1968); 'Human Rights in Armed Conflicts, Resolution XXIII of the International Conference on Human Rights, Teheran' A/CONF.32/41 (12 May 1968).

[107]  UN Human Rights Council, 'Resolution 5/1 of 18 June 2007, Annex: United Nations Human Rights Council: Institution-Building', para 2, endorsed by UNGA Resolution 62/219 A/RES/62/219 (28 February 2008).

[108]  ECHR article 15; ICCPR article 4; ACHR article 27.

[109]  ECHR article 15(2).

[110]  ibid article 2(2).

standards of proof that would never be sufficient to try a war criminal, but give the erroneous impression (and sometimes even explicitly state) that war crimes were committed.

## B. The ICRC Increasingly Refers to and Enforces IHRL

The main international body implementing IHL, the ICRC, has for a long time been engaged in activities in situations of internal violence similar to those it performs in IACs. During such situations, IHL does not apply. In the past, implicitly, and today more and more explicitly—while maintaining its pragmatic, cooperative, and victim-oriented approach—the ICRC must therefore refer to the applicable international standards in IHRL. Even in armed conflicts, the ICRC increasingly refers explicitly to IHRL where IHL provides no rules or insufficiently detailed rules, for example, on procedural principles and safeguards for internment or administrative detention in NIACs,[111] or on the rules applicable to law enforcement in armed conflicts.[112]

## 6. Concluding Observations

Some of the situations for which the interplay between IHL and IHRL are discussed are not armed conflicts and therefore only IHRL applies, subject to debate over its active personal and territorial scope of application. Today, genuine armed conflicts are mainly not of an international character. In such situations, the relationship between IHL and IHRL is particularly controversial and difficult to determine. Nevertheless, both IHL and IHRL lead, in most cases, to the same results. The few instances where the results differ reflect the characteristic problems the regimes were intended to govern. The applicable rules should therefore not be the same; otherwise they would be unrealistic and fail to meet with respect.

Even in those instances when results differ, states could do a lot to harmonize their obligations under both branches, by resorting to derogations permitted under IHRL, one of the means offered by international law to harmonize their IHRL obligations with their IHL obligations. Beyond this, legal reasoning allows for differentiated solutions on when and on which issues one or the other branch prevails. Whether this reasoning is labelled the search for the *lex specialis*, systemic integration or interpretation, or whether a new flexible sliding scale taking several factors into account is applied, the result is often the same.

Lawyers must, however, be careful to ensure that the results of such reasoning are realistic for those engaged on the ground. In an ideal world, armed forces and armed groups could apply one set of rules, or, after a binary, alternative determination, either IHL or IHRL. This ideal world does not exist in today's armed conflicts. Their feature is precisely that the full spectrum of laws applies to everyone involved: IHL, made for armed conflicts but leaving some questions open, in particular in NIACs; IHRL, made for the relations between a state

---

[111] Jelena Pejic, 'Procedural Principles and Safeguards for Internment: Administrative Detention in Armed Conflicts and Other Situations of Violence' (2005) 87 *IRRC* 375, 377–9, later published as ICRC, ICRC Guidelines, 'International Humanitarian Law and the Challenges of Contemporary Armed Conflicts', annex 1 to the ICRC's report, 'International Humanitarian Law and the Challenges of Contemporary Armed Conflicts', 30th International Conference of the Red Cross and Red Crescent (October 2007) 30IC/07/8.4.
[112] See ICRC, 'The Use of Force in Armed Conflicts' (above n 11).

and its citizens, but also applicable to (or at least containing values that must protect) people confronted with agents of a state acting outside its borders; not to mention domestic law (of the territorial state and the home state in case of action by international forces). It is also normal that there is no general answer as to how these laws interrelate and which one prevails. In my view, everything depends on where on the spectrum between the typical armed conflict problems for which IHL was made, and the typical peacetime problems for which IHRL was made, a certain event is situated. Therefore, the relationship between IHL and IHRL depends on many variables. The identity and weight of those variables is the subject of additional controversies among lawyers.

Many will consider this nuanced line, which I call the determination of the *lex specialis* (while others insist it has nothing to do with the principle), and which admittedly is unable to provide solutions and can only list arguments in relation to some important issues, as unrealistic. In my view, military operations—difficult to classify and often covering the full spectrum from hostilities to law enforcement—require those involved, at increasingly lower hierarchical levels, to apply, simultaneously, a patchwork of complicated and controversial rules. However, they are not and should not be left alone in working out solutions to practical problems. This is true for government forces, but even more so for armed groups; otherwise every hope that they respect IHL vanishes. All those involved need the best possible training and clear instructions for every sortie; instructions anyway do not simply translate the law, but are often—for tactical, policy, or perception reasons—more restrictive than the law would permit.

In addition, international lawyers and practitioners should meet, not to reaffirm their theories or to conclude that the old rules are not adequate for new situations, but to clarify the interplay between the existing rules agreed upon by states. This includes explaining the few issues on which there are genuine divergences of views, the (often rather limited) practical impact of those divergences, and exploring the possible solutions available. Although this may sound like heresy to state representatives obsessed with sovereignty, such a process must include representatives of armed groups and deal with the specific difficulties such groups are confronted with. States, NGOs, and in addition, when discussing the relationship between the two branches, scholars should not be driven by their preferred outcomes and preconceived ideas of their epistemic communities to characterize the solutions of the other branch either as unrealistic or as inhumane. IHRL can be realistic and IHL can be humane.

# 18

# Terrorism, Counter-Terrorism, and International Humanitarian Law

*Ben Saul*

## 1. Introduction

Despite much debate about the coverage, adequacy, and effectiveness of IHL in regulating 'terrorism', international humanitarian law (IHL) does not recognize any specific legal categories for, or special regime governing, terrorists and terrorist groups. Rather, the general norms of IHL, discussed in previous chapters, apply to terrorists according to their conduct. IHL was precisely developed as a kind of exceptional or emergency law comprehensively addressing all forms of violence in armed conflict, including that which is labelled 'terrorist' in other areas of law (international, regional, or national).

Particularly relevant to terrorism are the general IHL rules, discussed in other chapters, on the classification of violence as armed conflict, the categorization of persons during conflict, targeting, detention, criminal liability, and fair trial.[1] Thus, terrorist and counter-terrorist violence may constitute a non-international armed conflict (NIAC) to which IHL applies if the violence is sufficiently intense and organized; a 'terrorist' may be militarily targeted if s/he is a member of an organized armed group performing a continuous combat function, or is otherwise taking a direct part in hostilities (DPH); a 'terrorist' in a NIAC may be detained under national law (consistent with human rights law), and may be liable for war crimes, other international crimes, or crimes under national law (including terrorist offences implementing treaties or UN Security Council resolutions), in a fair trial in a regular court.

The application of all of these general rules in relation to terrorists has been controversial in one way or another, and has produced long-running debates (before and after 9/11) about the adequacy of IHL—whether from a military or humanitarian standpoint. Overall these debates have not produced fundamental normative changes in IHL, or exceptions to its application, even if they have sharpened—or divided—the interpretation of many of the above rules. Where formal normative change has ensued, thus far it has tended not to stiffen the law against perceived 'terrorists' but to relax constraints in their favour, as in the looser conditions of guerilla combatancy and the right to combatant status of liberation movements under Additional Protocol I (API) of 1977.[2] 'Soft law' processes have also sought to

---

[1] See generally Ben Saul, 'Terrorism and International Humanitarian Law', in Ben Saul (ed), *Research Handbook on International Law and Terrorism* (Edward Elgar 2014) 208–231; Andrea Bianchi and Yasmin Naqvi, *International Humanitarian Law and Terrorism* (Hart 2011).

[2] Protocol Additional to the Geneva Conventions of 12 August 1949, and Relating to the Protection of Victims of International Armed Conflicts (adopted 8 June 1977, entered into force 7 December 1978) 1125 UNTS 3 (API) articles 44(3) and 1(4), respectively.

clarify interpretation on some matters (such as the meaning of DPH)[3] or strengthen existing norms without creating new law (as with the protection of persons deprived of liberty, or compliance with IHL).[4]

This chapter does not reiterate or particularize the general rules, discussed in previous chapters (often including in the context of terrorism) as they apply to terrorism or terrorists. Instead, it focuses on three key legal issues of particular relevance and specificity to terrorism in armed conflict. First, it examines IHL's specific, narrow prohibitions on 'terrorism' in armed conflict and the connected war crime of intending to spread terror amongst a civilian population, which is distinct from peacetime legal notions of terrorism. The war crimes jurisprudence has been developed by the International Criminal Tribunal for the former Yugoslavia (ICTY) and the Special Court for Sierra Leone (SCSL), and has implications for criminal jurisdiction under customary IHL and before the International Criminal Court (ICC).

Second, the chapter analyses the varied and complicated relationships between IHL and different international counter-terrorism law (CTL) norms and instruments. Depending on the norm and context, CTL can apply, not apply, or partially apply in armed conflict, and there is no general international rule determining whether CTL or IHL is the more special law (*lex specialis*). Often CTL complements and extends IHL's focus on preventing and criminalizing attacks on civilians. Further, CTL often does not directly conflict with IHL. However, some aspects of CTL interfere with IHL's delicate balance between humanitarian protection and military necessity, by 'taking sides', undermining the equality of the parties, and ultimately reducing incentives for non-state armed groups (NSAGs) to comply with IHL.

The chapter concludes by exploring the related, adverse effects of CTL on humanitarian relief operations in armed conflict. National implementation of CTL has variously chilled, restricted, prohibited, and even criminalized humanitarian engagement by external actors with armed 'terrorist' groups. These measures have both inhibited effective humanitarian assistance to vulnerable civilian populations and undermined the confidence of NSAGs in humanitarian cooperation with the international community.

## 2. Prohibitions on and Criminal Liabilities for Terrorism in Armed Conflict

### A. Prohibitions on Terrorist-Type Conduct

Most terrorist-type conduct committed in any type of armed conflict is already criminalized as various war crimes.[5] This is because IHL prohibits and criminalizes deliberate attacks on civilians or civilian objects, including by indiscriminate attacks; reprisals; the use

---

[3] ICRC, *Interpretive Guidance on the Notion of Direct Participation in Hostilities under International Humanitarian Law* (ICRC 2009).

[4] 32nd International Conference of the Red Cross and Red Crescent, Resolution 1: Strengthening international humanitarian law protecting persons deprived of their liberty (32IC/15/R1) (8–10 December 2015). The outcome of an ICRC study and consultation from 2012–2015 was a directive to pursue further work to produce 'concrete and implementable outcomes' of a 'non-legally binding nature' para 8.

[5] See Hans Gasser, 'Acts of Terror, "Terrorism" and International Humanitarian Law' (2002) 84 *IRRC* 547.

of prohibited weapons (including incendiaries, cluster munitions, or chemical or biological weapons); attacks on cultural property, objects indispensable to civilian survival (such as food and water supplies), or works containing dangerous forces (including dams, dykes, and nuclear facilities); or through illegal detention, torture, or inhuman treatment (see chapters 6–12 in this book). In addition, the suite of crimes against humanity applies concurrently in armed conflict to protect civilian populations against widespread or systematic attack, which may be perpetrated by an organized non-state group.

In addition to such protections for civilians, IHL specifically prohibits terrorism. Article 33(1) of the Fourth Geneva Convention 1949 (GCIV) prohibits 'collective penalties and likewise all measures of intimidation or of terrorism' against protected persons 'in the hands of a Party' (as in detention or occupied territory) to an international armed conflict (IAC).[6] The provision was a response to the mass intimidation of civilians in occupied territory in the Second World War.

All civilians in IAC (including those not 'in the hands of' a party) are protected by article 51(2) of API, which prohibits 'acts or threats of violence the primary purpose of which is to spread terror among the civilian population'. The same acts are prohibited in NIAC by article 13(2) of Additional Protocol II (APII). Both provisions are part of wider prohibitions on attacking civilians.[7] Article 4(2)(d) of APII further prohibits 'acts of terrorism' in NIACs.


## B. The War Crime of Intending to Spread Terror amongst a Civilian Population

In the *Galić* case (2003), the ICTY was the first international tribunal to recognize 'the crime of terror as a violation of the laws or customs of war', based on a violation of article 51(2) of API.[8] The elements of the crime are as follows:

1. Acts of violence directed against the civilian population or individual civilians not taking direct part in hostilities causing death or serious injury to body or health within the civilian population.
2. The offender wilfully made the civilian population or individual civilians not taking direct part in hostilities the object of those acts of violence.
3. The above offence was committed with the primary purpose of spreading terror among the civilian population.[9]

The ICTY clarified that 'acts of violence' do not include legitimate attacks against combatants but only unlawful attacks against civilians.[10] On appeal it found that the crime encompasses both attacks and threats of attacks against civilians; and that it is not limited to direct

---

[6] Geneva Convention (IV) Relative to the Protection of Civilian Persons in Time of War (adopted 12 August 1949, entered into force 21 October 1950) 75 UNTS 287 (GCIV) article 4.

[7] API article 51(2) and Protocol Additional to the Geneva Conventions of 12 August 1949, and Relating to the Protection of Victims of Non-International Armed Conflicts (adopted 8 June 1977, entered into force 7 December 1978) 1125 UNTS 609 (APII) article 13(2).

[8] *Prosecutor v Galić* (Trial Chamber Judgment and Opinion) ICTY-98-29-T (5 December 2003) paras 65–66, 138; affirmed in *Prosecutor v Galić* (Appeals Chamber Judgment) IT-98-29-A (30 November 2006) paras 87–90.

[9] *Galić* (Trial Chamber Judgment) (above n 8) para 133.

[10] ibid para 135.

attacks or threats but includes indiscriminate or disproportionate ones.[11] Further, 'extensive trauma and psychological damage form part of the acts or threats of violence.'[12]

The distinctive feature of the war crime of terror is its mental elements. There must first be a general intent to wilfully make civilians the object of acts or threats of violence.[13] In addition, there must be a 'specific intent', that is, the primary purpose to spread terror amongst civilians, which necessarily excludes '*dolus eventualis* or recklessness.'[14] The accused must specifically intend terror to result and not merely be aware of its likelihood. The actual infliction of terror is not required.[15]

Terror was defined simply as 'extreme fear'.[16] The Appeals Chamber clarified that the offence is not concerned with the incidental fear civilians experience in war as a result of legitimate military actions, but rather with acts or threats that are specifically undertaken to spread terror.[17] Further, it observed that the intent to spread terror need not be the only purpose of the act or threat, as long as the intent to spread terror 'was principal among the aims'.[18] It noted that 'intent can be inferred from the circumstances of the acts or threats, that is from their nature, manner, timing and duration'.[19]

On the facts in *Galić*, the war crime of spreading terror was found to have been committed by a campaign of sniping and shelling of civilians in the besieged city of Sarajevo, as a result of 'the nature of the civilian activities targeted, the manner in which the attacks on civilians were carried out and the timing and duration of the attacks on civilians'.[20] The ICTY found that civilians were targeted 'while engaged in typical civilian activities or where expected to be found' throughout the city,[21] such as during funerals; in ambulances and hospitals; on trams and buses; when driving, cycling, or walking; at home or in school; while shopping; when gardening, tending fires, clearing rubbish, or collecting water or firewood; at suppertime; and at public festivals and funerals.[22] The vulnerable were especially targeted, including women, children, and the elderly.[23] Hundreds of civilians were killed and thousands injured.[24]

The attacks were found to have no military significance and could not be accounted for by targeting errors or cross-fire.[25] They were also not designed to exterminate or deplete the population.[26] Rather, the pattern of fire was random and indiscriminate, at unexpected places and times, calculated to achieve surprise and maximize the psychological effects.[27] Civilians responded by closing schools, hiding by day and living at night, rarely moving around, and creating barricades.[28] The ICTY concluded that the aim was to 'very clearly'

---

[11]  *Galić* (Appeals Chamber Judgment) (above n 8) para 102.
[12]  ibid.
[13]  *Galić* (Trial Chamber Judgment) (above n 8) para 136.
[14]  ibid.
[15]  ibid para 134; *Galić* (Appeals Chamber Judgment) (above n 8) paras 103–104.
[16]  *Galić* (Trial Chamber Judgment) (above n 8) para 137.
[17]  *Galić* (Appeals Chamber Judgment) (above n 8) para 103.
[18]  ibid para 104.
[19]  ibid.
[20]  *Galić* (Trial Chamber Judgment) (above n 8) paras 592, 596–597.
[21]  ibid para 593.
[22]  ibid paras 569, 584–585.
[23]  ibid paras 584, 593.
[24]  ibid para 591.
[25]  ibid paras 567, 593, 598.
[26]  ibid para 593.
[27]  ibid paras 563, 568, 570, 573, 589.
[28]  ibid para 586.

send the message 'that no Sarajevo civilian was safe anywhere, at any time of day or night'.[29] It found that 'the only reasonable conclusion in light of the evidence ... is that the primary purpose of the campaign was to instil in the civilian population a state of extreme fear'.[30]

The charges in the *Galić* case were based on the terrorism prohibitions in API, which applied by agreement between the parties in that conflict, and normally only applies to IACs. However, the ICTY also recognized that the prohibition on terror was a specific prohibition within IHL's general prohibition on attacks on civilians, which constitutes customary international law.[31] It further held that there is individual criminal responsibility for violations of the rule under customary international law,[32] including in NIACs.

In *Milošević* (2007),[33] the ICTY found another Bosnian Serb commander responsible for the war crime of spreading terror during the Sarajevo siege, again for a campaign of sniping and shelling of civilians, including by the use of inaccurate and indiscriminate modified air bombs. The ICTY has found a number of other defendants guilty of participation in a joint criminal enterprise (JCE) to carry out a campaign of sniping and shelling of civilians in Sarajevo, the primary purpose of which was to spread terror among the civilian population, namely in *Karadžić* (2016) (concerning the Bosnian Serb political leader and military commander in Bosnia-Herzegovina) and *Mladić* (2017) (the Bosnian Serb army commander).[34]

The SCSL has also followed the *Galić* jurisprudence to find numerous convictions for the war crime of spreading terror.[35] In *Brima et al* (2007),[36] it found that the war crime of terror was committed by violent attacks on civilians, including amputation and mutilation. Such acts constituted terrorism because they were committed against unarmed civilians repeatedly, brutally, and not for military advantage; they were often accompanied by perpetrator statements that they were done to cause fear; and they aimed to intimidate civilians not to support the adversary.

In *Sesay et al* (2009),[37] the SCSL found that terrorism was constituted by unlawful killings, rape, sexual violence and forced marriage, physical violence, abductions, enslavement and forced labour, threats, and looting and burning of property. Indications of the intent to spread terror included: the lack of a military or other legitimate objective; brutality (such as mutilations and amputations); the location of attacks (such as at public places, protests, homes, and schools); mass attacks to compel obedience; the scale of property destruction out of proportion to the effects of hostilities; the targeting of public officials or collaborators; public demonstration killings and publicizing attacks to intimidate others; indiscriminate attacks; threats, insults, or statements by perpetrators as to their intent; punishment to warn civilians not to support the adversary; evidence of a policy (*gori-gori*) to target and subdue, and seek revenge against, civilians; and civilian efforts to hide from fighters.

---

[29] ibid paras 592–93.

[30] ibid para 593.

[31] *Galić* (Appeals Chamber Judgment) (above n 8) paras 87–90.

[32] ibid paras 91–98.

[33] *Prosecutor v Milošević* (ICTY Trial Chamber Judgment) IT-98-29/1-T (12 December 2007).

[34] *Prosecutor v Karadžić* (ICTY Trial Chamber Judgment) IT-95-5/18-T (24 March 2016) paras 4632–4634; *Prosecutor v Mladić* (ICTY Trial Chamber Judgment) IT-09-92-T (22 November 2017) para 4921.

[35] The crime of 'acts of terrorism' in NIAC is expressly included in article 3(d) of the Statute of the Special Court for Sierra Leone (SCSL).

[36] *Prosecutor v Brima et al* (Trial Chamber Judgment) SCSL-0416-T (20 June 2007) paras 662, 666; also *Prosecutor v Taylor* (SCSL Trial Chamber Judgment) SCSL-03-1-T (26 April 2012) paras 112, 1430–1633.

[37] *Prosecutor v Sesay et al* (SCSL Trial Chamber Judgment) SCSL-04-15-T (2 March 2009) paras 1032–1036, 1124–1130, 1347–1352, 1357, 1361, 1491, 1596–1604.

Importantly, the SCSL found that rape, sexual slavery, 'forced marriages', and other outrages on personal dignity can constitute acts of terrorism.[38] It held that 'the nature and manner in which the female population was a target of the sexual violence portrays a calculated and concerted pattern on the part of the perpetrators to use sexual violence as a weapon of terror'. The 'deliberate and concerted campaign to rape women' constituted 'an extension of the battlefield to the women's bodies, a degrading treatment that inflicts physical, mental and sexual suffering to the victims and to their community'. Terror was evidenced by perverse methods of violence (including gang rape, rape of pregnant women, forced intercourse, and violence in front of family members); an intent beyond mere personal gratification; the targeting of the most vulnerable; the attendant destruction of the family nucleus, cultural values, and social relationships; the purposeful infliction of psychological injury; the atmosphere of terror, helplessness, and insecurity in the face of attacks and domination; and the shame and stigma resulting from forced marriages and sexual slavery.

In *Taylor* (2012),[39] the SCSL found that acts of terrorism had been committed through the burning of civilian property, unlawful killings, sexual violence (including rape and sexual slavery), and physical violence (including amputations and mutilations), with the intent to spread terror.[40] Such acts were typically done to intimidate civilians into leaving the area; to warn them not to resist; to demonstrate the repercussions of supporting the enemy; and, in the case of sexual violence, to destroy the traditional family nucleus, thus undermining the cultural values and relationships which held society together.[41] The intent to spread terror was inferred where there was no direct evidence of it but the acts followed a similar pattern.[42]

In a number of these cases, the SCSL found that certain acts of violence did not evidence an intent to spread terror, because the purpose of violence was utilitarian, military, punitive or disciplinary, for personal gain, or isolated.[43]

The Rome Statute of the ICC does not explicitly include a war crime of terrorism within its jurisdiction. However, as noted by the ICTY in *Galić*, such acts may be regarded as specific instances of the general prohibition of attacks on civilians, breaches of which are within the ICC's jurisdiction.[44] As noted, the war crime of terrorism is also part of customary IHL.

The war crime of terror is not, however, the same as certain peacetime legal conceptions of terrorism, namely violence committed to compel a government to do or refrain from doing something, or to advance a political, religious, or ideological cause.[45] The meaning of terrorism in IHL is thus more limited than definitions of terrorism outside of armed conflict. Certain terrorism offences within the jurisdiction of post-9/11 US military commissions were not IHL offences as the US asserted, but were peacetime terrorism offences retroactively applied to a particular armed conflict.[46] In addition to war crimes, domestic

---

[38]   ibid paras 1347–1352, 1602.

[39]   *Taylor* (above n 36) paras 402–410, 1964–2192.

[40]   ibid paras 2048, 2055, 2192.

[41]   ibid, respectively paras 2006, 2017; 2040; 2021, 2041; 2035.

[42]   ibid para 2026.

[43]   *Sesay* (above n 37) paras 1034, 1363, 1494, 1126, 1358–1359, 1362, 1128; *Taylor* (above n 36) paras 1969, 1971 1975–1977, 2047.

[44]   See eg Rome Statute of the International Criminal Court (adopted 17 July 1998, entered into force 1 July 2002) 2187 UNTS 3 (Rome Statute) articles 8(2)(b)(i)–(v) (IACs) and 8(2)(e)(i)–(v) (NIACs).

[45]   See Ben Saul, *Defining Terrorism in International Law* (OUP 2006) chapters 3–4.

[46]   US Department of Defense (DoD), 'Military Commission Instruction No 2: Crimes and Elements for Trials by Military Commission' (30 April 2003) clause 18 (terrorism as 'intended to intimidate or coerce a civilian

criminal (and/or military) law may apply to certain terrorist acts in armed conflict; terrorism offences under domestic law are discussed further in section D 'Security Council Counter-Terrorism Obligations' below.

## 3. Relationship between IHL and Counter-Terrorism Law

The interaction between IHL and CTL is complex and varies according to the context. CTL is not a unified field of international law[47] but comprises disparate norms emanating from multiple sources. Foremost are the nineteen 'sectoral' counter-terrorism instruments adopted since 1963,[48] which require states parties to criminalize particular methods of transnational violence commonly used by terrorists, establish extensive jurisdiction over the offences, and investigate, apprehend, and 'extradite or prosecute' or offenders. In

---

population, or to influence the policy of a government by intimidation and coercion'); Military Commission Act 2006 (US) s 950v(25)(A); see also DoD, *Military Commission Manual*, Part IV-18-19 (DoD 2007) 261–262 ('material support for terrorism'). The latter offence was found to be unlawfully retrospective in *Hamdan v United States* US Court of Appeals (DC Circuit) (16 October 2012) and *Hicks v Australia*, UN Human Rights Committee Communication No 2005/2010 (5 November 2015) para 4.8.

[47] Ben Saul, 'The Emerging International Law of Terrorism', in Ben Saul (ed), *Terrorism: Documents in International Law* (Hart 2012) 67.
[48] Convention on Offences and Certain Other Acts Committed on Board Aircraft (adopted 14 September 1963, entered into force 4 December 1969) 704 UNTS 219 (Tokyo Convention 1963); Convention for the Suppression of Unlawful Seizure of Aircraft (adopted 16 December 1970, entered into force 14 October 1971) 860 UNTS 105 (Hague Convention 1970); Convention for the Suppression of Unlawful Acts against the Safety of Civil Aviation 1971 (adopted 23 September 1971, entered into force 26 January 1973) 974 UNTS 178 (Montreal Convention 1971); Convention on the Prevention and Punishment of Crimes against Internationally Protected Persons, including Diplomatic Agents (adopted 14 December 1973, entered into force 20 February 1977) 1035 UNTS 167 (Protected Persons Convention 1973); International Convention against the Taking of Hostages (adopted 17 December 1979, entered into force 3 June 1983) 1316 UNTS 205 (Hostages Convention 1979); Convention on the Physical Protection of Nuclear Material (adopted 3 March 1980, entered into force 8 February 1987) 1456 UNTS 101 (Vienna Convention 1980); Protocol on the Suppression of Unlawful Acts of Violence at Airports Serving International Civil Aviation (adopted 24 February 1988, entered into force 6 August 1989) 974 UNTS 177 (Montreal Protocol 1988); Convention for the Suppression of Unlawful Acts against the Safety of Maritime Navigation (adopted 10 March 1988, entered into force 1 March 1992) 1678 UNTS 221 (Rome Convention 1988); Protocol for the Suppression of Unlawful Acts against the Safety of Fixed Platforms Located on the Continental Shelf (adopted 10 March 1988, entered into force 1 March 1992) 1678 UNTS 304 (Rome Protocol 1988); Convention on the Marking of Plastic Explosives for the Purpose of Detection (adopted 1 March 1991, entered into force 21 June 1998) 2122 UNTS 359 (Plastic Explosives Convention 1991); International Convention for the Suppression of Terrorist Bombings (adopted 15 December 1997, entered into force 23 May 2001) 2149 UNTS 256 (Terrorist Bombings Convention 1997); International Convention for the Suppression of the Financing of Terrorism (adopted 9 December 1999, entered into force 10 April 2002) 2178 UNTS 197 (Terrorist Financing Convention 1999); Protocol to the Convention for the Suppression of Unlawful Acts against the Safety of Maritime Navigation 1988 (adopted 14 October 2005; entered into force 28 July 2010) 1678 UNTS 201 (Protocol 2005 to the Rome Convention 1988, creating the consolidated Convention for the Suppression of Unlawful Acts against the Safety of Maritime Navigation 2005); Protocol 2005 to the Rome Protocol 1988 (adopted 14 October 2005, entered into force 28 July 2010) 1678 UNTS 201 (Protocol 2005 to the Rome Protocol 1988); Amendment to the Convention on the Physical Protection of Nuclear Material 1980 (adopted 8 July 2005, entered into force 8 May 2016) UN Registration No 24631 (Amendment 2005 to the Nuclear Material Convention 1980); International Convention for the Suppression of Acts of Nuclear Terrorism (adopted 13 April 2005, entered into force 7 July 2007) 2445 UNTS 89 (Nuclear Terrorism Convention 2005); Convention on the Suppression of Unlawful Acts Relating to International Civil Aviation 2010 (adopted 10 September 2010, entered into force 1 July 2018) ICAO Doc 9960 (Beijing Convention 2010, consolidating the Montreal Convention 1971 and Montreal Protocol 1988); Protocol Supplementary to the Convention for the Suppression of Unlawful Seizure of Aircraft, done at Beijing (adopted 10 September 2010, entered into force 1 January 2018) ICAO Doc 9959 (Beijing Protocol 2010); Protocol to Amend the Convention on Offences and Certain Other Acts Committed on Board Aircraft (adopted 4 April 2014, entered into force 1 January 2020) ICAO Doc 10034 (Montreal Protocol 2014).

addition, Security Council resolutions adopted since 1999 have imposed sanctions regimes on specific terrorist actors, while resolutions since 2001 have required broader legislative and enforcement measures to be taken by states against terrorist threats in general. There are also numerous 'soft law' norms on terrorism, including those in UN General Assembly resolutions[49] and the Assembly's Global Counter-Terrorism Strategy 2006.[50]

It is clear that CTL does not simply displace IHL or vice versa. UN Security Council and General Assembly resolutions have repeatedly emphasized that states must respect their obligations under IHL when countering terrorism.[51] There is, however, no further guidance from the UN organs on the precise relationship between CTL and IHL, nor any general rule of international law specifying the relationship.

The international law principle of *lex specialis derogat legi generali* (more specific law prevails over more general law) does not readily provide a definitive answer to potential conflicts of norms between the two areas, since both CTL and IHL could be viewed as the more specific norms addressing the same subject matter. At the regime level, CTL addresses the sub-set of violence described as terrorism, potentially whether within or outside of armed conflict. IHL addresses the sub-set of violence known as armed conflict, whether also qualifying as terrorism or not. Each could therefore be seen as best adapted to the overlapping, exceptional violence that they address. Beneath the abstract regime level, whether IHL or CTL is more specific may more pragmatically depend on the particular context and rules at issue.

In place of a general rule, different CTL norms themselves often specify various relationships to IHL. Some of the key interactions are discussed below. In broad terms, direct conflicts between international CTL norms and IHL are rare, although national CTL can be much more problematic (as discussion in section D below).

## A.  International Counter-Terrorism Conventions and IHL

The various sectoral CTL treaties are limited to transnational offences and thus exclude purely domestic violence.[52] In consequence, violence in NIACs that are purely domestic—such as classic civil wars involving nationals of a single state within the state's territory—will not be covered by the sectoral CTL treaties and instead will be solely regulated by IHL (as well as applicable international criminal law and international human rights law (IHRL)).

The sectoral CTL treaties specify five different relationships to armed conflict and IHL. First, the Hostages Convention 1979 effectively does not apply in IAC (while still applying to hostage taking with a transnational dimension in a NIAC). Specifically, the Convention provides that it does not apply to hostage taking in armed conflict where states parties are

---

[49]  See Saul (ed), *Terrorism: Documents in International Law* (above n 47) ch 4.

[50]  UNGA Resolution 60/288 (20 September 2006).

[51]  ibid para 3; UNSC Resolutions 1456 (20 January 2003) annex para 6 and 1624 (14 September 2005) para 4.

[52]  Specifically, the treaties typically do not apply where an offence is committed in a single state, the offender and victims are nationals of that state, the offender is found in the state's territory and no other state has jurisdiction under those treaties: Tokyo Convention 1963 article 5(1); Hague Convention 1970 article 3(3)–(4); Hague Convention 1970 article 3(5) as amended by the Beijing Protocol 2010; Montreal Convention 1971 articles 4(2)–(5); Rome Convention 1988 article 4(1)–(2); Rome Protocol 1988 article 1(2); Hostages Convention 1979 article 13; Vienna Convention 1980 article 14; Nuclear Terrorism Convention 2005 article 3; Terrorist Bombings Convention 1997 article 3; Terrorist Financing Convention 1999 article 3.

bound to prosecute or extradite a hostage-taker under the Geneva Conventions of 1949 and Additional Protocols of 1977.[53] IHL is thus accorded precedence as the *lex specialis*. The definition of hostage taking in peacetime and during armed conflict is similar.[54] IHL prohibits and criminalizes hostage taking in IACs and NIACs,[55] but only hostage taking in IAC is subject to an obligation on states to extradite or prosecute (being a 'grave breach' attracting individual criminal liability under the Geneva Conventions).

No such obligation arises in NIACs, whether under Common Article 3 of the four Geneva Conventions 1949 or APII, since none of those treaties recognizes hostage taking as a 'grave breach' war crime subject to extradition or prosecution. This is the case notwithstanding that hostage taking in NIAC is a war crime under customary IHL and under the Rome Statute of the ICC; neither custom nor the Rome Statute impose an 'extradite or prosecute' obligation, and even if custom did so, the Hostages Convention is only inapplicable where such obligations arise under IHL *treaties*. As such, the Hostages Convention applies to hostage taking in NIACs, criminalizing it and thereby supplementing the IHL treaty provisions that prohibit but do not criminalize it.

Second, some of the sectoral CTL treaties applying to transnational aviation and maritime safety do not apply to military, customs, or police aircraft or ships,[56] or do not apply to military air bases (instead only applying to civilian airports).[57] As a result, attacks on such targets during armed conflict (or indeed peacetime) are not covered by the CTL instruments and are instead exclusively regulated by IHL. On the other hand, transnational attacks on civilian aircraft, ships, or airports during armed conflict, whether by state military forces, NSAGs, or civilians taking a direct part in hostilities, fall within both the CTL treaties and IHL and could simultaneously constitute crimes under both regimes.

Third, in a related vein, the Terrorist Financing Convention 1999 prohibits the financing of terrorist acts, in peace or war, against civilians or others out of combat (such as prisoners of war), but not against persons taking an active part in hostilities.[58] There is no exclusion for acts by armed forces, such that it is a crime to finance attacks on civilians by state forces, NSAGs, disorganized groups, or individual civilians taking part in hostilities. By contrast, the Terrorist Bombings Convention 1997 prohibits bombings against civilian or military objectives alike,[59] whether in peace or war, but excludes the activities of armed forces (see below). In armed conflict it thus makes criminal isolated terrorist attacks on the military, but not those against the state's military committed by organized armed groups.

[53] Hostages Convention 1979 article 12.
[54] While IHL treaties do not define it, the *Elements of Crimes* of the Rome Statute of the International Criminal Court follows the definition of the Hostages Convention 1979 in requiring an intent 'to compel a State, an international organization, a natural or legal person or a group of persons to act or refrain from acting as an explicit or implicit condition for the safety or the release of such person or persons': Rome Statute: *Elements of Crimes* (2002): common element 3, article 8(2)(a)(viii) and (c)(iii).
[55] Four Geneva Conventions 1949, Common Article 3(1)(b); GCIV article 34; APII article 4(2)(c); Rome Statute article 8(2)(a)(viii) (IACs) and article 8(2)(c)(iii) (NIACs); Jean-Marie Henckaerts and Louise Doswald-Beck (eds), *Customary International Humanitarian Law, Vol I: Rules* (CUP 2005) (CIHL) rule 96.
[56] Tokyo Convention 1963 article 1(4); Hague Convention 1970 article 3(2); Montreal Convention 1971 article 4; Rome Convention 1988 article 2.
[57] Montreal Protocol 1988 article 2.
[58] Terrorist Financing Convention 1999 article 2(1)(b).
[59] Daniel O'Donnell, 'International Treaties against Terrorism and the Use of Terrorism during Armed Conflict and by Armed Forces' (2006) 88 *IRRC* 653, 684.

Fourth, the most recent CTL treaties (addressing nuclear terrorism, terrorist bombings, and aviation safety) exclude the 'activities of armed forces during armed conflict, as those terms are understood under international humanitarian law, which are governed by that law'.[60] 'Armed forces' under IHL—an expression used in Common Article 3 of the four Geneva Conventions concerning NIACs[61]—refers to both state military forces and organized NSAGs.[62] Military attacks (as well as other violent or dangerous activities) by such forces in IACs or NIACs are thus excluded from these CTL treaties. On the other hand, violence by disorganized armed groups or civilians sporadically taking a direct part in hostilities is still covered, and is simultaneously regulated by IHL's prohibitions and criminal liabilities.

A fifth issue relating to IHL does not strictly involve a CTL instrument but a treaty modelled on one such instrument and serving an indirect counter-terrorism purpose. The Convention on the Safety of United Nations and Associated Personnel 1994 is based on the Protected Persons Convention 1973 and similarly requires states to criminalize 'kidnapping or other attack on the person or liberty' of UN and associated personnel[63] (who include the military, police, or civilian components of a UN mission, and related UN officials or experts, secondees, contractors, and humanitarian non-governmental organizations (NGOs)).[64] The Convention explicitly excludes from its scope of application UN enforcement actions under Chapter VII of the UN Charter, where UN personnel are 'engaged as combatants against organised armed forces and to which the law of international armed conflict applies' (article 2(2)), namely in IACs. This clause thus excludes attacks on UN combatants, by state forces in IAC (but probably not by non-state forces in NIAC),[65] where UN forces are taking Chapter VII enforcement action. IHL will instead govern such situations.

However, the Convention still co-applies with IHL in a number of situations: (i) attacks on non-combatant UN personnel in IAC or NIAC; (ii) attacks by NSAGs on UN personnel taking a direct part in hostilities in an NIAC (even if authorized to do so by the Security Council); and (iii) attacks in IAC or NIAC on UN combatants who are not authorized in an enforcement action by the Security Council—for example where UN peacekeepers, deployed with the consent of a state, take a direct part in hostilities (and are not acting only in self-defence) in the course of their mission. Such attacks on UN personnel would come under the Convention whether committed by state armed forces, organized NSAGs, disorganized groups, or individual civilians.

---

[60] Nuclear Terrorism Convention 2005 article 4(2); Terrorist Bombings Convention 1997 article 19(2); Terrorist Financing Convention 1999 article 2(1)(b); Vienna Convention 1980 (as amended by the Amendment 2005) article 2(4)(b); Hague Convention 1970 (as amended by the Beijing Protocol 2010) article 3 bis; Rome Convention 1988 (as amended by the Protocol 2005) article 2 bis (2); Plastic Explosives Convention 1991 articles 3–4.

[61] Jelena Pejic, 'Armed Conflict and Terrorism', in Ana Maria Salinas de Frias, Katja Samuel, and Nigel White (eds), Counter-Terrorism: International Law and Practice (OUP 2012) 171, 189.

[62] O'Donnell (above n 59) 866.

[63] Convention on the Safety of United Nations and Associated Personnel (adopted 9 December 1994, entered into force 15 January 1999) 2051 UNTS 363 article 9(1).

[64] ibid article 1.

[65] The reference to 'the law of international armed conflict' in article 2(2) is not intended to limit the exclusion to IACs, given that article 2(2) also refers to UN combatancy against 'organized armed forces', thus encompassing NIACs. Rather, that phrase is intended to refer to the applicable body of law, namely IHL. On the drafting of the Convention, see Antoine Bouvier, 'Convention on the Safety of United Nations and Associated Personnel: Presentation and Analysis' (1995) 35 IRRC 638.

## B. The UN Draft Comprehensive Terrorism Convention

The UN Draft Comprehensive Terrorism Convention, under negotiation since 2000, initially proposed to replicate the above exclusionary provision, based on the consensus reflected in the Terrorist Bombings Convention 1997. The proposal was challenged by alternative proposals sponsored by the Organisation of Islamic Cooperation (OIC), which led to an impasse in the drafting from 2002 to the present (2020). The OIC proposed that a convention should exclude the activities of the 'parties'—rather than 'armed forces'—during armed conflict,[66] 'including in situations of foreign occupation'.[67] The alternative proposals reflect semantic, legal, and political considerations.

The OIC reference to the 'parties', a technical IHL term for both state and non-state forces, may be designed to counter those states (nowadays including the US, France, and Russia) that interpret 'armed forces' as only encompassing state militaries.[68] In that sense, it is unobjectionable and indeed preferable, in order that belligerent parties are equally exempted and so that states are not placed in a more favourable position. As already noted, however, properly interpreted 'armed forces' also means state and non-state forces, so the competition between the two formulations is more semantic than substantive.

On the other hand, some states fear that the OIC intends the term 'parties' to embrace a wider array of actors, such as disorganized armed groups[69] or occasional violence by civilians loosely affiliated with such groups (including those sporadically supporting terrorism). Self-determination movements, for example, typically comprise not only armed wings but wider (and larger) political memberships, whether the Palestine Liberation Organisation, Hamas, or Polisario. On the flipside, a wider range of state actors might also be excluded under the rubric of the 'parties' to a conflict, such as civilian police and intelligence agencies (although some states treat these as part of the 'armed forces' in armed conflict). On that approach, most violence during a conflict, with the exception of unaffiliated civilians committing isolated acts, would be excluded from a convention, not just acts by armed forces.

To some extent, the distinction is one without difference, since IHL applies to violence whether by armed forces or other actors (including individual civilians). Exempting conduct from a terrorism convention would not confer impunity, but would leave liability to war crimes law. The exclusion debate is thus partly a political struggle over labelling and the stigmatization and delegitimization it brings, rather than a push to evade liability whatsoever.

As discussed further below, there are sound policy arguments for leaving armed conflict to be exclusively regulated by IHL, and for reserving crimes of terrorism for peacetime. As noted earlier, however, existing CTL treaties do not preserve a neat separation, but endorse co-regulation of certain acts in conflict. There are also real questions of liability at stake. From a law enforcement standpoint, sweeping preventive offences and special powers may

---

[66] UNGA Sixth Committee (59th Session), 'Report of the Working Group on Measures to Eliminate International Terrorism' UN Doc A/C.6/59/L.10 (8 October 2004); UNGA, 'Report of the Ad Hoc Committee Established by UNGA Res 51/210' (17 December 1996) 8th Session UN Doc Supp No 37 (A/59/37) (2004) 11 para 6; see also UNGA, 'Report of the Ad Hoc Committee Established by UNGA Resolution 51/210' (17 December 1996) 7th Session UN Doc Supp No 37 (A/58/37) (2003) 11–12.

[67] OIC proposal, in UNGA, 'Report of the Ad Hoc Committee Established by UNGA Res 51/210' (17 December 1996) 6th Session UN Doc Supp No (A/57/37) (2002) annex IV, 17.

[68] Pejic (above n 61) 192.

[69] ibid 193.

accompany terrorism offences but not war crimes. The dual criminalization of attacks on civilians as a war crime or the crime of terrorism is largely (but not wholly) unobjectionable, even if hostilities between armed forces ought to be properly left to the exclusive domain of IHL.

The OIC's proposed exclusion of 'foreign occupation' is redundant in that an occupation is by definition an international armed conflict under Common Article 2 of the four Geneva Conventions 1949, regardless whether there are also hostilities involving state forces.[70] The view that occupation is NIAC[71] is legally incorrect. In addition, organized NSAGs involved in hostilities in occupied territory would still be 'armed forces' in a NIAC that are also excluded from the convention.

Notably, the OIC has not formally sought a wider exclusion of all self-determination violence, including that committed outside of armed conflict. In contrast, three recent regional counter-terrorism conventions, of the OIC, African Union, and Arab League, exempt altogether struggles for national liberation or self-determination. Pakistan also lodged a reservation purporting to exclude self-determination struggles from the application of the Terrorist Bombings Convention 1997, triggering formal objections from many states on the basis that it was contrary to the treaty's object and purpose.[72] UN General Assembly and Security Council resolutions have repeatedly affirmed that all acts of terrorism are 'criminal and unjustifiable, wherever and by whomever committed'.[73]

Sixth, some CTL instruments have a different kind of partial application in armed conflict. The Nuclear Material Convention 1980 establishes offences relating to interference in 'nuclear material used for peaceful purposes while in international nuclear transport'. It thus has no application to attacks (whether lawful or unlawful under IHL) on a military's nuclear weapons facilities during conflict. However, the offences of dealings with peaceful nuclear materials in ways that cause death or injury or substantial property damage (article 7) could still be committed during armed conflict, for instance by stealing nuclear material and dispersing it against civilian or military targets.[74]

## C.  Lesser Situations of Violence

Some CTL treaties raise a further issue at the margins of IHL. Recent treaties exclude the (peacetime) 'activities undertaken by military forces of a State in the exercise of their official duties, inasmuch as they are governed by other rules of international law'.[75] Official duties could include legitimate law enforcement and counter-terrorism operations (including hostage rescue), evacuation operations, peace or UN peacekeeping operations, or humanitarian relief. While the exemption arguably concerns only peacetime duties (though there is

---

[70]   ibid 189, 193.

[71]   O'Donnell (above n 59) 868.

[72]   Austria, Australia, Canada, Denmark, Finland, France, Germany, India, Israel, Italy, Japan, Netherlands, New Zealand, Norway, Spain, Sweden, UK, US.

[73]   UNGA Resolution 49/60 (9 December 1994) annex: Declaration on Measures to Eliminate International Terrorism para 1.

[74]   O'Donnell (above n 59) 862.

[75]   Nuclear Terrorism Convention 2005 article 4(2); Terrorist Bombings Convention 1997 article 19(2); Terrorist Financing Convention 1999 article 2(1)(b); Vienna Convention 1980 (as amended by the Amendment 2005) article 2(4)(b); Hague Convention 1970 (as amended by the Beijing Protocol 2010) article 3*bis*; Rome Convention 1988 (as amended by the Protocol 2005) article 2*bis* (2); Plastic Explosives Convention 1991 articles 3–4.

some ambiguity whether it also overlaps with the exclusion for armed forces in armed conflict, which is part of the same provision), situations such as peacekeeping can involve the application of military force approaching armed conflict.

The exclusion only extends to state military forces and not to other state entities (such as police, security, or civilian intelligence agencies) that might be similarly deployed and may also need to use coercive force (for instance, to control a riot at a food distribution centre or disorder within a displaced persons camp). The provision does, however, contemplate that state military forces may include 'persons acting in support of those armed forces who are under their formal command, control and responsibility', which could include police or other civilian personnel coopted by the military.

Violence outside of 'official duties' will still come within these conventions. The concept is undefined in the conventions but acts outside official duties would foremost include purely private conduct by military personnel. It is less clear whether 'official duties' would also exclude acts by military personnel that are unlawful under domestic law (for instance, for being outside the scope of authority, and even if performed under apparent authority). It is likely, however, that 'official duties' includes acts contrary to other rules of international law (thus carving out from the conventions, for example, France's bombing of the Greenpeace ship, *Rainbow Warrior*, in New Zealand in 1986, since the operation was carried out by French military intelligence[76] acting on orders of the French government).

In the Draft Comprehensive Terrorism Convention, the OIC has sought to restrict this exemption to state military forces that are 'in conformity' with, and not merely 'governed by', international law. The proposal thus aims to qualify excessive state violence as 'terrorism', notwithstanding the application of existing international law to state breaches. Again, political labelling is at stake, but also real legal consequences. Presently, state violations of international law (including human rights and state responsibility) do not always attract criminal liability, whereas non-state actors would be asymmetrically liable under a terrorism convention. At the same time, states enjoy special legal personality and are lawfully entitled to utilize force in circumstances where non-state actors are not. States and non-state actors are therefore not similarly situated, even if it is desirable, from a rule-of-law standpoint, to equally criminalize state and non-state conduct that can be sensibly equated.

## D.  Security Council Counter-Terrorism Obligations

Counter-terrorism obligations imposed on states by the UN Security Council also raise issues of interaction with IHL. First, individuals and entities listed, under Security Council sanctions resolutions, as associated with Al Qaeda, the Taliban (until the suspension of its listing in 2019), and Islamic State of Iraq and al-Sham (ISIS) are subject to those restrictive financial measures even if they are also NSAGs that are parties to a NIAC, or individual members of such armed groups, and are thus already governed by IHL. The implications of such designation for compliance with IHL is considered below.

Second, the decentralized national implementation of the Security Council's CTL norms has generated normative and policy-oriented friction between CTL and IHL. In resolution

---

[76] Direction générale des services spéciaux (DGSS).

1373 (2001), the Security Council required states to criminalize terrorist acts in domestic law but failed to provide a common international definition of such acts or stipulate the relationship of such offences to IHL (such as through any of the exemption-type clauses found in the sectoral CTL conventions). Further, in resolution 2178 (2014), the Security Council required states to criminalize certain conduct relating to so-called 'foreign terrorist fighters', again without defining the operative concept of terrorism.

Many states have duly enacted their own terrorism and foreign terrorist fighter offences under these resolutions. National approaches to the relationship between terrorism and IHL vary.

### 1. Exclusion of certain conduct in armed conflict

EU law largely reflects the exemption clauses found in the recent CTL treaties, by providing that EU terrorism offences do 'not govern the activities of armed forces during periods of armed conflict, which are governed by international humanitarian law'.[77] The EU law thus excludes acts by (state or non-state) armed forces regardless of whether they are IHL compliant or non-compliant. Various decisions of European national courts have applied the exemption.

For example, a Belgian law implementing the EU offences was applied by a Belgian court in 2019 to acquit Kurdistan Workers' Party (PKK) members charged with terrorism offences, on the basis that the PKK was a party to a NIAC and was not engaged in terrorist acts outside of it.[78] Likewise in an Italian case of 2011, the court held that the LTTE in Sri Lanka was a party to a NIAC and could not be qualified as a terrorist organization under international law (without more evidence that its acts were preponderantly terrorist, not militant), including because terrorism is not an international crime in armed conflict and the EU law on terrorist crimes excludes activities of armed forces in armed conflict.[79]

Also in 2011, a Dutch court dismissed charges of participation in a terrorist organization, namely the LTTE in Sri Lanka, on the basis that the LTTE was an armed group in a NIAC, and that 'incidental' terrorist acts by its members, without a nexus to the conflict, were not sufficient to qualify it as a terrorist organization.[80] The court implicitly incorporated the EU exemption into Dutch law, which had not expressly replicated it.

Canadian law (and similarly New Zealand law) more narrowly excludes 'an act or omission that is committed during an armed conflict' and that is in accordance with applicable international or customary or treaty law.[81] Violence consistent with IHL and committed by state or non-state forces is thus excluded, whereas state or non-state violence in breach of IHL may be treated as terrorist offences. Little difficulty arises where national laws duplicate or complement war crimes against civilians under IHL, or are otherwise limited to protecting civilians (such as by criminalizing the financing of attacks on civilians). International criminal law already enables certain underlying conduct to be qualified as different but overlapping crimes, whether war crimes, crimes against humanity, or genocide.

[77] EU Directive of 15 March 2017 on Combating Terrorism and replacing Council Framework Decision 2002/475/JHA and amending Council Decision 2005/671/JHA recital 37.
[78] Chamber of Indictments of the Court of Appeal of Brussels (8 March 2019) (applying the Belgian Criminal Code article 141 *bis*).
[79] *Republic of Italy v TJ (aka Kumar) and Twenty-Nine Others*, Court of Naples (23 June 2011) (there was also insufficient evidence that the defendants had raised funds specifically to finance terrorist acts).
[80] District Court of The Hague (Judgment) (21 October 2011) (ECLI: NL: RBSGR: 2011: BU2066 and BT8829).
[81] Criminal Code (RSC 1985 c C-46) (Canada) s 83.01(1); see also Terrorism Suppression Act 2002 (NZ) s 5(4).

## 2. No exclusion of conduct in armed conflict

More problematically, some national laws have criminalized violence in armed conflict without any exception whatsoever to accommodate armed conflict and the special regime of IHL, as in the UK, Australia, and the Netherlands.[82] Such laws may criminalize acts which are not prohibited or criminalized by IHL, such as proportionate attacks on state military forces or military objectives by NSAGs, or direct participation in hostilities by civilians. National laws may then trigger exceptional domestic powers of search, seizure, and surveillance; extend inchoate or preparatory criminal liability; or modify criminal procedure in favour of national security. They may also serve as a basis for transnational criminal cooperation with other states to suppress terrorism.

The UK and Dutch courts, and the EU Court of Justice, have accordingly upheld the co-application of national terrorism offences to armed conflicts governed by IHL. In 2004 the Dutch Supreme Court held that IHL does not apply exclusively in a NIAC to the exclusion of common criminal law; that the criminalization of war crimes in a NIAC does not preclude the punishment of such acts alternatively as common crimes; and that conduct not amounting to war crimes under IHL may also be punishable as common crimes.[83]

In *R v Gul* [2013],[84] the UK Supreme Court found that international law does not prohibit the national criminalization as terrorism of hostile acts in NIACs, even those confined to targeting military objectives. It found that the counter-terrorism treaties, and national laws, were inconsistent in regard to the existence and scope of exclusionary provisions, and did not establish a general rule excluding national terrorism offences.[85] It further noted that no combatant immunity exists in NIACs.[86] While international law may not prohibit such hostilities, nor does it positively authorize them.

In *Liberation Tigers of Tamil Eelam (LTTE) v Council of the European Union* (2014),[87] the Court of Justice of the EU (CJEU) held that the existence of an armed conflict under IHL does not preclude the application of EU counter-terrorism financing law; that terrorist acts are in fact expressly forbidden by IHL; and that there are no exceptions for 'freedom fighters' or those resisting 'oppressive government' under either EU or international law. The Court additionally observed that Security Council resolution 1373, which the EU financing measures implement, does not exempt activities of armed forces in armed conflict.[88]

The case illustrates, however, that even within regional law there are different approaches to the interaction between CTL and IHL. The case concerned the listing of the LTTE for the purpose of asset freezing under an EU CTL of 2001 which contained no exception for armed forces in armed conflict.[89] In contrast, as mentioned earlier, EU law establishing terrorism offences *does* exclude such acts,[90] including by non-state armed forces in NIAC,

---

[82]   Terrorism Act 2000 (UK) s 1; Criminal Code 1995 (Australia) s 100.1.
[83]   Dutch Supreme Court (Judgment) (7 May 2004) (ECLI: NL: HR: AF6988) paras 3.3.7–3.3.8.
[84]   *R v Gul (Appellant)* [2013] UKSC 64 (affirming *R v Gul* [2012] EWCA Crim 280).
[85]   ibid paras 48 and 50.
[86]   ibid para 51.
[87]   *Liberation Tigers of Tamil Eelam (LTTE) v Council of the European Union* (Judgment of the General Court) T-208/11 European Court of Justice (Sixth Chamber, Extended Composition) (16 October 2014) paras 54–83.
[88]   ibid para 74.
[89]   EU Common Position 2001/931/CFSP on the Application of Specific Measures to Combat Terrorism (OJ 2001 L 344, 93), as implemented by EC Regulation No 2580/2001 and Decisions 2001/927/EC and 2006/379.
[90]   EU Framework Decision 2002/475 on Combating Terrorism 2002/475/JHA (13 June 2002) (since replaced by the EU Directive of 15 March 2017 (above n 77)).

notwithstanding that they do not enjoy combatant immunity. EU terrorist financing measures thus apply to armed conflict where EU terrorist offences do not.

Complicating matters, in 2014, the District Court of the Hague approved of the above decisions of the CJEU and the Dutch Supreme Court (in 2004) in finding that IHL does not apply exclusively in armed conflict and that Dutch criminal law—*including its terrorist offences*—co-applied to a NIAC in Syria.[91] It found that members of organized armed groups do not enjoy combatant immunity in NIAC and that their mere participation in the conflict can be punished. It regarded such principles as flowing from IHL treaties, 'settled' case law, and authoritative writers. While the Dutch terrorism offences implemented the EU terrorism offences of 2002 (which exempt armed forces in armed conflict), the Dutch law does not *expressly* include such exemption. The Court did not discuss this discrepancy, despite the defendants invoking the above-mentioned Dutch case of 2011 which *had* excluded armed forces from the Dutch terrorism offences on the basis that they implemented the EU offences.

Setting aside jurisdiction- or treaty-specific exemptions for armed conflict, while applying national terrorism offences to hostilities in NIAC may otherwise be strictly lawful as a matter of general international law, an adverse policy impact of this approach may be to undermine the effectiveness of IHL and its humanitarian purposes. The International Committee of the Red Cross (ICRC) warns against criminalizing acts that are not already unlawful under IHL.[92] IHL does not prohibit attacks on military objectives.[93] Criminalizing fighting by NSAGs as terrorism undermines their incentive to comply with IHL, for there is no longer any difference in legal consequence between proportionately attacking the military or indiscriminately targeting civilians. All armed resistance to state forces becomes 'terrorism', regardless of how one fights or whether one respects IHL.

Admittedly, in NIACs the state has long been entitled to criminalize members of non-state armed forces for offences against national security, whether labelled terrorism or otherwise. There is no combatant immunity in NIACs and at most IHL encourages states to grant the widest possible amnesty at the end of the conflict for hostile acts that did not violate IHL.[94] The incentives for armed groups to comply with IHL have always been rather limited, resulting from state's concerns to protect their sovereign right to restore law and order within their territories.

However, the additional criminalization of non-state hostilities as terrorism accentuates the existing disincentives for armed groups to comply with IHL.[95] First, current national legislative efforts carry the imprimatur of implementing UN Security Council obligations, according them a greater legal authority than ordinary offences. Second, such measures are intended to enable transnational criminal cooperation on terrorism, whereas hostile acts in NIAC (which are not war crimes) were hitherto typically treated as non-extraditable, quintessentially 'political' offences. Foreign states are thereby encouraged to cooperate in the repression of domestic political rebellion.

---

[91] *Prosecutor v Maher H*, Case No 09/767116-14, District Court of The Hague (Judgment) (1 December 2014) para 3.
[92] ICRC, *Terrorism and International Law: Challenges and Responses: The Complementary Nature of Human Rights Law, International Humanitarian Law and Refugee Law* (ICRC 2002).
[93] Pejic (above n 61) 177.
[94] APII article 6(5).
[95] Pejic (above n 61) 185.

Third, the labelling of hostilities as terrorism carries a special stigma which widens political and social divisions between the parties and dampens the prospects for peace negotiations; disarmament, demobilization, and reintegration (DDR); and post-conflict reconciliation (including prospects for conferring amnesties at the end of the conflict for participation in hostilities, as recommended by IHL).[96] Fourth, the criminalization or proscription of terrorists may stimulate armed groups to distrust the international community and discourage them from engaging in humanitarian assistance to civilians, discussed in section 4 'Impact of Counter-Terrorism on Humanitarian Relief Operations' below.

Finally, there is also a broader international legal concern about the over-extension of domestic criminal jurisdiction. The right of a state to criminalize hostile acts by armed groups in a NIAC historically arose in the context of NIACs being civil wars; it was thus a simple exercise of prescriptive territorial criminal jurisdiction. In contrast, the internationalization of terrorism offences, flowing from national implementation of Security Council resolution 1373, has resulted in the expansive extraterritorial criminalization of conduct in NIACs by states other than the territorial sovereign of the place of the conflict.

The sovereign territorial jurisdictional nexus is thus no longer apparent. It is one thing for a state to suppress non-state violence which challenges its political authority in its own territory, but quite a different proposition for other states to suppress such violence. The latter interferes, on the side of the foreign government, in domestic political struggles in other states—which historically was avoided by, for example, the application of the political offence exception in extradition law and treaties. As such, there are good reasons to be cautious about criminalizing hostilities in foreign NIACs (other than that deliberately targeting civilians); military combat should arguably be left to regulation by IHL.

## E.  A Customary International Crime of Terrorism?

Finally, CTL norms in customary international law also relate to IHL. In identifying a customary international law crime of transnational terrorism, the Special Tribunal for Lebanon (STL) held that such crime only exists in peacetime and not in armed conflict.[97] As such, there can be no overlap between IHL and this CTL norm. The STL indicated, however, that 'a broader norm that would outlaw terrorist acts *during times of armed conflict* may also be emerging'.[98] The STL's decision that there exists a customary crime of terrorism at all is controversial and arguably unsupported by state practice.[99]

## 4.  Impact of Counter-Terrorism on Humanitarian Relief Operations

In armed conflict, humanitarian activities (including aid, assistance, relief, or protection) are essential to protect civilian lives, basic needs, and human rights (including such as food

---

[96] Protocol II article 6(5).
[97] *Prosecutor v Ayyash et al* (STL Appeal Chamber) (Interlocutory Decision on the Applicable Law: Terrorism, Conspiracy, Homicide, Perpetration, Cumulative Charging) (16 February 2011) para 85.
[98] ibid para 107.
[99] Ben Saul, 'Legislating from a Radical Hague: The United Nations Special Tribunal for Lebanon Invents an International Crime of Transnational Terrorism' (2011) 24 *LJIL* 677.

or medical care, or humane treatment in detention). Under IHL, parties to a conflict must allow and facilitate the rapid and unimpeded passage of impartial humanitarian relief for civilians in need,[100] subject to reasonable measures of control. The wounded and sick must also receive the necessary medical care,[101] and medical personnel, units, and activities are protected.[102] States may not override these obligations in countering terrorism.

In practice, however, many humanitarian actors have expressed concern at the impact of CTLs on their activities during armed conflict. Humanitarian actors often have to negotiate or cooperate with all parties to a conflict (including 'terrorist' groups) to undertake their humanitarian activities. International and national CTLs generally do not prohibit mere contact or engagement with non-state actors for humanitarian purposes.[103] However, since 9/11, some national laws and policies have restricted or even prohibited engagement with 'terrorist' groups in various ways,[104] particularly through expansive terrorism offences (such as financing, training, support, or association) as well as financial restrictions relating to charitable or humanitarian activities.

First, even purely humanitarian dealings with terrorist groups have been criminalized. For example, it is an offence under US law to provide 'material support or resources to a foreign terrorist organization',[105] which is defined to include any training, advice, finance, or other assistance to a group. In *Holder v Humanitarian Law Project* (2010),[106] the US Supreme Court interpreted this strictly to include training groups such as the Kurdistan Workers' Party (PKK) on how to use IHL and international law to peacefully resolve disputes and how to petition UN bodies for relief. Any support was thought to facilitate the terrorist activity of the group, even if it does not contribute to a specific attack. Thus, international law training could potentially lend a group legitimacy, strain the US' relationship with its allies, or enable the group to use the international legal system to buy time, 'threaten, manipulate, and disrupt', or seek humanitarian financial aid that could be diverted to terrorism.

Second, some donors have adopted 'no contact' policies, which prohibit humanitarian actors (such as aid agencies or NGOs) from dealing with certain groups (such as Hamas in Gaza), even to secure access or safety for humanitarian personnel, or the passage of relief supplies. Third, some donors have imposed restrictive conditions on funding, which require humanitarian actors, and their partners and contractors, to exercise due diligence in their operations, or which impose vetting and monitoring requirements, to prevent diversion of funds to terrorist activities.

Restrictive laws and policies have adversely impacted on humanitarian operations, for instance by limiting funding to particular places, populations, partners, or programmes. For example, after Al-Shabaab was labelled as a terrorist group, US aid to southern Somalia was reduced by almost 90 per cent between 2008 and 2010[107]—in the midst of a famine

---

[100] CIHL rule 55; see eg GCIV article 23; API article 70(2); APII article 18; Rome Statute article 8(2)(b)(xxv).

[101] CIHL rule 110.

[102] CIHL rules 25–30.

[103] See Kate Mackintosh and Patrick Duplat, 'Study of the Impact of Donor Counter-Terrorism Measures on Principled Humanitarian Action' (Commissioned by UN Office of the Coordination of Humanitarian Affairs and the Norwegian Refugee Council, July 2013).

[104] Kate Mackintosh and Ingrid Macdonald, 'Counter-Terrorism and Humanitarian Action' (2013) 58 *Hum Exch Mag* 23, 24.

[105] USC Title 18, Part I, Chapter 113B, para 2339B.

[106] *Holder v Humanitarian Law Project*, 561 US (2010) Nos 08-1498 and 09-89 (US Supreme Court) (21 June 2010).

[107] Mackintosh and Duplat (above n 103).

that killed 260,000 people by 2012.[108] Islamic charities have been particularly hard hit by restrictions.[109]

In addition to increasing the administrative burdens on humanitarian actors, restrictive laws and policies have led to self-limitation because of uncertainty about legal liabilities and the related chilling effect on humanitarian operations. It can result in actors refusing funding from some donors, ceasing operations in some places or to some populations, or passing on risk to partners and contractors. It can also impede information sharing, co-operation, and coordination between actors.

Some humanitarian actors, such as the ICRC and the United Nations, enjoy international immunities from national legal liabilities,[110] but NGOs, civil society actors, and contractors do not. Informal engagement is often tolerated in practice, although this can still leave organizations facing legal uncertainty or self-restriction.[111] In some cases, specific UN mandates enable limited engagement, as with Hamas in Gaza or Al Shabaab in Somalia,[112] but this does not necessarily immunize NGOs from their home states' laws. Restrictive measures have also affected NGOs and civil society actors working in conflict areas, such as human rights groups engaged in advocacy, monitoring, or fact-finding.

The designation of some armed groups as 'terrorist' also challenges the principles of humanitarianism.[113] The four principles of humanitarian action are humanity (addressing suffering wherever it is found); neutrality (not taking sides in hostilities or preferring some political, racial, religious, or ideological causes over others); impartiality (acting on the basis of need and without discrimination); and independence (remaining autonomous from the political, economic, military, or other agendas of other actors).[114] CTL, on the other hand, 'takes sides' by criminalizing and/or ostracizing some groups. Neutrality and independence can also be compromised by humanitarian actors being pressured to participate in multinational stabilization or counter-insurgency efforts,[115] in which humanitarian assistance is co-opted and militarized as part of strategies to win civilian 'hearts and minds'. Humanity and impartiality are further undermined by restrictive policies which discourage aid to certain populations or places even if they are in most need.

While the Security Council has emphasized that counter-terrorism must comply with international law (including IHL and human rights), which implicitly safeguards humanitarian activities, it has not expressly provided for humanitarian exceptions to states'

---

[108] 'Somalia Famine "Killed 260,000 people"' *BBC News* (London, 2 May 2013) www.bbc.com/news/world-africa-22380352.

[109] Mackintosh and Duplat (above n 103).

[110] Mackintosh and Macdonald (above n 104) 25.

[111] Naz Modirzadeh, Dustin Lewis, and Claude Bruderlein, 'Humanitarian Engagement under Counter-Terrorism: A Conflict of Norms and the Emerging Policy Landscape' (2011) 93 *IRRC* 1, 19–20.

[112] UNGA Resolution 46/182 (19 December 1991) para 35(d) mandated UN humanitarian actors to negotiate with relevant parties. On Somalia, see UNSC Resolution 1916 (19 March 2010) para 5 (creating a temporary humanitarian exception to counter-terrorism financing sanctions).

[113] Ashley Jackson and Eleanor Davey, 'From the Spanish Civil War to Afghanistan: Historical and Contemporary Reflections on Humanitarian Engagement with Non-State Armed Groups', Humanitarian Policy Group Working Paper (Overseas Development Institute, July 2014) 1, 2.

[114] UNGA Resolutions 46/182 (19 December 1991) and 58/114 (17 December 2003).

[115] Jackson and Davey (above n 113) 17; Ashley Jackson, 'Talking to the Other Side: Humanitarian Engagement with Armed Non-State Actors', Humanitarian Policy Group Brief 47 (Overseas Development Institute, June 2012) 3.

counter-terrorism obligations (as it has done, for instance, in relation to country or situation specific sanctions regimes). At most, in Resolution 2462 (2019), concerning terrorist financing, it:

> Urges States, when designing and applying measures to counter the financing of terrorism, to take into account the potential effect of those measures on exclusively humanitarian activities, including medical activities, that are carried out by impartial humanitarian actors in a manner consistent with international humanitarian law.[116]

Beyond financing, the UN Secretary General has likewise urged states 'to consider the potential humanitarian consequences of their legal and policy initiatives and to avoid introducing measures that have the effect of inhibiting humanitarian actors in their efforts to engage armed groups for... humanitarian purposes'.[117] An example of good practice in relation to counter-terrorism is in EU law, which excludes '[t]he provision of humanitarian activities by impartial humanitarian organisations recognised by international law, including international humanitarian law'.[118]

## 5. Conclusion

IHL has proved capable of accommodating the historical and contemporary challenges presented by terrorism and counter-terrorism. In part this is because IHL focuses on regulating objectively harmful conduct rather than being preoccupied by the pejorative and contested labelling of actors. IHL thus prefers neutral terminology like 'armed groups' or 'parties' over politically loaded and stigmatizing terms such as 'terrorist' or 'terrorist organization'. Many of its proscriptions apply equally to both parties to a conflict and in principle it aims to avoid 'taking sides', even if IHL's regulation of NIACs undoubtedly favours states and reduces incentives for any armed group, including 'terrorists' to comply with IHL.

Further, the generality and ambiguity in some IHL rules—such as the threshold of a NIAC or the meaning of DPH—have also enabled it to be flexibly, constructively, and dynamically interpreted to accommodate emerging concerns. Sometimes the cost of generality has been claims by certain states that there are gaps in IHL or that it is otherwise inadequate; it has also brought prolonged uncertainty about the precise content of norms and difficulty in achieving consensus. Proposals to ratchet down IHL's protections for 'terrorists' have not, however, gained serious currency and the fifteen years after 9/11 broadly affirmed IHL's applicability—despite serious non-compliance—and later course correction—by some powerful states.

Where IHL has developed terrorism-specific rules, these have been tightly focused on IHL's core business of protecting civilians, rather than taking sides with states against non-state adversaries. Thus IHL's prohibitions on terrorism, acts of terror, and intending to spread terror amongst a civilian population target state and non-state conduct alike. The

[116] UNSC Resolution 2462 (28 March 2019) para 24.
[117] UN Security Council, 'Report of the UN Secretary General on the Protection of Civilians in Armed Conflict', UN Doc S/2010/579 (11 November 2010) para 57.
[118] EU Directive of 15 March 2017 (above n 77) recital 38.

war crime of spreading terror recognizes the additional wrongfulness of attacking civilians for the ulterior purpose of psychologically intimidating or terrorizing them.

More problematic has been the overlaying of CTL instruments and norms on armed conflict, which take varied approaches to their interaction with IHL. While CTL instruments and norms often reinforce or complement IHL's protections for civilians, some have interfered in IHL's regulation of violence by prohibiting or criminalizing conduct that is not unlawful under IHL. The problem is most acute in those national laws, implementing Security Council obligations, that criminalize all war fighting by armed groups in NIACs. When CTL takes sides in this way, it can undermine the already weak incentives for armed groups to respect IHL. It can also inhibit humanitarian engagement and cooperation by external actors with armed groups—and thereby undermine IHL's guarantees of civilian protection in conflict.

# Index

Note: *For the benefit of digital users, indexed terms that span two pages (e.g., 52–53) may, on occasion, appear on only one of those pages.*